persian gulf war almanac

HARRY G. SUMMERS JR.
Colonel of Infantry

Facts On File®

AN INFOBASE HOLDINGS COMPANY

PERSIAN GULF WAR ALMANAC

Facts On File, Inc.
460 Park Avenue South
New York NY 10016

Library of Congress Cataloging-in-Publication Data
Summers, Harry G.
    The Persian Gulf War almanac / Harry G. Summers.
        p.   cm.
    Includes bibliographical references and index.
    ISBN 0-8160-2821-4 (alk. paper)
    1. Persian Gulf War, 1991.   I. Title.
    DS79.72.S862 1995
    956.7044'2—dc20   94-28450

Facts On File books are available at special discounts when purchased in bulk quantities for businesses, associations, institutions or sales promotions. Please call our Special Sales Department in New York at 212/683-2244 or 800/322-8755.

Text design by Ron Monteleone
Jacket design by Paul Agresti

Charts and map on page 3 by Marc R. Greene

Printed in the United States of America

RRD FOF 10 9 8 7 6 5 4 3 2 1

This book is printed on acid-free paper.

In Honor of
my daughter-in-law

Chief Warrant Officer

Kathy Summers

United States Army

and her fellow soldiers of the
3d Armored "Spearhead" Division
which led VII Corps's main attack in the Gulf
and in whose ranks a generation earlier I
began my military career

CONTENTS

MAP SYMBOLS

On a map, friendly military units are represented by a rectangle, enemy units by a double-lined rectangle. Symbols within the rectangle indicate the unit type. A "cannon ball" circle represents field artillery, crossed diagonal "pack straps" represent infantry, a single diagonal "sash" represents cavalry, an oval "tank tread" represents armor, and a footed "Y" "helicopter mast" represents army aviation.

The "tanks treads" are superimposed over the "pack straps" to represent mechanized infantry, and over the "sash" of a cavalry unit to represent armored cavalry. Likewise, the symbol for an aviation unit is superimposed over the infantry "pack straps" to symbolize air assault. Airborne units are symbolized by adding a "gull wing" to the symbol.

To symbolize their MAGTF (Marine Air Ground Task Force) composition, Marine Corps units combine the basic symbol for infantry with the propellor symbol for Marine aviation. Abbreviations within the rectangle are used to identify other units: "SF" for Special Forces, or "RGR" for Rangers.

Symbols above the rectangle denote the unit size. One vertical line represents a company, two a battalion and three a regiment or group. One "x" denotes a brigade, two a division, three a corps and four a field army. Numbers to the left of the rectangle designate the unit identification, and symbols or letters to the right provide additional data: a minus (-) if the unit is at less than full strength, or the country of origin if other than the United States. "SANG" is Saudi Arabian National Guard and "RSLF" is Royal Saudi Land Forces.

Unit symbols for the Persian Gulf War are shown on opposite page.

MAP SYMBOLS

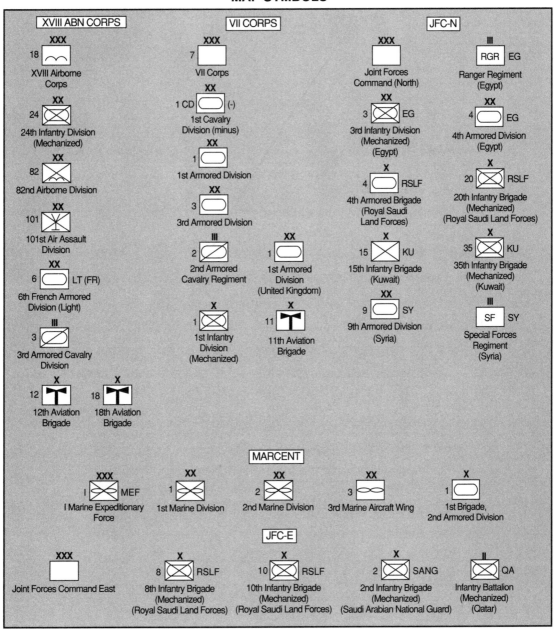

XVIII ABN CORPS

XXX
18
XVIII Airborne Corps

XX
24
24th Infantry Division (Mechanized)

XX
82
82nd Airborne Division

XX
101
101st Air Assault Division

XX
6 LT (FR)
6th French Armored Division (Light)

III
3
3rd Armored Cavalry Division

X
12
12th Aviation Brigade

X
18
18th Aviation Brigade

VII CORPS

XXX
7
VII Corps

XX
1 CD (-)
1st Cavalry Division (minus)

XX
1
1st Armored Division

XX
3
3rd Armored Division

III
2
2nd Armored Cavalry Regiment

XX
1
1st Armored Division (United Kingdom)

X
1
1st Infantry Division (Mechanized)

X
11
11th Aviation Brigade

JFC-N

XXX
Joint Forces Command (North)

XX
3 EG
3rd Infantry Division (Mechanized) (Egypt)

X
4 RSLF
4th Armored Brigade (Royal Saudi Land Forces)

X
15 KU
15th Infantry Brigade (Kuwait)

XX
9 SY
9th Armored Division (Syria)

III
RGR EG
Ranger Regiment (Egypt)

XX
4 EG
4th Armored Division (Egypt)

X
20 RSLF
20th Infantry Brigade (Mechanized) (Royal Saudi Land Forces)

X
35 KU
35th Infantry Brigade (Mechanized) (Kuwait)

III
SF SY
Special Forces Regiment (Syria)

MARCENT

XXX
I MEF
I Marine Expeditionary Force

XX
1
1st Marine Division

XX
2
2nd Marine Division

XX
3
3rd Marine Aircraft Wing

X
1
1st Brigade, 2nd Armored Division

JFC-E

XXX
Joint Forces Command East

X
8 RSLF
8th Infantry Brigade (Mechanized) (Royal Saudi Land Forces)

X
10 RSLF
10th Infantry Brigade (Mechanized) (Royal Saudi Land Forces)

X
2 SANG
2nd Infantry Brigade (Mechanized) (Saudi Arabian National Guard)

II
QA
Infantry Battalion (Mechanized) (Qatar)

MAPS AND FIGURES

ACKNOWLEDGMENTS

Unlike my earlier two almanacs on the Korean and Vietnam Wars, this book concerns a conflict in which I was not an active combat participant. My primary involvement with the Persian Gulf War was as a military analyst. In addition to my own writings and the hundreds of newspaper and radio interviews I gave to media in the United States and abroad, I made some 125 television appearances, primarily on NBC and CNN, but also on ABC, CBS, Fox, C-Span and Canada's CBC-Newsworld.

As a military analyst for NBC's *America at War* special reports during Operation Desert Storm, I was able to gain a unique insight into the war. For that, much thanks to NBC senior vice president Timothy J. Russert; to Nancy Nathan, Washington producer of the *TODAY* show; to the NBC Washington Bureau's Betty Nevins, Marcie Rickun and Colleen Halpin; and to Kristin Moore and Alison Rosenberg in New York. Special thanks also to Tom Brokaw and Jane Pauley of NBC News, and to the *TODAY* show's Bryant Gumbel, Deborah Norville, Faith Daniels and Katie Curic.

In the first months of Operation Desert Shield, courtesy of CNN Pentagon correspondent Wolf Blitzer, Washington bureau chief Bill Headline and CNN vice president Gail Evans in Atlanta, I served as the military analyst for CNN's *Crisis in the Gulf* reports. My appreciation to them and to news anchors Bernard Shaw, David French, Reid Collins and John Holliman, and to the hosts of CNN's several talk shows, including *Telemundo, Crossfire, Larry King Live* and *Newsmaker Sunday*.

In addition to writing my weekly syndicated newspaper column, I was asked by Shelby Coffee, the editor-in-chief of the *Los Angeles Times,* to be that paper's "Drew Middleton"—for many years the distinguished military correspondent for the *New York Times*—and to write a series of analyses of the strategic issues of the war. Special gratitude to him for that great honor, as well as to my editor, Tony Day, and the staff of the newspaper's War Desk for their help in that endeavor. Also most helpful, as usual, were the *Los Angeles Times Syndicate*'s managing editor, Steve Christiansen, and copy editors Connie Cloos and Tim Lange.

Another great honor was Congressman (later Secretary of Defense) Les Aspin's invitation to testify before his House Armed Services Committee on the situation in the Gulf, and Senator Herbert Kohl's invitation to testify before his Governmental Affairs Committee on media coverage of the Gulf War.

Unlike my earlier almanacs, whose data could be gleaned from years of accumulated research, this work was completed only two and one-half years after the Gulf ceasefire. Much of the data therefore comes from news accounts and official documents.

From the White House Office of Media Relations came copies of presidential speeches and announcements. Colonel F. William Smullen III and Lieutenant Colonel Larry Icenogel in the Office of the Chairman of the Joint Chiefs of Staff provided needed documentation, and the Army General Staff's Dennis Keating was most helpful in obtaining biographies and photos of key Army generals.

Department of Defense public affairs officers Colonel David H. Burpee, Major Doug Hart and Major Bryan Whitman, and U.S. Central Command's Lieutenant Colonels Robert T. Donnelly and John Olsen provided much useful information, as did the Military Airlift Command's Major Jim Bates. Colonels Bill Mulvey and Dave Kiernan, and Captain Linda Ritchie and others in Army public affairs were also most helpful, as were the public affairs officers of the Navy, Air Force, Marine Corps and Coast Guard.

Particular thanks to Cowles History Group's Jennifer S. Keen for her help in obtaining photographs for this work, and to an old friend, General Barry R. McCaffrey, for the briefing books and photographs of the Victory Division in action in the Gulf.

A final word of thanks to my editor, James Warren, who not only provided the original inspiration for this book, but also provided kind words and encouragement along the way; to copy editor Roger Labrie for his outstanding work; and to my wife Eloise and our two sons, Major Harry G. Summers III and Major David Cosgrove Summers, United States Army. And special thanks to our daughter-in-law, Chief Warrant Officer Kathy L. Summers, who served in the Gulf with the 3d Armored Division.

In expressing my thanks to those who provided comments and advice, I must add that the conclusions and such errors as the book may contain are solely my responsibility.

H.G.S.
Bowie, Maryland

INTRODUCTION

This almanac is designed to capture the incredible diversity and complexity of the Persian Gulf War, the first major military action in the post–Cold War world. Because it was written primarily for an American audience, U.S. military units and activities are given greater prominence than those of other nations. But the Persian Gulf War was a true coalition war, and every effort has been made to provide objective coverage of the many other participants.

The conflict developed in three distinct phases. The first was the buildup of tensions in the area following the end of the Iran-Iraq War; these tensions led to border disputes between Iraq and Kuwait that culminated in Saddam Hussein's invasion of Kuwait in August 1990 (see Part I). Then there was the forming of the allied coalition and the buildup of coalition forces in the Kuwaiti Theater of Operations during Operation Desert Shield (see especially DEPLOYMENT OF U.S. FORCES; LOGISTICS, U.S.; and MOBILIZATION, U.S. in part III). The third phase was the war itself during Operation Desert Storm (see AIR CAMPAIGN, GROUND CAMPAIGN and MARITIME CAMPAIGN in part III).

Part I of the almanac explores the geography of the Kuwaiti Theater of Operations, including such factors as the effects of time and distance and weather and terrain on military operations. The examination of the Gulf region's historical background includes its ancient roots as well as the rise of Islam and the Arabs, the ebb and flow of the Ottoman and British Empires, the Pan-Arab movement and the waxing and waning of U.S. influence in the area after World War II. The events and forces leading up to the Persian Gulf War are also described and assessed, including the 1980–1988 Iran-Iraq War and Saddam Hussein's invasion of Kuwait.

Part II, the chronology of the war, lists events in the order in which they unfolded, beginning with Saddam Hussein's February 1990 demands for recompense from the Gulf states for the costs of the Iran-Iraq War, and continuing through the cease-fire and the release of the allied prisoners of war (POWs) on March 5, 1991. Incidents occurring after the ceasefire and up to the departure of President George Bush from office in January 1993, such as the Kurdish and Shiite uprisings in Iraq, are covered in entries for those specific events in part III.

Because of the relatively short time lapse since the end of the war, much of the material in this almanac is drawn from contemporary news accounts. While there have been many complaints from the media about restrictions on their coverage, the truth is that the Persian Gulf conflict was the most thoroughly and competently reported wars in history. As this almanac is being published in the spring of 1995, no major new revelations have emerged in the more than four years since the March 1991 cease-fire.

This is not to say that the Gulf War is an uncontroversial conflict. One controversy raised by the war, particularly in the United States, concerns the role of the media in wartime. Another concerns the performance of the Patriot missile system used against Iraqi Scud missile attacks. Still another is the so-called Iraqgate affair concerning U.S. dealings with Iraq prior to the war. Arguments persist about how many Iraqis, military and civilian, were killed and wounded in the war (see CASUALTIES). Finally, with Saddam Hussein still in power in Iraq, there is debate over whether or not victory was actually achieved (see WAR TERMINATION).

All of these controversies are discussed in detail in part III. Also included, where possible, are suggestions for further reading on all sides of the issues. Other entries in that section explain why the former Soviet Union, even though it deployed no troops to the Gulf, was perhaps the most important coalition partner of the war (see SOVIET UNION).

For example, Iraqi president Saddam Hussein thought he could fight the Vietnam War all over again. And sure enough, he did. But with the sea change in U.S.-Soviet relations, he got to play the role not of North Vietnam's Ho Chi Minh, as he had intended, but rather South Vietnam's Nguyen Van Thieu—he was abandoned by the Soviets as Thieu had earlier been abandoned by the United States.

The critical changes in America's post-Vietnam warfighting doctrines, including the new AirLand battle doctrine, are highlighted as the little-known keys to battlefield victory. But most significant was the reversal of U.S. military strategy from the strategic defense to the strategic offense.

During the Korean War, as I discussed in my *Korean War Almanac* (Facts On File, 1990), U.S. national policy shifted from rollback and liberation, as in World War II, to containment. This proved to be a wise long-term choice, for as predicted, it allowed for the contradictions inherent in Marxist-Leninist dogmas to destroy communism from within. But the adoption of containment had an unforeseen effect on U.S. military strategy. It caused a shift from the strategic offensive to the strategic defensive, which continued through the Vietnam War. As the United States found to its sorrow in both Korea and Vietnam, the best possible result obtainable with the strategic defensive is stalemate.

But the end of the Cold War also spelled the end of containment. With the advent of the Persian Gulf War, for the first time since World War II the American military was back on the strategic offensive. That had a decisive impact on the conduct of military operations.

In addition to this shift in strategic policy, the Gulf War changed future U.S. military operational policies in four significant ways. One was the precedent set by the expanded role of women on the battlefield (see WOMEN IN THE MILITARY). Another was a renewed appreciation of the contribution of the reserve components to battlefield success and to national mobilization (see MOBILIZATION, U.S.). The third was the absolute necessity of joint interservice cooperation (see GOLDWATER-NICHOLS DEFENSE DEPARTMENT REORGANIZATION ACT). Finally, there was an awareness of the importance of combined operations with allies (see STRATEGY, COALITION).

Also featured in part III are articles on the weaponry of the war, including the M1A1 Abrams tank with its uranium-depleted armor; the Apache helicopter gunship and A-10 Warthog tank killers; the air campaign's fighters, fighter-bombers and bombers; and the high-technology reconnaissance and surveillance systems—AWACS, JSTARS and the like—that brought all of that firepower to bear.

The Persian Gulf War was one of the shortest wars in history. But in the application of high technology to the battlefield, it may well prove to be one of the most significant. We disregard its lessons at our peril.

Part I

the setting: the kuwaiti theater of operations

GEOGRAPHIC REALITIES

The Kuwaiti Theater of Operations (KTO) was defined by President George Bush on January 21, 1991, in Executive Order 12744, which designated the following locations, including the airspace above them, "as an area in which Armed Forces of the United States are and have been engaged in combat":

- the Persian Gulf
- the Red Sea
- the Gulf of Oman
- that portion of the Arabian Sea that lies north of 10 degrees north latitude and west of 68 degrees east longitude
- the Gulf of Aden
- the total land areas of Iraq, Kuwait, Saudi Arabia, Oman, Bahrain, Qatar, and the United Arab Emirates

Essentially, the Kuwaiti Theater of Operations encompassed the one-million-square-mile Arabian Peninsula and its adjacent waters, less the Republic of Yemen on its southern coast which, while supportive of Iraq, remained neutral during the conflict.

With peaks rising more than 14,000 feet, the Taurus and Zagros Mountains along Iraq's borders with Turkey and Iran form the northern and northeastern boundaries of the peninsula. To the east and southeast, the boundaries include the Shatt-al-Arab waterway in the delta of the Tigris and Euphrates Rivers, the Persian Gulf, the Strait of Hormuz, and the Gulf of Oman. Along the peninsula's southern coast lie the Arabian Sea and the Gulf of Aden. To the west lies the Red Sea. To the northwest, Syria and Jordan separate the peninsula from the Mediterranean Sea.

The Kuwaiti Theater of Operations included the total land area of seven nation-states: Iraq, Kuwait, Saudi Arabia, Oman, Bahrain, Qatar and the United Arab Emirates. A concise geographic survey of each follows.

The *Republic of Iraq*, with a land area of 167,924 square miles, is slightly larger than the state of California. Its July 1990 population was 18,781,770, of which approximately 75 to 80 percent were ethnic Arabs and 15 to 20 percent were Kurds. Roughly 97 percent of its people were Muslims, with 60 to 65 percent Shiites and 32 to 37 percent Sunnis. Iraq has a 100-billion-barrel oil reserve; in 1990, oil exports provided about 95 percent of Iraq's foreign exchange. Essentially landlocked during the Iran-Iraq war, Iraq relied on oil pipelines stretching across Turkey and Syria to the Mediterranean, and across Saudi Arabia to the Red Sea.

Most of Iraq is sparsely populated desert and steppes. The roughly 56,000 square miles of land that run along the Tigris and Euphrates Rivers comprise a relatively small part of the total land area of the country but contain about three quarters of its population. In 1990, approximately 20 percent of the population (3.6 million) lived in the capital city of Baghdad. Basra, the nation's second largest city and at one time its largest port, had a 1977 population of about 1.5 million, but that was reduced by half by the fighting in the Iran-Iraq War. Most of Iraq's other cities are also along the Tigris or Euphrates Rivers.

The *State of Kuwait*, with a land area of 6,880 square miles, is slightly smaller than New Jersey. Its July 1990 population was 2,123,711, of which about 37.9 percent were native Kuwaitis, 39 percent other Arabs, and the remainder Asians and other nationalities. About 85 percent of Kuwait's people were Muslims, (30 percent Shiites, 45 percent Sunnis and 10 percent other sects); the remaining 15 percent of its population were Christians, Hindus, Parsis and followers of other religions.

The economy of Kuwait was heavily dependent on foreign labor: Kuwaitis themselves accounted for less that 20 percent of the labor force. With a 98-billion-barrel reserve, the economy of Kuwait is totally dominated by oil and oil-related activities.

Kuwait shares a 240-kilometer land boundary with Iraq to the north and a 222-kilometer boundary with Saudi Arabia to the south. Although it has a 499-kilometer coastline along the Persian Gulf, Kuwait is flat, hot and very dry.

SOUTHWEST ASIA

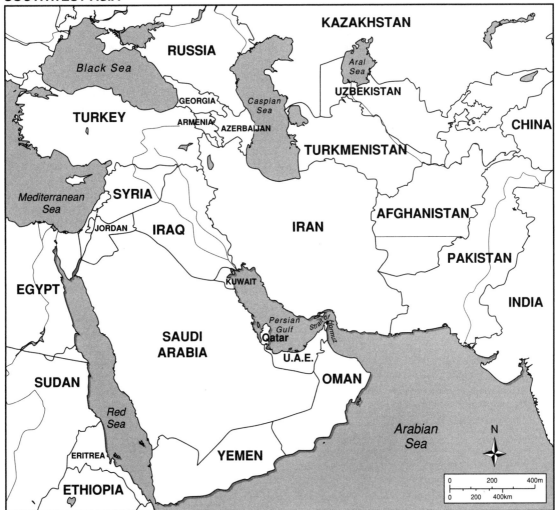

The *Kingdom of Saudi Arabia*, with a land area of 839,996 square miles, is about one-fourth the size of the contiguous United States and occupies most of the Arabian Peninsula. Its July 1990 population was 17,115,728, of which about 90 percent were Arabs and 10 percent Afro-Asians. Except for some of its foreign workers, who comprise 60 percent of its 4,200,000-man work force, Saudi Arabia is 100 percent Muslim.

With 260 billion barrels of oil, Saudi Arabia has the largest petroleum reserves in the world and is the world's largest exporter of oil. Its capital city,

Riyadh, had an estimated population of 1,386,000 in 1986. Jidda had an estimated population of 1,210,000, and Mecca 463,000. With a 2,510-kilometer coastline, Saudi Arabia has a number of major ports and airfields. From 9,000-foot highlands in the west, Saudi Arabia slopes across mostly uninhabited arid, barren sandy deserts to the Persian Gulf in the east. It has a harsh dry climate with great extremes in temperature.

The *Sultanate of Oman*, with a land area of 82,030 square miles, is about the size of New Mexico. Its July 1990 population was 1,457,064, almost entirely Arab.

Seventy-five percent of Omanis are Ibadhi Muslims, with the remainder Sunni and Shiite Muslims and some Hindus.

Oman has oil reserves of some 4 billion barrels, and oil dominates its economy. The capital city, Muscat, had an estimated 1990 population of 85,000; its enclave at the tip of Cape Musandam controls access to the Strait of Hormuz.

Located primarily along the southeastern side of the Arabian Peninsula, Oman has a narrow coastal plain up to 10 miles wide, a range of barren mountains reaching 9,900 feet and a wide, stony waterless plateau. Hot and humid along the coast, Oman is hot and dry in the interior.

The *State of Bahrain*, with a land area of 268 square miles, is smaller than New York City. An island in the Persian Gulf located between the Qatar Peninsula and Saudi Arabia, Bahrain's 1990 population was 520,286. Sixty-three percent of the people were Bahraini, with the remainder being Asian, Arab or Iranian; 70 percent were Shiite Muslims and 30 percent were Sunnis.

With estimated oil reserves of 173 million barrels in 1985, Bahrain's economy is dominated by oil production and processing, along with offshore banking. Its capital city, Manama, had an estimated 1988 population of 151,000. Bahrain has several ports and three major airfields. Mostly a low, arid desert plain, it is mild and pleasant in the winter but hot and humid in the summer.

The *State of Qatar*, with a land area of 4,247 square miles, is slightly smaller than Connecticut. Occupying a peninsula on the Persian Gulf on the east coast of Arabia, its 1990 population was 490,857. Forty percent Arab, Qatar's population also includes Pakistanis (18 percent), Indians, (10 percent) Iranians (10 percent) and other ethnic groups.

With reserves of 4.5 billion barrels, Qatar is heavily dependent on oil exports for most (80 percent) of its government revenues. Its capital city, Doha, had an estimated 1987 population of 250,000. Qatar has several ports and airfields. Humid and sultry in summer, hot and dry at other times, Qatar is mostly flat and barren, its desert covered with loose sand and gravel.

The *United Arab Emirates (UAE)*, with a land area of 32,000 square miles, is about the size of Maine. Formerly known as the Trucial States, these seven sheikdoms combined in 1971 to form the UAE. Located on the east coast of the Arabian Peninsula, the UAE had a 1990 population of 2,253,624, of which 19 percent were Emirians, 23 percent other Arabs, 50 percent South Asians, and the remainder other foreign nationals. Less than 20 percent of the population are UAE citizens. Ninety-six percent of the people are Muslims, of which 16 percent are Shiites.

Oil dominates the economy of the UAE, which has reserves of 98 billion barrels. Its capital city of Abu Dhabi had an estimated 1990 population of 722,000. The UAE has several ports and airfields. With the Hajar Mountains in the east, the UAE is primarily a barren flat coastal plain with a vast wasteland of uninhabited sand dunes.

Suggestions for further reading: *The World Factbook 1990* (Washington, D.C.: Central Intelligence Agency, 1990); and *The World Alamanac and Book of Facts* (New York: World Almanac, 1993).

METT-T

A framework for an appreciation of the effects of geography on military operations is provided by the acronym "METT-T," which stands for *Mission, Enemy, Terrain and weather* and *Troops available,* all affected by *Time.* Used by the U.S. military as a planning guide, these considerations can spell the difference between victory and defeat. As discussed below, the geography of the KTO had an impact on each of these factors.

Mission

The very decision to become involved in the Kuwaiti crisis in the first place, as will be discussed in more detail below, had to do with a geographic consideration: the fact that the Kuwaiti Theater of Operations (KTO) contained the world's largest oil reserves. Although other factors were also at play, oil was behind Saddam Hussein's seizure of Kuwait, and oil was behind the coalition's mission of reversing that takeover.

But while oil fueled the crisis, other geographic considerations posed what seemed at the beginning to be almost insurmountable obstacles to bringing coalition power to bear against Iraq.

Time and Troops Available

With Saddam Hussein's forces poised on the Saudi Arabian border, most U.S. military forces were half a world away. Even with inflight refueling, C-5 and

The terrain in the KTO was harsh and inhospitable.
USAF photo (SRA Rodney Kern) courtesy of OCJCS.

C-141 jet transport aircraft would take 15 to 16 hours to cover the 6,700 nautical miles between Fort Bragg, North Carolina, the home base of the Army's rapid-reaction 82d Airborne Division, and airfields in Saudi Arabia. At best, all that lightly equipped force could do was show the flag.

The heavy armored forces needed to stop an Iraqi attack on Saudi Arabia could only be moved by ship, as could the bulk of the ammunition, fuel and supplies necessary to sustain the forces. It would take some 20 to 24 days for the bulk of U.S. ground forces to cover the 8,850 nautical miles from the east coast of America to the Persian Gulf through the Suez Canal, or 28 to 33 days to travel the 11,990 nautical miles around the Cape of Good Hope.

Although U.S. Marine expeditionary forces could be flown the 7,600 nautical miles from their bases on America's west coast to Saudi Arabia in 17 to 18 hours, their heavy equipment would take 27 to 32 days to travel the 11,600 nautical miles from California. Even the tanks, artillery and other equipment from the Maritime Prepositioning Ships at Diego Garcia, in the Indian Ocean, 2,700 nautical miles

away from the Arabian Peninsula, would take six to eight days to reach Saudi ports.

One saving grace was the existence of modern port facilities such as those at Ad Damman and Al-Jubayl in Saudi Arabia, and a number of jet-capable airfields throughout the area. On August 8, 1990, for example, 24 F-15C Eagle air superiority fighters landed at Dhahran airfield in Saudi Arabia, having made the flight from Langley Air Force Base in Virginia in 15 hours.

Another blessing was that the Kuwaiti Theater of Operations was located on a peninsula, allowing sea power to be rapidly brought to bear. The USS *Independence* carrier air group was on station in the Arabian Sea when the crisis began. Two days later, the carrier USS *Dwight D. Eisenhower*, then in the Mediterranean, passed through the Suez Canal and into striking distance in the Red Sea.

Fortuitously, Saddam Hussein did not continue the attack after his seizure of Kuwait, and time was available for the massive buildup of allied coalition forces that followed. That buildup involved not only the air and sea movement into the KTO of hundreds of thousands of military personnel from around the world, but also the shipping of some 3.5 million tons of dry cargo and 6 million tons of fuel by sea, and another 500,000 tons of supplies by air.

Terrain and Weather

Initially, it was also feared that terrain and weather would severely hamper the allied conduct of military operations. As noted in the country surveys above, the Kuwaiti Theater of Operations was one of the most inhospitable regions of the world. Composed primarily of uninhabited steppes and deserts, it has a particularly fierce climate as well. From May to September, highs range from 110 to 120 degrees Fahrenheit, whereas winter lows are in the 30s and 40s.

A study prepared by the Congressional Research Service of the Library of Congress at the beginning of the crisis warned of the dangers posed by terrain and weather:

> Summer heat seriously degrades the performance of humans and machines everywhere in Iraq and adjacent Arab territory. Dehydration and heat prostration are constant dangers even for acclimatized troops, unless they take proper precautions that include shelter from the sun whenever possible and copious amounts of water. Sanitation problems can quickly become unmanageable under the hot sun. . . . Flies that feed on garbage and human waste broadcast disease.
>
> Metal is blistering hot to touch. Aircraft and vehicle maintenance is a clumsy process for mechanics who must wear gloves. Electronic equipment, including essential computers and sensors, is especially sensitive to intemperate temperatures. Malfunctions occur if air conditioning and other precautions prove insufficient. Heavyweight oil and other special lubricants are required. . . .
>
> Abrasive, windblown sand and silt clog machines, jam weapons, seep past engine filters, pit radar scopes, and contaminate food. Grit magnifies maintenance problems manyfold. Performance in emergency becomes problematic and service life of equipment shortens, despite all preventative measures. Logistics loads increase commensurately. . . .
>
> The value of water in the desert is well

known. . . . Water for personal consumption by U.S. forces—drinking, cooking, bathing, laundry—presently approximates 11 gallons per day. Vehicles demand 10–12 gallons more. . . .

In the early days of Desert Shield, critics claimed, for example, that the Army's M1 Abrams tank would not work in the desert and that the Apache tank-killer helicopters soon would become ineffective in combat because of the erosion of their rotor blades. Through a high level of personnel training and dedication, and intensive maintenance of arms and equipment, none of these dire predictions proved true.

Terrain and weather, of course, affected the Iraqi forces as well as those of the allies. But there were certain aspects of military geography that gave coalition forces an advantage.

Although roads as such are scarce in the desert, it was found that the trafficability of the hard, flat desert surface for wheeled and tracked vehicles was excellent. Unlike for foot-mobile infantry, distance per se was not an obstacle for mounted units, thus giving an edge to the highly mobile armored and mechanized forces that dominated the allied coalition. The U.S. 24th Infantry Division (Mechanized), for example, moved some 368 kilometers in four days to outflank the Iraqi defenders. Desert terrain also favored airmobile operations, as the U.S. 101st Airborne Division (Air Assault) demonstrated by its 250-kilometer deep air assault into the Euphrates Valley.

But the most decisive coalition advantage was in the air. The arid, flat desert landscape, virtually devoid of vegetation, provided almost no cover or concealment for defensive forces. As the Congressional Research Service study presciently observed:

> Aerial observers, able to claim clear views as far as the eye can see, have far easier tasks than those who tried to track enemy traffic in Korea's mountains and along the Ho Chi Minh Trail in Vietnam. Vehicular columns on the move. . . . raise telltale clouds of dust that mark their location and line of march. Formations at rest are also visible. The side able to establish air superiority early will have a huge advantage.

And that proved to be exactly the case. When it came to METT-T, geography was on the side of the allied coalition.

HISTORICAL REALITIES

The Kuwaiti Theater of Operations encompassed one of the most ancient areas of the world. It has been said that the biblical Garden of Eden was located in the Tigris and Euphrates River valleys. Be that as it may, the Arabian Peninsula, and Iraq in particular, have very deep historical roots.

BABYLONIA AND THE ANCIENT BEGINNINGS

Ancient Babylonia stretched from modern Baghdad to the Persian Gulf along the Tigris and Euphrates River valleys. Before the rise of the city of Babylon, the area to the southeast was known as Sumer and the area to the northwest as Akkad. Assyria lay north of Babylon, which was located about 55 miles south of modern Baghdad on the banks of the Euphrates.

The Sumerians, the first civilized inhabitants of the Babylonian plain, settled in the area near the Persian Gulf in about 5000 B.C. Their civilization was adopted by the Semites (Akkadians) to the northwest, but both peoples were overshadowed by a new Semite tribe, the Amorites, who established their capital at Babylon in about 1850 B.C. The influence of the Amorites spread through the Tigris-Euphrates Valley and beyond, culminating in the Babylonian Empire founded by Hammurabi in about 1700 B.C., which extended over Sumer, Akkad, Assyria and into what is now Syria. Sacked by the Hittites after Hummurabi's death, Babylonia in 1600 B.C. fell to the Kassites, who ruled the area for the next 400 years.

The Kassite Dynasty was succeeded by the Pashe Dynasty, which was succeeded in turn by the Assyrians in 1169 B.C. By 722 B.C., the Assyrians had entered a true imperial age, extending their empire as far west as Egypt and deporting the Israelites. After the fall of Assyria in 612 B.C., Babylonia enjoyed a short period of independence. Nebuchadnezzar, who ruled in Babylon from 605 to 562 B.C., is best remembered as the king who carried the Jews into their Babylonian captivity.

In 539 B.C., Babylonia was conquered by Cyrus the Great, and the Persians ruled the area for the next 200 years. Persian rule was overthrown by the Macedon-ian Alexander the Great, whose armies captured Babylon in 331 B.C. After Alexander died in Babylon in 323 B.C., he was succeeded by one of his Macedon-ian generals, Seleucus, who established a dynasty that would rule the area for the next 75 years. As the dynasty crumbled, Persian nationalists united against the Greeks and restored Persia's independence in about 250 B.C. Known as the Parthians, the nationalists swept into Babylonia and ruled there for the next 300 years.

Fierce warriors, the Parthians were nonetheless weakened by a series of battles with the Roman legions, and in A.D. 227 they fell to the Sassanian Persians. The Sassanians carried on the fight with the Roman Empire and its Byzantine successors, defeating and capturing the Roman emperor Valerian. But with the rise of a new people, the Arabs, who in the mid-7th century began to expand outside their homeland, the ancient period came to an end.

MESOPOTAMIA AND THE ARABS

Originating in the southwest part of the Arabian Peninsula in what is now Yemen, Arabs were first mentioned in Babylonian texts in 2450 B.C. During the same period, Bedouin Arabs were portrayed in Egyptian reliefs. The Minaean Kingdom in southwest Arabia existed from about 1200 to 650 B.C., and the Sabaean Kingdom, which eventually absorbed it, from 950 to 115 B.C. The third of these Arab kingdoms, the Himyarite Kingdom, lasted until A.D. 525, but in the century before the rise of Muhammad, Arabs were in a state of anarchy.

Born in 570 at Mecca in western Arabia, which is also the site of the Kaaba, a sacred Islamic shrine toward which believers worldwide turn when praying, Muhammad is buried nearby at Medina. Every Muslim is expected to make a pilgrimage, or hajj, to Mecca at least once in his or her lifetime. This gives what is now Saudi Arabia a special place in the Muslim world as the protector of the faith.

The prophet Muhammad, seen by believers as God's messenger, brought to the Arabs along the

Red Sea not only the Islamic faith, but unity and a sense of mission as well. This mission to propagate the faith sent the Arabs westward across North Africa to the Atlantic Ocean and into Spain; northward into Lebanon and Syria; and eastward across Babylonia and Persia into the Indian subcontinent and beyond.

Today, Morocco, Tunisia, Algeria and Libya in North Africa have predominantly Arab populations, as do Jordan, Lebanon and Syria in the Middle East, and Yemen, Saudi Arabia, Iraq, Kuwait, Oman, Qatar, Bahrain and the United Arab Emirates on the Arabian Peninsula. Islam has spread around the globe, with some 950,726,000 members worldwide and 8,000,000 in the United States.

Muhammad's successors were called caliphs, the temporal and spiritual heads of Islam. From 637 to 1258, Babylonia (then known as Mesopotamia, "the land between the rivers") flourished under the caliphates. The city of Baghdad was founded by the Abbasid caliph al-Mansur in 762, replacing Damascus as the center of the Muslim world. But by the 11th century the caliphates, in decline, came under the domination of the Seljuk Turks. From 1055 to 1194, a Seljuk sultan ruled in Baghdad.

Although the Mongol hordes under Genghis Khan swept across Mesopotamia between 1218 and 1222, it was his grandson, Hulagu, who put Baghdad to the sword in 1258 (some 800,000 noncombatants were reported to have been killed). For the next century and a half, Mesopotamia was under first Mongol and then Turkoman rule. In 1393, Baghdad was sacked again, this time by the Turkoman Tamerlane. The countryside was now in ruins: the irrigation systems essential to agriculture were destroyed, and much of the cultivated land was lost.

THE OTTOMAN EMPIRE

No sooner had the Mongols and Turkomans departed than Mesopotamia once again fell under foreign rule. In 1453, the Turks laid siege to Constantinople, at the time the capital of the Byzantine Empire. After its fall, it became the capital of the Ottoman Empire, which was to spread through Europe, Africa and the Middle East. In 1534, the great Ottoman sultan Suleiman the Magnificent extended his sway over Mesopotamia and the entire Arabian Peninsula.

Although the Turks' power was tenuous at times, especially in Arabia itself, for nearly 400 years the area remained essentially a Turkish possession. Yemen, however, reestablished its independence in 1635, and the nomadic Bedouins of the hinterlands never really lost theirs. But by the 19th century the Ottoman Empire was in decline. Known as "the sick man of Europe," the empire's undoing came with World War I. Allied with the Central Powers (Germany and Austria-Hungary), it went down with them in defeat.

Great Britain landed military forces at Basra in 1914. After an initial defeat at Kut-el-Amara on the Tigris River, they went on to capture Baghdad in 1917. Earlier, in eastern Arabia, Ibn Saud, who had been exiled at the court of the sheik of Kuwait, had begun a revolt against the Turks; he captured Riyadh in 1901 and the coastal cities along the Persian Gulf in 1913.

In western Arabia along the Red Sea, the British, including the famous "Lawrence of Arabia," Thomas Edward Lawrence, were working with Arab forces under Ibn Saud's chief rival, Husayn ibn Ali, and Faisal, the son of the sharif of Arabia. These forces captured Damascus in 1917, but Husayn became too demanding and lost allied support. Ibn Saud would become king of Saudi Arabia and Faisal, the king of Iraq.

The Treaty of Sèvres, signed on August 10, 1920, stripped Turkey of its non-Turkish provinces, including Arabia and Mesopotamia. The Ottoman Empire ended in 1922 with the creation of the modern Republic of Turkey by Kemal Ataturk. Turkey would not again involve itself in the Arabian Peninsula until the Persian Gulf War some 70 years later.

BRITISH IMPERIALISM

In October 1798, the British East India Company signed an agreement with the imam of Muscat (present-day Oman) to exclude the French from his territory. This was the beginning of a series of agreements through which most of the principalities on the southern and eastern coast of Arabia became dependent on Great Britain. In 1820, Oman and Bahrain agreed to aid Britain in suppressing piracy and slave trading in the area, leading to Britain's formal acceptance of responsibility for security in the Gulf region.

In 1839, Great Britain forcibly annexed Aden (in present-day Yemen) as a coaling station for its steamships; London retained it as a colony until 1967. As part of the "Great Game" with Russia (that is, the long-standing competition for influence in South Asia), Great Britain severed Afghanistan from Persia in 1857.

Built by A French-led consortium formed in 1858, the Suez Canal, which opened in 1869, facilitated sea transport from Europe via the Gulf of Suez to the Red Sea and the Arabian Ocean, opening up the area to more direct Western trade and influence. In 1875, Britain bought Egypt's shares in the Suez Canal Company and, since it also controlled its approaches, the canal came under British control.

As British influence grew, the sheik of Bahrain surrendered his country's external sovereignty to Great Britain in 1880; the sheik of Muscat (Oman) did the same in 1891, as did the sheik of Kuwait in 1899. Britain occupied Egypt in 1882, and at the outbreak of World War I, declared it a British protectorate.

During the war, Great Britain had promised Mesopotamia its independence. Granted a League of Nations trusteeship over that nation in 1920, Britain promoted and recognized Emir Faisal as king of the newly proclaimed Kingdom of Iraq in 1921.

Britain recognized Iraq as an independent state in 1927, and in 1932 Iraq was admitted to the League of Nations. That same year, the Kingdom of Saudi Arabia was formally established by Ibn Saud. In Persia, a young cavalry officer, Reza Pahlavi, one of the leaders of a nationalist uprising that had forced the British to withdraw from his country after the war, proclaimed himself shah in 1925 and began to rapidly modernize the economy. In recognition of this new direction, in March 1935 the name of Persia was changed to Iran.

Meanwhile, major oil deposits had been discovered on the Arabian Peninsula. In 1928, Britain and Iraq signed an agreement regulating the interests of the various oil companies in Iraq, and oil production began in 1930. In 1933, an American company, Standard Oil of California, obtained a 60-year oil concession in Saudi Arabia, and in 1934 the Arabian-American Oil Company (ARAMCO) was formed.

Although no fighting occurred east of Suez during World War II, British and Soviet troops were sent into Iran in 1941 to build supply lines for the movement of allied war matériel through the "back door" to the Soviet Union. The shah, considered pro-German by the British, was forced to abdicate in favor of his son, Mohammad Reza Pahlavi, who would rule until he was deposed in 1979.

In September 1941, the U.S. Military Iranian Mission was formed, becoming the Persian Gulf Command in December 1943. Some 4 million tons of war supplies were sent to the Soviet Union through Iran, including 45 percent of the 400,000 lend-lease trucks that the United States provided. Among those who served in Iran during the war were Brigadier General H. Norman Schwarzkopf Sr. and his young son, H. Norman Jr., who would return almost five decades later as commander of U.S. forces in the Gulf War.

One of the first crises of what was to become the Cold War occurred in March 1946, when the Soviet Union refused to honor its earlier pledge to withdraw its forces from the Iranian province of Azerbaijan after the end of World War II. Under pressure from the United States and the newly created United Nations (UN), the Soviets withdrew later that year.

Meanwhile, in 1942 the United States established diplomatic relations with Saudi Arabia, which was emerging as one of the major powers in the region. Through its Army Corps of Engineers, the United States began an enduring partnership with Saudi Arabia to aid in its modernization, including the construction of ports and airfields. In 1944, President Franklin Roosevelt and Prime Minister Winston Churchill of Great Britain met with King Saud to discuss Arab contributions to the war effort. But as the war ended, there emerged new issues that would complicate U.S.-Arab relations. Among them were the question of who would govern Palestine, the creation of a Jewish homeland there, and the emerging Cold War between the United States and the Soviet Union.

PAN-ARABISM

The unity imposed on the Middle East by the Ottoman Empire had disappeared during World War I. After World War II, the unity provided by Great Britain disappeared as well. The Arab League, formed at the end of that war, was an attempt to fill the void and hold the Arab world together.

Concerned about increased Jewish immigration into Palestine and calls by Zionist leaders to establish a Jewish homeland there, Arab leaders met in Cairo beginning in August 1943, and in February-March

1945 formulated the covenant that established the Arab League, consisting originally of Saudi Arabia, Egypt, Transjordan (now Jordan), Syria, Lebanon, Iraq and Yemen. The league was a symbol of increased Arab nationalism in the Middle East, and of Pan-Arabism throughout the world.

Also attempting to foster Arab unity was the Baath (Renaissance) Socialist Party founded in Damascus, Syria, in 1940–1941. It preached an all-encompassing Arab nation under a great leader. Using a Leninist revolutionary model of tight central control to gain and maintain power, Baathist military officers would take over the governments of Syria in 1963 and Iraq in 1968, where Baathists continue in office to this day.

Britain, which had established Transjordan in 1921 as an autonomous part of its Palestinian Mandate, withdrew its troops in 1946, and an independent Transjordan was declared. British troops were withdrawn from the rest of Palestine following a 1947 United Nations resolution on the partition of Palestine.

Likewise, France, which had a League of Nations mandate over Lebanon and Syria, withdrew its troops from Lebanon in 1946. In April of that year, Syria became an independent state.

Israel proclaimed itself an independent state in 1948 and was immediately recognized by the United States. A special relationship between the two countries was created that endures to this day. The Arab nations, however, did not recognize Israeli independence and sought unsuccessfully to restore Arab control of Palestine by force of arms. During the fighting that followed Israel's declaration of independence, Transjordan seized part of what had been Palestine, causing dissension within the ranks of the Arab League. To underscore its new acquisition, Transjordan proclaimed itself the Kingdom of Jordan in April 1949.

In Egypt, Pan-Arabism reached its zenith under Gamal Abdel Nasser, who took part in the military revolt that forced the abdication of King Farouk in 1952. The Republic of Egypt was proclaimed, and Nasser assumed the presidency. British domination of Egypt and the entire Middle East was at an end. The Anglo-Egyptian Evacuation Agreement was signed in October 1954, leading to the end of the 75-year British occupation.

Rejecting a mutual security pact with the United States, Nasser concluded an arms deal with the Soviet Union and Czechoslovakia in September 1955, establishing ties between Egypt and the Soviet Union that would endure until 1972. The next year, when the United States refused to grant Nasser a loan to build the Aswan High Dam, the Soviets stepped into the breach and offered to finance the project.

Disaffected with the West, Nasser seized and nationalized the Suez Canal in July 1956. In October, Israel, joined by Britain and France, invaded Egypt, which on November 1 blocked the canal. In a surprise move, the United States sided with Nasser rather that with its British, French and Israeli allies. Following intense U.S. pressure, a cease-fire was declared on November 6. Not only did Nasser emerge a hero throughout the Arab world, but the decline in French and British power to influence events in the region was duly noted. After the Suez crisis, the United States assumed a more active role in Middle Eastern affairs.

To monitor the cease-fire, a UN force was sent into the Sinai desert, which lies between Israel and the Suez Canal. In May 1967, Nasser demanded that this force be withdrawn. After its departure, Egyptian forces reoccupied the Sinai and closed the Gulf of Aqaba to Israeli shipping. On June 5, 1967, Israel launched the so-called Six Day War. In a series of attacks on Egypt, Jordan, and Syria, Israel occupied the Sinai up to the canal and seized the Gaza Strip, lying on the Mediterranean coast and occupied by Egypt since 1948, and captured Jerusalem and Jordan's West Bank, as well as Syria's Golan Heights.

Meanwhile, in October 1947, the last British troops left Iraq, marking the real beginning of Iraqi independence. On July 14, 1958, King Faisal II was murdered and the Republic of Iraq was proclaimed. After the country experienced a long period of instability in 1968 a Baathist Army officer, Ahmad Hasan al-Bakr, became head of state, with his cousin, Saddam Hussein, as his deputy. Relations with fellow Baathists in Syria were cool, however, and became poisonous after Saddam Hussein succeeded al-Bakr in July 1979.

Earlier, in 1953, the shah of Iran had been temporarily deposed by the radical Mohammad Mossadegh, but thanks to the efforts of the United States—particularly the Central Intelligence Agency—the shah was soon restored to power.

But the revolutionary fervor continued to sweep the area, and in September 1962 the monarchy in Yemen was overthrown. In 1967, after Britain granted Aden its independence, two factions vied for power. South Yemen (officially the People's Democratic Republic of Yemen, the Arab world's only Marxist state) was supported by Egypt and the Soviet Union; in 1970, it signed a 20-year friendship treaty with the Soviet Union that allowed for the stationing of Soviet troops in the area. North Yemen (officially the Yemen Arab Republic) was supported by Saudi Arabia and the United States. The dispute between North and South flared into open war twice in the 1970s. An Arab League-sponsored agreement on unification was signed in March 1979, but it was not until May 22, 1990, that the two Yemens were formally reunited.

Ironically, the last major coordinated Arab military effort before the Persian Gulf War was the so-called Yom Kippur War, which began with an Egyptian-Syrian attack on Israel on October 6, 1973. After some initial successes, especially by Egyptian forces in the Sinai, the attacks were repulsed and Israeli forces crossed the Suez Canal into Egypt. A ceasefire went into effect on October 24, and a disengagement agreement was signed on January 18, 1974.

The preconditions for the Gulf War were now set. The Middle East's colonial era was at an end. Nationalism was on the rise, and the discovery of oil in the region had added an economic dimension to the ferment. The cries for Arab unity rekindled the ancient enmities between the Persians of present-day Iran and the Arabs that would later explode into war. And the shaky territorial foundations of the Gulf states, originally created by British fiat, would serve as a pretext for the Iraqi invasion of Kuwait.

THE UNITED STATES WAXES AND WANES

"Empires wax and wane," begins the ancient Chinese classic *The Romance of the Three Kingdoms*, "they have their ends and their beginnings." What had been true of the Ottoman and British Empires in the Middle East seemed true of the United States as well. The Eisenhower administration's deliberate humiliation of Britain and France during the 1956 Suez crisis was evidence of the waxing of American power in the area.

As the Cold War between democracy and communism progressed, a kind of zero-sum game developed, wherein each side competed for client states in the Middle East. In 1955, Britain had proposed the Baghdad Pact, whereby the United States would come together with Iran, Pakistan, and Great Britain to form a "northern tier" alliance against the spread of Communist influence. But instead of uniting the area, the pact further divided it, as the treaty became the focus of Arab nationalist resentment. Its successor, CENTO (the Central Treaty Organization), a Middle Eastern version of the North Atlantic Treaty Organization (NATO) in Europe, fared no better.

With Egypt already in the Soviet orbit, in early 1957 the "Eisenhower Doctrine" was announced: The United States would defend any country in the Middle East "requesting assistance against armed aggression from any country controlled by international Communism." In July 1958, Lebanon's president, Camille Chamoun, requested just such U.S. help.

Claiming that "events in Iraq [i.e., the assassination of King Faisal by Arab radicals] demonstrate a ruthlessness of aggressive purpose which tiny Lebanon cannot combat without further evidence of support from friendly nations," Eisenhower sent 14,000 U.S. troops into Lebanon, ordered a worldwide alert of U.S. forces, including the Strategic Air Command, and dispatched a Marine Regimental Combat team into the Persian Gulf to guard against a possible Iraqi attack on Kuwait, then a British protectorate.

According to former National Security Council staffer William Quandt in *Force Without War* (Washington, D.C.: Brookings Institution, 1978), as a further indication that the United States was not bluffing, Eisenhower ordered the chairman of the Joint Chiefs of Staff "to be prepared to employ, subject to my personal approval, *whatever* means might become necessary to prevent any unfriendly force from moving into Kuwait." It was later acknowledged by insiders that "whatever means" referred specifically to the use of nuclear weapons.

Eisenhower's was a message not lost on the Iraqis, who tempered their revolution accordingly. After Kuwait declared its independence from Great Britain in 1961, Iraq's military leader, Abdul Kareim Qassim, massed troops on the Kuwaiti border but pulled back after British and Arab League troops were sent into the area. When Qassim was overthrown by the Baathists in 1963, Iraq's relations with Kuwait were normalized, reportedly in exchange for an $85 million Kuwaiti "loan."

Meanwhile, U.S. attention had been diverted by the Vietnam War. In 1969, the "Nixon Doctrine" was announced: The United States would move from direct intervention to the use of proxies to enforce its policy of containing the Soviets.

During the Nixon administration, Iran and Saudi Arabia were established as the "twin pillars" of U.S. defense policy in the Middle East. U.S. military advisors were sent to both nations to help in the training of their armed forces, and from 1970 to 1979 Iran alone reportedly spent some $8.3 billion on U.S. arms. During that same period, Saudi Arabia purchased $3.2 billion worth of U.S. arms; in addition, 675 U.S. military personnel and some 10,000 U.S. civilian contractors were building military installations there.

In 1973, prior to launching his attack against Israel, Egyptian president Anwar Sadat had expelled all Soviet advisors from Egypt. The United States would soon fill that vacuum, and the first steps were made by President Jimmy Carter through his Camp David peace initiatives to promote a peaceful settlement between Egypt and Israel.

In March 1977, Sadat made a surprise visit to Israel to talk peace. The high-water mark of U.S. influence in the Middle East was the Camp David accords of 1978. A year later, on March 26, 1979, Eqypt and Israel signed a formal peace agreement and established diplomatic relations, ending 30 years of hostilities.

But elsewhere in the Middle East things were not so rosy. Although not noted at the time, the waning of U.S. power in the region actually began on June 16, 1976, with the assassination of the U.S. ambassador to Lebanon, Francis C. Meloy, by Arab fanatics.

Although the identity of the murderers was known, according to a 1990 investigative report "the U.S. government engaged in a deliberate cover-up of the real facts in order to avoid public or congressional pressure to retaliate against those responsible for the murders." Instead of deterring aggression, this behavior "laid the groundwork for the subsequent deaths of other Americans in Lebanon during the 1980s as terrorists—emboldened by American timidity in the face of repeated attacks—grew even

more aggressive." (Neil Livingstone and David Halevy, *Inside the PLO* [New York: William Morrow, 1990].)

American pusillanimity, coupled with militant nationalism in the region, also contributed to the collapse of one of the "twin pillars" of U.S. security policy in the Middle East. In 1978, riots against the shah broke out in Iran, and martial law was declared that September. The United States stood by idly while the shah came under increasing political attack, and on January 16, 1979, he left the country, ostensibly to receive medical treatment abroad; in fact, he knew his government was about to fall.

On January 31, 1979, Ayatollah Ruholla Khomeini, an exiled fundamentalist religious leader, named a provisional government for Iran, and the next month he seized power in Tehran. American fecklessness was rewarded on November 4, 1979, when the U.S. Embassy in Tehran was seized and 62 Americans were taken hostage. The United States would be subjected to more than a year of humiliation as the Iranian government ignored all pleas for the hostages' release. Perceptions of American impotence were enhanced by the failure of a military rescue mission in April 1980: eight Americans died and five were injured when the operation was bungled before reaching Tehran. The hostages would not be released until January 21, 1981, as President Carter left office.

The year 1979 also marked the coming to power of Saddam Hussein, who took control of the Iraqi government on July 16. But that event was overshadowed by the Soviet invasion of Afghanistan later that year. Moscow's action was a major escalation of the Cold War, for it marked the first time in that conflict that the Soviet Union had deployed forces outside the geographic boundaries of the Soviet bloc.

Earlier, in 1973, as revolutionary fervor swept through the area, the kingdom of Afghanistan had been overthrown and a republic proclaimed. Five years later, leftist leaders of a bloody coup took power and concluded an economic and military treaty with the Soviet Union. But relations between the two countries became strained, and in December 1979 a massive Soviet airlift into the capital of Kabul began. The Afghan government was toppled on December 27 and replaced with one that was more pro-Soviet. A nine-year anti-Soviet guerrilla war followed, during which more than 15,000 Soviet soldiers were killed in battle. After a UN-mediated agreement was reached in 1988, the last Soviet troops withdrew from Afghanistan on February 15, 1989.

By its weak initial response to the Soviet invasion, the United States humiliated itself once again. Far from Eisenhower's strong action in 1958 to block perceived Soviet designs in the Middle East, President Carter at first limited himself largely to cancelling American participation in the Olympic Games that were to be held in Moscow in the summer of 1980.

After reaching its nadir, U.S. Middle East policy soon began its fitful recovery in January 1980 when the "Carter Doctrine" was announced. "An attempt by any outside force to gain control of the Persian Gulf region will be regarded as an assault on the vital interests of the United States," said President Carter in his State of the Union address, "and such an assault will be repelled by any means necessary, including military force."

Putting teeth into that doctrine began with the formation of the military's Rapid Deployment Joint Task Force (RDJTF) in March 1980. Tellingly, however, a lack of faith in U.S. commitments was revealed when no country in the region allowed the RDJTF's headquarters to be established on its soil. Instead, the task force was located at MacDill Air Force Base in Florida.

In September 1980, political-military relationships in the Middle East were transformed even further when Iraq invaded Iran. Ostensibly triggered by arguments over access to the Shatt-al-Arab waterway in the delta formed by the Tigris and Euphrates Rivers, Iraq's invasion marked the beginning of a bloody eight-year war.

One immediate consequence was the formation in 1981 of the Gulf Cooperation Council (GCC), which brought together Saudi Arabia, Kuwait, Bahrain, Qatar, Oman and the United Arab Emirates for their mutual protection and, incidentally, to serve as a conduit for their financial aid to Iraq. Another consequence of the Iran-Iraq War was the increased influence of the Soviet Union, which became Iraq's main arms supplier. Between 1983 and 1987, the Soviets supplied 47 percent of Iraq's weapons at a cost of $13.9 billion.

Yet another consequence of the war was renewed American concern for the security of the Gulf region. In 1983, the Reagan administration redesignated the

RDJTF the U.S. Central Command (CENTCOM), making it one of the Defense Department's major geographic commands. Still without a Middle East headquarters, CENTCOM nonetheless oversaw the deployment of maritime prepositioning ships (MPS) loaded with war matériel to Diego Garcia, a British island in the Indian Ocean.

A number of combat units, including the Army's XVIII Airborne Corps and the Ninth Air Force, were also earmarked for CENTCOM in the event of a Middle East crisis. Egypt, Bahrain and Oman allowed the United States limited use of their military facilities, and joint training exercises began in the area, including the "Bright Star" exercises in Egypt in 1983.

"Over the course of the decade," noted the editors of *Middle East Report* in their January-February 1991 issue, "Saudi Arabia poured nearly $50 billion into building a Gulf-wide air defense system. . . . By 1988, the U.S. Army Corps of Engineers had designed and constructed a $14 billion network of military facilities across Saudi Arabia, including military cantonments at Khamis Mushayat, Tabuk and King Khalid Military City [and] port facilities at Ras al-Mish'ab, Jidda and Jubayl." These installations would prove critical during the Gulf War.

Finally, there was Operation Earnest Will, in which the United States reflagged 11 Kuwaiti oil tankers in the Persian Gulf in 1987–1988, allowing them to fly the U.S. flag in order to prevent their being attacked by Iran in its "tanker war" with Iraq. The U.S. Joint Task Force Middle East (JTFME), which only recently had become part of CENTCOM, deployed 22 Navy combatants and support ships to the Gulf region. The U.S. effort also included deploying four Airborne Warning and Control System (AWACS) aircraft, eight KC-135 and KC-10 aerial refueling tankers, two mobile sea bases used for operations against the Iranian Revolutionary Guard Corps Navy, five P-3 surface surveillance aircraft, eight attack helicopters, eight mine clearing helicopters, a Marine Air Ground Task Force (MAGTF) of approximately 400 Marines, as well as approximately 800 Air Force crewmen and support personnel.

These actions should have provided clear signs of America's resolve to protect its interests in the Middle East, but they were obscured by vacillation between the twin pillars of "Irangate" and "Iraqgate."

Officially, the United States "tilted" toward Iraq during the Iran-Iraq War, so much so that there have been postwar charges that the United States gave Iraq much of the wherewithal for its later attack on Kuwait. U.S. diplomatic relations with Iraq, which had been broken after the 1967 Arab-Israeli war, were reestablished in 1984.

For its part, Iraq saw itself as playing a heroic role. Calling the war with Iran *Qadisiyyah Saddam,* after the 7th-century battle of Qadisiyyah in which the Arabs drove the Persians from Mesopotamia, Iraqis believed they had blocked the "Eastern Gateway" through which the Iranians—the latter-day Persians—would have overrun the region. Saddam Hussein would later demand recompence from the Gulf states for the terrible sacrifices that effort had entailed.

Ironically, it was the inadvertent Iraqi attack on the frigate USS *Stark* in the Persian Gulf on May 17, 1987, costing 37 American lives, that pushed the United States into direct military intervention on the side of Iraq in its "tanker war" with Iran. Another tragedy occurred on July 3, 1988, when the cruiser USS *Vincennes* shot down an Iranian civilian airliner that was misidentified as an attacking military aircraft, killing all 290 passengers on board.

But in fact the United States was playing both sides of the street. In November 1986, a U.S. delegation had secretly visited Iran to make a deal to swap American arms through Israel for Iranian help in obtaining the release of American hostages held in Lebanon. The Israeli connection was particularly offensive to Iraq because in 1981 Israel had staged an air attack that destroyed Iraq's nuclear reactor. On July 25, 1990, on the eve of the Persian Gulf War, Saddam Hussein would complain to U.S. Ambassador April Glaspie about what he called "Irangate." Saddam would describe it as the worst rift in U.S.-Iraqi relations since diplomatic relations had been restored, and would note that it came at the low point in Iraq's war with Iran, when the Iranians occupied the Fao Peninsula.

U.S. moral authority was strained not only by this duplicity but also by a whole series of events that called American will and resolve into question. When terrorists blew up the Marine barracks in Beirut, Lebanon, in 1983, killing 241 American servicemen, the United States withdrew its forces without taking punitive action for fear of offending Syria, a

Soviet client state and a mortal enemy of fellow Baathist Saddam Hussein's Iraq. By then, the kidnapping of U.S. nationals in Lebanon by Islamic terrorists was a common occurrence. In 1985, when Syrian-backed terrorists, reportedly at the behest of the Soviet KGB (intelligence service), kidnapped William Buckley, an agent of the U.S. Central Intelligence Agency (CIA), and tortured him to death, once again the United States did not respond.

An even stronger signal of U.S. impotence was sent on July 31, 1989, when Middle East terrorists flaunted their cold-blooded murder of U.S. Marine Colonel William Higgins, an official emissary of the United States seconded to the United Nations, by releasing a grisly videotape of his corpse hanging from a rope. Although he issued a mild rebuke, President Bush went ahead with a planned dinner party on the White House lawn.

The fall of the Berlin Wall in November 1989 and the imminent collapse of communism would create a sea change in the international strategic environment, but that was not immediately discernible. No wonder, then, that when in July 1990 Ambassador Glaspie presented to Saddam Hussein the feeble U.S. remonstrances about his military buildup on the Kuwaiti border, he paid them scant heed. Despite its considerable military strength, America had created the impression that it was a paper tiger, more fierce in appearance than in action.

Events would soon prove that perception to be false, but at the time it seemed reasonable. Instead of deterring war, the United States had unwittingly encouraged it.

THE CRISIS ERUPTS
Without the United States to worry about, Saddam Hussein evidently felt he had a free hand to bully Kuwait. Perhaps genuinely believing, as was discussed earlier, that in Iraq's struggle with Iran he had fought the good fight for the entire Arab world, Saddam Hussein revived old border disputes with Kuwait as a means of coercing it to help pay off Iraq's more than $37 billion war debts. If not rescheduled, the annual principal and interest on the non-Arab debt alone would have taken more than half of Iraq's estimated 1989 oil revenues of $13 billion. By mid-1990, Iraq had only enough cash reserves for three months of imports, as well as an inflation rate of 40 percent. In addition, its $12.9 billion military budget

was consuming $700 of the average citizen's annual income of $1,950.

Hussein demanded money from Kuwait, and when it refused he renewed his claims to the islands of Bubiyan and Warbah, which dominated Iraqi access to the Persian Gulf. He also claimed that Kuwait had been stealing oil from the al-Rumaylah oil field that straddled the Iraqi-Kuwaiti border, and that Kuwait and the United Arab Emirates had conspired to drive down the price of oil.

Kuwait sought to ease the crisis by making concessions at the negotiating table, including guaranteeing loans to the Iraqi government and sharing revenues from the al-Rumaylah oil field. Egyptian president Hosni Mubarak and Saudi king Fahd ibn Abdul Aziz offered to help settle the crisis, but at a meeting in Jidda, Saudi Arabia, on August 1, 1990, the Iraqi representative walked out, complaining of Kuwait's failure to discuss Iraqi territorial claims or to forgive Iraq's debts.

But by this time, Iraq had already massed some eight divisions on the Kuwaiti border, and at 1:00 A.M. (Kuwaiti time) on August 2, the Iraqi invasion of Kuwait began. It is obvious in retrospect that Iraq never intended to negotiate an end to the crisis. Its political maneuverings were designed to buy time for its final military preparations and to give an air of legitimacy to the invasion.

Iraq justified its aggression in terms of claims dating back to 1961, when Great Britain ended its protectorate over Kuwait. At that time, Iraq claimed that Kuwait was an integral part of Iraq because it had been part of the former Ottoman province of Al-Basrah. But by reviving such old claims, Saddam Hussein almost guaranteed the enmity of the Gulf Cooperation Council states, because the territorial boundaries of all of those countries rested on equally shaky grounds. And by threatening the industrialized nations' access to Middle East oil, he guaranteed the intervention of the United States, Great Britain and France. His blatant cross-border invasion of a peaceful neighbor, in direct violation of the United Nations Charter, helped mobilize almost the entire world against him.

See also LISTINGS FOR INDIVIDUAL COUNTRIES; ARAB LEAGUE; BAATH PARTY; BRIGHT STAR EXERCISES; CARTER DOCTRINE; CENTCOM; GLASPIE; APRIL; GULF COOPERATION COUNCIL; INVASION OF KUWAIT; IRAN-IRAQ WAR; IRAQGATE; ISLAM; LAND TRANSPORTATION NETWORK; SOVIET UNION.

Suggestions for further reading: For geographic factors, see Lt. Gen. John Yeosock, "Army Operations in the Gulf Theater," *Military Review,* September 1991; John Collins, "Military Geography of Iraq and Adjacent Arab Territory," *CRS Report for Congress,* September 7, 1991. For historical background, see Halim Barakat, *The Arab World: Society, Culture and State* (Berkeley: University of California Press, 1993); Michah L. Sifry and Christopher Serf, eds., *The Gulf War Reader* (New York: Times Books, 1991).

Part II

the persian gulf war: chronology 1990–1991

1990

February 19

At Arab Cooperation Council (ACC) meeting, President Saddam Hussein of Iraq says he will take $30 billion debt forgiveness for granted, but expects $30 billion more as Gulf states' share of cost of Iran-Iraq War.

May 28–30

At Arab League summit in Baghdad, Saddam Hussein complains that overproduction of oil by Kuwait and United Arab Emirates (UAE) is "economic warfare" against Iraq.

July 15

Iraq accuses Kuwait of stealing oil from al-Rumaylah oil field, which straddles the Iraqi-Kuwaiti border.

July 17

Saddam Hussein warns of military action if Kuwait does not desist from "econmic warfare" against Iraq.

July 18

Kuwait calls military alert.

July 22

Iraqi military buildup against Kuwait begins.

July 23

Saudi Arabia places its armed forces on alert.

July 24

U.S. Navy warships and aircraft begin a "short-notice exercise" with United Arab Emirate warships in the Persian Gulf.

July 25

Saddam Hussein summons U.S. Ambassador April Glaspie for talks in Baghdad. According to Glaspie, he informs her that Iraq will not use force against Kuwait, and that he wants improved relations between Baghdad and Washington. According to Hussein, she assures him that the United States has no

interest in Iraq's long-standing border dispute with Kuwait.

July 31

Iraq masses more than 100,000 troops on Kuwaiti border.

August 1

Iraq breaks off talks with Kuwait.

August 2

At 1:00 A.M. (Gulf time), Iraq invades and occupies Kuwait, seizing Kuwaiti oil fields. Kuwait's emir flees to Saudi Arabia. Iraq masses troops along the Saudi border.

United Nations Security Council (UNSC) meets in New York, and by a vote of 14 to 0 (Yemen abstaining) passes UNSC Resolution 660, condemning Iraq's invasion of Kuwait and demanding immediate withdrawal. U.S. National Security Council (NSC) meets in Washington. President George Bush condemns Iraq's invasion as an act of naked aggression and orders extra warships to the Gulf.

August 3

U.S.-USSR joint statement condemns Iraqi invasion.

USSR freezes arms shipments to Iraq.

Iraq promises to withdraw from Kuwait by August 5.

August 4

U.S. Central Command (CENTCOM) at MacDill Air Force Base in Tampa, Florida, is alerted for possible operations in the Gulf.

Fifty U.S. Navy ships are ordered to the Gulf region.

British and French warships steam toward the Gulf.

August 6

UN Security Council, by a vote of 13 to 0 (Cuba and Yemen abstaining), passes UNSC Resolution 661, imposing trade embargo on Iraq.

U.S. Secretary of Defense Dick Cheney meets with Saudi Arabian government to pledge U.S. support and to secure access to bases. Saudi king Fahd formally asks the United States and other friendly states to provide military assistance.

U.S. Navy Carrier Battle Group Independence arrives in Gulf of Oman.

Several hundred Westerners in Kuwait, including 28 Americans, are taken to Baghdad.

August 7 (C-Day)

At Saudi Arabia's request, U.S. troops are ordered to Saudi Arabia to defend against a possible Iraqi attack.

The 1st Tactical Fighter Wing begins deployment from Langley Air Force Base in Virginia.

XVIII Airborne Corps, 24th Infantry Division (Mechanized), 101st Airborne Division (Air Assault), 1st Cavalry Division with 1st Brigade, 2d Armored Division and 3d Armored Cavalry Regiment are alerted.

The 82d Airborne Division begins deploying from Fort Bragg, North Carolina.

Turkey cuts off Iraqi oil pipelines.

August 8

Iraqi president Saddam Hussein proclaims annexation of Kuwait.

August 9

First U.S. military forces arrive in Saudi Arabia.

UN Security Council, by a vote of 15 to 0, passes UNSC Resolution 662, declaring the Iraqi annexation of Kuwait to be void.

August 10

Arab League votes 12 to 9 to send Arab troops to Saudi Arabia.

Saddam Hussein declares a "jihad," or holy war, against the United States and Israel.

Iraq gives foreign governments until August 24 to close their embassies in Kuwait.

General H. Norman Schwarzkopf, commander in chief, U.S. Central Command (CENTCOM), is named commander of Operation Desert Shield, the code name for the defensive or buildup phase of the Gulf War.

August 11

First contingent of Egyptian troops arrives in Saudi Arabia.

August 12

Naval blockade of Iraq begins. All shipments of Iraqi oil are halted.

August 13

FSS (Fast Support Ship) Capella, the first of 10 ships, sails from Savannah, Georgia, with armored vehicles of the 24th Infantry Division (Mechanized).

August 14

U.S. Transportation Command activates the Fleet Ready Reserve, 71 standby cargo ships manned by civilian merchant mariners.

The First Marine Expeditionary Force arrives in Saudi Arabia.

August 15

In a bid to win Iranian support, Saddam Hussein withdraws Iraqi troops from all Iranian territories seized during the 1980–1988 Iran-Iraq War, releases all Iranian prisoners of war, and renounces his claim to the Shatt-al-Arab waterway, the very reason for the Iran-Iraq War.

August 16

U.S. Navy establishes "interception zones" in Red Sea, Gulf of Aden, Gulf of Oman and Persian Gulf to prevent prohibited cargo from reaching or leaving Iraqi and Kuwaiti ports or Al-Aqabah, Jordan.

August 17

Saddam Hussein's government declares all Westerners in Iraq "members of aggressive countries" and announces that it has moved Western captives to vital military installations, where they will be used as human shields.

For the first time, President Bush calls Westerners held captive in Iraq "hostages."

U.S. Transportation Command activates the Civil Air Reserve Fleet.

USS *John I. Hall* intercepts the Iraqi tanker *Al-Fao* in the Red Sea; USS *England* intercepts *Al-Abid* and *Al-Byaa* in the Persian Gulf.

First elements of 101st Airborne Division (Air Assault) begin deploying from Fort Campbell, Kentucky, to Saudi Arabia.

August 18

UN Security Council, in a unanimous vote, passes UNSC Resolution 664, demanding the immediate release of hostages.

August 19

Egyptian troop strength in Saudi Arabia reaches 5,000; Morocco has 1,000 troops deployed there as well.

August 20

United Arab Emirates grant U.S. forces access to bases.

A U.S. Air Force F-117 squadron arrives in Saudi Arabia.

August 22

President Bush signs an Executive Order authorizing the call-up of up to 200,000 reservists.

The United States orders 40,000 reservists to active duty.

Saudi Arabia agrees to provide fuel for U.S. forces on its territory.

August 23

Saddam Hussein appears on television with Western hostages, including children.

August 24

Six Iraqi Republican Guard armored divisions regroup in strategic reserve south of Basra in southern Iraq after withdrawing from forward positions in kuwait.

Iraqi forces in Kuwait begin construction of defensive positions.

August 24

United States and other nations defy Iraqi ultimatum to close embassies in Kuwait. Iraqi troops ring Western embassies in Kuwait, including the U.S. mission, and detain some 100 U.S. Embassy staff members and their dependents.

August 25

UN Security Council, by a vote of 13 to 0 (Cuba and Yemen abstaining), passes UNSC Resolution 665, authorizing the use of force to enforce trade sanctions against Iraq.

August 26

U.S. Central Command relocates its command post from MacDill Air Force Base, Florida, to Riyadh, Saudi Arabia.

Three Spanish ships set sail for Persian Gulf.

The USSR announces it will not deploy its military forces in the Gulf.

August 28

Iraq declares Kuwait its 19th province and renames Kuwait City al-Kadhima.

Saddam Hussein says he will release women and children hostages.

United States announces that its goal is Iraqi withdrawal from Kuwait "without violence."

August 30

President Bush stops short of demanding the removal of Saddam Hussein from power.

September 6

Total number of Western hostages held by Iraq reported to be 11,000.

September 7

Two brigades of 24th Infantry Division (Mechanized), with tanks and armored vehicles, are deployed in Saudi Arabia.

September 13

United Nations Security Council, by a vote of 13 to 2 (Cuba and Yemen against), passes UNSC Resolution

666, reaffirming Iraqi responsibility for safety of foreign nationals.

September 14

United Kingdom (UK) announces it will send 6,000 troops and 129 tanks to the Gulf.

September 15

France announces it will send 4,000 troops to the Gulf.

United States is reported to have more than 150,000 troops, 420 combat aircraft and 250 support aircraft in the Gulf.

September 16

United Nations Security Council, by unanimous vote, passes UNSC Resolution 667, condemning Iraq for violation of embassies in Kuwait and committing UN members to "further actions."

September 17

General Michael J. Dugan is relieved as Air Force chief of staff for making unauthorized public comments on how the United States will fight the war.

September 18

Pentagon reports Iraqi military buildup in Kuwait totals 365,000 troops, 2,800 tanks, 1,800 other armored vehicles and 1,450 artillery pieces.

Argentina announces it will send troops to the Gulf.

September 23

French Foreign Legion's 1st Parachute Regiment and 2,600 men of French Army's 6th Light Armored Division arrive in Saudi Arabia as part of the French Rapid Intervention Force.

September 24

United Nations Security Council, by unanimous vote, passes UNSC Resolution 669, stating that only its Special Sanctions Committee can authorize food and aid shipments to Iraq or Kuwait.

September 25

United Nations Security Council, by a vote of 14 to 1 (Cuba against), passes UNSC Resolution 670, expanding the trade embargo to include air traffic and calling on UN members to detain Iraqi ships that could be used to break the embargo.

September 26

U.S. Transportation Command announces that only 14 of 41 Ready Reserve Fleet ships met their activation schedule, forcing the leasing of foreign cargo ships.

Egyptian 3d Mechanized Division arrives in Saudi Arabia.

September 27

United Kingdom and Iran reestablish diplomatic relations.

September 30

French Rapid Intervention Force's 4,000 men are deployed in Saudi Arabia.

October 1

U.S. House of Representatives votes 380 to 20 for resolution supporting President Bush's actions in the Gulf.

U.S. Marines practice assault landings on Arabian Peninsula.

October 2

U.S. Senate votes 90 to 3 for resolution supporting President Bush's actions in the Gulf.

October 8

Israel begins distributing gas masks to its citizens after Iraq's warning that it has a new missile, the "Hijara," that can reach deep within Israel.

October 15

Iran and Iraq restore diplomatic relations.

October 17

First elements of UK 7th Armoured Brigade arrive in Saudi Arabia.

October 20

Antiwar marches occur in 15 major cities across United States.

October 23

Pentagon reports United States has more than 210,000 troops in Gulf region, including 100,000 Army personnel and 45,000 Marines, 11,000 of whom are on ships offshore.

President Bush warns Iraq that no compromise is possible on UN Security Council Resolution requiring Iraqi withdrawal from Kuwait.

October 29

UN Security Council, by a vote of 13 to 0 (Cuba and Yemen abstaining), passes UNSC Resolution 674, condemning Iraq's mistreatment and repression of Kuwaitis.

November 1

U.S. Marines conduct second amphibious landing exercise in the Gulf.

President Bush compares Saddam Hussein to Adolf Hitler.

November 4

Syrian 9th Armored Division begins arriving in Saudi Arabia.

November 6

Saddam Hussein relieves General Nazir Khazara as chief of staff of Iraqi armed forces.

President Bush announces allied coalition will be reinforced to provide for an adequate offensive military option; he orders some 200,000 additional U.S. troops to the Gulf.

VII Corps—including 1st Armored Division, 2d Armored Division (Forward), 3d Armored Division and 2d Armored Cavalry Regiment—is ordered to deploy from Germany to the Gulf.

November 8

The 1st Infantry Division (Mechanized), stationed at Fort Riley, Kansas, is ordered to the Gulf.

The 2d Marine Division at Camp Lejeune, North Carolina, is ordered to the Gulf.

The 5th Marine Expeditionary Brigade is ordered to the Gulf.

Reserve call-up time extended from 90 days to 180 days.

November 14

Defense Department authorizes call-up of 72,500 additional reservists.

November 15

Imminent Thunder, an amphibious assault exercise involving U.S. Navy and Marine forces and U.S. and Royal Saudi Air Forces, is conducted 100 miles south of Kuwaiti border.

Catholic bishops caution that offensive action in Gulf may not be a "just war."

National Council of Churches rebukes U.S. Gulf policy.

November 18

U.S. Embassy in Baghdad reports that 104 Americans are being used as human shields by Iraq.

November 19

Iraq announces mobilization of reserves and deployment of 250,000 more troops to Kuwait, including up to 150,000 reservists.

November 20

Iraq announces release of all German hostages.

Forty-five congressmen seek U.S. District Court injunction to prevent President Bush from ordering attack without Congressional approval.

November 21

President Bush arrives in Saudi Arabia for visit with troops.

U.S. National Guard combat brigades ordered to active duty.

November 22

United Kingdom announces it will send 14,000 more troops and additional combat aircraft to the Gulf, raising its total troop strength there to 30,000.

November 23

In a leadership battle within England's Conservative Party, Margaret Thatcher resigns as prime minister.

November 27

Senate Armed Services Committee begins hearings on Gulf crisis.

November 28

John Major officially appointed British prime minister.

UN Security Council, by unanimous vote, approves UNSC Resolution 677, demanding that Iraq cease altering Kuwait's demographic composition and stop destroying Kuwaiti civil records.

In Senate Armed Services Committee hearings, two former chairmen of the Joint Chiefs of Staff, Admiral William Crowe and General David Jones of the Air Force, counsel waiting for sanctions to soften Iraqi intransigence.

November 29

UN Security Council, by a vote of 12 to 2 (Cuba and Yemen against, China abstaining), approves UNSC Resolution 678, authorizing UN members to use "all necessary means" to enforce previous UNSC resolutions if Iraq does not leave Kuwait by January 15, 1991.

December 1

United States and Iraq agree to talks on Kuwait crisis.

December 3

Secretary of Defense Cheney announces U.S. force levels in Saudi Arabia have reached 240,000. Iraqi forces in Kuwaiti Theater of Operations (KTO) are estimated at 450,000.

December 4

House Armed Services Committee begins hearings on the crisis in the Persian Gulf.

U.S. Army's 2d Armored Cavalry Regiment becomes first of VII Corps forces to depart Germany for Saudi Arabia.

December 5

Secretary of States James Baker tells House Armed Services Committee that sanctions alone will not compel Iraq to withdraw from Kuwait.

Central Intelligence Agency (CIA) director William H. Webster tells House Armed Services Committee that sanctions could take nine more months to become effective, but gives no assurance of success.

December 6

Saddam Hussein announces release of all Western hostages.

December 11

Saddam Hussein fires Defense Minister General Abdel-Jabbar Shanshal; Major General Saadi Tuma Abbas is named defense minister.

United States announces that all American hostages who wanted to leave Iraq and Kuwait have now left; about 500 voluntarily chose to remain.

December 12

French government sends more aircraft and an additional 4,000 men to the Gulf, where 6,000 French troops are already deployed.

December 14

U.S. Ambassador Nathaniel Howell closes U.S. Embassy in Kuwait.

December 17

British Embassy, the last functioning Western embassy in Kuwait, is closed.

UN deadline for Iraqi withdrawal from Kuwait is fixed at 2100 hours (9:00 P.M.) on January 15, 1991.

December 18

Saddam Hussein rejects all UN resolutions, saying "Kuwait will remain an integral part of Iraq forever."

UN General Assembly votes 144 to 1 to condemn Iraqi human rights violations in Kuwait.

Naval blockade forces have intercepted 5,500 ships, boarded more than 500 and turned back 24.

December 19

Lieutenant General Calvin A. H. Waller, deputy commander in chief, U.S. Central Command, reports that "every unit will not be combat ready until after February 1."

Turkey asks North Atlantic Treaty Organization (NATO) to send air forces to bolster its defenses.

December 22

In an accident, USS *Saratoga* launch ferrying sailors to shore for liberty sinks off Haifa, Israel, killing 21 sailors.

December 26

Defense Department reports that 300,000 U.S. military personnel are in Gulf, including 180,000 in Army, 50,000 in Marine Corps, 35,000 in Navy and 35,000 in Air Force.

December 28

USS *Roosevelt* and USS *America* carrier battle groups sail for Gulf.

December 29

Poland sends two ships and a medical team to the Gulf.

1991

January 2

Turkey's request for reinforcements is approved by NATO.

U.S. Fifth Marine Expeditionary Brigade sets sail from San Diego, California, for the Gulf.

UK 4th Armoured Brigade becomes operational in Saudi Arabia.

January 3

U.S. Congress reconvenes.

Defense Department issues press rules on war coverage.

January 7

Speaker of the House of Representatives Thomas S. Foley announces that on January 10 the House will begin debating a resolution authorizing the use of force in the Gulf.

Defense Department announces estimates of Iraqi forces in Kuwaiti Theater of Operations (KTO): 537,000 men, 4,000 main battle tanks, 2,700 armored fighting vehicles, 3,000 artillery pieces and 700 combat aircraft plus helicopters.

Defense Department imposes censorship on war reporting by the press.

Six U.S. Special Operations helicopters returning to Saudi Arabia from covert operations in Kuwaiti Theater of Operations are mistakenly reported as being Iraqi defectors.

January 8

President Bush sends to Congress a letter asking for endorsement of the "all necessary means" language of UNSC Resolution 678, which authorized member nations to use military force to enforce UN resolutions on Kuwait.

January 9

Six-hour meeting in Geneva between Secretary of State James Baker and Foreign Minister Tariq Aziz of Iraq ends in stalemate.

Pakistan sends 5,000 more troops to Gulf, raising its total there to 10,000.

Iraq reiterates that it will attack Israel in the event of war.

U.S. Central Command acknowledges that none of VII Corps's three divisions will be fully deployed by January 15.

January 10

U.S. House and Senate begin debate on use of force in Gulf.

Air elements of NATO's Allied Command Europe (ACE) Mobile Force arrive in Turkey.

January 12

Congress, by votes of 250 to 183 in the House of Representatives and 52 to 47 in the Senate, grants President Bush the authority to "use all necessary means" (i.e., to wage war) to enforce UN resolutions against Iraq.

United States closes its embassy in Baghdad.

January 16

French National Assembly approves French participation in military action in the Gulf. French forces are placed under U.S. operational control.

Greece approves U.S. use of its bases and ports for logistical support.

H-hour for Operation Desert Storm is set for 1900 hours (7:00 P.M.) eastern standard time (0300 [3:00 A.M.] Baghdad time, January 17).

January 17 (D-Day)

Coalition air campaign begins with preliminary strikes at early-warning radar control stations throughout Iraq at 2:51 A.M. Baghdad time.

Operation Desert Storm officially begins at 3:00 A.M. Baghdad time.

Senate passes resolution commending President Bush and troops.

January 18

Coalition planes drop 2,500 tons of ordnance in first 24 hours of Gulf War.

Allied air sortie rate is 2,000 per day.

U.S. B-52 bombers strike Iraqi Republican Guard positions.

Iraq launches Scud missiles at Israel and Saudi Arabia.

World leaders condemn Iraqi missile attacks on Israel.

Egypt says it would tolerate Israeli retaliation against Iraq for missile attacks. Syria indicates it also might tolerate Israeli retaliation.

President Bush signs an Executive Order authorizing the retainment of reserves on active duty beyond 180 days and a call-up of an additional 1 million reserves if needed.

U.S. House of Representatives approves resolution of support for Gulf War.

United States launches air strikes against Iraq from Incirlik Air Base in Turkey.

January 19

Scud missiles strike Israel.

United States deploys two Patriot surface-to-air missile batteries to Israel.

Coalition naval forces recapture nine Kuwaiti oil platforms in the Gulf and capture 12 Iraqis.

Approximately 25,000 antiwar protestors march in Washington, D.C.

Iraq orders all foreign correspondents except Peter Arnett of Cable News Network (CNN) to leave the country.

January 20

Scud missiles strike Israel and Saudi Arabia.

Iraqis parade blindfolded allied prisoners of war (POWs) through Baghdad's streets; seven POWs are interviewed on Iraqi television.

Defense Department announces call-up of an additional 20,000 reservists.

January 21

Iraq announces it will use allied POWs as human shields.

Coalition air sorties flown to date number 8,100.

Scud missiles are fired at Riyadh and Dhahran, Saudi Arabia; none hits targets.

President Bush declares the KTO a combat zone.

Syria says it will not quit alliance against Iraq if Israel retaliates for Iraqi Scud attacks.

January 22

U.S. Navy reports Iraqi minelayer was sunk in Persian Gulf.

Patrol of U.S. 3d Armored Cavalry Regiment captures six Iraqis.

Iraq begins blowing up oil wells in Kuwait.

Scud missiles strike Israel and Saudi Arabia.

Iraq reports its civilian casualties to date are 41 killed and 191 wounded in coalition air attacks.

Iraq displays two more allied POWs on television.

January 23

Allied air attacks on Iraqi aircraft shelters begin.

CNN's Peter Arnett claims that United States bombed "baby milk factory" in Baghdad; United States says it struck a biological warfare facility.

January 24

A Saudi Arabian F-15C aircraft shoots down two Iraqi Mirage FC-1s.

Allied sorties flown to date total 15,000; losses include 11 U.S., one UK, one Kuwaiti and one Italian aircraft.

Coalition forces in Gulf total 624,000 military personnel, including 487,000 U.S. troops.

Kuwaiti island of Qaruh is recaptured, with 51 Iraqis taken prisoner.

January 25

Iraqi Air Force and Air Defense commanders are reportedly executed.

Iraq sabotages Kuwait's Sea Island supertanker terminal and begins "environmental war," pumping millions of gallons of crude oil into the Gulf.

Seven Scud missiles strike Israel.

Coalition air sorties to date total 17,500.

Qatari F-1 Mirage aircraft join coalition air campaign.

January 26

Iraqi Air Force planes begin fleeing to Iran; by war's end, some 109 fixed-wing Combat Aircraft will have sought sanctuary there.

Scud missiles are fired at Riyadh, Saudi Arabia.

The last of VII Corps's heavy equipment arrives in Saudi Arabia.

In their first use in combat, army tactical missile system (ATACMS) missiles attack an Iraqi surface-to-air missile (SAM) site.

January 27

U.S. aircraft target oil-pumping facilities in Kuwait to halt discharge of oil into the Gulf.

Two U.S. F-15s shoot down four Iraqi MiG-23s.

Twenty-three Iraqi aircraft flee to Iran, bringing the total there to 39. Iran say all Iraqi aircraft will be confiscated.

Four Scud missiles aimed at Israel are reportedly intercepted by U.S. Patriot missiles.

One Scud missile aimed at Riyadh is reportedly intercepted by a Patriot missile.

January 28

Coalition air force announces achievement of "air supremacy" over the region and "air superiority" on a local basis.

Coalition air sorties total 24,000.

Iraqi aircraft in Iran total more than 80.

Iraq claims its civilian casualties have reached 324 killed and more than 400 wounded.

Coalition naval forces report that 15 Iraqi naval vessels have been destroyed to date.

Scud are fired at Israel and Saudi Arabia.

January 29

President Bush gives State of the Union address to Congress, including report on progress of Desert Storm.

Iraqi aircraft in Iran total 90.

January 30

First major ground battle of war takes place at Khafji, Saudi Arabia, between Iraqi forces and coalition forces of Saudi Arabia, Qatar and U.S. Marines. Iraqi forces briefly occupy the town.

Coalition naval forces report the sinking of three Iraqi vessels near Bubiyan Island; 35 Iraqis are taken prisoner.

January 31

Saudi forces recapture Khafji.

UK Royal Air Force (RAF) Tornado aircraft destroys Scud launcher in first use of BL-755 cluster bomb.

UK 1st Armoured Division is declared operational.

Army Specialist Melissa A. Rathbun-Nealy is first female U.S. soldier taken prisoner by Iraqi forces.

February 1

Coalition air sorties to date total 35,000, including 19,000 flown by U.S. planes.

France allows U.S. B-52 bombers enroute from bases in UK to Persian Gulf to overfly French airspace.

Secretary of Defense Dick Cheney warns that the United States will retaliate with "strong measures" if Iraq uses chemical weapons or other weapons of mass destruction.

Radio Iraq says captured allied airmen should be treated as war criminals, not POWs.

February 2

Coalition air forces have destroyed 100 Iraqi aircraft on the ground.

Scud missiles are fired at Israel and Saudi Arabia; two hit Arab-populated West Bank.

U.S. Defense Department spokesman says the Bush administration "does not want, will not ask Congress for, and does not feel we need the draft."

February 3

Bomb tonnage dropped on Iraq exceeds the 2,150,000 total tons dropped during all of World War II by U.S. forces.

U.S. B-52 bomber crashes in Indian Ocean; three crewmen are missing in action.

Scud missiles are fired at Israel and Saudi Arabia.

More than 600 Iraqi POWs are in allied hands.

February 4

The 16-inch guns of the battleship USS *Missouri* fire on targets in Kuwaiti Theater of Operations.

Iraq severs diplomatic ties with Egypt, France, United Kingdom and Saudi Arabia.

Coalition air sorties flown to date total 44,000, of which 27,000 are combat missions.

U.S. Marines engage Iraqi forces in skirmish at Umm Gadar on Saudi-Kuwaiti border.

State Department advises all U.S. citizens to leave Jordan.

February 5

President Bush says he is skeptical that airpower alone can prevail in Gulf War.

President Bush says he has "absolutely no intention of reinstating the draft."

One third of the bridges over Euphrates and Tigris Rivers reportedly have been destroyed by coalition air strikes.

Syrian forces skirmish with Iraqi troops along Kuwaiti border.

Saudi naval patrol boats destroy one Iraqi patrol boat and damage two others off the coast near Khafji, Saudi Arabia.

Iraq says its civilian casualties from allied bombing now total more than 428 killed and 650 wounded.

February 6

Iraqi aircraft that have fled to Iran now total 115, including 33 civil aircraft.

Coalition naval forces report the destruction of 41 Iraqi ships to date, including 23 combatants, and the damaging of 42 others, including 34 combatants.

Two U.S. F-15s shoot down four Iraqi jets fleeing to Iran.

February 7

Iraq begins destroying Kuwaiti oil fields.

Coaltion air forces report the destruction of 31 of the 38 bridges leading into the Kuwaiti Theater of Operations, the most recent being the al-Jomhouriya bridge over the Tigris River.

A Scud missile is intercepted by a Patriot missile over Riyadh.

The 16-inch guns of the battleship USS *Wisconsin* engage Iraqi targets.

UK Royal Navy Sea Lynx helicopters destroy an Iraqi patrol vessel.

A U.S. A-10 aircraft shoots down an Iraqi helicopter.

Iran reports that five Iraqi planes crashed while trying to reach safety there.

February 8

Secretary of Defense Dick Cheney and Joint Chiefs of Staff chairman General Colin Powell arrive in Saudi Arabia to finalize plans for ground campaign.

U.S. troop strength in Gulf now totals 505,228.

Six hundred Iraqi main battle tanks and 400 Iraqi artillery pieces reportedly have been destroyed to date.

Iraqi POWs in allied hands total 936.

Thirteen Iraqi jets flee to Iran; total number there is 147.

A Scud missile is fired at Saudi Arabia.

February 9

Coalition estimates that 750 of 4,000 Iraqi tanks have been destroyed, in addition to 600 of 4,000 armored fighting vehicles and 650 of 3,200 artillery pieces.

A Scud missile fired at Israel injures 26 people.

Iraq formally notifies United States of break in diplomatic relations.

February 10

Soviet president Mikhail Gorbachev says United States is overstepping UN mandate in its attacks on Iraq.

Air sorties of coalition forces now total 60,000.

February 11

President Bush approves plan for launching ground attack within a given "window of opportunity," saying allies will also continue with "very, very effective" air campaign "for a while."

Three hundred Afghan Mujahedeen join allied forces in Gulf.

Iraq calls its 17-year-olds to military service.

Scuds are fired at Israel and Saudi Arabia.

February 12

U.S., UK and French defense ministers meet in Washington, D.C.

Heavy air bombardment of Baghdad takes place.

Three major bridges over Tigris and Euphrates Rivers are destroyed.

Scud missiles are fired at Israel and Saudi Arabia.

U.S. and UK aircraft destroy an Iraqi patrol boat near Faylakah Island.

More than 50 oil fires burn in Kuwait.

February 13

Iraq claims coalition bombing of air raid shelter in Baghdad killed 400 persons, many of them members of families of ruling Baath Party elite. United States claims the target that was destroyed was a military command center.

Estimated Iraqi losses now total 1,320 main battle tanks, 800 armored fighting vehicles and 1,100 artillery pieces.

February 14

Scud missiles fired at Israel explode in air.

French premier Michel Rocard visits Saudi Arabia.

February 15

Coalition air forces begin using 10,000-pound BLU-82 "daisy cutters" and fuel air explosive (FAE) bombs against Iraqi entrenchments.

German Air Force air defense units deploy to Turkey.

President Bush announces "42 Scuds engaged [by Patriot missiles], 41 intercepted" since start of war.

Iraq announces that CBS newsman Bob Simon and his crew were captured on January 21 and are being held as POWs in Baghdad.

February 16

U.S. troop strength in Gulf reaches 535,000.

All U.S. ground forces are now in position to begin ground offensive.

Estimated Iraqi losses now total 1,400 tanks, 800 armored fighting vehicles and 1,200 artillery pieces.

Scud missiles are fired against Israel and Saudi Arabia.

U.S. attack helicopters make first cross-border strikes into Kuwait and Iraq.

February 17

Iraqi foreign minister Tariq Aziz arrives in Moscow to confer with Soviet president Mikhail Gorbachev.

Scuds fired at Israel's Dimona nuclear facility land harmlessly in Negev Desert.

Air sorties flown by coalition forces total 80,000 thus far.

In a "friendly fire" incident during a border skirmish, a U.S. helicopter kills two U.S. soldiers and wounds six.

February 18

A Soviet-Iraqi "Eight-Point Plan for Peace" is announced in Moscow.

Thirty-five Scud missiles have been fired at Israel thus far in the war, resulting in 2 deaths and 230 injuries.

U.S. 1st Infantry Division fires massive artillery barrage at Iraqi fortifications.

Persian Gulf oil spill now extends 100 miles to the south.

Coalition air sorties flown thus far total 82,000.

U.S. VII and XVIII Corps continue deploying westward to initial attack positions.

Cruiser USS *Princeton* and amphibious assault ship USS *Tripoli* are damaged by Iraqi mines in Persian Gulf.

February 19

President Bush says Soviet peace plan "falls well short" of UN demand for unconditional Iraqi withdrawal from Kuwait.

A Scud missile is fired at Israel.

Oil spill in Gulf estimated to be 1.5 million barrels.

February 20

Coalition air losses now total 36 aircraft, including 23 fixed-wing lost in combat and 5 fixed-wing and 8 helicopters lost in noncombat actions.

Coalition air sorties flown thus far total 86,000, including 3,500 flown from Turkey.

February 21

Iraq accepts Soviet peace proposal.

Saddam Hussein announces: "We will win the Mother of all Battles against the forces of Satan."

Allies bomb Baghdad in daylight.

Scud and Frog missiles are fired at Saudi Arabia.

National Defense Service Medal is awarded to all U.S. military personnel on active duty worldwide.

February 22

President Bush issues 24-hour ultimatum: Iraq must withdraw from Kuwait by 1200 eastern standard time February 23 (2000 hours [8:00 P.M.] Baghdad time) in order to avert a ground war.

Coalition air sorties flown thus far total 90,000.

A Scud missile hits Bahrain.

One hundred and forty Kuwaiti oil wells have been set afire by Iraq.

Soviet president Gorbachev announces a new "Six-Point Plan for Peace."

Between 50,000 tons and 54,000 tons of bombs reportedly have been dropped on Iraq and Kuwait since the start of air campaign. "Smart" bombs are said to account for 5 to 10 percent of total.

Allies use napalm strikes to set Iraqi "fire trenches" ablaze.

February 23

The Soviets' last-minute peace initiative collapses.

President Bush authorizes General Schwarzkopf to begin ground campaign.

February 24 (G-Day)

At 0400 (4:00 A.M.) Gulf time (2000 hours [8:00 P.M.] eastern standard time 23 February) the ground campaign begins.

With an amphibious presence afloat off the Kuwaiti coast, 4th Marine Expeditionary Brigade ties down four Iraqi divisions in coastal defense.

The 5th Marine Expeditionary Brigade disembarks to become a reserve for First Marine Expeditionary Force.

First Marine Expeditionary Force attacks north through Iraqi barrier system toward Kuwait.

Arab coalition forces attack north through barrier system toward Kuwait.

VII Corps, with UK 1st Armoured Division, and XVII Airborne Corps conduct wide turning movement to west.

In a heliborne air assault, U.S. 101st Airborne Division (Air Assault) establishes forward operating base Cobra 93 miles behind Iraqi lines.

The 6th French Armored Division and a brigade of U.S. 82d Airborne Division attack to seize Alcimon Airfield and to screen coalition's western flank.

More than 10,000 Iraqis are taken prisoner in first 24 hours of ground war.

February 25 (G +1)

Coalition ground forces continue their rapid movement with light casualties.

In a heliborne assault, elements of 101st Airborne Division (Air Assault) establish blocking positions 155 miles behind enemy lines to cut Iraqi main supply route in Euphrates Valley.

An Iraqi Scud missile scores a direct hit on U.S. barracks in Dhahran, Saudi Arabia: 28 U.S. soldiers are killed, including the first American enlisted women ever killed in combat, and 100 are wounded.

February 26 (G +2)

Marines reach outskirts of Kuwait City and hold in place to await coalition forces that will liberate the city.

At 1120 hours (11:20 A.M.) Gulf time (0320 hours [3:20 A.M.] eastern standard time), Saddam Hussein announces Iraqi's withdrawal from Kuwait.

At 9:45 A.M. eastern standard time, President Bush rejects Saddam Hussein's announcement as "an outrage" and says "coalition will continue to prosecute the war with undiminished intensity."

The 2d Armored Cavalry Regiment fights the battle of 73 Easting (a north-south map grid-line location in Iraq near the Kuwaiti border) with the Iraqi Republican Guard's Tawakalna Division.

VII Corps attacks Iraqi Revolutionary Guard divisions along Kuwait's western border.

Forces of XVIII Corps reach Euphrates Valley.

Iraqi forces are in massive disorganized retreat. Coalition intelligence reports 21 Iraqi divisions have been rendered combat ineffective, with losses of 2,085 tanks and 1,005 artillery pieces.

More than 30,000 Iraqis are POWs.

More than 600 oil wells are set afire by retreating Iraqis.

February 27 (G +3)

Coalition forces enter Kuwait City in triumph.

In one of the largest battles of the war, 2d Brigade of U.S. 1st Armored Division fights battle of "Medina Ridge" against 2d Brigade of Iraqi Republican Guard's Medina Division in Iraq.

U.S. 2d Armored Division (Forward) fights battle of "Norfolk" in Iraq.

U.S. 24th Infantry Division (Mechanized) conducts the fastest moving attack in the annals of warfare, having covered 368 kilometers in four days.

A U.S. A-10 aircraft mistakenly kills nine UK soldiers.

Army Major Rhonda Cornum becomes the second female U.S. POW when her helicopter is shot down behind Iraqi lines.

At 2100 hours (9:00 P.M. eastern standard time), President Bush declares that Kuwait is liberated and Iraq is defeated. He announces that coalition will suspend ground combat operations 100 hours after they began.

At 2300 hours (11:00 P.M. eastern standard time), Iraq delivers letter to UN, saying it will comply with all 12 UNSC resolutions.

February 28 (G +4)

At 0800 (8:00 A.M.) Gulf time (2400 hours [12:00 P.M. eastern standard time] 27 February), coalition forces suspend operations.

Coalition air sorties flown to date: 110,000.

U.S. combat casualties to date: 89 killed in action, 213 wounded in action, 44 missing in action (MIA).

Estimated number of Iraqi POWs held by coalition: 80,000.

March 1

Two U.S. servicemen are killed by mines.

Army helicopter pilot Major Marie T. Rossi becomes the 13th U.S. female service member killed in the Persian Gulf War when her helicopter hits an unlit tower in bad weather and crashes.

A total of 148 allied military personnel, including 89 Americans, have died in combat during the war.

March 2

Retreating Iraqi armor engages U.S. forces: 140 Iraqi armored vehicles are destroyed or captured.

Two more U.S. servicemen are killed by mines. Death toll for American military personnel is now 91.

At request of Soviet Union, Iraq releases CBS News correspondent Bob Simon and his crew, who were held as POWs for 40 days.

March 2

Security Council, by a vote of 11 to 1 (Cuba against, Yemen, China and India abstaining), adopts UNSC Resolution 686, demanding that Iraq cease hostile action, release all POWs and detainees, rescind its annexation of Kuwait, accept liability for damages to Kuwait, return property stolen from Kuwait and disclose locations of mines.

March 3

General Schwarzkopf meets with Iraqi generals, who agree to provide information about location of minefields and to release prisoners.

Iraqi foreign minister Tariq Aziz sends letter to UN, agreeing to the cease-fire terms of UNSC Resolution 686.

Iraq has blown up 535 Kuwaiti oil wells; 800 of Kuwait's 1080 wells are inoperable.

March 5

Thirty-five allied POWs, 15 of them Americans, are repatriated, including the two U.S. female POWs.

All allied MIAs are accounted for. With recovery of bodies, the total number of Americans killed in action stands at 123.

U.S. aircraft dropped a total of 88,500 tons of bombs, including 6,520 tons of "smart" weapons, in the war.

Coalition reports capturing or destroying 3,900 Iraqi tanks, 1,500 Iraqi armored fighting vehicles and 3,000 Iraqi artillery pieces.

For information on events following the ceasefire, see KURDS; MINESWEEPING; SANCTIONS; SHIITE REVOLT; TOMAHAWK LAND ATTACK MISSILE; WAR TERMINATION.

Part III

---

the persian
gulf war: a to z

A

A-10 THUNDERBOLT II "WARTHOG"

The A-10 Thunderbolt II, affectionately known as the "Warthog" because of its ugly appearance, was the U.S. Air Force's chief antitank weapon in the Persian Gulf War. With a top speed of 423 miles per hour and a combat radius of 288 miles, the A-10 was designed specifically for close air support (CAS) of ground forces. The OA-10 has the same airframe, modified for forward air control.

The cockpit area, flight control systems and engines are encased in titanium armor plating for protection, and a 700-pound titanium tub protects the pilot. The twin jet engines are mounted so as to make them less vulnerable to ground fire, and they have no hot exhaust or afterburners that heat-seeking ground-to-air missiles could home in on.

The seven-barrel GAU-8/A Avenger 30 mm nose-mounted cannon can shoot 70 rounds of depleted-uranium armor-piercing ammunition per second from its 1,174-round magazine. The A-10's eleven external wing points can carry an additional 16,000-pound weapon load, including the tank-killing Maverick air-to-ground precision-guided missile, conventional and laser-guided bombs, rocket pods, gun pods, or Sidewinder air-to-air missiles.

Based at King Fahd International Airport and using King Khalid Military City as their forward operating base, the 136 A-10s and 12 OA-10s were

The war's premier tank-killer aircraft, the A-10 flew more than 8,000 combat sorties.
Central Command Public Affairs.

flown primarily by U.S. Air National Guard and Air Force Reserve pilots called to active duty.

During the course of the war, these aircraft flew 8,077 combat sorties, of which fewer than 1,000 were CAS missions. Scud missile and tank hunting, suppression of enemy air defenses, and armed road reconnaissance were among their other duties.

A-10s fired 4,801 Maverick missiles with a 94 percent reliability rate. In one action, two A-10 pilots destroyed 23 enemy tanks in 6 sorties. Overall, A-10 pilots claimed 1,000 enemy tanks, 2,000 other vehicles and 1,200 artillery pieces destroyed, and two enemy helicopters shot down.

Five A-10s were lost to enemy fire, and a sixth was so badly damaged it could not be repaired.

See also ARMOR; DEPLETED URANIUM; FRIENDLY FIRE; MAVERICK ANTITANK MISSILE.

Suggestions for further reading: Department of Defense, *Conduct of the Persian Gulf War: Final Report to the Congress,* "Appendix T: Performance of Selected Weapons Systems" (Washington, D.C.: USGPO, 1992); Eliot A. Cohen et al., *Gulf War Airpower Survey* (Washington, D.C.: USGPO, 1993); William L. Smallwood, *Warthog: Flying the A-10 in the Gulf War* (MacLean, Va.: Brassey's, 1993); Richard P. Hallion, *Storm Over Iraq: Air Power and the Gulf War* (Washington, D.C.: Smithsonian Institution Press, 1992); Fred Kaplan, "Beast of Battle," *Boston Globe Magazine,* July 21, 1991.

ABCCC (AIRBORNE BATTLEFIELD COMMAND AND CONTROL CENTER)

Growing out of the Vietnam War, the Airborne Battlefield Command and Control Center (ABCCC) was intended as the ground-strike equivalent of the Airborne Warning and Control System (AWACS) that controls air-to-air operations. A command, control, communications and computer system with 12 battle-management workstations (each with four megabytes of random-access memory (RAM), real-time access to a suite of tactical databases, and a four-disk optical storage subsystem with 1.6 gigabytes of mass memory, ABCCC received data both by voice and from such electronic sources as the Joint Surveillance Target Attack Radar System (JSTARS).

Mounted in EC-130E aircraft, the two ABCCCs deployed to the Persian Gulf flew more than 40 missions and logged more than 400 flight hours. They were used to provide tactical information, in-

cluding target description, target location and position of friendly forces. ABCCCs also furnished target acquisition data to ground commanders and assisted in search and rescue (SAR) operations.

The Central Command (CENTCOM) Air Force commander reportedly also used ABCCC as a command-and-control platform from which to fight the air-to-air and air-to-ground battles. Workstations were manned by battle managers drawn from the U.S. Army, Marines and Air Force, as well as from allied personnel; they followed the battle on digitalized maps displayed on high-resolution-graphics monitors. When a soldier on the ground called for air support, the ABCCC could divert a flight to the location and pass on to the pilot all-source target details.

See also ATO (AIR TASKING ORDER); AWACS (AIRBORNE WARNING AND CONTROL SYSTEM); COMPUTER WAR; JSTARS (JOINT SURVEILLANCE TARGET ATTACK SYSTEM).

Suggestions for further reading: Norman Friedman, *Desert Victory: The War for Kuwait* (Annapolis, Md.: Naval Institute Press, 1991).

ABRAMS M1A1 TANK

The Abrams M1A1 main battle tank was the primary U.S. ground offensive weapon in the Gulf War, and as such it spearheaded the drive into Iraq. Two models were deployed to the Gulf: the M1A1, which incorporates a protective NBC (nuclear-biological-chemical) overpressure package and a microclimatic cooling system, as well as thermal sights, laser rangefinders and full shoot-on-the-move stabilization; and the M1A1 Heavy Armor (HA) model, which has additional depleted-uranium armor plating.

With a weight of 67 tons and a crew of four, the Abrams has a 1,500-horsepower turbine engine and an improved suspension system that allow it to traverse the battlefield at top speeds of 41.5 miles per hour. Its main shortcoming is its low fuel mileage. With a 498-gallon fuel capacity, the Abrams has a cruising range of about 280 miles and an operational range of about 130 miles.

The Abrams's main armament is the M256 120-mm smooth bore cannon. The tank carries a basic load of 40 cannon rounds, including the kinetic-energy M829 armor-piercing, fin-stabilized discarding sabot with tracer (APFSDS-T), which features a combustible cartridge case, a one-piece depleted ura-

The world's best main battle tank, the Abrams led the ground attack in the Gulf War.
Central Command Public Affairs.

nium penetrator and a discarding aluminum sabot. As the shell flies toward its target, the aluminum sabot falls away and the penetrator, a dense metal dart, continues at a speed of about one mile per second and penetrates the enemy's armor with brute force.

The other standard round used by the Abrams is the M830 high-explosive anti-tank multipurpose with tracer (HEAT-MP-T), also with a combustible cartridge case, whose shaped-charge warhead explodes as it hits the target. The force of the explosion is concentrated at the round's tip, creating a jet of molten metal that can burn through armor plate. The Abrams also mounts one M2 .50-caliber and two M240 7.62-mm machine guns.

The improved M1A1 version of the Abrams tank had been furnished to Army units in Germany, including VII Corps, which spearheaded the main attack in the Gulf War. But armor units in the United States such as the 1st Cavalry Division, the 24th Infantry Division (Mechanized) and the 3d Armored Cavalry Regiment that ultimately deployed to the

Gulf were equipped with an earlier model of the Abrams tank, the M1, which mounted a 105-mm gun and lacked the NBC protective system and other upgrades. Marine units were equipped with an even earlier tank, the M60A3, which also carried a 105-mm gun, as were some of the coalition forces.

Before the ground war began, a major effort was made to reequip all U.S. units with the newer M1A1s in order to meet the Iraqi armor and chemical threat. The Army fielded 1,178 M1A1s and 594 M1A1s (HA), and the Marine Corps 16 M1A1s and 60 M1A1s (HA).

In the opening days of Desert Shield, there was much speculation that the Abrams tanks would not be able to function effectively in the deserts. This proved not to be the case. Combat readiness rates were greater than 90 percent. The 3d Armored Division, for example, moved more than 300 tanks at night across 200 kilometers without any breakdowns. The tanks' combat effectiveness was phenomenal: the median target detection range of their thermal-imaging systems was 2,600 meters, and as a result M1A1 crews were able to "see first, shoot first" and engage well beyond the range of the Iraqi T-72 tanks.

Many of the Abrams tanks' first-round hits occurred on the move at 15 to 25 kilometers per hour, and the 120-mm ammunition achieved catastrophic kills against the enemy's T-72 tanks even when the latter were behind thick berms. At the battle of Medina Ridge, for example, the 2d Brigade, 1st Armored Division destroyed 100 Iraqi tanks and more than 30 BMPS (armored fighting vehicles) in a 45-minute battle.

Only three Abrams tanks were damaged by enemy fire during Desert Storm. According to reports, several M1A1s received direct hits from enemy 125-mm armor-piercing ammunition without a single penetration. Nine of the 18 combat damage incidents involving the Abrams were the result of friendly fire, and most of the others were caused by mines.

See also ARMOR; DEPLETED URANIUM; FRIENDLY FIRE.

Suggestions for further reading: Department of Defense, *Conduct of the Persian Gulf War: Final Report to the Congress,* "Appendix T: Performance of Selected Weapons Systems" (Washington, D.C.: USGPO, 1992); *Weapons Systems of the United States Army* (Washington, D.C.: USGPO, 1989); Orr Kelly, *King of the Killing Zone: The Story of the M1, America's Super Tank* (New York: W. W. Norton, 1989); Richard P. Hallion, *Storm Over Iraq: Air Power and the Gulf War* (Washington, D.C.: Smithsonian Institution Press, 1992).

ACE

See AERIAL COMBAT.

ADVISORY EFFORT, U.S.

Although there was no U.S. advisory effort in the Gulf comparable to that of KMAG (Korean Military Advisory Group) in the Korean War or MACV (Military Assistance Command Vietnam) in the Vietnam War, the United States did provide some combat training and assistance to allied forces in the Gulf War. The majority of such operations were conducted by SOCCENT (Special Operations Command, CENTCOM) and subordinate SOF (special operations forces) units. As discussed elsewhere (see SPECIAL OPERATIONS COMMAND CENTRAL COM-

MAND), these specially trained Army, Navy and Air Force units are organized for just such missions.

One mission was to train Royal Saudi Forces and set up combined surveillance teams along the border. Another was to reconstitute the Kuwaiti armed forces and to train a Special Forces (SF) battalion and a commando brigade organized from former Kuwaiti military personnel. With a training site at KKMC (King Khalid Military City) in Saudi Arabia, SOCCENT's 5th Special Forces Group began the training program in mid-September 1990. The mission was expanded to encompass four new Kuwaiti infantry brigades. On February 26, 1991, the SF battalion, the Al-Tahir Commando Brigade, and the Al-Khulud, Al-Haq, Fatah and Badr Infantry Brigades, totalling 6,357 personnel, joined coalition forces for the ground offensive.

The reconstitution of the Kuwaiti Navy also began in September 1990. SOCCENT's SEAL (sea-air-land) and SBU (Special Boat Unit) personnel from Navy Special Warfare Task Group Central (NSWTG-CEN) played a key role in preparing the warships *Sawahil, Istiglal* and *Sambovk* for combat operations.

Specially tailored Coordination and Training Teams (CTTs) were also created by SOCCENT to work with coalition forces. Initially limited to the Royal Saudi Land Forces and the Saudi Arabian National Guard, the program was later expanded to include forces from Egypt, Syria, Oman, Morocco, Bahrain, the United Arab Emirates, Qatar and France. Eventually, 109 CTTs were created.

Language-qualified SOF liaison teams also linked the CENTCOM manuever planning staff and the Arab-Islamic units. The teams passed situation reports through the U.S. chain of command and provided coordination between adjacent coalition forces.

One of the more unusual advisory efforts was that of training female recruits for the United Arab Emirates (UAE) Army. At the UAE's request, the United States organized the first all-female technical assistance field team at Fort Bragg, North Carolina. Under the command of Major Janis Karpinski of the Army, the 10-woman team arrived in Abu Dhabi in October 1990, and each member spent two days living with an Emirate family to begin her adjustment to the Arab culture.

Seventy-five Emirate women were selected from the 1,200 volunteers for the program. Fifteen

**Operation Desert Storm Air-to-Air Victories by Coalition Air Forces, 17 January to 28 February.
Source: Joint Staff/J3 (Joint Operations Division).**

Date	Shooter Aircraft	Type Downed	Weapon Used
Jan. 17	F-15C	MIG-29	AIM 7
Jan. 17	F-15C	F-1 Mirage	AIM 7
Jan. 17	F-15C	2 F-1 Mirages	AIM 7
Jan. 17	F-15C	MIG-29	AIM 7
Jan. 17	F-15C	MIG-29	AIM 7
Jan. 17	F/A-18	MIG-21	AIM 9
Jan. 17	F/A-18	MIG-21	AIM 7
Jan. 19	F-15C	MIG-25	AIM 7
Jan. 19	F-15C	MIG-25	AIM 7
Jan. 19	F-15C	MIG-29	AIM 7
Jan. 19	F-15C	MIG-29	AIM 7
Jan. 19	F-15C	F-1 Mirage	AIM 7
Jan. 19	F-15C	F-1 Mirage	AIM 7
Jan. 24	F-15C	2 F-1 Mirages	AIM 9
Jan. 26	F-15C	MIG-23	AIM 7
Jan. 26	F-15C	MIG-23	AIM 7
Jan. 26	F-15C	MIG-23	AIM 7
Jan. 27	F-15C	2 MIG-23s	AIM 9
Jan. 27	F-15C	MIG-23	AIM 7
Jan. 27	F-15C	F-1 Mirage	AIM 7
Jan. 28	F-15C	MIG-23	AIM 7
Jan. 29	F-15C	MIG-23	AIM 7
Feb. 2	F-15C	IL-76	AIM 7
Feb. 6	F-15C	2 SU-25s	AIM 9
Feb. 6	F-15C	2 MIG-21s	AIM 9
Feb. 6	A-10	Helo	Gun
Feb. 6	F-14A	Helo	AIM 9
Feb. 7	F-15C	2 SU-7/17s	AIM 7
Feb. 7	F-15C	SU-7/17	AIM 7
Feb. 7	F-15C	Helo	AIM 7
Feb. 11	F-15C	Helo	AIM 7
Feb. 15	A-10	MI-8 Helo	Gun

dropped out during the first weeks because of the rigorous American-style basic training, but the remainder did well; two were selected to attend the British military academy at Sandhurst. After their graduation, 25 of the women were selected as cadres to train new recruits, and the American female soldiers reverted to an advisory role.

One of the factors that made cooperation between the United States and its Arab allies easier was the existence of long-standing U.S. military assistance and military training programs with most of the Arab nations. Many of the senior Arab officers had trained at U.S. military schools. For example, Saudi Arabian Lieutenant General Khalid Bin Sultan Bin Abdulaziz, the commander of Joint Forces/Theater of Operations (i.e., General Schwarzkopf's Arab counterpart), had attended the U.S. Air War College in Alabama.

See also SPECIAL OPERATIONS COMMAND CENTRAL COMMAND (SOCCENT).

Suggestions for further reading: Department of Defense, *Conduct of the Persian Gulf War: Final Report to the Congress*, "Annex I: Coalition Development, Coordination and Warfare," and "Annex J: Special Operations Forces" (Washington, D.C.: USGPO, 1992); Geraldine Brooks, "The Metamorphosis: Women Warriors Join an Arab Army," *Wall Street Journal*, August 8, 1991.

AERIAL COMBAT

"Air superiority," the dominance of a group of aircraft in a given time and space without prohibitive interference by the opposing force, and preferably "air supremacy," the degree of air superiority in which the enemy is incapable of effective interference, are the prerequisites for successful ground combat operations. To that end, coalition air forces gained air superiority within the first hours of the start of the air campaign on January 17, 1991, and air supremacy was announced on January 27, 1991. The Iraqi Air Force had been swept from the skies.

Forty-one Iraqi aircraft—35 fixed-wing and 6 helicopters—were shot down during Operation Desert Storm, including two Su-22 fighter-bombers destroyed in March 1991 after the informal cease-fire had been declared. Of these 41 "kills" 33 (and 1 probable) were by U.S. Air Force F-15C Eagles, 16 (and 1 probable) were by the 33d Tactical Fighter Wing (TFW) from Eglin Air Force Base (AFB) in

Florida, 15 were by the 36th TFW from Bitburg Air Base in Germany, one was by aircraft of the 1st TFW from Langley AFB in Virginia and one was by aircraft of the 32d Tactical Fighter Group (TFG) from Soesterberg Air Base in the Netherlands.

Two Iraqi helicopters were shot down by 30-mm cannon fire from A-10 Warthogs of the Air Force Reserve's 926th TFG from New Orleans, Louisiana. Three Iraqi aircraft were shot down by Navy pilots—two MiG-21s by F/A-18 Hornets from the USS *Saratoga* and one helicopter by an F-14A Tomcat from the USS *Ranger*. The only non-U.S. air-to-air kills were by a Royal Saudi Air Force F-15 Eagle that shot down two Iraqi Mirage fighters with AIM-9 Sidewinder missiles.

Although Sidewinder missiles were responsible for many U.S. Air Force and Navy kills, the AIM-7 Sparrow missile was the most frequently used Air Force weapons system. For the first time in warfare, nearly half of the Sparrow kills were made beyond visual range, the pilots relying on cockpit electronics and AWACS (airborne warning and control system) aircraft for target location.

Although one critic has claimed that a Navy F/A-18 Hornet was shot down by an Iraqi MiG-25 (the loss was officially blamed on a surface-to-air missile), the Department of Defense has stated that no U.S. aircraft were lost in air-to-air combat.

There were no "aces" (i.e., pilots credited with five or more kills) in the Persian Gulf War, but one pilot reportedly had three kills and two others each had two shoot-downs.

See also A-10 THUNDERBOLT II "WARTHOG"; AIR CAMPAIGN; AIRCRAFT CARRIERS; AIR FORCE, IRAQI; AIR FORCES, COALITION; AIR FORCE, U.S.; FIGHTERS AND FIGHTER-BOMBERS; SIDEWINDER (AIM-9) AIR-TO-AIR MISSILE; SPARROW (AIM-7) AIR-TO-AIR MISSILE.

Suggestions for further reading: Department of Defense, *Conduct of the Persian Gulf War: Final Report to the Congress*, "Chapter VI: The Air Campaign" and "Appendix T: Performance of Selected Weapons Systems" (Washington, D.C.: USGPO, 1992); Richard P. Hallion, *Storm Over Iraq: Air Power and the Gulf War* (Washington, D.C.: Smithsonian Institution Press, 1992); Bruce W. Watson, ed., *Military Lessons of the Gulf War* (Novato, Calif.: Presidio Press, 1991); Mark Crispin Miller, "Death of a Fighter Pilot," *New York Times*, September 15, 1992.

Air Force KC-135 Stratotankers, such as the one refueling this Navy A6-E Intruder squadron, were indispensable to the air effort in the Gulf. U.S. Navy photo (CDR John Leenhouts), Empire Press.

AERIAL REFUELING

Aerial refueling played a critical role in the Gulf War air campaign. Originally developed by the Strategic Air Command (SAC) to refuel its intercontinental nuclear bombers, aerial refueling actually proved its worth in Vietnam. SAC tankers refueled B-52 bombers en route to Vietnam from bases in Guam and Okinawa, and they also refueled fighters and fighter-bombers over both North and South Vietnam.

The most common aerial refueling tanker in the Gulf War was the KC-135 Stratotanker, the military version of the Boeing 707 airliner, which began operations in 1957. There was also the newer KC-10 Extender, a military version of the McDonnel-Douglas DC-10, which entered service in 1981. The KC-10 has four times the range of the KC-135. Both can haul troops and cargo as well as fuel, and in the Gulf, KC-135s flew 913 airlift sorties.

During Operation Desert Storm and Operation Desert Shield, 262 KC-135s and 46 KC-10s were committed. In addition to the SAC tankers, air refueling groups and air refueling wings from the Air National Guard and Air Force Reserve were also mobilized for service in the Gulf; aircraft from these units made up some 37 percent of the coalition's tanker fleet.

Facilitating the Air Force's response at the beginning of the Gulf crisis was the fact that during a training exercise with Gulf nations in July 1990, SAC had moved two KC-10 and 72 KC-135 tanker aircraft into the area; these were in place at the outset of the crisis, and they made possible the strategic air bridge between the United States and Saudi Arabia.

Tactically, aerial refueling tankers played an equally key role. For example, when the air war began on January 17, 1991, some 160 tankers—including U.S. KC-10s and KC-135s, British Victors and Tristars and VC1OKs, and Royal Saudi Air Force KE-3Bs—were already aloft and flying multiple refueling tracks outside of Iraqi radar.

In addition to refueling the aircraft of the Air Force, Navy and Marines, U.S. aerial tankers also refueled aircraft of the armed forces of Italy, Oman, Bahrain, Saudi Arabia and the UAE. The KC-135 tankers alone flew almost 23,000 refueling sorties, delivering more than 136 million gallons of fuel to more than 69,000 receivers.

See also AIR CAMPAIGN; STRATEGIC AIR COMMAND (SAC); TRANSPORTATION COMMAND (TRANSCOM).

Suggestions for further reading: Department of Defense, *Conduct of the Persian Gulf War: Final Report to the Congress,* "Appendix T: Performance of Selected Weapons Systems" (Washington, D.C.: USGPO, 1992); Richard P. Hallion, *Storm Over Iraq: Air Power and the Gulf War* (Washington, D.C.: Smithsonian Institution Press, 1992); Bruce W. Watson, ed., *Military Lessons of the Gulf War* (Novato, Calif.: Presidio Press, 1991), which has an appendix listing the Air Refueling Groups and Wings mobilized for the Gulf War; James Blackwell, *Thunder in the Gulf* (New York: Bantam, 1991).

AEROMEDICAL EVACUATION

See MEDICAL CARE AND EVACUATION, COALITION.

AFGHANISTAN

See COALITION FORCES.

AFLOAT PREPOSITIONING SHIPS (APS)

In strategic terms, the United States is a world island, and one of its major problems is bringing its military power to bear overseas. Although airlift can rapidly move troops into distant crisis areas, it takes weeks to transport their tanks, artillery and other heavy equipment by sea.

The solution for reinforcement of NATO forces was POMCUS (prepositioned material configured for unit sets), an acronym for the stockpiling of a unit's heavy equipment in Europe for immediate issue to troops coming in by air. At the outbreak of the Kuwaiti crisis, the Army had POMCUS stockpiles for two armored divisions, three mechanized divisions, a light infantry division and an armored cavalry regiment stored in Europe (70 percent of the equipment was in Germany). Much of this materièl was later moved to the Gulf to upgrade the units there.

But prior to the war, POMCUS was not a viable alternative in the Gulf. For political reasons, none of the countries in the region would permit such stockpiling on their territory. The solution was to preposition equipment on merchant ships, some of them anchored at the island of Diego Garcia, a British possession in the Indian Ocean. The Navy and Marines maintained 13 such ships, which were organized into three maritime prepositioning squadrons

(MPS). The Army and the Air Force kept their equipment aboard 11 afloat prepositioning ships (APS).

When the crisis began, there were at Diego Garcia two APS tankers with water and fuel; four lighter-aboard ships (LASH), including two with Air Force ammunition; two break-bulk cargo ships; and one float-on-float-off (FloFlo) ship with small harbor craft and barges. These ships set sail at the beginning of the crisis and arrived in Saudi Arabia on August 17, 1990. Their cargo included subsistence, ammunition, construction and barrier material, packaged fuel and medical supplies.

See also LOGISTICS, U.S.; MARITIME PREPOSITION-ING SQUADRONS (MPS).

Suggestions for further reading: Department of Defense, *Conduct of the Persian Gulf War: Final Report to the Congress,* "Appendix E: Deployment" and "Appendix F: Logistical Buildup and Sustainment" (Washington, D.C.: USGPO, 1992); Norman Friedman, *Desert Victory: The War for Kuwait* (Annapolis, Md.: Naval Institute Press, 1991); "The United States," in *The Military Balance 1990–1991* (London: International Institute for Strategic Studies, 1990).

AGM (AIR-TO-GROUND MISSILE)
See MAVERICK ANTITANK MISSILE (AGM-65).

AIR ASSAULT:
See 101ST AIRBORNE DIVISION (AIR ASSAULT).

AIR CAMPAIGN
The 43-day air campaign waged by coalition air forces during the Gulf War was an integral part of the overall CENTCOM (Central Command) campaign plan to oust Iraqi forces from Kuwait. Planned, coordinated and executed by the CENTAF (Air Force Central Command) commander, U.S. Air Force Lieutenant General Charles A. Horner, and his staff, it was one of the most brilliantly executed air campaigns in history.

One of the reasons for its success was that, unlike the fragmented command structures of air campaigns of past wars, unity of command (and hence unity of effort) was achieved in the Gulf War through the formal establishment of the AFCENT commander as the joint forces air component commander (JFACC). As such, he was in charge of more than 2,700 coalition aircraft representing 14 separate national or service components.

Another reason why the campaign was successful was its detailed planning. At the very beginning of the Gulf crisis, a Pentagon Air Staff planning group called "Checkmate" prepared a concept plan labeled "Instant Thunder." The title was meant to convey that the Gulf War air campaign would differ radically from the prolonged, graduated "Rolling Thunder" campaign of the Vietnam War, which was intended to send "signals" to the enemy. "Instant Thunder" would concentrate instead on warfighting. It was designed to quickly paralyze the Iraqi leadership, degrade its military capability and neutralize its will to fight. In addition, the Navy Operational Intelligence Center's Strike Projection Evaluation and Antiair Research (SPEAR) team helped to complete the picture of Iraq's integrated air defenses.

In the fall of 1990, the JFACC's planners merged CENTAF's predeployment concept of operations with the Air Staff's "Instant Thunder" concepts to form the foundation for the Operation Desert Storm air campaign. A special planning group (SPG) was formed at CENTAF headquarters in the Royal Saudi Air Force (RSAF) building in Riyadh.

Working in what came to be known as the "Black Hole" because of the extreme secrecy surrounding its activities, the SPG was headed by Brigadier General Buster C. Glossen (USAF). Although U.S. Air Force personnel predominated, the 30-member staff included representatives of the U.S. Army, Navy and Marines as well as of the British Royal Air Force. It was also augmented by the Air Force and Navy's "Checkmate" and SPEAR planners.

The plan for the air campaign was aimed at achieving five primary military objectives. The first was to isolate and incapacitate the Iraqi regime. The second objective was to gain and maintain air supremacy. The third was to destroy Iraq's NBC (nuclear-biological-chemical) warfare capability. The fourth objective was to eliminate Iraq's offensive military capability by destroying key military production and power-projection capabilities and infrastructure. The final task was to render ineffective the Iraqi Army and its mechanized equipment.

The JFACC's objectives in the air campaign were set forth in a Master Attack Plan (MAP) and further refined in the Air Tasking Order. Taking the enemy centers of gravity identified by CINCCENT (commander in chief, Central Command) whose destruction was deemed essential for achieving the war's stated objectives, JFACC identified 12 target sets. These included Iraq's leadership command facilities; electricity production facilities; telecommunications and command, control and communication nodes; the strategic integrated air defense system; air forces and airfields; nuclear, biological and chemical weapons research, production and storage facilities; Scud missiles, launchers, and production and storage facilities; naval forces and port facilities; oil refining

Navy attack aircraft such as these A-6E Intruders and F/A-18 Hornets on the carrier USS *Saratoga* **(CV-60) flew 23 percent of the strike missions.**   Navy photo (CWO Ed Bailey), Empire Press.

Vietnam-War vintage F-111 Aardvarks flew from bases in Saudi Arabia and Turkey in support of the air campaign. Central Command Public Affairs.

and distribution facilities; railroads and bridges; Iraqi army units, including Republican Guard forces in the Kuwaiti Theater of Operations (KTO); and military storage and production sites.

A JFACC master strategic target list was then developed, based on these 12 categories as well as on timely analysis of bomb damage assessment (BDA), changing target priorities and other political and combat developments. Constraints were also imposed on the targets that could be struck, including avoiding collateral damage, minimizing civilian casualties, and scrupulously avoiding damage to mosques, religious shrines and archeological sites.

"The result of this planning," according to the official Department of Defense report on the war, "was a relatively compact document . . . that integrated all attacking elements into force packages and provided strategic coherency and timing. . . . The MAP drove the process."

The air campaign was divided into four phases. The strategic air campaign made up Phase I. Achieving air superiority and suppressing or eliminating Iraqi ground-based air defenses in the KTO were the focus of Phase II. Preparation of the battlefield and reducing Iraqi combat efficiency, and particularly the efficiency of the Republican Guard, were the objective of Phase III. Phase IV was support of the ground offensive.

H-Hour for the air campaign, 3:00 A.M. local time, January 17, 1991, was marked by an attack on Baghdad itself by F-117 Stealth aircraft and Tomahawk cruise missiles, as well as by strikes on strategic targets throughout Iraq by coalition aircraft. By D+10 (January 27), the Iraqi Air Force was no longer an effective combat force: air supremacy had been achieved by the coalition.

By January 31, the beginning of the third week of the campaign, the focus of attack shifted from strategic objectives to the Iraqi Republican Guard in the KTO. Having learned that infrared sensors could detect buried Iraqi armor, aircraft began "tank plinking" with GBU-12 500-pound laser-guided bombs. PSYOPS (Psychological Operations), such as the dropping of millions of leaflets over enemy positions, were also conducted.

Prior to the beginning of the ground campaign on February 24, 1991 (G-Day), coalition aircraft had flown nearly 100,000 sorties, 60 percent of which were combat missions. In addition, 288 Tomahawk missiles and 35 ALCMs (air-launched cruise missiles) had been launched at strategic targets. Damage to Iraqi forces was extensive. Coalition estimates were that the combat effectiveness of the Republican Guard had been reduced by 25 percent, and that of frontline forces by about 50 percent.

To assist in the breaching of enemy defenses, B-52 bombers bombed the Iraqi minefields with 750-pound M-117 and 500-pound Mk-82 bombs, while MC-130 aircraft dropped 15,000-pound BLU-82 bombs to create overpressure to detonate the mines. Fuel-air explosives were also used. Marine AV-8Bs dropped napalm on Iraqi fire trenches (i.e., barrier trenches filled with oil that would be ignited to foil an attack) to burn off the fuel.

During the four days before G-Day, nearly 90 percent of the combat sorties were directed at enemy armor, artillery and combat fortifications. Pilots reported destroying 178 tanks, 92 armored personnel carriers, 290 other vehicles, 201 artillery pieces or multiple rocket launchers, 66 revetments and bunkers and two AAA/SAM (antiaircraft artillery/surface-to-air missile) sites.

When the ground campaign began, coalition aircraft struck frontline Iraqi positions, continued their interdiction of the battlefield, and began providing close air support for the attacking forces. Because of the coalition's rapid ground advance, however, more of the air effort was expended on interdiction than on close air support.

"My private conviction is that this is the first time in history that a field army has been defeated by air power," said Air Force chief of staff General Merrill A. McPeak in the aftermath of the Gulf War. As discussed elsewhere (see AIRPOWER), the overwhelming success of the air campaign revived the argument about whether airpower alone can be decisive in winning a war.

But no one doubts that the Gulf War air campaign was critical to Desert Storm's ultimate success.

See also A-10 THUNDERBOLT II "WARTHOG"; ABCCC (AIRBORNE BATTLEFIELD COMMAND AND CONTROL CENTER); AERIAL COMBAT; AERIAL REFUELING; AFLOAT PREPOSITIONING SHIPS (APS); AIR CAMPAIGN; AIRCRAFT CARRIERS; AIR DEFENSES; AIRFIELDS; AIR FORCE CROSS; AIR FORCE, IRAQ; AIR FORCES, COALITION; AIR-LAUNCHED CRUISE MISSILE; AIRLIFT; AIR MEDAL; AIRPOWER; ATO (AIR TASKING ORDER); AWACS (AIRBORNE WARNING AND CONTROL SYSTEM); B-52 STRATOFORTRESS BOMBER; CHIEF OF STAFF, U.S. AIR FORCE; CLOSE AIR SUPPORT (CAS); COMPUTER WAR; CRAF (CIVIL RESERVE AIR FLEET); DRONES AND DECOYS; EW ELECTRONIC WARFARE (EW); FAC (FORWARD AIR CONTROLLER); FIGHTERS AND FIGHTER-BOMBERS; FRIENDLY FIRE; GROUND CAMPAIGN; GUNSHIPS; HIGH TECHNOLOGY; JSTARS (JOINT SURVEILLANCE TARGET ATTACK SYSTEM); JUST WAR; MOBILIZATION, U.S.; NINTH U.S. AIR FORCE; RECONNAISSANCE; SCUD MISSILES; SEARCH AND RESCUE (SAR); SMART BOMBS; SORTIES; SPECIAL OPERATIONS COMMAND CENTRAL COMMAND (SOCCENT); STEALTH AIRCRAFT; STRATEGIC AIR COMMAND (SAC); 3D MARINE AIRCRAFT WING; TRANSPORTATION COMMAND (TRANSCOM); WILD WEASEL.

Suggestions for further reading: Department of Defense, *Conduct of the Persian Gulf War: Final Report to the Congress,* "Chapter VI: The Air Campaign" (Washington, D.C.: USGPO, 1992); Department of the Air Force, *Reaching Globally, Reaching Powerfully: The United States Air Force in the Gulf War* (Washington, D.C.: USGPO, September 1991); Eliot A. Cohen et. al., *Gulf War Airpower Survey* (Washington, D.C.: USGPO, 1993); Norman Friedman, *Desert Victory: The War for Kuwait* (Annapolis, Md.: Naval Institute Press, 1991); Richard P. Hallion, *Storm Over Iraq: Air Power and the Gulf War* (Washington, D.C.: Smithsonian Institution Press, 1992), which has a detailed analysis of the air campaign, Bruce W. Watson, ed., *Military Lessons of the Gulf War* (Novato, Calif.: Presidio Press, 1991); Captain Lyle G. Bien, USN, "From the Strike Cell," *U.S. Naval Institute Proceedings,* June 1991; Commander Daniel J. Muir, USN, "A View from the Black Hole," *U.S. Naval Institute Proceedings,* October 1991. For the air campaign's genesis, see

John A. Warden III, *The Air Campaign: Planning for Combat* (Washington, D.C.: National Defense University Press, 1989). The best concise analysis is Michael A. Palmer, "The Storm in the Air: One Plan, Two Air Wars?" *Air Power History,* Winter 1992.

AIRCRAFT CARRIERS

Although the French aircraft carrier *Clemenceau* was used to transport troops and helicopters to the Gulf, and British Sea King and Lynx helicopter Naval Air Squadrons were deployed on Royal Navy destroyers

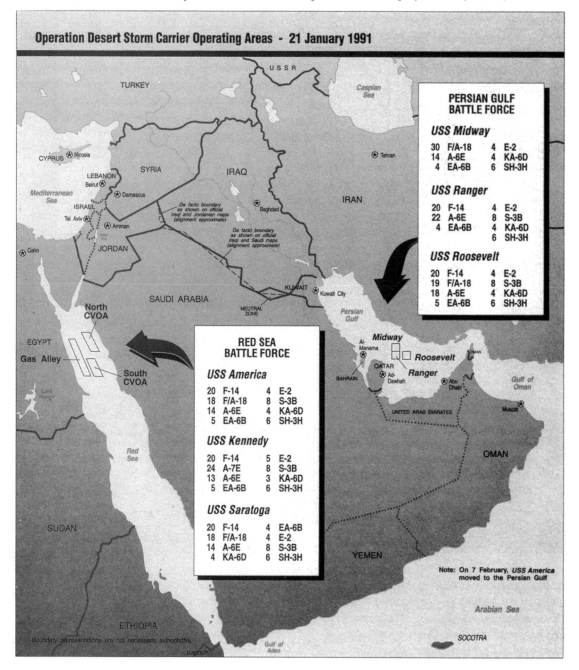

Operation Desert Storm Carrier Operating Areas - 21 January 1991

PERSIAN GULF BATTLE FORCE

USS Midway

30	F/A-18	4	E-2
14	A-6E	4	KA-6D
4	EA-6B	6	SH-3H

USS Ranger

20	F-14	4	E-2
22	A-6E	8	S-3B
4	EA-6B	4	KA-6D
		6	SH-3H

USS Roosevelt

20	F-14	4	E-2
19	F/A-18	8	S-3B
18	A-6E	4	KA-6D
5	EA-6B	6	SH-3H

RED SEA BATTLE FORCE

USS America

20	F-14	4	E-2
18	F/A-18	8	S-3B
14	A-6E	4	KA-6D
5	EA-6B	6	SH-3H

USS Kennedy

20	F-14	5	E-2
24	A-7E	8	S-3B
13	A-6E	3	KA-6D
5	EA-6B	6	SH-3H

USS Saratoga

20	F-14	4	EA-6B
18	F/A-18	4	E-2
14	A-6E	8	S-3B
4	KA-6D	6	SH-3H

Note: On 7 February, *USS America* moved to the Persian Gulf

Boundary representations are not necessarily authoritative.

and frigates, the United States was the only nation to provide operational aircraft carriers in the Persian Gulf War. Before the crisis began, U.S. aircraft carriers were on station to "show the flag" and to demonstrate the degree of U.S. interest in the region. And when the crisis began, they were there to provide air support to coalition forces.

On August 7, 1990, when President George Bush made the decision to commit U.S. forces in the Middle East, the USS *Dwight D. Eisenhower* (CVN-69) and the USS *Independence* (CV-62) carrier battle groups were already on station in the Red Sea. Relieved by the USS *John F. Kennedy* (CV-67), *Saratoga* (CV-60) and *America* (CV-66) carrier battle groups before the air campaign began on January 17, 1991 (local time), these Red Sea carriers concentrated their attacks on targets in western Iraq and in the Baghdad area. From the Persian Gulf, strikes were launched on targets in southeastern Iraq from the USS *Midway* (CV-41) and *Ranger* (CV-61); these were joined on January 19 by the USS *Theodore Roosevelt* (CVN-71) and on February 7 by the *America*, which shifted from the Red Sea to the Gulf to add strike support for the ground campaign.

Directed by the air tasking orders (ATOs) of the Joint Forces Air Component Commander (JFACC), Navy carrier-based aircraft took part in all phases of the air campaign. Navy E-2C Hawkeyes assisted Air Force E-3C Sentry aircraft warning and control (AWACS) in directing the complex air effort, while Navy EA-6B Prowlers assisted in the jamming of enemy radars. F-14 Tomcats equipped with TARPS (tactical air reconnaissance pod systems) flew BDA (bomb damage assessment) and battlefield reconnaissance. F-14s also flew combat air patrols against Iraqi interceptors (MiGCAP), and A-6E *Intruders* and F/A-18 Hornets suppressed enemy air defenses, interdicted enemy lines of supply and communication and helped sweep the Iraqi Navy from the Gulf. Three Iraqi aircraft were shot down by Navy planes—two MiG-21s by F/A-18s from the *Saratoga,* and one helicopter by an F-14 from the *Ranger.*

Seven Navy aircraft were lost in combat: two F/A-18s, one F-14A, and four A-6E. Four additional aircraft were lost due to noncombat causes, including one A-6E, one F/A 18, one SH-60 Sea Hawk helicopter and one CH-46 Sea Knight helicopter.

In the first 48 hours of the air war, Navy pilots flew 60 percent of the air defense suppression missions.

The USS *Independence* (CV-62) was one of six carrier action groups deployed to the KTO.
Central Command Public Affairs.

Overall, they flew some 18,624 sorties, 23 percent of the coalition's total combat missions.

See also AERIAL COMBAT; AIR CAMPAIGN; AIR DEFENSES; AIR FORCE, U.S.; AIRPOWER; ATO (AIR TASKING ORDER); FIGHTERS AND FIGHTER-BOMBERS; MARITIME CAMPAIGN; NAVY, U.S.

Suggestions for further reading: Department of Defense, *Conduct of the Persian Gulf War: Final Report to the Congress,*"Chapter VI: The Air Campaign," "Chapter VII: The Maritime Campaign," "Appendix T: Performance of Selected Weapons Systems" (Washington, D.C.: USGPO, 1992); Norman Friedman, *Desert Victory: The War for Kuwait* (Annapolis, Md.: Naval Institute Press, 1991), which has a vigorous defense of carrier-based aircraft; Richard P. Hallion, *Storm Over Iraq; Air Power and the Gulf War* (Washington, D.C.: Smithsonian Institution Press, 1992), which is critical of Naval aviation; Bruce W. Watson, ed., *Military Lessons of the Gulf War* (Novato, Calif.: Presidio Press, 1991); Michael A. Palmer, "The Navy Did Its Job," *U.S. Naval Institute Proceedings,* 1991 Naval Review issue, which has a listing of the embarked aircraft squadrons; Rear Admiral Riley D. Mixon, USN, "Where We Must Do Better," *U.S. Naval Institute Proceedings,* August 1991.

AIR DEFENSES

Iraq had one of the world's most sophisticated air defense networks at the beginning of the Persian Gulf War. According to the official Department of Defense (DOD) analysis, "the multi-layered, redundant, computer-controlled air defense network around Baghdad was . . . several orders of magnitude greater than that which had defended Hanoi during the later stages of the Vietnam War."

Redesigned after the Israeli raid on the Osirak nuclear reactor in 1981, the Iraqi integrated air defense system (IADS) featured a network of radars, surface-to-air missiles (SAMs) and antiaircraft artillery (AAA) concentrated primarily around key facilities in the Baghdad area. Controlled by the national air defense operations center (ADOC) in Baghdad, which maintained an overall picture of the air war in Iraq and established priorities for air defense engagements, the IADS was linked to sector operations centers (SOCs) that controlled specific geographic areas.

The heart of Iraq's IADS was the modern, computerized, French-built Kari command and control (C^2) system. Kari provided linkage between the ADOC and the SOCs and the diverse Iraqi inventory of Soviet and Western radar and air defense weaponry, as well as a redundant C^2 capability. Weaponry included some 16,000 SA-2, SA-3, SA-6 and Roland surface-to-air-missile (SAM) systems; interceptor aircraft; and organic Army AAA weapons such as SA-7/14, SA-8, SA-9/13 and SA-16 missiles, and the self-propelled ZSU-23/4.

In addition, to defend targets of value, the Iraqi IADS had more than 7,500 AAA pieces, some deployed on the roofs of government buildings in Baghdad. These 37-mm and 57-mm AAA guns, ZSU-23/4 and ZSU-57/2 self-propelled AAA systems, and hundreds of 14.5- mm and 23-mm light antiaircraft weapons formed the backbone of Iraq's integrated defense system, which was lethal to aircraft operating below 10,000 feet.

Suppression of enemy air defenses (SEAD) was critical to the coalition's prosecution of the war. In the weeks before the air campaign began, the U.S. Navy's Operational Intelligence Center put together a Strike Projection Evaluation and Antiair Research (SPEAR) team to make a detailed analysis of Iraq's IADS. Working closely with the U.S. Air Force (USAF) and national agency teams (i.e., the Central Intelligence Agency, the Defense Intelligence Agency, the National Security Agency), SPEAR identified the key IADS nodes whose destruction would neutralize the Kari system.

Neutralizing the Kari system was accomplished in the opening hours of the air campaign. Even before H-Hour on January 17, 1991, Special Operations Command (SOCCENT) helicopters attacked early-warning radar sites in southern Iraq. The low-altitude air- launched cruise missile (ALCM) and Tomahawk cruise missile attacks and the medium-altitude F-117A stealth fighter strikes on Baghdad that officially opened the air campaign created gaps in the Iraqi radar coverage and C^2 networks for the non-stealth aircraft that followed. USAF, Navy, U.S. Marine Corps (USMC), Army and other coalition attack aircraft closed in on Iraq's IADS and C^2 infrastructure.

"At one time during that first hour," according to the official DOD analysis, the lead F-4G (i.e., "Wild

Weasel") flight countered more than 15 radar sites and several different type SAMs. More than 200 HARMs (high-speed antiradiation missiles) were fired against Iraqi radars, 100 by USMC F/A-18s alone. USAF EF-111s and F-4Gs, Navy and USMC EA-6Bs, A-7s and F/A-18s determined threat locations [and] then jammed enemy radar installations or attacked them with HARMs, while EC-130 Compass Call aircraft jammed enemy communications.

One effective tactic to fool enemy air defenses involved Navy and Marine Corps tactical air launched decoys (TALDS). The decoys caused Iraqi defenders to turn on their radars, revealing their locations and making them vulnerable to Coalition SEAD aircraft.... The joint SEAD effort also used 10 long-range Army tactical missile system (ATACMS) missiles to attack Iraqi air defense sites with good success....

Within hours of the start of combat operations, Iraq's IADS had been fragmented and individual air defense sectors (IOC) forced into autonomous operations. Most hardened SOC and IOC were destroyed or neutralized within the first few days.... After the first week (when 17 aircraft were lost, most in low-level attacks on air fields) coalition aircraft were able to operate at medium and high altitudes with virtual impunity. . . . During the next three weeks only seven coalition aircraft were lost to Iraqi defenses.

Although the Iraqi medium- and high-altitude threat had been neutralized, Iraq's low-level air defenses were still deadly. These included the heat-seeking, hand-held SAMs such as the Soviet-made SA-7s, SA-14s and SA-16s, and the French-made Mistrals; vehicle-mounted SA-9s and SA-13s; the Soviet-supplied ZSU 57-2, ZSU 23-4 and 14.55-mm AA guns; and the Swiss-made Skyguard with its twin 35-mm radar-controlled guns.

Except when Iraqi radars were operating, they were difficult to detect and therefore almost impos-

Although Iraqi missiles and interceptors were taken out early in the air campaign, their AAA guns, such as this ZSU-23-4 23-mm quad-barreled machine gun, were deadly against low-flying aircraft.
U.S. Army photo courtesy of 24th Infantry Division (Mechanized).

sible to counterattack. Some success was gained through the use of Army and Marine observation and attack helicopters to locate and destroy such sites with laser-designated missiles such as Hellfire and Copperhead.

When coalition aircraft moved into the ground attack phase, Iraqi low-level defenses took their toll. Ten coalition aircraft were lost to enemy ground fire in the last 10 days of the war. In all, 15 aircraft were lost to AAA fire and heat-seeking, hand-held surface-to-air missiles.

As a result of the coalition's successful SEAD operations, air superiority was achieved early. From that point on, coalition forces were free of the danger of Iraqi air attack. But the coalition did deploy its own air defenses, most notably the Hawk antiaircraft missile system and the Patriot air defense system, as well as the gun and short-range missile air defense systems organic to the air defense battalions of the various combat divisions.

Saudi Arabia had 33 SAM batteries (including 16 with Hawk missiles), Egypt had 12 Hawk batteries and the United Arab Emirates had 5; Kuwait had 6 Hawk batteries that fell into Iraqi hands but were never used against coalition aircraft.

The U.S. Army deployed the 11th Air Defense Artillery Group, which included Hawk and Patriot battalions, and the Marine Corps deployed the 2d and 3d Light Antiaircraft Missile Battalions with Hawk missile systems. Although none of these air defense systems were called upon to defend against Iraqi aircraft, the Patriot system did play a major role against Scud missile attacks.

See also AIR CAMPAIGN; AIRFIELDS; AIR-LAUNCHED CRUISE MISSILE; DECOYS AND DRONES; ELECTRONIC WARFARE; HARM; PATRIOT MISSILE; SCUD MISSILES; STEALTH AIRCRAFT; TOMAHAWK LAND ATTACK MISSILE; WILD WEASEL.

Suggestions for further reading: Department of Defense, *Conduct of the Persian Gulf War: Final Report to the Congress* (Washington, D.C.: USGPO, 1992), chapters 1 through 8; Norman Friedman, *Desert Victory: The War for Kuwait* (Annapolis, Md.: Naval Institute Press, 1991), which has a detailed listing of coalition aircraft losses; Richard P. Hallion, *Storm Over Iraq: Air Power and the Gulf War* (Washington, D.C.: Smithsonian Institution Press, 1992); Bruce W. Watson, ed., *Military Lessons of the Gulf War* (Novato, Calif.: Presidio Press, 1991); *The Military Balance*

1990–1991 (London: International Institute for Strategic Studies, 1990).

AIRFIELDS

As was discussed in part I, there had been extensive airfield construction in the Persian Gulf region prior to the Gulf War. Thus, when U.S. forces began to deploy there in August 1990, they found a considerable number of airfields already in being, especially in Saudi Arabia. Among others, these included the Dhahran and Huffaf Royal Saudi Air Force Bases (RSAFB) near Dhahran, and the Al-Jabayl RSAFB near Jubayl in eastern Saudi Arabia; airfields at the capital, Riyadh, in central Saudi Arabia; at Tabuk, Jidda and Taif in western Saudi Arabia; and at Khamis-Mushayt in the south.

Coalition aircraft also used Muharraq in Bahrain, airfields in Qatar and Oman, and Al-Dhafra and Al-Mindhat in the United Arab Emirates, as well as Incirlik and Diyarbakir air bases in Turkey. B-52 bombers launched strikes from bases in the United States, Great Britain and Spain, as well as from the island of Diego Garcia in the Indian Ocean.

Iraqi aircraft were deployed at more than 24 primary and 40 dispersal airfields across the country. Most were placed under hardened shelters. In the north were bases at Mosul, Tall Afar, Irbil, Qayyarah West and Qayyarah South, Kirkuk, As-Sulaymaniyah, Tel Ashtah, Tikrit, Tikrit East and Tikrit South. In the Baghdad area were bases at Balad, Salum, Al-Muhammadi, Al-Taji, Ba'qubah, Habbaniyah, Al-Fallujah, Al-Ramadi, Al-Taqaddum, Muthenna, Rasheed, Salam Pak, Al-'Aziziya, Al-Iskandariyah, Al-Numaniyah, Karbala, Karbala East and Saddam International Airport in Baghdad.

Airfields in southern Iraq were located at Al-Jarrah, Al-Hayy, Najef, Al-Diwaniyah, Qal'at Sukkar, Kut al-Hayy, Amara, Qal'at Salih, Nasiriya, Tallil, Samawah, Wadi al-Khirr, Ghalaysan, As-Salman, Al-Ubayyid, and Jalibah. And in the southeast and in occupied Kuwait, there were airfields at Al-Qurna, Basra, Al-Basra, Al-Rumaylah, Shaiban, Safwan, Ali al-Salem, Ahmed al-Jaber and Kuwait International Airport.

To shut down these air bases, runways became prime targets for attack. British Royal Air Force (RAF) Tornado fighter-bombers accounted for two-thirds of runway attacks; they used the JP233 Low

Altitude Airfield Attack System, which was designed specifically to neutralize enemy airfields by cratering runways and laying delayed explosives that posed a continuing threat to repair crews and vehicles. Tornados could carry two JP233 systems, each with 30 SG357 cratering weapons and 215 HB876 denial weapons. In four days, Tornados had closed eight Iraqi airfields and severely hampered activities at other fields. But these successes came at a terrible price when 6 of Britain's 42 Tornados were lost to enemy ground fire.

Later in the war, the RAF Tornados were fitted with thermal-imaging laser designators that enabled them to use laser-guided bombs. In a strike against the Iraqi base at Shaibah, the Tornado bomb runs were so accurate that, according to RAF Group Captain Andrew Vallance, they "put paid to the last possibility that the Iraqi Air Force [could appear] over the battlefield."

See also AIR CAMPAIGN; AIRCRAFT CARRIERS; AIR DEFENSES; AIR FORCE, IRAQ; AIR FORCES, COALITION; AIR FORCE, U.S.

Suggestions for further reading: Department of Defense, *Conduct of the Persian Gulf War: Final Report to the Congress,* "Appendix E: Deployment" (Washington, D.C.: USGPO, 1992); Richard P. Hallion, *Storm Over Iraq: Air Power and the Gulf War* (Washington, D.C.: Smithsonian Institution Press, 1992), which has maps of the locations of coalition and Iraqi airfields; James Blackwell, *Thunder in the Desert: The Strategy and Tactics of the Persian Gulf War* (New York: Bantam, 1991), which has a map and a list of Iraqi airfields; Bruce W. Watson, ed., *Military Lessons of the Gulf War* (Novato, Calif.: Presidio Press, 1991); Norman Friedman, *Desert Victory: The War for Kuwait* (Annapolis, Md.: Naval Institute Press, 1991).

AIR FORCE CROSS

First authorized during the Vietnam War, the Air Force Cross is the equivalent of the Army's Distinguished Service Cross and the Navy and Marine Corps's Navy Cross; they are the United States's second highest awards for bravery.

The Air Force Cross is awarded in the name of the president of the United States for extraordinary heroism in an action against the enemy. The act of heroism, although not justifying the award of the Medal of Honor, has to be so notable and to involve

a risk of life so extraordinary as to set the individual apart from his comrades.

During the Persian Gulf War, two Air Force Crosses were awarded for such extraordinary heroism.

See also DECORATIONS, U.S.; NAVY CROSS; SERVICE MEDALS, U.S.

AIR FORCE, IRAQ

On the eve of the Gulf War, the Iraqi Air Force was the largest in the Middle East and the sixth largest in the world. Compared to most coalition aviators, however, Iraqi pilots were of marginal quality, and those flying older aircraft were poorly trained. The elite Iraqi pilots were French-trained and flew Mirage F-1s. (It was an Iraqi Mirage F-1 that fired two Exocet antiship missiles at the USS *Stark* (FFG-31) in 1987.)

Although estimates of the number of aircraft in Iraq's inventory when the war began vary widely, the official U.S. Department of Defense (DOD) report on the war gives a figure of 750-plus. Fewer than half of Iraq's aircraft, however, were modern combat aircraft. These included some 50 Soviet-supplied MiG-23 Floggers, 20 MiG-25 Foxbats and 116 French Mirage F-1s that were on a par with the third-generation, Vietnam-era U.S. F-4 Phantom; and 48 Soviet-built MiG-29 Fulcrums and 20 Su-24MK Fencers, which were equivalent to the fourth-generation U.S. F-15 Eagle.

The rest of Iraq's inventory consisted of aircraft whose technology dated from the 1950s and 1960s. These included 40 Soviet/Chinese-built MiG-19/Xian F-6 fighter-bombers, 150 MiG-21/Xian F-7 interceptors, 20 MiG-27 fighter-bombers, 80 Su-20/22 Fitter fighter-bombers, 30 Su-25 ground-attack aircraft, and 5 Tu-22 Blinder, 12 Tu-16 Badger and 4 Chinese H-6 bombers.

Because of the ferocity of the coalition air campaign, most Iraqi planes never got off the ground. By January 27, 1991, the CINCCENT (commander in chief, Central Command) was able to announce that the Iraqi Air Force was combat ineffective, and that air superiority had been achieved. As Richard Hallion put it in *Storm Over Iraq,* "The Iraqi Air Force died ignominiously."

"By the war's end," according to the DOD report, "324 of the original 750-plus Iraqi fixed-wing combat aircraft were reported destroyed, captured, or relocated outside Iraq." The report cites CENTAF (Central Command Air Force) estimates that "109 Iraqi combat fixed-wing aircraft flew to Iran; 151 were destroyed on the ground; 33 were shot down by Coalition fighter aircraft [not including 2 helicopters and 2 Su-22s that were shot down after the preliminary cease-fire had been announced]; and 31 were captured or destroyed by ground forces (the status of others was unknown)."

The DOD report concluded that "fewer than 300 [aircraft] were believed to remain in Iraq and their combat readiness was doubtful. . . . Of the 594 Iraqi aircraft shelters, 375 were severely damaged or destroyed. Within six weeks, the world's sixth largest air force had been decimated."

See also AERIAL COMBAT; AIR CAMPAIGN; AIRFIELDS.

Suggestions for further reading: Department of Defense, *Conduct of the Persian Gulf War: Final Report to the Congress,* "Chapter VI, The Air Campaign" (Washington, D.C.: USGPO, 1992); Norman Friedman, *Desert Victory: The War for Kuwait* (Annapolis, Md.: Naval Institute Press, 1991); Richard P. Hallion, *Storm Over Iraq: Air Power and the Gulf War* (Washington, D.C.: Smithsonian Institution Press, 1992); Bruce W. Watson, ed., *Military Lessons of the Gulf War* (Novato, Calif.: Presidio Press, 1991); *The Military Balance 1990–1991* (London: International Institute for Strategic Studies, 1990).

AIR FORCES, COALITION

Coalition partners other than the United States provided more than 700 combat and combat support aircraft to the Persian Gulf War. Although the figures varied during the course of the war, the numbers given in the following table provide a close approximation of the contributions. (The national airlines of Italy, Kuwait, Luxembourg, the Netherlands and South Korea made available civilian aircraft to assist in the logistics effort of the coalition partners.)

Eleven coalition aircraft were lost in combat during the war, including one Kuwaiti Vietnam-era A-4 KU Skyhawk fighter, one French Jaguar A fighter, one Italian Tornado fighter, two Royal Saudi Air Force fighters (an F-5E and a Tornado), and six British Royal Air Force (RAF) Tornados, most of which were lost in low-level bombing attacks on enemy airfields. A seventh RAF Tornado was lost in a noncombat flying accident.

Coalition Air Forces

Country	Type	Number	Total
Argentina	Boeing 707-320 transport	1	
	C-130H transport	2	3
Bahrain	F-5 fighter	12	
	F-16 fighter	12	24
Canada	CF-18 fighter	24	
	EC-144A EW	2	
	CH-124A helicopter	5	31
France	Jaguar A fighter	25	
	Mirage 2000 fighter	12	
	Mirage F-1C fighter	8	
	Mirage F-1CR	4	
	C-135R tanker	5	
	C-160G EW jammer	1	
	C-160F transport	3	
	C-160HG transport	6	
	DC-8 Sarigue ELINT	1	
	SA-130 ECM helicopter	2	67
Italy	Tornado fighter	10	
	C-130 transport	1	
	G-222 transport	1	12
Kuwait	A-4 fighter	24	
	Mirage F-1 fighter	16	
	transport	3	
	armed helicopter	24	67
New Zealand	C-130 transport	3	3
Oman	Jaguar fighter	20	20
Qatar	Mirage F-1 fighter	14	
	Alfa fighter	6	20
Saudi Arabia	Tornado F.3 fighter	24	
	Tornado GR.1 fighter	36	
	F-5E/B fighter	76	
	F-15C fighter	63	
	E-3 AWACS	3	

Coalition Air Forces

Country	Type	Number	Total
	tanker	15	
	transport	38	255
United Arab Emirates	Mirage fighter	50	50
United Kingdom	Tornado GR.1 fighter	45	
	Tornado GR.1A reconnaissance	6	
	Tornado F.3 air superiority	18	
	Jaguar GR Mk 1 A fighter	12	
	Buccaneer S.2B	12	
	Nimrod maritime patrol	4	
	C-130 transport	7	
	HS-125 transport	1	
	Puma helicopter	19	
	Chinook helicopter	17	
	Victor Tristar and VC10 K	17	
	tankers		158
TOTAL			710

All of the coalition aircraft taking part in the air campaign were integrated into the ATO (Air Tasking Order) prepared by AFCENT (Air Forces Central Command). As a result, there were no "friendly fire" aircraft shoot-downs, even though some coalition aircraft were identical to those of Iraq.

The foundation of the coalition's successful partnership, according to U.S. Lieutenant General Charles Horner, the AFCENT commander, was absolute equality and absolute trust among its members. An example of the cooperation among coalition air forces was the target identification of two Iraqi F-1 Mirage fighters by a USAF AWACS (airborne warning and control system) aircraft and their subsequent shoot-down by a Royal Saudi Air Force F-15 fighter on January 24, 1991.

There were a number of exchange pilots among the coalition air forces. For example, two British RAF officers on exchange with the U.S. 3d Marine Aircraft Wing were awarded Air Medals in the name of the president of the United States for their actions in the Gulf War.

See also AERIAL COMBAT; AIR CAMPAIGN; AIR DEFENSES; AIRFIELDS; AIRLIFT; ATO (AIR TASKING ORDER); COALITION FORCES.

Suggestions for further reading: Department of Defense, *Conduct of the Persian Gulf War: Final Report to the Congress,* "Appendix I: Coalition Development, Coordination and Warfare" (Washington, D.C.: USGPO, 1992); Norman Friedman, *Desert Victory: The War for Kuwait* (Annapolis, Md.: Naval Institute Press, 1991), which has a listing of coalition air forces; Richard P. Hallion, *Storm Over Iraq: Air Power and the Gulf War* (Washington, D.C.: Smithsonian Institution Press, 1992), which has a listing and a discussion of coalition air actions; Bruce W. Watson, ed., *Military Lessons of the Gulf War* (Novato, Calif.: Presidio Press, 1991), which also has a listing of coalition air forces.

AIR FORCE, U.S.

The United States Air Force (USAF), including the Air Force Reserve and the Air National Guard, was the most powerful air force in the world at the time of the Gulf War, and remains so today. During the Persian Gulf War, it played a crucial, some would say a decisive, role in bringing that conflict to a swift and successful conclusion.

Although figures vary slightly, depending on the source, of the 1,376 U.S. fixed-wing combat aircraft committed to the war, the USAF provided 820. These included 144 A-10 "Warthogs," 120 F-15C Eagles and 48 F-15E Strike Eagles, 246 F-16 Fighting Falcons, 82 F-111E/F and 18 F-111 Aardvarks, 42 F-117 stealth fighters, 48 F-4G and 24 RF-4C Phantom EW "Wild Weasels" and reconnaissance aircraft, and some 80 B-52G Stratofortress bombers. USAF Special Operations aircraft, such as the AC-130H Spectre fixed-wing gunships, also played an active role.

The USAF also provided almost all of the 285 aerial refueling tankers used in the war, including KC-10 Extenders and KC-135 Stratotankers, as well as the bulk of the 175 strategic inter-theater airlift transports, including C-5A Galaxys and C-141 Starlifters and the tactical C-130 Hercules.

The USAF flew 29,393 combat sorties, 67 percent of the approximately 44,145 U.S. combat sorties flown in the war. The USAF dropped 60,624 tons of bombs, 72 percent of the 82,000 tons of bombs dropped during the war.

More than 50,000 USAF personnel deployed to the Gulf, including 5,300 women and 10,800 National Guard and Air Force Reserve personnel mobilized for the war. Another 22,000 reservists supported the war from bases outside the KTO. (Kuwaiti Theater of Operations). Twenty were killed in action, six died in fatal accidents, nine were wounded in action and eight were taken prisoner and subsequently released.

Fourteen USAF aircraft were lost in combat operations, including two F-15E Strike Eagles, five F-16A Fighting Falcons, one F-4G Wild Weasel, one AC-130H Spectre gunship and five A-10 Thunderbolt "Warthogs." Four additional aircraft were non-combat losses, including two F-16C Fighting Falcons, one EF-111 Raven and one B-52 Stratofortress.

Two Air Force Crosses were awarded to USAF personnel for extraordinary heroism, and 50 Silver Stars were awarded for gallantry in action. In addition, 864 Distinguished Flying Crosses and 15,938 Air Medals were given to USAF personnel.

During the Gulf War, the USAF was organized into three major components. SAC (Strategic Air Command) was charged with the nuclear strike mission, with strategic (non-nuclear) air attacks on the enemy's homeland, and with aerial refueling. TAC (Tactical Air Command) was charged with fighting the tactical air war, including air interdiction, close air support of ground forces, and intra-theater airlift. MAC (Military Airlift Command), under the operational control of U.S. TRANSCOM (Transportation Command), was charged with intercontinental airlift.

The anomaly in the Gulf War, as in the Vietnam War, was that in actual practice the warfighting missions of

The 820 U.S. Air Force combat aircraft committed to the war flew 29,393 combat sorties.
Central Command Public Affairs.

TAC and SAC were reversed. TAC fighter-bombers became the primary instrument of the strategic air war against Iraq, while SAC B-52 bombers were used primarily in a tactical ground-support role and SAC tankers were used to sustain tactical air strikes even more than they were used to refuel SAC bombers. As a result, the USAF's internal chain of command had to be jury-rigged to deal with these conflicting lines of authority.

While this ad hoc command system worked, it had the potential for disaster. Following the Persian Gulf War, therefore, the USAF was reconfigured to reflect wartime reality. SAC, TAC and MAC were disestablished. The nuclear strike mission was assigned to the U.S. Strategic Command (STRATCOM), which is directly subordinate to the Department of Defense. Combat aircraft (the "shooters") were organized into composite squadrons of bombers, fighters and tankers, and assigned to the newly formed Air Combat Command (ACC) headquartered at Langley Air Force Base (AFB) in Virginia. Transport aircraft (the "movers") were assigned to the new Air Mobility Command (AMC) at Scott AFB in Illinois.

See also A-10 THUNDERBOLT II "WARTHOG"; ABCCC (AIRBORNE BATTLEFIELD COMMAND AND CONTROL CENTER); AERIAL COMBAT; AERIAL REFUELING; AFLOAT PREPOSITIONING SHIPS (APS); AIR CAMPAIGN; AIRCRAFT CARRIERS; AIR DEFENSES; AIRFIELDS; AIR FORCE CROSS; AIR FORCE, IRAQ; AIR FORCES, COALITION; AIR-LAUNCHED CRUISE MISSILE; AIRLIFT; AIR MEDAL; AIRPOWER; ATO (AIR TASKING ORDER); AWACS (AIRBORNE WARNING AND CONTROL SYSTEM); B-52 STRATOFORTRESS BOMBER; CHIEF OF STAFF, U.S. AIR FORCE; CLOSE AIR SUPPORT; COMPUTER WAR; CRAF (CIVIL RESERVE AIR FLEET); DRONES AND DECOYS ELECTRONIC WARFARE (EW); FIGHTERS AND FIGHTER-BOMBERS; FRIENDLY FIRE; GROUND CAMPAIGN; GUNSHIPS; HORNER, CHARLES A.; JSTARS (JOINT SURVEILLANCE TARGET ATTACK SYSTEM); JUST WAR; MOBILIZATION; U.S.; NINTH U.S. AIR FORCE; RECONNAISSANCE; SAC (STRATEGIC AIR COMMAND); SCUD MISSILES; SEARCH AND RESCUE (SAR); SORTIES; SPECIAL OPERATIONS COMMAND CENTRAL COMMAND (SOCCENT); STEALTH AIRCRAFT; STRATEGIC AIR COMMAND (SAC); 3D MARINE AIRCRAFT WING; TRANSPORTATION COMMAND (TRANSCOM); WILD WEASEL.

Suggestions for further reading: Department of Defense, *Conduct of the Persian Gulf War: Final Report to the Congress*, "Chapter VI: The Air Campaign" (Washington, D.C.: USGPO, 1992); Department of the Air Force, *Reaching Globally, Reaching Powerfully: The United States Air Force in the Gulf War* (Washington, D.C.: USGPO, September 1991); *Air Force Manual (AFM) 1-1: Basic Aerospace Doctrine of the United States Air Force* (Washington, D.C.: USGPO, 1984); *Air Force Manual (AFM) 1-1: Basic Aerospace Doctrine of the United States Air Force* (Washington, D.C.: USGPO, 1992); Eliot A. Cohen et al., *Gulf War Airpower Survey* (Washington, D.C.: USGPO, 1993); Norman Friedman, *Desert Victory: The War for Kuwait* (Annapolis, Md.: Naval Institute Press, 1991); Richard P. Hallion, *Storm Over Iraq: Air Power and the Gulf War* (Washington, D.C.: Smithsonian Institution Press, 1992); Bruce W. Watson, ed., *Military Lessons of the Gulf War* (Novato, Calif.: Presidio Press, 1991), which lists the active, Air Force Reserve and Air National Guard units deployed to the Gulf; *The Military Balance 1990–1991* (London: International Institute for Strategic Studies, 1990).

AIRLAND BATTLE DOCTRINE

"AirLand Battle" was the official U.S. Army warfighting doctrine during the Persian Gulf War. First announced in 1982, it was formulated at the Army's Training and Doctrine Command (TRADOC) at Fort Monroe, Virginia, and at the Army Command and General Staff College (CGSC) at Fort Leavenworth, Kansas. Revised in 1986, the AirLand Battle doctrine reintroduced the concept of "operational art," the intermediate level of war between military strategy and tactics, that was to define the nature of the modern battlefield.

Under this new formulation, combat consisted not only of fighting along the line of contact—now called *close operations*—but also of *deep operations* "directed against enemy forces not in contact [to] create the conditions for future victory," and of *rear operations*, "rearward of elements in contact designed to assure freedom of manuever and continuity of operations, including continuity of sustainment and command and control" (FM 100-5, 1986).

Coordinated with the Air Force's Tactical Air Command, AirLand Battle envisioned not just Army-Air Force cooperation and support, but also simultaneous battles on the forward line and deep in the enemy's rear echelon in close concert with airpower. Rejecting the conceits of the atomic theorists that conventional war was obsolete in the nuclear age, the AirLand Battle doctrine marked a return to the fundamental principles of ground combat. Emphasizing campaign planning, manuever and fluidity of action, AirLand Battle was validated in the Gulf War.

See also AIRPOWER; ARMY, U.S.; CAMPAIGN PLAN; DOCTRINE; GROUND CAMPAIGN; MARITIME STRATEGIC DOCTRINE, U.S.

Suggestions for further reading: "AirLand Battle Doctrine," in Colonel Harry G. Summers Jr., *On Strategy II: A Critical Analysis of the Gulf War* (New York: Dell, 1991); *Field Manual 100-5: Operations* (Washington, D.C.: USGPO, 1982); *Field Manual 100-5: Operations* (Washington, D.C.: USGPO, 1986); John L. Romjue, *From Active Defense to AirLand Battle: The Development of Army Doctrine, 1973–1982* (Fort Monroe, Va.: U.S. Army Training and Doctrine Command, 1984).

AIR-LAUNCHED CRUISE MISSILE (AGM-86C)

At 6:36 A.M. on January 16, 1991, seven Strategic Air Command (SAC) B-52 bombers took off from Barksdale Air Force Base in Louisiana en route to Iraq. Repeatedly refueled by SAC tankers during their 12-hour flight, and some two hours after the air campaign began, the bombers launched 35 AGM-86C air-launched cruise missiles (ALCMs) at eight critical Iraqi communications, power generation and transmission facilities, the first and only time these missiles were used in the Persian Gulf War.

The ALCM incorporates a global positioning system and an internal navigation system to guide it to its target. With a 1,000-pound high-explosive blast/fragmentation warhead and a turbofan engine, it has a cruising speed of 500 miles per hour and a maximum range of 1,550 miles. The B-52 Stratofortress can carry 12 ALCMs externally and 8 missiles internally.

Although all of the missiles were launched successfully, their effectiveness was difficult to determine because of incomplete battle damage assessment and the inability to distinguish damage caused by other munitions that struck some of the same targets.

See also AIR CAMPAIGN; B-52 STRATOFORTRESS BOMBER; STRATEGIC AIR COMMAND (SAC); TOMAHAWK LAND-ATTACK MISSILE.

Suggestions for further reading: Department of Defense, *Conduct of the Persian Gulf War: Final Report to the Congress,* "Appendix T: Performance of Selected Weapons Systems" (Washington, D.C.: USGPO, 1992); Richard P. Hallion, *Storm Over Iraq: Air Power and the Gulf War* (Washington, D.C.: Smithsonian Institution Press, 1992).

AIRLIFT

Airlift was critical to the coalition's success in the Persian Gulf War. Inter-theater *strategic* airlift between the United States, Europe and the Middle East was the key to the rapid buildup of forces within the KTO (Kuwaiti Theater of Operations). Intra-theater *tactical* airlift enabled CENTCOM (Central Command) to quickly shift troops and supplies within the KTO to influence the battlefield situation.

Strategic airlift was the responsibility of the USAF Military Airlift Command (MAC), part of the U.S. Transportation Command (TRANSCOM) at Scott Air Force Base in Illinois. Primary jet transport aircraft included the C-141B Starlifter and the C-5 Galaxy. The C-141 could carry 200 troops or 34 tons of cargo, while the C-5 could carry 340 troops or 130 tons of cargo. Both were air refuelable and therefore had an unlimited range.

Two weeks after the crisis began, 118 of the 126 C-5s in the Air Force were committed to the Gulf, as were 195 of the 265 C-141s. Most of these were aircraft of the Air National Guard and Air Force Reserve, whose 7 C-5 squadrons and 11 C-141 squadrons composed 86 percent of the Air Force's airlift assets. Two-thirds of the aerial port personnel and 90 percent of the aeromedical evacuation personnel deployed to the Gulf were also from the reserve components. Prior to mobilization, more than 5,000 reservists volunteered for duty with MAC, including the 9-man crew of the only MAC aircraft that was lost in the war, a C-5 that crashed in Germany en route to the Gulf.

MAC was further reinforced by civilian aircraft from the Civil Reserve Air Fleet (CRAF), which was mobilized for the first time in its history. Four of the Navy's Reserve Transportation Squadrons were also recalled to active duty, and their C-9 aircraft, which carried passengers and cargo between Europe and the Middle East, flew more than 9,000 hours.

Making this intercontinental airlift possible were the Strategic Air Command's aerial refueling tankers and the en route air bases in Germany, Italy, Portugal and Spain. For example, 84 percent of the airlift missions flowed through Torrejón in Spain and Rhein-Main in Germany.

Flying some 16,400 missions as of March 1991, strategic airlift delivered to the Gulf some 562,000 tons of cargo, only about 5 percent of the total, but it delivered approximately more than 544,000 personnel, approximately 99 percent of the total. Also created was a "Desert Express," which rapidly moved some 2,500 tons of critical items, such as high-priority spare parts, to the Gulf.

Although jet transports made up the strategic airlift, the tactical in-country airlift consisted primarily of propeller-driven C-130 Hercules aircraft from the active Air Force, Air Guard and Reserve, and from active and reserve Navy and Marine units (other coalition partners also contributed aircraft for tactical airlift). Delivering more than 300,000 tons of cargo and moving 209,000 troops, these tactical aircraft flew 22,064 intra-theater airlift sorties, according to the *Gulf War Airpower Survey*.

As part of the intra-theater airlift, two scheduled airlift operations were conducted. "STAR" (Scheduled Theater Airlift Route) had the primary mission of moving people and mail among the operating bases on the Arabian Peninsula. "Camel" missions provided a daily cargo service throughout the KTO.

In the weeks preceding the ground war, the tactical airlift fleet supported VII Corps's and XVIII Airborne Corps's shift to their jump-off positions to the west. Flying some 1,200 missions, most at low altitudes to avoid Iraqi radar, and averaging one takeoff and landing every seven minutes, 24 hours a day, during the first 13 days of the redeployment, the fleet delivered 14,000 persons and more than 9,000 tons of equipment to the new assault positions.

See also AERIAL REFUELING; AIR FORCES, COALITION; AIR FORCE, U.S.; CRAF (CIVIL RESERVE AIR FLEET); DEPLOYMENT OF U.S. FORCES; MEDICAL CARE AND EVACUATION, COALITION; MOBILIZATION, U.S.; SEALIFT.

Suggestions for further reading: Department of Defense, *Conduct of the Persian Gulf War: Final Report to the Congress* (Washington, D.C.: USGPO, 1992); Eliot A. Cohen et al., *Gulf War Airpower Survey* (Washington, D.C.: USGPO, 1993) Norman Friedman, *Desert Victory: The War for Kuwait* (Annapolis, Md.: Naval Institute Press, 1991); Richard P. Hallion,

Storm Over Iraq: Air Power and the Gulf War (Washington, D.C.: Smithsonian Institution Press, 1992).

AIR MEDAL

First authorized in 1942, the Air Medal is awarded in the name of the president of the United States for aerial valor (denoted by a "V" device worn on the ribbon) of a lesser degree than that required for the Distinguished Flying Cross; for single acts of meritorious service beyond that normally expected, again to a lesser degree than that required for the Distinguished Flying Cross; and for sustained distinctive achievement in regular and frequent flights over enemy territory. Subsequent awards of the Air Medal are denoted by a metal numeral worn on the ribbon.

During the Persian Gulf War, 5,741 Air Medals were awarded to Army personnel, including 694 for valor, 555 for meritorious service and the remaining 4,492 for meritorious achievement. The Marine Corps awarded a total of 2,950 Air Medals, including two to British Royal Air Force exchange officers. The Navy awarded 4,850 Air Medals, including 1,482 for service and 3,368 for strike operations. As of April 1993, the Air Force had awarded a total of 15,938 Air Medals for Desert Shield and Desert Storm and for the continuing air operations to enforce UN-designated no-fly zones in Iraq.

See also DECORATIONS, U.S.; DISTINGUISHED FLYING CROSS; SERVICE MEDALS, U.S.

AIRPOWER

Landpower, seapower and airpower have traditionally combined to achieve battlefield victory, and that was the case in the Persian Gulf War as well. "Operation Desert Shield/Desert Storm was certainly the classic example of a multi-service operation," said General H. Norman Schwarzkopf, the U.S. commander in the Gulf, "a truly joint operation" (*U.S. Naval Institute Proceedings*, August 1991).

Some authorities believed, however, that airpower alone could have won the war. "Airpower is the only answer available to our country in this circumstance," said Air Force Chief of Staff General Michael J. Dugan in an interview on September 17, 1990, before the air campaign began. "Ground forces may be needed to reoccupy Kuwait," he was quoted as saying, "but only after airpower has so shattered enemy resistance that soldiers can walk in and not have to fight a pitched battle." (John Broder, "U.S.

War Plans in Iraq," *Los Angeles Times,* September 16, 1990). For these and other remarks, Dugan was summarily relieved from his post by Defense Secretary Dick Cheney. "As a matter of general policy," Cheney said, "I don't think we want to be demeaning the contributions of other services" (DOD News Conference, September 17, 1990).

The roots of this argument go back to the Italian general Giulio Douhet's influential 1921 book, *Command of the Air,* which argued that wars could be won by airpower alone, an argument that was also made in the United States by General Billy Mitchell in the 1930s. Although airpower played a major role in World War II and in the Korean and Vietnam Wars, in none of those was it decisive. But in the Gulf War, argued the architect of the air campaign, Air Force Brigadier General Buster C. Glosson, in an interview with the historian Michael A. Palmer, "technology had 'caught up with Billy Mitchell's vision' and . . . air power alone could defeat Saddam Hussein" (*Air Power History,* Winter 1992).

Many believe it did just that. "My private conviction," said General Dugan's successor, Air Force Chief of Staff General Merrill A. McPeak, in the wake of the Gulf victory, "is that this is the first time in history that a field army has been defeated by air power" (quoted in Michael A. Palmer, *Air Power History,* Winter 1992). As Colonel Dennis M. Drew of the Air Force's Center for Aerospace Doctrine put it, the Gulf War was "clear evidence to all the doubters of airpower in warfare. . . . Airpower now dominates land warfare" (*Jane's Defense Weekly,* June 29, 1991).

Other airmen, however, disagree. "Despite the overwhelming success of the allied air forces in the Gulf War," said British Air Chief Marshall Sir Brendan Jackson, "there should be no assumption that air alone can win wars . . . but air power is a vital component of any joint operation" (*RUSI Journal,* August 1992).

General Dugan had the first word on airpower in the Gulf War. He may have had the last word as well. In an address to the Royal United Service Institute for Defence Studies on February 14, 1992, General Dugan concluded that "Nations . . . will keep a flexible mix of modern, ready air, ground, and naval forces, sized to meet the extent of its interests. When that day comes, whether airmen will stand in the front rank, I do not know. They may or may not be decisive; they will surely be indispensable" (*RUSI Journal,* August 1992).

See also AIR CAMPAIGN; DOCTRINE; STRATEGY, COALITION.

Suggestions for further reading: "Aerospace Doctrine," in Colonel Harry G. Summers Jr., *On Strategy II: A Critical Analysis of the Gulf War* (New York: Dell, 1992); Eliot A. Cohen, "The Mystique of U.S. Air Power," *Foreign Affairs,* January/February 1994; *Air Force Manual (AFM) 1-1, Basic Aerospace Doctrine of the United States Air Force* (Washington, D.C.: USGPO, March 16, 1984); Eliot A. Cohen et al., *Gulf War Airpower Survey* (Washington, D.C.: USGPO, 1993); John A. Warden III, *The Air Campaign: Planning for Combat* (Washington, D.C.: National Defense University Press, 1989). Richard P. Hallion, *Storm Over Iraq: Air Power and the Gulf War* (Washington, D.C.: Smithsonian Institution Press, 1992) has an excellent discussion of airpower in the Gulf, as does Michael A. Palmer, "The Storm in the Air: One Plan, Two Air Wars?" *Air Power History,* Winter 1992. For Colonel Drew's remarks, see Bill Sweetman, "Catching Up with Doctrine," *Jane's Defense Weekly,* June 29, 1991. See also Air Chief Marshal Sir Brendan Jackson, "Air Power," and General Michael J. Dugan, "Operational Experience and Future Applications of Air Power," in *The RUSI Journal,* August 1992.

ALARM ANTI-RADAR MISSILE

The British ALARM anti-radar missile used during the Gulf War has been described as a "miniature Wild Weasel," the U.S. military's anti-radar system. Resembling "a vaulting pole with fins," the ALARM has radar-finding sensors that enabled it to be fired from Tornado strike aircraft as an air-to-ground self-protection weapon, rather than, as with the "Wild Weasel," from a special-purpose electronic warfare plane.

Under development when the war began, the missile was rushed to the Gulf battlefield where it proved devastatingly effective. As Richard Hallion noted in *Storm Over Iraq,* "the Iraqis soon learned that turning on a radar was tantamount to suicide." ALARM would home in on an enemy radar and destroy it, but if the missile did not find a target immediately, it would deploy a parachute and loiter over the battlefield. When it detected a target, it shed its parachute and attacked.

A Tornado strike aircraft could carry three ALARM missiles. During the course of the war, 123 such missiles were fired.

See also HARM; WILD WEASEL.

Suggestions for further reading: Richard P. Hallion, *Storm Over Iraq: Air Power and the Gulf War* (Washington, D.C.: Smithsonian Institution Press, 1992); Norman Friedman, *Desert Victory: The War for Kuwait* (Annapolis, Md.: Naval Institute Press, 1991).

ALLIES

See COALITION FORCES.

AMPHIBIOUS TASK FORCE (ATF)

U.S. Navy and Marine Corps amphibious forces played a key role in the Persian Gulf War. Under the commander of NAVCENT (Naval Forces, Central Command), who was concurrently the Commander, Seventh Fleet, amphibious forces consisted of the Amphibious Task Force (ATF), Task Force 156, under the command of Rear Admiral J. B. LaPlante, and the Landing Force, Task Force 158, commanded by Marine Major General Harry W. Jenkins Jr., who also commanded the 4th Marine Expeditionary Brigade (MEB).

Stationed at Little Creek, Virginia, the first elements of Amphibious Group Two/4th MEB shipped out for the KTO (Kuwaiti Theater of Operations) on August 17, 1990 (C + 10). Like all Marine Air-Ground Task Forces (MAGTAF), the 4th MEB consisted of a ground element, the 2d Marine Regiment; an air element, Marine Air Group 40, which consisted of 160 helicopters and 26 AV-8B Harrier jump jets; and a 1,500-man Brigade Service Support Group, BSSG-4. By September 17, these elements were on station in the Gulf of Oman.

By December 1990, this 8,000-man force had conducted rehearsals for five amphibious assaults, for four amphibious raids, for one amphibious withdrawal, and one amphibious demonstration. Staged from Oman, these amphibious exercises included Imminent Thunder in November 1990, which convinced the Iraqis that they could not take their eyes off the sea.

In September 1990, the ATF was reinforced by Amphibious Squadron Five/13th MEU (SOC). This 2,400 man Marine Expeditionary Unit (MEU), consisting of the 1st Battalion, 4th Marine Regiment, Medium Helicopter Squadron 164, and Marine Ser-

vice Support Group 13, was trained for special operations (SOC).

Amphibious Group Three, with the 7,500-man 5th MEB from Camp Pendleton, California, was commanded by Marine Brigadier General Peter J. Rowe; it reinforced the Task Force in January 1991. It had a ground element, the 5th Marine Regiment; an air element, Marine Air Group 50 (MAG 50), which included HMA-773, a reserve AH-IJ Cobra helicopter gunship squadron from Atlanta, Georgia, HMM-265, a CH-46 Sea Knight helicopter squadron, and AV-8B Harriers; and a Brigade Service Support Group, BSSG-50. As the largest amphibious task force since World War II, the ATF now numbered some 17,000 Marines, 31 amphibious ships, five Military Sealift Command ships, 17 LCACs (Landing Craft Air Cushion), 13 LCUs (Landing Craft Utility) and 115 AAVs (Assault Amphibian Vehicles).

The 13th MEU (SOC) was assigned the task of conducting advanced force operations and raids, with the 4th and 5th MEB remaining capable of attacking separate objectives or joining together for a single mission.

"In addition to exercises," states the official Department of Defense (DOD) report to the Congress.

> the ATF conducted five amphibious operations during Desert Storm. . . . On 29 January, the 13th MEU (SOC) raided Umm Al-Maradim Island off the Kuwaiti coast. Amphibious operations supporting the ground offensive were conducted from 20 to 26 February against Faylaka Island, the Ash Shuaybah port facility and Bubiyan Island. . . .
>
> The largest direct contribution to the ground offensive by amphibious forces came from the 5th MEB, which began landing through Al-Mish'ab and Al-Jubayl, Saudi Arabia, on 24 February to assume the mission of I MEF [Marine Expeditionary Force] reserve. Although experiencing little active combat, the MEB assisted in mopping up operations, EPW [enemy prisoner of war] control and security duties, while providing the MEF commander, whose two Marine divisions were fully committed, additional tactical and operational flexibility.

Meanwhile, beginning four days before G-Day (the start of the ground campaign), the ATF's Harriers began flying combat missions from the landing assault ship *Nassau* (LHA-4).

"The ATF's contribution to the theater campaign cannot be quantified," says the DOD report, yet it was significant to the Coalition's success. . . . The amphibious invasion was not an idle threat. . . .

The decision not to conduct that assault is a tribute to the success of the theater deception efforts. Since the ATF's presence was sufficient, the ATF accomplished its mission without having to fight. . . . Iraq's reactions, and refusal to evacuate coastal defenses even when ground forces were encircling the rear, testified to the effectiveness of these operations.

The ATF pinned down four Iraqi divisions that were dug in along the coast in defensive positions, plus two Iraqi armored divisions that were held in reserve. Of the enemy's 1,100 artillery pieces, more than half were pointed toward the sea.

See also ASSAULT AMPHIBIAN VEHICLE (AAV7A1); BATTLESHIPS; DECEPTION; FIRST MARINE EXPEDITIONARY FORCE; HARRIER (AV-8B) STOVL MARINE CORPS, U.S.; MARITIME CAMPAIGN; SEVENTH U.S. FLEET.

Suggestions for further reading: Department of Defense, *Conduct of the Persian Gulf War: Final Report to the Congress,* "Chapter VII: The Maritime Campaign" (Washington, D.C.: USGPO, 1992); Norman Friedman, *Desert Victory: The War for Kuwait* (Annapolis, Md.: Naval Institute Press, 1991); See also Brig. Gen. Edwin Simmons, "Getting Marines to the Gulf"; "Interview with MGen Harry W. Jenkins, USMC"; "Interview with BGen Peter J. Rowe, USMC," all in *Naval Institute Proceedings,* Naval Review Issue, 1992.

ANTIAIRCRAFT ARTILLERY (AAA)

See AIR DEFENSES.

ANTIWAR MOVEMENT

The antiwar movement was not a significant force during the Persian Gulf War. A *Newsweek* poll published on February 4, 1991, after the air campaign had begun, showed that 86 percent of the American people supported the president's policy in the Gulf.

"The problem with the peace movement," said Senator Paul Wellstone (Dem. Minn.), "is that besides 'peace now,' it has not presented a real alternative. It's a movement without a coherent message." But it was not for lack of trying.

Some protestors hoped to strengthen the movement by resurrecting the fear of the draft among college students, which had proved to be a strong motivation for the antiwar movement during the Vietnam War. Rep. John Conyers [Dem. MI] predicted . . . that [President] Bush would soon have to reactivate the draft—and if so, he added, "we want it to be fair and there'll be no exemptions for college students." This, said *Newsweek,* "was a shrewd tactic for stampeding young people, and their parents, into the peace movement." But the stampede never started.

A coordinated campus protest scheduled for February 21, 1991, and organized by the National Student and Youth Campaign for Peace in the Middle East, for example, turned out to be a fizzle. "It was pathetically small, pathetically small," George Washington University history professor Leo Ribuffo told the *Washington Post* On February 22, 1992. "It's sad, but I guess it does show that the prevailing attitude is that the war is not at the center of consciousness for students."

A main reason why the antiwar movement was weak was that rumors of a draft had no basis in fact. Both Secretary of Defense Dick Cheney and President Bush made it clear that they had no intention of reinstituting the draft. Instead, the nation relied on the all-volunteer forces of the active military and the reserve components, which had been mobilized for the war. When activists made an example of those few volunteers who tried to renege on their military commitments, the public showed little sympathy for their protestations (see CONSCIENTIOUS OBJECTORS, U.S.).

Attempts were also made to revive the Vietnam War-era claims that blacks and other minorities would bear the brunt of the casualties and were being victimized by the Gulf crisis. As is discussed elsewhere in more detail (see BLACK U.S. MILITARY FORCES), these claims bore little effect. It was hard to portray such black Americans as General Colin Powell, the Chairman of the Joint Chiefs of Staff, or Lieutenant General Calvin Waller, the CENTCOM Deputy Commander, as "victims." As it turned out, black casualties were not disproportionate: White Americans, who made up 66 percent of the force, sustained 78 percent of the casualties, whereas black Americans, who made up 24.5 percent of the force, sustained 15 percent of the deaths.

Activists also claimed that the news media had been so manipulated, shackled and suppressed by the White House and the Pentagon that the "truth" about the war had been deliberately concealed from the American public. Capitalizing on justifiable media complaints about military-media relations in the Gulf, some activists seized on these shortcomings to write antiwar editorials. But the public for the most part was not impressed.

Finally, and again reminiscent of the Vietnam era, some antiwar activists charged that the "hyperwar" in Iraq had inflicted casualties, both military and civilian, so severe as to constitute war crimes. Leading this effort was the radical activist Ramsey Clark, who traveled to Baghdad at the height of the air war in February 1991. Clark further charged (see *The Fire This Time*) a conspiracy by the United States to provoke the war in the first place, so as to control the Middle East. His allegations have gained little support outside of the antiwar community.

Although the antiwar movement held a 100,000-strong rally in Washington, D.C., in January 1991, it was largely dismissed by the media because it attracted fewer first-time protestors than did the Vietnam War rallies. According to the *Washington Post*, 9 out of 10 participants had previously attended a protest on some political or social issue: 1 out of 3 were veterans of the anti–Vietnam War demonstrations.

Why did the antiwar movement have such a small impact on most Americans? New York University Professor Mitchell Stephens put forward one answer: "Despite all the debate about 'just wars,' the American people typically seem to base their support or opposition on another consideration: how well a war is going. The Persian Gulf War went well. The protest movement fizzled." (*Long Island Newsday*, March 27, 1991.) *Tikkun* editor Michael Lerner saw the movement as "60's nostalgia at its worst," and the *New Republic*'s Jacob Weisberg noted that even the demonstrators' signs "looked like mildewed relics from old rallies." Antiwar veteran Sam Brown commented that "Generals are always accused of fighting the last war, and maybe the antiwar movement is fighting against the last" (*VFW Magazine*, August 1991).

Many Americans were particularly offended by antiwar protests after the war started. An ABC News poll found that 71 percent disapproved of the protests, and a *Wall Street Journal*/NBC News poll indicated that 60 percent lost respect for antiwar demonstrators once Americans were engaged in actual fighting.

Saddam Hussein also undercut the antiwar movement with his public praise for U.S. protestors. "He immediately made it into a situation where anyone who was against the war was supporting him," said Rochester University professor John Mueller, an expert on wartime public opinion. Indeed, Mueller may also have hit on the real reason for the ineffectiveness of the antiwar movement: "It got outclassed by the war."

See also BLACK U.S. MILITARY FORCES; BOMBING; CASUALTIES: CONSCIENTIOUS OBJECTORS, U.S.; JUST WAR; MEDIA; WAR CRIMES.

Suggestions for further reading: Micah L. Sifry and Christopher Cerf, eds., *The Gulf War Reader* (New York: Times Books, 1991); Ramsey Clark, *The Fire This Time: U.S. War Crimes in the Gulf* (New York: Thunder's Mouth Press, 1992); John MacArthur, *Second Front: Censorship and Propaganda in the Gulf War* (New York: Hill and Wang, 1992), a prime example of an antiwar screed masquerading as a media critique; Todd Gitlin, "Student Activism Without Barricades," *Los Angeles Times*, December 23, 1990. For the *Newsweek* poll and Senator Wellstone's and Representative Conyers's remarks, see Jerry Adams, "The War Within," *Newsweek*, February 4, 1991. Joan E. Rigdon, "Students Prepare To Dodge a Draft That Doesn't Exist," *Wall Street Journal*, February 27, 1991. For Professor Ribuffo's remarks, see Kenneth J. Cooper and Elsa Walsh, "On U.S. Campuses, a Faint Anti-War Cry," *Washington Post*, February 22, 1991. For statistics on the January 1991 marchers, see Richard Morin, "Marchers in D.C. Liberal, Educated, Survey Finds," *Washington Post*, January 27, 1991. See also John B. Judis, "The Strange Case of Ramsey Clark," *New Republic*, April 22, 1991; Mitchell Stephens, "Why the Protest Against the Gulf War Fizzled," *Long Island Newsday*, March 27, 1991. For Michael Lerner's comments, see Jacob Weisberg, "Means of Dissent," *New Republic*, February 25, 1991. For Sam Brown's comments and the ABC and *Wall Street Journal*/NBC polls, see "The Failed Anti-War Movement," *VFW Magazine*, August 1991. For John Mueller's remarks, see Elsa Walsh, "Anti-War Movement Is Fighting a Losing Battle," *Washington Post*, March 5, 1991. See also Peter Collier, "The Other War They Lost," *Second Thoughts*, Spring 1991.

The AH-64 Apache attack helicopter proved to be one of the most effective weapons of the war.
U.S. Army photo courtesy of U.S. Army Ordnance Museum.

APACHE ATTACK HELICOPTER (AH-64)

One of the most effective weapons of the Gulf War, the AH-64 Apache attack helicopter was initially one of the U.S. Army's most controversial weapons systems. Denigrated by critics as "too sophisticated," "unreliable" and "unmaintainable," during the war the Apaches actually flew more than 18,700 hours with a mission-capable rate exceeding 90 percent.

An outgrowth of the Army's experience with helicopter gunships during the Vietnam War, the Apache was developed as part of the postwar advanced attack helicopter (AAH) program to create an antitank helicopter to offset the then Warsaw Pact's advantage in tanks and armored vehicles.

Armed with up to 16 laser-guided HELLFIRE antitank missiles and a nose-mounted 30-mm chain gun, the Apache entered the Army's inventory in December 1983. Survivability was one of its main features, and its cockpit and critical systems were designed to absorb hits from 23-mm and 12.7-mm antiaircraft guns. Among its other avionic features are forward-looking infrared (FLIR), target acquisition and designation sights, an integrated helmet

and display system that automatically aims the guns in the direction the pilot is looking, and a pilot night vision system (PNVS).

With a combat radius of 162 miles and a speed of 145 knots, the Apache is the Army's primary attack helicopter, and 274 were deployed to the Kuwaiti Theater of Operations.

Used to conduct deep attacks, raids, and close battle and armed reconnaissance missions, the Apaches made the first strike of the Gulf War. At 0238 hours (H-22) on January 17, 1991, eight AH-64A Apache attack helicopters from the 101st Airborne Division destroyed two Iraqi early-warning radar sites some 500 nautical miles deep within enemy territory. Credited with destroying numerous Iraqi tanks, trucks and armored vehicles, only one Apache was lost to enemy action, and even then the crew was recovered uninjured.

See also HELICOPTERS; HELLFIRE MISSILE.

Suggestions for further reading: Department of Defense, *Conduct of the Persian Gulf War: Final Report to the Congress,* "Appendix T: Performance of Selected Weapons Systems" (Washington, D.C.:

USGPO, 1992); Department of the Army, *Weapons Systems of the United States Army* (Washington, D.C.: USGPO, 1989); Richard P. Hallion, *Storm Over Iraq: Air Power and the Gulf War* (Washington, D.C.: Smithsonian Institution Press, 1992); "The Soldier Armed: AH-64A Apache Attack Helicopter," *Army,* April 1991; Charles R. Babcock, "Temperamental Helicopter Joins Battle," *Washington Post,* February 20, 1991.

ARAB LEAGUE

Established by the 1945 Pan-Arab Protocol, the 21-member Arab League played an important part in the Persian Gulf War, for it was under the League's auspices that Arab troops were deployed to the Gulf.

At an emergency summit meeting in Cairo, Egypt, on August 4, 1990, the Arab League passed a resolution condemning the Iraqi invasion of Kuwait and calling for restoration of the prewar Kuwaiti government. On August 10, the League voted to ratify United Nations economic sanctions against Iraq and to send an Arab force to Saudi Arabia and other Gulf states to protect them against further attack. The vote was 12 in favor (Egypt, Saudi Arabia, Kuwait, Morocco, Qatar, Bahrain, Somalia, Lebanon, Oman, the United Arab Emirates, Syria and Djibouti), 3 against (Iraq, Libya and the Palestine Liberation Organization), 2 abstaining (Yemen and Algeria), 3 expressing reservations (Jordan, Sudan, and Mauritania) and 1 absent (Tunisia).

Egyptian and Syrian special operations forces were among the first to deploy, arriving in Saudi Arabia in August 1990. Other Arab League forces would soon follow. They would serve not under the U.S. Central Command (CENTCOM) but under its Arab counterpart, the Joint Forces Command (JFC), headed by Lieutenant General Khalid bin Sultan of Saudi Arabia.

Although initially there was some speculation that Arab League forces were dispatched to the Gulf only for defensive purposes and would not attack fellow Arabs, all did in fact take part in the final offensive.

See also COALITION FORCES; GULF COOPERATION COUNCIL (GCC); JOINT FORCES COMMAND (JFC).

Suggestions for further reading: Department of Defense, *Conduct of the Persian Gulf War: Final Report to the Congress* (Washington, D.C.: USGPO, 1992); Micah L. Sifry and Christopher Cerf, eds., *The Gulf War Reader* (New York: Times Books, 1991); Norman Friedman, *Desert Victory: The War for Kuwait* (Annap-olis, Md.: Naval Institute Press, 1991); The staff of U.S. News & Word Report, *Triumph Without Victory: The Unreported History of the Persian Gulf War* (New York: Times Books, 1992); Sterett Pope and Raghida Dergham, "Shifting Sands: Arab Alliances and the Gulf Crisis," *the inter dependent,* November 4, 1990.

ARCENT (ARMY FORCES, CENTRAL COMMAND)

See THIRD U.S. ARMY.

ARGENTINA

See COALITION FORCES.

ARMED FORCES RECREATION CENTER BAHRAIN

Unlike in the Korean and Vietnam Wars, an out-of-theater R&R (Rest and Recuperation) program was not instituted for U.S. service personnel during Operations Desert Shield and Desert Storm. To provide the troops with some relief from the region's arduous conditions, however, a cruise ship, the *Cunard Princess,* was chartered by the United States and docked at Bahrain. It began its first R&R cycle on December 24, 1990.

With a berthing capacity of 900 in 393 cabins, the ship made available a four-day, three-night R&R package to more than 50,000 mainly junior-grade service men and women in its first six months of operation. Lodging, dining, sports, recreation activities and local tour packages were provided free of charge.

Officially called the "Armed Forces Recreation Center Bahrain," the program ceased operation on September 23, 1991, and the *Cunard Princess* was released from its contract.

Suggestions for further reading: Department of Defense, *Conduct of the Persian Gulf War: Final Report to the Congress,* "Appendix I: Coalition Development, Coordination, and Warfare" (Washington, D.C.: USGPO, 1992). For a satirical view, see G. B. Trudeau, *Welcome to Club Scud* (Kansas City: Andrews and McMeel, 1991).

ARMIES, COALITION

"The contribution of the 160,000 non-U.S. Coalition forces," states the official Department of Defense report to the Congress, "was essential to the success of the ground operation."

Among the major coalition ground forces were Egypt's II Corps, consisting of its 3d Mechanized Division, 4th Armored Division and 1st Ranger Regiment; France's 6th Light Armored Division; Syria's

9th Armored Division and 45th Commando Brigade; the United Kingdom's 1st Armoured Division; Saudi Arabia's five armored and mechanized brigades; Pakistan's 7th Armored Brigade; and brigades and battalions from Bangladesh, Kuwait, Morocco, Oman, Qatar, Senegal and the United Arab Emirates.

While figures varied during the course of the war, the following is a close approximation of allied land force contributions:

Country	Contribution
Afghanistan	300 Mujahedeen soldiers
Australia	2 surgical teams
Bahrain	3,500 soldiers
Bangladesh	6,000-man Bangladesh Brigade
	1st East Bengal Infantry Battalion
Czechoslovakia	200-man chemical defense unit
	150-man field hospital
Egypt	40,000-man II Corps
France	20,000-man 6th Light Armored Division
Honduras	150 soldiers
Hungary	Medical team
Kuwait	Al-Fatah, Haq and Khulud Brigades
	15th and 35th Mechanized Brigades
Morocco	6th Mechanized Battalion
Netherlands	Field hospital
	3 Patriot Missile Batteries
New Zealand	Field hospital
Niger	480-man infantry battalion
Oman	Omani Brigade
Pakistan	7th Armored Brigade
	Infantry battalion
Poland	Field hospital
Qatar	7,000-man mechanized task force
Romania	Medical team
Saudi Arabia	5 armored and mechanized brigades
Senegal	Infantry battalion
Sierra Leone	Medical team
South Korea	Medical team
Sweden	Field hospital
Syria	9th Armored Division
	45th Commando Brigade
United Arab Emirates (UAE)	Mechanized battalion
United Kingdom	1st Armoured Division

Unlike the Joint Forces Air Component Commander in the air campaign, there was no unity of command for coalition forces in the ground campaign. Instead, there were parallel command structures: the U.S. Central Command (CENTCOM) controlled all U.S. ground forces as well as the British 1st Armoured Division and the French 6th Light Armored Division; and the Joint Forces/Theater of Operations Command, headed by a Saudi general, controlled all Islamic forces. Unity of effort was nonetheless achieved by mutual cooperation. Both commanders agreed that any military action or operation would be subject to their discussion and approval.

See also ARMOR; COALITION FORCES; COMMAND AND CONTROL; GROUND CAMPAIGN.

Suggestions for further reading: Department of Defense, *Conduct of the Persian Gulf War: Final Report to the Congress,* "Appendix I: Coalition Development, Coordination and Warfare" (Washington, D.C.: USGPO, 1992); Norman Friedman, *Desert Victory: The War for Kuwait* (Annapolis, Md.: Naval Institute Press, 1991), which has a listing of coalition ground forces; Bruce W. Watson, ed., *Military Lessons of the Gulf War* (Novato, Calif. Presidio Press, 1991), which also has a listing of coalition ground forces. See also Frank Chadwick, *Gulf War Fact Book* (Bloomington, Ill.: GDW Publications, 1991).

ARMOR

The ground war in the Kuwaiti Theater of Operations was primarily an armor war dominated on both sides by tanks, armored fighting vehicles (AFVs) and armored personnel carriers (APCs). At the outset of the ground compaign, Iraq was credited with some 5,500 main battle tanks, 1,500 AFVs and 6,000 APCs organized into seven armored/mechanized divisions, six Republican Guard Force divisions and two armored brigades.

U.S. armored/mechanized units included the 1st and 3d Armored Divisions, the 1st Cavalry Division, the 1st and 24th Infantry Divisions (Mechanized), the 2d and 3d Armored Cavalry Regiments, and brigades of the 2d Armored Division, as well as the tanks, assault amphibian vehicles (AAVs) and light armored vehicles (LAVs) of the First Marine Expeditionary Force.

Among other coalition armored forces were Egypt's II Corps with its 3d Mechanized Division and 4th Armored Division, the United Kingdom's 1st Armoured Division, France's 6th Light Armored Division, Syria's 9th Armored Division, Pakistan's 7th Armored Brigade, Kuwait's 35th Mechanized Brigade, Morocco's 6th Mechanized Battalion, the United Arab Emirates' (UAE) mechanized battalion, Qatar's mechanized battalion task force, and Bahrain's motorized infantry company, as well as the several armored and mechanized brigades of the Royal Saudi Land Forces and the Saudi Arabian National Guard.

The M1A1 Abrams, with its 120-mm gun, was the primary U.S. tank in the Persian Gulf War. Some 2,300 M1A1-series tanks were deployed, with the Army fielding 1,178 M1A1s and 594 M1A1 heavy armor (HA) models with depleted uranium armor, and the Marine Corps deploying 16 M1A1s and 60 M1A1 HAs (the remainder was kept in theater reserve). As discussed elsewhere in more detail (see

Soviet-supplied Iraqi tanks and armored vehicles were no match for U.S. tanks and the deadly variety of U.S. antitank weaponry.
U.S. Army photo courtesy of 24th Infantry Division (Mechanized).

ABRAMS M1A1 TANK) the Abrams was by far the most effective tank on the battlefield.

The United States also deployed the Marines' M60-series tanks with their 105-mm guns, as did Bahrain, Saudi Arabia and Egypt. The standard British tank in the Gulf was the Challenger, whose 120-mm rifled cannon has great long-range accuracy. One Royal Scots Guard gunner reported destroying an Iraqi tank with a first-round hit at 5,100 meters.

The French AMX-30, more a tank destroyer than a tank, was also fielded by the Saudis, Qataris and UAE forces; it mounted a 105-mm gun but was less heavily armored, and less effective, than its U.S. and British equivalents. Other coalition tanks included Oman's and Kuwait's British-built Chieftain, with a 120-mm gun, and Kuwait's 125-mm-gun M-84, a Yugoslav-built version of the Soviet T-72. Syria also fielded Soviet-built T-72s as well as 115-mm-gun T-62s.

For its part, Iraq had some 1,000 Czech- or Polish-built 125-mm-gun T-72s, 1,600 Soviet-built 115-mm-gun T-62s, 1,000 Chinese-built 100-mm-gun Type 69s, 500 105-mm-gun Type 59s (a Chinese-built version of the Soviet T-54) and some 1,400 Soviet-built 100- mm-gun T-55 main battle tanks.

Tanks were not the only armored forces on the battlefield. Armored fighting vehicles (AFVs) also played a major role. The mainstay for the U.S. Army were the 2,200 Bradley fighting vehicles. Discussed in more detail elsewhere (see BRADLEY M2/M3 FIGHTING VEHICLE), the tracked M2 Infantry Fighting Vehicle (IFV) and the M3 Cavalry Fighting Vehicle (CFV) mount a 25-mm cannon, TOW antitank missiles, and a 7.62-mm machine gun. The IFV carries a nine-man infantry squad, whereas the CFV is designed for a six-man reconnaissance team.

Also discussed in more detail elsewhere (see ASSAULT AMPHIBIAN VEHICLE) were the Marine Corps's tracked Assault Amphibian Vehicles (AAVs) and wheeled Light Armored Vehicles (LAVs). The more than 500 AAVs deployed to the Gulf were armed with a .50-caliber or a 40-mm machine gun and could carry 21 combat-equipped Marines. The 350 LAVs in the Gulf, armed with 25-mm chain guns and two 7.62-mm machine guns, came in an antitank version mounting a TOW missile, a mortar version mounting an 82-mm mortar, logistics, command-and-control and recovery versions, and the basic scout/reconnaissance version with a commander, driver, gunner and four scouts.

The primary British AFV was the tracked Warrior, armed with a 30-mm Rarden cannon and carrying 7 to 8 troops. Also deployed were the tracked Scorpion and Scimitar light reconnaissance vehicles. The Scorpion, which was also fielded by Oman and the UAE, was armed with a 76-mm gun, while the Scimitar mounted a 30-mm gun.

The French fielded the tracked AMX-10P AFV armed with a 20-mm gun, but it can also mount a Milan antitank missile. With a capacity of eight troops, the AMX-10 was also used by Saudi Arabia, Qatar and the UAE. The French also deployed the AMX-10RC with a 105-mm gun; a wheeled armored car, it was employed more as a light tank or tank destroyer than as the reconnaissance vehicle it was designed to be.

Also prominent on the battlefield was the venerable Vietnam-era American-built M-113 Armored Personnel Carrier (APC). Fully tracked, armed with a .50-caliber machine gun, and in some cases mounting additional applique armor, the M113, which can carry 11 combat-equipped troops, was fielded by the United States, Saudi Arabia, Kuwait, Egypt and Morocco.

Both Syria and Kuwait deployed Soviet-built Bronevaya Maschina Piekhota (BMP) AFVs. The prototype of all modern infantry fighting vehicles, the tracked BMP is armed with a 30-mm gun, mounts an AT-4 missile and can carry 7 troops. The 1,000 Soviet- and Czech-supplied BMP-1s fielded by the Iraqi Republican Guard were armed with a 73-mm gun and an AT-3 Sagger antitank missile, and could carry 8 troops. Other Iraqi units were equipped with the more than 1,000 Chinese-supplied, tracked Type 354s, which the Iraqis called the BTR-63; armed with a 12.7-mm machine gun, it could carry 13 troops.

Wheeled AFVs were also in the Iraqi inventory, including the French-supplied ERC-90 Panhard armored car, mounting a 90-mm gun, and the more than 1,000 Soviet-supplied BTR-60 armored personnel carriers. The latter, each armed with a 12.7-mm machine gun, can carry eight troops.

One major U.S. advantage in the Persian Gulf War was the superiority of the new composite armor incorporated into the design of the Abrams tank. Another innovation was the use of Chobham armor, developed by the British at their Chobham arsenal and incorporated into their armored vehicles. A blend of ceramic blocks sandwiched between sheets of conventional armor, Chobham armor is extremely effective against shaped-charge antitank rounds.

Yet another innovation was the use of depleted uranium in the armor plating of the heavy armor version of the M1A1 Abrams tank. By one account, seven M1s were hit by Iraqi T-72 rounds and none received discernible damage.

See also ABRAMS M1A1 TANK; ASSAULT AMPHIBIAN VEHICLE; BRADLEY M2/M3 FIGHTING VEHICLE; DEPLETED URANIUM; GROUND CAMPAIGN.

Suggestions for further reading: Department of Defense, *Conduct of the Persian Gulf War: Final Report to the Congress;* "Appendix T: Performance of Selected Weapons Systems" (Washington, D.C.: USGPO, 1992); Norman Friedman, *Desert Victory: The War for Kuwait* (Annapolis; Md.: Naval Institute Press, 1991), especially Appendix A, which has a listing of ground force units. Particularly useful is Frank Chadwick, *Gulf War Fact Book* (Bloomington, Ill.: GDW Publications, 1991). See also *The Armored Fist* (Alexandria, Va.: Time-Life Books, 1991).

ARMORED FIGHTING VEHICLE (AFV)

See ARMOR; ASSAULT AMPHIBIAN VEHICLE; BRADLEY M2/M3 FIGHTING VEHICLE.

ARMY

In military circles, the term "army" has both a general and a specific meaning. In its general sense, it is synonymous with ground forces—that is, "a large, organized body of soldiers for waging war, especially on land." In the U.S. military, "army" specifically refers to an organizational entity composed of two or more corps and usually commanded by a lieutenant general.

The Third U.S. Army, which incorporated the U.S. VII and XVII Corps, the British 1st Armoured Division and the French 6th Light Armored Division, was the only army per se on the Persian Gulf battlefield. It also served as the ARCENT (Army Component, Central Command) headquarters.

See also ARMIES, COALITION; ARMY, IRAQ; ARMY, U.S.; CENTCOM (CENTRAL COMMAND); ORGANIZATION FOR COMBAT, U.S.; THIRD U.S. ARMY.

ARMY, IRAQ

At the beginning of the Gulf crisis, Iraqi's ground forces were the largest in the Persian Gulf and the fourth largest army in the world. Battle-tested in the Iran-Iraq war, this 955,000-man army was equipped with more than 5,000 main battle tanks, 5,000 armored fighting vehicles and 3,000 artillery pieces.

The regular army consisted of some 50 divisions organized into Corps I through VIII. Most were infantry divisions, but there were also seven armored or mechanized divisions. Equipped mainly with 1960s-vintage Soviet and Chinese equipment, the divisions ranged in combat effectiveness from good in the case of those that existed before the Iran-Iraq war, to poor in the largely conscript infantry divisions.

The elite, eight-division Republican Guard Forces Command (RGFC) was Iraq's most capable and loyal force, and had the best equipment. Organized into two corps, it consisted of the 1st Hammurabi and 2d Medina Armored Divisions, the 3d Tawakalna and 5th Baghdad Mechanized Divisions, the 4th al-Faw, 6th Nebuchadnezzar and 7th Adnan Motorized Divisions and an 8th special forces division.

Five new Guard divisions were announced in January 1991, including the al-Nidala division (the Iraqi name for Kuwait City), the al-Abed and the al-Mustafa divisions. The RGFC also included some independent brigades.

Comprising almost 20 percent of Iraq's ground forces, the RGFC was equipped with state-of-the-art Soviet T-72 tanks, Soviet BMP armored fighting vehicles, French GCT self-propelled howitzers and Austrian GHN-45 towed howitzers. Subordinate to the State Special Security Apparatus, not the Defense Ministry, the RGFC was under GHQ (General Headquarters) operational control during combat.

The initial invasion of Kuwait was conducted by the RGFC (less the 5th Baghdad Division, which continued its garrison duties), but Guard Forces were soon withdrawn and held in reserve. The 10-division III Corps was deployed along the Kuwaiti-Saudi border, and the newly formed 5-division VIII Tank Corps was deployed in central Kuwait. The 7-division IV Corps was committed to coastal defenses, and the 6-division VII Corps was deployed in southern Iraq, as was the 3-division IX Reserve Corps.

In January 1991, the U.S. Defense Intelligence Agency estimated that Iraq had 42–43 divisions in the Kuwaiti Theater of Operations, including 540,000

troops, more than 4,200 tanks, 2,800 armored fighing vehicles and approximately 3,100 artillery pieces. "In retrospect," according to the 1993 *Gulf War Airpower Survey*, "postwar analysis confirmed the presence of this number of divisions but concluded that the number of troops, armor and artillery in these units was overstated. . . . A revised estimate [found] no more than 336,000 Iraqi troops in the theater on 17 January 1991. . . . The Iraqi Army had approximately 800 fewer tanks and 600 fewer artillery pieces [in the theater] at the beginning of the air war than originally thought—approximately 20 percent fewer."

But Iraq was still a formidable foe, and it was initially feared that the entrenched Iraqi Army would offer stiff resistance. In fact, however, the army had been decimated by the air campaign and was annihilated by the 100-hour ground campaign.

Official Department of Defense estimates are that 3,847 Iraqi tanks were destroyed or captured, as were 1,450 armored fighting vehicles and 2,917 artillery pieces. The U.S. Central Command estimated that at war's end, only seven of Iraq's combat divisions remained capable of offensive action. An estimated 86,000 Iraqi prisoners had been taken (64,000 by U.S. forces), and initial reports were that 10,000 Iraqi soldiers had been killed. Subsequent analysis revealed that these initial casualty figures were drastically overstated.

See also AIR CAMPAIGN; ARMOR; CASUALTIES; FIELD ARTILLERY; GROUND CAMPAIGN; INFANTRY.

Suggestions for further reading: Department of Defense, *Conduct of the Persian Gulf War: Final Report to the Congress,* "Chapter I: The Invasion of Kuwait," "Chapter VIII: The Ground Campaign" (Washington, D.C.: USGPO, 1992); Norman Friedman, *Desert Victory: The War for Kuwait* (Annapolis, Md.: Naval Institute Press, 1991), whose Appendix A has a detailed breakdown of Iraqi ground forces; Richard P. Hallion, *Storm Over Iraq: Air Power and the Gulf War* (Washington, D.C.: Smithsonian Institution Press, 1992). Bruce W. Watson, ed., *Military Lessons of the Gulf War* (Novato, Calif.: Presidio Press, 1991) has a listing of Iraqi ground forces; Frank Chadwick, *Gulf War Fact Book* (Bloomington, Ill.: GDW Publications, 1991) lists the Iraqi Order of Battle. See also *The Military Balance 1990–1991* (London: International Institute for Strategic Studies, 1990). For revised estimates of Iraqi strength, see Eliot A. Cohen et al.,

The coalition air and ground campaigns inflicted terrible losses on the Iraqi Army.
U.S. Army photo courtesy of 24th Infantry Division (Mechanized).

Gulf War Airpower Survey (Washington, D.C.: USGPO, 1993).

ARMY, U.S.

The United States Army, including the Army Reserve and the Army National Guard, is the most formidable ground force in the world. During the Persian Gulf War—and in conjunction with the U.S. Air Force, Navy, Marine Corps, and coalition allies—it played the decisive role, bringing the war to an end in a lightning 100-hour ground campaign.

A total of 306,730 U.S. Army, Army Reserve and National Guard soldiers, including 26,000 women, were deployed to the Kuwaiti Theater of Operations (KTO). In the first wave was the 82d Airborne Division, which arrived on August 8, 1990, within 31 hours of the initial alert. The 82d was followed in mid-September by the 24th Infantry Division (Mechanized) and its attached 197th Infantry Brigade, and in October by the 101st Airborne Division (Air Assault), the 1st Cavalry Division with its attached 1st Brigade of the 2d Armored Division, and the 3d Cavalry Regiment.

Also included in the initial deployment were XVII Airborne Corps, III Corps Artillery, the 11th Air Defense Brigade, the I and XIII Corps Support Commands and, from Germany, the 7th Medical Command and the 12th Combat Aviation Brigade.

Under the command of the Third U.S. Army, which doubled as the ARCENT (Army Component, Central Command), the nondivisional combat support and combat service support units were organized under the newly formed 22d Theater Army Support Command.

On November 8, 1990, President Bush ordered the deployment of the U.S. VII Corps from Europe and the 1st Infantry Division (Mechanized) from Fort Riley, Kansas. Among VII Corps's units were the 1st Armored Division, the 3d Armored Division, the 2d Armored Cavalry Regiment, the 2d Brigade of the 2d Armored Division, and the VII Corps's Support Command.

More than 1,040 units and more than 140,000 personnel of the Army Reserve Component were mobilized for the war, including more than 60,000 soldiers from the Army National Guard and more than 79,000 from the Army Reserve. In all, some 78,000 reservists actually served in the Gulf. Although most reservists served in combat support and combat service support units, reserve combat units were also mobilized: the 142d Field Artillery Brigade from the Arkansas/Oklahoma National Guard, and the Tennessee/Kentucky/West Virginia National Guard's 196th Field Artillery Brigade were deployed to the Gulf. Also mobilized were the 48th Infantry Brigade from Georgia, the 155th Armored Brigade from Mississippi, and the 256th Infantry Brigade from Louisiana, each of which was in predeployment training when the war ended.

Army AH-64 Apache attack helicopters from the 101st Aviation Brigade struck the first blow of the war when, early on the night of January 17, 1991, they attacked two Iraqi early-warning radar sites. Army Patriot missiles were also active from the beginning of the war, countering Scud attacks in both Saudi Arabia and Israel.

Between January 17 and February 16, under air cover, some 200,000 troops of the VII Corps and the XVIII Airborne Corps were shifted to attack positions along the Saudi-Iraqi border, and Army Special Forces teams were inserted deep into Iraq to perform strategic reconnaissance.

At 0400 hours (Gulf time) on February 24, 1991, the coalition's ground campaign was launched. Across a 300-mile front, U.S. Army, Marine and allied coalition forces launched the largest ground campaign since World War II. With the 8,508 armored vehicles of VII Corps forming the main attack, the XVIII Airborne Corps with 2,769 tracked vehicles and 1,026 aircraft attacking along multiple axes, and the First Marine Expeditionary Force (with the "Tiger" Brigade of the Army's 2d Armored Division attached) and Arab coalition forces attacking along the coast, the ground war was over 100 hours after it began. The world's fourth largest army had been decisively defeated.

U.S. Army losses were gratifyingly light. Of the approximately 300,000 soldiers that were deployed, 96 were killed in action, another 84 died from nonbattle causes, and 354 were wounded in action. Remarkably, only three M1A1 Abrams tanks and five M2/M3 Bradley fighting vehicles were damaged by enemy fire. Five Army helicopters were lost in action, including two UH-60 Blackhawks, one AH-64 Apache, one UH-1 Huey and one OH-58 Kiowa.

Seventy-four Silver Stars were awarded for gallantry in action during the war; 24 Legions of Merit were awarded for distinguished service; 23 Distinguished Flying Crosses were awarded for valor, and 74 for meritorious service; 37 Soldier's Medals were awarded for noncombat heroism; and 891 Bronze Star Medals were awarded for heroism, 20,005 for meritorious achievement, and 6,327 for meritorious service.

For wounds received in action, 396 Purple Hearts were awarded, 97 of them posthumously. In addition, 694 Air Medals were awarded for valor, 4,494 for achievement, and 555 for service; 976 Army Commendation Medals were awarded for valor, 68,693 for achievement, and 12,009 for service. Combat Infantryman Badges were awarded to 21,775 soldiers, as were 3,136 Combat Medical Badges.

See also listings for specific units; ABRAMS M1A1 TANK; AIRLAND BATTLE DOCTRINE; APACHE AT-TACK HELICOPTER; ARMOR; ATACMS (M39 ARMY TACTICAL MISSILE SYSTEM); BLACK U.S. MILITARY FORCES; BRADLEY M2/M3 FIGHTING VEHICLE; CAVALRY; COMBAT INFANTRYMAN BADGE; COMBAT MEDICAL BADGE; FIELD ARTILLERY; GROUND CAMPAIGN; HELICOPTERS; INFANTRY; MLRS (MULTIPLE LAUNCH ROCKET SYSTEM); MOBILIZATION, U.S.; PATRIOT MISSILE; WOMEN IN THE MILITARY; YEOSOCK, JOHN J.

Suggestions for further reading: Department of Defense, *Conduct of the Persian Gulf War: Final Report to the Congress,* "Chapter VIII: The Ground Campaign" (Washington, D.C.: USGPO, 1992); Lt. Gen. Richard L. West, USA (Ret.) et al., *Special Report: The US Army in Operation Desert Storm* (Arlington, Va.: Association of the United States Army, 1991); Lt. Gen. John J. Yeosock, USA, "H+100: An Army Comes of Age in the Persian Gulf," *Army,* October 1991; Charles E. Kirkpatrick, *Building the Army for Desert Storm* (Arlington, Va.: The Institute of Land Warfare, AUSA, 1991); Colonel Harry G. Summers Jr., *On Strategy II: A Critical Analysis of the Gulf War* (New York: Dell, 1992); *Field Manual 100-5: Operations* (Washington, D.C.: USGPO, 1986); Norman Friedman, *Desert Victory: The War for Kuwait* (Annapolis, Md.: Naval Institute Press, 1991); Bruce W. Watson, ed., *Military Lessons of the Gulf War* (Novato, Calif., Presidio Press, 1991).

ARNETT, PETER

See CNN (CABLE NEWS NETWORK).

ARTHUR, STANLEY R(OGER), VICE ADMIRAL, USN (1935–)

Commander of the U.S. Seventh Fleet and Commander, U.S. Naval Component Central Command (COMUSNAVCENT) during Operation Desert Storm, Admiral Stanley Arthur entered the United States Navy through the Naval Reserve Officer Training Corps (NROTC) at Miami University in Oxford, Ohio, and was commisioned in June 1957.

Designated a naval aviator in 1958, he flew more than 500 combat missions in the A-4 Skyhawk during the Vietnam War. He holds a Bachelor of Science degree in aeronautical engineering from the Naval Postgraduate School and a Master of Science degree in administration from George Washington University.

Among his significant assignments were command of the USS *Coral Sea* (CV 43); commander, Rapid Deployment Naval Forces; and a peacetime tour in COMUSNAVCENT, commander, Carrier Group SEVEN. After his promotion to vice admiral in February 1988, he served as deputy chief of naval operations (logistics).

On December 1, 1990, Admiral Arthur replaced Vice Admiral Henry Mauz as Commander, U.S. Seventh Fleet and concurrently COMUSNAVCENT. He directed the operations and tactical movements of more than 96,000 Navy and Marine Corps personnel and the largest U.S. naval armada since World War II. The 130 U.S. Navy and other coalition ships in-

Vice Admiral Arthur (right) assumes command of the U.S. Seventh Fleet from Vice Admiral Mauz.
U.S. Navy photo courtesy of U.S. Naval Institute.

cluded 6 aircraft carrier battle groups, 2 battleships, 2 hospital ships, 4 minesweepers and numerous combat and amphibious ships.

On April 24, 1991, Admiral Arthur relinquished command of USNAVCENT but continued as commander of the Seventh Fleet until July 1992. Promoted to full admiral (i.e., four stars), he assumed duties as vice chief of naval operations on July 6, 1992.

Admiral Arthur has been awarded the Navy Distinguished Service Medal (3 awards), the Legion of Merit (4 awards, including 1 with combat "V"), the Distinguished Flying Cross (11 awards), the Meritorious Service Medal, the individual Air Medal (4 awards), the Strike/Flight Air Medal (47 awards), the Navy Commendation Medal (2 awards, including 1 with combat "V") as well as numerous other service medals and foreign decorations.

See also CENTCOM (CENTRAL COMMAND); MARITIME CAMPAIGN; NAVY, U.S.; SEVENTH U.S. FLEET.

ARTILLERY

See AIR DEFENSES; ATACMS (M39 ARMY TACTICAL MISSILE SYSTEM); BULL, GERALD V.; FIELD ARTILLERY; MLRS (MULTIPLE LAUNCH ROCKET SYSTEM).

ASSAULT AMPHIBIAN VEHICLE (AAV7A1)

The Assault Amphibian Vehicle (AAV7A1) is the U.S. Marine Corps equivalent of the U.S. Army's M113 Armored Personnel Carrier (APC) and Bradley Fighting Vehicle. It is designed to carry the surface assault elements of the landing force from amphibious ships to inland objectives. Once ashore, it acts as an infantry assault vehicle to carry troops into the attack.

The AAV has three variants. The AAVP7A1 is the baseline infantry fighting vehicle, but it also carries combat engineer teams and special mission kits for minefield breeching. The AAVC7A1 is fitted with additional communications equipment and is used as a mobile command post. The AAVR7A1 is a recovery and maintenance vehicle.

With a crew of 3, the AAV can carry 21 combat-equipped Marines or 10,000 pounds of cargo. It has a 300-mile land cruising range and a 7-hour water cruising time, and can travel at 25–30 miles per hour (mph)on land and 6 mph in the water. With 1.4 to 1.75 inches of aluminum armor plating, the AAV is armed with a M85 .50-caliber machine gun in its

electric-drive turret or a Mk 19 MOD-3 40-mm machine gun and a M2HB .50-caliber machine gun.

Although the AAV proved to be effective in the desert environment, its firing sights had no night- or low-visibility capability; thus, the vehicle was unable to engage targets beyond its visual range. The AAV also lacked the speed to keep up with the M1A1 Abrams tank.

During Operation Desert Storm, 473 AAVP7A1s, 40 AAVC7A1s and 19 AAVR7A1s were committed, and an additional 93 AAVP7A1s, 6 AAVC7A1s and 4 AAVR7A1s were aboard the amphibious task force.

See also AMPHIBIOUS TASK FORCE; ARMORED FIGHTING VEHICLES.

Suggestion for further reading Department of Defense, *Conduct of the Persian Gulf War: Final Report to the Congress,* "Appendix T: Performance of Selected Weapons Systems" (Washington, D.C.: USGPO, 1992).

ATACMS (M39 ARMY TACTICAL MISSILE SYSTEM)

Launched from the MLRS (multiple launch rocket system) M270 launcher, the M39 ATACMS (army tactical missile system) is a solid-rocket-propelled conventional ballistic missile designed to strike deep battlefield targets. With a range of more than 100 kilometers, it can carry the M74 antipersonnel/anti-material warhead with a "footprint" of about 600 square feet. Each of the M74's 944 bomblets produces some 1,200 splinters with a kill radius of 15 meters. A submunition warhead is also under development.

Two ATACMS-capable batteries and some 105 ATACMS missiles were deployed to the Gulf by the U.S. Army; 33 missiles were actually fired.

According to the official Defense Department account, during one ATACMS strike more than 200 unarmored vehicles were destroyed as they attempted to cross a bridge.

See also FIELD ARTILLERY; MLRS (MULTIPLE LAUNCH ROCKET SYSTEM).

Suggestions for further reading Department of Defense, *Conduct of the Persian Gulf War: Final Report to the Congress,* "Appendix T: Performance of Selected Weapons Systems" (Washington, D.C.: USGPO, 1992); Richard P. Hallion, *Storm Over Iraq: Air Power and the Gulf War* (Washington, D.C.: Smithsonian Institution Press, 1992); "M39 Army Tactical Missile System (ATACMS)," *Army,* January 1992.

ATO (AIR TASKING ORDER)

The Air Tasking Order (ATO) was the daily schedule providing the details and guidance that aircrews needed to execute the coalition air campaign's Master Attack Plan (MAP). Target assignments, route plans, altitudes, refueling tracks, fuel offloads, call signs, IFF (identification friend or foe) and other details for every coalition sortie were included in the ATO.

The ATO was a two-part document. The first part focused on targeting and mission data and on EW/SEAD (electronic warfare/suppression of enemy air defenses) support. The second part contained special instructions on such topics as communications frequencies, tanker and reconnaissance support, AWACS (airborne warning and control system) coverage, combat search and rescue (CSAR) resources, and routes into and out of enemy airspace.

The ATO provided a single script for air attacks, allowing command and control (C^2) elements to orchestrate combat and support operations. Although it included Navy flights over Kuwait and Iraq, the ATO excluded Navy sorties over water.

Once approved by the JFACC (Joint Forces Air Component Commander), the ATO, which could run to more than 300 pages of text, was entered into the computer-aided force management system (CAFMS) and transmitted electronically each day to those units equipped to receive it. Because aircraft carriers were not so equipped, a hard-copy ATO was sent to them by courier. According to the official Department of Defense (DOD) report to the Congress, "There were acknowledged difficulties with the mechanics of disseminating the ATO because of the lack of interoperability between the carrier data systems and CAFMS. . . . Planners rarely changed Navy sorties because of planning and communications concerns. Initially, this limited the flexible use of Navy air assets."

The DOD report went on to note:

> Planners built flexibility and responsiveness into operations by delegating most detailed mission planning to the wing and unit level. Some aircraft were held . . . on ground alert to allow quick response to combat developments. . . . Many aircraft were assigned to generic or regional target locations, such as kill boxes in the KTO where they might receive detailed attack instructions from air controllers."

Despite these shortcomings, the DOD report concluded that "it would have been impossible to achieve the air campaign's successes and conduct combat operations as they were fought without the . . . ATO."

See also AIR CAMPAIGN.

Suggestions for further reading: Department of Defense, *Conduct of the Persian Gulf War: Final Report to the Congress*, "Chapter VI: The Air Campaign" (Washington, D.C.: USGPO, 1992). Norman Friedman, *Desert Victory: The War for Kuwait* (Annapolis, Md.: Naval Institute Press, 1991) is very critical of the ATO concept; for a more favorable view, see Richard P. Hallion, *Storm Over Iraq: Air Power and the Gulf War* (Washington, D.C.: Smithsonian Institution Press, 1992). In "From the Strike Cell," *US Naval Institute Proceedings*, June 1991, Captain Lyle G. Bien, the Navy liaison officer to JFACC, analyzes the ATO from a Navy perspective.

ATROCITIES
See WAR CRIMES.

AUSTRALIA
See COALITION FORCES; MINESWEEPING.

AWACS (AIRBORNE WARNING AND CONTROL SYSTEM)

The E-3 AWACS is a land-based, airborne early warning and control aircraft used by the U.S. Air Force (USAF), the Royal Saudi Air Force and NATO (North Atlantic Treaty Organization). With a cruising speed of 460 knots, a flight crew of 4, and 19 to 29 onboard mission specialists, this air-refuelable aircraft's flight time is limited only by the crew's requirement for rest.

AWACS provides all-altitude surveillance of airborne targets over land and water, with the mission of detecting enemy aircraft, controlling defensive friendly fighters, controlling strike aircraft and tankers, and providing the long-range air picture.

In order to maintain a surveillance station around the clock by using multiple aircraft in sequence, the USAF deployed 5 E-3s to the Kuwaiti Theater of Operations (KTO) at the beginning of the crisis and established an orbit 110–125 miles from the borders of Kuwait and Iraq on August 9, 1990. By the commencement of the air campaign on January 17, 1991, 11 AWACS were in the KTO and 3 had been deployed to Incirlik, Turkey, where, together with NATO AWACS aircraft, they helped maintain sovereignty over Turkish airspace.

At the start of Operation Desert Storm, four USAF E-3s were airborne over Saudi Arabia (three forward, one to the rear) and one was over southern Turkey. The rearmost E-3 was used primarily to manage aerial refueling operations. A Saudi E-3 over southern Saudi Arabia was used primarily for relaying communications.

During the war, AWACS aircraft flew 448 sorties for a total of 5,546 hours. Supporting all daily air-tasking-order activities, they controlled some 2,240 sorties a day, for a total of more than 90,000 sorties.

Throughout the war, AWACS provided the primary air picture to commanders. In addition, AWACS helped to ensure that there were no mid-air collisions between coalition aircraft. No AWACS were damaged and no AWACS personnel were injured as a result of enemy action.

See also ABCCC (AIRBORNE BATTLEFIELD COMMAND AND CONTROL CENTER); AIR CAMPAIGN; ATO (AIR TASKING ORDER).

Suggestions for further reading: Department of Defense, *Conduct of the Persian Gulf War: Final Report to the Congress,* "Chapter VI: The Air Campaign;" "Appendix T: Performance of Selected Weapons Systems" (Washington, D.C.: USGPO, 1992); Norman Friedman, *Desert Victory: The War for Kuwait* (Annapolis, Md.: Naval Institute Press, 1991); Richard P. Hallion; *Storm Over Iraq: Air Power and the Gulf War* (Washington, D.C.: Smithsonian Institution Press, 1992).

AWARDS, COALITION FORCES

In addition to U.S. service medals, those members of the U.S. Armed Forces who served in the Persian Gulf War were also awarded the Kuwait Liberation Medal by the Government of Saudi Arabia. As required by law, the U.S. has approved acceptance of this foreign award and its wear on the military uniform.

Those eligible include those who served in or flew over the Kuwait Theater of Operations (KTO) between January 17, 1991 and February 28, 1991.

See also KTO (KUWAITI THEATER OF OPERATIONS); SERVICE MEDALS, U.S.

AWARDS, U.S.

See DECORATIONS, U.S.; SERVICE MEDALS, U.S.

B

B-52 STRATOFORTRESS BOMBER

Conceived and built in the 1950s as a strategic intercontinental nuclear bomber, the B-52 Stratofortress instead proved its worth in both the Vietnam and Persian Gulf Wars as a tactical bomber armed with conventional bombs and missiles.

First entering operational service on June 29, 1955, the B-52 was originally designed as a high-level bomber. But in the 1960s, in order to contend with advances in Soviet air defenses, it switched to low-level penetration, flying as low as 200 feet above the ground at 400 knots.

The G model, which entered service in 1959, was used both to launch conventional ALCMs (air-launched cruise missiles) and as a conventional bomber. With a crew of six, the B-52 has an un-refueled range of 5,016 miles with a 70,000-pound bomb load.

Seven B-52Gs carrying a total of 35 ALCMs took off from Barksdale Air Force Base (AFB) in Louisiana prior to H-Hour and struck eight strategic targets in Iraq. Their round-trip sorties—over a distance of more than 14,000 miles and aloft for 35 hours—were the longest combat missions in time and distance in military history.

Forty-one B-52Gs, modified to improve their conventional bombing capability, flew more than 1,600 combat sorties during the war. They dropped more than 72,000 weapons and delivered more than 27,000 tons of munitions on targets in the Kuwaiti Theater of Operations. Making up only 3 percent of the combat aircraft, they delivered 30 percent of the air munitions.

Flying from bases in England, Spain, the Indian Ocean island of Diego Garcia and Saudi Arabia, three of the four B-52 bomber wings routinely flew 14- to 16-hour missions. The Stratofortress could carry a variety of bomb loads, including 45 250-pound bombs, 51 500-pound or 750-pound bombs, or 18 2,000-pound bombs.

One B-52G sustained minor damage when it was hit while leaving a target area, but there were no casualties. Returning from a raid over Iraq, another B-52G developed mechanical difficulties and crashed in the Indian Ocean, killing three crewmen.

See also AIR-LAUNCHED CRUISE MISSILE; BOMBING.

Sugggestions for further reading: Department of Defense, *Conduct of the Persian Gulf War: Final Report to the Congress,* "Appendix T: Performance of Selected Weapons Systems" (Washington, D.C.: USGPO, 1992; Norman Friedman, *Desert Victory: The War for Kuwait* (Annapolis, Md.: Naval Institute Press, 1991); Richard P. Hallion, *Storm Over Iraq: Air Power and the Gulf War* (Washington, D.C.: Smithsonian Institution Press, 1992); Jeffrey L. Ethell, *B-52 Stratofortress* (London: Arms & Armour Press, 1989).

BAATH PARTY

Founded in the early 1940s in Damascus, Syria, by three school teachers—the Greek Orthodox Christian Michel Aflaq, the Sunni Muslim Salah al-Din al-Bitar, and the Alawite Zaki al-Arsuzi—the Baath (literally "Resurrection" or "Renaisance") Party was inspired by the vision of a radiant Arab future.

Refusing to recognize the legitimacy of modern Arab states, the Baaths preached that all had to be replaced by a united Arab nation under its leadership. The intellectual appeal of the party was heightened when it merged with the Arab Socialist Party in the late 1940s, becoming officially the Arab Baath Socialist Party.

Intensely popular among young Syrian army officers, the Baath Party came to power in Syria in 1963, and Baathism was made the official ideology of the state. Baathism was also strong among the Iraqi army officers who seized power in Baghdad in 1963, but they were deposed when a split developed within the party.

On July 30, 1969, the Baath Party again seized power in Baghdad. Saddam Hussein, who had joined the party in 1957, served as deputy to his older cousin, the then head of state Ahmas Hasan al-Bakr. When al-Bakr retired in 1979, he was succeeded by Saddam Hussein, who was named president of Iraq and served concurrently as secretary general of the Iraqi Baath Party.

Although Syria and Iraq share a common Baathist ideology, relations between them have been acrimonious, so much so that Syria joined the anti-Iraq coalition in the Gulf War.

See also SYRIA.

Suggestions for further reading: Elis Kedourie, "What's Baathism Anyway?" *Wall Street Journal,* October 17, 1990; Micah L. Sifry and Christopher Cerf, eds., *The Gulf War Reader* (New York: Times Books, 1991).

BAGHDAD

The capital of Iraq and its largest city, Baghdad had a prewar population of some 3.4 million. As the country's leadership center, telecommunications hub, and strategic integrated air defense command center, Baghdad was the focus of the coalition's strategic air campaign.

At 3:00 A.M. on January 17, 1991, the Persian Gulf War began with air strikes on Baghdad by ALCMs (air-launched cruise missiles) launched from B-52 Stratofortress bombers, by Tomahawk cruise missiles fired from ships at sea, and by F-117A Stealth aircraft. Within hours of the first attack, key parts of the Iraqi leadership, command and control network, strategic air defense system and nuclear-biological-chemical capabilities were neutralized. Electrical production grids, telecommunications facilities, bridges and rail nets were also hard hit.

Baghdad had one of the most sophisticated air defense systems in the world, several orders of magnitude greater than the defenses around Hanoi during the Vietnam War. For that reason, strikes on Baghdad were limited to cruise missiles and F-117A Stealth aircraft, none of which were lost to enemy action.

Particular care was taken by coalition forces to avoid inflicting civilian casualties, but some civilians were killed nonetheless. There were wildly inflated claims of civilian bombing casualties by antiwar activists, but their figures did stand up to more dispassionate analysis. "If projections of civilian casualties in Baghdad are based on the highest estimates for the worst hit areas," wrote Erika Munk in the May 6, 1991, edition of *The Nation*, "the American 'clean' bombing of Baghdad was the direct cause of 3,000 civilian casualties. . . . the *lowest* number of civilian

deaths from bombing of a major city in the history of modern war."

See also BIOLOGICAL WARFARE; BOMBING; BOMB SHELTER CONTROVERSY; CASUALTIES; CNN (CABLE NEWS NETWORK); NUCLEAR WEAPONS; WAR CRIMES.

Suggestions for further reading: Michael Kelly, *Martyrs' Day: Chronicle of a Small War* (New York: Random House, 1993) has an account of Baghdad before, during and after the war. Major General Perry M. Smith, USAF (Ret.), *How CNN Fought the War: A View from the Inside* (New York: Birch Lane Press, 1991) has an account of CNN's news coverage from Baghdad. For an account of the air campaign, see Department of Defense, *Conduct of the Persian Gulf War: Final Report to the Congress,* "Chapter VI: The Air Campaign" (Washington, D.C.: USGPO, 1992). For the claims of antiwar activists, see Ramsey Clark, *The Fire This Time: U.S. War Crimes in the Gulf* (New York: Thunder's Mouth Press, 1992).

BAHRAIN

A member of both the Arab League and the Gulf Cooperation Council (GCC), the State of Bahrain played an important part in the Persian Gulf War.

An island in the Gulf of Bahrain between the Qatar Peninsula and Saudi Arabia, Bahrain's 1990 population was 520,286. With a land area of 268 square miles, it is smaller than New York City. A British protectorate from 1861, it declared its independence on August 15, 1971. Long ruled by the Khalifa family, its head of state is Amir Isa bin Sulman al-Khalifa.

With oil reserves estimated to be 173 million barrels in 1985, Bahrain has an economy dominated by oil production and processing and by offshore banking. Its capital city, Manama, had an estimated 1988 population of 151,000. Bahrain has several ports and three major airfields. Primarily a low arid desert plain, the country is mild and pleasant in the winter but hot and humid in the summer.

In July 1977, the United States and Bahrain concluded an agreement for continued leasing of docking and shore facilities by the U.S. Middle East Force, which had been stationed at Manama since 1949. Before the Gulf War, some $1 billion in U.S. Air Force prepositioned assets were stored there, including fuel, ammunition and equipment sufficient to support 1,200 personnel at 14 aircraft bed-down facilties. The U.S. Navy also maintained forward logistics sites in Bahrain and established a sea port of debarkation there.

During the Gulf War, Bahrain hosted a large part of the coalition's fighter and tanker force, and provided important port activities to maintain coalition shipping. It also provided lodging, food and facilities for the personnel and equipment based there, including the fighters, transports and tankers of the Marine Corps's MAG (Marine Air Group) 11 at Bahrain International Airport; the U.S. Navy-staffed 350-bed hospital; and the Navy's E-2 Hawkeye aircraft. A rest-and-recreation (R&R) center aboard the cruise ship Cunard Princess was also established in Bahrain.

Bahrain's naval forces, including its Maritime Intercept Force (MIF), participated in the maritime operations of Desert Storm. Its air force joined the coalition's air campaign, and the Bahraini Infantry Company was part of Task Force Othman, one of the task forces comprising JFC-E (Joint Forces Command-East). According to U.S. Central Command, two Bahraini soldiers were wounded in action during the Persian Gulf War.

See also AIR FORCES, COALITION; ARMED FORCES RECREATION CENTER BAHRAIN; ARMIES, COALITION; COALITION FORCES; GULF COOPERATION COUNCIL (GCC); NAVY, COALITION.

Suggestion for further reading: Department of Defense, *Conduct of the Persian Gulf War: Final Report to the Congress* (Washington, D.C.: USGPO, 1992).

BAKER, JAMES A. III
See STATE DEPARTMENT, U.S.

BALLISTIC LASER PROTECTIVE SPECTACLES (BLPS)
Part of the protective gear issued to U.S. soldiers in the Persian Gulf were what appeared to be wraparound sunglasses. But these "sunshades" were much more than that. Officially known as "ballistic laser protective spectacles (BLPS)," these safety goggles provided protection against sand, small shell fragments and lasers.

A relatively new battlefield danger, lasers are now commonly used as range finders by tanks and other direct-fire weapons. Even low-level lasers can damage the retina of unprotected eyes.

Costing about $40.00 each, the BLPS are made of polycarbonate plastic that is resistant to high-speed shrapnel. They also include a green polycarbonate frontsert to protect eyes from the two common laser wavelengths.

BANGLADESH
See COALITION FORCES.

BATTALION
Under the command of a lieutenant colonel and normally consisting of two or more companies or batteries, the battalion is a basic organizational unit in most of the world's ground forces. The comparable unit in the cavalry is the "squadron."

Infantry and armor battalions are normally organized into brigades or regiments. Artillery battalions may be separate or organized into groups. The size of a battalion varies widely, depending on its type. For example, a U.S. Army infantry battalion may include almost 900 officers and men, whereas an artillery or armor battalion may be less than half that size.

Iraqi battalions were smaller than U.S. battalions. The nominal strength of an Iraqi infantry battalion was 450 officers and men, with 170 in a tank battalion. Except for Republican Guard Force units, the actual battlefield strength of Iraqi battalions was even less.

See also BATTERY; BRIGADE; COMPANY; GROUP; ORGANIZATION FOR COMBAT, U.S.; REGIMENT.

BATTERY
Consisting of six or more towed or self-propelled howitzers, guns or rocket launchers, and under the command of a captain, the battery is a basic element of most of the world's artillery organizations. The comparable unit outside of the artillery organization is the "company," but in the cavalry it is called a "troop."

Normally an integral part of an artillery battalion, the battery varies in size depending on the number of firing sections, but it usually consists of about 100 officers and men.

See also COMPANY; FIELD ARTILLERY; GROUP; ORGANIZATION FOR COMBAT, U.S.

BATTLESHIPS
The United States deployed two battleships during the Persian Gulf War, the Iowa-class USS *Missouri* (BB 63) and the USS *Wisconsin* (BB 64). Both played a major role in providing naval gunfire support.

The battleship USS *Wisconsin* (BB-64) is resupplied at sea by the combat stores ship USNS *Spica.*
Navy photo (CWO Ed Bailey), Empire Press.

With a crew of 1,537 men and a speed of more than 27 knots, each battleship was armed with nine 16-inch guns that could fire a 2,700-pound armor-piercing shell more than 23 miles.

During Operation Desert Storm, these two battleships fired 1,102 16-inch shells during 83 naval gunfire support missions. Their targets included field artillery and antiaircraft artillery batteries, ammunition storage sites and command posts.

The battleships were also armed with Tomahawk cruise missiles. On January 17, 1991, the USS *Wisconsin* launched one of the first cruise missile attacks of the war.

After the war, both battleships were decommissioned, the USS *Wisconsin* in September 1991, and the USS *Missouri* in March 1992.

See also MARITIME CAMPAIGN; NAVY, U.S.

Suggestion for further reading: Department of Defense, *Conduct of the Persian Gulf War: Final Report to the Congress,* "Appendix T: Performance of Se-

lected Weapons Systems" (Washington, D.C.: USGPO, 1992).

BDA (BATTLE DAMAGE ASSESSMENT)

BDA (battle damage assessment) is a necessary wartime function to determine if the desired effects are being achieved by the application of force. BDA is essential at all levels of warfare. At the national level, it is used to determine which options are to be pursued. At the theater of war or operational level, it is employed to determine whether the required damage has been done to a target. At the tactical or battlefield level, it is used to validate tactics and weapons performance.

CENTCOM J-2 (i.e., Central Command's intelligence staff) developed a BDA methodology that incorporated information from national systems, such as space satellite, and information from mission reports, deserter reports and gun camera film. Since the United States directed the air war, BDA was primarily a U.S. concern.

General H. Norman Schwarzkopf, the Commander in Chief, Central Command (CINCCENT), complained that BDA was abysmal. One problem was the lack of automatic data processing software to handle the massive volume of information that had to be collated. Another had to do with changes in battlefield weaponry. For example, the official Department of Defense (DOD) report states that

> precise targeting and striking of sections of buildings or hardened shelters complicated the assessment process. In many cases, all that was available to imagery analysts was a relatively small entry hole . . . with no indication of the extent of internal damage. Another example involves damage to individual tanks or vehicles, such as mobile missile launchers.
>
> Unless the destruction was catastrophic, a destroyed tank might still appear operational. Even if secondary explosions accompanied the destruction of a suspected missile launcher, it was not possible to conclude with a high degree of certainty that a Scud had been destroyed.

Noting that "BDA is not a precise science," the DOD report acknowledged that "BDA in the Gulf War, as a whole, has been criticized as too slow and inadequate. It is quite possible that assessments of Iraqi losses at various times overestimated or underestimated actual results . . ." As a consequence, "even though there was enough general information to enable CINCCENT to prosecute the war, some targets that had been destroyed may have been struck again and some that had not been destroyed may have been neglected. Targeting at the theater and tactical levels was less effective in the absence of more precise damage assessment."

See also INTELLIGENCE.

Suggestion for further reading: Department of Defense, *Conduct of the Persian Gulf War: Final Report to the Congress,* "Chapter VI: The Air Campaign," and "Appendix C: Intelligence" (Washington, D.C.: USGPO, 1992).

BELGIUM

See COALITION FORCES.

BIN SULTAN BIN ABDULAZIZ, KHALID, LIEUTENANT GENERAL (1950–)

The son of the Saudi Arabian defense minister, a member of the Saudi royal family and a lieutenant general in the Royal Saudi military, Prince Khalid Bin Sultan Bin Abdulaziz commanded all Arab/Islamic forces in the Persian Gulf War.

A 1968 graduate of the United Kingdom's Royal Military Academy at Sandhurst, General Khalid received a Master's Degree in military arts and science from the U.S. Army Command and General Staff College in 1979, and a Master of Arts degree from Auburn University in Alabama in 1980. He is also a graduate of the U.S. Army's Air Defense Artillery School at Fort Bliss, Texas, and the U.S. Air Force's Air War College at Maxwell Air Force Base, Alabama.

When the Kuwaiti crisis began in August 1990, General Khalid was commander of the Saudi Royal Air Defense Force Command. On August 10, he was named commander of the Joint Forces Command by King Fahd ibn Abdul Aziz, thereby becoming the dual commander, with General H. Norman Schwarzkopf, the commander in chief, U.S. Central Command (CINCCENT), of the entire coalition war effort. In the ground campaign, General Khalid's two corps-size ground units, Joint Forces Command-East and Joint Forces Command-North, breached the Iraqi fortifications and continued their attack to liberate Kuwait City.

Promoted to four-star general in September 1991, Khalid retired from active duty shortly thereafter.

See also COALITION COORDINATION, COMMUNICATIONS AND CONTROL INTEGRATION CENTER; JOINT FORCES COMMAND; SAUDI ARABIA.

Suggestions for further reading: General H. Norman Schwarzkopf, *It Doesn't Take a Hero* (New York: Bantam Books, 1992) discusses his joint command with General Khalid, but within days of its publication Khalid publicly complained that Schwarzkopf "gives himself all the credit for the victory over Iraq while running down just about everyone else." See General Khalid Bin Sultan, "Schwarzkopf Did Not Win the War Alone," *Defense News,* October 26–November 1, 1992, reprinted in *Chicago Tribune,* November 7, 1992.

BIOLOGICAL WARFARE (BW)

One of the coalition's major concerns during the Persian Gulf War was Iraq's biological warfare capability. Intelligence agencies had concluded that Saddam Hussein had developed and stockpiled anthrax bacteria and botulism toxin. Large-scale production of these agents was thought to have begun in 1989 at four facilities near Baghdad. After the war, United Nations inspections teams found evidence that both toxins had been manufactured.

Anthrax was consided the more dangerous of the two. An animal disease, anthrax is a relatively fast-acting agent that is almost always fatal to human beings. It can affect anyone exposed to it in a matter of hours. Because methods for rapidly detecting biological warfare agents in the field do not exist, as a precaution a massive inoculation campaign was launched to immunize U.S. personnel.

In addition to immunizing troops and issuing individual protective clothing and equipment, the United States deployed a CW/BW (chemical warfare/biological warfare) defense force structure that included 45 units with 6,028 soldiers and more than 450 vehicles for reconnaissance, detection and decontamination.

Iraqi plants capable of manufacturing biological weapons were identified and attacked during the air campaign. The most controversial attack was the bombing of what the United States labeled a biological warfare production facility but what Iraq claimed to be a milk factory producing formula for babies.

During the air campaign, all of Iraq's known key biological warfare research and development facilities were destroyed, most of its refrigerated storage facilities were knocked out, and all known production facilities were rendered unusable.

See also AIR CAMPAIGN; CHEMICAL WARFARE; CNN (CABLE NEWS NETWORK); NUCLEAR WEAPONS.

Suggestions for further reading: Department of Defense, *Conduct of the Persian Gulf War: Final Report to the Congress*, "Appendix Q: Chemical and Biological Warfare Defense" (Washington, D.C.: USGPO, 1992); Norman Friedman, *Desert Victory: The War for Kuwait* (Annapolis, Md.: Naval Institute Press, 1991); Richard P. Hallion, *Storm Over Iraq: Air Power and the Gulf War* (Washington, D.C.: Smithsonian Institution Press, 1992.) Bruce W. Watson, ed., *Military Lessons of the Gulf War* (Novato, Calif., Presidio Press, 1991). See also Alfonso Rojo, "Bombed Plant 'Nuclear Site Not Milk Factory,'" *The Guardian* (London), March 11, 1991.

BLACK U.S. MILITARY FORCES

Black Americans have served with distinction in all of America's wars. Until the Korean War they served in all-black units, but that ended in 1951 when black service personnel were integrated into previously all-white units. Blacks accounted for 12.1 percent of American fatalities in the Vietnam War. During the Gulf War, black Americans occupied the highest ranks of the military, with General Colin Powell serving as chairman of the Joint Chiefs of Staff, Lieutenant General Calvin Waller serving as the deputy CENTCOM (Central Command) commander, and many others serving in positions of authority.

Although black Americans make up only about 12 percent of the U.S. population, they made up 24.5 percent of the U.S. military force in the Kuwaiti Theater of Operations, including 73,000 soldiers (29.8 percent of the total), 12,500 Marines (16.7 percent), 13,000 sailors (21.7 percent) and 6,000 airmen (13.3 percent). These numbers raised concerns among some Americans that blacks would account for a disproportionate share of the casualties in the war.

As it turned out, white Americans, who made up 66 percent of the force, sustained 78 percent of the deaths. Hispanics, who accounted for 5 percent of the force, sustained 4 percent of the deaths; Asians, who were 2 percent of the force, sustained less than 1 percent of the fatalities; and black Americans, who made up 24.5 percent of the force, sustained 15 percent of the deaths. In actual numbers, of the 182 U.S. soldiers who were killed, 142 were white, 27 were black, 8 were Hispanic, 1 was Asian and 4 were of "other" races.

Many of the arguments raised against the relatively high proportion of blacks serving in the Gulf were disingenuous. In the pages of the *Washington Post*, a distinguished black soldier, retired Army Brigadier General Dallas Brown, asked: "Do we wish to have limits or quotas on the number of blacks who can serve in combat? We had this in World War II until black leaders . . . raised such a commotion that black combat units . . . were started. In other words those who are complaining about too many blacks in combat are actually spouting the old segregationist attitudes—strange bedfellows."

Dismissing the critics, General Powell told the *Washington Post* that he was "proud of the fact that

A 24th Infantry Division soldier spikes an Iraqi machine gun with an American flag.
U.S. Army photo courtesy of 24th Infantry Division.

African Americans have seen fit to volunteer to join the armed forces." Most Americans would appear to agree.

See also ANTIWAR MOVEMENT; CASUALTIES.

Suggestions for futher reading Isabel Wilkerson, "Blacks Wary of Their Big Role in Military," *New York Times,* January 25, 1991; Lynn Duke, "General Powell Notes Military Enlistment Remains Matter of Individual Choice," *Washington Post,* November 28, 1990; Dallas Brown, "Too Many Blacks in Combat?" *Washington Post,* July 30, 1991.

BLOCKADE
See MARITIME INTERCEPTION OPERATIONS; SANCTIONS.

BMP (BRONEVAYA MASCHINA PIEKHOTA)
See ARMOR.

BOMBING
To many observers, the coalition's bombing campaign in the Persian Gulf War was exemplified by the pinpoint accuracy of "smart" bombs.

The shrinkage of the CEP (circular error probable, or the radius in which on average 50 percent of the bombs will fall) has been dramatic. British bombers at the beginning of World War II had a CEP of more than four miles, making their chance of even hitting a city, much less a specific building, problematical. By the end of the war, the CEP of U.S. B-17 bombers had been reduced only to thousands of feet, still necessitating many sorties and much bomb tonnage to guarantee a target's destruction. During the Vietnam War, improved technology reduced the CEP to hundreds of feet, but until the introduction of "smart bombs" late in that war, accuracy was still a major problem.

Smart bombs came of age during the Persian Gulf War, when they could literally be placed through windows. This meant far fewer combat aircraft losses, far fewer civilian casualties and far less collateral damage. But impressive as the technological advances were, they did not mean that an era of "surgical" strikes was at hand.

For one thing, most of the 88,500 tons of bombs dropped on Iraq were "dumb" iron bombs; "smart" bombs accounted for only 6,520 tons, or about 7 percent of the total. As Air Force chief of staff General Merrill A. McPeak disclosed after the war, 70 percent of the bombs that were dropped missed their target. "Smart" bombs had an accuracy rate of 90 percent, while the rate for unguided bombs was only about 25 percent. Such calculations are somewhat misleading, however, for even these rates were an enormous improvement over those in past wars.

Among the "smart" bombs used in the war was the GBU-28, a 4,700-pound laser-guided bomb fashioned out of an eight-inch artillery barrel and designed specifically to penetrate deep shelters. At the other end of the spectrum were the 500-pound GBU-12 laser-guided bombs that were used against Iraqi tanks and vehicles; these constituted 50 percent of the "smart" bombs dropped during the conflict. Other "smart" bombs included the laser-guided 2,000-pound GBU-24 and the GBU-15, which utilized either television (TV) guidance or an imaging infrared (IIR) system rather than lasers. Of the 80 TV or IIR GBU-15s that were dropped, 79 hit their aim points.

See also: AIR CAMPAIGN; CASUALTIES; HIGH TECHNOLOGY.

Suggestions for further reading: Department of Defense, *Conduct of the Persian Gulf War: Final Report to the Congress,* "Chapter VI: The Air Campaign" (Washington, D.C.: USGPO, 1992); Richard P. Hallion, *Storm Over Iraq: Air Power and the Gulf War* (Washington, D.C.: Smithsonian Institution Press, 1992), especially Appendix E, "The 'Smart' Bomb"; Douglas Pasternak, "Minimizing Casualties: Technology's Other Payoff," *U.S. News & World Report,* February 11, 1991; Barton Gellman, "U.S. Bombs Missed 70% of Time," *Washington Post,* March 16, 1991.

BOMB SHELTER CONTROVERSY

One of the major controversies of the Gulf War was the bombing of what was purported to be the Al-Amariyah civilian air raid shelter (sometimes referred to as the Al-Firdus bunker) in Baghdad on February 13, 1991. Listing it as one of the "war crimes" committed by the United States in the Gulf War, antiwar activist Ramsey Clark claims in his book *The Fire This Time* that although "media and Iraqi government accounts report that 300–400 people were killed in the shelter," his sources revealed that "the number killed was closer to 1,500."

The U.S. decision to bomb the bunker, reports *Washington Post* war correspondent Rick Atkinson in *Crusade: The Untold Story of the Persian Gulf War,* was based on a report from a spy who was a top official in the Iraqi government. In the second week of February, the spy reported that Iraqi intelligence had begun using the bunker as an alternative command post.

"The tragedy caused such negative publicity," notes Richard Hallion in *Storm Over Iraq,* "that the senior military leadership in Washington severely curtailed bombing in downtown Baghdad after February 16.

Much of the negative reporting came from Peter Arnett of Cable News Network (CNN), who accepted uncritically Iraq's contention that the shelter was purely a civilian facility. But CNN's military analyst, retired Air Force Major General Perry Smith, took great exception. "What I saw on the television monitor," Smith said, "appeared to be a classic command bunker, heavily fortified with reinforced concrete, camouflaged on the roof and surrounded by a perimeter fence. A standard civilian bomb shelter does not have a perimeter fence, because people

have to be able to get into a bomb shelter quickly when the siren warning of an air raid goes off."

According to the official Defense Department report to the Congress, the cause of the incident was Iraq's commingling of military objects with the civilian population.

> Undoubtedly, the most tragic result of this commingling . . . occurred on the 13 February attack on the Al-Firdus Bunker . . . in Baghdad. Originally constructed during the Tran-Iraq War as an air-raid shelter, it had been converted into a military C2 [i.e., command and control] bunker in the middle of a populated area. . . . Knowing Coalition air attacks on targets in Baghdad took advantage of the cover of darkness, Iraqi authorities permitted selected civilians—apparently the families of officer personnel working in the bunker—to enter the Al-Amariyah Bunker at night to use the former air raid shelter part of the bunker on a level above the C2 center. . . .

> . . . . [T]he Coalition forces had evidence the bunker was being used as an Iraqi command and control center and had no knowledge it was concurrently being used as a bomb shelter for civilians. Under the rules of international law known as military necessity, which permits the attack of structures used to further an enemy's prosecution of a war, this was a legitimate military target."

The "truth" is still elusive and will probably remain so. The incident is yet another testament to the "fog of war," which throughout history has obscured battlefield events.

See also BAGHDAD; BIOLOGICAL WARFARE; WAR CRIMES.

Suggestions for further reading: Department of Defense, *Conduct of the Persian Gulf War: Final Report to the Congress,* "Appendix O: The Role of the Law of War" (Washington, D.C.: USGPO, 1992); Rick Atkinson, *Crusade: The Untold Story of the Persian Gulf War* (New York: Houghton- Mifflin, 1993); Richard P. Hallion, *Storm Over Iraq: Air Power and the Gulf War* (Washington, D.C.: Smithsonian Institution Press, 1992); Major General Perry Smith, USAF (Retired), *How CNN Fought the War: A View From Inside* (New York: Birch Lane Press, 1991); Ramsey Clark, *The Fire This Time: U.S. War Crimes in the Gulf* (New York: Thunder's Mouth Press, 1992).

BOOMER, WALTER E(UGENE) LIEUTENANT GENERAL, USMC (1938–)

Commander of the First Marine Expeditionary Force (I MEF) and concurrently MARCENT (Marine

Marine Gulf War generals meet with General Schwarzkopf and their commander, Lieutenant General Boomer, second from Schwarzkopf's left.
Marine Corps photo courtesy of U.S. Naval Institute.

Forces, Central Command) commander during Operation Desert Storm, General Walter E. Boomer was commissioned a second lieutenant in the United States Marine Corps upon graduation from Duke University in Durham, North Carolina, in 1960.

In 1966–1967, Captain Boomer saw combat action in Vietnam as the commanding officer of Company H, 2d Battalion, 4th Marine Regiment, 3d Marine Division. Promoted to major in 1968, he returned to Vietnam in 1971 as an advisor to a South Vietnamese Marine infantry battalion.

Returning to the United States in 1972, Boomer attended American University in Washington, D.C. Awarded a Master of Science degree in technology of management in 1973, he then served as a management instructor and as chairman of the Department of Management at the United States Naval Academy.

Subsequent assignments include command of the 2d Battalion, 3d Marines; director of the Fourth Marine Corps District; director of Marine Corps Public Affairs; and commanding general, Fourth Marine

Division. After being promoted to lieutenant general, on August 15, 1990, General Boomer deployed to Saudi Arabia as I MEF commander. His command included the 1st and 2d Marine Divisions, the 3d Marine Aircraft Wing and the Tiger Brigade from the Army's 2d Armored Divison.

Returning to the United States with the First Marine Expeditionary Force in April 1991, Boomer later served as commander of the Marine Corps Combat Development Command at Quantico, Virginia, until his promotion to four-star general in September 1992, when he became assistant commandant of the Marine Corps.

General Boomer has been awarded the Distinguished Service Medal, two Silver Stars for gallantry in action, the Legion of Merit, two Bronze Star Medals with combat "V," the Navy Commendation Medal with combat "V," the Combat Action Ribbon and numerous other service medals and foreign decorations.

See also FIRST MARINE EXPEDITIONARY FORCE (I MEF); GROUND CAMPAIGN; MARINE CORPS, U.S.

Suggestions for further reading: Lt. Gen. Walter E. Boomer, USMC, "Special Trust and Confidence Among the Trail Breakers," *U.S. Naval Institute Proceedings,* November 1991; Molly Moore, "Storming the Desert with the Generals," *Washington Post,* April 14, 1991; Molly Moore, *A Woman at War* (New York: Charles Scribner's Sons, 1993).

BRADLEY M2/M3 FIGHTING VEHICLE

The battlefield infantry/cavalry complement to the M1A1 Abrams tank was the Bradley fighting vehicle. The M2 IFV (infantry fighting vehicle) and the M3 CFV (cavalry fighting vehicle) provided tactical mobility, limited armor protection and an antiarmor capability to the infantry and scout squads respectively. In addition to the Bradley's basic model, three improved models were also deployed, the A1 (-), the A1 and the A2.

The IFV carries a nine-man infantry squad while the CFV carries a five-man scout section. In both, three of the members comprise the vehicle's crew. With a cross-country speed of 30–35 miles per hour and a cruising range of 275–300 miles, the Bradley is capable of keeping pace with the Abrams tank.

The Bradley's main armament was the M242 25-mm cannon. Its secondary armament included an M240C 7.62-mm coaxial machine gun, two-tube

TOW (Tube-launched, Optically-tracked, Wire-guided) antitank missile launchers and M231 5.56-mm firing ports. Thermal-imaging systems allowed TOW gunners to acquire and engage targets through smoke and sand both day and night at ranges of up to 3,500 meters. The 25-mm cannon proved effective against light armor, trucks and bunkers.

Although criticized before the war as being mechanically unreliable, the Bradley fleet maintained an availability rate of more than 90 percent during the high-speed ground campaign, with some units moving 100–300 miles cross-country with no major breakdowns. Criticism was also directed at the vehicle's armor protection. Yet during the war, several vehicles took significant hits without experiencing flash fires or catastrophic loss; most of the damage was found to be penetrator-related, with little resulting from spall. Two 3d Armored Division

soldiers were killed and three were wounded when their Bradley was hit at point-blank range by an Iraqi T-72 tank, but more Bradleys were lost to friendly fire than to enemy action.

Most U.S.-based units initially deployed to the Gulf with the basic Bradley model, but the Army opted to modernize the fleet in-theater. In addition to those Europe-based units already equipped with the newer models, some 692 A2 models, which incorporated add-on armor, an interior spall liner, a larger engine and improved ammunition storage, were shipped to the Gulf. Of the 2,200 Bradleys that were in-theater during the ground campaign, the A1 and A2 models accounted for 33 percent and 48 percent respectively.

See also ARMOR; FRIENDLY FIRE.

Suggestions for further reading: Department of Defense, *Conduct of the Persian Gulf War: Final Report*

The Bradley armored fighting vehicle carried either a nine-man infantry squad or a five-man cavalry scout team.
U.S. Army photo courtesy of U.S. Army Ordnance Museum.

Leading the way into Iraq, Bradley armored fighting vehicles provided protection from enemy artillery.
U.S. Army photo courtesy of 24th Infantry Division (Mechanized).

to the Congress, "Appendix T: Performance of Selected Weapons Systems" (Washington, D.C.: USGPO, 1992); Evelyn Richards and Charles R. Babcock, "Half-Tank, Half-Taxi Bradley Proves Worth in Battle," *Washington Post,* March 15, 1991.

BREACHING OPERATIONS

Given the extent of Iraqi entrenchments and field fortifications in the Kuwaiti Theater of Operations, land-mine countermeasures (LCM) and obstacle-breaching operations took on great importance.

Among the systems deployed by U.S. and other coalition forces were the antipersonnel obstacle breaching system (APOBS), an explosive device that blasts a continuous 0.6 x 45-meter footpath through an enemy minefield; the M58 single-shot line charge/mine-clearing line charge (MICLIC), a rocket-propelled explosive that blasts a continuous 8 x 100-meter path; and the Mk 154 triple- shot line charge, which is fired from an AAV (Assault Amphibian Vehicle) and uses an explosive to clear an 8 x 300-meter path.

Other devices included the track-wide mine roller (TWMR), consisting of two reinforced weighted rollers mounted in front of a tank to activate mines in its path, and the full-width mine rake (FWMR), mounted on the dozer blade of an M-60 tank or an M728 Combat Engineer Vehicle (CEV). The FWMR could clear mines on the surface or buried up to 12 inches in sandy soils across the full width of an armored vehicle's path. Pipe fascines were also used to fill in antitank ditches and other gaps.

Breaching vehicles included the M-9 Armored Combat Earthmover (ACE), the M728 Combat Engineer Vehicle (CEV) and the Armored Vehicle Launched Bridge, a 60-foot span transported on an M-48 or M-60 tank chassis.

In the course of their breaching operations the U.S. Marine Corps fired 49 single-shot and 55 triple-shot line charges and the U.S. Army used a limited number of MICLICs. The U.S. Air Force also dropped

15,000-pound "Daisy Cutter" bombs and fuel-air explosives to blast paths through enemy minefields, but these explosives had only limited success, as did the track-wide mine roller, which was difficult to transport and bogged down in soft sand.

Most effective were the 59 full-width mine rakes, which created easily visible lanes for follow-on forces. Also effective was the armored combat earth-mover, 151 of which were deployed to the Gulf for use by both the Army and the Marine Corps. Unlike civilian bulldozers, which have a top speed of about 5 miles per hour, the ACE has a top speed of 30 miles per hour and a range of some 200 miles, enabling it to keep pace with combat manuever forces.

One of the minor controversies of the war concerns the rumor that bulldozers were used during breaching operations to bury Iraqi soldiers alive in their trenches. Evidently the rumor grew out of pre-assault plans to use ACE bulldozers to fill in enemy trenchlines to enable assault elements to continue the attack. Officers who were on the scene have stead-fastly denied that bulldozers were so used, and there is no evidence to contradict their assertions.

See also ENGINEERS; FORTIFICATIONS; GROUND CAMPAIGN; MINES, LAND; WAR CRIMES.

Suggestions for further reading: Department of Defense, *Conduct of the Persian Gulf War: Final Report to the Congress,* "Appendix T: Performance of Selected Weapons Systems" (Washington, D.C.: USGPO, 1992); Department of the Army, *Weapons Systems of the United States Army* (Washington, D.C.: USGPO, 1989). For the "buried alive" controversy, see Barton Gellman, "Reaction to Tactic Baffles 1st Division," *Washington Post,* September 13, 1991; Michael Hedges, "Trench-burial Story 'Exaggerated,'" *Washington Times,* September 13, 1991.

BRIGADE

Normally consisting of two or more battalions, and under the command of a colonel (or, in the case of an independent brigade, a brigadier general), the brigade is a basic organizational element in most of the world's militaries, including those of the United States, its coalition partners and Iraq.

Unlike the regiment, which it has largely replaced (except in the U.S. Marine Corps), the brigade has no fixed structure and is usually organized to accomplish specific missions. A mechanized infantry brigade, for example, may include tank battalions, and an armor brigade may include mechanized infantry battalions.

Brigades are normally an integral part of divisions but may also operate as independent units. The U.S. Army's 2d Armored Division's "Tiger Brigade" was a case in point. Detached from its parent division, during the Gulf War it served under the operational control of the First Marine Expeditionary Force. The Iraqi Republican Guard Force Command also deployed a number of independent brigades around Baghdad and on the Syrian and Turkish borders.

See also DIVISION; ORGANIZATION FOR COMBAT, U.S.; REGIMENT.

BRIGHT STAR EXERCISES

"Bright Star" was the code name for a series of pre–Gulf War U.S. Central Command (CENTCOM) training exercises conducted in the Middle East in 1983, 1985, 1987 and 1990.

As part of "Bright Star," U.S. Army and Air Force units deployed from bases in the United States to Egypt, Oman, Jordan, Somalia and Kenya, where they joined with host-nation forces to train on the ground and in the air. U.S. Marine Expeditionary units also conducted amphibious landings, and Maritime Prepositioning Forces unloaded supplies and equipment. Navy carrier battle groups participated at sea and in strikes on shore. Several small Special Operations Force deployment exercises were also conducted.

According to the official Department of Defense report to the Congress, such high-quality training "was one of the more important contributors to the preparedness of US forces and subsequent success in the Gulf operation."

See also COMBAT TRAINING CENTERS.

Suggestion for further reading: Department of Defense, *Conduct of the Persian Gulf War: Final Report to the Congress,* "Appendix D: Preparedness of United States Forces" (Washington, D.C.: USGPO, 1992).

BRONZE STAR MEDAL

Initially conceived as the equivalent of the Air Medal, which recognized the wartime sacrifices of aircrews, the Bronze Star Medal was created in World War II to recognize the battlefield sacrifices of the ground forces. It was later extended to Navy and Air Force personnel as well. The medal is awarded in the name of the president of the United States for heroic or meritorious achievement or service in military operations against an armed enemy not involving participation in aerial flight.

The Bronze Star Medal is awarded for valor (denoted by a metallic "V" device worn on the medal ribbon) performed under circumstances not as hazardous as those required for the awarding of the Silver Star. It is also awarded (without the "V") for meritorious achievement in a combat zone or for sustained meritorious performance of duty. Subsequent awards are denoted by an oak-leaf cluster (or a gold star for Navy and Marine Corps personnel) worn on the medal ribbon.

During the Persian Gulf War, 891 Army personnel were awarded the Bronze Star Medal for valor, 20,005 received the medal for achievement, and 6,327 were awarded the medal for service.

See also DECORATIONS, U.S.

BULL, GERALD V(INCENT) (1928–1990)

An artillery wizard, Gerald V. Bull earned a doctorate in aerodynamics from the University of Toronto in 1950. Working with the U.S. military, in the 1960s he designed a 120- foot-long gun that fired a projectile 112 miles into outer space.

Founding his own company, Space Research Corporation (SRC), in 1968, Bull set out to design and market conventional artillery. He developed a new 155-mm artillery shell and a towed 155-mm howitzer with a range of 24 miles. Sold to Austria's Voest Alpine steelworks, the howitzer was marketed as the GHN-45.

Working with both South Africa and China to develop new artillery weapons, Bull was jailed in the United States in 1981 for violating arms-export laws. In 1988, Bull signed a contract with Iraq to produce conventional artillery as well as a 450-foot-long supergun with a muzzle diameter of 1,000 millimeters (more than three feet) and a potential range of 1,000 miles. Forty-four segments of 1,000-mm steel tubing were eventually sent to Iraq, and eight more segments were later confiscated by British authorities.

"Of an estimated 3,700 Iraqi artillery pieces," said a 1991 *Washington Post* article, "some 520 are Bull-designed long-range 155s: 200 South African G-5s and G-6s, 200 Austrian GHN-45s, and about 120 Chinese WAC 21s. All the guns, many with inter-changeable shells and barrels, can outshoot U.S. and Coalition guns." A prototype of the 1,000-mm super-gun was found by United Nations inspectors at Jabal Hamrayn, north of Baghdad, after the war.

On March 22, 1990, Bull was shot down in cold blood by two assassins as he left his Brussels apartment. Allegedly, his murder was ordered by the Israeli government to prevent him from continuing to work with Iraq on "Project Babylon," as the super-gun project was called. No suspects in Bull's murder have ever been publicly identified, and the Israeli government has refused comment.

See also FIELD ARTILLERY.

Suggestions for further reading: William Lowther, *Arms and the Man: Dr. Gerald Bull, Iraq and the Supergun* (Novato, Calif.: Presidio Press, 1991); Dale Grant, *Wilderness of Mirrors* (Toronto: Prentice-Hall of Canada, 1991); D'Arcy Jenisn and Dale Grant, "The Man With the Golden Gun," *Macleans,* April 22, 1991; Kevin Toolis, "The Man Behind Iraq's Super-gun," *New York Times Magazine,* August 26, 1990; William Scott Malone, David Halevy and Sam Hemingway, "The Guns of Saddam," *Washington Post,* February 10, 1991; Christopher F. Foss, "Exposing the Secrets of Jabal Hamrayn," *Jane's Defense Weekly,* September 14, 1991.

BUSH, GEORGE H(ERBERT) W(ALKER) (1924–)

The 41st president of the United States, George Bush was commander in chief of the American armed forces during the Persian Gulf War.

The son of U.S. Senator Prescott Bush (Rep. Conn.), George Bush served as a naval aviator in World War II, earning the Distinguished Flying Cross and three Air Medals for service in the Asian-Pacific Theater of Operations. Elected to the U.S. House of Representatives in 1966 and 1968, he served as U.S. ambassador to the United Nations from 1971 to 1973, headed the U.S. liaison office in China from 1974 to 1975, and was director of the Central Intelligence Agency (CIA) from 1976 to 1977.

From 1981 to 1989, Bush served as vice president of the United States under President Ronald Reagan. In 1988, he won the Republican Party's nomination and was elected president, taking office in January 1989.

In December 1989, President Bush ordered U.S. troops to Panama to overthrow the regime of the strongman Manuel Noriega. Following the Iraqi invasion of Kuwait in August 1990, he ordered U.S. forces to the Persian Gulf.

Belonging to what Defense Secretary Dick Cheney called the "don't screw around school of military strategy," Bush as commander in chief took firm control of the conduct of U.S. military operations. Unlike during the Vietnam War, when a nebulous "national command authority" had been ostensibly in charge, President Bush personally presided over the building of a powerful allied coalition to combat Iraqi aggression: he set the objectives and made the key decisions on the Gulf War.

When the war ended, Bush enjoyed one of the highest presidential approval ratings in history. But a prolonged postwar economic recession and his perceived indifference to domestic affairs eroded that support. Plagued by "Iraqgate" charges of hav-ing conducted improper prewar relations with Iraq, in November 1992 Bush was defeated for reelection by Governor William Jefferson (Bill) Clinton of Arkansas.

One of Bush's final acts as president was to order U.S. air strikes on Iraq on January 13, 1993, for violation of the terms of the United Nations ceasefire agreements.

See also COMMAND AND CONTROL; IRAQGATE; STRATEGY, COALITION.

Suggestions for further reading: Bob Woodward, *The Commanders* (New York: Simon & Schuster, 1991) has an excellent account of Bush's wartime leadership. For a more critical view, see Roger Hilsman, *George Bush vs. Saddam Hussein* (Novato, Calif.: Lyford Books, 1992). See also Fred Barnes, "The Unwimp," *The New Republic,* March 6, 1991.

CAMPAIGN MEDAL

See AWARDS, COALITION FORCES; SERVICE MEDALS, U.S.; SOUTHWEST ASIA SERVICE MEDAL.

CAMPAIGN PLAN

One of the major post–Vietnam War developments in the U.S. military has been the reemphasis on "operational art" at the theater-of-war level. While tactics are concerned with winning an individual battle, operational art focuses on winning a series of interrelated battles that, in their totality, would achieve the strategic political ends for which the war is being waged.

The link between tactics and strategy, the key to the operational level of war in the Persian Gulf War, was the campaign plan. The theater campaign plan of Central Command (CENTCOM) had three major components—the air campaign, the ground campaign and a maritime campaign that provided for sea control and maritime interdiction, aircraft and naval gunfire support as part of the air and ground campaigns, and an amphibious invasion force that evolved into part of CENTCOM's deception operation.

CENTCOM's campaign plan, coordinated with the campaign plan of the Arab Joint Forces Command, was divided into four phases. Phase I, the strategic air campaign, was designed to paralyze the Iraqi leadership and command structure by striking Iraq's most critical centers of gravity simultaneously. Phase II was focused on suppressing or eliminating Iraqi ground-based air defenses in the Kuwaiti Theater of Operations (KTO). Phase III emphasized direct air attacks on Iraqi forces in the KTO, including the Republican Guard Forces Command (RGFC) and the Iraqi Army in Kuwait. Phases I through III made up the air campaign. Phase IV, the ground campaign to liberate Kuwait, employed air attacks and sea bombardment on concentrations of Iraqi forces remaining in the KTO in addition to ground attacks.

Campaign planning provided the blueprint for success in the Persian Gulf War. As General Crosbie E. Saint, commander of U.S. Army Europe and the Seventh Army, noted: "Looking back, we should have known from the outset that the Iraqis were probably a pretty good tactical army, but not playing in our league. After all, Saddam spent his time talking about 'the Mother of all battles,' clearly a tactical event, while we were talking about the campaign, an operational set of sequenced events."

See also AIR CAMPAIGN; DECEPTION; GROUND CAMPAIGN: MARITIME CAMPAIGN; STRATEGY, COALITION.

Suggestions for further reading: Department of Defense, *Conduct of the Persian Gulf War: Final Report to the Congress* (Washington, D.C.: USGPO, 1992). For the evolution of operational art and the source of General Saint's remarks, see Colonel Harry G. Summers Jr., *On Strategy II: A Critical Analysis of the Gulf War* (New York: Dell, 1992).

CAMPAIGNS, U.S. MILITARY

The U.S. military divides each war into campaigns, each of which is a series of military operations forming a distinct phase of the war. The units involved in these operations display, along with their colors (i.e., a unit's official flag), a streamer embroidered with the name of the particular campaign. Personnel are authorized to wear on the ribbon of their service medal a bronze battle star for each campaign in which they take part.

Three campaigns were authorized for the Persian Gulf War. As of 1994, the "cease-fire campaign" is still in progress for those involved in enforcing United Nations cease-fire resolutions.

Campaign	Inclusive Dates
Defense of Saudi Arabia	August 2, 1990–January 16, 1991
Liberation of Kuwait	January 17, 1991–April 11, 1991
Southwest Asia Cease-Fire	April 12, 1991–

See also SERVICE MEDALS, U.S.

CANADA

See COALITION FORCES.

The U.S. Navy maintained six carrier action groups in the KTO, including the USS *Independence* (CV-62) with F/A-18 Hornets embarked.
U.S. Navy photo (PH1 Scott Allen), Empire Press.

CARRIER BATTLE GROUPS (CVBG)

The U.S. Navy deployed six aircraft carrier battle groups (CVBGs) during the Persian Gulf War. Each consisted of an aircraft carrier, one or two Aegis cruisers, several destroyers and frigates, a station replenishment ship and in some cases an oiler and an ammunition ship.

For example, the USS *America* battle group consisted of the carrier itself, accompanied by the cruisers USS *Normandy* (CG 60) and *Virginia* (CGN 38), the destroyers USS *Preble* (DDG 46) and *William V. Pratt* (DDG 44), the frigate USS *Halberton* (FFG-40), the station replenishment ship USS *Kalamazoo* (AOR 6) and the ammunition ship USS *Nitro* (AE 23).

See also AIRCRAFT CARRIERS; NAVY, U.S.

Suggestion for further reading: Norman Friedman, *Desert Victory: The War for Kuwait* (Annapolis, Md.: Naval Institute Press, 1991, Appendix C, which lists the composition of each of the CVBGS.

CARTER DOCTRINE

In his January 1980 State of the Union address, President Jimmy Carter enunciated what came to be known as the "Carter Doctrine." Issued in the wake of the December 1979 Soviet invasion of Afghanistan, it affirmed that the Persian Gulf region was an area of vital interest to the United States. The doctrine specifically stated that "any attempt by any outside force to gain control of the Persian Gulf region will be regarded as an assault on the vital interests of the USA and will be repelled by any means necessary, including military force."

The Carter Doctrine prompted the establishment of the Rapid Deployment Joint Task Force (RDJTF) on March 5, 1980. This in turn sparked contingency planning for operations in Southwest Asia, the beginning of the Bright Star training exercises with Egypt and other nations in the region, the start of prepositioning of logistical supplies on land and at sea in the area, and the establishment of Army and Marine desert training centers.

Ultimately, the Carter Doctrine led to the formation of the U.S. Central Command (CENTCOM), which succeeded the RDJTF on January 1, 1983.

See also CENTCOM.

CASUALTIES

"Casualty reports . . . are never accurate, seldom truthful, and in most cases deliberately falsified." So wrote the great military philosopher Carl von Clausewitz more than 160 years ago. Time has revalidated the truth of his observation. Casualty figures for the Korean and Vietnam Wars remain controversial, as the erstwhile enemies of the United States still refuse to release official figures on their battlefield losses. And Iraqi casualty figures for the Gulf War remain a matter for argument as well.

Allied casualty figures are more precise, and U.S. casualty figures are a matter of public record. According to the U.S. Central Command, 146 U.S. service men and women were killed in action during the Persian Gulf War. The Army lost 96; the Air Force 20, the Marines 24 and the Navy 6. An additional 121 Americans died from accidents or other nonbattle causes, including 84 Army personnel, 25 Marines, 6 Air Force personnel and 6 Navy personnel. Four Army and 3 Navy civilian contractors also died. The 467 Americans wounded in action included 354 from the Army, 9 from the Air Force, 12 from the Navy and 92 from the Marines.

Not including those who died from accidents and other nonhostile causes, 98 other coalition service personnel were killed in action, including 47 from Saudi Arabia, 25 from the United Kingdom, 12 from Egypt, 10 from the United Arab Emirates (UAE), 2 from Syria and 2 from France.

Another 427 coalition military personnel were wounded in action, including 220 from Saudi Arabia, 95 from Egypt, 45 from the United Kingdom, 38 from France, 17 from the UAE, 8 from Senegal, 2 from Bahrain and 1 each from Syria and Oman.

But Iraqi casualties remain a subject of wild speculation. As in the Vietnam War, antiwar activists attempted to use charges of large numbers of civilian casualties to inflame public opinion.

In his acclaimed *Vietnam: A History* (New York: Viking, 1983), the journalist Stanley Karnow told how U.S. antiwar activists in North Vietnam during the so-called Christmas bombing in 1972 tried to get the mayor of Hanoi to claim that 10,000 civilians had been killed. The mayor refused, telling the activists that his government's credibility was at stake. The official North Vietnamese figure for civilian bombing casualties in Hanoi at the time was 1,318.

The same drama played itself out in the Persian Gulf War. Again U.S. antiwar activists claimed a civilian death toll of 10,000 in Baghdad. But this time the voice of truth came from one of their own. "If projections of civilian casualties in Baghdad are based on the highest estimates for the worst hit areas," wrote Erika Munk in the May 6, 1991, issue of the *The Nation*, "the American 'clean' bombing of Baghdad was the direct cause of 3,000 civilian casualties. . . . the *lowest* number of civilian deaths from bombing of a major city in the history of modern war."

Iraqi military casualties were also grossly exaggerated, initially by the U.S. Defense Intelligence Agency (DIA) itself. In May 1991, DIA released preliminary figures showing that 100,000 Iraqi soldiers had been killed and 300,000 had been wounded during the war. DIA acknowledged, however, that its error factor was 50 percent or greater.

Later disavowed completely by the Pentagon, these figures were revised downward by Lieutenant General Charles Horner, the CENTAF (Central Command Air Force) commander during the war. In a January 1992 speeech, he said that "eyewitness accounts on the battlefield support probably less than 10,000 [Iraqi] casualties."

A 1993 study claimed that Iraqi military casualties were even lower. John G. Heidenrich, a former DIA analyst, estimated that Iraqi military casualties were no more than 9,500 dead and 26,000 wounded; minimum casualties were 1,500 killed and 3,000 wounded, about one-third during the air campaign and two-thirds during the ground campaign. Yet another 1993 study, this one by University of Rochester professor John Mueller, found that less than 1,000 Iraqi soldiers were killed in the war.

Although exact figures are still unknown, there is general agreement that Iraqi military casualties were nowhere near the "megadeaths" originally reported.

See also ANTIWAR MOVEMENT; BLACK U.S. MILITARY FORCES; BOMB SHELTER CONTROVERSY; FRIENDLY FIRE; WOMEN IN THE MILITARY.

Suggestions for further reading: For a listing of U.S. personnel who died in the Persian Gulf War, see "The Fallen," *Washington Post*, March 10, 1991. See also Department of Defense, *Conduct of the Persian Gulf War: Final Report to the Congress*, "Appendix A: List of US Fatalities and Prisoners of War During Operations Desert Shield and Desert Storm" (Washington, D.C.: USGPO, 1992). For casualty estimates, see Patrick E. Tyler, "Iraq's War Toll Estimated by U.S.," *New York Times,* June 5, 1991; Ronald A. Taylor, "Greenpeace Outlines War's Toll," *Washington Times,* May 30, 1991; and John G. Heidenrich, "The Gulf War: How Many Iraqis Died?" *Foreign Policy,* Spring 1993, and the rebuttals and Heidenrich's response in the Summer 1993 issue. See also Peter N. Kochansky, "3 Years Later, Gulf War Toll Unknown," *San Francisco Examiner,* July 31, 1993; The Staff of U.S. News & World Report, *Triumph Without Victory: The Unreported History of the Persian Gulf War* (New York: Times Books, 1992); and Eliot A. Cohen et al., *Gulf War Airpower Survey* (Washington, D.C.: USGPO, 1993) for a discussion of Gulf War casualties.

CAVALRY

Cavalry returned to the ranks of the U.S. Army during the Vietnam War, its horses replaced by helicopters and armored fighting vehicles (AFV). Cavalry played a major role in the Persian Gulf War as well.

Both the 2d and 3d Armored Cavalry Regiments were deployed to the Kuwaiti Theater of Operations (KTO). Each had three ground cavalry squadrons (i.e., battalions) equipped with Bradley M3 cavalry fighting vehicles, and an air cavalry squadron with OH-58D Kiowa scout helicopters. All of the Army divisions deployed to the KTO had an organic cavalry squadron with both ground troops (i.e., companies) and air cavalry troops.

The United Kingdom and France also deployed cavalry units. The British units included the 16/5th Queen's Royal Lancers, augmented by elements of the 1st Queen's Dragoon Guards and the 9/12th Lancers with Scimitar AFVs. The French units included the 1st Foreign Legion Armored Regiment and the 1st Regiment de Spahis with AMX-10RC AFVs.

See also ARMOR; BRADLEY M2/M3 FIGHTING VEHICLE; HELICOPTERS; 2D ARMORED CAVALRY REGIMENT; 3D ARMORED CAVALRY REGIMENT.

C-DAY

The day on which a deployment operation begins or is scheduled to begin. In the case of Operation Desert Shield, C-Day was August 7, 1990.

CEASE-FIRE

In what remains a controversial decision, President George Bush ordered an informal battlefield cease-fire on February 28, 1991, 100 hours after the ground campaign had begun. The official cease-fire for the Persian Gulf War, however, came on April 11, 1991.

United Nations Security Council (UNSC) Resolution 686, approved on March 2, 1991, by a vote of 11 for, 1 against (Cuba) and 3 abstentions (Yemen, China and India), set the initial terms of the cease-fire. It was followed on April 4, 1991, by Resolution 687, which was approved by a vote of 12 for, 1 against (Cuba) and 2 abstentions (Ecuador and Yemen), dictating the actual terms of the permanent cease-fire.

Among other actions, Resolution 687 required Iraqi acceptance of all previous UNSC resolutions, which called for withdrawal from Kuwait and renunciation of all claims on Kuwaiti territory. It also authorized a UN observer team to monitor a demilitarized zone between the two countries.

UNSC Resolution 687 also required total destruction of all Iraqi ballistic missiles with a range of more than 150 kilometers, and of all chemical, biological and nuclear agents, including all research, development, support and manufacturing facilities, and requested the director general of the International Atomic Energy Agency (IAEA) to monitor Iraq's compliance.

By the time the cease-fire went into effect, more than 86,000 Iraqi soldiers had surrendered.
U.S. Army photo courtesy of 24th Infantry Division (Mechanized).

On April 6, 1991, in a 23-page letter to the UN Security Council, the Iraqi parliament unconditionally agreed to these terms, and on April 11, 1991, the formal cease-fire went into effect. Since then, however, there have been numerous Iraqi violations of the agreement, in particular with respect to nuclear weapons.

A separate issue, deliberately not part of the cease-fire agreement, was Iraq's brutal suppression of a postwar Kurdish uprising in northern Iraq and a Shiite revolt in southern Iraq, which led to the establishment of "no-fly" zones and other restrictions on Iraqi military action in those regions.

See also KURDS; NUCLEAR WEAPONS; SHIITE REVOLT; UNITED NATIONS; WAR TERMINATION.

Suggestion for futher reading: The Staff of U.S. News & World Report, *Triumph Without Victory: The Unreported History of the Persian Gulf War* (New York: Times Books, 1992), Appendix A, which contains the complete texts of the UN Security Council resolutions.

CENSORSHIP
See MEDIA.

CENTAF (CENTRAL COMMAND AIR FORCE)
See NINTH U.S. AIR FORCE.

CENTCOM (CENTRAL COMMAND)
The military headquarters for the conduct of U.S., French and British operations in the Persian Gulf War, U.S. Central Command (CENTCOM) is one of the several geographic commands (European Command [EUCOM], Pacific Command [PACOM], Southern Command [SOUCOM]) into which the American armed forces are organized. Although their forces are drawn from the Army, Navy, Air Force and Marine Corps, the commanders in chief (CINCs) of these commands are independent of those services and report directly to the

U.S. COMMAND RELATIONSHIPS

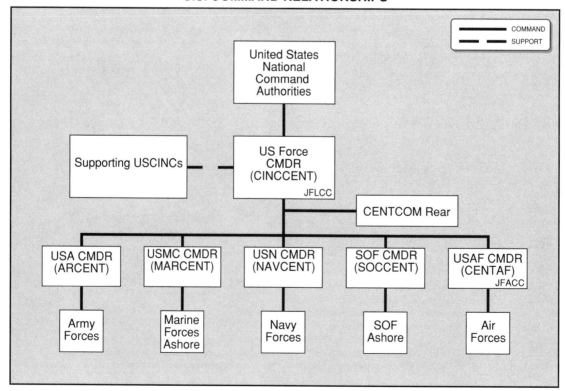

secretary of defense through the chairman of the Joint Chiefs of Staff.

Formed on January 1, 1983, as the successor to the Rapid Deployment Joint Task Force (RDJTF) and with the mission of protecting U.S. national interests in Southwest Asia (SWA), CENTCOM's headquarters is at MacDill Air Force Base in Tampa, Florida. During the Gulf crisis, an advanced command post was deployed to Saudi Arabia on August 6, 1990, and on August 26, 1990, CENTCOM's headquarters moved to Riyadh, Saudi Arabia.

During the war, CENTCOM was commanded by Army General H. Norman Schwarzkopf; the deputy CENTCOM commander was Army Lieutenant General Calvin A. H. Waller. Subordinate to CENTCOM were the four service component commanders as well as the commander of SOCCENT (Special Operations Command Central Command), who retained operational control of all Army, Navy and Air Force special operations forces in the Kuwaiti Theater of Operations (KTO).

Lieutenant General John J. Yeosock, the Army component commander (ARCENT), concurrently commanded the U.S. Third Army. His forces included the VII Corps and the XVIII Airborne Corps as well as the 22d Theater Army Support Command and other support units. The CENTCOM Air Force component commander (CENTAF), Lieutenant General Charles A. Horner, not only commanded the Ninth U.S. Air Force but also served as the JFACC (joint forces air component commander), coordinating all coalition air forces.

Also the commander of the U.S. Seventh Fleet, the NAVCENT (Naval component commander) was initially Vice Admiral Henry Mauz, but he was replaced on December 1, 1990, by Vice Admiral Stanley R. Arthur. Lieutenant General Walter E. Boomer was the MARCENT (Marine component commander, CENTCOM) and also the commander of the First Marine Expeditionary Force (I MEF).

CENTCOM had no command authority over non-U.S. coalition forces, but during the air campaign the JFACC coordinated all U.S. and coalition air operations. Maritime interception operations were coordinated by NAVCENT. During the ground campaign, the British 1st Armoured Division was under the operational control of VII Corps, and the French 6th Armored Division was under the tactical control of XVIII Airborne Corps.

Arab forces were under the Saudi-led Joint Forces Command (JFC) and were coordinated through the Coalition Coordination, Communications and Control Integration Center (C^{3}IC).

See also AIR CAMPAIGN; CAMPAIGN PLAN; CO-ALITION COORDINATION, COMMUNICATIONS AND CONTROL INTEGRATION CENTER (C^{3}IC); FIRST MARINE EXPEDITIONARY FORCE (I MEF); GROUND CAMPAIGN; JOINT FORCES COMMAND; MARITIME CAMPAIGN; NINTH U.S. AIR FORCE; SCHWARZKOPF, H. NORMAN; SEVENTH U.S. FLEET; SPECIAL OPERATIONS COMMAND CENTRAL COMMAND; THIRD U.S. ARMY.

Suggestions for further reading: Department of Defense, *Conduct of the Persian Gulf War: Final Report to the Congress,* "Appendix K: Command, Control, Communications (C3), and Space" (Washington, D.C.: USGPO, 1992); General H. Norman Schwarzkopf, *It Doesn't Take a Hero* (New York: Bantam Books, 1992).

CHAIRMAN, JOINT CHIEFS OF STAFF

During the Persian Gulf War the chairman of the Joint Chiefs of Staff (CJCS) of the United States was Army General Colin L. Powell. By law the senior officer of the U.S. armed forces and a statutory advisor to the National Security Council, the CJCS presides over the Joint Chiefs of Staff (JCS).

At one time only the first among equals, the chairman was elevated above the other service chiefs by the Goldwater-Nichols Defense Reorganization Act of 1986 and became the principal advisor to the secretary of defense, the National Security Council and the president. Whereas in the past, the chairman by law represented only the views of the JCS, now—and during the Persian Gulf War—he is required to give only his own views. This arrangement has greatly enhanced the chairman's authority.

Like other members of the JCS, the chairman is not legally in the operational chain of command. Nonetheless, the chairman in fact has considerable operational authority. The Goldwater-Nichols Reorganization Act permits the president to direct that communications from the combatant commands be transmitted through the chairman, and it allows the secretary of defense to assign the chairman responsibility for overseeing the activities of the combatant commands.

Touring facilities in Saudi Arabia, General Powell familiarizes himself with the battlefield situation.
USAF photo (SRA Rodney Kerns) courtesy of OCJCS.

This was the case during the Persian Gulf War. As General H. Norman Schwarzkopf, the CINCCENT (commander in chief, Central Command), noted in his autobiography, "Officially, as a commander in chief, I reported to Secretary [of Defense Dick] Cheney, but Colin Powell was virtually my sole point of contact with the Administration."

See also COMMAND AND CONTROL; GOLDWATER-NICHOLS DEFENSE DEPARTMENT REORGANIZATION ACT; JOINT CHIEFS OF STAFF, U.S.; POWELL, COLIN L.

Suggestions for further reading: Richard P. Hallion, *Storm Over Iraq: Air Power and the Gulf War* (Washington, D.C.: Smithsonian Institution Press, 1992); General H. Norman Schwarzkopf, *It Doesn't Take a Hero* (New York: Bantam Books, 1992).

CHAPLAINS
See RELIGIOUS SERVICES.

CHEMICAL WARFARE (CW)
The chemical warfare (CW) threat in the Kuwaiti Theater of Operations (KTO) was taken very seriously by coalition forces. For one thing, Iraq had the largest chemical agent production capability in the Third World, each year producing thousands of tons of the blister agent mustard gas and both the nonpersistent and persistent nerve agents Sartin (GB) and GF.

In addition to missile warheads, Iraq's means for delivering chemical agents included aerial bombs, artillery shells, rockets and aircraft-mounted spray tanks. And Iraq had shown that it was not hesitant about using them. In 1984, during the Iran-Iraq War, Iraq became the first nation in history to use nerve agents on the battlefield. Although these were not effective initially, by 1988 Iraq had developed an offensive doctrine that fully integrated CW into its fire-support plans.

Both blister and nerve agents were used successfully in 1988 in Iraq's final offensive that led to the Iranian defeat. Further, in the spring of 1988 Iraqi troops used CW against Kurdish insurgents in the town of Halabjan, killing thousands of civilian men, women and children.

Given the gravity of the threat, Iraq's CW weapons and their delivery systems were specified targets during the coalition's air campaign. According to the official Department of Defense (DOD) report to the Congress, "At least 75 percent of Iraq's CW production capability was destroyed." At Samarra, for example, coalition forces "destroyed or severely damaged most known primary CW production, processing or production support buildings. . . . All three precursor chemical facilities at Habbaniyah were seriously damaged."

In addition to taking offensive military action against Iraqi CW facilities, the coalition undertook an enormous defensive effort. Individual protective clothing and equipment—including protective masks, boots, gloves, battle dress overgarments, agent antidote injectors and personal decontamination equipment—were issued to the troops, and there was constant CW training in their use. As the official DOD report states, "Many units donned protective chemical clothing at the start of Desert Storm and continued to wear some items throughout the ground offensive."

More than 1,300 chemical agent monitors were deployed to the KTO, and 10 developmental XM-21 remote-sensing agent alarms were fielded by the end of December 1990. The most effective contamination detection system was the German-donated Fuchs (FOX) NBC (nuclear-biological-chemical) reconnaissance vehicle. Czechoslovakia also provided chemical detection and analysis equipment, along with trained operators.

Why Iraq did not use CW is still a matter of conjecture. United Nations postwar inspectors confirmed that Iraq did have some 30 chemical warheads for its Scud missiles, but none were fired. Almost no chemical munitions were distributed to Iraqi forces in the KTO.

Iraq did indeed have an extensive CW arsenal, however. UN inspectors found a stockpile of some 46,000 chemical munitions of various types. According to a report in the *Christian Science Monitor,* "Chemicals stored in barrels at Al-Muthanna . . . include[d] 225 tons of nerve agents and 280 tons of mustard gas."

See also BIOLOGICAL WARFARE; NUCLEAR WEAPONS.

Suggestions for further reading: Department of Defense, *Conduct of the Persian Gulf War: Final Report to the Congress,* volume I and volume II, "Appendix Q: Chemical and Biological Warfare Defense," (Washington, D.C.: USGPO, 1992); Norman Friedman, *Desert Victory: The War for Kuwait* (Annapolis, Md.: Naval Institute Press, 1991); Bruce W. Watson, ed., *Military Lessons of the Gulf War* (Novato, Calif.: Presidio Press, 1991). For the Fox NBC reconnaissance vehicle, see Philip Shenon, "Vehicles Roam the Front to Detect Gas Attacks," *New York Times,* February 24, 1991. For Iraq's CW capability, see John J. Goldman, "Iraq Tells of Chemical Arms Cache," *Los Angeles Times,* April 19, 1991; Peter Grier, "Iraq's Chemical Weapons Found to be Potent," *Christian Science Monitor,* January 23, 1992.

CHENEY, RICHARD B. (DICK), SECRETARY OF DEFENSE (1941–)

The secretary of defense during the Persian Gulf War, Dick Cheney was the de facto commander of the U.S. armed forces and responsible to President George Bush for the conduct of the war.

Born in Lincoln, Nebraska, but raised in Wyoming, Cheney did not serve in the Vietnam War. Instead, he used student deferments to earn Bachelor of Arts and Master of Arts degrees from the University of Wyoming in 1965 and 1966. Cheney later served in the Nixon and Ford administrations and was White House chief of staff under President Gerald Ford. Elected to Congress from Wyoming in 1979, he served 10 years in the U.S. House of Representatives before being named secretary of defense in March 1989.

During the Gulf War Cheney had two distinct roles. One was to manage the $300 billion Pentagon budget and oversee the more than 2 million uniformed personnel and 1 million civilian employees of the Defense Department. As such, the *New York Times* awarded him a "hero's medal" for canceling the Navy's A-12 stealth bomber. "If we cannot spend the taxpayer's money wisely," Cheney said, "we will not spend it" (*The Economist,* January 25, 1991).

His other role was to lead the armed forces in the Persian Gulf War. Enjoying the full confidence of President Bush, Cheney also had a smooth working relationship with General Colin Powell, the chairman of the Joint Chiefs of Staff.

In sharp contrast to the acrimony that plagued the Pentagon in the course of Robert S. McNamara's regime during the Vietnam War, Cheney had the full confidence and support of his military subordinates. He did not hesitate to enforce his will, however, when things did not suit him. At the beginning of the conflict, he fired Air Force chief of staff General Michael J. Dugan for making unauthorized remarks about U.S. strategy (see CHIEF OF STAFF, U.S. AIR FORCE), and he reportedly bluntly criticized some of General Powell's early plans for the war. There was much "intense interaction that was even more intense during the period when our forces were engaged in combat," Cheney told the *New York Times* after the end of the war. But it paid off in clear and precise guidance to the forces in the field.

Most observers would agree that Dick Cheney was the most capable wartime secretary of defense in the history of that office.

See also COMMAND AND CONTROL; DEFENSE DEPARTMENT, U.S.; POWELL, COLIN L.

Suggestions for further reading: Bob Woodward, *The Commanders* (New York: Simon & Schuster, 1991); "Dick Cheney's Pentagon," *The Economist,*

January 25, 1991; Patrick E. Tyler, "The Powell-Cheney Relationship: Blunt Give-and- Take Early in Crisis," *New York Times*, March 15, 1991.

CHIEF OF NAVAL OPERATIONS (CNO)

The chief of naval operations (CNO) is the senior officer of the United States Navy. He is responsible for the recruiting, training, arming, equipping and overall readiness of naval forces. A statutory member of the Joint Chiefs of Staff, the CNO is precluded by law from exercising operational command.

During the Persian Gulf War the chief of naval operations was Admiral Frank B. Kelso II.

See also JOINT CHIEFS OF STAFF, U.S; NAVY, U.S.

CHIEF OF STAFF, U.S. AIR FORCE (CSAF)

The chief of staff, U.S. Air Force (CSAF) is the senior officer of the United States Air Force. He is responsible for the recruiting, training, arming, equipping and overall readiness of air forces. A statutory member of the Joint Chiefs of Staff, the CSAF is precluded by law from exercising operational command.

When the Persian Gulf crisis began, the chief of staff, U.S. Air Force was General Larry Welch. When his tour of duty expired in mid-August 1990, he was replaced by General Michael J. Dugan. During an inspection trip to Saudi Arabia in September 1990, Dugan told a press conference that in the battle to come, airpower alone would be decisive.

Secretary of defense Dick Cheney relieved General Dugan as Air Force chief of staff and replaced

Army chief of staff General Carl Vuono talks with 82d Airborne Division commander Major General James Johnson during a visit to the Gulf.
U.S. Army photo courtesy of Lieutenant General James Johnson.

him with General Merrill A. McPeak, who served for the remainder of the Persian Gulf War.

See also AIR FORCE, U.S.; AIRPOWER; JOINT CHIEFS OF STAFF, U.S.

Suggestions for further reading: For accounts of the relief of General Dugan, see Bob Woodward, *The Commanders* (New York: Simon & Schuster, 1991); Richard P. Hallion, *Storm Over Iraq: Air Power and the Gulf War* (Washington, D.C.: Smithsonian Institution Press, 1992.

CHIEF OF STAFF, U.S. ARMY (CSA)

The Chief of Staff, U.S. Army (CSA) is the senior officer of the United States Army. He is responsible for the recruiting, training, arming, equipping and overall readiness of army forces. A statutory member of the Joint Chiefs of Staff, the CSA is precluded by law from exercising operational command.

During the Persian Gulf War the chief of staff, U.S. Army, was General Carl E. Vuono.

See also ARMY, U.S.; JOINT CHIEFS OF STAFF, U.S.

CHINA, PEOPLE'S REPUBLIC OF

Although not a member of the allied coalition, the People's Republic of China played a major role in the Persian Gulf War. As a permanent member of the United Nations Security Council (UNSC), China had the power to veto any proposed UNSC resolution on Iraq. If it had chosen to do so, the legal basis for the war would have been undermined and UN action would have been precluded.

Because China had been a major prewar supplier of military aircraft, arms and equipment to Iraq, such a veto would not have been unexpected. Although China abstained on UNSC Resolution 678 authorizing the use of military force, it did not exercise its veto and in fact voted in favor of the majority of the UNSC resolutions, including those that imposed the trade and financial embargo on Iraq and that enforced the sanctions.

See also UNITED NATIONS.

Suggestions for further reading: Bob Woodward, *The Commanders* (New York: Simon & Schuster, 1991) has a brief discussion of U.S. diplomatic efforts toward China. A more thorough examination is in Yitzhak Shichor, "China and the Gulf Crisis: Escape From the Predicaments," *Problems of Communism*, November/December 1991.

CIA (CENTRAL INTELLIGENCE AGENCY)

See INTELLIGENCE.

CIVIL AFFAIRS

"Civil Affairs units played an important role throughout Operations Desert Storm and Desert Shield," according to the official Department of Defense report. Missions included coordinating and facilitating host nation support; providing emergency services and support to the civilian sector; minimizing civilian interference and casualties; providing for movement and control of civilians; providing emergency water, food, shelter and medical care for displaced civilians and enemy prisoners of war; and providing emergency services and reconstruction assistance to Kuwait.

Operating under U.S. Central Command (CENT-COM) U.S. civil affairs units included the Army's 96th Civil Affairs (CA) Battalion (the only active Army unit); 16 Army Reserve civil affairs units and 2 Marine Reserve civil affairs groups.

In October 1990, the government of Kuwait requested U.S. assistance in postwar recovery. In early December 1990, the Kuwait Civil Affairs Task Force or "Task Force Freedom," was formed around the personnel of the 352d CA Command, an Army Reserve unit from Riverdale, Maryland. Working with representatives of the Kuwaiti government-in-exile to formulate plans for the necessary services, supplies and equipment needed for postwar reconstruction, the unit deployed to Saudi Arabia in January 1991 to complete CA planning and to execute the plan.

Task Force Freedom reached a peak strength of 3,650 persons and included British engineers and U.S. Navy, Air Force and Marine Corps personnel as well as the Army Reserve's 416th Engineer Command and elements from France, Canada, Saudi Arabia and Kuwait.

More than 12,500 metric tons of emergency food were provided to Kuwait, along with 12.8 million liters of water, 2.8 million liters of diesel fuel, 64 generators, 1,250 tons of medical supplies and 764 vehicles. In April 1991, Task Force Freedom handed off its ongoing projects to the newly created Kuwaiti Defense Restoration Assistance Organization.

Suggestions for further reading: Department of Defense, *Conduct of the Persian Gulf War: Final Report to the Congress,* "Appendix J: Special Operations Forces" (Washington, D.C.: USGPO, 1992); *Civil Affairs in the Persian Gulf: A Symposium,* U.S. Army JFK Special Warfare Center, Fort Bragg, N.C., October 1991; Major General Robert S. Frix and Captain Archie L. Davis III, "Task Force Freedom and the Restoration of Kuwait," *Military Review,* October 1992.

CIVILIAN CASUALTIES

See CASUALTIES.

CIVILIAN TECHNICIANS

Because they were operating in their home territories, the Arab Gulf Cooperation Council states made extensive use of their civilian labor force to support the war effort. Although civilian technicans accompanied other coalition forces, the United States had a major civilian contingent in the Kuwaiti Theater of Operations (KTO).

U.S. civilian employees have served with military forces in the field in previous wars, but far more served in the Persian Gulf War, both as career civil service employees and, indirectly, as contractor employees.

At the close of the war, some 4,500 U.S. government civilian employees were serving in the KTO, including 500 merchant mariners employed by the Military Sealift Command. A large number of U.S. civilian contractors also served in the KTO. General Dynamics Service Company, for example, fielded six-man maintenance teams with VII Corps and XVIII Airborne Corps units, while FMC Corporation fielded maintenance teams for the Bradley fighting vehicles.

Army civilian employees received a five-day indoctrination and training program prior to deployment. The Army Material Command, which was the principal source of in-theater civilian support, involved some 1,500 government and 3,000 contractor civilians in the issuing of new equipment and the maintaining of complex technical systems. The Army Corps of Engineers also had a large number of civilian employees in the KTO.

Approximately 200 Air Force civilian employees served in the KTO; these were mostly logistics support personnel from the Air Force Logistics Command, but also included 44 engineering and technical service personnel from Tactical Air Command.

On average, the Navy had 500 to 600 civilian employees in the KTO; these were drawn from the Navy's aircraft depots, shipyards and other field activities, and engaged primarily in aircraft and ship repair. A similar number of Military Sealift Command (MSC) civilian mariners served aboard ships. Additionally, technical representatives from aircraft contractor firms accompanied the 3d Marine Aircraft Wing.

The Defense Communications Agency, the Defense Intelligence Agency, the Defense Mapping Agency and, in particular, the Defense Logistics Agency also deployed civilian employees to the Gulf.

Four Army civilian contractor employees and three Navy civilian contractor employees are listed among the Americans killed in Operations Desert Shield and Desert Storm. The entire Military Sealift Command was awarded the Navy Unit Commendation for its support in the KTO, and civilian merchant mariners who served with the MSC between August 2, 1990, and March 9, 1991, are authorized to wear that award. Additionally, a new Merchant Marine Expeditionary Medal has been authorized, as has a Defense Department civilian service medal.

Suggestions for further reading: Department of Defense, *Conduct of the Persian Gulf War: Final Report to the Congress,* "Appendix N: Civilian Support" (Washington, D.C.: USGPO, 1992); James C. Hyde, "Defense Contractors Serve on the Front Lines of Operation Desert Storm," *Armed Forces Journal,* March 1991; James Kitfield, "Civilian War," *Government Executive,* 1990.

CLOSE AIR SUPPORT (CAS)

Close air support (CAS) is a term that refers to aerial fire support of ground forces. Pioneered in World War II, it played a major role in both the Korean and Vietnam Wars.

During the Persian Gulf War, forward air controllers (FACs) and air naval liaison company (ANGLICO) personnel were attached to U.S. ground manuever battalions and to other coalition ground forces. Their task was to select and identify targets and to guide strike aircraft to them.

Airborne FACs were also used extensively. The Marines employed Fast FAC F/A-18 Hornets and slower OV-10 Broncos, while the Air Force used the OV-10s and Fast FAC F-16 Fighting Falcons called "Killer Scouts." These airborne FACs marked targets with a white phosphorus rocket or a laser designator

in order that attack pilots could find and strike the targets. Aircraft designed for CAS operations included the A-10 Warthog, the AV-8B Harrier II and other combat aircraft.

Despite these capabilities, CAS was not as critical in the Gulf War as it had been in past wars. As the official Department of Defense report notes, "The effects of Coalition operations against Iraqi forces before G-Day and the overall light resistance by Iraqi forces, limited the amount of CAS [that] Coalition ground forces needed."

See also A-10 THUNDERBOLT II "WARTHOG"; AIR CAMPAIGN; GROUND CAMPAIGN; HARRIER (AV-8B) STOVL (SHORT TAKE OFF AND VERTICAL LAND) AIRCRAFT.

Suggestion for further reading: Department of Defense, *Conduct of the Persian Gulf War: Final Report to the Congress,* "Chapter 4: The Air Campaign" (Washington, D.C.: USGPO, 1992).

CNN (CABLE NEWS NETWORK)

The most spectacular television coverage of the Gulf War was probably CNN's (Cable News Network's) footage of the bombing of Baghdad during the opening hours of the air campaign on January 17, 1991. Reported live by CNN news anchor Bernard Shaw and correspondent John Holliman from the Rashid Hotel in downtown Baghdad, the coverage was truly spectacular.

CNN was formed in 1980 by Ted Turner as an international news network. Based in Atlanta, Georgia, CNN by its 10th anniversary in 1990 was being received in 53 million American homes and in 84 countries around the world. It was estimated that approximately 1 billion people in 108 nations watched CNN at some time during the war.

With war correspondents such as Christiane Amanpour and Charles Jaco, and military analysts such as retired Air Force Major General Perry M. Smith and retired Army Major James Blackwell, most of CNN's coverage of the war was balanced and well informed. Peter Arnett's reporting from Baghdad, however, was controversial, especially his accounts of the bombing of the "baby milk factory" and the "civilian bomb shelter," which caused many to view him as a propaganda conduit for Saddam Hussein.

See also BOMB SHELTER CONTROVERSY; MEDIA.

Suggestions for further reading: Perry M. Smith, *How CNN Fought the War: A View From Inside* (New York: Birch Lane Press, 1991); Vern E. Smith, "The Whole World Is Watching," *London Sunday Times Magazine,* October 7, 1990; Michael Schwellen, "CNN: Television for the Global Village," *World Press Review,* December 1990; Richard Zoglin, "Live From the Middle East," *Time,* January 28, 1991. For how Iraq was using the Western media, including Arnett, see Lee Hockstader, "Media Ouster Cuts Off West's View of Iraq," *Washington Post,* March 9, 1991.

COALITION COORDINATION, COMMUNICATIONS AND CONTROL INTEGRATION CENTER (C³IC)

Because of political sensitivities, unity of command—the appointment of a single commander for the conduct of the coalition's military operations—was not possible in the Kuwaiti Theater of Operations (KTO). To overcome this deficiency, the commander of ARCENT (Army Component Central Command), Lieutenant General John Yeosock, drawing on his previous experience working with the Saudi Arabian National Guard, assumed responsibility for establishing an organization to coordinate multinational activities, facilitate the combined planning process and integrate coalition operations. This combined operations center, officially called the Coalition Coordination, Communications and Control Integration Center, or C³IC, was established on August 13, 1990, in Riyadh at the National Defense Operations Center, in the same building housing CENTCOM (Central Command) headquarters.

As the official Department of Defense report on the Persian Gulf War notes,

> The C³IC served as the link between the two major command structures that developed during Operation Desert Shield—the American, British and French (as well as air units from Italy and Canada) on the one hand, and the Arab/Islamic (the JFC [Joint Forces Command]) forces on the other. The 24-hour center exercised no command authority, but was the conduit for all coordination between the Western and Arab/Islam forces. It proved crucial to the success of Operation Desert Storm.
> The Vice Deputy Commanding General ARCENT and the Saudi JFC, each representing his command structure, directed the C³IC. The center was organized into Ground, Air Force, Naval, Air Defense, Special Operations, Logistics and Intelligence sec-

tions, each jointly manned by Saudi and American officers. They were the point of contact between their CENTCOM and Saudi General Staff functional elements.

See also COMMAND AND CONTROL.

Suggestion for further reading: Department of Defense, *Conduct of the Persian Gulf War: Final Report to the Congress,* "Appendix K: Command, Control, Communications (C3) and Space" (Washington, D.C.: USGPO, 1992).

COALITION FORCES

Unlike the Korean and Vietnam Wars, the Persian Gulf War was a true coalition effort. In Korea, there were some 39,000 "United Nations" ground forces compared with 302,483 Americans. In Vietnam, there were more than 68,000 "free world military forces" compared with 543,400 Americans. But in the Persian Gulf War, there were 205,000 other coalition forces compared with 532,000 Americans. The coalition included forces of the members of the Gulf Cooperation Council (Saudi Arabia, Kuwait, Bahrain, Qatar, the United Arab Emirates [UAE] and Oman) and major contingents from France, Egypt, Syria and the United Kingdom; these are discussed in more detail in other articles.

Overall, nearly 50 countries contributed to the coalition's war effort.

Aside from the United States, 38 countries deployed air, sea or ground forces: together, they committed more than 200,000 troops, more than 60 warships, 750 aircraft and 1,200 tanks. In addition, U.S. allies provided $54 billion in financial contributions against the estimated $61 billion of incremental costs of the war.

Saudi Arabia also provided approximately 4,800 tents; 1.7 million gallons of packaged petroleum, oil and lubricants; more than 300 heavy-equipment transporters (HET); about 20 million meals; an average of more than 20.5 million gallons of fuel each day; and bottled water for personnel throughout the theater. Other nations provided logistical support as well.

Afghanistan, Australia, Bahrain, Bangladesh, Czechoslovakia, Egypt, France, Honduras, Hungary, Kuwait, Morocco, the Netherlands, New Zealand, Niger, Oman, Pakistan, Poland, Qatar, Romania, Saudi Arabia, Senegal, Sierra Leone, South Korea, Sweden, Syria, the UAE and the United Kingdom sent land forces or field hospitals to the Kuwaiti Theater of Operations (KTO).

Argentina, Australia, Belgium, Canada, Denmark, France, Greece, Italy, Kuwait, the Netherlands, Norway, Poland, Portugal, Spain and the United Kingdom sent naval vessels to join in naval operations in the Persian Gulf.

Argentina, Bahrain, Canada, France, Italy, Kuwait, New Zealand, Oman, Qatar, Saudi Arabia, the UAE and the United Kingdon sent combat and transport aircraft.

Not including those who died from accidents and other nonhostile causes, 98 non-U.S. coalition service personnel were killed in action, including 47 from Saudi Arabia, 25 from the United Kingdom, 12 from Egypt, 10 from the UAE, 2 from Syria and 2 from France. Another 427 non-U.S. coalition military personnel were wounded in action, including 220 from Saudi Arabia, 95 from Egypt, 45 from the United Kingdom, 38 from France, 17 from the UAE, 8 from Senegal, 2 from Bahrain and 1 each from Syria and Oman.

See also AIR FORCES, COALITION; ARMIES, COALITION; BAHRAIN; CASUALTIES; COALITION COORDINATION, COMMUNICATIONS AND CONTROL INTEGRATION CENTER; COMMAND AND CONTROL; EGYPT; FRANCE; GULF COOPERATION COUNCIL; KUWAIT; NAVY, COALITION; OMAN; QATAR; SAUDI ARABIA; SOVIET UNION; STRATEGY, COALITION; SYRIA; TURKEY; UNITED ARAB EMIRATES; UNITED KINGDOM.

Suggestions for further reading: Department of Defense, *Conduct of the Persian Gulf War: Final Report to the Congress,* "Appendix I: Coalition Development, Coordination and Warfare" (Washington, D.C.: USGPO, 1992). Norman Friedman, *Desert Victory: The War for Kuwait* (Annapolis, Md.: Naval Institute Press, 1991) has an appendix listing all coalition forces, as does Bruce W. Watson, ed., *Military Lessons of the Gulf War* (Novato, Calif.: Presidio Press, 1991). See also Colonel R. M. Connaughton, "The Principles of Multilateral Military Intervention and the 1990–1991 Gulf Crisis," *British Army Review,* August 1991.

COAST GUARD, U.S.

By law one of the five U.S. armed services, the U.S. Coast Guard (USCG) is part of the Department of Transportation (before 1977, it was part of the Department of the Treasury) in peacetime. In wartime,

if so directed by the president, the USCG becomes a service of the United States Navy.

A trained military-force-in-being, the Coast Guard maintains a constant military capability and readiness. Since 1981, a Navy–Coast Guard Board of senior flag officers has met semiannually to coordinate policy and programs of mutual interest. In 1984, a Maritime Defense Zone (MDZ) was established around the United States; the Coast Guard Atlantic and Pacific Area commanders are responsible to their Navy fleet commanders in chief for port security and coastal defense operations within the 200-mile MDZ.

Although it remained under the control of the Department of Transportation during the war, the USCG played a major role in Operations Desert Shield and Desert Storm.

In the United States, the USCG provided security at 14 major ports of embarkation. In August 1990, for example, the Coast Guard cutter (CGC) *Key Largo* and three port security boats, aided by local USCG reservists, provided security at the port of Savannah, Georgia, for the outloading of the 24th Infantry Division (Mechanized).

Meanwhile 10 USCG LEDETS (law enforcement detachments), each consisting of one officer and three enlisted men, were ordered to the Gulf to use their ship-boarding experience as part of the Navy's maritime interdiction operation to enforce the United Nations economic sanctions against Iraq. From September 20, 1990, to April 1, 1991, some 25,000 vessels were monitored and tracked, 1,500 were intercepted, 400 were boarded and 40 were seized.

During the war, 877 USCG reservists were called to active duty, including, for the first time in history, the members of three 100-man Coast Guard Reserve Port Security Units (PSU). PSU 301 from Buffalo, New York, PSU 302 from Cleveland, Ohio, and PSU 303 from Milwaukee, Wisconsin, were each deployed to the Persian Gulf. Assigned to the Al-Jubayl and Ad Dammam ports of embarkation in Saudi Arabia and to Manama in Bahrain, the PSUs had as their mission establishing surveillance and port security and enabling the safe transport of military and civilian cargo.

In addition to these duties, in January 1991 a Coast Guard team was ordered to the Kuwaiti Theater of Operations to advise the Saudi Arabian government on its efforts to clean up the massive oil pollution of the Persian Gulf caused by Iraq.

See also COMMANDANT, U.S. COAST GUARD; ECO-LOGICAL WARFARE; MARITIME INTERCEPTION OPERATIONS; NAVY, U.S.; SANCTIONS.

Suggestions for further reading: Department of Defense, *Conduct of the Persian Gulf War: Final Report to the Congress,* "Chapter 4: Maritime Interception Operations" (Washington, D.C.: USGPO, 1992); "The USCG's Forward-Deployed LEDETs," *Seapower,* February 1991; "Patrolling the Persian Gulf," *Bulletin: The United States Coast Guard Magazine,* March 1991; "The Coast Guard Patrols the Persian Gulf," *U.S. Naval Institute Proceedings,* April 1991; Carmond C. Fitzgerald and John R. Olson, "Answering the Call," *U.S. Naval Institute Proceedings,* December 1992.

COMBAT ACTION RIBBON

First authorized by the secretary of the Navy in 1969, the Combat Action Ribbon of the Navy, Marine Corps and Coast Guard is similar to the Army's Combat Infantryman's Badge and Combat Medical Badge in that it recognizes those who have actively participated in ground or surface combat.

The recipient must have participated in a bona fide ground or surface firefight or other action in which he or she was under enemy fire and performed satisfactorily. Personnel assigned to areas subjected to sustained mortar and artillery attack and who actively participated in retaliatory or offensive actions, and personnel aboard a ship whose safety and crew were endangered by enemy attack—such as a ship struck by a mine or engaged by shore, surface, air or subsurface elements—were also eligible.

During the Persian Gulf War, this criterion was expanded to include ships that passed safely through waters sown with enemy mines. In addition to the crews of the USS *Tripoli* and the USS *Princeton,* which struck enemy mines, and the crews of the USS *Missouri* and the USS *Jarrett,* which came under fire from Iraqi Silkworm missiles, the crews of some 26 other warships that operated in the mine-infested waters of the northern Persian Gulf were also authorized to wear the Combat Action Ribbon.

Ten female Marine radio operators, wiremen and truck drivers (one of whom struck a mine but was not injured) from the 1st Marine Division's 11th Marine Regimental Headquarters Battery earned the Combat Action Ribbon as they crossed the Iraqi obstacle belt with their unit on G-Day under indirect enemy fire. Four other female Marines from the 2d Marine Division received the Combat Action Ribbon for having been engaged by, and returning fire against, bypassed Iraqi troops.

See also COMBAT INFANTRYMAN BADGE; COMBAT MEDICAL BADGE.

Suggestions for further reading: Department of Defense, *Conduct of the Persian Gulf War: Final Report to the Congress,* "Appendix R: Role of Women in the Theater of Operations" (Washington, D.C.: USGPO, 1992); David Evans, "Just Standing By Earns a Combat Ribbon," *Chicago Tribune,* June 20, 1992. Information on the 10 female Marines from the 11th Marine Regiment was received from their commander, Major J. M. Seng, USMC.

COMBAT INFANTRYMAN BADGE (CIB)

One of the most prized U.S. Army awards because it signifies participation in frontline combat, the Combat Infantryman Badge (CIB) was first authorized in World War II to distinguish those Army infantrymen who had engaged in ground combat.

During World War II and the Korean and Vietnam Wars, the CIB was restricted to infantrymen in the grades of colonel and below (although combat advisors regardless of branch were included during the Vietnam War) who had served 30 days on the front lines. This requirement was subsequently changed to "any period" during which an infantry unit had engaged in ground combat.

The CIB consists of a silver musket on a rectangular blue background surmounted by a silver oak wreath. Subsequent awardings of the CIB are depicted by a star centered on the top of the badge between the points of the oak wreath. However, only one awarding of the CIB was authorized for individuals who served in Vietnam, Laos, the Dominican Republic, Grenada, Panama or the Persian Gulf, regardless of whether their service consisted of one or more tours in one or more of these countries or regions.

During the Persian Gulf War, 21,775 Combat Infantryman Badges were awarded by the Army.

See also COMBAT ACTION RIBBON; COMBAT MEDICAL BADGE.

COMBAT MEDICAL BADGE (CMB)

The Combat Medical Badge (CMB) is the Army Medical Department's equivalent of the Combat Infantryman Badge. It was authorized during World War II to recognize those Army combat medical personnel (and attached Navy and Air Force combat medical personnel) in the ranks of colonel or Navy captain and below who performed medical duties in support of an infantry unit that was in actual contact with the enemy.

Thirty days of service on the front lines were required for the awarding of the CMB during World War II and the Korean and Vietnam Wars. That requirement was subsequently changed to "any period" in which an individual is assigned to a medical unit (of company or smaller size) organic to an infantry unit of brigade, regimental or smaller size that is engaged in active ground combat.

Subsequent awardings are denoted by a silver star superimposed on the badge. However, only one awarding of the CMB was authorized for service in Vietnam, Laos, the Dominican Republic, Grenada, Panama or the Persian Gulf, regardless of whether an individual had served one or more tours in one or more of these areas.

During the Persian Gulf War, 3,136 Combat Medical Badges were awarded.

See also COMBAT ACTION RIBBON; COMBAT INFANTRYMAN BADGE; MEDICAL CARE AND EVACUATION, COALITION.

COMBAT TRAINING CENTERS

Realistic combat training was one of the more important factors in the U.S. military's success in the Persian Gulf War. Part of this high-quality training was

Combat training at the National Training Center in the Mohave Desert proved to be ideal preparation for the Gulf War.
U.S. Army photo courtesy of Department of the Army Public Affairs.

conducted at the several Army, Navy, Air Force and Marine combat training centers.

The Army maintains several combat training centers to enhance the warfighting capability of its combat units. These include the National Training Center (NTC) at Fort Irwin, California, for desert training of armor and mechanized units; the Joint Readiness Training Center (JRTC) at Fort Chaffee/Little Rock Air Force Base, Arkansas, for light units; the Combined Manuever Training Center (CMTC) in Hohenfels, Germany; and the Battle Command Training Program (BCTP) at Fort Leavenworth, Kansas.

A warfighting seminar followed by a battle-simulation command post exercise, the BCTP was designed to train division and corps commanders and their staffs. A BCTP team was deployed to Saudi Arabia and, using operational plans developed in-theater, war-gamed the various courses of action with the actual corps and division commanders.

In addition to providing close air support for Army training exercises, the Air Force conducts numerous exercises at its own training centers. "Green Flag," at the Tonopah Electronic Combat Range in Nevada, trains aircrews in electronic warfare and SEAD (suppression of enemy air defenses). "Red Flag," at Nellis Air Force Base in Nevada, exposes aircrews to a realistic combat environment. It focuses on the integration of various types of combat aircraft with supporting air-refueling tankers and electronic jammers, while opposing systems provide a credible air threat.

The Navy Strike Warfare Center at the Fallon Naval Air Station in Nevada exposes Navy aircrews to realistic combat conditions. In addition, the Navy's Fleet Combat Tactical Training Center at Dam Neck, Virginia, and the Battle Group Tactical Training Continuum at San Diego, California, provide training for carrier battle groups.

The Marine Corps Air-Ground Combat Center at 29 Palms, California, conducts realistic combat training for Marine battalion- and regimental-size air-ground task forces, integrating ground, aviation and combat service support elements.

Originally designed to prepare American ground, naval and air units to fight against Soviet forces and equipment, the services' combat training centers provided ideal training for waging war against Iraqi forces trained in Soviet tactics and equipped with Soviet arms.

Suggestion for further reading: Department of Defense, *Conduct of the Persian Gulf War: Final Report to the Congress,* "Appendix D: Preparedness of United States Forces" (Washington, D.C.: USGPO, 1992).

COMMAND AND CONTROL

At the highest levels, "command and control" is the means by which a nation's political leaders ensure that the military remains responsive to their authority and operates under their control. This mechanism, the so-called chain of command, extends from top to bottom throughout the military structure.

All of the nations involved in the Persian Gulf War had chains of command. Saddam Hussein, for example, was not only the president of Iraq, he was also the supreme commander of the Iraqi Armed Forces and chairman of the Revolutionary Command Council. The Iraqi chain of command ran from Hussein through the General Headquarters (GHQ) to the Defense Ministry (State Special Security Apparatus for the Republican Guard Forces Command), and then to the Air Force, Navy and Army corps commanders in the field.

As for the allied coalition, Saudi Arabia invited foreign Islamic forces to serve with the understanding that they would operate under Saudi operational control (see JOINT FORCES COMMAND). The United Kingdom (UK) arranged with Saudi Arabia for British forces to be under the tactical control of the commander in chief, U.S. Central Command (CINCCENT) while remaining under the overall command of the UK government. French forces also remained under the command of the French government while ultimately coming under the tactical control of CINCCENT.

Command and control of U.S. military forces in the Persian Gulf was relatively straightforward. President George Bush, in his constitutional capacity as commander in chief, exercised overall command of Operations Desert Storm and Desert Shield through his secretary of defense, Dick Cheney, who was the de facto commander of all U.S. military forces worldwide.

Secretary Cheney transmitted his orders to the field through General Colin Powell, the chairman of the Joint Chiefs of Staff (CJCS). Although by law not in the formal chain of command, the CJCS wielded enormous influence and served as the direct interface between Washington and the U.S. field commander in Riyadh, General H. Norman Schwarzkopf.

As CINCCENT (commander in chief, U.S. Central Command), General Schwarzkopf commanded all U.S. military forces in the KTO (Kuwaiti Theater of Operations). His Army component commander (ARCENT) was Lieutenant General John Yeosock, the commanding general of the Third U.S. Army. His Navy component commander (NAVCENT) was initially Vice Admiral Henry Mauz and later Vice Admiral Stanley Arthur, the commander of the U.S. Seventh Fleet. Schwarzkopf's Air Force component commander (CENTAF) and joint forces air component commander (JFAAC) was Lieutenant General Charles Horner, the commanding general of the Ninth U.S. Air Force. His Marine component commander was Lieutenant General Walter Boomer, the commanding general of the First Marine Expeditionary Force.

These component commanders in turn exercised command and control over their respective forces. Lieutenant General Yeosock, for example, commanded the U.S. VII Corps and the XVIII Airborne Corps as well as exercising operation control over the British 1st Armoured Division and tactical control over the French 6th Light Armored Division.

Although unity of command through the appointment of a single battlefield commander was not politically feasible, unity of effort was nevertheless achieved through mutual cooperation between CINCENT and the commander of all Arab/Islamic forces in the Gulf, Lieutenant General Khalid Bin Sultan of Saudi Arabia. Making that success possible was the Coalition Coordination, Communications and Control Integration Center (C^3IC).

Chairman of the Joint Chiefs of Staff General Colin Powell, with XVIII Airborne Corps commander Lieutenant General Gary Luck, makes a first-hand assessment of the military situation.
USAF Photo (SRA Rodney Kerns) courtesy of OCJCS.

COALITION COMMAND RELATIONSHIPS FOR OPERATION DESERT STORM

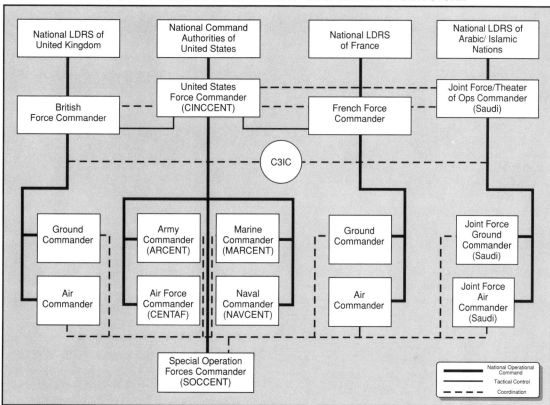

See also GOLDWATER-NICHOLS DEFENSE DE-PARTMENT REORGANIZATION ACT; ORGANIZATION FOR COMBAT, U.S.

Suggestions for further reading: Department of Defense, *Conduct of the Persian Gulf War: Final Report to the Congress,* "Appendix I: Coalition Development, Coordination and Warfare"; "Appendix K: Command, Control, Communications" (Washington, D.C.: USGPO, 1992); Bob Woodward, *The Commanders* (New York: Simon & Schuster, 1991); John H. Cushman, "Command and Control in the Coalition," *U.S. Naval Institute Proceedings,* May 1991; John M. Collins, *High Command Arrangements Early in the Persian Gulf Crisis,* Congressional Research Service, 1990.

COMMANDANT, U.S. COAST GUARD

By law the senior officer of the U.S. Coast Guard, the commandant, reports to the secretary of transporta-tion in peacetime. In wartime, if so directed by the president, he reports to the secretary of the navy.

Although the Coast Guard remained under the Department of Transportation during the Persian Gulf War, Coast Guard units did provide security for U.S. ports of embarkation while active and reserve Coast Guard units deployed to the Persian Gulf.

During the Persian Gulf War the commandant of the Coast Guard was Admiral J. William Kime.

See also COAST GUARD, U.S.

COMMANDANT, U.S. MARINE CORPS

The commandant of the Marine Corps is by law the senior officer of the United States Marine Corps, responsible for the recruiting, training, arming, equipping and overall readiness of Marine forces. A statutory member of the Joint Chiefs of Staff, the commandant of the Marine Corps is precluded by law from exercising operational command.

During the Persian Gulf War the commandant of the Marine Corps was General Alfred M. Gray.

See also FIRST MARINE EXPEDITIONARY FORCE; JOINT CHIEFS OF STAFF (JCS), U.S.; MARINE CORPS, U.S.

COMMENDATION MEDAL

The Commendation Medal was first authorized during World War II as the Commendation Ribbon with Medal Pendant to give visual recognition to those who had received Letters of Commendation for exemplary performance. The Army, Navy, Air Force or (after 1967) Joint Service Commendation Medal is usually awarded in the name of the secretary of the Army, Navy or Air Force or, for the Joint Service Commendation Medal, the secretary of defense for peacetime or wartime meritorious achievement. As such, it ranks below the Distinguished Service Medal, the Legion of Merit, and the Meritorious Service Medal.

In wartime, the Commendation Medal can also be awarded for acts of valor of lesser degree than those required for the awarding of the Bronze Star Medal. Commendation Medals for valor are denoted by a metallic "V" worn on the medal's ribbon.

Numbers for the other services are not available, but 81,678 Army Commendation Medals were awarded during the Persian Gulf War for meritorious achievement.

See also DECORATIONS, U.S.

COMMUNICATIONS AND ELECTRONICS

"Shoot, move and communicate" are the three essentials of battlefield operations, and when it came to communications, the Iraqi forces in the Persian Gulf War were totally outclassed. More than 60 percent of their military landline communications, for example, passed through the civilian telephone system, making them especially vulnerable to air attack. Iraqi microwave relay towers, telephone exchanges, switching rooms, fiber-optic nodes and bridges that carried coaxial communications cables were specifically targeted by the coalition air forces.

Telecommunications sites in Baghdad and elsewhere were attacked heavily during the first three days of the air war, and by the beginning of the ground campaign Iraq's regular means of communication had been reduced dramatically. The Iraqi government had a reduced capacity to broadcast outside the country and only a sporadic ability to broadcast inside the country.

But it was another story when it came to the coalition's communications and electronics capabilities.

The communications network established by coalition forces for Operations Desert Shield and Desert Storm was the largest in history. It was installed in record time and had a remarkable 98 percent readiness rate. At the height of the war, it supported 700,000 telephone calls and 152,000 messages a day.

Among the first U.S. units to deploy to Saudi Arabia on August 8, 1990, were those of the Joint Communications Support Element (JCSE). Formed in 1962, the JCSE has the capability to deploy a contingency support package within 24 hours and an entire unit within 72 hours. Included in the initial package sent to Saudi Arabia were a super-high-frequency (SHF) multichannel satellite terminal, several ultra-high-frequency (UHF) single channel tactical satellite (TACSAT) terminals and associated terminal equipment to provide secure voice and facsimile communications and connectivity to the Worldwide Military Command and Control System (WWMCCS).

The Saudi national telephone service augmented the communications equipment of the XVIII Airborne Corps, the First Marine Expeditionary Force (I MEF) and the Ninth U.S. Air Force, which also began arriving in Saudi Arabia. By November 1990, according to the Department of Defense report on the war, there were more circuits, telephone trunks and radio links in the Kuwaiti Theater of Operations (KTO) than in Europe.

For the first time in history, satellites played a major role in both inter- and intra-theater communications. Military Satellite Communications (MILSATCOM) formed the command and control backbone. Two satellites were moved to the KTO to support intra-theater communications for VII Corps and I MEF, while United Kingdom (UK) satellites were used to support U.S. and UK forces. Commercial satellites were leased as well. Satellite communications (SATCOM) provided communication channels for command and control, intelligence dissemination and logistics support, especially over long distances where conventional FM radios did not have the needed range.

At the battlefield level, the Army's all-digital Mobile Subscriber Equipment (MSE), which interfaced with tactical satellite and tropospheric scatter communications equipment, performed well. MSE-equipped units moving through the desert could be reached by direct dialing from the United States.

The new electronic counter-countermeasures-capable Single Channel Ground and Airborne Radio System (SINCGARS) also worked well, but only 1,000 units were deployed. The *Gulf War Airpower Survey* found that the Secure Telephone Unit (STU-III) was one of the most useful new technologies employed in the war. The more than 350 STU-IIIs enabled commanders and planners worldwide to discuss top secret matters without worrying about interception.

But even these capabilities were not sufficient. With responsibility for managing all 35,000 radio frequencies used by U.S. and coalition forces, CENTCOM (Central Command) was hampered by a shortage of communications security (COMSEC) and cryptographic keys as well as by delays in preparing and fielding the joint communications-electronics operating instructions (JCEOI). A more sophisticated Iraqi electronic warfare effort initially could have caused serious communications problems for the coalition.

Lack of compatibility between Army and Air Force communications equipment and the U.S. Navy's equipment was also a problem, as was the lack of new SINCGARS radios to equip all tactical ground units. Those units equipped with the older Vietnam-era radios frequently had trouble communicating over the long distances that are inherent in desert warfare.

See also ELECTRONIC WARFARE (EW); SATELLITES.

Suggestions for further reading: Department of Defense, *Conduct of the Persian Gulf War: Final Report to the Congress*, "Appendix K: Command, Control, Communications (C3) and Space" (Washington, D.C.: USGPO, 1992); Eliot A. Cohen et al., *Gulf War Airpower Survey* (Washington, D.C.: USGPO, 1993); "Gulf War Emphasizes Communications Shortfalls," *International Defense Review*, December 1991; Dave Schad and Chuck Vinch, "Low-tech Woes Plagued Some Units," *Stars & Stripes*, March 20, 1991.

COMPANY

A company is the basic organizational unit in the U.S. Army and Marine Corps, as well as in most foreign military organizations (including those of other coalition members and Iraq). Commanded by a captain, a company has two or more platoons commanded by lieutenants.

Normally part of a battalion, a company varies widely in size depending on its type and mission. A mechanized rifle company in the U.S. Army, for example, is authorized to have six officers and 152 men, whereas a tank company is authorized to have five officers and 85 men.

In the U.S. military, companies that are part of a battalion have letter designations (i.e., "A" Company, "B" Company), whereas unattached companies have numerical designations.

A company-sized unit is called a "battery" in the artillery and a "troop" in the cavalry.

See also ORGANIZATION FOR COMBAT, U.S.

COMPUTER WAR

Walking along the "Highway to Hell" north of Kuwait in the closing days of Operation Desert Storm, war correspondent Michael Kelly and two American officers came across a slide rule lying next to an abandoned Iraqi howitzer. "It must have belonged to the howitzer's gunner, who would have used it to calculate range, as American gunners did 40 years ago," writes Kelly in *Martyrs' Day: Chronicle of a Small War* (New York: Random House, 1993). "Incredible," said Army Special Forces Major Bob Nugent. "Imagine an army using slide rules up against an army using computers and AWACS. Incredible." In those few words, Kelly captured one of the untold stories of the Persian Gulf War.

Among U.S. and most other coalition forces, computers were ubiquitous. They were used by artillerymen for fire direction and control, by tank crews to aim their main guns while on the move, by pilots for navigating and bombing, and by logisticians to feed and supply the forces. They were critical to the operations of the airborne battle command and control center (ABCCC), the airborne warning and control system (AWACS) and the joint surveillance target attack radar system (JSTARS).

Computers made the air war possible. The computer-aided force management system (CAFMS), an interactive computer system that also allows on-line

Military Airlift Command computers track the movement of personnel and supplies over the "aluminum bridge" to the Gulf.
USAF photo courtesy of Military Airlift Command.

discussion, was used to transmit the daily air tasking order (ATO) as well as real-time changes in plans to land-based units in the Kuwaiti Theater of Operations (KTO).

Fully integrated and secure computer networks were also at the heart of the Army's command and control information system and of the 22d Support Command's logistic system. For the coalition forces, the Persian Gulf War was truly a computer war.

"We had some problems with computers," Lieutenant General Charles A. Horner, the CENTAF (Air Force Component, Central Command) commander told the Business Executives for National Security Education Fund on May 8, 1992. "The problem there is that we underestimated the role of the computer in modern warfare."

See also COMMUNICATIONS AND ELECTRONICS; ELECRONIC WARFARE (EW); HIGH TECHNOLOGY.

Suggestions for further reading: Department of Defense, *Conduct of the Persian Gulf War: Final Report to the Congress,* "Appendix K: Command, Control, Communications (C3) and Space" (Washington, D.C.: USGPO, 1992); Major Timothy J. Gibson, "Command, Control System Abets Victory in Gulf War," *Signal,* March 1992.

CONGRESS, U.S.

Article I, Section 8 of the Constitution of the United States specifically gives Congress and Congress alone the power to declare war, to raise and support armies, to provide and maintain a navy, to make laws for the government and regulation of the land and naval forces, to provide for organizing, arming and disciplining the militia, and for governing such part of them as may be employed in the service of the United States.

During the Korean War, Congress abdicated these responsibilities by allowing President Harry Truman to send American forces into sustained combat without first having obtained the permission of Congress. In the Vietnam War, both Presidents Lyndon Johnson and Richard Nixon declared that they did not need congressional authority to take America to war. Instead of issuing a bill of impeachment or cutting off all funds for the war, Congress passed a watered-down substitute for its constitutional war powers—the 1973 War Powers Act. Yet Congress lacked the will to enforce even that.

This situation changed during the Gulf crisis. Congress demanded to play its proper role in the war-making process. Both the House of Representatives and the Senate held hearings on the Gulf crisis, and on November 21, 1990, 45 members of Congress filed a lawsuit to bar President George Bush from waging war without first obtaining a declaration of war or other explicit authority from Congress. Specifically citing the Constitution, the leader of the congressional delegation filing the suit, California Democratic Representative Ronald Dellums (the current chairman of the House Armed Services Committee) dismissed the War Powers Act as "a meaningless piece of legislation."

The court action was rendered moot when on January 8, 1991, President Bush formally asked Congress to approve United Nations Resolution 678, which authorized member states to use "all necessary means" to force Iraqi troops out of Kuwait. After three days of debate, on January 12, 1991, Congress voted to grant President Bush the authority to go to war against Iraq. The "Authorization for Use of Military Force Against Iraq Resolution" passed the Senate by a vote of 52 to 47, and the House of Representatives by a vote of 250 to 183.

Although some members of Congress voted against the January 12 resolution because they wanted to give more time for United Nations sanctions to work, the majority of members overwhelmingly supported the war once it began. "The Congress commends and supports the efforts and leadership of the President as Commander-in-Chief in the Persian Gulf hostilities," read a January 18, 1991, House and Senate concurrent resolution, "and unequivocally supports the men and women who are carrying out their missions with professional excellence, dedicated patriotism and exemplary bravery." The vote on this resolution was 98 to 0 in the Senate and 399 to 6 in the House.

Although Congress never issued a formal declaration of war during the Persian Gulf crisis, its "Au-thorization for Use of Military Force Against Iraq Resolution" did reassert the constitutional war-making powers it had surrendered in both the Korean and Vietnam Wars.

Suggestions for further reading: Senate Committee on the Armed Services, Hearings, *Crisis in the Persian Gulf Region: U.S. Policy Options and Implications,* 101st Cong., 2d sess., 1990; House Committee on The Armed Services, Hearings, *Crisis in the Persian Gulf: Sanctions, Diplomacy and War,* 101st Cong., 2d sess., 1991. See also "Chapter 2: The Vietnam Syndrome and the Government," in Colonel Harry G. Summers Jr., *On Strategy II: A Critical Analysis of the Gulf War* (New York: Dell, 1992).

CONSCIENTIOUS OBJECTORS, U.S.

The right of conscientious objection to military service is older than the Republic itself. As Eliot A. Cohen pointed out in his study *Citizen Soldiers: The Dilemmas of Military Service* (Ithaca, N.Y.: Cornell University Press, 1985), "The Virginia convention held before the ratification of the American Constitution proposed that the Bill of Rights include the statement 'that any person religiously scrupulous of bearing arms ought to be exempted, upon payment of an equivalent to employ another to serve in his stead.'"

During World War II, when more than 10 million Americans were inducted into the armed forces, only 72,000 filed claims as conscientious objectors (COs). But, as Cohen noted, in the closing days of the Vietnam War in 1970–1971, when only 153,000 were inducted, more than 120,000 conscientious objector claims were filed. "In other words," wrote Cohen, "the rate . . . was one hundred times that of World War II."

During the Persian Gulf War, all of the members of the armed forces, active and reserve, were volunteers. Since genuine pacifists as a matter of principle would never have enlisted in the armed forces, those who claimed conscientious objector status during Operations Desert Shield and Desert Storm did so only when war seemed likely.

Some COs were undoubtedly sincere. According to the Pentagon, 400 applications for conscientious objector status were received in 1991, and 217 were approved. Antiwar activists, however, contended that there were many more CO claims that were blocked by local commanders before reaching the Pentagon.

During the Vietnam War, those members of the armed forces claiming CO status were held in the United States while their cases were adjudicated. During the Persian Gulf War, CO applicants were required to deploy overseas with their units while their paperwork was being processed. Those who deliberately refused to deploy or missed shipping out with their units were subsequently brought to trial. Military courts tended to be harsh on these erstwhile volunteers. An Army reserve doctor, Captain Yolanda Huet-Vaughn, for example, served eight months in prison for refusing to deploy to the Gulf.

Although antiwar groups tried to stir up public sentiment, there was little sympathy for those who had volunteered to serve and then changed their mind when the shooting started.

See also ANTIWAR MOVEMENT.

CORPS

In military establishments throughout the world, "corps" has both a general and a specific meaning. In its general sense, it means a body of men and women who share similar functions, such as the Marine Corps or the Signal Corps or the Corps of Engineers.

In its specific sense, "corps" means a large military organization—in the U.S. military it comprises two or more divisions and is commanded by a lieutenant general. It may include a corps support command (COSCOM) for logistical support and such corps combat forces as artillery brigades and an armored cavalry regiment.

In the Persian Gulf War, the United States fielded three corps-size units, the Army's VII Corps and XVIII Airborne Corps and the Marines' First Marine Expeditionary Force. Another comparable coalition unit was the II Egyptian Corps.

Iraq's Army consisted of the I through VII Corps and the two-corps Republican Guard Force Command.

See also ARMY, IRAQ; EGYPT; XVIII AIRBORNE CORPS; FIRST MARINE EXPEDITIONARY FORCE; OR-GANIZATION FOR COMBAT, U.S.; VII CORPS.

COST

One of the unique aspects of the Persian Gulf War was that many of the financial costs incurred by the United States during the conflict were offset by monetary contributions from allies.

According to the Pentagon's final accounting, the incremental costs for the U.S. war effort totaled $61.1 billion. Contributions from other countries added up to $53.6 billion, including $48 billion in cash and $5.6 billion in materials or services, leaving the cost to American taxpayers at $7.2 billion.

The two largest contributors were Saudi Arabia at $16.8 billion and Kuwait at $16 billion. Japan contributed $10 billion, Germany $6.5 billion, the United Arab Emirates $4 billion and South Korea $355 million. Other nations contributed a total of $29 million.

Suggestions for further reading: Department of Defense, *Conduct of the Persian Gulf War: Final Report to the Congress,* "Appendix P: Responsibility Sharing" (Washington, D.C.: USGPO, 1992); Dick Cheney, "The Cost of Desert Storm," *Defense Issues,* vol. 6, no. 7, March 1991.

CRAF (CIVIL RESERVE AIR FLEET)

Established in 1952, the Civil Reserve Air Fleet (CRAF) is a program in which commercial airlines agree to make aircraft available for Defense Department deployments in exchange for peacetime military business. Administered by the Transportation Command's Military Airlift Command (MAC), CRAF was activated for the first time in its history for the Persian Gulf War.

Phase I of the Civil Reserve Air Fleet operation began on August 18, 1990, when 18 long-range passenger aircraft and 21 cargo aircraft were added to MAC's inter-theater airlift capability. Phase II began on January 17, 1991, when an additional 59 passenger aircraft and 17 cargo aircraft were put into service.

Some 34 commercial air carriers took part in the CRAF program. In addition, the national airlines of Italy, Kuwait, Luxembourg, the Netherlands and South Korea contributed aircraft to the CRAF program.

CRAF aircraft, including the foreign carriers, flew 2,585 passenger missions and 2,870 cargo missions during the course of the war.

See also AIRLIFT.

Suggestions for further reading: Department of Defense, *Conduct of the Persian Gulf War: Final Report to the Congress,* "Appendix E: Deployment" and "Appendix F: Logistical Buildup and Sustainment" (Washington, D.C.: USGPO, 1992); Eliot A. Cohen et al., *Gulf War Airpower Survey* (Washington, D.C.: USGPO, 1993). For a listing of carriers and the missions they flew, see "Civil Reserve Fleet Missions Flown in Operation Desert Shield and Operation Desert Storm," *Airforce,* March 1992.

CRUISE MISSILES
See AIR-LAUNCHED CRUISE MISSILE; TOMAHAWK LAND-ATTACK MISSILE.

CZECHOSLOVAKIA
See CHEMICAL WARFARE; COALITION FORCES.

D

DAGUET DIVISION (6TH LIGHT ARMORED DIVISION)

See FRANCE.

DECEPTION

Under the laws of war, deception includes measures designed to mislead the enemy—such as manipulation, distortion or falsification of evidence—in order to induce him to react in a manner prejudicial to his interests.

The 1977 Laws of War Protocol to the Geneva Conventions of August 12, 1949, deals with the laws of war in international armed conflicts. Article 37(2) states that "ruses of war are not prohibited. Such ruses are acts which are intended to mislead an adversary or to induce him to act recklessly. . . . The following are examples of ruses: the use of camouflage, decoys, mock operations and misinformation."

All of these ruses were used in the Persian Gulf War. According to the official Department of Defense report on the war,

> Coalition actions that convinced Iraqi military leaders that the ground campaign to liberate Kuwait would be focused in eastern Kuwait, and would include an amphibious assault, are examples of legitimate ruses. These deception measures were crucial to the Coalition's goal of minimizing the number of Coalition casualties and, in all likelihood, resulted in fewer Iraqi casualties as well.

Another example of the coalition's use of deception was the employment of tactical air-launched decoys (TALDs), which mimic the radar signature of incoming attack aircraft. Drawing Iraqi antiaircraft fire, TALDs exposed Iraqi radar to attack by anti-radar missiles.

Iraq also conducted deception operations. Its forces made extensive use of camouflage and shelters to hide aircraft and tanks from coalition air attack. And like the United States, Iraq had made a heavy investment in decoy technology. According to Richard Hallion in *Storm Over Iraq,*

Before the war, Iraq had contracted with an Italian company for delivery of thousands of dummy tanks, artillery and even aircraft.

Unlike the famous "rubber tanks" of World War II . . . modern decoys not only visually look like the real thing, but could in many cases mimic the infrared and even radar signature of a genuine item, forcing intelligence analysts to employ sophisticated cross-checks to ensure that a target was genuine.

Nevertheless, reported Hallion, "occasional decoy bombing occurred."

One of the strangest aspects of the coalition's deception operation was its use of the media, which, of necessity, was not made privy to the coalition ruses and complained bitterly that it had been deceived. Yet as retired Marine Lieutenant General Bernard Trainor, the director of Harvard University's National Security Program, observed: "For senior American editors to complain it was unfair or unethical for the U.S. military to make use of the press—to advance American interests and to save American lives in wartime—must make the American public question the editors' common sense. . . . Most Americans probably view it as petulant grousing."

See also AMPHIBIOUS TASK FORCE (ATF); DRONES AND DECOYS; 1ST CAVALRY DIVISION; FIRST MARINE EXPEDITIONARY FORCE (I MEF).

Suggestions for further reading: Department of Defense, *Conduct of the Persian Gulf War: Final Report to the Congress,* "Chapter 7: The Maritime Campaign," "Chapter 8: The Ground War," "Appendix O: The Role of the Laws of War" (Washington, D.C.: USGPO, 1992); Richard P. Hallion, *Storm Over Iraq: Air Power and the Gulf War* (Washington, D.C.: Smithsonian Institution Press, 1992). See also Sean Piccoli, "Decoy," *Washington Times,* January 25, 1991; Barton Gellman, "Allies Prevented War of Attrition With Deception," *Washington Post,* February 28, 1991; Bernard E. Trainor, "A Case for 'Strategic Deception' in Wartime," *San Diego Union,* July 21, 1991; Tim Weiner, "The Desert Storm Mirage: Waging a War of Deception," *Philadelphia Inquirer,* June 30, 1991.

DECLARATION OF WAR

See CONGRESS, U.S.

DECORATIONS, U.S.

U.S. military wartime decorations include a series of medals awarded to individuals for bravery or for especially meritorious acts. They are distinguished from service medals, which, as the name implies, are awarded to denote service during a particular period of time or at a particular place.

Three decorations are awarded in the name of the president of the United States solely for valor. They are the Medal of Honor; the Army, Navy, or Air Force Distinguished Service Cross; and the Silver Star.

During the Persian Gulf War, no Medals of Honor or Army Distinguished Service Crosses were awarded. Two Air Force Crosses, however, were awarded for acts of exceptional bravery, and two Marines won the Navy Cross. Seventy-four Silver Stars were awarded to members of the Army for gallantry in action, 11 to Navy personnel, 11 to members of the Marine Corps, and 50 to Air Force personnel.

Three other decorations are awarded in the name of the president for lesser acts of valor or for exceptional meritorious service. They include the Distinguished Flying Cross, the Bronze Star Medal and the Air Medal. A metallic "V" is worn on the ribbon of the Bronze Star Medal and the Air Medal to denote an award for valor.

Finally, for yet lesser acts of valor or meritorious service, the Commendation medals of the various services are awarded in the name of the secretary of defense or the service secretaries. In a category by itself is the Purple Heart Medal, which is awarded exclusively for wounds received in action.

See also AIR FORCE CROSS; AIR MEDAL; BRONZE STAR MEDAL; COMMENDATION MEDAL; DISTINGUISHED FLYING CROSS; NAVY CROSS; PURPLE HEART; SERVICE MEDALS, U.S.; SILVER STAR.

DEFENSE DEPARTMENT, U.S.

The National Security Act of 1947 created the cabinet post of secretary of defense and relegated the secretary of war (renamed the secretary of the Army), the secretary of the Navy and the newly created post of the secretary of the Air Force to subcabinet status. On August 10, 1949, an amendment to the National Security Act of 1947 created the Department of Defense, whereupon the president delegated (some say abdicated) operational command of the armed forces to the secretary of defense, making him the de facto commander of the United States military.

Over the years many military functions have been assigned to agencies controlled by the Defense Department, including the Defense Communications Agency (DCA) [renamed the Defense Information Systems Agency in June 1991], the Defense Intelligence Agency (DIA) and the Defense Logistics Agency (DLA), each of which played a major role in the Persian Gulf War.

During the Gulf War, the chain of command ran from President George Bush, the commander in chief, to Secretary of Defense Dick Cheney, through General Colin Powell, the chairman of the Joint Chiefs of Staff, to General H. Norman Schwarzkopf, the commander in chief, U.S. Central Command (CINCCENT).

Among the best secretaries of defense ever, Dick Cheney was able to maintain firm control of the military while garnering maximum cooperation from the services.

See also COMMAND AND CONTROL.

Suggestions for further reading: Bob Woodward, *The Commanders* (New York: Simon & Schuster, 1991); Colonel Harry G. Summers Jr., *On Strategy II: A Critical Analysis of the Gulf War,* (New York: Dell, 1992). For historical background, see Douglas Kinnard, *The Secretary of Defense* (Lexington, Ky.: University of Kentucky Press, 1980).

DE LA BILLIERE, GENERAL SIR PETER

See UNITED KINGDOM.

DENMARK

See COALITION FORCES.

DEPLETED URANIUM

A strong, heavy metal two and one-half times as dense as steel, depleted uranium (DU) is a by-product of the process for enriching uranium. After the fissile isotope uranium 235 is concentrated, only depleted uranium remains. DU has about the same level of radioactivity as natural uranium.

DU was present in the armor plating of the 654 heavy-armor (HA) M1A1 Abrams tanks used by the Army and the Marine Corps in the Gulf War. It was also used to enhance the penetration capability of the M1A1's armor-piercing 120-mm ammunition and of 30-mm antitank shells.

DU armor-plating proved highly effective. The crews of seven M1A1 HA tanks reported no damage after being hit by Iraqi T-72 tank rounds. But the DU ammunition presented some risks. Approximately 4,000 DU tank rounds were fired, as well as 940,000 DU- tipped 30-mm antitank rounds by A-10 Warthog aircraft.

Those at risk from DU ammunition include 35 U.S. soldiers who were exposed to uranium poisoning when their vehicles were hit by friendly DU rounds, plus the maintenance and salvage crews who worked on vehicles hit by DU rounds. According to a January 27, 1993, reply of the Defense Department to a General Accounting Office study of DU poisoning, beginning in July 1993 the affected soldiers were to be "medically evaluated . . . to determine the presence of uranium" in their bodies, and the health of the soldiers will be monitored for years because little is known about the long-term effects of uranium in the body.

After the Gulf War, the concern about depleted uranium was used to discredit the Bush administration's war policy. William M. Arkin, Greenpeace International's director of military research, debunked the more outlandish claims about the danger of DU in the pages of the *Bulletin of the Atomic Scientists*. Responding to the antiwar critic Ramsey Clark's claim that because DU-tipped shells litter the battlefield, "entire regions in Iraq and Kuwait may be deadly and uninhabitable forever," Arkin pointed out that to be injured by a shell "an individual . . . would have to carry the bullet constantly for a month to have a one percent chance of incurring a cancer from this exposure."

See also A-10 THUNDERBOLT II "WARTHOG"; ABRAMS M1A1 TANK; ECOLOGICAL WARFARE; FRIENDLY FIRE; VETERANS.

Suggestions for further reading: The best account of the depleted uranium controversy is William M. Arkin, "The Desert Glows—With Propaganda," *Bulletin of the Atomic Scientists,* May 1993. See also Thomas W. Lippman, "Gulf War Vets Were Exposed to Uranium From Friendly Fire," *Washington Post,* January 28, 1993; Eric Hoskins, "Making the Desert Glow," *New York Times,* January 21, 1993; Ramsey Clark, *The Fire This Time* (New York: Thunder's Mouth Press, 1992).

DEPLOYMENT OF U.S. FORCES

Among the nations of the world, only the United States had the capability to move more than half a million men and women, together with their aircraft, helicopters, tanks, artillery, arms and equipment, almost halfway around the world, as well as the tons of ammunition and supplies needed to sustain them in combat. As Lieutenant General William G. (Gus) Pagonis, CENTCOM's (Central Command's) chief logistician noted, the effort was like transporting the entire population of Alaska, along with personal belongings, to the other side of the globe.

The credit for this remarkable achievement goes to one of the newest and least known of the several Defense Department unified commands, the U.S. Transportation Command (TRANSCOM), headquartered at Scott Air Force Base in Illinois. Since becoming operational on October 1, 1988, TRANSCOM's mission has been to coordinate air, land and sea transportation to meet operational needs.

Commanded during the Gulf War by Air Force General Hansford T. Johnson, with Navy Vice Admiral Paul Butcher as his deputy, TRANSCOM included the Navy's Military Sealift Command (MSC), the Air Force's Military Airlift Command (MAC) and the Army's Military Traffic Management Command (MTMC).

With a logistics lifeline of approximately 9,000 miles, the task was truly herculean. As detailed elsewhere (see AIRLIFT), MAC flew some 16,000 missions as of March 1991, delivering some 562,000 tons of cargo and 544,000 passengers. Meanwhile, MTMC routed 83,000 passengers, 27,360 trucks and 15,827 railcars to stateside ports, loaded some 560 ships carrying 945,000 vehicles and arranged transport for 37,000 containers.

Using 23 ships prepositioned at the Indian Ocean island of Diego Garcia and elsewhere, 8 Navy fast-sealift ships, 6 ships already under charter, 55 ships from the Ready Reserve Fleet, 39 U.S.-flagged charter ships and 94 foreign-flagged ships, as well as 7 ships on loan from Japan, MSC moved more than 3 million short tons of cargo and 6 million tons of petroleum to the Persian Gulf.

Army Bradley fighting vehicles move by rail to the port of Savannah for sealift to the KTO.
U.S. Army photo (Dan Mock) courtesy of 24th Infantry Division (Mechanized).

Early in the crisis, CINCCENT (commander in chief, Central Command) made a crucial decision to deploy combat elements first and to temporarily defer the deployment of theater logistics forces. Tank-killing Air Force A-10 Warthog units, the 3d Cavalry Regiment and the 24th Infantry Division (Mechanized) had priority of movement so as to get more antiarmor units into Saudi Arabia as soon as possible. Thus, some units were dependent on host nation (i.e., Saudi Arabian) support for sustainment until November 1990, when the theater logistics elements were finally in place.

Marine and Air Force units were not as severely affected as Army units by the CINCCENT's decision

to deploy ground-combat units before their logistics. The Marine Air-Ground Task Force (MAGTF) includes an organic logistics element at each force level, and thus units were able to draw on up to 30 days of supplies from Maritime Prepositioning Ships. Air Force squadrons also deployed with organic 30-day aviation support packages. Still, as the official Department of Defense (DOD) report notes, "by C +60 both the USAF and USMC suffered from a lack of common support items normally provided by a theater logictics structure."

Deployment of U.S. forces in Operation Desert Shield occurred in two phases. Phase I began on C-Day (August 7, 1990) and lasted until mid-Novem-

Although most soldiers deployed to the Gulf by air, their heavy equipment had to be moved by sea in ships such as the fast sealift ship USNS Algol.
U.S. Navy photo (PH1 Scott Allen), Empire Press.

ber. As noted above, this phase was designed to deploy enough forces to deter further Iraqi aggression and to prepare for defensive operations. Ultimately, during Phase I the United States deployed about 1,030 aircraft, 60 Navy ships, an amphibious task force and 240,000 military personnel.

Deployed during Phase I, the Third U.S. Army included the XVIII Airborne Corps's 82d Airborne Division, 101st Airborne Division (Air Assault) and 24th Infantry Division (Mechanized), as well as the 3d Armored Cavalry Regiment and logistical support forces. By the end of Phase I, more that 700 tanks, 1,000 armored combat vehicles, 145 Apache helicopters and 299 155-mm howitzers had arrived.

The first Air Force combat elements arrived in Riyadh, Saudi Arabia, on August 8, 1990. These were

from the 1st Tactical Fighter Wing (TFW)—24 F-15C Strike Eagles from the 71st Tactical Fighter Squadron at Langley Air Force Base (AFB) in Virginia—supported by five AWACS (airborne warning and control system) aircraft from Tinker AFB in Oklahoma. By August 14, 1990, more than 200 Air Force combat aircraft had deployed to the Kuwaiti Theater of Operations (KTO), including three squadrons of air-to-air superiority fighters and eight squadrons of air-to-ground fighters. By the end of Phase I, the Ninth U.S. Air Force had more than 1,030 aircraft in the KTO, including more that 590 combat aircraft deployed from the United States and Europe.

The 7th Marine Expeditionary Brigade (MEB) began arriving in the KTO on August 14, 1990, linking up with its equipment that had arrived at the Saudi port of Al-Jubayl from Diego Garcia aboard Maritime Prepositioning Ships. The 7th MEB was ready for combat by August 26, 1990, providing Central Command (CENTCOM) with its first mechanized ground-combat capability. On September 11, 1990, the 7th MEB was joined by the 1st MEB; both were then incorporated into the First Marine Expeditionary Force's 1st Marine Division, which had arrived on September 4, 1990.

The Seventh U.S. Fleet's forces included the six-ship Middle East Force, which was already on station. During Phase I it was joined by four carrier action groups (those of the USS *Independence*, the *Eisenhower* [relieved by the *John F. Kennedy* in mid-August], the *Saratoga* and the *Midway)* and the battleship USS *Wisconsin.* The Seventh Fleet also included an Amphibious Task Force (ATF), which consisted initially of Amphibious Group Two with the 4th MEB embarked and later included Amphibious Group Alfa with the special-operations-capable 13th MEU (Marine Expeditionary Unit) embarked.

Phase II of the deployment began with President George Bush's November 8, 1990, announcement that the U.S. presence in the KTO would be reinforced by approximately 200,000 personnel.

Forces moved during the second phase included the Army's 1st Infantry Division (Mechanized) from Fort Riley, Kansas; the Europe-based VII Corps, consisting of the 1st and 3d Armored Divisions; and the 2d Armored Cavalry Regiment. Substantial numbers of Army Reserve and Army National Guard combat-support and combat-service-support units were also deployed.

During Phase II, three additional carrier action groups—the USS *Ranger*'s (which relieved that of the *Independence*, the *Roosevelt*'s and the *America*'s—were deployed, as was the battleship USS *Missouri*.

Amphibious Group Three, with the 5th MEB embarked, was also deployed, bringing the Amphibious Task Force to 31 amphibious ships and 17,000 Marines. With the addition of the 2d Marine Division, which arrived on January 8, 1991, I MEF's strength ashore reached more than 70,000 personnel.

As the official DOD report concluded: "Iraq's failure to move into Saudi Arabia allowed sufficient time to deploy substantial countervailing forces. The success of the deployment was dependent on the availability of aircraft, ships, and crews; timely decisions to augment active force lift assets with the Selected Reserve, CRAF (Civil Reserve Air Fleet), RRF (Ready Reserve Fleet); ability to load effectively; forward staging bases for international flights; forward deployed forces; superb Saudi port facilities; cooperation of European allies; and TRANSCOM's effectiveness."

See also AIRLIFT; CRAF (CIVIL RESERVE AIR FLEET); FIRST MARINE EXPEDITIONARY FORCE (I MEF); LOGISTICS, U.S.; MOBILIZATION, U.S.; NINTH U.S. AIR FORCE; SEALIFT; SEVENTH U.S. FLEET; THIRD U.S. ARMY.

Suggestions for further reading: Department of Defense, *Conduct of the Persian Gulf War: Final Report to the Congress,* "Chapter 3: The Military Option—Operation Desert Shield," and "Appendix E: Deployment" (Washington, D.C.: USGPO, 1992); Eliot A. Cohen et al., *Gulf War Airpower Survey* (Washington, D.C.: USGPO, 1993); Lieutenant General William G. Pagonis with Jeffrey L. Cruikshank, *Moving Mountains* (Cambridge, Mass.: Harvard Business School Press, 1992); Richard P. Hallion, *Storm Over Iraq: Air Power and the Gulf War* (Washington, D.C.: Smithsonian Institution Press, 1992); Douglas Frantz, "Military Gets to the Gulf 'Fastest with the Mostest,'" *Los Angeles Times,* December 31, 1990; Katherine Butler, "Operation Desert Storm: The Logistical Story," *Government Executive,* May 1991.

DESERT SHIELD

The code name for the initial phase of the Persian Gulf War, Operation Desert Shield coincided with the official "Defense of Saudi Arabia" campaign. Beginning on C-Day, August 7, 1990, Operation Desert Shield ended on the eve of D- Day, January 17, 1991, when Operation Desert Storm began.

See also CAMPAIGNS, U.S. MILITARY; DESERT STORM.

DESERT STORM

The code name for the second phase of the Persian Gulf War, Operation Desert Storm began on D-Day, January 17, 1991. Coinciding with the official "Liberation of Kuwait" campaign, Operation Desert Storm ended on April 11, 1991, when the "Southwest Asia Cease-Fire" campaign began.

See also CAMPAIGNS, U.S. MILITARY; DESERT SHIELD.

DIEGO GARCIA

Located in the Chagos Archipelago in the Indian Ocean about 1,900 miles from the Strait of Hormuz, Diego Garcia is part of the British Indian Ocean Territory. The largest island in the archipelago, it has a total land area of some 10.5 square miles (6,720 acres), or about 0.3 times the area of Washington, D.C. Diego Garcia is the site of joint United Kingdom–United States defense facilities, including a 12,000-foot runway and a lagoon large enough to accommodate an entire carrier action group.

Since 1980, Diego Garcia has been an anchorage for the U.S. Air Force's (USAF's) afloat prepositioning ships (APS) and the U.S. Navy/Marine Corps's maritime prepositioning ships (MPS). During the Persian Gulf War, Diego Garcia was used as a base for USAF aerial refueling tankers and B-52 Stratofortress bombers.

Suggestion for further reading: P. Lewis Young, "Diego Garcia: Its Role in the US Gulf Security Policy," *Asian Defense,* July 1992.

DISCIPLINE
See LAW AND ORDER.

DISTINGUISHED FLYING CROSS

Authorized in 1926, the Distinguished Flying Cross (DFC) is awarded in the name of the president of the United States for heroism or extraordinary achievement while participating in aerial flight. The act of heroism has to be a voluntary action above and beyond the call of duty. The extraordinary achievement has to be so exceptional and outstanding as to clearly set the individual apart from his or her comrades or other persons in similar circumstances.

During the Persian Gulf War the Army awarded 97, 23 for valor and 74 for achievement. The Navy awarded a total of 130 DFCs, the Air Force 864 and the Marine Corps 8.

See also DECORATIONS, U.S.

DISTINGUISHED SERVICE CROSS

See DECORATIONS, U.S.

DIVISION

In the U.S. Army and Marine Corps, as well as in most foreign military organizations, the division is the basic combined-arms organization for waging war.

Normally commanded by a major general, a division consists of two or more manuever (i.e., infantry or armor) brigades or regiments plus supporting artillery, aviation, engineer and logistical support units. Its size is not fixed, but divisions may include up to 20,000 men and women.

The U.S. Army deployed seven divisions to the Kuwaiti Theater of Operations (KTO): the 1st Armored Division, the 1st Cavalry Division, the 1st Infantry Division (Mechanized), the 3d Armored Division, the 24th Infantry Division (Mechanized), the 82d Airborne Division and the 101st Airborne Division (Air Assault), plus elements of the 2d Armored Division and the 3d Infantry Division (Mechanized). The U.S. Marine Corps deployed its 1st and 2d Marine Divisions.

Other coalition allies also deployed divisions. The British deployed their 1st Armoured Division and the French their 6th Light Armored Division. Other coalition divisions included the Egyptian 3d Mechanized and 4th Armored Divisions and the Syrian 9th Armored Division.

Iraq deployed some 50 infantry, armored and mechanized divisions as well as eight Republican Guard Force Command (RGFC) divisions. Five more RGFC divisions were added during the war. Except for those in the RGFC, Iraqi divisions varied widely in size, equipment and training.

The term "division" is also used by the U.S. Air Force to designate a unit smaller than a numbered air force (such as the Ninth Air Force) but larger than an air wing. In December 1990, the commander of CENTAF (Central Command Air Force), who was concurrently the Ninth U.S. Air Force commander, created four provisional Air Divisions to clarify command relationships. The 14th Air Division consisted of all Tactical Air Command (TAC) fighter aircraft. EW (electronic warfare) and command and control aircraft made up the 15th Air Division. The 17th Air Division consisted of the aerial tankers and B-52 bombers of the Strategic Air Command (SAC), while the 1610th Air Lift Division was made up of Military Airlift Command (MAC) transports.

See also ORGANIZATION FOR COMBAT, U.S.

DOCTRINE

The Persian Gulf War was fought according to a design, what the military calls "doctrine." "At the heart of warfare lies doctrine," wrote the late Air Force General Curtis E. LeMay in the introduction to the Air Force's doctrinal manual, AFM 1-1. "It represents the central beliefs for waging war."

After the Vietnam War, the U.S. military underwent an enormous renaissance, unnoticed outside its own ranks, as it rethought the very fundamentals of military operations. Begun under Vice Admiral Stansfield Turner at the Naval War College in 1972, this rethinking soon spread to the other services.

Among the results of this renaissance were new warfighting doctrines for the Army, Navy, Air Force and Marine Corps. From the Army came the Airland Battle doctrine, a manuever-oriented, multidimensional conception of how to fight. The Maritime Strategy was the Navy's blueprint for the future. It put the Navy back on the offensive and emphasized the importance of building a sea bridge so that America's mobilization capabilities could be brought to bear. Air Force doctrine emphasized the decisive role of airpower, whereas the Marine Corps's Amphibious Warfare Strategy, with its reemphasis on campaigning as well as its revolutionary new Marine Air-Ground Task Force (MAGTF) organization, marked a return to basic principles.

"The U.S. military victory in the Gulf was above all a victory for doctrines developed and tested within the Services," wrote the Naval War College's Mackubin Owens. "It was effective doctrine that shaped the battlefield and transformed what could have been a formidable adversary into a disorganized and almost completely ineffective force."

See also AIRLAND BATTLE DOCTRINE; AIRPOWER; MARITIME STRATEGIC DOCTRINE, U.S.

Suggestions for further reading: For an account of the military renaissance see Colonel Harry G.

Summers Jr., *On Strategy II: A Critical Analysis of the Gulf War* (New York: Dell, 1992). See also Lt. Col. Price T. Bingham, USAF, "Air Power in Desert Storm," *Airpower Journal,* Winter 1991; Mackubin Thomas Owens, "Desert Storm and the Renaissance in Military Doctrine," *Strategic Review,* Spring 1991; Stephen S. Rosenfeld, "Military Doctrine Today," *Washington Post,* March 22, 1991.

DRAFT

Contrary to popular opinion, the U.S. Army has never drafted anyone in its entire history. The reason is simple: The Constitution of the United States gives Congress the sole power to "raise and support armies" and to "provide and maintain a navy," and only Congress can conscript citizens into military service. Congress did so in the Civil War with the Enrollment Act of 1863, in World War I with the Selective Service Act of 1917, and, for the first time in peacetime, on the eve of World War II with the Selective Training and Service Act of 1940.

In March 1947, the World War II Selective Service Act expired, but a new Selective Service Act was passed in 1948, followed by the Universal Military Training and Service Act of 1951 that provided manpower for the Korean War and extended into the Vietnam War as well. In 1973, military conscription officially came to an end, but following the Soviet invasion of Afghanistan in 1979, President Jimmy Carter asked Congress to reinstate draft registration, which it did in 1980. As the requirement now stands, all men must register within 30 days of their 18th birthday.

At the outbreak of the Gulf crisis, the U.S. armed forces were an all-volunteer force. Ample active and reserve forces were available, and a revival of the draft was never considered.

See also ANTIWAR MOVEMENT.

Suggestions for further reading: For background on the draft, see Eliot A. Cohen, *Citizens and Soldiers: The Dilemmas of Military Service* (Ithaca, N.Y.: Cornell University Press, 1985), and Charles E. Moskos, *A Call to Civic Service* (New York: The Free Press, 1988). See also Bill McAllister, "Officials Deny Plan to Revive Draft, But Rumors Persist," *Washington Post,* February 3, 1991; Joan E. Rigdon, "Students Prepare to Dodge a Draft That Doesn't Exist," *Wall Street Journal,* February 27, 1991.

DRONES AND DECOYS

"Unmanned Aerial Vehicles (UAV) performed superbly during Desert Shield/Storm," said the U.S. Navy in its after-action report on the Gulf War. UAVs were used for real-time battle damage assessment, artillery and naval gunfire adjustment, reconnaissance, and coordination of ground and air operations.

Approximately 88 Pioneer UAVs were used by the battleships USS *Wisconsin* (BB-64) and *Missouri* (BB-63); by the 1st, 2d and 3d Marine RPV (remote-piloted vehicle) Companies; and by the Army's 1st UAV Platoon. These gasoline-engine UAVs have a 17-foot wingspan, weigh 420 pounds, and have a maximum speed of 115 miles per hour and a maximum altitude of 15,000 feet. Mounting a video camera that can take detailed pictures from 2,000 feet and transmit them to a distance of 100 miles, the Pioneer was typically flown four hours at a time within a 100-mile radius of its launch point.

Fifty-five Pointer FQM-151A UAVs were also used by the Army and the Marines. Little more than a model airplane, the battery-operated Pointer has a 9-foot wingspan, weighs 9 pounds and has a maximum speed of 40 knots over a 5.6 kilometer range. It carries a camera for black and white electro-optic imagery.

The number of Pointer UAVs used in the Gulf War is not available, but it is known that 522 Pioneer sorties were flown during some 1,640 mission hours. Twelve Pioneer UAVs were lost, one to hostile fire and three due to electomagnetic interference.

Another type of drone used in the Gulf War is the ADM-41 tactical air-launched decoy (TALD). This small, unpowered decoy approximates the size and weight of a 500-pound bomb, and up to eight can be carried by a tactical aircraft.

Mimicking the radar signature of incoming strike aircraft, TALDs caused Iraqi defenders to switch on their radars, thus giving radar-hunters something to shoot at. "At one point, following a shower of drones near Baghdad," reports Richard Hallion, "over 200 HARM antiradar missiles were launched, homing in on Iraqi radars."

According to the offical Department of Defense report on the Gulf War, "pilots reported SAMs (surface-to-air missiles) were launched in response to TALD launches. Furthermore, it is likely that TALD contributed to Iraqi claims of massive Coalition aircraft losses early in the theater air campaign."

Suggestions for further reading: Department of Defense, *Conduct of the Persian Gulf War: Final Report to the Congress,* "Appendix C: Intelligence," "Appendix T: Performance of Selected Weapons Systems" (Washington, D.C.: USGPO, 1992); Richard P. Hallion, *Storm Over Iraq: Air Power and the Gulf War* (Washington, D.C.: Smithsonian Institution Press, 1992); Eliot A. Cohen et al., *Gulf War Airpower Survey* (Washington, D.C.: USGPO, 1993); Robert J. Roy, "Combat Operations Garner Unmanned Aerial Support," *Signal,* April 1991.

DUGAN, MICHAEL J., GENERAL, USAF

See AIRPOWER; CHIEF OF STAFF, U.S. AIR FORCE.

DUNE BUGGIES

U.S. military forces in the Persian Gulf used not only standard-issue equipment, they also took advantage of civilian off-the-shelf items for special tasks and missions.

Among such items were the dune buggies made by Chenowth Racing Products in California. Sturdier than the civilian models and modified by adding a gunner's cage to the back and racks for carrying gear to the side, these lightweight tubular recreational vehicles can reach speeds of up to 100 miles per hour.

Ideally suited for desert reconnaissance, the dune buggies were used by Navy SEALS (sea-air-land commandos) for special missions; they were also used in the retaking of the American Embassy in Kuwait.

Suggestion for further reading: Julie Pitts, "Totally Tubular, Dude," *Forbes,* May 13, 1991.

ECOLOGICAL WARFARE

Although the term is new, "ecological warfare"—the deliberate destruction of the ecosystem as an act of war—is as old as warfare itself, dating at least to 146 B.C. and the Third Punic War, when the Roman general Scipio the Younger sacked Carthage, exiled the inhabitants and plowed the ground with salt. What Scipio did with salt, Iraqi dictator Saddam Hussein would do with oil.

In what the U.S. State Department called an "indiscriminate environmental war," on January 25, 1991, Iraq dumped into the Persian Gulf an estimated 4–6 million barrels of oil from the Kuwaiti crude oil tanker-loading terminal at Sea Island. Iraq also drained five oil tankers in the Kuwaiti port of Mina al-Ahmadi, and pumped oil from on-shore storage tanks into the Persian Gulf.

Two days later, U.S. Air Force F-111F Aardvarks using GBU-15 guided bombs managed to destroy the oil manifolding from the storage tanks to the Sea Island terminal, thereby drastically cutting the flow of oil into the Gulf. But the damage had already been done. The oil slick eventually covered some 600 square miles of the Persian Gulf and 300 miles of its shoreline. The U.S. Coast Guard assisted in skimming about 1.5 million barrels of oil off of Gulf waters

Burning Kuwaiti oil wells set afire by the Iraqis did not slow the coalition's advance.
U.S. Army photo courtesy of 24th Infantry Division (Mechanized).

after the war, but serious long-term environmental damage had been done to marine life, including water birds, plankton and fish larvae.

On February 22, 1991, in a systematic attempt to destroy Kuwait, Iraq forces intentionally dynamited 732 producing oil wells, more than 650 of which caught fire. The 80-odd wells that did not catch fire continued to pour oil into the countryside. Some of the blazes reached 200 feet into the air, and oil-laden clouds rose as high as 22,000 feet, literally turning day into night. At their peak, these oil fires burned about 5 million barrels of oil daily, generating more than half a million tons of aerial pollutants.

Some 10,000 workers from 27 fire-fighting teams,—including teams from the United States, Canada, China, France, Hungary, Iran, Kuwait, Romania and the Soviet Union—battled the blazes. Texans, such as Red Adair, and firms such as "Boots and Coots," "Wild Well Control" and Canada's "Safety Boss," put out more than 80 percent of the fires.

Although initial estimates were that it would take two to three years to extinguish the fires, it actually took only eight months. The last blaze was ceremoniously snuffed out on November 6, 1991, by the Kuwaiti emir. It would be several additional months, however, before the 25–50 million barrels of oil in the pool lakes created by the Iraqi dynamiting could be recovered.

After the war, antiwar activists charged that the U.S. use of depleted uranium (DU) in its tank armor and especially as armor-penetrators in the 30-mm ammunition of the A-10 Warthog aircraft also constituted ecological warfare. For example, Ramsey Clark claimed that because thousands of DU-tipped shells littered the battlefield, "entire regions in Iraq and Kuwait may be deadly and uninhabitable forever." But according to Greenpeace International's director of military research, William M. Arkin, "an individual . . . would have to carry [such a] bullet constantly for a month to have a one percent chance of incurring a cancer from this exposure."

See also DEPLETED URANIUM; VETERANS; WAR CRIMES.

Suggestions for further reading: Department of Defense, *Conduct of the Persian Gulf War: Final Report to the Congress,* "Appendix O: The Rules of War" (Washington, D.C.: USGPO, 1992); T. M. Hawley, *Against the Fires of Hell: The Environmental Disaster of the Gulf War* (New York: Harcourt, Brace Jovanovich, 1992); Richard P. Hallion, *Storm Over Iraq: Air Power and the Gulf War* (Washington, D.C.: Smithsonian Institution Press, 1992). See also Walter G. Sharp Sr., "The Effective Deterrence of Environmental Damage During Armed Conflict: A Case Analysis of the Persian Gulf War," *Military Law Review,* Summer 1992 (from which portions of the above information was extracted); Robert Hutchison and Sean Ryan, "Saddam's Oil 'Time Bomb' Ravages Fish and Bird Life," *The Sunday Times* (London), February 21, 1993. For the depleted-uranium controversy, see Eric Hoskins, "Making the Desert Glow," *New York Times,* January 21, 1993; Ramsey Clark, *The Fire This Time* (New York: Thunder's Mouth Press, 1992), and the rebuttal by William M. Arkin, "The Desert Glows— With Propaganda," *Bulletin of the Atomic Scientists,* May 1993.

EGYPT

One of the primary coalition partners, Egypt played a major role, both politically and militarily, in the Persian Gulf War.

With an estimated 1991 population of 54,451,000, Egypt is the most populous Arab nation in the world. Located at the northeast corner of Africa, Egypt covers an area of 386,650 square miles, about the size of Texas, Oklahoma and Arkansas combined. Egypt's 103-mile-long Suez Canal, which links the Mediterranean Sea and the Indian Ocean, was of great strategic importance during the war, allowing for the quick transport of supplies and the use of the Red Sea by carrier strike forces.

Beginning in November 1980, Egypt had participated in U.S. Central Command's "Bright Star" manuevers, wherein U.S. and Egyptian troops took part in a series of joint training exercises in order to improve their capabilities for combined operations. The Egyptian Air Force had also participated in the U.S. Air Force's "Red Flag" training exercises. Moreover, Egypt had bought substantial amounts of U.S. military weapons and equipment, and in the course of the war the United States wrote off some $6.7 billion of Egypt's debt.

President Hosni Mubarak of Egypt was instrumental in gaining the Arab League's condemnation of the Iraqi invasion of Kuwait at the League's meeting in Cairo on August 4, 1990. He also played a key role in the League's August 10, 1990, ratification of

The unrestricted passage of warships, underway replenishment ships and transports through Egypt's Suez Canal was vital to the war effort.
U.S. Navy photo (PH3 Frank Marquart), Empire Press.

the United Nations sanctions against Iraq, and in its decision to send an Arab force to Saudi Arabia and the other Gulf states. Egyptian special operations forces drawn from the 1st Ranger Regiment were among the first foreign troops to deploy to Saudi Arabia, arriving in early August 1990. Egypt also opened its ports and airfields in support of Operations Desert Shield and Desert Storm.

Egypt deployed its II Corps, commanded by Major General Salah Mohammed Attia Halaby, to Saudi Arabia. The 40,000-strong corps consisted of the 3d Mechanized Division and the 4th Armored Division. These units were equipped with some 400 U.S.-supplied M-60 tanks as well as M113 armored personnel carriers.

Along with Saudi Arabia, Egypt was one of the designated planners for the Arab/Islamic forces. Egyptian forces were part of the Arab-Islamic Joint Task Force North, commanded by Saudi Major General Abdulrahman al-Kammi, that formed the western flank of the Joint Forces Command attack.

The Egyptian II Corps jumped off on February 24, 1991 (G-Day), attacking between the U.S. XVIII Corps on its left and the U.S. First Marine Expeditionary Force on its right. Advancing through Iraqi fire trenches, fortifications and mine fields, by February 26 II Corps had captured some 1,500 Iraqis, and by February 27 it had liberated 'Ali As-Salim airfield in Kuwait. By February 28, the Egyptian Ranger Regiment had secured the Egyptian Embassy in Kuwait City; the 6th Brigade, 4th Armored Division was clearing the western part of Kuwait City; and the 3d Mechanized Division was screening north from its position at Al-Abraq.

According to the U.S. Central Command, 12 Egyptian soldiers were killed in action (KIA) during the fighting, and 95 were wounded in action (WIA). Egypt reported its casualties as 14 KIA and 120 WIA.

See also ARAB LEAGUE; BRIGHT STAR EXERCISES; GROUND CAMPAIGN; JOINT FORCES COMMAND.

Suggestions for further reading: Department of Defense, *Conduct of the Persian Gulf War: Final Report to the Congress* (Washington, D.C.: USGPO, 1992); General H. Norman Schwarzkopf, *It Doesn't Take a Hero* (New York: Bantam Books, 1992). Norman Friedman, *Desert Victory: The War for Kuwait* (Annapolis, Md.: Naval Institute Press, 1991) has an appendix on coalition land forces. See also Michael Kelly, *Martyr's Day* (New York: Random House, 1993): Kelly, a war correspondent for *The New Republic*, accompanied Egyptian forces in their attack to liberate Kuwait. An excellent overview of Egyptian mili-

tary operations is David B. Ottoway, "For Saudi Military, New Self-Confidence," *Washington Post*, April 20, 1991.

XVIII AIRBORNE CORPS

Among the first U.S. military units to deploy to the Kuwaiti Theater of Operations (KTO), XVIII Airborne Corps's assault command post and lead elements of its 82d Airborne Division left Fort Bragg, North Carolina, on August 8, 1990. Commanded by Lieutenant General Gary E. Luck, the XVIII Airborne Corps was the major ground force unit in Saudi Arabia during Phase I (August–November 1990) of the U.S. deployment to the Gulf.

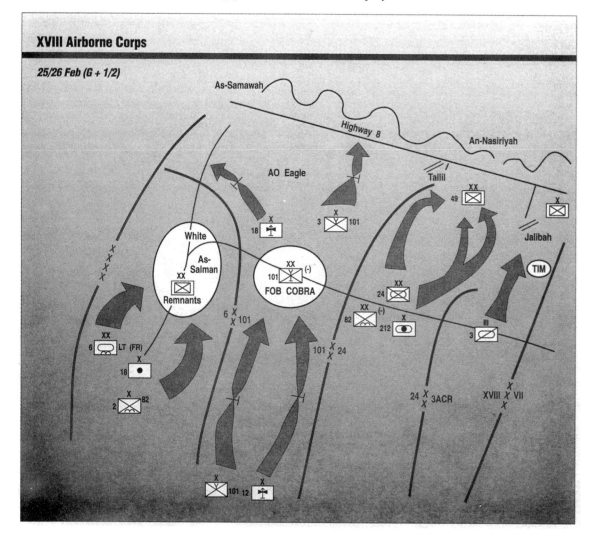

Tanks of the XVIII Airborne Corps's 24th Infantry Division (Mechanized) race to cut off the enemy's retreat.
U.S. Army photo courtesy of 24th Infantry Division (Mechanized).

One of the Third U.S. Army's two combat corps, the XVIII Airborne Corps on the eve of the ground war consisted of the 24th Infantry Division (Mechanized), the 82d Airborne Division and the 101st Airborne Division (Air Assault). The French 6th Light Armored Division was also under XVIII Corps's tactical control. Other corps units included the 3d Armored Cavalry Regiment; the 12th and 18th Aviation Groups; the XVIII Airborne Corps Artillery and the attached III Corps Artillery's 7th, 212th and 214th Field Artillery Brigades; and the 196th Field Artillery Brigade from the Tennessee-West Virginia-Kentucky National Guard.

After shifting some 300 miles to the west to its attack positions near Rafha, Saudi Arabia, XVIII Airborne Corps formed the left flank of the coalition's attack. Its objectives were to penetrate approximately 260 kilometers to the Euphrates River, cut the Iraqi lines of communication along Highway 8 to Baghdad, isolate Iraqi forces in the KTO and help destroy the Republican Guards, Iraq's theater reserve.

By February 26, 1991, XVIII Airborne Corps had achieved all of its objectives. Still protecting the western and northern flanks, the corps advanced east into the Euphrates River valley. When offensive operations ended at 8:00 A.M. on February 28, the lead elements of the XVIII Airborne Corps's 24th Infantry Division (Mechanized) stood only 30 miles west of Basra, Iraq.

After the cease-fire, XVIII Airborne Corps withdrew from the KTO and returned to its home base at Fort Bragg, North Carolina.

See also LISTINGS FOR INDIVIDUAL UNITS; ARMY, U.S.; FRANCE; GROUND CAMPAIGN; LUCK, GARY E.; THIRD U.S. ARMY.

Suggestions for further reading: Department of Defense, *Conduct of the Persian Gulf War: Final Report to the Congress,* "Chapter 8: The Ground Campaign" (Washington, D.C.: USGPO, 1992); Major James Blackwell, *Thunder in the Desert: The Strategy and Tactics of the Persian Gulf War* (New York: Bantam Books, 1991); General H. Norman Schwarzkopf, *It Doesn't Take a Hero* (New York: Bantam Books, 1992); The Staff of U.S. News & World Report, *Triumph*

Without Victory: The Unreported History of the Persian Gulf War (New York: Times Books, 1992).

82D AIRBORNE DIVISION

One of the more famous units in the U.S. Army, the 82d Airborne "All American" Division fought in World War I as an infantry division and in World War II as an airborne division. It sent its 3d Brigade to Vietnam in 1968 and took part in Operation Urgent Fury in Grenada in 1983 and Operation Just Cause in Panama in 1988.

The 82d Airborne Division was the first Army ground combat unit to arrive in Saudi Arabia; the lead elements of its 2d Brigade were on the ground on August 8, 1990. The 82d Airborne Division's initial mission was to defend Saudi Arabia until the rest of its parent XVIII Airborne Corps could arrive in-country.

Commanded by Major General James H. Johnson Jr., the 82d Airborne Division consisted of the 1st, 2d and 4th Battalions of the 325th Infantry; the 1st, 2d and 3d Battalions of the 504th Infantry; and the 1st, 2d and 3d Battalions of the 505th Infantry. Organized into three maneuver brigades, these units were supported by an Aviation Brigade and a Division Artillery.

The Aviation Brigade consisted of a battalion of UH-60 Blackhawk assault helicopters, a battalion of AH-64 Apache attack helicopters, and the 1st Squadron, 17th Air Cavalry equipped with OH-58 Kiowa scout helicopters. The 1st, 2d and 3d Battalions of the 319th Airborne Artillery, each with 18 towed 105-mm howitzers, made up the Division Artillery, which was also augmented with MLRS (multiple launch rocket systems) medium artillery. Also part of the division was the 2d Battalion of the 73d Armor, which was equipped with M-551 Sheridan light tanks that fired either 152-mm low-velocity rounds or Shillelagh missiles.

Along with the French 6th Light Armored Division, the 82d Airborne Division had as its mission sealing the western flank of the coalition's ground attack. Its 2d Brigade was attached to the French unit, which had as its objective seizing the crossing points along the Saudi-Iraqi border and assisting in clearing the main route north to the initial objective, the Iraqi airfield at As-Salman. After seizing Al-Salman, the French 6th Light Armored Division was left to screen the western flank while the main body of the 82d

Airborne Division turned northeast to seize the Iraqi airfield at Tallil near the Euphrates River.

During its 350-mile advance, the 82d Airborne Division took more than 2,700 prisoners and destroyed 10 armored vehicles, 124 artillery and mortar tubes, 341 trucks, 19 fighter aircraft on the ground, and thousands of antitank and air defense weapons as well as small arms and ammunition.

Following the cease-fire, the 82d Airborne Division returned to its home station of Fort Bragg, North Carolina.

See also XVIII AIRBORNE CORPS; FRANCE; GROUND CAMPAIGN.

Suggestions for further reading: Department of Defense, *Conduct of the Persian Gulf War: Final Report to the Congress,* "Chapter 8: The Ground Campaign" (Washington, D.C.: USGPO, 1992); Major James Blackwell, *Thunder in the Desert: The Strategy and Tactics of the Persian Gulf War* (New York: Bantam Books, 1991); General H. Norman Schwarzkopf, *It Doesn't Take a Hero* (New York: Bantam Books, 1992); The Staff of U.S. News & World Report, *Triumph Without Victory* (New York: Times Books, 1992). See also Katherine McIntire, "Speed Bumps: 82d Airborne's Shaky Line in the Sand," *Army Times,* October 21, 1991.

ELECTRONIC WARFARE (EW)

Electronic warfare (EW) and its companion, electronic countermeasures (ECM), were vital to the coalition's success in the Persian Gulf War. EW completely disrupted Iraq's command, control, communications and intelligence (C^3I) systems. With its EW capabilities, the coalition could see and hear deep within Iraq, while at the same time, with its ECM, the coalition could deny Iraq the same advantage.

Electronic warfare was one of several areas in which the Iraqis found themselves hopelessly outclassed. It is not that they were without EW equipment. Iraq had an extensive array of air defense radars as well as some Soviet- and Western-designed electronic support measures (ESM) that allowed it to monitor coalition communications and to detect stand-off jamming as coalition aircraft neared a target area.

When it came to ECM, Iraq's active jamming with Soviet-designed systems and 1970s-vintage French systems was focused mainly on ground systems with little effect. Iraqis did make extensive use of emission control to minimize the vulnerability of their radios and air defense radars, but as long as those systems were not emitting they were useless. As Richard Hallion noted in *Storm Over Iraq,* "The Iraqis soon learned that turning on a radar was tantamount to suicide."

As a result, noted Lieutenant General Charles A. Horner, the CENTAF (Central Command Air Component) commander, in an interview with *Airforce* senior editor James Canan in June 1991, "our losses to surface-to-air missiles were something like ten planes," even though the enemy "fired thousands and thousands of surface-to-air missiles [which] would tell you automatically that . . . electronic countermeasures . . . [were] certainly effective. . . . In fact the only kills [the enemy] got were probably flukes."

EW and ECM systems that are discussed elsewhere in more detail include ABCCC (Airborne Battlefield Command and Control Center), the ALARM antiradar missile, AWACS (Airborne Warning and Control System), drones and decoys, the Global Positioning System (GPS), HARM (high-speed anti-radiation missiles), JSTARS (Joint Surveillance Target Attack System), LANTIRN (Low-Altitude Navigational and Targeting Infrared for Night), reconnaissance, satellites, Stealth aircraft and the Wild Weasel aircraft.

Other coalition EW and ECM systems included aircraft countermeasure pods that jammed enemy missile guidance radars; among these systems were the ALQ-119, the ALQ-126B, the ALQ-131, the ALQ-137, the ALQ-164 (which combines the ALQ-126 and the ALQ-162 into a single pod to counter both pulses and continuous-wave radar threats), the new ALQ-184 and the internal ALQ-135. Helicopters were protected by ALQ-144 and ALQ-156 missile-warning systems that jammed enemy missile guidance radars and, in the case of the ALQ-156, triggered flares, chaff and other expendable ECM gear.

Coalition aircraft were also equipped with radar warning receivers (RWRs) such as the ALR-56A and the ALR-56C, which warn of the approach of a radar-guided missile. Some coalition aircraft also carried a newer missile warning system (MWS) that could detect all kinds of missiles, including those using infrared and electro-optic sensors.

Area jamming aircraft such as the U.S. Air Force F-4G Wild Weasel and EF-111 Raven, and the Navy's

EA-6B Prowler, poured electrons into the enemy's target acquisition radars, causing their screens to go blank. And EC-130 Compass Call aircraft disrupted Iraqi military communications. Also used on Tomahawk cruise missiles were a limited number of high-powered microwave warheads, which convert the energy of a conventional explosion into a pulse of radio energy that can penetrate computerized weapons systems and disrupt or even burn out their electronic components.

Listening in on enemy communications was the mission of the Air Force's RC-135 Rivet Joint aircraft. While the E-3 AWACS was called the "eyes of the storm," the RC-135s were the "ears of the storm." Specially built versions of the KC-135 Stratotanker, the RC-135V and RC-135W were part of the 38th and 1700th Strategic Reconnaissance Squadrons. Arriving in the Kuwaiti Theater of Operations (KTO) on August 11, 1990, they maintained a continuous 24-hour orbit along the Saudi-Iraqi border. Their mission was to use their sensors to locate, identify and catalogue Iraqi electronic emissions. The RC-135s were also used in search and rescue (SAR) operations.

In addition to these Air Force, Navy and Marine Corps systems, the Army's Quick Fix helicopter-mounted jamming system, Quick Look electronic intelligence system mounted in RV-1D Mohawk aircraft, and Guardrail communications intercept system also played an important part in the EW/ECM effort. On the ground, the Army's vehicle-mounted TACJAM AN/MLQ-34 Trailblazer special-purpose countermeasures set and the smaller Trafficjam system were used to jam enemy communications.

Thirteen Trojan Spirit mobile satellite communications systems were also deployed to the KTO to handle sensitive compartmentalized intelligence. Three units were used by ARCENT (Army Component Central Command) headquarters, another was located at the main XVIII Corps command post (CP), two were at the VII Corps CP and its Military Intelligence Brigade operations center, and one was provided to MARCENT (the Marine Corps Component commander).

The coalition's EW efforts were so effective that it became almost suicidal for the Iraqis to turn on a radar or radio transmitter. It was rumored that some Iraqi soldiers were even afraid to turn on their radio receivers, fearing that this action, too, would trigger an attack.

Much of the coalition's EW/ECM effort remains highly classified. But one thing is clear: as the defense analyst David Isby put it, "Control of the battlefield means control of the electromagnetic spectrum."

See also ABCCC (AIRBORNE BATTLEFIELD COMMAND AND CONTROL CENTER); AIR CAMPAIGN; AIR DEFENSES; ALARM ANTI-RADAR MISSILE; AWACS (AIRBORNE WARNING AND CONTROL SYSTEM); DRONES AND DECOYS; GLOBAL POSITIONING SYSTEM (GPS); HARM (HIGH-SPEED ANTI-RADAR MISSILE); JSTARS (JOINT SURVEILLANCE TARGET ATTACK SYSTEM); LANTIRN (LOW-ALTITUDE NAVIGATIONAL AND TARGETING INFRARED FOR NIGHT); RECONNAISSANCE; SATELLITES; STEALTH AIRCRAFT; TURKEY; WILD WEASEL.

Suggestions for further reading: Department of Defense, *Conduct of the Persian Gulf War: Final Report to the Congress*, "Chapter 6: The Air Campaign;" "Appendix T: Performance of Selected Weapons Systems" (Washington, D.C.: USGPO, 1992); Richard P. Hallion, *Storm Over Iraq: Air Power And The Gulf War* (Washington, D.C.: Smithsonian Institution Press; 1992); David C. Isby, "Electronic Warfare Lessons," in *Military Lessons of the Gulf War*, ed. Bruce W. Watson (Novato, Calif.: Presidio Press, 1991); Neil Munro, *The Quick and the Dead: Electronic Combat and Modern Warfare* (New York: St. Martin's Press, 1991). See also Wayne P. Gagner, "Black Art Electronic Systems Prove Merit in Gulf Air War," *Signal*, April 1991; James W. Canan, "The Electronic Storm," *Air Force*, June 1991; Robert S. Hopkins III, "Ears of the Storm," *Air Force*, February 1992; Robert Holzer and Neil Munro, "Microwave Weapon Stuns Iraqis," *Defense News*, April 13–19, 1992.

ENGINEERS

Engineers on both sides played a vital role in the Persian Gulf War. For example, after their invasion of Kuwait, Iraqi engineers constructed an elaborate fortification system, including strong points, fire ditches and minefields along the Kuwaiti-Saudi Arabian border, in record time to bar a coalition attack.

Engineering units were an integral part of the forces of every coalition partner, the United States being no exception. American engineering units included Army combat and construction engineer commands, brigades, battalions and separate com-

panies; Navy Seabee amphibious construction battalions; Marine Force Service Support Group (FSSG) engineer support battalions; and Air Force Prime BEEF (Base Emergency Engineering Force), RED HORSE (Rapid Engineer Deployable, Heavy Operations Repair Squadrons, Engineer) and Prime RIBS (Readiness In Base Services) teams.

The U.S. Army Corps of Engineers has had a long-term relationship (dating back to 1951) with the Saudi Arabian government, and the Middle East/Africa Project office of the Corps of Engineers acted as the Defense Department's agent on construction projects during the Persian Gulf crisis. In addition, approximately $110 million worth of leases were signed, providing sleeping accommodations for more than 45,000 troops, supply warehouses, cold storage buildings and medical facilities.

Under the Army Reserve's 416th Engineer Command, some 11,000 engineers from the active force, the Army Reserve and the Army National Guard built, upgraded or maintained more than 2,000 miles of road; installed approximately 200 miles of coupled pipeline; developed seven major logistical bases in the desert; and within 30 days constructed four large camps capable of holding up to 100,000 enemy prisoners of war (POWs).

Meanwhile, approximately 3,700 Air Force engineers and 1,450 service personnel were the key to base-support programs that bedded down more than 1,200 aircraft and 55,000 Air Force personnel at more than 25 locations, including 21 airfields. In the course of the crisis, Air Force engineers erected more than 5,000 tents, paved more than two million square feet of land to expand aircraft parking areas, constructed 39 facilities totaling 192,000 square feet and built 200 aircraft revetments.

The Air Force's most notable engineering success was the construction of Al-Khari, the largest base ever built by Air Force combat engineers, from the ground up. Working around the clock, they constructed a fully operational combat base in less than 40 days. Al-Khari housed more than 5,000 personnel and five fighter squadrons.

More than 5,000 Navy Seabees, including 1,000 from the Navy Reserve, expanded airfields, set up berthing facilities and built ammunition storage bunkers, roads and defensive barriers. They also built a 500-bed fleet hospital, a 400-bed Army hospital, 14 mess facilities capable of feeding 75,000 peo-

Constructing airfields and bases was only one of the tasks of engineers in the Gulf.
U.S. Army photo courtesy of 24th Infantry Division (Mechanized).

ple, and 4,750 other buildings. The Seabees also improved and maintained 200 miles of unpaved desert four-lane highways; these roads were used as main supply routes (MSRs) and played a vital role in the coalition's flanking movement.

At Al-Khanjar, U.S. Marine Corps engineers built 24 miles of berm in seven days; constructed a 768-acre ammunition supply point with 150 cells, the largest in Marine Corps history; built in 10 days a fuel farm with a capacity of 4.8 million gallons; completed 26 miles of road to the Kuwait border; and built a 4,000-person POW camp. At Al-Kibrit, they built more than 2,000 bunkers and fighting positions, transformed a one-lane desert track into an eight-lane MSR, and upgraded an abandoned airstrip to handle C-130 aircraft.

As discussed elsewhere (see BREACHING OPERATIONS), breaching the Iraqi-built fortifications along

the Kuwaiti-Saudi border was also a task of U.S. Army and Marine Corps combat engineers.

See also BREACHING OPERATIONS; FORTIFICATIONS.

Suggestions for further reading: Department of Defense, *Conduct of the Persian Gulf War: Final Report to the Congress,* "Appendix F: Logistical Buildup and Sustainment" (Washington, D.C.: USGPO, 1992); Douglas Jehl, "Rommel's Ghost Haunts Army Engineers' Work," *Los Angeles Times,* November 18, 1990; Katherine McIntyre, "Road Warriors," *Army Times,* April 6, 1992.

EUROPE

Although not per se a member of the coalition, Europe played a major role in the Persian Gulf War. France and the United Kingdom (UK) furnished substantial combat forces to the coalition. Other nations in both Eastern and Western Europe furnished land, sea and air forces or shared in the cost of the coalition's war effort. And although the Soviet Union made no tangible contribution to the coalition, its political support was crucial.

B-52 Stratofortress bombers flew strikes from Morón Air Base (AB) in Spain and Royal Air Force Base Fairford in the United Kingdom. Eighty-four percent of the airlift to the Gulf staged through either Rhein-Main AB in Germany or Torrejón *AB* in Spain. Ramstein *AB* in Germany, Sigonella AB in Italy, and Rota Naval Base and Zaragoza AB in Spain were also used, as were bases in France, Greece and Portugal. Luxembourg and Italy also donated airlift support. Overflight rights were granted by all European countries, as were landing rights at 90 European airfields.

Germany sent no military forces to the Gulf but did donate 60 Fuchs NBC (nuclear-biological-chemical) reconnaissance vehicles and 118 HETs (heavy equipment transports) that formerly belonged to East Germany. Germany also provided 120-mm tank ammunition to the United States, and its six C-160 transports flew for nearly 3,500 hours, carrying U.S. cargo within Western Europe.

The North Atlantic Treaty Organization (NATO) Allied Command Europe Mobile Force (Air) deployed some 60 combat aircraft as well as Patriot, I-Hawk and Roland air defense units from Belgium, Germany, Italy and the Netherlands to five Turkish air bases as a deterrent to Iraqi attack. NATO aircraft also flew some 1,600 sorties along the Turkish-Iraqi border.

Czechoslovakia not only provided chemical detection and analysis equipment along with trained operators, it also sold to the United States 40 HETs that proved invaluable in moving heavy equipment from ports of entry to staging areas and in the long offensive drive into Iraq. Hungary, Romania and Poland sent medical teams to Saudi Arabia.

See also COALITION FORCES; COST; FRANCE; SOVIET UNION; UNITED KINGDOM.

Suggestions for further reading: Department of Defense, *Conduct of the Persian Gulf War: Final Report to the Congress* (Washington, D.C.: USGPO, 1992); "European Security and the Gulf Crisis," Document 1244, *Assembly of Western European Union*, November 14, 1990.

FAC (FORWARD AIR CONTROLLER)
See CLOSE AIR SUPPORT.

FAHD IBN ABDUL AZIZ, KING OF SAUDI ARABIA
See SAUDI ARABIA.

FAST SEALIFT SQUADRON
See SEALIFT.

FIELD ARTILLERY
Ground combat is characterized by firepower and manuever. Field artillery, the "King of Battle," is responsible for providing the fire support for the infantry, armor and cavalry manuever units. Augmented by aerial fire support, the coalition's field artillery played a key role in the Persian Gulf War.

For its part, the U.S. Army deployed two Corps Artilleries, seven Division Artilleries and seven Army and Army National Guard Field Artillery Brigades. Among the latter were the six field artillery battalions of the 148th Field Artillery Brigade from the Arkansas-Oklahoma Army National Guard and the 196th Artillery Brigade from the Tennessee-West Virginia-Kentucky Army National Guard.

All told, the Army deployed 108 M102 105-mm towed howitzers, 642 M109 self-propelled 155-mm howitzers, 96 M110 self-propelled 203-mm (8-inch) howitzers and 189 M270 227-mm Multiple-Launch Rocket System (MLRS) launchers, including 18 capable of firing the long-range Army Tactical Missile System (ATACMS) missile. In addition, the 10th and 11th Marine Regiments, augmented with howitzer

The backbone of the coalition's field artillery was the 155-mm M109 self-propelled howitzer.
U.S. Army photo (SP Jack Gordon), Department of the Army Public Affairs.

batteries from the reserve 14th Marine Regiment, deployed a mix of towed and self-propelled 155-mm and 8-inch howitzers reinforced by attached Army MLRS batteries.

Among the forces of other coalition partners, some Egyptian and Syrian units were equipped with Soviet-supplied 122-mm and 152-mm towed howitzers and 122-mm 2S1S and 152-mm 2S3S self-propelled howitzers. Saudi Arabian forces were equipped with FH72 NATO (North Atlantic Treaty Organization) howitzers.

France fielded the 11th and 68th Marine Artillery Regiments, each with four batteries of towed 155-mm howitzers. The United Kingdom deployed the 2d, 26th and 40th Regiments of the Royal Artillery (RA), each with 24 M109 155-mm howitzers; and the 32d and 39th Heavy Regiments, each with 8-inch howitzers and Multiple-Launch Rocket Systems.

On paper, Iraq, with some 3,500 tubes and launchers, had more than twice as many artillery pieces as the coalition. Moreover, Iraq's 300–400 Austrian-supplied GHN-45 and South African-supplied G-5 155-mm howitzers outranged any howitzer in the coalition's inventory. Designed by artillery wizard Dr. Gerald V. Bull, the GHN-45s and G-5s have a range of up to 23 miles, far greater than the 14-mile range of the standard U.S. M109 howitzer. But according to the *Gulf War Airpower Survey*, the Iraqi Army actually had approximately 600 fewer artillery pieces than the coalition had originally estimated, and most were towed rather than self-propelled. And as discussed elsewhere (see COMPUTER WAR), Iraqi artillery lacked the sophisticated targeting and fire-control systems of most coalition artillery.

Pounded from the skies during the air campaign, Iraqi artillery was also out-maneuvered and out-fought by the coalition's artillery during the ground campaign. By the end of the war, the Iraqi Army had suffered 90 percent attrition in its artillery units.

See also AIR CAMPAIGN; ATACMS (M39 ARMY TACTICAL MISSILE SYSTEM); BULL, GERALD V.; GROUND CAMPAIGN; MLRS (MULTIPLE-LAUNCH ROCKET SYSTEM).

Suggestions for further reading: Department of Defense, *Conduct of the Persian Gulf War: Final Report to the Congress* (Washington, D.C.: USGPO, 1992); Eliot A. Cohen et al., *Gulf War Airpower Survey* (Washington, D.C.: USGPO, 1993); Norman Friedman, *Desert Victory: The War for Kuwait* (Annapolis,

Md.: Naval Institute Press, 1991); *The Military Balance 1990–1991* (London: International Institute for Strategic Studies, 1990); Sean D. Naylor, "Iraqi Fire: Big Guns, Bad Aim," *Army Times*, January 14, 1991; Harry G. Summers Jr., "When It Comes to Artillery, U.S. Is Outgunned by Enemy's Weaponry," *Los Angeles Times*, January 21, 1991; "Field Artillery Desert Facts," *Field Artillery*, October 1991.

FIGHTERS AND FIGHTER-BOMBERS

Coalition fighter-bombers played a key role in the Persian Gulf War. They quickly gained air superiority and then air supremacy over the Iraqi Air Force. Tactical fighter-bombers also conducted most of the strategic attacks on the enemy homeland, while "strategic" bombers were used primarily to support tactical ground operations.

The primary fighters and fighter bombers in the U.S. Air Force were the F-15C and F-15E Eagle fighters, the F-16 Fighting Falcon multirole aircraft, the F-111 Aardvark strike aircraft and the F-117A Nighthawk Stealth fighter.

The F-15C was among the first aircraft to deploy to the Kuwaiti Theater of Operations (KTO). Eventually, a total of 118 F-15Cs were sent to Saudi Arabia. Within 10 days of the start of the air war, they had achieved air superiority over the entire theater. Flying 5,906 offensive counter-air and defensive counter-air (OCA/DCA) missions, F-15Cs accounted for 33 of the 38 air-to-air kills made by coalition aircraft. No F-15Cs were lost to enemy action.

Forty-eight F-15Es also participated in the war. Equipped with LANTIRN (Low-Altitude Navigational and Targeting Infrared for Night) pods, the F-15Es flew 2,210 sorties, most at night, and dropped some 1,700 GBU-10 and GBU-12 bombs. On one occasion, 16 enemy armored vehicles were destroyed by two F-15Es each carrying eight GBU-12s. Two F-15E Eagles were lost in combat to enemy ground fire.

A total of 251 F-16s took part in the war. They flew more than 13,480 combat sorties against enemy airfields, Republican Guard positions and strategic targets near Baghdad, including a 56-plane raid on the Nuclear Research Center there. They were also used for "killer scout" armed reconnaissance missions. Five F-16 Flying Falcons were lost in combat.

Both the F-111E and F-111F models took part in the war, the main difference between the two being the F model's Pave Tack pod, which provides an infrared target-acquisition and laser-designator capability to attack point targets. Flying from bases in Saudi Arabia and from Incirlik, Turkey, F-111s flew some 4,000 sorties. Using a GBU-15 TV-guided bomb, an F-111 destroyed the Sea Island oil facility, which was pumping oil into the Persian Gulf (see ECOLOGICAL WARFARE). Although one F-111 received slight battle damage, no Aardvarks were lost in combat.

The newest aircraft in the U.S. Air Force's inventory, the F-117A Nighthawk was instrumental in knocking out Iraq's integrated air defense system. Taking advantage of its "stealth" technology, it was the only aircraft to strike targets in downtown Baghdad. Flying only 2 percent of the coalition sorties, the F-117 struck 40 percent of the strategic targets. During the war, the F-117A Nighthawk flew 1,296 sorties against heavily defended targets without the loss of a single aircraft.

One of the oldest fighters in the U.S. inventory is the Navy's and Marine Corps's Vietnam War–vintage A-6E Intruder. Taking advantage of its night and all-weather capabilities, it was flown exclusively during periods of darkness or low visibility. Navy and Marine A-6s flew more than 4,700 sorties against strategic and high-value targets. Five A-6 Intruders were lost or damaged during the war, two during low-level attacks.

The aircraft carrier-based F-14 Tomcat was designed as an air-superiority fighter but was never challenged in that role during the Gulf War. Used in fighter sweeps, combat air patrols and escort missions, the 99 F-14s in the KTO flew 4,182 sorties, more than any other Navy fixed-wing aircraft. The 16 F-14s configured to carry the Tactical Air Reconnaissance Pod System (TARPS) flew 751 sorties. F-14s intercepted six enemy aircraft and one Iraqi helicopter. One F-14 Tomcat was lost, possibly to an Iraqi surface-to-air missile.

Three models of the F/A-18 Hornet were flown in the Gulf War. Ninety Navy F/A-18 A/Cs operated from four aircraft carriers in KTO waters while 72 Marine F/A-18 A/Cs operated from Shaikh Isa, Bahrain. Use in all phases of the air campaign, F/A-18s delivered more than 17,500 tons of ordnance against

The Air Force's F-15 Eagle made 33 of the 38 air-to-air kills during the war.
Central Command Public Affairs.

a variety of targets. F/A-18s intercepted 10 hostile aircraft and shot down two Iraqi planes. One F/A 18 A/C Hornet was lost in combat.

Meanwhile, the two-seater F-18D Hornet was used by the Marines in tactical air coordinator and airborne forward air control (Fast FAC) roles. Flying some 557 sorties, the F-18Ds provided 24-hour battlefield coverage for close air support missions.

Other coalition fighters and fighter-bombers included F-15 Eagles from Saudi Arabia; F-16 Flying Falcons from Bahrain; CF-18 Hornets from Canada; Tornados from the United Kingdom (UK), France, Italy, and Saudi Arabia; Jaguars from the UK, France and Oman; Mirages from France and the United Arab Emirates; Buccaneers from the UK; A-4s from Kuwait; and F-5s from Bahrain and Saudi Arabia.

Iraqi fighters and fighter-bombers included J-6 (Chinese MiG-19) and J-7 (Chinese Mig-21) fighters, MiG-23s, Mig-25s, MiG-29s, Mirage EQ5/2000s, Mirage F-1s, Su-7s, Su-20s, Su-24s and Su-25s. Dominated from the start by the coalition's airpower, the Iraqi Air Force played no appreciable part in the war.

See also A-10 THUNDERBOLT II "WARTHOG"; AERIAL COMBAT; AIR CAMPAIGN; AIR DEFENSES; AIR FORCE, IRAQ; AIR FORCES, COALITION; AIR FORCE, U.S.; AIRPOWER; BOMBING; HARRIER (AV-8B) STOVL (SHORT TAKE OFF AND VERTICAL LAND) AIRCRAFT.

Suggestions for further reading: Department of Defense, *Conduct of the Persian Gulf War: Final Report to the Congress,* "Appendix T: Performance of Selected Weapons Systems" (Washington, D.C.: USGPO, 1992); Bruce W. Watson, ed., *Military Lessons of the Gulf War* (Novato, Calif.: Presidio Press, 1991).

1ST ARMORED DIVISION

Stationed at Ansbach, West Germany, as part of the NATO (North Atlantic Treaty Organization) defense against a Warsaw Pact attack across the Iron Curtain, the 1st Armored "Old Ironsides" Division had not seen combat since World War II.

Commanded by Major General Ronald Griffith, the 1st Armored Division was reorganized for combat before it departed for the Persian Gulf. Leaving behind its 3d Brigade, which was still equipped with old M113 armored personnel carriers, the 1st Armored Division was augmented by the Aschaffenburg-based 3d Brigade, 3d Infantry Division (Mechanized).

Part of the Phase II deployment ordered by President George Bush in November 1990, the 1st Armored Division consisted of more than 22,000 soldiers and 9,000 vehicles. It was organized into three armor-heavy manuever brigades equipped with M1A1 Abrams tanks and M2 Bradley infantry fighting vehicles; an aviation brigade with AH-64 Apache and AH-1 Cobra attack helicopters and UH-60 Blackhawk assault helicopters; and a reconnaissance squadron, the 1st Squadron, 1st Cavalry, with M1A1 tanks, M3 Bradley cavalry fighting vehicles and OH-58 Kiowa scout helicopters.

Division artillery consisted of three battalions of M109 self-propelled 155-mm howitzers, a battery of Multiple-Launch Rocket Systems (MLRS) and an air defense artillery battalion. Division troops included a support command, a signal battalion, an engineer battalion and a military intelligence battalion.

Part of VII Corps's main attack, the 1st Armored Division had as its initial objective the crossroads at the ancient town of Al-Busayyah in the Euphrates River valley 150 miles deep within Iraq. After encountering light resistance, the division seized the town and made a 90-degree turn to complete the envelopment of the enemy forces in Kuwait.

Ahead were the Tawakalna Division and the Medina Armored Division of the Iraqi Republican Guard Forces Command (RGFC), which had moved into blocking positions in the 1st Armored Division's sector. The first contact was made with the 3d Brigade of the Tawakalna Division, and from then until the cease-fire two days later, "Old Ironsides" was in continuous contact with the enemy. Its biggest battle was the fight for Medina Ridge on February 27, 1991.

The RGFC's Medina Division, reinforced by elements of the Iraqi 10th, 12th, 17th and 52d Armored Divisions, was dug in for six miles along a north-south ridgeline. Attacking with three brigades abreast, the 1st Armored Division's Abrams tanks registered hits at ranges of up to 3,000 meters. The division's battle damage assessment showed 186 enemy tanks and 127 enemy armored fighting vehicles destroyed, including 137 destroyed in less than an hour, in one of the biggest battles of the war. "Old Ironsides" had destroyed two brigades of the RGFC's Medina Division, one brigade of the Tawakalna Division plus elements of several other Iraqi divisions.

After the cease-fire, the 1st Armored Division returned to Germany where, as of June 1994, it remains part of the residual U.S. military presence in NATO.

See also GROUND CAMPAIGN; VII CORPS.

Suggestions for further reading: Tom Carhart, *Old Ironsides: How the Men of "Old Ironsides" Destroyed the Iraqi Republican Guard During Operation Desert Storm* (New York: Pocket Books, 1994); Department of Defense, *Conduct of the Persian Gulf War: Final Report to the Congress,* "Chapter 8: The Ground Campaign" (Washington, D.C.: USGPO, 1992); Major James Blackwell, *Thunder in the Desert: The Strategy and Tactics of the Persian Gulf War* (New York: Bantam Books, 1991); General H. Norman Schwarzkopf, *It Doesn't Take a Hero* (New York: Bantam Books, 1992); The Staff of *U.S. News & World Report, Triumph Without Victory* (New York: Times Books, 1992). See also Steve Vogel, "Desert Storm After Action Review: Metal Rain," *Army Times,* September 16, 1991.

1ST ARMOURED DIVISION, UNITED KINGDOM

See UNITED KINGDOM.

1ST CAVALRY DIVISION

When it was organized in 1921, the 1st Cavalry Division brought together several famous horse cavalry regiments that had distinguished themselves during the Indian wars on the Western plains. During World War II, it was reorganized to fight on foot, and it fought that war and the Korean War as an infantry division.

During the Vietnam War, the division was again reorganized, this time as an airmobile division, and it pioneered that concept beginning with the battle of the Ia Drang in 1965. After Vietnam, it was reorganized yet again, this time as an armored division.

Stationed at Fort Hood, Texas, the 1st Cavalry Division was one of several that were supposed to be rounded-out by brigades from the Army National Guard. But when the "First Team" was alerted for movement to the Persian Gulf on August 7, 1990, its round-out brigade, the 155th Armored Brigade from the Mississippi Army National Guard, had not yet been mobilized. Instead, the 1st Brigade of the 2d Armored Division (the "Tiger Brigade") was attached to the division.

As reconstituted, the 1st Cavalry Division consisted of three armor-heavy manuever brigades, an aviation brigade with AH-64 Apache and AH-1 Cobra attack helicopters and UH-60 Blackhawk assault helicopters, and a reconnaissance squadron, the 1st Squadron, 7th Cavalry, with M1A1 tanks, M3 Bradley cavalry fighting vehicles and OH-58 Kiowa scout helicopters.

Division artillery consisted of three battalions of M109 self-propelled 155-mm howitzers, a battery of Multiple-Launch Rocket Systems (MLRS), and an air defense artillery battalion. Division troops included a support command, a signal battalion, an engineer battalion and a military intelligence battalion.

Commanded by Major General John Tilelli Jr., the 1st Cavalry Division began deploying to the Persian Gulf on September 16, 1990, and completed its move there in mid-October as part of XVIII Airborne Corps's defensive force. The "Tiger Brigade," upgraded with new M1A1 Abrams tanks and M2/M3 Bradley armored fighting vehicles drawn from prepositioned stocks in Germany, was detached to reinforce the First Marine Expeditionary Force in December 1990.

Meanwhile, the "First Team" was transferred from XVIII Airborne Corps to VII Corps control on the eve of the ground campaign. Thirty days before that campaign began, the "First Team" had been given the mission of conducting a series of deception operations to convince the Iraqis that the main coalition attack would be directed at the Wadi al-Batin in western Kuwait, well away from the actual VII Corps attack, thereby holding five Iraqi infantry divisions and an armored division in place. This series of ground feints and artillery raids included the brigade-size Operation Knight Strike on February 19–20, 1991, four days before G-Day (February 24, 1991). The operation succeeded in penetrating some 10 kilometers into the Iraqi lines.

Designated as the VII Corps's reserve, the 1st Cavalry Division moved some 300 kilometers in 24 hours and was poised to attack an Iraqi Republican Guard division when the cease-fire was declared.

After the war the 1st Cavalry Division returned to its home station at Fort Hood, Texas.

See also GROUND CAMPAIGN.

Suggestions for further reading: Department of Defense, *Conduct of the Persian Gulf War: Final Report to the Congress,* "Chapter 8: The Ground Campaign" (Washington, D.C.: USGPO, 1992); Major James Blackwell, *Thunder in the Desert: The Strategy and Tactics of the Persian Gulf War* (New York: Bantam

Books, 1991); General H. Norman Schwarzkopf, *It Doesn't Take a Hero* (New York: Bantam Books, 1992); The Staff of *U.S. News & World Report, Triumph Without Victory* (New York: Times Books, 1992). See also J. Paul Scicchitano, "Night Strikes," *Army Times,* September 23, 1991.

1ST INFANTRY DIVISION (MECHANIZED)

One of the most distinguished divisions in the U.S. Army, the 1st Infantry Division fought in World War I, World War II and the Vietnam War as a regular infantry division. Returning to its home station at Fort Riley, Kansas, after its withdrawal from Vietnam in 1970, the "Big Red One" became an armor-heavy mechanized division.

The 1st Infantry Division was assigned the role of reinforcing NATO (North Atlantic Treaty Organization) in the event of a war with the Soviet Union; its 3d Brigade, known as 1st Infantry Division (Forward), was stationed in Germany and was in the process of deactivation when the Persian Gulf crisis began. When the 1st Infantry Division was alerted to move to the Kuwaiti Theater of Operations (KTO) in November 1990 as part of President George Bush's Phase II deployment, the 3d Brigade, 2d Armored Division from Garlstedt, Germany, which was equipped with the depleted-uranium heavy armor version of the M1A1 tank, was attached to the division in place of its 3d Brigade.

As reconstituted, the division consisted of three armor-heavy manuever brigades equipped with M1A1 Abrams tanks and M2 Bradley infantry fighting vehicles, an aviation brigade with AH-64 Apache and AH-1 Cobra attack helicopters and UH-60 Blackhawk assault helicopters, and a reconnaissance squadron, the 1st Squadron, 4th Cavalry, with M1A1 tanks, M3 Bradley cavalry fighting vehicles and OH-58 Kiowa scout helicopters.

Division artillery consisted of three battalions of M109 self-propelled 155-mm howitzers, a battery of Multiple-Launch Rocket Systems (MLRS) and an air defense artillery battalion. Division troops included a support command, a signal battalion, an engineer battalion and a military intelligence battalion.

Commanded by Major General Thomas G. Rhame, the 1st Infantry Division began deploying to the Gulf in November 1990 and completed its move there in January 1991, joining the U.S. VII Corps, which had deployed to the KTO from Germany.

The 1st Infantry Division was tasked to breach the Iraqi fortifications in preparation for the VII Corps's attack. The division's engineer battalion was reinforced by the 9th and 317th Engineer Battalions from Germany, the 588th Engineer Battalion from Fort Polk, Louisiana, and the 176th Engineer Group from the Virginia National Guard.

Cutting some 24 assault lanes through the Iraqi defenses, the Big Red One by late afternoon on G-Day (February 24, 1991, the start of the ground campaign) had destroyed the Iraqi 26th Infantry Division and taken more than 2,000 prisoners. On G +3, the division passed through the U.S. 2d Armored Cavalry Regiment to engage and destroy the Iraqi Republican Guard's Tawakalna Division.

By the last day of the war, the Big Red One was astride the Basra–Kuwait City road, cutting off the fleeing Iraqi army. It had moved 260 kilometers, destroyed more than 500 tanks and taken more than 11,400 prisoners of war.

Meanwhile, its 3d Brigade, under the command of Brigadier General William Mullen, had also moved to the Gulf to provide manpower for the 22d Support Command. Serving as the Port Security Activity, its troops helped unload ships, coordinated contract food services, staged outgoing convoys and played host to more than 100,000 VII Corps soldiers who passed through the ports.

After the war the 1st Infantry Division (Mechanized) returned to its home station at Fort Riley, Kansas.

See also BREACHING OPERATIONS; GROUND CAMPAIGN.

Suggestions for further reading: Department of Defense, *Conduct of the Persian Gulf War: Final Report to the Congress,* "Chapter 8: The Ground Campaign" (Washington, D.C.: USGPO, 1992); Major James Blackwell, *Thunder in the Desert: The Strategy and Tactics of the Persian Gulf War* (New York: Bantam Books, 1991); General H. Norman Schwarzkopf, *It Doesn't Take a Hero* (New York: Bantam Books, 1992). See also Steve Vogel, "Fast and Hard," *Army Times,* March 25, 1991; Jim Tice, "'Coming Through,'" *Army Times,* August 25, 1991; Lt. Col. Gregory Fontenot, "The 'Dreadnaughts' Rip the Saddam Line," *Army,* January 1992. For 3d Brigade activities, see Major William L. Brame, "From Garrison to Desert Offensive in 97 Days," *Army,* February 1992.

1ST MARINE DIVISION

No stranger to combat, the 1st Marine Division fought in World War II, the Korean War and the Vietnam War. Its 7th Marine Expeditionary Brigade (MEB) from Twentynine Palms, California, included the 1st and 2d Battalions, 7th Marine Regiment; the 1st Battalion, 5th Marine Regiment; and the 3d Battalion, 9th Marine Regiment. Stationed at Camp Pendleton, California, the 1st Marine Division was among the first units to deploy to the Kuwaiti Theater of Operations (KTO). Along with the 1st MEB from Hawaii, it deployed by air, marrying with its heavy equipment that was delivered to Saudi Arabia aboard Maritime Prepositioning Ships (MPS). MPS Squadron 2 sailed from Diego Garcia with the 7th MEB's equipment and MPS Squadron 3 sailed from Guam with the 1st MEB's supplies.

Commanded by Major General J.K. Myatt, the 1st Marine Division arrived in the KTO on September 5, 1990, taking command of the MEBs already there. The 1st Marine Division was reinforced by combat elements from the 3d Marine Division on Okinawa, the reserve 1st Battalion, 25th Marine Regiment and two artillery batteries from the reserve 3d Battalion, 14th Marine Regiment. The division also included the 1st and 3d Tank Battalions with M60A1 tanks, the 1st and 3d Light Armored Infantry Battalions with light armored vehicles (LAVs), an Assault Amphibian Battalion with assault amphibian vehicles (AAVs), and a combat engineer battalion.

The division's fire support included the 155-mm and 8-inch towed and self-propelled howitzers and Multiple-Launch Rocket System (MLRS) missiles of its 11th Marine Artillery Regiment, and the Harrier A-8B fighters and AH-1 Cobra helicopter gunships of the 3d Marine Aircraft Wing.

Under the command of the corps-level First Marine Expeditionary Force, on G-Day (February 24, 1991) the 1st Marine Division, in coordination with the 2d Marine Division on its left flank, attacked north through the Iraqi defensive fortifications. On that first day, and against sometimes stiff resistance, the division succeeded in breaching two fortified trench lines and in establishing a solid foothold inside Kuwait.

On G +1, near the Al-Burgan oil field, the division encountered a strong enemy counterattack that penetrated to within 300 meters of the division's command post. In the end, however, the attacking forces were destroyed. More than 100 Iraqi armored vehicles were destroyed and 1,500 enemy prisoners were taken. Following the battle, the division completed consolidation of Ahmed Al-Jaber airfield and moved within 10 miles of Kuwait City.

On G +2 (February 26), the division turned toward Kuwait International Airport. Running into a desperate enemy armor defense there, the division fought throughout the night, assisted by naval gunfire from the USS *Wisconsin*. The airport was finally seized at 3:30 A.M. on February 27 (G +3). Enemy losses included more than 250 tanks and 70 armored fighting vehicles. The division then held in place awaiting the arrival of the Arab/Islamic Joint Forces Command that would liberate Kuwait City.

Following the war the division returned to its home station at Camp Pendleton, California. In 1992–1993, it took part in United Nations relief operations in Somalia.

See also FIRST MARINE EXPEDITIONARY FORCE (I MEF); GROUND CAMPAIGN; MARINE CORPS, U.S.

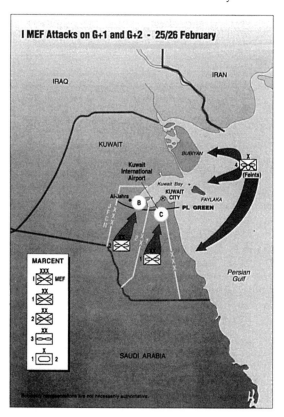

Suggestions for further reading: Department of Defense, *Conduct of the Persian Gulf War: Final Report to the Congress,* "Chapter 8: The Ground Campaign" (Washington, D.C.: USGPO, 1992); Major James Blackwell, *Thunder in the Desert: The Strategy and Tactics of the Persian Gulf War* (New York: Bantam Books, 1991); General H. Norman Schwarzkopf, *It Doesn't Take a Hero* (New York: Bantam Books, 1992); The Staff of *U.S. News & World Report, Triumph Without Victory* (New York: Times Books, 1992). See also Maj. Gen. J. M. Myatt, USMC, "The 1st Marine Division in the Attack," *U.S. Naval Institute Proceedings,* November 1991.

FIRST MARINE EXPEDITIONARY FORCE (I MEF)

Serving as headquarters for MARCENT (Marine Forces, Central Command), and thus on the same level as the U.S. Third Army (ARCENT), the Ninth U.S. Air Force (CENTAF) and the U.S. Seventh Fleet (NAVCENT), the First Marine Expeditionary Force (I MEF) was also a tactical corps-level command during the Persian Gulf War.

Commanded by Lieutenant General Walter E. Boomer, I MEF arrived in Saudi Arabia from its home station at Camp Pendleton, California, in early August 1990 to assume command of Marine forces already in-country.

I MEF consisted of the 1st and 2d Marine Divisions, the 3d Marine Aircraft Wing, the 1st and 2d Force Service Support Groups and the "Tiger Brigade" from the Army's 2d Armored Division. By the end of the war, I MEF had more than 92,900 Marines, including 13,066 Marine reservists and more than 1,000 female Marines in the Kuwaiti Theater of Operations (KTO).

According to the Department of Defense (DOD) report on the Gulf War, "CINCCENT [commander in chief, Central Command] chose to retain the Joint Force Land Component Command responsibility [and] directed the ground service components. . . . However ARCENT and MARCENT had primary responsibility for developing and analyzing courses of action for their respective ground offensives." The air operations of the 19 fixed-wing and 21 helicopter squadrons in the KTO were coordinated by the Joint Forces Air Component Commander (JFACC).

While Marine aircraft were taking part in the air campaign, beginning on January 17, 1991, the eve of the ground campaign, I MEF conducted Operation Troy, a deception operation in which for 10 days the impression was created that a much larger force was about to launch an attack. On G-Day (February 24, 1991), I MEF's 24 Marine infantry battalions, with supporting air, armor and artillery, attacked north through the Iraqi fortifications toward Kuwait City. With the Arab/Islamic Joint Task Force (JTF) North on its left flank and JTF East on its right flank, I MEF had as its mission holding the Iraqi forces in place while the Third U.S. Army conducted an envelopment to destroy the Iraqi Republican Guard.

By G +3 (February 27), I MEF had seized all of its objectives and was holding in place outside Kuwait City to allow Arab/Islamic forces to conduct the actual liberation.

See also LISTINGS FOR INDIVIDUAL UNITS; AMPHIBIOUS TASK FORCE (ATF); BOOMER, WALTER E.; CENTCOM (CENTRAL COMMAND); GROUND CAMPAIGN; LOGISTICS, (U.S.); MARINE CORPS, U.S.; MOBILIZATION, U.S.

Suggestions for further reading: Department of Defense, *Conduct of the Persian Gulf War: Final Report to the Congress,* "Chapter 8: The Ground Campaign" (Washington, D.C.: USGPO, 1992); Molly Moore, *A Woman at War: Storming Kuwait with the Marines* (New York: Scribner's, 1993); Major James Blackwell, *Thunder in the Desert: The Strategy and Tactics of the Persian Gulf War* (New York: Bantam Books, 1991); General H. Norman Schwarzkopf, *It Doesn't Take a Hero* (New York: Bantam Books, 1992); The Staff of *U.S. News & World Report, Triumph Without Victory* (New York: Times Books, 1992). See also Lt. Gen. Walter E. Boomer, "Special Trust and Confidence Among the Trail Breakers," *U.S. Naval Institute Proceedings,* November 1991; Brig. Gen. Edwin H. Simmons, "Getting the Job Done," *U.S. Naval Institute Proceedings,* May 1991.

FORTIFICATIONS

As the official Department of Defense (DOD) report on the Persian Gulf War noted, "The Iraqis prepared for the expected assault into Kuwait in a manner that reflected the successes of their defensive strategy during the Iranian war." In a remarkable engineering effort, they constructed hundreds of miles of roads within Kuwait, dug in their command posts, buried their telephone lines and prepared two major defensive belts paralleling the Kuwaiti-Saudi border.

IRAQI DEFENSE IN DEPTH

The first belt, roughly five to 15 kilometers within Kuwait, was composed of continuous minefields varying in width from 100 to 200 meters, with barbed wire, antitank ditches, berms and oil-filled fire trenches blocking key avenues of approach. Covering the first belt were Iraqi platoon- and company-size strong points to provide early warning and to delay an attack.

The second obstacle belt, up to 20 kilometers behind the first, began north of Khafji and proceeded northwest of the Al-Wafrah oil fields until it joined with the first belt near Al-Manaqish. It too was covered by an almost unbroken line of mutually supporting brigade-size defensive positions that included trench lines, strong points and antitank and antipersonnel minefields.

The Iraqi plan was to slow the attackers at the first belt, then trap them in prearranged killing zones between the belts, and finally use armor reserves to counterattack those who broke through.

The tanks and artillery pieces of this armor reserve were spread out, revetted, dug in up to their turrets, sandbagged and surrounded by berms to protect them from coalition air attack.

The Iraqis also built elaborate fortifications along the Kuwaiti coast to guard against an amphibious attack. In the area closest to the shore, the Iraqis placed underwater obstacles, mines and barbed wire to ensnare landing craft. Additional mines and barbed wire were laid between the high- and low-water marks, and behind the beaches the Iraqis dug trench lines and bunkers. Berms, antitank ditches and dug-in tanks blocked the beach exits.

But this static defense posture had its drawbacks. Even before the air campaign began in January 1991, noted the DOD report, "obstacles dug in September and October [1990] had been neglected in the following weeks. Some minefields had been exposed by wind, and mines could be seen from the air or by

With sand bulldozed into a berm, U.S. units in Saudi Arabia hastily construct field fortifications.
U.S. Army photo courtesy of 24th Infantry Division (Mechanized).

approaching ground troops. Many alternate positions and trenches had filled with sand."

Pounded during the coalition's air campaign and by artillery raids, the elaborate Iraqi fortifications collapsed in the face of the coalition's ground assault. Contrary to earlier concerns, defensive fortifications posed no serious obstacle to the allied advance.

See also AMPHIBIOUS TASK FORCE (ATF); BREACHING OPERATIONS; ENGINEERS; STRATEGY, IRAQ.

Suggestions for further reading: Department of Defense, *Conduct of the Persian Gulf War: Final Report to the Congress*, "Chapter 8: The Ground Campaign" (Washington, D.C.: USGPO, 1992); Major James Blackwell, *Thunder in the Desert: The Strategy and Tactics of the Persian Gulf War* (New York: Bantam Books, 1991); General H. Norman Schwarzkopf, *It Doesn't Take a Hero* (New York: Bantam Books, 1992); The Staff of *U.S. News & World Report, Triumph Without Victory* (New York: Times Books, 1992).

FRANCE

France played a major role in the Persian Gulf War. France being a permanent member of the United Nations Security Council, its political support was critical but clouded at first by the opposition of French defense minister Jean-Pierre Chevènement, who had been a founding member of the French-Iraqi Friendship Society. Chevènement was eventually overruled by President François Mitterrand and resigned on January 21, 1991.

Early on, while Mitterrand pursued separate peace proposals in the United Nations, French military forces in the Kuwaiti Theater of Operations (KTO) were not under the control of CINCCENT (commander in chief, U.S. Central Command). But on January 16, 1991, the day before the war began, Mitterrand agreed to put French forces under CENTCOM while retaining ultimate command authority himself.

Unlike during United States' 1986 raid on Libya, when the French government refused to grant U.S. aircraft overflight rights over French territory, during the Gulf War U.S. KC-135 Stratotankers were based at Mont-de-Marsan Air Base in southwestern France to refuel B-52 Stratofortress bombers en route to the KTO from their bases in the United Kingdom.

French forces in the KTO were under the overall command of Lieutenant General Michel Roquejeoffre. France sent substantial military forces for maritime interdiction (which the French called Operation Artimon) and for Operations Desert Shield and Desert Storm (called Operation Daguet).

Although there were some changes in the composition of the French naval contingent, for most of the maritime interception operation the contingent consisted of the destroyers *Du Chayla, Jeanne de Vienne,* and *La Motte-Picquet;* the frigates *Cadet Bory, Doudart de Lagree* and *Protet;* and the corvette *Premier Maitre L'Her.* These vessels were supported by the replenishment ships *Durance* and *Marne,* the maintenance ship *Jules Verne* and the tug *Buffle.* France also sent two hospital ships, the *Rance* and the *Foudre,* which operated in the Red Sea.

France deployed elements of four combat air wings (escadres) to the Gulf, including 12 Mirage 2000s from the 5th escadre de chasse, 25 Jaguar As from the 11th escadre de chasse, 8 Mirage F-1Cs from the 12th escadre de chasse and 4 Mirage F-1CRs from the 33d escadre de chasse. Also deployed were 5 C-135R tankers, 1 C-160G electronic warfare jammer, 1 DC-8 Sarigue electronic intelligence aircraft and 9 C-160 transports.

Although France has a large Army, most of it could not be deployed to the Gulf. Composed primarily of draftees, under French law it cannot be made to serve overseas. The French government therefore had to assemble an ad hoc division around the 6th Light Armored Division, manning it with Foreign Legionnaires, Marines and troops from the Force d'Action Rapide (FAR).

From the Foreign Legion came the 1st Foreign Legion Armored Regiment with some 35 AMX-10RC wheeled armored cars, and the 2d Foreign Legion Infantry Regiment. From the Marines came the 2d Marine Regiment, a detachment from the 3d Marine Regiment, the 21st Marine Infantry Regiment and the 11th and 68th Marine Artillery Regiments (each with four batteries of towed 155-mm howitzers).

Also included in the 6th Light Armored Division were the 1st Régiment de Spahis with 35 AMX-10RCs, the 1st Infantry Regiment (Airmobile), the 5th Combat Helicopter Regiment and the 4th Dragoon Regiment with 40 AMX-30B2 main battle tanks mounting a 105-mm gun.

Under the command of Brigadier General Jean-Charles Mouscardes, the 6th French Light Armored Division came under the tactical control of the U.S. XVIII Corps and was given the mission of screening the coalition's entire left flank.

With a brigade of the U.S. 82d Airborne Division attached to it, at 4:00 A.M. on February 24, 1991 (G-Day), the 6th Light Armored Division attacked north toward Iraq's As-Salman Air Base some 90 miles deep into Iraqi territory. Overruning elements of the Iraqi 45th Infantry Division, and taking some 2,500 prisoners in the process, the 6th Light Armored Division secured its objectives in seven hours. The left flank of the coalition's ground campaign was secure.

"I would . . . like to say that the French did an absolutely superb job of moving out rapidly to take their objectives," said CINCCENT General H. Norman Schwarzkopf in his postvictory briefing, "and they were very, very successful." Two French servicemen were killed during the war, and 38 were wounded.

See also AIR CAMPAIGN; AIR FORCES, COALITION; ARMIES, COALITION; XVIII AIRBORNE CORPS; 82D AIRBORNE DIVISION; GROUND CAMPAIGN; MARITIME INTERCEPTION OPERATIONS; NAVIES, COALITION; UNITED NATIONS.

Suggestions for further reading: James J. Cooke, *100 Miles From Baghdad: With the French in Desert Storm* (Westport, Conn.: Praeger, 1993); Department of Defense, *Conduct of the Persian Gulf War: Final Report to the Congress* (Washington, D.C.: USGPO, 1992); Major James Blackwell, *Thunder in the Desert: The Strategy and Tactics of the Persian Gulf War* (New York: Bantam Books, 1991); Rick Atkinson, *Crusade: The Untold Story of the Persian Gulf War* (New York: Houghton-Mifflin, 1993). See also Denis Jeambar and Christian Makarian, "Le 'Scandale' Chevènement," *Le Point,* September 10, 1990; William Drozdiak and R. Jeffrey Smith, "French Decision Makes Coalition Complete," *Washington Post,* January 17, 1991; "The Gulf Crisis," *France Magazine,* Spring 1991.

FRANKS, FREDERICK M(ELVIN), JR., LIEUTENANT GENERAL, USA (1936–)

Commander of VII Corps during the Persian Gulf War, General Frederick M. Franks Jr. entered the U.S. Army through the United States Military Academy at West Point, New York, and was commissioned a second lieutenant of armor in 1959. He received a Master of Arts degree from Columbia University in 1966, and served from 1969 to 1970 with the 11th Armored Cavalry Regiment in Vietnam, where he lost a leg in a land mine explosion. After serving on the Army General Staff, he returned to Columbia University, where he was awarded a Master of Philosophy degree in 1975.

Among his significant assignments were commander, 1st Squadron, 3d Armored Cavalry Regiment at Fort Bliss, Texas; commander, 11th Armored Cavalry Regiment in Germany; commander, Seventh Army Training Command; deputy comman-

dant of the Army Command and General Staff College at Fort Leavenworth, Kansas; director, J-7 (Operational Plans and Interoperability), Organization of the Joint Chiefs of Staff in Washington, D.C.; and commander, 1st Armored Division in Germany. He assumed command of VII Corps in 1989.

The major Army component of President George Bush's November 1990 Phase II buildup of an offensive capability in the KTO (Kuwaiti Theater of Operations), General Franks's VII Corps made the main attack of the coalition's ground campaign.

The 146,000-strong VII Corps consisted of the 1st Armored Division, the 1st Infantry Division (Mechanized), the 1st Cavalry Division, the 3d Armored Division, the 2d Armored Cavalry Regiment (ACR), the 11th Aviation Brigade, corps field artillery (FA) units (including the 142d FA Brigade from the Arkansas-Oklahoma National Guard) and the attached British 1st Armoured Division.

Lieutenant General Fred Franks (left) reviews the tactical situation with Major General Thomas Rhame, commander of the U.S. 1st Infantry Division.
U.S. Army photo courtesy of Training and Doctrine Command.

A sweeping envelopment, VII Corps's attack was designed to avoid most fixed defenses and drive deep into Iraq from the west, attacking and destroying Iraq's strategic reserve—the armored and mechanized forces of the elite Republican Guard Forces Command. "In 90 hours of continuous movement," according to the official Department of Defense report on the war, "VII Corps achieved devastating results against the best units of the Iraqi Army. VII Corps reported destroying more that a dozen Iraqi divisions; an estimated 1,300 tanks, 1,200 fighting vehicles and APCs [armored personnel carriers], 285 artillery pieces, and 100 air defense systems; and captured nearly 22,000 enemy soldiers."

General Franks's awards and decorations include the Silver Star for gallantry in action, the Defense Distinguished Service Medal, the Army Distinguished Service Medal, two Legions of Merit, the Distinguished Flying Cross, Bronze Star Medals with "V" device for heroism, two Purple Hearts for wounds received in action, two Meritorious Service Medals, 43 Air Medals and the Army Commendation Medal with "V" device.

After the Gulf War, General Franks was promoted to four-star rank and selected to command the Army's Training and Doctrine Command (TRADOC) at Fort Monroe, Virginia.

See also VII CORPS.

Suggestions for further reading The Staff of *U.S. News & World Report, Triumph Without Victory* (New York: Times Books, 1992); Major James Blackwell, *Thunder in the Desert: The Strategy and Tactics of the Persian Gulf War* (New York: Bantam Books, 1991); General H. Norman Schwarzkopf, *It Doesn't Take a Hero* (New York: Bantam Books, 1992). For a commentary on relations between Schwarzkopf and Franks, see Rick Atkinson, *Crusade: The Untold Story of the Persian Gulf War* (New York: Houghton-Mifflin, 1993).

FRIENDLY FIRE

Deaths from friendly fire—that is, from the inadvertent firing on one's own troops—were one of the great tragedies of the Persian Gulf War. Sadly, they are not a new battlefield phenomenon. During the Civil War, Confederate Lieutenant General Thomas J. Jackson was fatally shot by his own men at Chancellorsville when they failed to recognize him, and during World War II Lieutenant General Leslie J. McNair, the chief of Army Ground Forces, was killed by U.S. bombs that fell short at St. Lô in France.

Of the 613 U.S. battle casualties during the Gulf War, 146 were killed in action, including 35 killed by friendly fire. Of the 467 wounded in action, 78 were by friendly fire. Nine British soldiers were also killed by U.S. friendly fire, and another 11 were wounded.

All friendly fire casualties were among ground forces. Despite the more than 100,000 sorties flown by some 2,700 coalition aircraft from 14 separate components, there were no cases of "blue-on-blue" fratricide. Of the 28 U.S. incidents of friendly fire, 16 occurred in ground-to-ground engagements, in which 24 were killed and 27 were wounded. Nine friendly fire incidents occurred in air-to-ground engagements, in which 11 were killed and 15 were wounded. Of these 9, 1 involved an Army AH-64 Apache attack helicopter, 4 involved Air Force aircraft and 1 involved a Marine aircraft; the other three involved HARM (high-speed anti-radar missile) attacks from undetermined sources. Of the remaining friendly fire incidents, one was ship-to-ship, one was shore-to-ship and one was ground-to-air; no casualties occurred in any of these incidents.

Of the 21 Army soldiers killed by friendly fire, 1 was a tank crewman, 15 were armored fighting vehicle (AFV) crewmen, 1 was an armored personnel carrier crewman and 4 were foot soldiers. Of the 65 Army soldiers wounded, 49 were AFV crewmen, 7 were tank crewmen and 9 were foot soldiers. Most crew member casualties were from high-velocity nonexplosive tanks rounds that rely on the force of impact to destroy the target.

Of the 14 Marines killed by friendly fire, 11 were light armored vehicle (LAV) crewmen and 3 were foot soldiers. Of the 6 Marines wounded, 2 were LAV crewmen and 4 were foot soldiers or in trucks. One sailor was wounded while serving with a Marine reconnaissance unit.

Approximately 39 percent of the friendly fire incidents (11 out of 28) appeared to be the result of target misidentification. Coordination problems accounted for 29 percent of the incidents (8 out of 28), and of the remaining 9 cases, 6 were due to technical or ordnance malfunctions and 3 remain unsolved.

To improve ground-to-ground and air-to-ground identification, an inverted "V" was painted on the sides of coalition vehicles and a VS-17 fluorescent cloth panel was displayed. These devices were only marginally effective, and a postwar research and development effort was launched to find a better method of battlefield identification.

Making the friendly fire incidents even more damaging were delays in notifying the families of those killed or wounded, and charges that the incidents had been covered up.

One of the worst incidents was a mistaken identity attack by two U.S. Air Force A-10 Warthogs on the United Kingdom's (UK) 8 Platoon, Company "C," 3d Royal Regiment of Fusiliers; 9 British soldiers were killed and 11 were wounded. Prohibited from flying below 8,000 feet because of the intensity of Iraqi antiaircraft fire, the A-10s each fired a Maverick infrared-guided antitank missile at what the pilots thought were Iraqi vehicles, striking instead two UK Warrior armored fighting vehicles (AFVs).

Such incidents led to the formation of the Combat Identification Task Force by Army Chief of Staff General Gordon Sullivan in 1991. "If I had to write down the top five major missions given to me by the Army Chief of Staff," said General Jimmy Ross, the head of the Army Material Command in 1993, "combat identification would be in the top two." The goal is to field a noncooperative target recognition system such as an IFF (interrogate-friend-or-foe) system (i.e., a system that automatically electronically identifies friendly or hostile vehicles or aircraft) by the year 2000.

A new complication in the friendly fire issue concerns the depleted uranium used in tank ammunition and in the A-10's 30-mm Gatling guns. Some studies indicate that the uranium can cause serious health problems among those exposed to friendly fire from such weapons.

See also DEPLETED URANIUM.

Suggestions for further reading: Department of Defense, *Conduct of the Persian Gulf War: Final Report*

The inverted "V" on the side of coalition vehicles was one of the means used to identify allied forces and avoid friendly fire incidents.
U.S. Army photo courtesy of 24th Infantry Division (Mechanized).

to the Congress, "Appendix M: Fire From Friendly Forces" (Washington, D.C.: USGPO, 1992); Sean D. Naylor, "Friendly Fire: The Reckoning," *Army Times,* August 26, 1991; Charles R. Shrader, "Friendly Fire: The Inevitable Price," *Parameters,* Autumn 1992; Dennis Steele, "New Technologies Target Friendly Fire Deaths," *Army,* April 1993; Malcolm Brown, "Steps to Avoid Own Side's Fire Studied by U.S.," *New York Times,* May 18, 1993.

G

GBU-28 BOMB

The only bomb developed by the United States specifically for the Persian Gulf War, the GBU-28 was a 4,700-pound laser-guided bomb designed to penetrate deeply buried targets. It was conceived, designed, tested and fielded in just over a month by the U.S. Air Force.

Aerospace companies were contacted by the Air Force on January 27, 1991, and a prototype was fabricated from Army surplus 8-inch artillery tubes on February 1. Operational tests at the Tonopah Range in Nevada revealed that it could penetrate more than 100 feet of earth and 30 feet of concrete.

The first two operational bombs were delivered to the Kuwaiti Theater of Operations (KTO) on February 27, and they were used in combat by F-111F Aardvarks just before the cease-fire. Striking a bunker at Al-Taji Air Base north of Baghdad that had survived earlier attacks, the GBU-28s created a huge explosion and destroyed the target.

See also BOMBING.

Suggestions for further reading: Department of Defense, *Conduct of the Persian Gulf War: Final Report to the Congress,* "Chapter 6: The Air Campaign" (Washington, D.C.: USGPO, 1992); Richard P. Hallion, *Storm Over Iraq: Air Power and the Gulf War* (Washington, D.C.: Smithsonian Institution Press, 1992); "'Cutting to the Case,'" *Indianapolis News,* July 10, 1991.

G-DAY

G-Day is the first day of a ground campaign. For Operation Desert Shield, G-Day was February 24, 1991.

GERMANY

See CHEMICAL WARFARE; COST; EUROPE; TURKEY.

GLASPIE, APRIL C(ATHERINE), U.S. AMBASSADOR (1942–)

A career Foreign Service officer, April C. Glaspie was nominated by President George Bush in the fall of 1987 to be the U.S. ambassador to Iraq. Confirmed by the Senate in March 1988, she became the first American female ambassador to an Arab country.

When nominated, Ms. Glaspie was serving as director of the Office of Jordan, Lebanon and Syria Affairs in the State Department's Bureau of Near East and South Asian Affairs. With degrees from Mills College and Johns Hopkins University's School of Advanced International Studies, Glaspie had entered the Foreign Service in 1966.

Described by Ambassador Hume Horan, one of America's leading experts on the Middle East, as "a first-class Arabist," Glaspie served as a political officer in the U.S. embassy in Cairo in the 1970s, as director of the language institute in Tunis, and as deputy chief of mission (DCM) in Damascus, Syria, from 1983 to 1985. As the ranking U.S. envoy in Damascus during the crisis over the sky-jacking of TWA Flight 847 in June 1985, Glaspie was credited with persuading Syria to help free the 104 U.S. hostages.

Arriving in Baghdad just after the end of the Iran-Iraq War, Glaspie had little opportunity to influence events. With the exception of the Soviets, Saddam Hussein never met with any foreign ambassadors and severely limited their contact with Iraqi officials.

On July 25, 1990, Glaspie was unexpectedly summoned to a private meeting with Saddam Hussein to discuss his demands on Kuwait. It was her first meeting with the Iraqi leader in the two years she had been in Iraq.

Emerging from the meeting with the belief that the Kuwait crisis had been defused, Glaspie left for Washington on July 30 to attend a series of briefings. After Iraq's invasion of Kuwait, she was kept in Washington to show U.S. displeasure with Iraq's actions. On September 11, Iraq released a taped version of her July 25 conversation with Hussein that purported to show that the United States had condoned the invasion. The tape was heavily edited to remove all of Glaspie's remonstrances to Hussein. It began with a long and unclear message from Hussein to President Bush, stating the Iraqi position on the crisis with Kuwait. Glaspie is then quoted as saying, "I have a direct instruction from the president to seek better relations with Iraq." After a discussion about oil prices, she allegedly stated, "We have no opinion on the Arab-Arab conflicts, like your border disagreement with Kuwait." (The tape was used by those who opposed U.S. intervention as a tool with which to berate the administration.)

Although Glaspie had been reiterating official State Department policy on the peaceful settlements of disputes, she was criticized for being too soft on Iraq. Instead of defending her, Secretary of State James A. Baker III used Glaspie as a scapegoat to cover the department's own failings on Iraq.

Glaspie was shunted aside to a low-level post in the U.S. mission to the United Nations. In January 1993, insult was added to injury when she was given five hours to leave that position by Madeleine K. Albright, the incoming Clinton administration ambassador to the United Nations. At her own suggestion, Glaspie was then posted to Somalia to work with the U.S. humanitarian relief effort there. In May 1993, it was announced that Ambassador Glaspie would return to Washington to serve as the director of the Office of Southern African Affairs in the Department of State.

See also IRAQGATE; STATE DEPARTMENT, U.S.

Suggestions for further reading: For the text of Saddam Hussein's version of his meeting with Ambassador Glaspie, see "The Glaspie Transcript: Saddam Meets the U.S. Ambassador (July 25, 1990)," in *The Gulf War Reader,* eds. Micah L. Sifry and Christopher Cerf (New York: Times Books, 1991). See also Jake Thompson, "Glaspie Twisting Slowly, Slowly in the Wind," *Washington Times,* March 13, 1991; Roxanne Roberts, "The Silence of the Diplomat," *Washington Post,* March 15, 1991; Robert D. Kaplan, "Tales From the Bazaar," *Atlantic Monthly,* August 1992; H. D. S. Greenway, "Gulf Cover-up Evidence Said Lacking," *Boston Globe,* October 21, 1992.

GLOBAL POSITIONING SYSTEM (GPS)

During the Persian Gulf War, the United States deployed 16 GPS (Global Positioning System) satellite-based radio-navigation systems to the Persian Gulf region. They provided precise world-wide, three-dimensional position, velocity and timing data to improve the navigation of air crews and other forces in the air and on the ground.

The system was an unqualified success, and demand for the SLGRs (small lightweight ground receivers, or "Sluggers") far exceeded the 842 receivers available. As a result, some 4,490 commercial GPS receivers were procured and distributed to the field.

Unlike the military SLGRs, the commercial ones could not receive encrypted data, which limited the range of GPS capabilities. That shortcoming aside, GPS provided a sure means of navigation in a featureless desert for helicopter pilots, truck drivers, tank crews and other members of the armed forces.

See also SATELLITES.

Suggestions for further reading: Department of Defense, *Conduct of the Persian Gulf War: Final Report to the Congress,* "Appendix T: Performance of Selected Weapons Systems" (Washington, D.C.: USGPO, 1992); Richard P. Hallion, *Storm Over Iraq: Air Power and the Gulf War* (Washington, D.C.: Smithsonian Institution Press, 1992).

GOLD STAR

The U.S. Navy, Marine Corps and Coast Guard equivalent of the Army and Air Force Oak Leaf Cluster, the small metallic Gold Star is worn on a medal ribbon to denote a subsequent awarding of the same decoration.

The term is also used, as in "Gold Star mother," to refer to a small flag with a gold star emblem that is given to the next of kin of servicemen and women killed in wartime.

GOLDWATER-NICHOLS DEFENSE DEPARTMENT REORGANIZATION ACT

Named after former Senator Barry Goldwater (Rep. Ariz.) and the late Representative Bill Nichols (Dem. Ala.) who sponsored the bill in Congress, the Goldwater-Nichols Defense Department Reorganization Act of 1986 has been hailed as one of the keys to victory in the Persian Gulf War.

A reaction to the confused and convoluted chain of command during the Vietnam War, the Goldwater-Nichols Reorganization Act (GNA) strengthened civilian control and oversight of military operations; improved the military advice provided to civilian authority; established the chairman of the Joint Chiefs of Staff (CJCS) as the principal military advisor to the president and the secretary of defense; and gave the military commanders in chief (CINCs) of the several unified commands the necessary authority to accomplish their assigned missions.

In the Persian Gulf War, GNA simplified the chain of command and the lines of communication running from the president and the secretary of defense through the CJCS to the commander in chief, U.S. Central Command. The CJCS's role was much strengthened, increasing his ability to give timely military advice. The role of the services—i.e., the Army, Navy, Air Force and Marine Corps—in supporting and sustaining the forces in the field was clarified, as was the supporting role of the several Defense Department logistic agencies and the other world-wide military commands.

See also COMMAND AND CONTROL.

Suggestions for further reading: Department of Defense, *Conduct of the Persian Gulf War: Final Report to the Congress,* "Appendix K: Command, Control, Communications (C3) and Space" (Washington, D.C.: USGPO, 1992); Senator Sam Nunn, "Military Reform Paved the Way for Gulf Triumph," *Atlanta Constitution,* March 31, 1991; Katherine Boo, "How Congress Won the War in the Gulf," *Washington Monthly,* October 1991.

GORBACHEV, MIKHAIL

See SOVIET UNION.

GREAT BRITAIN

See UNITED KINGDOM.

GREECE

See COALITION FORCES.

GROUND CAMPAIGN

G-Day for the coalition's ground campaign against Iraqi forces occupying Kuwait was February 24, 1991. After more than 180 days of maritime interdiction operations and 38 days of aerial bombardment, the Gulf War's final phase began.

"The ground offensive's objectives," according to the official Department of Defense (DOD) report on the war, "were to eject Iraqi Armed Forces from Kuwait, destroy the Republican Guard in the KTO [Kuwaiti Theater of Operations], and help restore the legitimate government of Kuwait."

The ground attack began with five coalition corps or corps-size equivalents on a line stretching from the western desert to the shores of the Persian Gulf. Occupying some two-thirds of the line was

CENTCOM's (Central Command) Third U.S. Army. The XVIII Airborne Corps with the French 6th Light Armored Division was on the far left, and VII Corps with the United Kingdom's (UK) 1st Armoured Division was to its right.

Next in line was the Arab/Islamic Joint Forces Command-North (JFC-N), including the Egyptian II Corps, the Syrian 9th Armored Division and two Royal Saudi Land Force (RSLF) Brigade Task Forces. To JFC-N's right was CENTCOM's First Marine Expeditionary Force (I MEF), and on the far right of the line, along the coast, was the Arab/Islamic Joint Forces Command-East (JFC-E) with units from all six of the Gulf Cooperation Council states.

The plan envisioned a supporting attack by I MEF, JFC-E and JFC-N straight into the Iraqi fortifications, in order to hold forward Iraqi forces in place. At the same time, the main attack by the Third U.S. Army's VII Corps and XVIII Airborne Corps would envelop the Iraqi defenses, strike deep into Iraq, cut the Iraqi lines of communication and destroy the Republican Guard forces.

An essential prelude to the attack was the movement of the 258,701 soldiers, 11,277 tracked vehicles, 487,449 wheeled vehicles and 1,619 aircraft of VII Corps and XVIII Airborne Corps, together with 60 days' worth of food, ammunition and supplies, from the Corps' assembly areas in the east to their attack positions in the west—a distance of some 150 miles for VII Corps and 260 miles for XVIII Corps. It was an enormous task. Just one of the five heavy armored and mechanized divisions, for example, needed 3,223 heavy-equipment transporters, 445 "lowboys" and 509 flatbed loads to move its heavy equipment. The movement, which continued 24 hours a day for more than three weeks, was one of the largest and longest in the history of warfare.

As part of the effort to prepare the battlefield, coalition air forces had flown more than 35,000 sorties against various targets in the KTO, including more than 5,600 sorties against the Iraqi Republican Guard Forces Command (RGFC). The battleships USS *Missouri* and *Wisconsin* also bombarded Iraqi coastal positions.

As described in more detail elsewhere (see listings for specific units), the execution of the plan was virtually flawless. By the end of G-Day (February 24), all of the coalition forces had achieved their initial objectives. By the end of G +1 (February 25), the forward Iraqi corps were assessed as combat ineffective. Baghdad radio reported that Saddam Hussein had ordered his forces to withdraw from Kuwait.

By G +2 (February 26), I MEF and JFC forces were on the outskirts of Kuwait City, XVIII Airborne Corps was astride the Iraqi lines of communication in the Euphrates River valley, and VII Corps had turned to the east and was in the process of destroying the Republican Guard divisions on its front.

On G +3 (February 27), I MEF forces seized Kuwait International Airport and held in place, awaiting the arrival of JFC forces that would liberate Kuwait City. XVIII Airborne Corps units were prepared to continue their attack into Basra, Iraq, while VII Corps units continued the destruction of the Republican Guard.

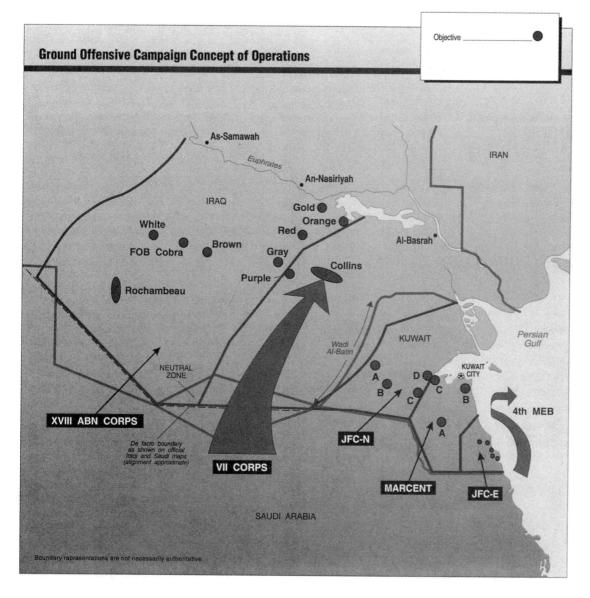

Ground Offensive Campaign Concept of Operations

Objective

Boundary representations are not necessarily authoritative.

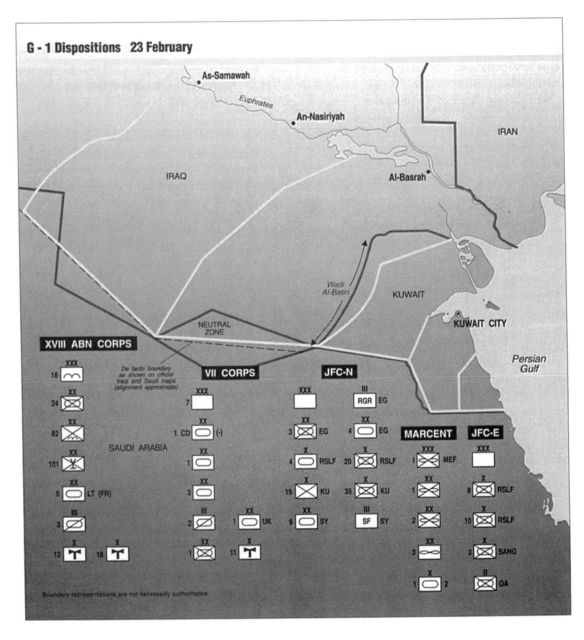

G - 1 Dispositions 23 February

Offensive operations ended at 8:00 A.M. on G +4 (February 28). After just 100 hours, the ground campaign had achieved its objectives. The official DOD report cites CENTCOM estimates that only five of Iraq's 43 combat divisions remained combat effective, and that more than 86,000 prisoners had been taken. The coalition had won one of the fastest and most complete victories in military history.

See also LISTINGS FOR INDIVIDUAL CORPS AND DIVISION UNITS; AIR CAMPAIGN; MARITIME CAMPAIGN; THIRD U.S. ARMY.

Suggestions for further reading: Department of Defense, *Conduct of the Persian Gulf War: Final Report*

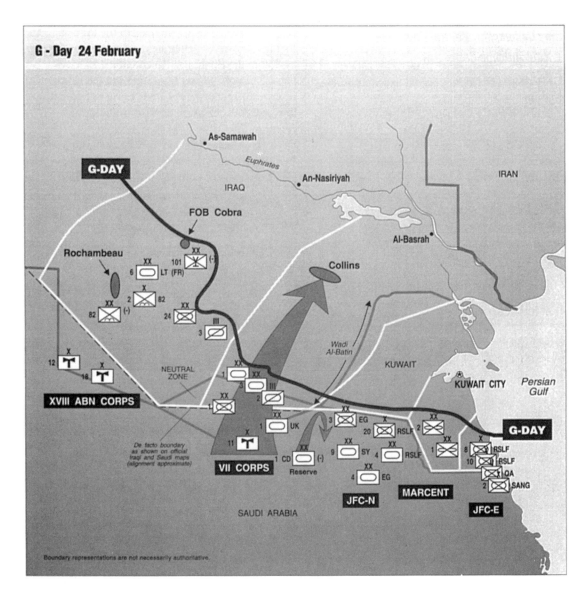

G - Day 24 February

to the Congress, "Chapter 8: The Ground Campaign" (Washington, D.C.: USGPO, 1992); Major James Blackwell, *Thunder in the Desert: The Strategy and Tactics of the Persian Gulf War* (New York: Bantam Books, 1991); General H. Norman Schwarzkopf, *It Doesn't Take a Hero* (New York: Bantam Books, 1992); The Staff of *U.S. News & World Report, Triumph Without Victory* (New York: Times Books, 1992). For General Schwarzkopf's account, see the appendix in Colonel Harry G. Summers Jr., *On Strategy II: A*

Critical Analysis of the Gulf War (New York: Dell, 1992). See also "Schwarzkopf; Strategy Behind Desert Storm," *Washington Post*, February 28, 1991.

GROUP

In the U.S. Army, a "group" is an organizational entity normally consisting of two or more battalions. Commanded by a colonel, a group is primarily a headquarters for artillery, engineer and combat support and combat service support units.

In the U.S. Navy, "group" designates a carrier battle group or a battleship action group commanded by a Navy captain. Each group includes a number of warships organized for a specific task. The commander of a cruiser/destroyer group is a rear admiral, and his group is divided into squadrons commanded by captains.

GULF COOPERATION COUNCIL (GCC)

The Gulf Cooperation Council (GCC), consisting of Saudi Arabia, Bahrain, Qatar, the United Arab Emirates (UAE), Oman and Kuwait was formed in 1988 in reaction to the Iran-Iraq War.

The GCC played a major role in the Persian Gulf War. Not only was its political support critical, it also provided the ports, airfields and military bases that were essential to the conduct of military operations. Moreover, its members also deployed their own armed forces.

The GCC states provided warships and combat aircraft as well as logistical and operational support for the air and naval campaigns. Ground forces from all six GCC member states comprised Joint Forces Command East, which was under the command of Lieutenant General Khalid Bin Sultan of Saudi Arabia.

Task Force Omar consisted of the Royal Saudi Land Force's (RSLF) 10th Infantry Brigade and a motorized UAE infantry battalion. Task Force Othman consisted of the RSLF's 8th Mechanized Infantry Brigade, an Omani motorized infantry battalion, an infantry company from Bahrain, and the Kuwaiti Al-Fatah Brigade. Task Force Abu Bakr was made up of the 2d Saudi Arabian National Guard Motorized Infantry Brigade and a Qatar mechanized battalion.

Not counting Kuwaiti military personnel killed in the initial Iraqi invasion, 47 troops from Saudi Arabia and 10 from the UAE were killed in action during the war, and 220 from Saudi Arabia, 17 from the UAE, 2 from Bahrain and 1 from Oman were wounded in action.

See also LISTINGS FOR INDIVIDUAL STATES; AIR CAMPAIGN; AIR FORCES, COALITION; ARMIES, COALITION; COALITION FORCES; GROUND CAMPAIGN; MARITIME INTERCEPTION OPERATIONS; NAVIES, COALITION.

Suggestions for further reading: Department of Defense, *Conduct of the Persian Gulf War: Final Report to the Congress* (Washington, D.C.: USGPO, 1992); Joseph Wright Twinam, *The Gulf, Cooperation and the Council* (Washington, D. C.: Middle East Policy Council, 1993).

GUNSHIPS

Pioneered in the Vietnam War by U.S. forces, fixed-wing and helicopter gunships were used to great effect in the Persian Gulf War by coalition forces.

The U.S. Air Force's fixed-wing gunships, the AC-130 Spectres, were provided by the 16th Special Operations Squadron of the 1st Special Operations Wing (SOW) of SOCCENT (Special Operations Command, Central Command). Built around the workhorse C-130 Hercules propeller-driven transport, the AC-130 is armed with 20-mm, 40-mm and 105-mm cannons. Unlike a jet fighter, the AC-130 has

an enormous loiter time and was able to provide effective fire on enemy positions for several hours at a time. For example, three AC-130 gunships delivered minigun and cannon fire against Iraqi wheeled vehicles and armored personnel carriers during the battle for Khafji on January 29–31, 1991. One AC-130 was shot down during the fighting.

The principal helicopter gunships used by U.S. forces were the Army's and Marine Corps's AH-1 Cobras, which were first used in the Vietnam War, and the Army's newer AH-64 Apaches. Two hundred seventy-four AH-64s and 221 AH-1s were deployed to the Gulf. Four squadrons of AH-1Ws were active-duty Marine units, two squadrons of AH-1Js were from the Marine reserve, and 145 AH-1Fs were from the Army.

Armed with antitank, Hellfire, Sidewinder and Sidearm missiles, and with 2.75 and 5-inch rockets and a 20-mm cannon, Marine helicopter gunships flew some 8,278 hours and Army gunships flew more than 10,000 hours of antiarmor, armed reconnaissance and screening missions. The AH-1Ws were credited with destroying 97 enemy tanks, 104 armored personnel carriers and other vehicles, 16 bunkers and 2 antiaircraft artillery sites. AH-1Fs prevented an Iraqi Republican Guard division from crossing a causeway over the Euphrates River by knocking out the lead vehicles with TOW missiles. Small- and large-scale Iraqi surrenders were common after the gunships had fired missiles at enemy armor or fortified positions.

Although the United States deployed the majority of the coalition's gunships, the United Kingdom deployed Lynx antitank helicopters armed with antitank missiles, and the French fielded Gazelle helicopters armed with antitank missiles and 20-mm guns. Iraq was credited with having 40 Soviet-supplied Mi-24 Hind gunships, 33 French-supplied Gazelles and 56 German-made Bo-105s, but none appeared in combat against coalition forces.

See also APACHE ATTACK HELICOPTER (AH-64).

Suggestions for further reading: Department of Defense, *Conduct of the Persian Gulf War: Final Report to the Congress*, "Appendix T: Performance of Selected Weapons Systems" (Washington, D.C.: USGPO, 1992); Major James Blackwell, *Thunder in the Desert: The Strategy and Tactics of the Persian Gulf War* (New York: Bantam Books, 1991).

HARM (HIGH-SPEED ANTI-RADAR MISSILE)

The High-Speed Anti-Radar Missile (HARM) was the primary weapon used against Iraqi radars. First used in the U.S. raid on Libya in 1986, HARM homes in on operating radars and destroys them with its 146-pound warhead. It can be used to home in on preselected radar signals, as a self-defense missile against air defense radars that lock onto the attacker's aircraft, and against targets of opportunity.

Approximately 1,000 HARMs were fired during the Gulf War, the majority by U.S. Navy and Marine Corps aircraft.

Suggestion for further reading: Norman Friedman, *Desert Victory: The War for Kuwait* (Annapolis, Md.: Naval Institute Press, 1991).

HARRIER (AV-8B) STOVL (SHORT TAKE-OFF AND VERTICAL LAND) AIRCRAFT

The U.S. Marine Corps's AV-8B Harrier jump-jet has a short takeoff and vertical landing capability that allows it to operate where other aircraft cannot, including the decks of amphibious assault ships (LHA) at sea.

Eighty-six AV-8Bs were deployed to the Persian Gulf by the U.S. Marines. Sixty aircraft (three squadrons) were shore-based, six were deployed on the

These Marine Corps Harrier jump jets aboard the USS *Nassau* (LHA-4), along with their counterparts on the *Tarawa* (LHA-1) and ashore, flew 3,342 sorties during the war.
U.S. Navy photo (PH1 Scott Allen), Empire Press.

USS *Tarawa* (LHA-1) and 20 on the USS *Nassau* (LHA-4). Some 3,342 sorties were flown from the LHAs and forward bases in the Kuwaiti Theater of Operations (KTO) against such targets as artillery, tanks, armor vehicles, ammunition storage bunkers, convoys, logistic sites, troops locations, airfields and antiaircraft artillery and surface-to-air missile locations.

Four AV-8B Harriers were lost to enemy ground fire and one crashed in a training accident.

Suggestions for further reading: Department of Defense, *Conduct of the Persian Gulf War: Final Report to the Congress*, "Appendix T: Performance of Selected Weapon Systems" (Washington, D.C.: USGPO, 1992); Norman Friedman, *Desert Victory: The War for Kuwait* (Annapolis, Md.: Naval Institute Press, 1991); Greg Ferguson, "Harrier: The Airpower Revolution Continues," *Marine Corps Gazette,* May 1991.

HELICOPTERS

Pioneered in the Korean War by the U.S. military and used extensively in the Vietnam War, helicopters were an integral part of coalition military organizations in the Persian Gulf War.

In addition to the helicopter-borne 101st Airborne Division (Air Assault), each U.S. Army division had an aviation brigade with AH-64 Apache attack helicopters, OH-58D Kiowa scout helicopters and UH-60 Blackhawk assault helicopters. Some older AH-1 Cobra gunships and UH-1 Huey utility helicopters were also deployed. In addition, the 12th and 18th Combat Aviation Groups provided helicopter support to the VII Corps and XVIII Airborne Corps.

Helicopter gunships are discussed elsewhere (see GUNSHIPS). Four hundred eighty-six UH-60 Blackhawks were deployed to the Kuwaiti Theater of Operations (KTO). Logging more than 44,000 hours, the UH-60s were used in combat and support missions, including emplacement of artillery, evacuation of enemy prisoners of war, and medical evacuation to and from hospital ships.

Also deployed were 10 Army medium helicopter companies with some 163 CH-47D Chinook transport helicopters, which flew more than 13,700 hours. The Marines deployed 9 active and 1 reserve medium helicopter squadrons with some 120 CH-46E See Knight transport helicopters, as well as CH-53 Sea Stallion Transports.

The U.S. Navy deployed 42 CH/HH-46D models in 21 two-ship detachments. Together, they flew some 15,000 miles, moved more than 37,000 passengers, delivered 4.6 million pounds of mail and flew 313 search-and-rescue and medical evacuation missions.

In addition, the Navy deployed one reserve and six active helicopter squadrons with 39 SH-3H Sea King multimission helicopters. Thirty-four Sea Kings were embarked on six aircraft carriers, two were aboard a Spruance-class destroyer at a search-and-rescue station in the northern Persian Gulf and three were stationed outside the KTO. Logging more than 5,781 hours, the Sea Kings supported maritime interception operations, maintained surface surveillance and conducted combat search-and-rescue operations.

The United States also deployed special operations helicopter units, including the Air Force's 20th Special Operations Squadron with MH-53J Pave Lows, the 55th Special Operations Squadron with MH-60G models and the 71st Special Operations Squadron with HH-3s.

The United Kingdom deployed 19 SA-330 Puma light helicopters, 17 Chinook medium helicopter transports, and Lynx antitank helicopters. France deployed 139 helicopters with the 5th Helicopter Regiment and the 1st Transport Helicopter Regiment, including SA-341 and SA-342 Gazelle antitank helicopters and SA-330 Puma utility helicopters.

The Arab members of the coalition also fielded a number of helicopters, including 85 Italian/U.S.-made Bell AB-205s, AB-206s and AB-212s; 37 French-made SA-332F Super Pumas, SA-316 Alouettes, SA-365 Dauphins and SA-342 Gazelles; 4 German-made Bo-105s; 12 U.S.-made UH-60 Blackhawks; 8 British-made Commandos; 7 Japanese-made KV-107s; and 4 German-made Bo-105s.

At the outbreak of the war, Iraq was credited with some 160 armed helicopters, including 40 Soviet-supplied Mi-24 Hinds, 20 French-made SA-342 Gazelles, 13 SA-321s, 30 SA-316Bs and 56 German-made Bo-105s. Iraq also had heavy, medium and light transport helicopters.

During the Gulf War, one U.S. AH-64 Apache helicopter was lost in combat and six Iraqi helicopters were shot down by coalition aircraft.

See also APACHE ATTACK HELICOPTER (AH-64); GUNSHIPS.

A CH-46A Sea Knight helicopter lifts supplies to the battleship USS *Wisconsin* underway in the Persian Gulf.
U.S. Navy photo (CWO Ed Bailey), Empire Press.

Suggestions for further reading: Department of Defense, *Conduct of the Persian Gulf War: Final Report to the Congress,* "Appendix T: Performance of Selected Weapon Systems" (Washington, D.C.: USGPO, 1992); Major James Blackwell, *Thunder in the Desert: The Strategy and Tactics of the Persian Gulf*

War (New York: Bantam Books, 1991); *The Military Balance 1989–1990* (London: International Institute for Strategic Studies, 1989).

HELLFIRE MISSILE (AGM-114)

The name "Hellfire" is derived from the fact that the missile is fired from a helicopter. The AGM-114 Hellfire is the current standard helicopter antitank missile used by U.S. forces. It replaced the slower BGM-71 TOW (tube-launched, optically tracked, wire-guided) missile that during the Gulf War was mounted on land vehicles and some older helicopters.

With a range of five miles and a warhead that sends a jet of molten metal to penetrate armor, the Hellfire was also used against Iraqi radars. It is guided by lasers that are carried by either the firing helicopter or ground forces. The Hellfire missile was carried by Army AH-64 Apache and Marine Corps AH-1W Cobra attack helicopters.

See also TOW.

Suggestion for further reading: Norman Friedman, *Desert Victory: The War for Kuwait* (Annapolis, Md.: Naval Institute Press, 1991).

HEMTT (HEAVY EXPANDED MOBILITY TACTICAL TRUCK)

The HEMTT is one of a new series of U.S. Army tactical trucks. An 8x8 diesel-powered 10-ton truck, the HEMTT provided fuel and ammunition to armor, artillery and infantry units. With a range of 300 miles, the tanker version has a capacity of 2,500 gallons and the truck has a towing capacity of 40,000 pounds.

Some 4,410 HEMTTs were deployed to the Persian Gulf, augmenting or replacing the old tankers and semitrailers in the divisions and armored cavalry regiments. Able to keep pace with armored vehicles, the HEMTT also operated superbly in terrain that became a quagmire when it rained.

See also HET (HEAVY EQUIPMENT TRANSPORTER); HMMWV (HIGH-MOBILITY MULTIPURPOSE WHEELED VEHICLE); LAND TRANSPORTATION NETWORK; LOGISTICS, U.S.

Suggestion for further reading: Department of Defense, *Conduct of the Persian Gulf War: Final Report to the Congress*, "Appendix T: Performance of Selected Weapons Systems" (Washington, D.C.: USGPO, 1992).

HET (HEAVY EQUIPMENT TRANSPORTER)

With a range of 420 miles, the M911 HET tractor has an 8x6 diesel engine. Its companion M747 trailer is rated at 60 tons.

Because of the coalition's ground campaign attack plan, wherein the U.S. VII Corps had to shift some 150 miles and the U.S. XVIII Airborne Corps some 260 miles from their assembly areas to their attack positions in the west, HETs played a critical role in the Gulf War. To move just one division's equipment required 3,223 HET loads.

The Army's initial deployment of 497 HETs was woefully inadequate. Moreover, the HETs were overloaded when carrying the M1A1 Abrams tank. Thus, a worldwide search was made for additional assets. Some 1,404 HETs were provided by Egypt, Italy, Germany and Saudi Arabia, while the United States leased or bought additional off-the-shelf HETs.

See also HEMTT (HEAVY EXPANDED MOBILITY TACTICAL TRUCK); HMMWV (HIGH-MOBILITY MULTIPURPOSE WHEELED VEHICLE); LAND TRANSPORTATION NETWORK; LOGISTICS, U.S.

Suggestion for further reading: Department of Defense, *Conduct of the Persian Gulf War: Final Report to the Congress*, "Appendix T: Performance of Selected Weapons Systems" (Washington, D.C.: USGPO, 1992).

HIGH TECHNOLOGY:

See AIR-LAUNCHED CRUISE MISSILE; AWACS (AIRBORNE WARNING AND CONTROL SYSTEM); BOMBING; COMPUTER WAR; ELECTRONIC WARFARE; GLOBAL POSITIONING SYSTEM; JSTARS (JOINT SURVEILLANCE TARGET ATTACK SYSTEM); LANTIRN (LOW-ALTITUDE NAVIGATIONAL AND TARGETING INFRARED FOR NIGHT); SATELLITES; STEALTH AIRCRAFT; TOMAHAWK LAND-ATTACK MISSILE.

HIGHWAY OF DEATH

Also called the "highway to hell," a seven-mile strip of road leading north from Kuwait City to Basra, Iraq, was dubbed by the media the "highway of death."

Beginning within the city as the Jahra Road, within Kuwait the road is a modern, six-lane divided highway. It climbs Mutlah Ridge at the sixth ring of the Kuwaiti beltway, angles northwest to the city of Al-Jahra, then goes on some 60 miles to Safwan on

Burning Iraqi vehicles clogged the road north of Kuwait City as their escape route was cut.
U.S. Army photo courtesy of 24th Infantry Division (Mechanized).

the Iraqi-Kuwaiti border, and then makes its way to the Iraqi city of Basra.

On the night of G +2 and in the early morning of G +3 (February 25–26, 1991), as coalition forces closed in on Kuwait City, thousands of Iraqi occupiers fled in panic in a convoy of some 1,500 vehicles. Iraqi military vehicles, including some 200 tanks, were interspersed with stolen Kuwaiti trucks and automobiles crammed with loot from the ransacked city.

As it retreated northward, the convoy was attacked by coalition aircraft, which knocked out the lead vehicles and dropped aerial mines at the convoy's head and tail to immobilize the column. On the afternoon of G +3, the "Tiger Brigade" of the U.S. Army's 2d Armored Division (then attached to the U.S. 2d Marine Division) closed off the road at the Mutlah Ridge police station. Unable to move and under intense air and ground attack, the column was turned into a raging inferno.

Attacking a retreating enemy force is fully consistent with the laws of war, but television coverage of the carnage was especially graphic. These pictures were reportedly one of the reasons why President George Bush halted the war when he did, fearing that public revulsion at the slaughter would undermine political support for the war. Foreign Secretary Douglas Hurd of the United Kingdom later wrote that once it became apparent that the Iraqi forces had lost the capacity to defend themselves, many coalition pilots "were reluctant to continue the fight."

But the pictures may have been worse than the reality. Having toured the area shortly after the cease-fire, war correspondent Michael Kelly concluded that "the precise number of Iraqis killed . . . is unclear, but it is smaller than one might expect, certainly under a thousand and probably only several hundred. . . . So fierce were the bombings that most of the Iraqis that survived the first waves gave no thought to fighting back, but ran away into the desert."

See also CASUALTIES; WAR CRIMES.

Suggestions for further reading: Department of Defense, *Conduct of the Persian Gulf War: Final Report to the Congress,* "Appendix O: The Role of the Law of War" (Washington, D.C.: USGPO, 1992); Michael Kelly, *Martyrs' Day: Chronicle of a Small War* (New York: Random House, 1993); "Why the War Had to

Stop at Mutlah Ridge," *The [London] Times,* August 2, 1991.

HMMWV (HIGH-MOBILITY MULTIPURPOSE WHEELED VEHICLE)

Pronounced "humvee," the HMMWV high-mobility multipurpose wheeled vehicle became the U.S. military's workhorse in the Gulf War, replacing most of the "Jeeps" that had held that role since World War II.

The HMMWV is a light, highly mobile diesel-powered tactical vehicle that uses a common quarter-ton payload chassis. The 20,000 HMMWVs deployed to the Gulf included cargo/troop carriers, armament carriers, communications center carriers, ambulances, TOW missile carriers and light artillery prime movers.

As the official Department of Defense report on the war concluded, "The HMMWV was the light vehicle of choice for soldiers in Operations Desert Shield and Desert Storm because of its superb performance. . . . It proved to be a rugged cross-country vehicle."

See also HEMTT (HEAVY EXPANDED MOBILITY TACTICAL TRUCK); HET (HEAVY EQUIPMENT TRANSPORTER); LAND TRANSPORTATION NETWORK; LOGISTICS, U.S.

Suggestions for further reading: Department of Defense, *Conduct of the Persian Gulf War: Final Report to the Congress,* "Appendix T: Performance of Selected Weapons Systems" (Washington, D.C.: USGPO, 1992); Guy Gugliotta, "The Desert Storm Dune Buggy—It's a Humdinger," *Washington Post,* January 28, 1991.

HONDURAS

See COALITION FORCES.

HORNER, CHARLES A(LBERT), LIEUTENANT GENERAL, USAF (1936–)

The commander of the Ninth U.S. Air Force and concurrently the CENTAF (Air Force Component, Central Command) commander, General Charles A. Horner was also the JFACC (Joint Force Air Component Commander), controlling the combat operations of all coalition aircraft during Operation Desert Storm.

Commissioned a second lieutenant in the U.S. Air Force upon graduation from the University of Iowa

in 1958, Horner earned his pilot wings the following year. From June to December 1964, as a F-105 Thunderchief pilot, he flew 41 combat missions over North Vietnam. Returning to Southeast Asia in May 1967, he flew 70 more combat missions over North Vietnam as an F-105 Wild Weasel pilot.

Subsequent assignments included commanding the 58th and 405th Tactical Training Wings, the 833d Air Division and the North American Aerospace Defense Command's (NORAD) 23d Air Division, and serving as deputy chief of staff for plans for the Tactical Air Command.

In March 1987, General Horner became commander of the Ninth U.S. Air Force and of CENTAF, and he served in those positions during the Gulf War. He is credited with conducting one of the most effective air campaigns in history, forging a 2,700-aircraft coalition that was based, in his words, on "absolute trust and equality" among 14 separate national or service components.

In charge of all coalition airpower in the Gulf War, General Horner ran the most successful air campaign in history.
USAF photo courtesy of Air Force Space Command.

General Horner's decorations include two Distinguished Service Medals, two Silver Stars for gallantry in action, the Legion of Merit, the Distinguished Flying Cross, three Meritorious Service Medals and eleven Air Medals. He has also received Canada's Meritorious Service Cross and awards from France, Pakistan, Bahrain, Kuwait, Saudi Arabia and the United Arab Emirates.

Returning to the United States after the war, he was promoted to four-star general in June 1992. That same month, he was appointed commander in chief of NORAD and concurrently commander in chief of U.S. Space Command and commander of the Air Force Space Command.

See also AIR CAMPAIGN; AIR FORCE, U.S.; AIRPOWER; NINTH U.S. AIR FORCE.

Suggestions for further reading: Department of Defense, *Conduct of the Persian Gulf War: Final Report to the Congress,* "Chapter 6: The Air Campaign" (Washington, D.C.: USGPO, 1992); Eliot A. Cohen et al., *Gulf War Airpower Survey* (Washington, D.C. USGPO, 1993); Richard P. Hallion, *Storm Over Iraq: Air Power and the Gulf War* (Washington, D.C.: Smithsonian Institution Press, 1992); Robert D. McFadden, "General Who Planned Air Assault with Lessons of Vietnam," *New York Times,* January 19, 1991.

HOSPITAL SHIPS

See MEDICAL CARE AND EVACUATION, COALITION.

HOSTAGES

At the time of the Iraqi invasion of Kuwait in early August 1990, there were an estimated 3,000 Americans and thousands of other foreigners living there. Shortly after seizing power, Iraqi officials began rounding up these primarily Western and Japanese nationals and either detained them in hotels in Kuwait or transported them to Baghdad.

During the second week of August, the U.S. Embassy in Baghdad was informed that some 500 Americans without diplomatic status in Iraq were to be taken to strategic sites to be used as "human shields."

On August 19, Saddam Hussein, the president of Iraq, announced that as many as 10,000 Westerners would be sent to strategic sites to deter attack. Some Westerners were actually moved to power plants, oil production facilities and military installations, including the 350 passengers of a commercial British Airways 747 that had been en route to India when it landed at Kuwait's International Airport for refueling. On August 20, President George Bush labeled the detainees "hostages" and demanded their immediate release.

In response to negative worldwide publicity, on August 28 Saddam Hussein announced that he would release all women and children, and their departures began on September 6. On November 18, Hussein announced that all hostages would be freed between December 25 and March 25, 1991, "if peace continued in the area." On December 6, 1990, he announced that all hostages would be freed. The exodus began on December 9 and was completed within the next few days.

One of the remarkable aspects of the hostage-taking was the American reaction. Saddam Hussein undoubtedly believed that his taking of hostages would have the same effect on the U.S. government and on American public opinion as did the taking of 52 American hostages by Iran in 1979. But it did not.

The lesson of the Iran crisis, the World Policy Institute's Walter Russell Mead told the *Washington Post* on December 17, 1990, was, "Don't let hostages drive your policy. . . . To be fixated by hostages is to be permanently paralyzed." Not only President Bush but many other Americans agreed. In an October 1990 *Washington Post*–ABC News poll, 51 percent of the respondents said the United States should bomb Iraqi military targets even if hostages might be killed as a result.

See also WAR CRIMES.

Suggestion for further reading: E. J. Dionne Jr., "This Time, No Fixation on Hostages," *Washington Post,* December 17, 1990.

HUNGARY

See COALITION FORCES.

HUSSEIN, IBN TALAL, KING OF JORDAN

See JORDAN.

HUSSEIN, SADDAM (1937–)

The president of Iraq and the commander in chief and field marshal of its armed forces, Saddam Hussein was the chief architect of his nation's invasion of Kuwait in August 1990 and Iraq's leader during the 1990–1991 Persian Gulf War.

Raised in the home of his maternal uncle after the breakup of his parents' marriage, Saddam Hussein joined the Baath Party in 1957. Wounded in the abortive assassination attempt on the ruler of Iraq in 1959, Hussein fled to Syria and then, in 1961, to Egypt where he reportedly attended college.

Returning to Iraq in 1963 after an initially successful Baathist takeover, he was imprisoned that same year when the coup ultimately collapsed. Two years later he escaped and went underground, helping to plan the successful July 17, 1968, coup.

Saddam Hussein then became vice chairman of the government's Revolutionary Command Council (RCC). By ruthlessly eliminating all opposition, he became the de facto ruler of Iraq. In July 1979, he convinced his older cousin, President Ahmad Hassan Al-Bakr, to step down. Saddam Hussein went on to be named president of the Republic; chairman of the RCC, ostensibly the highest authority in the country; supreme commander and field marshal of the armed forces; and secretary general of the Baath Party.

Obsessed with security, Hussein runs four separate intelligence services, employing tens of thousands of people. His dictatorship is maintained by a small inner circle of relatives from Takrit, a town of Sunni Muslims north of Baghdad. According to a report in *The Economist*, jobs in intelligence and internal security, for which Hussein requires iron loyalty, are filled by members of his father's Al-Majid family, his mother's Tulfah family and his cousin's Al-Rahshid family. The Maktab Al-Khas (i.e., an internal security special bureau), packed with his relatives, is more powerful than the RCC and in effect runs Iraq.

Shrewd in his maintaining of power within Iraq, Hussein is less adept at dealing with the outside world. As discussed elsewhere (see STRATEGY,

IRAQ), his whole conduct of the Persian Gulf War was marked by a series of miscalculations. He misread the world's reaction to his aggression, he misread his ability to manipulate public opinion abroad, he overestimated the strength of the "Israeli card" and he misjudged his ability to withstand the strength of the coalition's military response.

After the war, General H. Norman Schwarzkopf, the commander in chief, U.S. Central Command, succinctly summed up Field Marshal Hussein's military abilities: "As far as Saddam Hussein being a great military strategist, he is neither a strategist nor is he schooled in the operational art, nor is he a tactician, nor is he a general, nor is he a soldier. . . ."

But he is a survivor. President George Bush had insisted on Hussein's ouster before trade sanctions against Iraq could be lifted, but in March 1993 the Clinton administration quietly dropped that precondition. It is just as well, for as of this writing Saddam Hussein remains in power.

See also INVASION OF KUWAIT; STRATEGY, IRAQ; WAR TERMINATION.

Suggestions for further reading: Halim Barakat, *The Arab World: Society, Culture and State* (Berkeley: University of California Press, 1993); Efraim Karsh and Inari Rautsi, *Saddam Hussein: A Political Biography* (New York: The Free Press, 1991); Judith Miller and Laurie Mylroie, *Saddam Hussein and the Gulf Crisis* (New York: Random House, 1990); Samir Al-Khalil, *Republic of Fear* (Berkeley: University of California Press, 1990): Elaine Sciolino, *The Outlaw State: Saddam Hussein's Quest for Power and the Gulf Crisis* (New York: John Wiley & Sons, 1991); Michah L. Sifry and Christopher Cerf, eds., *The Gulf War Reader* (New York: Times Books, 1991); "The House Saddam Built," *The Economist*, September 29, 1990; R. Jeffrey Smith and Julia Preston, "U.S. Drops Demand for Saddam's Ouster," *Washington Post*, March 30, 1993.

IMMINENT THUNDER OPERATION
See AMPHIBIOUS TASK FORCE.

INFANTRY
Infantry has been the decisive force on most battlefields throughout history, but the "Queen of Battle" played a secondary role in the Persian Gulf War. Although infantry's mission to "close with the enemy and destroy it by fire and manuever" remained unchanged, the nature of the Gulf War battlefield favored armor operations.

With the exception of the 82d Airborne Division (which was in fact truck-mounted for most of its attack into Iraq) and the helicopter-mounted 101st Airborne Division (Air Assault), U.S. Army infantry in the Gulf War was mechanized, mounted on M2 Bradley infantry fighting vehicles (IFVs). Once the Iraqi fortifications were breached, most of the fighting was done from tanks and IFVs.

Although not as mechanized as the Army's, U.S. Marine Corps infantry was equipped with assault amphibian vehicles (AAV7A1s). Other coalition ground forces were also mechanized, including the infantry units of the 1st Armoured Division from the United Kingdom, the 6th Armored Division from France, the 3d Mechanized Division and the 4th Armored Division from Egypt, the 9th Armored Division from Syria, and mechanized brigades from Saudi Arabia and the other Gulf states.

Although most of Iraq's infantry divisions were dismounted, the infantry of the elite Republican Guard Forces Command were mounted in Soviet-supplied BMP infantry fighting vehicles.

See also ARMOR; ASSAULT AMPHIBIAN VEHICLE; BRADLEY M2/M3 FIGHTING VEHICLE; COMBAT ACTION RIBBON; COMBAT INFANTRYMAN BADGE; GROUND CAMPAIGN,

Suggestions for further reading: Department of Defense, *Conduct of the Persian Gulf War: Final Report to the Congress*, "Chapter 8: The Ground Campaign" (Washington, D.C.: USGPO, 1992); Major James Blackwell, *Thunder in the Desert: The Strategy and Tactics of the Persian Gulf War* (New York: Bantam Books, 1991); General H. Norman Schwarzkopf, *It Doesn't Take a Hero* (New York: Bantam Books, 1992); The Staff of *U.S. News & World Report, Triumph Without Victory* (New York: Times Books, 1992).

INTELLIGENCE
Intelligence is the eyes and ears of the battlefield commander, providing him with information about enemy strengths and dispositions, and insights into the enemy's intentions. Early in the air campaign, the coalition literally blinded the Iraqi military. According to General H. Norman Schwarzkopf, the commander in chief of U.S. Central Command, "We knew that he had very very limited reconnaissance means, and therefore when we took out his Air Force for all intents and purposes we took out his ability to see what we were doing down here in Saudi Arabia."

The United States, on the other hand, had massive intelligence coverage of Iraq and Kuwait. Although coalition intelligence assets contributed to the overall intelligence picture, it was U.S. technical intelligence that provided most of the input.

"I was blessed with an intelligence staff whose work was so good," General Schwarzkopf wrote in his autobiography, "that the military intelligence community in Washington usually let Central Command [CENTCOM] take the lead, seconding our assessments of developments in the Middle East." But in his testimony before Congress after his return from the Gulf, Schwarzkopf complained that as a theater commander he had not been well served by the intelligence community. National intelligence estimates were so heavily caveated as to be "useless," and the quality of battle damage assessments done in Washington, he felt, left much to be desired.

This seeming anomaly reflects the fact that "intelligence" is not a single entity but has many different parts. "The record of intelligence in the air war is a mixed one," concluded the *Gulf War Airpower Survey*, "with remarkable successes as well as notable (but far from fatal) failures.

The accurate strategic assessment of Iraqi intent and capabilities following the August [1990] crisis, and the mass of detailed information about a wide range of targets acquired from August 1990 through February 1991 contributed immensely to the air campaign. The overall misestimate of Iraqi order of battle and inadequate bomb damage assessment were the largest failures.

While much of the intelligence effort, especially HUMINT (human intelligence) and SIGINT (signal intelligence), remains secret, the official Department of Defense (DOD) report on the war notes the contributions of national intelligence agencies, including the Central Intelligence Agency (CIA), the Defense Intelligence Agency (DIA) and the National Security Agency (NSA). Mapping, charting and geodesy support was critical, and eventually 90 million maps were furnished to the Kuwaiti Theater of Operations (KTO).

The CIA established 24-hour task forces in its Operations and Intelligence Directorates, and all national intelligence organizations eventually deployed intelligence operations specialists, area specialists and analysts to augment CENTCOM's intelligence staffs. DIA, for example, deployed 11 National Military Intelligence Support Teams (NMISTs) to the KTO.

At the theater level, CENTCOM's Joint Intelligence Center (JIC) was created as the senior intelligence organization; it acted as the clearinghouse for intelligence requirements and as the collection manager for theater intelligence assets. Among the JIC's subordinate units was the Combat Assessment Center, which provided an assessment of enemy intentions 24 to 96 hours into the future. Another was the Joint Reconnaissance Center, which managed the reconnaissance and airborne intelligence collection effort, including the use of JSTARS (Joint Surveillance Target Attack Radar System).

At the tactical level, ARCENT (Army Component, Central Command—i.e., the Third U.S. Army) was supported by the 513th Military Intelligence (MI) Brigade, which conducted all-source intelligence operations. Each corps had its own MI brigade as well as an armored cavalry regiment and aviation groups for tactical intelligence collection. Each division had an assigned Combat Electronic Warfare and Intelligence (CEWI) Battalion as well as armored and air-cavalry reconnaissance units.

CENTAF (Air Component, Central Command—i.e., the Ninth U.S. Air Force) was supported by the 9th Tactical Intelligence Squadron, the 6975th Electronic Security Squadron and a detachment of the Air Force Special Activities Center NAVCENT (Naval Component, Central Command—i.e., the U.S. Seventh Fleet) was supported by the intelligence staff of the command ship USS *Blue Ridge* (LCC 19).

MARCENT (Marine Forces, Central Command—i.e., the First Marine Expeditionary Force) was supported by the 1st Surveillance, Reconnaissance and Intelligence Group (SRIG), while Special Operations Command (SOC) was supported by a heavily augmented intelligence staff.

Suggestions for further reading: Department of Defense, *Conduct of the Persian Gulf War: Final Report to the Congress,* "Appendix C: Intelligence" (Washington, D.C.: USGPO, 1992); Eliot A. Cohen et al., *Gulf War Airpower Survey* (Washington, D.C.: USGPO, 1993); General H. Norman Schwarzkopf, *It Doesn't Take a Hero* (New York: Bantam Books, 1992).

INTERDICTION

See AIR CAMPAIGN; MARITIME INTERCEPTION OPERATIONS.

INVASION OF KUWAIT

On July 17, 1990, Iraqi president Saddam Hussein accused Kuwait and the United Arab Emirates (UAE) of conspiring with the United States to cheat on oil production quotas, thereby driving down the price of oil and costing Iraq billions of dollars in lost revenue. He demanded money from Kuwait and raised the question of ownership of the islands of Warbah and Bubiyan at the head of the Persian Gulf.

Efforts by Egypt and Saudi Arabia to peacefully resolve the crisis were unsuccessful, and by July 21 an Iraqi Republican Guard Forces Command (RGFC) armored division had deployed just north of Kuwait. By August 1, there were eight RGFC divisions between Basra and the Kuwaiti border, comprising some 140,000 troops supported by more than 1,500 tanks, infantry vehicles and artillery. Attack fighter-bomber aircraft and helicopters moved onto southern bases.

At 1:00 A.M. (Kuwait time) on August 2, three Iraqi RGFC divisions attacked across the Kuwaiti frontier. A mechanized infantry division and an armored division conducted the main attack into Kuwait, driving south for the Al-Jahra Pass. Another ar-

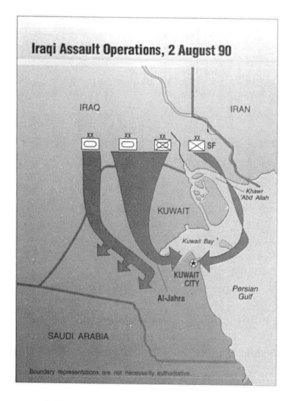

Iraqi Assault Operations, 2 August 90

mored division conducted a supporting attack farther west.

An Iraqi special operations force conducted the
first attack on Kuwait City—a heliborne assault
against key government facilities—at 1:30 A.M.
Meanwhile, commando teams made amphibious assaults against the emir's palace and other key facilities. The emir was able to escape to Saudi Arabia, but
his brother was killed in the Iraqi assault on the
Dasman Palace.

Supported by combat aircraft, the three attacking
armored and mechanized divisions linked up at the
Al-Jahra Pass. The two divisions conducting the
main attack then continued east to Kuwait City,
where they joined the special operations forces by
5:30 A.M. By 7:00 P.M. on August 2, Iraqi forces had
secured the city.

Despite individual acts of bravery, the Kuwaiti
military was hopelessly outmatched and its resistance was uncoordinated. Some Kuwaiti forces successfully retreated across the Saudi border as
defenses collapsed. Kuwait Air Force pilots flew
limited sorties against attacking Iraqi units but were

forced to recover in Saudi Arabia and Bahrain because the two Kuwaiti air bases had been overrun.
All, however, would return to fight another day.

See also COALITION FORCES; KUWAIT.

Suggestions for further reading: Department of
Defense, *Conduct of the Persian Gulf War: Final Report
to the Congress* (Washington, D.C.: USGPO, 1992);
Efraim Karsh and Inari Rautsi, "Why Saddam Hussein Invaded Kuwait," *Survival*, January/February
1991; Laurie Mylroie, "Why Saddam Hussein Invaded Kuwait," *Orbis*, Winter 1993; Norman Cigar,
"Iraq's Strategic Mindset and the Gulf War: Blueprint for Defeat," *Journal of Strategic Studies*, March
1992; Major James Blackwell, *Thunder in the Desert:
The Strategy and Tactics of the Persian Gulf War* (New
York: Bantam Books, 1991); John Bulloch and Harvey Morris, *Saddam's War: The Origins of the Kuwait
Conflict and the International Response* (New York:
Faber, 1991).

IRAN-IRAQ WAR (1980–1988)

The animosity between the Persians (the latter-day
Iranians) and the Arabs dates back more than a
thousand years. Iraq's very name for its 1980–1988
war with Iran is the Qadisiyyah Saddam, after the
7th-century battle of Qadisiyyah, where the Arabs
drove the Persians from Mesopotamia (today's Iraq).
As discussed in part 1, this ancient history had real
meaning, for Saddam Hussein would claim that in
the Iran-Iraq War he had blocked the "eastern gateway," saving the region from being overrun by the
Iranians. Part of Iraq's demands on Kuwait in 1990
were for recompense for the terrible suffering Iraq
had suffered in that conflict.

The Iran-Iraq War, which began in September
1980 with an Iraqi invasion of Iran, was rooted in the
calls of Iranian fundamentalist Ayatollah Ruholla
Khomeini for the overthrow of Iraq's Baath Party
and in his active support of anti-Baathist groups
within Iraq, as well as in Iraq's desire to abrogate the
1975 Algerian Treaty that had established joint Iraqi-
Iranian control over the Shatt-Al-Arab waterway
between the two countries. When the much-hoped-
for quick victory failed to materialize, Iraq fell back
to its border and adopted a defensive strategy. For
the next six years, Iraq inflicted heavy losses on the
Iranians as they attempted to breach the Iraqi fortifications. Iraq's strategy changed, however, with the

loss of the Faw Peninsula to Iran in 1987 and the threatened loss of Basra.

Between April and August 1988, four major battles were fought in which the Iranian forces were routed. In the first offensive, "Blessed Ramadhan," Iraqi Republican Guard units, using nerve and blister gas chemical warfare (CW) agents, recaptured the Faw Peninsula. Farther north, in the last of these operations, Iraqi forces penetrated deep into Iran, capturing three-quarters of Iran's armor inventory and almost half of its artillery.

Iran sued for peace in August 1988 and a cease-fire was declared. Iraq had suffered an estimated 375,000 casualties but emerged with the largest military force in the Gulf region and, except for Israel's, in the entire Middle East. Two years later, on August 15, 1990, in a desperate attempt to win Iran's support in the Kuwait crisis, Saddam Hussein released all Iranian prisoners of war, returned all the land taken during the Iran-Iraq War, and accepted the prewar agreements for control of the Shatt-al-Arab waterway.

But the Iraqi leader's gambit did not work. Iran remained resolutely neutral, impounding and later confiscating the more than 130 Iraqi aircraft that sought refuge there during the Gulf War.

See also IRAQGATE.

Suggestions for further reading: Dilip Hiro, *The Longest War: The Iran-Iraq Military Conflict* (New York: Routledge, 1991); Stephen C. Pelletiere and Douglas V. Johnson II, *Lessons Learned: The Iran-Iraq War* (Carlisle, Pa.: Strategic Studies Institute, U.S. Army War College, 1990); Michah L. Sifry and Christopher Cerf, eds., *The Gulf War Reader* (New York: Times Books, 1991).

IRAQ:

See AIR CAMPAIGN; AIR FORCE, IRAQ; ARMY, IRAQ; BIOLOGICAL WARFARE; BOMB SHELTER CONTROVERSY; CHEMICAL WARFARE; GROUND CAMPAIGN; HUSSEIN, SADDAM; INVASION OF KUWAIT; IRAN-IRAQ WAR; IRAQGATE; LOGISTICS, IRAQ; MARITIME CAMPAIGN; MARITIME INTERCEPTION OPERATION; NAVY, IRAQ; NUCLEAR WEAPONS; SCUD MISSILES; STRATEGY, IRAQ; WAR CRIMES; WAR TERMINATION.

IRAQGATE

Playing off "Watergate," the name of the scandal that brought down the Nixon administration in 1974,

"Iraqgate" was the label given to charges that the Bush administration had, through mismanagement, encouraged Iraq's aggression and precipitated the Persian Gulf War.

Concerned with Iranian-sponsored Islamic fundamentalism and outraged over the Iran hostage crisis, in which U.S. diplomats had been held captive inside the American Embassy in Tehran, the United States "tilted" toward Iraq during the 1980–1988 Iran-Iraq War. When President George Bush took office in January 1989, he ordered a postwar review of U.S. relations with Iraq. Completed in June 1989, the resulting National Security Directive (NSD) 26 was approved by the president on October 2 of that year and became the basic policy statement for U.S.-Iraqi relations. According to a secret State Department memorandum written at that time, NSD 26 spoke of "the new political, military and economic importance of Iraq" and emphasized "the need for a cautious step-by-step approach to broadening and deepening our bilateral relations."

Four days after NSD 26 was signed, Secretary of State James A. Baker III met with Foreign Minister Tariq Aziz of Iraq. Referring to a secret memorandum of the meeting, the *Washington Post* reported on June 29, 1992, that "the two sides committed themselves to work for an improved long-term relationship" and expressed their mutual belief that "there was reason to continue and where possible expand cooperation."

Critics later charged that the United States had ignored Iraq's abysmal record of human rights violations, including its use of poison gas against its own Kurdish dissidents; had ignored evidence that Iraq was in the process of building a nuclear bomb; and had overlooked Iraq's increasing belligerency in the area. Critics further charged that Bush's policies had helped make Iraq a regional menace. The Commerce and Defense Departments had been pressured into approving the sale of sensitive military technology to Iraq, and the White House had pressed for federal loan guarantees that had encouraged banks to lend money to Iraq. The result was that the U.S. Treasury had had to make good on some $1.5 billion in bad loans. Critics also charged that the administration had been involved in the Italian Banca Nazionale del Lavoro (BNL) scandal, in which Iraq defaulted on $350 million in loans backed by U.S. Department of Agriculture guarantees.

The Bush administration vehemently denied any wrongdoing. "To give Saddam incentives to moderate his behavior," said National Security Advisor Brent Scowcroft, "the Bush administration, with considerable Congressional support, authorized $1 billion in credit guarantees—not loans or cash—to exporters selling grain to Iraq." Scowcroft went on to claim that

> The U.S. government export controls toward Iraq were tougher that those of any other industrial country. We followed a strict policy of denying the export of weapons to Iraq. . . . During Desert Storm, coalition forces did not encounter any U.S.-supplied weapons on the battlefield, and the more than 40 inspections conducted . . . by the International Atomic Energy Agency . . . demonstrate conclusively that U.S. technology made no significant contribution to Iraq's military capability.

As the Ambassador Glaspie affair makes clear, there is no doubt that the Bush administration continued to tilt toward Iraq long after it should have regained its balance. Her reported remark to Saddam Hussein on the eve of his invasion of Kuwait that she had "a direct instruction from the president to seek better relations with Iraq" has been cited as evidence of the shortsightedness of U.S. policy.

To many observers, however, the whole affair appeared to be partisan politics. A month before the November 1992 presidential election, Iraqgate was much in the news, but as soon as the election was over and Bush was defeated, the issue receded. With some justification, Brent Scowcroft called Iraqgate "an attempt to turn a legitimate policy debate into a criminal conspiracy."

See also GLASPIE, APRIL C.; NUCLEAR WEAPONS.

Suggestions for further reading: Richard Lacayo, "Did Bush Create This Monster?" *Time,* June 8, 1992; R. Jeffrey Smith and John Goshko, "Ill-Fated Policy Originated Shortly After Bush Took Office," *Washington Post,* June 27, 1992; Brent Scowcroft, "We Didn't 'Coddle' Saddam," *Washington Post,* October 10, 1992; Kenneth R. Timmerman, *Death Lobby: How the West Armed Iraq* (New York: Houghton Mifflin, 1991).

ISLAM

One of the world's major faiths, Islam is a monotheistic religion that preaches that there is but one God, Allah, and Mohammed is his prophet. Born in Mecca in what is now Saudi Arabia in A.D. 570, Mohammed became the founder of Islam, which spread rapidly throughout the Arab world and now has more than 950 million adherents worldwide (see part I).

Islam is not just a matter of personal faith; it also embraces political theory and social conduct. Just as Christianity is split into Protestants and Roman Catholics, so Islam is split into two major groups, the Shias, or Shiites, and the Sunnis who outnumber them by nine to one. Growing out of disagreement over the succession to the Prophet Mohammed, the Shiites believe that Ali, Mohammed's son-in-law, was divinely appointed as the successor, while the Sunnis believe that leadership should pass to those best qualified.

Much like the difference between Protestants and Catholics, Shiites invest their religious leaders (imams) with spiritual authority, whereas Sunnis do not venerate their religious leaders. Everywhere in the Islamic world, Shiism is a cult associated with the poor. Historically passive, Shiites were stirred to action by Ayatollah Ruholla Khomeini of Iran, where Shiism has been the state religion since the 16th century.

Spreading what has been labeled "Islamic fundamentalism" throughout the Muslim world, Khomeini championed the oppressed and preached the need for a "just struggle" to overthrow "corrupt regimes." One regime targeted by Khomeini was the Baathist government of Saddam Hussein in Iraq, and this was one of the factors leading to the 1980–1988 Iran-Iraq War.

Khomeini's calling for his overthrow was potentially dangerous for Hussein, because 60 percent of Iraq's population consists of Shiites. But the Iraqi Shiites are Arabs, not Persians (i.e., Iranians), and most remained loyal to Saddam Hussein. After the Gulf War, however, there was a Shiite uprising in southeast Iraq, in the Basra area and among "marsh Arabs" in the Tigris-Euphrates Delta. That uprising continues to smolder.

See also SHIITE REVOLT; WAR TERMINATION.

Suggestions for further reading: Halim Barakat, *The Arab World: Society, Culture and the State* (Berkeley: University of California Press, 1993); John L. Esposito, *The Islamic Threat: Myth or Reality?* (New York: Oxford University Press, 1992); Michael Colins Dunn, "The Peoples of Iraq," *The Estimate,* May 9, 1991; "Islamic Resurgence," *Background Brief* (London: Foreign and Commonwealth Office, April 1990).

ISRAEL

Israel remained neutral during the Persian Gulf War despite the best efforts of Saddam Hussein to provoke its involvement. Given the long-standing Arab hostility toward Israel, he believed that Israeli involvement would fracture the allied coalition.

To that end, beginning at 3:03 A.M. on January 18, 1991, Iraq launched the first in a series of Scud missile attacks on Israel. The last Iraqi missile struck Israel on the night of February 24–25, 1991. During the course of the war some 42 Scud missiles were fired at Israel.

According to a March 1993 study by the Center for International Studies at the Massachusetts Institute of Technology, Scud attacks on Israel caused 2 deaths, 11 serious injuries and about 220 slight injuries. A total of 4,100 buildings were damaged and at least 28 were destroyed.

In response the first Iraqi attacks, President George Bush ordered U.S. Army Patriot missile batteries to Israel to defend it against Scud missiles. The first battery, sent from Europe, became operational on January 21, 1991. Ultimately, six Patriot batteries were deployed, two being manned by Israeli Defense Force crews. Although the figure is disputed, it is estimated that the Patriot systems had a 40 percent success rate in intercepting incoming Scuds.

In any event, Saddam Hussein's attempt to "play the Israeli card" and split the allied coalition failed.

It failed not only because of Israeli restraint but also because of the nature of coalition warfare itself. A common threat not only brings a coalition into being, but also provides the glue that holds it together under stress.

The threat posed by Iraq's aggression against its Arab neighbors was so strong, it brought such former enemies as Syria and Saudi Arabia together in common cause. A glue that strong would arguably have held the coalition together even if Israel had intervened in the war. In fact, after Iraq began its Scud attacks against Israel, both Syria and Egypt publicly stated that every nation had an inherent right to self-defense.

One of the results of the Gulf War has been the start of peace talks between Israel and its Arab neighbors.

See also PATRIOT MISSILE; SCUD MISSILES; STRATEGY, IRAQ.

Suggestions for further reading: by C. J. D. Lewis, "How Israel Saw Iraq During the Gulf War," *RUSI Journal,* Winter 1991; Amatzia Baram, "Israeli Deterrence, Iraqi Responses," *Orbis,* Summer 1992; Joseph Alpher, ed., *War in the Gulf: Implications for Israel* (Boulder, Colo.: Westview Press, 1993).

ITALY

See COALITION FORCES; PRISONERS OF WAR.

ARAB/ISLAMIC COALITION COMMAND RELATIONSHIPS

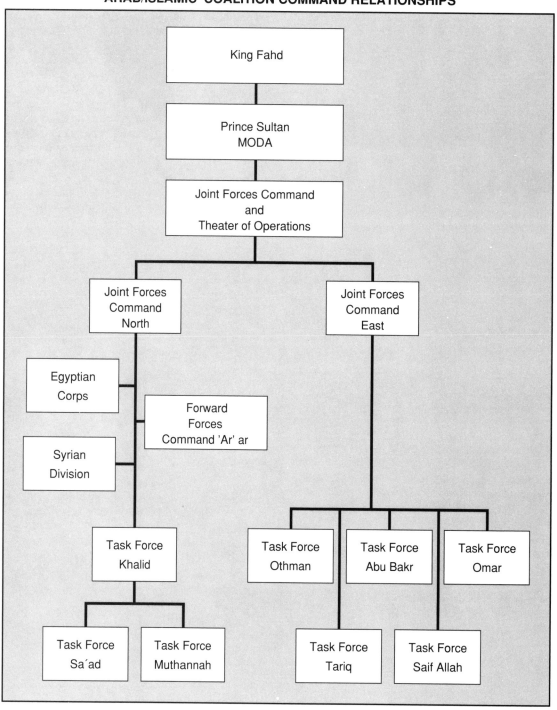

JAPAN

See COST; LAND TRANSPORTATION NETWORK.

JEDI KNIGHTS

In mid-September 1990, at the request of General H. Norman Schwarzkopf, the commander in chief, Central Command, a J-5 (Strategic Plans and Policy) Special Planning Group was formed, consisting of Army officers who had graduated from the School of Advanced Military Studies at the Army Command and General Staff College at Fort Leavenworth, Kansas. Nicknamed the "Jedi Knights" after the characters in the movie *Star Wars,* the officers had completed an intensive post–staff college yearlong study of the theory and practice of warfare at the operational level. Their mission was to develop courses of action for the ground offensive.

Suggestions for further reading: Department of Defense, *Conduct of the Persian Gulf War: Final Report to the Congress,* "Chapter 8: The Ground Campaign" (Washington, D.C.: USGPO, 1992); The Staff of *U.S. News & World Report, Triumph Without Victory* (New York: Times Books, 1992).

JFACC (JOINT FORCES AIR COMPONENT COMMANDER)

See AIR CAMPAIGN.

JOINT CHIEFS OF STAFF (JCS), U.S.

Including a chairman, a vice chairman, the Army and Air Force chiefs of staff, the chief of naval operations and the commandant of the Marine Corps, the Joint Chiefs of Staff are the senior military advisors to the president, the National Security Council and the secretary of defense. Although the chairman is the principal advisor, the other members may provide additional information upon request and may also submit their own advice when it does not coincide with that of the chairman.

The JCS formally came into being after World War II as part of the reorganization of the U.S. defense establishment that placed a secretary of defense between the president and his military advisors. Prior

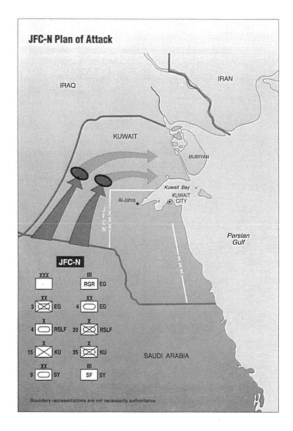

JFC-N Plan of Attack

to the Gulf War, the JCS was restructured by the Goldwater-Nichols Defense Department Reorganization Act of 1986, which added a vice chairman and strengthened the role of the chairman at the expense of the other members.

By law the JCS has no command authority over forces in the field. In theory, its members merely pass on the orders of the president and the secretary of defense to the military commander in chief of the unified command conducting combat operations, in the Gulf War, General H. Norman Schwarzkopf, the CINCENT (commander in chief, Central Command). In reality, however, members of the JCS exert considerable influence on the course of events.

During the Gulf War the six members of the Joint Chiefs of Staff were the chairman, Army General Colin L. Powell; the vice chairman, Navy Admiral David E. Jeremiah; the Army chief of staff, General Carl E. Vuono; the chief of naval operations, Admiral Carlisle A. H. Trost; the Air Force chief of staff, General Merrill A. McPeak (who replaced General Michael J. Dugan in September 1990); and the commandant of the Marine Corps, General Alfred M. Gray.

See also Listings for service chiefs; DEFENSE DEPARTMENT, U.S.; GOLDWATER-NICHOLS DEFENSE DEPARTMENT REORGANIZATION ACT; ORGANIZATION FOR COMBAT, U.S.; POWELL, COLIN L.

Suggestions for further reading: The best account of the inner workings of the JCS is Bob Woodward, *The Commanders* (New York: Simon & Schuster, 1991). See also General H. Norman Schwarzkopf, *It Doesn't Take a Hero* (New York: Ban-

tam Books, 1992). For the decline of the JCS, see Colonel Gordon D. Batcheller, USMC (Ret.), "The Eclipse of the Joint Chiefs," *Marine Corps Gazette*, July 1991.

JOINT FORCES COMMAND (JFC)

The Joint Forces Command (JFC) was the Arab/Islamic counterpart of the U.S. Central Command (CENTCOM). Appointment of one overall commander for coalition forces in the Persian Gulf War was not politically possible. Instead, a dual command was created with all U.S., United Kingdom and ultimately French forces under the operational command of CENTCOM, and all Arab/Islamic forces under the Joint Forces Command. Tying them together was the Coalition Coordination, Communications and Control Integration Center.

Commanded by Lieutenant General Khalid Bin Sultan of Saudi Arabia, the JFC was organized into

In the gun turret of the battleship USS *Wisconsin* (BB-64) in the Persian Gulf, chairman of the Joint Chiefs of Staff General Colin Powell checks on the readiness of the force.
U.S. Navy photo (PH1 Scott Allen) courtesy of OCJCS.

General Schwarzkopf (left), the U.S. commander in the Gulf, visits his Joint Forces Command Arab/Islamic counterparts in the field.
Central Command Public Affairs.

two corps-sized units, JFC-North and JFC-East, and the Forward Forces Command 'Ar'ar. Forward Forces Command 'Ar'ar consisted of the Royal Saudi Land Forces' (RSLF) 5th Airborne Battalion, the Saudi Arabian National Guard (SANG) King Faisal Brigade and the Pakistani 7th Armored Brigade.

Joint Forces Command-North (JFC-N) consisted of the 3d Egyptian Mechanized Division, the 4th Egyptian Armored Division, the 9th Syrian Armored Division, the Egyptian Ranger Regiment, the Syrian Special Forces Regiment, the RSLF 4th Armored and 20th Mechanized Brigades, the Kuwaiti 15th Infantry Brigade and 35th Mechanized Brigade and a Niger infantry battalion.

Joint Forces Command-East (JFC-E), organized into three task forces, consisted of units from all six Gulf Cooperation Council states. Task Force (TF) Omar consisted of the RSLF 10th Infantry Brigade and a United Arab Emirates (UAE) motorized infantry battalion. In TF Othman was the RSLF 8th Mechanized Infantry Brigade, an Omani motorized infantry battalion, a Bahraini infantry company and the Kuwaiti Al-Fatah Brigade. TF Abu Bakr included

the SANG 2d Motorized Infantry Brigade and a Qatari mechanized battalion. Also included in JFC-E were the Moroccan 6th Mechanized Battalion, the Pakistani 1st East Bengal Infantry Battalion and the Senegalese 1st Infantry Battalion.

Deployed on the right flank along the Gulf coast, JFC-E anchored the coalition's line. To its left was the U.S. First Marine Expeditionary Force (I MEF), and to I MEF's left was JFC-N. Together, these three corps-size units made up the coalition's supporting attack, driving straight ahead through the Iraqi fortifications to fix the Iraqi defenders in place while the Third U.S. Army's main attack enveloped the Iraqis from the west (see GROUND CAMPAIGN).

Seventy-one JFC personnel were killed in action, including 47 from Saudi Arabia, 12 from Egypt, 10 from the UAE and 2 from Syria. Another 344 were wounded in action, including 220 from Saudi Arabia, 95 from Egypt, 17 from the UAE, 8 from Senegal, 2 from Bahrain and 1 each from Syria and Oman.

See also ARMIES, COALITION; BAHRAIN; BIN SULTAN BIN ABDULAZIZ, KHALID; CENTCOM (CENTRAL COMMAND); COALITION COORDINATION,

COMMUNICATIONS AND CONTROL INTEGRATION CENTER; EGYPT; GROUND CAMPAIGN; KUWAIT; OMAN; QATAR; SAUDI ARABIA; SYRIA; UNITED ARAB EMIRATES; YEMEN.

Suggestions for further reading: Department of Defense, *Conduct of the Persian Gulf War: Final Report to the Congress,* "Appendix I: Coalition Development, Coordination and Warfare" (Washington, D.C.: USGPO, 1992); Major James Blackwell, *Thunder in the Desert: The Strategy and Tactics of the Persian Gulf War* (New York: Bantam Books, 1991); General H. Norman Schwarzkopf, *It Doesn't Take a Hero* (New York: Bantam Books, 1992); Frank Chadwick, *Gulf War Fact Book* (Bloomington, Ill.: GDW, 1991).

JOINT TASK FORCE MIDDLE EAST, U.S.

Dating back to 1949 when the commander, Middle East Force (CMEF) took up station in the Persian Gulf, the U.S. Joint Task Force Middle East (JTFME) maintained a permanent presence in the region. Becoming part of CENTCOM (Central Command) in 1988, JTFME normally consisted of less than a dozen ships. For more than 40 years it served as a symbol of U.S. interests in the Gulf, and on several occasions, such as Operation Earnest Will in 1987–1988 (the reflagging of Kuwaiti oil tankers during the Iran-Iraq War), as a base for larger U.S. operations.

JTFME gave the United States a head start in the Persian Gulf War. It provided the operational experience needed to establish patrol areas and rendezvous points, making possible the rapid organization of the maritime interception program.

When the Kuwaiti crisis began, there were six U.S. Navy ships on station in the Gulf, and JTFME was designated Naval Component, Central Command (NAVCENT). On August 15, 1990, the commander of the Seventh U.S. Fleet assumed command of NAVCENT and the JTFME was disbanded.

See also BAHRAIN; NAVY, U.S.; SEVENTH U.S. FLEET.

Suggestion for further reading: Department of Defense, *Conduct of the Persian Gulf War: Final Report to the Congress,* "Appendix D: Preparedness" (Washington, D.C.: USGPO, 1992).

JORDAN

A member of the Arab League, Jordan was one of the few Arab states that supported Iraq during the Persian Gulf War. It ostensibly remained neutral but, in contravention of the United Nations-mandated sanctions, turned a blind eye to the massive smuggling of contraband to Iraq through its territory.

Formed out of the old British protectorate of Transjordan, Jordan gained its independence in 1946. During the Arab-Israeli war of 1948, it annexed the west bank of the Jordan River and the city of Jerusalem, but lost both in the next Arab-Israeli war in 1967. Jordan was then flooded with Palestinian refugees. A 1974 Arab summit conference designated the Palestine Liberation Organization (PLO) as the refugees' sole representative, and until the Gulf War, Jordan received an annual subsidy from Arab oil- producing nations.

Bordering Israel to the west, Iraq to the east, Syria to the north and Saudi Arabia to the south, Jordan is slightly larger than the state of Indiana. Sixty percent of its 3,412,000 people are Palestinian refugees. Its port on the Gulf of Aqaba was Iraq's main maritime outlet, handling an average of 2,300 tons of cargo each day from some 500 ships each year. In return, Jordan received a daily shipment of 35,000 barrels of Iraqi oil.

King ibn Talal Hussein, Jordan's ruler since 1952, succeeded his grandfather, King Abdullah, who was assassinated by a Palestinian radical. In order to survive, his government had to take into account the sensitivities of the Palestinian refugees. Saddam Hussein's immense popularity among this group, and the PLO's endorsement of Iraqi aggression, was a primary factor in Jordan's "tilt" toward Iraq. In compliance with United Nations demands, however, Jordan did close its port at Aqaba to Iraqi shipping.

Suggestions for further reading: For a discussion of the dilemma that King Hussein faced, see Scott MacLeod, "In the Wake of Desert Storm," *New York Review of Books,* March 7, 1991. For Jordanian public attitudes during the war, see Michael Kelly, *Martyrs' Day: Chronicle of a Small War* (New York: Random House, 1993).

JSTARS (JOINT SURVEILLANCE TARGET ATTACK SYSTEM)

Still in development by the Grumman Aerospace Corporation and not due to be fielded until 1997, two prototype Joint Surveillance Target Attack Systems (JSTARS) aircraft were deployed to the Kuwaiti Theater of Operations (KTO) with their civilian technicans on January 12, 1991, and began flying operational missions two days later.

A modified E-8A aircraft, a military version of the Boeing 707, JSTARS carries a flight crew of four plus 17 to 25 mission specialists. JSTARS is a joint Army-Air Force program designed to provide a near-real-time wide-area surveillance and deep targeting capability to ground and air commanders.

The JSTARS radar provides information on both moving and fixed targets. A frequency-hopping Ku-band surveillance control data link (SCDL) provides ground station module (GSM) operators the same radar data that are available to onboard operators, for processing, analyzing and dissemination to tactical ground commanders.

Six interim ground station modules (IGCM), each mounted on a five-ton truck, were deployed to Saudi Arabia. One was allocated to the Third Army, one to the Ninth Air Force, one to the First Marine Expeditionary Force, one to the Third Army forward and one each to VII Corps and XVIII Airborne Corps.

By all reports, JSTAR proved enormously successful during the Persian Gulf War. It was credited with detecting, locating and tracking enemy supply depots, troop assembly areas and convoys. On January 29, 1991, for example, it detected an Iraqi convoy moving south from Kuwait City and called in coalition air strikes, which destroyed 58 of its 61 vehicles.

Also important was what JSTARS did not see. During the battle for Khafji, JSTARS did not see the Iraqis reinforcing their initial attack elements, and its reports of the lack of enemy activity greatly facilitated the Arab Joint Forces Command East's counterattack.

Suggestions for further reading: Department of Defense, *Conduct of the Persian Gulf War: Final Report to the Congress,* "Appendix T: Performance of Selected Weapon Systems" (Washington, D.C.: USGPO, 1992); Richard P. Hallion, *Storm Over Iraq: Air Power and the Gulf War* (Washington, D.C.: Smithsonian Institution Press, 1992.)

JUST WAR

Derived from the 4th-century writings of Saint Augustine as refined by Saint Thomas Aquinas in the 13th century, classic just-war theory has two main parts, *jus ad bellum,* the decision to go to war, and *jus in bello,* the conduct of war itself.

In order for a war to be "just," the decision to go to war must be made by a *proper authority,* it must involve a *just cause* and it must have the *right intentions.* Further, the war must have a *reasonable chance of success,* the good that might be achieved has to be *proportionate* to the evil that would be caused, and the war must be waged only as a *last resort.*

In the conduct of war, excessive use of military force is to be avoided and the means used must be in *proportion* to the ends to be achieved and in accordance with the positive rules of war. Finally, *discrimination* must be used to avoid harming nonbelligerents and civilians.

Acknowledging the relevance of just-war theory to the modern world, the official U.S. Department of Defense report on the Gulf War includes an appendix on the role of the law of war, covering the concepts of *jus ad bellum* and *jus in bello.*

See also WAR CRIMES.

Suggestions for further reading: Department of Defense, *Conduct of the Persian Gulf War: Final Report to the Congress,* "Appendix O: The Role of the Law of War" (Washington, D.C.: USGPO, 1992); Jean Bethke Elshtain et al., *But Was It Just? Reflections on the Morality of the Persian Gulf War* (New York: Doubleday, 1992); James Turner Johnson and George Weigel, *Just War and the Gulf War* (Lanham, Md.: University Press of America, 1991). See also Richard John Neuhaus, "Just War and This War," *Wall Street Journal,* January 29, 1991; Tom Roberts and Gary O'Guinn, "Persian Gulf Makes 'Just War' Debate No Longer Academic," *Washington Post,* February 2, 1991; Nicholas G. Fotion, "The Gulf War: Cleanly Fought," and George A. Lopez, "The Gulf War: Not So Clean," *Bulletin of the Atomic Scientists,* September 1991.

K

KHAFJI, BATTLE OF

The first major ground engagement of the Persian Gulf War occurred on January 29, 1991, with a surprise attack by elements of Iraq's 5th Mechanized Division and 3d Armored Division on Ras Al-Khafji, a small undefended town on the Saudi-Kuwaiti border that had been evacuated earlier in the crisis. A small U.S. Marine reconnaissance team was in the town at the time but remained concealed during the subsequent action.

The attack on Khafji was part of a larger Iraqi probe of coalition defenses that involved five separate attacks. The first cross-border attack, by an Iraqi armored brigade 17 miles west of Al-Wafrah, was repulsed by a U.S. Marine light armored infantry (LAI) battalion supported by coalition tactical air; the Iraqis lost 10 tanks, and four of their soldiers were taken prisoner. That probe was followed by an attack by an Iraqi mechanized infantry battalion north of Khafji, where it met a screening force of the 2d Saudi Arabian National Guard (SANG) that was also supported by coalition tactical air. Outnumbered, the screening force broke contact with the enemy and withdrew to the south after destroying 13 Iraqi vehicles. Elements of the Iraqi battalion then occupied Khafji.

In the early morning of January 30, additional Iraqi mechanized infantry and tanks crossed the Saudi border 20 miles northwest of Khafji and were met by a Marine LAI battalion supported by coalition tactical air, which drove them back across the border. Later that morning, another force of 40 Iraqi tanks crossed the border west of Al-Wafrah, where it also was engaged and thrown back by a Marine LAI battalion supported by additional tactical air. The Marines destroyed 15 enemy tanks and captured nine prisoners without suffering any losses. On the afternoon of January 30, yet another Iraqi mechanized infantry battalion was reported on the Saudi border north of Khafji, but it withdrew after coming under coalition air and ground attack.

The counterattack to retake Khafji began at 2:30 A.M. on January 31. Qatari forces blocked to the north

and the 8th Royal Saudi Land Forces (RSLF) Brigade blocked to the south while the 2d SANG Task Force—supported by U.S. Marine artillery, U.S. naval gunfire and coalition tactical air—launched a ground attack to expel the enemy. After several hours of intense fighting, and at a cost of 29 Saudis killed and 36 wounded, the Saudi forces cleared the town. Continuing the attack, they engaged the remaining Iraqi armored forces seven miles to the north, taking 160 prisoners. The battle ended on February 2 with the Arab forces repulsing an Iraqi company-size armor attack.

According to the official DOD report, the battle of Khafji had three major consequences. It exposed the limitations of the Iraqi ground forces and confirmed their vulnerability to coalition tactics. It bolstered the morale and self-confidence of the Arab coalition forces. And, most importantly, it "erased any misperception there may have been on the part of other Coalition members as to the quality of the Arab troops."

See also JSTARS (JOINT SURVEILLANCE TARGET ATTACK SYSTEM).

Suggestions for further reading: Department of Defense, *Conduct of the Persian Gulf War: Final Report to the Congress,* "Chapter 6: The Air Campaign" and "Appendix I: Coalition Development, Coordination and Warfare" (Washington, D.C.: USGPO, 1992); Richard P. Hallion, *Storm Over Iraq: Air Power and the Gulf War* (Washington, D.C.: Smithsonian Institution Press, 1992); Major James Blackwell, *Thunder in the Desert: The Strategy and Tactics of the Persian Gulf War* (New York: Bantam Books, 1991).

KOREA, REPUBLIC OF

See COALITION FORCES; COST.

KTO (KUWAITI THEATER OF OPERATIONS)

Established by White House Executive Order 12744, January 21, 1991, the KTO (Kuwaiti Theater of Operations) included the following locations, including the airspace above such locations:

- the Persian Gulf
- the Red Sea
- the Gulf of Oman
- that portion of the Arabian Sea that lies north of 10 degrees north latitude and west of 68 degrees east longtitude
- the Gulf of Aden
- the total land areas of Iraq, Kuwait, Saudi Arabia, Oman, Bahrain, Qatar, and the United Arab Emirates

KURDS

Still unresolved, the Kurdish crisis both preceded and followed the Persian Gulf War.

Numbering more than 27 million, the Kurds have existed as a tribal people with their own culture and tradition and language for at least 3,000 years. But despite their strong desire for independence, they have never been united under a single ruler, and "Kurdistan" remains only a dream.

Some 4.8 million Kurds live in the mountainous regions of northern Iraq, some 6.7 million in north-western Iran, and approximately 14 million in south-eastern Turkey. There are about 1.4 million Kurds in Syria and Lebanon, and about half a million in the Transcaucasian states of the former Soviet Union. Most are Sunni Muslims, their ancestors having been converted to Islam in the 7th century.

The Kurds have often revolted against the governments of the countries in which they reside. In the 1970s, the Kurds in Iraq battled the Baghdad government and supported Iran in the 1980–1988 Iran-Iraq War. In late 1987, Saddam Hussein exacted his revenge, razing 3,000 Kurdish villages and using poison gas to kill thousands of Kurdish men, women and children.

In March 1991, following Iraq's defeat in the Persian Gulf War, the Kurds in Iraq again rose in revolt, capturing much of northeastern Iraq. When the Iraqi military counterattacked in the spring of 1991, about 1.5 million Kurds took refuge in the mountains of Iraq, Turkey and Iran. With the Kurds living in appalling conditions and with many dying every day from cold and hunger, pressure was put on the international community to intervene.

From April to July 1991, the United Kingdom, the Netherlands, Turkey, France and the United States deployed air and ground forces to provide short-term security and relief supplies to the Kurds. Called Operation Provide Comfort by the United States and Operation Haven by the Europeans, this "armed relief effort" provided protection and humanitarian aid to some 800,000 Kurdish refugees.

By June 1991, most of the Iraqi Kurds had returned to their homes and the allied troops had begun to withdraw. A residual allied Combined Task Force remained in Turkey, however, and a "no-fly" zone over the area north of the 36th parallel, established in April 1991 to protect the Kurds from Iraqi air attack, has remained in effect into the Clinton administration. As recently as August 1993, U.S. warplanes attacked Iraqi antiaircraft artillery positions and air defense radar sites in the area.

A similar "no-fly" zone has been established in southern Iraq to protect the Shiites.

See also SHIITE REVOLT.

Suggestions for further reading: "The Kurdish Problem in Iraq," *Background Briefs* (London: Foreign and Commonwealth Office, May 1992); John Bulloch and Harvey Morris, *No Friends but the Mountains: The Tragic History of the Kurds* (New York: Oxford University Press, 1992). Michael Kelly, *Martyrs' Day: Chronicle of a Small War* (New York: Random House, 1993). For the allied relief effort, see Major General R. Ross, "Some Early Lessons From Operation Safe Haven," *RUSI Journal,* Winter 1991; and Tim Ripley, "Operation Provide Comfort II," *International Defense Review,* October 1991.

KUWAIT

A member of both the Arab League and the Gulf Cooperation Council (GCC), Kuwait was invaded by Iraq on August 2, 1990, triggering the Persian Gulf War.

With a land area of 6,880 square miles, Kuwait is slightly smaller than New Jersey. With its capital at Kuwait City, the country is flat, very dry and extremely hot. Located at the head of the Persian Gulf, it is bordered by Iraq to the north and Saudi Arabia to the south.

Kuwait has been ruled by the Sabah dynasty since 1789; its current head of state is the emir Sheik Jabir al-Ahmad al-Sabah. Kuwait was a British protectorate from 1899 until it declared its independence in 1961. Kuwaitis are a minority in their own country, making up only 28 percent of Kuwait's 1991 population of 2,024,000; other Arabs, mainly Palestinians, make up 39 percent, with the remainder being Iranians, Indians, and Pakistanis.

With oil reserves estimated at 94 billion barrels, Kuwait is one of the world's major oil producing nations. It was a dispute over oil production that precipitated the war, although Iraq had long harbored designs on its neighbor.

Kuwait suffered brutally during the Iraqi occupation. An estimated 1,082 civilians were murdered, and several thousand remain missing (see WAR CRIMES). "The crushing weight of Iraqi military superiority did not deter thousands of brave [Kuwaiti] men and women who chose to resist the invaders and fight on from inside Kuwait," notes the official Department of Defense report on the war. "Despite acts of vicious retribution by the occupying force—often including the abuse or murder of Kuwaitis in the presence of their family members—the Resistance tied down an estimated two divisions of Iraqi occupation troops in Kuwait City. . . ."

Unable to hold off the Iraqi attack, the Kuwaiti armed forces had fallen back and regrouped in Saudi Arabia. They would take an active part in the fight to liberate their country. Two Kuwaiti naval craft, the *Istiqlal* and the *Al Sanbouk,* retook oil platforms and some of the Gulf islands. The Kuwaiti Air Force, including some 24 A-4 fighters and 16 Mirage F-1 fighters, were part of the coalition's air campaign, while Kuwaiti Army units were part of the Arab/Islamic Joint Forces Command that liberated Kuwait City on February 27, 1991. The 15th Infantry and 35th Mechanized Brigades were part of Joint Forces Command-North, and the Al-Fatah Brigade was part of Task Force Othman in Joint Forces Command-East.

See also AIR FORCES, COALITION; ARAB LEAGUE; ARMIES, COALITION; GULF COOPERATION COUNCIL; INVASION OF KUWAIT; JOINT FORCES COMMAND; NAVIES, COALITION; PRISONERS OF WAR; WAR CRIMES.

Suggestions for further reading: Department of Defense, *Conduct of the Persian Gulf War: Final Report to the Congress,* "Appendix I: Coalition Development, Coordination and Warfare" (Washington, D.C.: USGPO, 1992), Michael Kelly, "The Rape and Rescue of Kuwait City," *The New Republic,* March 25, 1991. See also Michael Kelly, *Martyrs' Day: Chronicle of a Small War* (New York: Random House, 1993); Jill Crystal, *Kuwait: The Transformation of an Oil State* (Boulder, Colo.: Westview Press, 1992); Jadranka Porter, *Under Siege in Kuwait* (New York: Houghton Mifflin, 1991); Jean P. Sasson, *The Rape of Kuwait: The True Stories of Iraqi Atrocities Against a Civilian Population* (New York: Knightsbridge Publishing Company, 1991).

LAND TRANSPORTATION NETWORK

Because of the absence of railroads and inland waterways in the Kuwaiti Theater of Operations, a huge burden was placed on the region's roads and highways during the Persian Gulf War. Although intratheater airlift moved many coalition passengers (see AIRLIFT), it could not move the enormous tonnages of ammunition and supplies. The only railroad in Saudi Arabia was a single track between the port of Ad-Dammam and Riyadh. While helpful, it played only a minor role, as did U.S. Army watercraft and coastal barges, which moved cargo from the primary seaports to other ports on the Persian Gulf coast of Saudi Arabia.

In addition to the trucks of the deploying units, some 2,600 vehicles were distributed from pre-positioned supplies. The arrival of the U.S. Army's 7th Transportation Command in August 1990 gave short-term relief, but it, too, was soon overwhelmed and a serious backup developed at the port areas.

On-the-spot contracting of trucks and buses helped ease the burden, as did the hiring of more than 2,000 civilian drivers, who, along with commercial vehicles, were organized into battalions with cadres of American soldiers. Concerned about the civilians' wartime reliability, the Army Support Command arranged for 3,000 American soldiers to act as backup drivers, and the Marine Corps made similar arrangements for its civilian truck fleet.

"Contracting and host-nation-support solved much of the transportation problem," according to the official Department of Defense report on the war. "Eventually more than half of the heavy transportation assets were either contracted commercial trucks or trucks provided by other nations. Japan contributed almost 2,000 4x4s, water trucks, refrigerator vans, and fuel vehicles."

Another complication was the highway system itself. Although there were modern roads along the Saudi coast and around the major cities, the inland transportation network was meager. There were only two east-west highways capable of handling the large volume of traffic needed to shift the Third U.S.

Despite the deployment of thousands of vehicles to the Gulf, trucks were always in short supply.
U.S. Army photo courtesy of 24th Infantry Division (Mechanized).

Army, and the supplies needed to sustain it, the hundreds of miles from its eastern assembly areas to its attack positions in the west.

The northern MSR (Main Supply Route) was the Tapline Road, a paved highway that crosses northern Saudi Arabia parallel to the Trans-Arabian Pipeline. The southern MSR ran from the port at Dhahran southwest through Riyadh and then northwest to the theater logistics base at King Khalid Military City (KKMC).

The distances over both MSRs were extensive. From the port of Dhahran to KKMC along the northern MSR was 334 miles, and 528 miles along the southern route. The forward attack positions of the westernmost unit, the U.S. XVIII Airborne Corps, were more than 500 miles from the ports by the northern route and 696 miles by the southern road.

The northern MSR was restricted to tactical support, including the transportation of combat troops, tanks, armored vehicles, weapons and ammunition. C-130 transports also used portions of The Tapline Road as an airstrip. All other supplies, including the bulk of the fuel and ammunition, were transported along the southern MSR. In addition, U.S. engineers and Saudi contractors helped expand the limited road network by constructing or maintaining more than 2,150 miles of secondary roads. To increase the road network's efficiency, 24-hour truck stops with fuel, latrines, food, sleeping tents and limited repair facilities were established along the MSRs.

According to the official DOD statistics, during the three weeks before the commencement of the ground campaign some 1,400 U.S. Army and 2,100 Saudi vehicles logged more than 35 million miles, including more than 1,700 moves by Heavy Equipment Transporters, 5,800 moves by lowboys and 10,100 trips by flatbed trucks. Moving 24 hours a day and often departing at 15-second intervals, these convoys moved two entire combat corps hundreds of miles to their initial attack positions.

The coalition's transportation effort was one of the most extensive in history.

See also HEMTT (HEAVY EXPANDED MOBILITY TACTICAL TRUCK); HET (HEAVY EQUIPMENT TRANSPORTER); LOGISTICS, U.S.

Suggestions for further reading: Department of Defense, *Conduct of the Persian Gulf War: Final Report to the Congress,* "Chapter 8: The Ground Campaign" "Appendix F: Logistics Buildup and Sustainment" (Washington, D.C.: USGPO, 1992); Lt. Gen. William G. Pagonis with Jeffrey L. Cruikshank, *Moving Mountains* (Cambridge: Harvard Business School Press, 1992).

LANTIRN (LOW-ALTITUDE NAVIGATIONAL AND TARGETING INFRARED FOR NIGHT)

Still under development when the Gulf War began, ·LANTIRN (Low-Altitude Navigational and Targeting Infrared for Night) provided U.S. Air Force aircraft with a previously unavailable capability for night operations.

The total package consisted of a wide field-of-view heads-up display (i.e., flight, navigational and attack information was superimposed on the pilot's forward field of view); a navigational pod housing a terrain-following radar and a wide field-of-view forward-looking infrared (FLIR) system; and a targeting pod with a high-resolution FLIR, a missile boresight correlator and a laser ranging and designation system.

The complete LANTIRN system was mounted on F-15E Eagle fighters, whose targeting pods were shipped to them after they had arrived in the Kuwaiti Theater of Operations (KTO). Flying almost entirely at night, the 48 F-15E aircraft of the two squadrons deployed to the Gulf flew 2,210 sorties and dropped 1,700 GBU-10 2,000-pound laser-guided bombs and GBU-12 500-pound laser-guided bombs and other munitions.

The LANTIRN system was extremely effective. For example, on one occasion 16 enemy armored vehicles were destroyed by two F-15Es carrying eight GBU-12s each.

LANTIRN navigational pods were also mounted on some F-16 Fighting Falcon aircraft, but because only a limited number of targeting pods were available, no F-16s were equipped with them.

See also NIGHT VISION DEVICES.

Suggestions for further reading: For the performance of the F-15E and F-16, see Department of Defense, *Conduct of the Persian Gulf War: Final Report to the Congress,* "Appendix T: Performance of Selected Weapon Systems" (Washington, D.C.: USGPO, 1992). For details on LANTIRN, see Richard P. Hallion, *Storm Over Iraq: Air Power and the Gulf War* (Washington, D.C.: Smithsonion Institution Press, 1992).

LAV (LIGHT ARMORED VEHICLE)
See ARMOR.

LAW AND ORDER
Although no statistics are available for other coalition forces, misconduct and indiscipline among U.S. servicemen and women during the Persian Gulf War were remarkably infrequent. There were some courts-martial in the United States for desertion and for mutiny, but even these were rare compared with those during previous wars.

Among the more than 532,000 U.S. military personnel deployed to the Persian Gulf, there were 3,506 reported cases of wrongdoing, only 191 of which were serious enough to be tried by courts-martial. This indiscipline rate of 3.7 per 10,000 compares with a normal peacetime rate of 71 per 10,000. One reason for this low rate of indiscipline was the absence among U.S. troops of alcoholic beverages, which were prohibited by Islamic law. Another reason was the relative isolation of most units from civilian population centers. A third reason was that the personnel serving in the Gulf War were more mature, better educated and better trained than their counterparts in previous wars.

Because of this low rate of indiscipline, the infractions that did occur received widespread publicity. One news story headlined the fact that among the more than 300,000 soldiers serving in the Gulf there were 13 cases of malingering—trying to harm oneself to avoid combat—all but 2 of which occurred before the shooting started. Another news story reported that 12 male and 4 female soldiers (again out of a force of more than 300,000 Army personnel) were prosecuted for homosexual activities while in the Kuwaiti Theater of Operations (KTO). Yet of the more than 33,000 women deployed to the KTO, only 24 were reportedly sexually assaulted.

"The phenomenal thing about this operation has been the exceptionally low level of acts of indiscipline," said Colonel Raymond C. Ruppert, the CENTCOM (Central Command) judge advocate general, in a 1991 interview with the *Los Angeles Times*. "The number of offenses that have occurred [is] remarkably low."

See also CONSCIENTIOUS OBJECTORS, U.S.; MOBILIZATION, U.S.; WAR CRIMES.

Suggestions for further reading: Tracy Wilkinson, "In Alcohol-Free Gulf, GIs Stayed Out of Hot Water," *Los Angeles Times*, April 1, 1991; John Lancaster, "24 Women Assaulted on Gulf Duty," *Washington Post*, July 21, 1991; Greg Seigle, "Gulf War Malingering Probed," *Army Times*, August 3, 1992; Greg Seigle, "16 Gays in Army Tried in Gulf War," *Washington Times*, June 28, 1993.

LOGISTICS, IRAQ

Wartime logistics includes not only maintaining sufficient quantities of the means for waging war—tanks, aircraft, spare parts, ammunition, petroleum, food and the like—but also the means for delivering those supplies to the troops at the front in a timely manner. The tonnages involved in military logistics are enormous. As logistics analysts have pointed out, each day an armored division can use up to 600,000 gallons of fuel, and a mechanized division can consume up to 75 tons of food, 108,000 gallons of water and 3,500 tons of ammunition.

Despite the United Nations embargo on trade with Iraq (see SANCTIONS), the supplies themselves

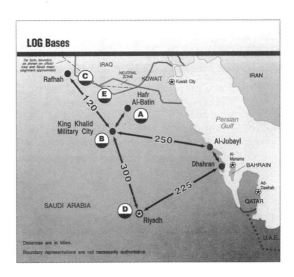

were not a problem. Iraq had its own petroleum refineries and produced some artillery and ammunition in its own factories. Iraq was estimated to have stockpiled at least a year's supply of spare parts, ammunition and food prior to the outbreak of hostilities.

Delivering these supplies to the battlefield ought to have been simple. Unlike the United States, which had to transport most of its supplies some 8,000 miles overseas to reach the battlefield (see LOGISTICS, U.S.), Iraq had to supply its military in its own homeland and in a neighboring country. When it came to supplying its troops in or near Kuwait, Iraq could take advantage of four major highways and a rail line running from central Iraq and converging at Az Zubayr, south of Basra; three airfields within southern Iraq (Safwan, Shaibah and Jalibah); and three airfields in Kuwait.

Iraqi logistics employed a "push" system in which supplies were managed by the General Headquarters (GHQ) in Baghdad. When a need arose, GHQ delivered the supplies to a forward depot, which then distributed them to the forward corps. Forward depots were located south and west of Basra, and it is likely that Kuwait City was used as a corps support area. Other depots were located along Kuwait's northern border and along Highway 8 on the south bank of the Euphrates River.

Below the corps level, units used a "pull" system in which supplies were requested from the corps depots; divisions assigned a transportation battalion and brigades a transportation company to the resupply operations. Since the corps depots were 100 to 200 kilometers from frontline troops, however, the supply routes were particularly vulnerable to air interdiction.

By February 11, 1991, according to the American logistics expert Joel Nadel, coalition air interdiction had reduced Iraqi supply routes to 30 percent of their prewar capacity. Although air strikes did not completely cut them off, convoys were reduced in size from 200 vehicles to about 20–30 vehicles. "The bombing campaign had completely wrecked the Iraqi distribution system," Nadel concluded, "because Coalition forces overran significant stockpiles of food and ammunition in Kuwait and Iraq, indicating that supplies were available, but Iraq could not get them to its soldiers."

See also LOGISTICS, U.S.

Suggestion for further reading: Joel H. Nadel, "Logistics Lessons," in *Military Lessons of the Gulf War,* ed. Bruce W. Watson (Novato, Calif.: Presidio Press, 1991).

LOGISTICS, U.S.

Logistics are the very sinews of war and thus played a critical role in the Persian Gulf War (Iraqi logistics are discussed elsewhere; see LOGISTICS, IRAQ). Non-Arab coalition forces were supported in the main by the United States while Arab coalition forces drew from their own local supplies. As discussed below, Arab coalition partners also provided host-nation support to U.S. forces.

Logistics had always been viewed as the greatest constraint on the ability of U.S. Central Command (CENTCOM) to accomplish its mission in the Middle East. One reason was the enormous distance involved and the relative inaccessibility of the area. Another reason was the reluctance of the nations in the region to allow the prepositioning of wartime arms and equipment on their soil.

Although U.S. Army and Air Force Afloat Prepositioned Ships (APS) and Navy and Marine Corps Maritime Prepositioning Squadrons (MPS) were anchored at the nearby island of Diego Garcia in the Indian Ocean, these provided only an initial combat capability. And while the U.S. Transportation Command's Military Airlift Command (MAC) could move personnel and supplies rapidly into the area, it did not have the lift capability to move the tanks

and other heavy equipment and the enormous tonnages of ammunition, supplies and equipment that would be needed.

Another complicating factor in the Gulf War was the fact that when the crisis began, the threat of an imminent Iraqi invasion of Saudi Arabia prompted a decision to give priority to the deployment of combat troops at the expense of their logistic support units. An additional complication was the fact that most combat support and combat service support units are in the Reserve components, which require a presidential order calling them to active duty before they can provide the logistic support needed to sustain the forces in the field.

These were the challenges facing Major General William G. Pagonis, CENTCOM's chief logistician, when he arrived in Riyadh on August 8, 1990. Doctrine called for establishing a Theater Army Area Command (TAACOM), and on August 18, ARCENT (Army Component, CENTCOM—i.e, the Third U.S. Army) created the ARCENT SUPCOM (Support Command), later designated the 22d Theater Army Support Command, with Pagonis at its head.

As the APS and MPS arrived from Diego Garcia and began to unload their cargo, the logistics system began to improve. In early September, the Saudi Arabian government agreed to provide at no cost all the food, fuel, water facilities and local transportation for all U.S. forces in the Kuwaiti Theater of Operations (KTO). This host-nation support (HNS), which was also extended by other Gulf nations, greatly eased the logistics burden. Saudi Arabia alone provided approximately 4,800 tents; 1.7 million gallons of packaged petroleum, oil and lubricants; more than 300 heavy equipment transporters; approximately 20 million meals; on average more than 20.5 million gallons of fuel per day; and bottled water for personnel in the entire theater.

Also in September 1990, XVIII Airborne Corps's 1st Corps Support Command (COSCOM) arrived in-theater, followed in November by VII Corps's 2d COSCOM. Each Army division also had its own division support commands (DISCOMs) for internal support.

SUPCOM (the 22d Theater Army Support Command), which at the height of the war drew more than 70 percent of its personnel from the Reserve components, not only provided logistical support for U.S. Army forces, it was also the executive agent for

More than 220,000 120-mm tank rounds were sealifted to the Gulf.
U.S. Army photo (George Proctor) courtesy of 24th Infantry Division (Mechanized).

food, water, bulk fuel, common ground munitions, port operations, inland cargo transportation, construction support and graves registration for all U.S. forces and for some other coalition forces as well.

In preparation for the ground offensive, the SUPCOM support plan included five phases. Phase Alpha involved repositioning support units and stocks to newly constructed large logistics bases along the northern main supply route. Phase Bravo involved the simultaneous movement of VII Corps and XVIII Airborne Corps to their attack positions (see LAND TRANSPORTATION NETWORK). Phase Charlie entailed support of the ground campaign, including transport of supplies—especially fuel, water and ammunition—as well as construction of new logistics bases deep in Iraq to sustain the offensive. Phase Delta involved support of the restoration of facilities in Kuwait, and Phase Echo focused on preparations for the long-term defense of Kuwait.

Beyond the common items drawn from the Army, Air Force and Navy, units were generally self-sustaining. Air Force units deployed with 30-days' worth of supplies and were sustained by prepositioned stocks and a series of bare-base "Harvest" contingency packages. "Harvest Falcon," for example, was designed to support 55,000 people and 750 aircraft at 14 separate locations. It included hard-wall shelters, tents, vehicles, material handling equipment, power generating and distribution equipment, kitchens, water purification equipment and airfield support equipment.

Much as they do in peacetime, Combat Logistics Force (CLF) ships supported the Navy's battle groups in the Persian Gulf and the Red Sea; they also supported more than 100 other coalition ships in the Persian Gulf. CLF ships, along with various MSC (Military Sealift Command) and RRF (Ready Reserve Force) ships, were responsible for the logistics support of more than 115 combatants. The CLF ships, in turn, were resupplied from such forward expeditionary logistics sites as Jidda on the Red Sea coast of Saudi Arabia, Fujairah in the United Arab Emirates, Masirah in Oman, Hurghada in Egypt, and ports in Djibouti and Bahrain.

Marine Corps logistics elements are integral parts of the Marine Air Ground Task Force (MAGTF) organization, which at all levels includes air, ground and logistics elements. Supporting the First Marine Expeditionary Force (I MEF) were the 1st and 2d Force Service Support Groups (FSSGs). The 1st FSSG, under the command of Brigadier General James A. Brabham, assumed the general support role for I MEF and for Marine elements of the Amphibious Task Force, as well as the job of maintaining the port of Al-Jubayl. When the 2d FSSG, under the command of Brigadier General Charles C. Krulak, arrived in the KTO, it assumed the responsibility for running the direct support logistics for the forthcoming battle. At the height of Desert Storm, I MEF's supply lines stretched more than 250 miles from the logistics center at Al-Jubayl.

In war the bottom line for logisticians, as for strategists and tacticians, is victory on the battlefield. By that criterion alone, U.S. logistics in the Gulf War was a success. In the course of the war, 4 million tons of equipment and supplies were moved into position, more than 122 million meals were prepared and distributed, 31,880 tons of mail were delivered and 1.3 billion gallons of gasoline were pumped.

But all was not as rosy as it appeared. According to December 1991 General Accounting Office (GAO) report on the war, "a major factor in the successful buildup of U.S. forces was that Iraq's defensive military tactics allowed the U.S. to (1) dictate when the war would commence and (2) prosecute the war on U.S. terms." U.S. military planners also failed to anticipate the vast distances involved in the war. "Under military doctrine," noted the GAO report, "the Army and Marine Corps are equipped to operate up to 90 miles and 30 miles respectively from their main supply bases." During Operation Desert Storm, however, the Army supported operations more than 600 miles from its main logistics bases, and the Marines supported operations more than 250 miles away.

Yet, as a Senate staff member concluded, "when you look at the number of miles they moved, and

how quickly they were able to move and go deep into Iraq and be sustained with fuel and ammunition, it is what I think future historians will call a logistical miracle."

See also DEPLOYMENT OF U.S. FORCES; LAND TRANSPORTATION NETWORK; LOGISTICS, IRAQ; PAGONIS, WILLIAM G.

Suggestions for further reading: Department of Defense, *Conduct of the Persian Gulf War: Final Report to the Congress,* "Appendix F: Logistics Buildup and Sustainment" (Washington, D.C.: USGPO, 1992); Lt. Gen. William G. Pagonis with Jeffrey L. Cruikshank, *Moving Mountains* (Cambridge: Harvard Business School Press, 1992); Brig. Gen. Charles C. Krulak, "CSS in the Desert," *Marine Corps Gazette,* October 1991; John Lancaster, "Logistical Shortcomings of 'Desert Storm' Cited," *Washington Post,* December 31, 1991.

LUCK, GARY E(DWARD), LIEUTENANT GENERAL, USA (1937–)

The commander of XVIII Airborne Corps during the Persian Gulf War, General Gary E. Luck entered the U.S. Army through the Reserve Officer Training Corps program at Kansas State University and was commissioned a second lieutenant of armor in 1960.

He was a Special Forces "A" Team commander in Vietnam, and later commanded a troop of the 3d Squadron, 17th Air Cavalry in combat there. After returning from Vietnam, he gained a Master of Business Administration degree from Florida State University and a Doctor of Philosophy degree in business administration from George Washington University in Washington, D.C.

Among his significant assignments are chief of staff, 8th Infantry Division in Germany; assistant division commander, 101st Airborne Division at Fort Campbell, Kentucky; commanding general, 2d Infantry Division in Korea; commanding general, Joint Special Operations Command; and commanding general, U.S. Army Special Operations Command at Fort Bragg, North Carolina.

General Luck deployed the XVIII Airborne Corps to the KTO (Kuwaiti Theater of Operations) in August 1990 as part of the United States's immediate reaction to the Iraqi invasion of Kuwait. Until November 1990 his corps was the major U.S. ground force in Saudi Arabia.

Holding down the left flank of the coalition attack, General Luck's XVIII Airborne Corps hooked around the enemy to cut off his lines of retreat.
U.S. Army photo courtesy of XVIII Airborne Corps.

XVIII Airborne Corps consisted of the 24th Infantry Division (Mechanized), the 82d Airborne Division, the 101st Airborne Division (Air Assault) and the 6th French Light Armored Division. Corps troops included the 3d Armored Cavalry Regiment, the 12th and 18th Aviation Groups, the XVIII Airborne Corps Artillery, the III Corps Artillery and the 196th Field Artillery Brigade from the Tennessee-West Virginia-Kentucky National Guard.

XVIII Airborne Corps formed the left flank of the coalition's ground attack. It penetrated some 260 miles to the Euphrates River, cut the Iraqi lines of communication along Highway 8 to Baghdad, isolated Iraqi forces in the KTO and helped to destroy the Iraqi Republican Guard Forces Command.

General Luck's awards and decorations include the Combat Infantryman Badge, the Defense Distinguished Service Medal, 2 Army Distinguished Service Medals, 2 Legions of Merit, 3 Distinguished Flying Crosses, 2 Bronze Star Medals, a Purple Heart for wounds received in action, the Meritorious Service Medal, 16 Air Medals with "V" device, and the Army Commendation Medal. He also holds the Senior Army Aviation Badge, the Master Parachutist Badge and the Special Forces tab.

In June 1993, General Luck was promoted to four-star rank and assigned as commander in chief, United Nations Command in Korea.

See also XVIII AIRBORNE CORPS.

Suggestions for further reading: The Staff of *U.S. News & World Report, Triumph Without Victory* (New York: Times Books, 1992); Major James Blackwell, *Thunder in the Desert: The Strategy and Tactics of the Persian Gulf War* (New York: Bantam Books, 1991); General H. Norman Schwarzkopf, *It Doesn't Take a Hero* (New York: Bantam Books, 1992). For a commentary on relations between Schwarzkopf and Luck, see Rick Atkinson, *Crusade: The Untold Story of the Persian Gulf War* (New York: Houghton Mifflin, 1993).

MARCENT (MARINE FORCES CENTRAL COMMAND)

See FIRST MARINE EXPEDITIONARY FORCE (I MEF).

MARINE CORPS, U.S.

"There are four kinds of Marines," noted Marine Corps commandant General Alfred M. Gray at the height of the buildup for Operation Desert Storm. "Those in Saudi Arabia, those going to Saudi Arabia, those who want to go to Saudi Arabia, and those who

don't want to go to Saudi Arabia and are going anyway."

By January 17, 1991, on the eve of the ground war, the Marine Corps had close to 84,000 troops in the KTO (Kuwaiti Theater of Operations), almost half of its entire active duty strength. Included were 13,066 of the more than 28,000 Marine Corps reservists who had been called to active duty. Some 66,000 Marines (including some 2,200 female Marines) were ashore with the First Marine Expeditionary Force (I MEF),

Marines of the 4th Marine Expeditionary Brigade prepare to embark on the amphibious ship USS *Shreveport* (LPD-12).
U.S. Navy photo (PH3 Joe Cina), Empire Press.

and 18,000 were afloat with the Amphibious Task Force (ATF) in the Persian Gulf.

The first unit to arrive, on August 12, 1990, was the 7th Marine Expeditionary Brigade (MEB) from Twentynine Palms, California. The next day it married up with its heavy equipment, which had arrived from Diego Garcia aboard the ships of Maritime Prepositioning Squadron (MPS) 2. By August 20, the 7th MEB was in northeast Saudi Arabia, in position to repel an Iraqi attack.

On August 25, 1990, the 1st MEB began to arrive in Saudi Arabia from Hawaii by air. Its heavy equipment arrived from Guam on August 26 aboard MPS-3 ships. Elements of the 3d Marine Aircraft Wing (MAW) also arrived in-country on August 26.

On September 2, 1990, Lieutenant General Walter E. Boomer, the commander of the First Marine Expeditionary Force (I MEF), also became the commander of MARCENT (Marine Forces, Central Command), overseeing all Marine forces ashore in the KTO. On September 5, the 1st Marine Division became operational, incorporating the 1st MEB's and the 7th MEB's ground forces.

The three major elements of I MEF were now in place: the 1st Marine Division, the 3d Marine Aircraft Wing, and the 1st Force Service Support Group (FSSG). Offshore with the Amphibious Task Force was the 4th MEB and the special-operations-trained 13th Marine Expeditionary Unit (MEU).

On November 8, 1990, President George Bush announced a major reinforcement of U.S. forces in the Gulf. Marine reservists from the 4th Marine Division and the 4th Marine Aircraft Wing were called to active duty, and the 5th MEB in San Diego was ordered to the Gulf to join the Amphibious Task Force. The 2d Marine Division from Camp Lejeune, North Carolina, was also ordered to the KTO, along with the 2d FSSG and elements of the 2d Marine Aircraft Wing, which would join the already deployed 3d Marine Aircraft Wing. MPS-1 with the 2d Marine Division's heavy equipment, arrived on December 12. Completing I MEF's ranks was the "Tiger Brigade" (the Army's 1st Brigade, 2d Armored Division), which replaced the United Kingdom's 1st Armoured Division, which was detached from the Marines to join VII Corps's main attack.

I MEF's organic combat battalions now included the 1st Marine Division's 1st, 3d and 7th Marine Infantry Regiments; the 11th Marine Artillery Regi-

ment; the 1st Light Armored Infantry (LAI) Battalion; the 1st Reconnaissance Battalion; the 3d Assault Amphibian Battalion; and the 1st and 3d Tank Battalions. Also included were the 2d Marine Division's 6th and 8th Marine Infantry Regiments, the 10th Marine Artillery Regiment, the 2d LAI Battalion, the 2d Reconnaissance Battalion, the 2d Assault Amphibian Battalion and the 2d and 8th Tank Battalions.

The Third Marine Aircraft Wing consisted of the 19 fixed-wing squadrons of Marine Air Groups (MAGs) 11 and 13, and the 21 helicopter squadrons of MAGs 16 and 26.

For the most part, units of the U.S. Marine Corps Reserve (USMCR) fought as integral components of active-duty units. The USMCR 8th Tank Battalion, for example, fought with the 6th Marine Regiment, and artillery units from the USMCR 14th Marine Artillery were integrated into 10th and 11th Marine Artilleries. The USMCR units were combat-ready. Company "B" of the USMCR 4th Tank Battalion arrived in Saudi Arabia on February 19, 1991, went into action on February 25, and destroyed more than 90 Iraqi armored vehicles.

Marine F/A-18 Hornets, A-6E Intruders and AV-8 Harrier IIs flew some 18,000 sorties during the air campaign, and even before the ground campaign officially began, Marine units engaged Iraqi forces during the battle of Khafji.

At 4:00 A.M. (Gulf time) on February 24, 1991, the ground campaign began. Across a 300-mile front, U.S. Army, U.S. Marine and other coalition forces launched the largest ground campaign since World War II. While the Marine Amphibious Task Force tied down Iraqi forces in coastal defense, the First Marine Expeditionary Force, in conjunction with the Arab/Islamic Joint Forces Command, launched the supporting attack straight through the Iraqi fortifications toward Kuwait City. The ground campaign was over 100 hours after it had begun. The world's fourth largest army had been decisively defeated.

Marine Corps losses were light. Of the 84,000 Marines deployed to the KTO, 24 were killed in action and another 25 died in accidents or of other nonbattle causes. Another 92 Marines were wounded in action.

Among the decorations awarded to Marines were 2 Navy Crosses for extraordinary heroism, 11 Silver Stars for gallantry in action, 8 Distinguished Service Medals, 36 Legions of Merit, 8 Distinguished Flying Crosses and

2,950 Air Medals (2 Air Medals were also awarded to exchange officers from the United Kingdom's Royal Air Force). Fourteen female Marines won the Combat Action Ribbon after they were engaged by and returned the fire of bypassed Iraqi troops. They were the first women to win the Ribbon since the award was created during the Vietnam War.

See also AIR CAMPAIGN; AMPHIBIOUS TASK FORCE; BOOMER, WALTER E.; DECEPTION; 1ST MARINE DIVISION; FIRST MARINE EXPEDITIONARY FORCE; GROUND CAMPAIGN; KHAFJI, BATTLE OF; LOGISTICS, U.S.; MARITIME PREPOSITIONING SQUADRONS; MARITIME STRATEGIC DOCTRINE, U.S.; 2D MARINE DIVISION; 3D MARINE AIRCRAFT WING.

Suggestions for further reading: Department of Defense, *Conduct of the Persian Gulf War: Final Report to the Congress* (Washington, D.C.: USGPO, 1992); Norman Friedman, *Desert Victory: The War for Kuwait* (Annapolis, Md.: Naval Institute Press, 1991); Brig. Gen. Edwin H. Simmons, USMC (Ret.), "Getting Marines to the Gulf," and "Getting the Job Done," *U.S. Naval Institute Proceedings*, May 1991; Louis G. Caporale, "Marine Corps Historical Notes From the Gulf War," *Marine Corps Gazette*, December 1991.

MARITIME CAMPAIGN

Like the air and ground campaigns, the maritime campaign was designed to support the coalition's overall campaign plan. The maritime campaign, under the control of NAVCENT (Naval Component, Central Command—i.e., the commander, Seventh Fleet), had several dimensions. The first was the use of carrier-based aircraft to support the air campaign. Another was supporting the deception campaign by developing and maintaining an amphibious invasion capability. Yet another dimension was conducting a maritime campaign itself.

The maritime campaign involved antisurface warfare (ASUW), antiair warfare (AAW), mine countermeasures (MCM), naval gunfire support (NGFS) and amphibious warfare.

Responsible for defending the coastlines of Saudi Arabia, the United Arab Emirates (UAE), Qatar and Bahrain, and especially the critical ports of Ad-Dammam and Al-Jubayl through which most of CENTCOM's war material flowed, NAVCENT—with assistance from the United Kingdom's (UK) Royal Navy, the Royal Saudi Naval Forces and the Kuwaiti Navy—mounted an aggressive ASUW of-fensive that found and destroyed the Iraqi Navy. One hundred and forty-three Iraqi naval vessels were destroyed or damaged, and all oil platforms in the northern Persian Gulf were searched and secured. As a result, there were no attacks by Iraqi surface vessels against coalition forces.

Mindful of the Iraqi attack on the USS *Stark* with Exocet missiles during the Iran-Iraq War, NAVCENT made antiair warfare an important part of the maritime campaign. Commanded alternatively by the cruisers USS *Bunker Hill* (CG 52) and USS *Worden* (CG 18), the mission of AAW was to establish and maintain air superiority over the Persian Gulf.

Of the approximately 18,120 sorties flown by carrier-based aircraft during the war, roughly 21 percent were devoted to defensive counter-air missions. Canadian CF-18 Hornet squadrons played an important part by manning one of the northern Persian Gulf CAP (combat air patrol) stations.

The only aircraft attack attempted by the Iraqis came on January 24, 1991, when two F-1 Mirages began to attack the port of Ad-Dammam. Detected by a U.S. AWACS (Airborne Warning and Control System) aircraft, the Iraqi planes were shot down by a Saudi Royal Air Force pilot flying an F-15 Eagle.

Two Iraqi Silkworm missiles were fired at the USS *Missouri* (BB 63) on February 25, 1991. One missed and the other was shot down by Sea Dart surface-to-air missiles launched by the UK's HMS *Gloucester*.

The principal mission of the coalition's mine countermeasures (MCM) operations was to clear a path to the Kuwaiti coast for naval gunfire support and for a possible amphibious landing.

Naval gunfire support was mainly the responsibility of the two battleships deployed to the Gulf, the USS *Wisconsin* and the USS *Missouri*. The battleships fired 1,102 rounds of 16-inch shells in 83 missions.

The Marine Amphibious Task Force (ATF) accomplished its mission without having to fight. As the Department of Defense report on the war concluded, "The ATF played a vital and integral role in Operation Desert Storm." And that was precisely what the maritime campaign was designed to ensure.

See also AIR CAMPAIGN; AMPHIBIOUS TASK FORCE; BATTLESHIPS; CAMPAIGN PLAN; DECEPTION; GROUND CAMPAIGN; MARITIME INTERCEPTION OPERATIONS; MINESWEEPING; NAVY, U.S.

Suggestions for further reading: Department of Defense, *Conduct of the Persian Gulf War: Final Report*

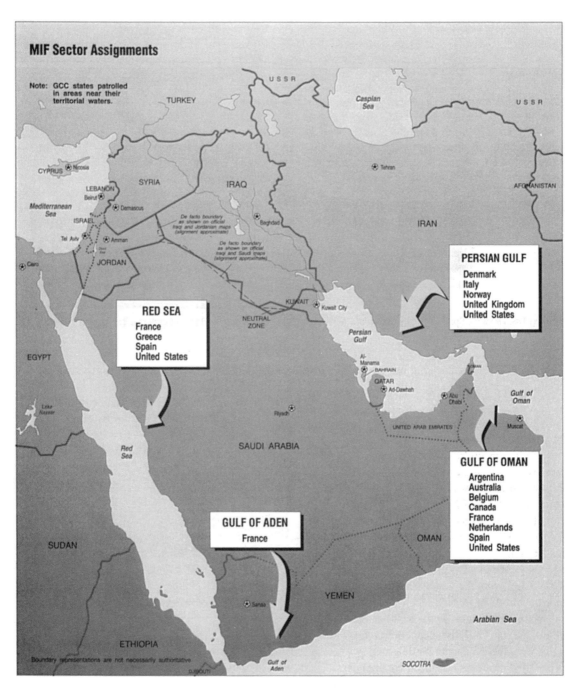

MIF Sector Assignments

Note: GCC states patrolled in areas near their territorial waters.

RED SEA
France
Greece
Spain
United States

PERSIAN GULF
Denmark
Italy
Norway
United Kingdom
United States

GULF OF OMAN
Argentina
Australia
Belgium
Canada
France
Netherlands
Spain
United States

GULF OF ADEN
France

to the Congress, "Chapter 7: The Maritime Campaign" (Washington, D.C.: USGPO, 1992); Norman Friedman, *Desert Victory: The War for Kuwait* (Annapolis, Md.: Naval Institute Press, 1991).

MARITIME INTERCEPTION OPERATIONS (MIO)

Authorized on August 25, 1990, by United Nations Security Council (UNSC) Resolution 665, maritime interception operations (MIO) were the primary means used by the coalition to enforce UNSC Resolution 661 of August 6, 1990, which mandated economic sanctions against Iraq.

Although NAVCENT (Naval Component, Central Command—i.e., the commander, Seventh U.S. Fleet) was charged with developing an operational plan for the multinational MIO, unity of effort was achieved through mutual cooperation rather than through unity of command under a single commander. Each participating country operated under its own national command authority.

In addition to the six Gulf Cooperation Council states, 13 other nations provided ships for the Maritime Interception Force (MIF). They included Argentina, Australia, Belgium, Canada, Denmark, France, Greece, Italy, the Netherlands, Norway, Spain, the United Kingdom (UK) and the United States.

MIO involved primarily surveillance of commercial shipping in the Persian Gulf, the Gulf of Oman, the Gulf of Aden, the Red Sea and the eastern Mediterranean Sea. When merchant ships were intercepted, they were queried as to their identity, their destination and their cargo. Suspect vessels were boarded for visual inspection, and if found to be

The chief, Middle East Force, whose SH-3G Sea King command helicopter is shown here, was charged with the U.S. effort to enforce United Nations economic sanctions.
U.S. Navy photo (JO2 Joe Bartlett), Empire Press.

carrying prohibited cargo, were diverted. If necessary, warning shots were fired and then a hostile takeover was conducted.

Because of their experience with similar operations, U.S. Coast Guard Law Enforcement Detachments proved invaluable in conducting the MIO. But because of the risk of potential combat with hostile crew members, forcible takeovers were carried out by Navy SEAL (sea-air-land) special operations forces and special U.S. Marine Corps teams.

During the seven months of the Persian Gulf crisis, more than 165 ships from 19 coalition navies challenged more than 7,500 merchant vessels, boarded 964 ships to inspect cargo holds, and diverted 51 ships carrying more than 1 million tons of contraband. Only 11 warning shots were fired, and only 11 hostile takeovers were necessary.

Commerce through Iraqi and Kuwaiti ports was eliminated and virtually all Iraqi oil revenues were cut off. By severely restricting Iraq's seaborne trade, MIO played a major role in intercepting materials required to sustain that country's war effort; for example, Iraq could no longer obtain arms and war material to replace its combat losses.

After the war ended, Maritime Interception Operations were continued in order to ensure Iraq's compliance with the terms of the cease-fire. Iraqi adherence has been reviewed every 60 days since then, and as of January 1994 Iraq remains in violation of the human rights provisions of the cease-fire agreement as well as of the requirement to submit to international monitoring of its weapons production facilities.

See also SANCTIONS.

Suggestion for further reading: Department of Defense, *Conduct of the Persian Gulf War: Final Report to the Congress,* "Chapter 4: Maritime Interception Operations" (Washington, D.C.: USGPO, 1992).

MARITIME PREPOSITIONING SQUADRONS (MPS)

Logistics was the Achilles' Heel of the U.S. Rapid Deployment Joint Task Force (RDJTF), and so it has been for the RDJTF's successor, U.S. Central Command (CENTCOM). An interim solution was the Near Term Prepositioning Ships (NTPS) program. By July 1980, NTPS ships loaded with wartime supplies were on station at the island of Diego Garcia in the Indian Ocean.

In 1984, the NPTS program was divided, with some ships going to the Army's and Air Force's Afloat Prepositioning Ship (APS) program and the remainder into the newly formed Navy–Marine Corps Maritime Prepositioning Squadrons (MPS). Each squadron carried vehicles and equipment for a Marine Expeditionary Brigade (MEB), including a 30-day supply of food and water.

By 1987, 13 ships organized into three MPS had been commissioned, including newly built or converted RO/RO (roll-on/roll-off) and break-cargo ships crewed by civilian mariners. MPS-1 was deployed in the western Atlantic Ocean, MPS-2 was anchored at Diego Garcia and MPS-3 was deployed at the Pacific Ocean islands of Guam and Saipan.

On August 7, 1990, the order was given for MPS 2 to set sail from Diego Garcia, and its first ships arrived in Saudi Arabia on August 15. MPS-3 sailed from Guam-Saipan and arrived in September, and MPS-1, supporting the 2d Marine Division, arrived in Saudi Arabia on December 12. After unloading their cargo, two MPS RO/RO ships were reloaded with Assault Follow-on Echelon supplies to support the Marine Corps's Amphibious Task Force.

See also AFLOAT PREPOSITIONING SHIPS (APS); DEPLOYMENT OF U.S. FORCES.

Suggestions for further reading: Department of Defense, *Conduct of the Persian Gulf War: Final Report to the Congress,* "Appendix E: Deployment" (Washington, D.C.: USGPO, 1992); Norman Friedman, *Desert Victory: The War for Kuwait* (Annapolis, Md.: Naval Institute Press, 1991).

MARITIME STRATEGIC DOCTRINE, U.S.

The strategic doctrine for U.S. naval operations in the Persian Gulf War was spelled out in the "Maritime Strategy," first announced in January 1986. That strategy took the naval services—the Navy and the Marine Corps—out of the Vietnam War doldrums and reoriented them to offensive operations and forward projection of power. The naval services' equivalent of the Air Force's airpower doctrines (see AIRPOWER) and the Army's warfighting doctrine (see AIRLAND BATTLE DOCTRINE), the Maritime Strategy provided the fundamentals for Navy and Marine Corps combat operations.

Much of the philosophy behind the Maritime Strategy was obscured by the ballyhoo over the Reagan administration's goal of a "600-ship Navy."

Although that goal was never achieved, on the eve of the Gulf War the Navy did have 534 warships, among them 14 aircraft carriers (13 attack carrier air wings), 4 battleships, 43 cruisers, 59 destroyers, 100 frigates, 65 amphibious warfare ships and 63 underway support, maintenance and logistics ships.

In the event of hostilities, the Maritime Strategy envisioned that the Navy would quickly seize control of the high seas, making possible the creation of a sea bridge to Europe so that the mobilization capabilities of the United States could be brought to bear on the critical North Atlantic Treaty Organization (NATO) central front. Fortuitously, it also called for projecting military power on NATO's flanks. Thus, the Navy was on the scene when the Gulf crisis began, both physically and mentally prepared to quickly project U.S. military power from warships in the Red Sea and the Persian Gulf. The Navy was also ready to begin building the sea bridge to the Gulf upon which the success of the entire operation would depend.

The Marine Corps, too, had returned to fundamentals. "We are pulling our heads out of the jungle and getting back into the amphibious business," said the Marine Corps commandant, General Robert E. Cushman, in 1972. As a subset of the Maritime Strategy, the Amphibious Warfare Strategy became the basic doctrine of the Marine Corps and led to the formation of the Marine Air Ground Task Force (MAGTF). Each MAGTF consists of a headquarters element, a ground combat element, an aviation combat element and a combat service support element.

The smallest MAGTF, the Marine Expeditionary Unit (MEU), is built around an infantry battalion. The largest, the Marine Expeditionary Force (MEF), is built around one or more divisions, a Marine Aircraft Wing and a Force Service Support Unit. Battle-tested by the First Marine Expeditionary Force (I MEF), the MAGTF concept was validated in the Gulf War.

The Marine Corps's warfighting doctrine centered on manuever and the operational level of war, the intermediate level that links strategy and tactics.

The success of the Maritime Strategy and its Amphibious Warfare Strategy led to a new post–Gulf War strategy to take the naval services into the 21st century. Called ". . . From the Sea," it deemphasizes traditional "blue water" Navy operations in favor of "brown water" operations along the world's littorals.

See also AIRLAND BATTLE DOCTRINE; AIRPOWER; MARITIME CAMPAIGN.

Suggestions for further reading: "Maritime Strategy and Amphibious Warfare," in Colonel Harry G. Summers Jr., *On Strategy II: A Critical Analysis of the Gulf War* (New York: Dell, 1992); Admiral James D. Watkins, "The Maritime Strategy," and General P. X. Kelley, "The Amphibious Warfare Strategy," *U.S. Naval Institute Proceedings,* January 1986. See also FMFM 1-1, *Warfighting* (Washington, D.C.: USMC, March 1989); FMFM 1-1, *Campaigning* (Washington, D.C.: USMC, January 1990).

MAVERICK ANTITANK MISSILE (AGM-65)

The standard antitank missile for U.S. fighter aircraft, the Maverick was carried by the F-16 Fighting Falcon, the F/A-18 Hornet and the A-10 Warthog. Guided by television, laser or imaging infrared (IIR), and carrying either a 125-pound or a 300-pound warhead, the Maverick has a maximum range of about 14 miles. During the Gulf War some 5,500 Mavericks were launched.

See also HELLFIRE MISSILE.

Suggestions for further reading: Norman Friedman, *Desert Victory: The War for Kuwait* (Annapolis, Md.: Naval Institute Press, 1991); Richard P. Hallion, *Storm Over Iraq: Air Power and the Gulf War* (Washington, D.C.: Smithsonian Institution Press, 1992).

MEDIA

The Persian Gulf War was one of the most thoroughly and competently reported conflicts in history. Nevertheless, the relationship between the military and the press was highly contentious, with the media complaining bitterly about the restrictions placed on their ability to cover the war.

A fundamental dichotomy was at work. On the one hand was the public's right to know about the progress of the war. On the other was the need to protect the details of military operations and troop movements that could provide aid to the enemy.

In the Gulf War security was maintained; for example, the press did not learn of the massive shift of ground combat units prior to the ground campaign. But while the public's right to know was ultimately maintained as well (four years after the war, there

have been no major revelations of Gulf War coverups), military restrictions did unduly inhibit the timeliness of news reporting. "Although plans called for expeditious handling" of news reporting, the Defense Department report on the war admits, "much of it moved far too slowly. The JIB [Joint Information Bureau] Dhahran reviewed 343 pool reports filed during or immediately after the ground war and found [that] approximately 21 percent arrived at the JIB in less than 12 hours, 69 percent arrived in less than two days, and 12 percent arrived in more than three days. Five reports . . . arrived at the JIB more than six days after they were filed."

There were several major areas of contention between the military and the media. Initially there was the matter of reporters' access to the crisis area. Saudi Arabia, long closed to the Western media, was reluctant to allow reporters to enter the country. At the urging of the U.S. government, these restrictions were eased. On August 11, 1990, the Saudi government agreed to allow entry to a pool of U.S. reporters, and later, visas to individual reporters were granted as well. More than 1,600 news media representatives eventually entered Saudi Arabia.

Ironically, one of the organizations created as a result of media complaints about the military's restrictions on reporting the Grenada operation in 1983 became a major point of contention. After discussions between the Department of Defense (DOD) and representatives of the media, the DOD National Media Pool was created in 1985 to guarantee the press immediate access to crisis areas. The pool was to deploy immediately to a crisis area and share its "pool reports" with other news agencies. As military operations progressed, the pool would eventually disband and open coverage would prevail.

In the Gulf crisis, the media pool initially worked as planned. Seventeen pool members—representing the Associated Press, United Press International, Reuters, Cable News Network (CNN), National Public Radio, *Time,* Scripps-Howard, the *Los Angeles Times* and the *Milwaukee Journal*—were alerted on August 11, 1990. But instead of being disbanded once the crisis had stabilized, the pool system remained in effect throughout the war. Access to combat units was restricted to pool members only. Although ground combat news media pools were formed, in which 159 reporters and photographers accompanied front-line units during the ground campaign (as opposed to the 27 reporters who were allowed to accompany the D-Day invasion force in Normandy in 1944), those who were not part of such pools were furious about their exclusion.

Another point of contention was the requirement that military public affairs escort officers accompany reporters in the field. "While many [escort officers] received praise from the media," noted the DOD report, "others overzealously performed their duties . . . isolated incidents such as . . . stepping in front of cameras to stop interviews, telling reporters they could not ask questions about certain subjects, and attempting to have some news media reports altered to eliminate unfavorable information were reported."

Finally, there was the imposition of censorship ("security review") for the first time since the Korean War. Driving that decision was the fact that satellite dishes and other electronic equipment made this the first major American war in which the news media could broadcast reports directly to the world, including to the enemy. The plan called for all pool media material to be examined on the scene by a public affairs escort officer, and if no agreement could be reached on releasing the material for dissemination, the material would be forwarded to the JIB in Dhahran. If the issue could not be resolved there, it would be referred to the Pentagon for resolution. According to the DOD report, only five of more than 1,300 print media pool stories were appealed to Washington. But the prospect of having to go through that process was chilling to reporters.

A unique feature of the war was the media's reporting from behind enemy lines, specifically CNN's television reporting from Baghdad. Another unusual occurrence was the capture of CBS television reporter Bob Simon and three crewmen by the Iraqis and their confinement for 40 days as prisoners of war.

For its part, to facilitate media coverage of U.S. forces in the KTO (Kuwaiti Theater of Operations) the military established a Joint Information Bureau in Dhahran and later another in Riyadh. The JIB coordinated with reporters and arranged visits to Saudi bases and to U.S. units in the field. The military also conducted extensive news briefings on the war, including those by Secretary of Defense Dick Cheney, General Colin Powell, the chairman of the Joint Chiefs of Staff (JCS), and General H. Norman Schwarzkopf, the commander in chief, Central Command (CINCCENT).

At the Pentagon, Army Lieutenant General Thomas W. Kelly, the JCS J-3 (director of operations), gave 35 televised news briefings, and in the Gulf, Marine Brigadier General Richard I. Neal, the CENTCOM deputy J-3, gave daily news briefings as well. In addition, CENTCOM provided 98 briefings (53 on-the-record and 45 on background) by those military personnel charged with the planning and execution of military operations.

One unintended result of the televised press briefings was to cast some of the less professional reporters in a particularly unfavorable light. NBC TV's satirical *Saturday Night Live* did a devastating skit on the posturing and pretentions of the reporters. But the most damning critique came from *Washington Post* reporter Henry Allen, himself a Marine combat rifleman in the Vietnam War:

> The Persian Gulf press briefings are making reporters look like fools, nit-pickers and egomaniacs; like dilettantes who have spent exactly none of their lives on the end of a shovel; dinner party commandos, slouching inquisitors, collegiate spitball artists; people who have never been in a fistfight much less in combat; a whining, self-righteous, upper-middle-class mob. . . . It is a silly spectacle.
>
> It is so silly that 80 percent of Americans say they approve of all the military restrictions on the reporting of the war, and 60 percent think there should be more.

On May 21, 1992, following eight months of discussion between the Pentagon and the news media, new Pentagon guidelines were adopted for media coverage of future conflicts. Addressing the specific media complaints about the Gulf War, the guidelines emphasized that "open and independent reporting will be the principal means of coverage of U.S. military operations," that "journalists will be provided access to all major military units" and that "military public affairs officers should . . . not interfere with the reporting process."

See also ANTIWAR MOVEMENT; CNN (CABLE NEWS NETWORK); DECEPTION; PRISONERS OF WAR.

Suggestions for further reading: Department of Defense, *Conduct of the Persian Gulf War: Final Report to the Congress,* "Appendix S: Media Policy" (Washington, D.C.: USGPO, 1992); Senate Committee on Governmental Affairs, *Pentagon Rules on Media Access to the Persian Gulf War,* 102d Cong., 1st sess., 1991.

Among the best books on media coverage of the war are *Wall Street Journal* war correspondent John J. Fialka's *Hotel Warriors: Covering the Gulf War* (Washington, D.C.: Woodrow Wilson Center Press, 1991); and Hedrick Smith's anthology, *The Media and the Gulf War* (Washington, D.C.: Seven Locks Press, 1992).

See also Henry Allen, "The Gulf Between Media and Military," *Washington Post,* February 21, 1991; Malcolm W. Browne, "The Military vs. the Press," *New York Times Magazine,* March 3, 1991; and Pete Williams, "The Press and the Persian Gulf War," *Parameters,* Autumn 1991. For historical perspectives on military-media relations, see Peter Braestrup, *Battle Lines: Report of the Twentieth Century Fund Task Force on the Military and the Media* (New York: Priority Press Publications, 1985); Colonel Harry G. Summers Jr., "Western Media and Recent Wars," *Military Review,* May 1986; and Lloyd J. Matthews, ed., *Newsmen and the National Defense* (Washington, D.C.: Brassey's, 1991).

MEDICAL CARE AND EVACUATION, COALITION

In the Gulf War, the largest medical force since World War II was established in one of the harshest environments in the world.

Each of the coalition partners, including the United States, provided for the medical care and evacuation of its own personnel. The Gulf Cooperation Council states had their own medical facilities in-theater. In addition, France deployed the hospital ships *Rance* and *Foudre,* which operated in the Red Sea; Italy provided the helicopter assault ship *San Marco,* which also served as a hospital ship; Poland sent the hospital ship *Wodnik;* and the United Kingdom sent the RFA (Royal Fleet Auxiliary) *Argus,* which also served as a hospital ship. Czechoslovakia, New Zealand, the Netherlands and Sweden provided field hospitals. Australia sent two surgical teams, and Hungary, Romania, Sierra Leone and South Korea sent medical teams.

The U.S. Army, which had by far the largest medical force in the field, established five levels of medical care, with the level provided being determined by the severity of the patient's disability. In the battle area, evacuation of patients from one level of care to another was by ground ambulance or helicopter air ambulance. Farther to the rear within the Kuwaiti Theater of Operations (KTO), evacuation was by Air Force medically configured C-130 Hercules transports. Evacuation to hospitals in Europe and in the United States was by C-140 Starlifters from the Military Airlift Command.

Level I medical care was given at the unit level by Army medical aidmen and Navy medical corpsmen attached to frontline Army and Marine platoons and companies. Here the emphasis was on emergency lifesaving and on stabilizing the patient sufficiently to permit his or her evacuation to a Level II facility, usually located at Army division clearing stations and Marine Force Service Support Groups. At Level II facilities, patients received a more thorough examination. A surgical capacity was available for emergency resuscitation and stabilization, but normally care did not go beyond immediate treatment and evacuation farther to the rear.

Level III facilities provided initial wound surgery and postoperative treatment. These facilities included MASH (Mobile Army Surgical Hospitals), which can provide intensive care for 60 patients; Combat Support Hospitals, which can provide care for up to 200 patients; and Evacuation Hospitals, which can care for up to 400 patients. Level III care was also provided by the Navy hospital ships USS *Mercy* and *Comfort,* each with 1,000 beds.

Level IV care, provided by field hospitals, station hospitals and general hospitals, involved general, specialty and surgical care as well as rehabilitation of patients for their return to duty. Field hospitals can accommodate up to 400 patients, while station and general hospitals have no fixed capacity.

Long-term reconstructive, rehabilitative and specialized care for the most serious wounds, such as burns and spinal injuries, was provided at Level V facilities, including civilian and Veterans Administration hospitals in the continental United States (CONUS) and U.S. military hospitals in European Command (EUCOM).

The Air Force used some 6,600 reservists to fill positions in CONUS medical facilities when active-duty personnel were deployed to the Gulf. The Army called up more than 4,200 Reserve medical personnel and deployed 199 medical teams to facilities in the KTO, EUCOM and CONUS. The Navy activated more than 10,500 medical and support personnel to staff its two hospital ships and two reserve Fleet Hospitals.

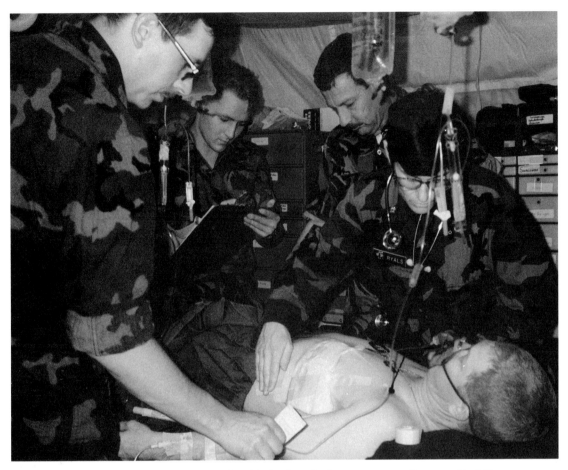

Reserve U.S. Navy medical personnel and a New Zealand medical team run a practice casualty drill.
U.S. Navy photo (CWO Ed Bailey), Empire Press.

Given the estimated 5,000 to 10,000 casualties that could have resulted from an attack on Iraqi fortified positions, Central Command (CENTCOM) established an initial requirement for 7,350 hospital beds in the KTO and 5,500 beds in EUCOM. An additional requirement for 17,000 to 22,000 beds in CONUS was also established.

When the air campaign began on January 17, 1991, 6,160 hospital beds were fully staffed and operational in the KTO. In preparation for the ground campaign, the requirement for in-country beds was increased to 18,530, of which 4,600 were to be provided through host-nation agreements with Saudi Arabia, Bahrain, the United Arab Emirates, Qatar and Oman. When the land campaign began on February 24, 1991, 15,430 beds were operational. The remainder were kept loaded on trucks that would follow the combat forces.

CENTCOM's entire health care delivery system ultimately included 65 hospitals, including two Navy hospital ships, three Navy Fleet Hospitals, 44 Army hospitals and 16 Air Force hospitals. The Army alone fielded 1,460 physicians.

"Disease, non-battle injury (DNBI) rates were markedly lower than expected," concluded the Department of Defense report on the war, and "the number of combat casualties experienced during Operation Desert Storm did not test the capacities of the medical units supporting forces in the theater."

What was tested, albeit not taxed, was the evacuation system. During Desert Storm, CENTCOM used more that 220 dedicated medical helicopters and more than 1,000 ground ambulances, including 60 German ambulances and 100 medical evacuation buses. In addition, 12 Army medical evacuation helicopters were used to transport patients to and from Navy hospital ships in the Gulf. During Desert Shield, 242 C-130 intra-theater aeromedical evacuation missions were flown, transporting 2,136 patients. During Desert Storm, 173 C-130 missions were flown, transporting 2,375 patients, including coalition and Iraqi wounded. Military Airlift Command flew more than 200 inter-theater missions, moving 3,400 litter patients and 5,200 ambulatory patients from the KTO to hospitals in EUCOM and CONUS.

A 1992 General Accounting Office (GAO) report was quite critical of the Army's medical preparedness in the Gulf War. The report cited physicians with no training in combat medicine; shortages of basic supplies, such as drugs and X-ray film; outdated hospital tents that could not be cooled below 100 degrees Fahrenheit; and a shortage of trucks to move hospitals forward. Acknowledging these problems, the Army surgeon general, Lieutenant General Frank F. Ledford Jr., said such difficulties were to be expected in the largest medical deployment since World War II. Ledford added that under the circumstances, "we can be very proud of what we did. . . . I'm convinced we could have taken care of casualties."

See also CASUALTIES; COMBAT MEDICAL BADGE; VETERANS.

Suggestions for further reading: Department of Defense, *Conduct of the Persian Gulf War: Final Report to the Congress,* "Appendix G: Medical Support" (Washington, D.C.: USGPO, 1992); John Lancaster, "GAO Study Says Army Dodged Medical Bullet," *Washington Post,* February 6, 1992.

MIA (MISSING IN ACTION)

There were no U.S. military personnel unaccounted for after the Gulf War. Although 22 Americans were reported missing in action (MIA) during the war, all were later found either to be prisoners of war who were subsequently released or to have been killed in action (KIA) in operations behind enemy lines. For example, after the cease-fire Air Force divers found the wreckage of a Special Operations Command AC-130 Spectre gunship that had gone down in the Persian Gulf with 14 crewmen aboard.

The last MIA to be accounted for was Navy Lieutenant Commander Michael Scott Speicher from the USS *Saratoga.* After the war, it was determined that his F/A-18 Hornet had blown up in the air after being hit by an Iraqi surface-to-air missile (SAM) near Baghdad on the first day of the air war. His remains were never found.

See also CASUALTIES; PRISONERS OF WAR (POW).

MILITARY AIRLIFT COMMAND (MAC)
See AIRLIFT; DEPLOYMENT OF U.S. FORCES.

MILITARY SEALIFT COMMAND (MSC)
See DEPLOYMENT OF U.S. FORCES; SEALIFT.

MILK PLANT CONTROVERSY
See BIOLOGICAL WARFARE; CNN (CABLE NEWS NETWORK).

MINES, LAND
Iraqi military forces made wide use of land mines in their extensive field fortifications.

It was reported that Iraq had some 10 million mines in its inventory at the start of the war, and that more than 500,000 antipersonnel and antitank land mines were laid by the Iraqis in the KTO (Kuwaiti Theater of Operations) to hold back the coalition's ground attack. These include the Soviet PMN and PMD-6 pressure-sensitive antipersonnel mines with half-pound explosives; the Soviet OZM bounding mine, which jumps two to eight feet in the air before exploding; the tiny scatterable European-made SB-33, a plastic mine that is difficult to detect; and U.S.-made "Claymore" mines containing hundreds of ball bearings that can cut a 150-foot swath. Antitank mines included the Soviet-supplied TM-46 with 12.1 pounds of TNT and the TM-57 with 20 pounds of TNT.

As discussed elsewhere (see BREACHING OPERATIONS), these mines failed to slow, much less stop, the coalition's ground attack. They did, however, pose a continuing threat to civilians after the war. Kuwait was divided into six areas for postwar mine cleanup, with teams from the United States, Great Britain, Bangladesh, Egypt, France and Pakistan hired to perform the work.

See also BREACHING OPERATIONS; GROUND CAMPAIGN.

MINESWEEPING

During the five months of Operation Desert Shield, Iraq laid 1,167 sea mines in the northern Persian Gulf. They were of 11 types, ranging from pre–World War I Russian-designed contact mines to high-technology magnetic and acoustic mines such as the Soviet KMD and UDM and the Italian Manta.

Having cooperated in minesweeping operations to clear shipping channels during the Iran-Iraq War, the United States and the United Kingdom (UK) were responsible for mine countermeasures (MCM) during the Persian Gulf War. The flagship for the U.S. Mine Countermeasures Group (USMCMG) was the amphibious ship USS *Tripoli,* which had on board more than 20 U.S. explosive ordnance demolition (EOD) teams and a 23-man Australian EOD team.

Also embarked on the Tripoli were six MH-53E aviation mine countermeasures (AMCM) helicopters. The MH-53Es towed a cable with a mechanical cutting device that severed a mine's mooring cable and brought the mine to the surface where it could be destroyed. The helicopters also towed acoustic and magnetic sleds that simulated a ship's propeller and magnetic signature in order to detonate mines.

U.S. surface mine countermeasure (SMCM) ships included the minesweepers USS *Impervious* (MSO 449) and *Adroit* (MSO 509) from the Naval Reserve Force; and the USS *Leader* (MSO 490), which used AN/SQQ-14 MCM sonar to detect bottom and moored mines, and mechanical minesweeping gear to cut mine cables. Also deployed was the newest and most capable MCM ship, the USS *Avenger* (MCM-1). It had a sophisticated AN/SQQ-32 minehunting sonar to detect moored and bottom mines, and an AN/SLQ-48 mine neutralization system (MNS) to locate, examine and destroy the detected mines. The MNS consisted of a remotely piloted submersible vehicle equipped with sonar and two television cameras for locating mines; with explosives for neutralizing them; and with cable cutters to sever their mooring lines.

The UK took responsibility for most surface-mine countermeasure operations. The Royal Navy first deployed the mine hunters HMS *Atherstone* (M38),

HMS *Cattistock* (M31), and HMS *Hurworth* (M 39), along with the support ship HMS *Herald* (AGSH 138). These were later joined by the minehunters HMS *Ledbury* (M30) and HMS *Dulverton* (M 35).

Saudi Arabia's MCM ships included the minesweepers *Addriyah, Al-Quysuman, Ak-Wadi'ah* and *Safwa.* Belgium contributed the mine hunters *Iris* and *Myosotis* and the support ship *Zinnia,* all three of which operated primarily in the Gulf of Oman.

On February 18, 1991, the USS *Tripoli* struck a moored contact mine, injuring four crewmen. Three hours later, the nearby cruiser USS *Princeton* triggered two Manta acoustic/magnetic mines, injuring three crewmen and severely damaging the ship. The minefield in which the *Tripoli* and the *Princeton* were damaged was one of six that stretched in a 150-mile arc in the Persian Gulf from Faylakah Island off the coast of Kuwait City south to the Saudi-Kuwaiti border. After the war, mine countermeasure assets from France, Germany, Italy, Japan and the Netherlands joined in the effort to clear these mines from the Gulf. Paths were swept to Kuwait's ports, and Persian Gulf mine clearing operations came to an end on September 10, 1991.

Mine countermeasures was one of the coalition's least effective capabilities. As the *Navy Times* noted, Iraqi mines were able to block the coalition's navies from taking control of the northern Persian Gulf. The mines kept the battleships USS *Missouri* and *Wisconsin* from maneuvering freely to provide naval gunfire support to Marine forces ashore. Floating mines interfered with the coalition's sealift operations, and obsolete equipment, poor logistical support and poor planning proved to be major hindrances in battling mines in the Gulf.

In the wake of Operation Desert Storm, the U.S. Navy ordered an extensive review of its mine and mine countermeasures programs. Mine warfare hampered coalition maritime operations in the Persian Gulf. The difficulty in coping with Iraqi minefields was one of the reasons why an amphibious invasion of Kuwait was not conducted.

See also AMPHIBIOUS TASK FORCE; MARITIME CAMPAIGN.

Suggestions for further reading: Department of Defense, *Conduct of the Persian Gulf War: Final Report to the Congress,* "Chapter 7: The Maritime Campaign" (Washington, D.C.: USGPO, 1992); Tamara Moser Melia, *"Damn the Torpedoes": A Short History of U.S.*

Naval Mine Countermeasures, 1777–1991 (Washington, D.C.: Naval Historical Center, 1991). Also, Capt. J. M. Martin, USNR, "We Still Haven't Learned"; CDR Frank Evans, USN, "Princeton Leaves the War"; and LCDR A. G. Rankin, RAN, and Lt. R. G. Smith, RAN, "Australian Divers Clear Mines," *U.S. Naval Institute Proceedings,* July 1991. See also Tom Philpott and David S. Steigman, "Navy's Mine Warfare Capabilities Surface to Controversy After Desert Storm Test," *Navy Times,* September 2, 1991.

MISSILES

See AIR DEFENSES; AIR-LAUNCHED CRUISE MISSILE; ALARM ANTI-RADAR MISSILE; ATACMS (M39 ARMY TACTICAL MISSILE SYSTEM); HARM (HIGH-SPEED ANTI-RADAR MISSILE); HELLFIRE MISSILE; MAVERICK ANTITANK MISSILE; PATRIOT MISSILE; SCUD MISSILES; SIDEWINDER (AIM-9) AIR-TO-AIR MISSILE; SLAM (AGM-84E) STANDOFF LAND ATTACK MISSILE; SPARROW (AIM-7) AIR-TO-AIR MISSILE; TOMA-HAWK LAND ATTACK MISSILE; TOW (TUBE-LAUNCHED, OPTICALLY TRACKED, WIRE-GUIDED ANTITANK MISSILE).

MLRS (MULTIPLE-LAUNCH ROCKET SYSTEM)

Fielded by U.S. forces in 1983 and used for the first time in combat in the Gulf War, the Multiple-Launch Rocket System (MLRS) is a long-range free rocket system that provides general support artillery fire to division- and corps-level units. Each Army division had a nine-launcher MLRS battery, and corps artillery MLRS battalions had 27 launchers each.

The MLRS's self-propelled M270 loader-launcher, a variant of the Bradley armored fighting vehicle chassis, is able to keep pace with other armored vehicles on the battlefield. The MLRS's two rocket pods each carry six M77 rockets whose warheads contain 644 dual-purpose grenades. All 12 rockets can be fired in less than one minute, covering a target area of more than 30 acres.

Firing a 227-mm rocket with a range of more than 30 kilometers, the MLRS played a major role in the war.
U.S. Army photo courtesy of U.S. Army Ordnance Museum.

During Operation Desert Storm, 189 MLRS launchers were deployed to the Kuwaiti Theater of Operations (KTO). They fired 9,660 rockets at artillery, convoys, logistic sites and troop positions. In addition to the MLRS's raw destructive power, its "steel rain" reportedly had a powerful psychological effect on Iraqi soldiers.

The Iraqi Astros II multiple-rocket launcher had almost double the range (60 kilometers) of the MLRS, but better U.S. ground and air target acquisition overcame this disadvantage.

See also ATACMS (M39 ARMY TACTICAL MISSILE SYSTEM); FIELD ARTILLERY.

Suggestions for further reading: Department of Defense, *Conduct of the Persian Gulf War: Final Report to the Congress,* "Appendix T: Performance of Selected Weapons Systems" (Washington, D.C.: USGPO, 1992); Department of the Army, *Weapons Systems of the United States Army* (Washington, D.C.: USGPO, 1989).

MOBILIZATION, U.S.

"Operations Desert Shield and Desert Storm required the largest mobilization and deployment of Reserve Component (RC) forces since the Korean Conflict," according to the official Department of Defense (DOD) report on the Gulf War. More than 230,000 reservists from the Army and Air National Guard and from the Army, Navy, Air Force, Marine Corps and Coast Guard Reserves were ordered to active duty during the Gulf crisis. More than 105,000 of these men and women served in the KTO (Kuwaiti Theater of Operations).

The comparison with the Korean War is apt, for that war would have been lost without the Reserves. And the same is true of the war in the Persian Gulf: Active-duty military units simply would have been overwhelmed. For example, much of the U.S. airlift capability was provided by Air National Guard and Air Reserve units, and a large proportion of the Army's logistics units came from the Reserve components.

The mobilization of the Reserve component was a validation of the Total Force concept that grew out of the Vietnam War experience. Although there had been a token partial mobilization during the Vietnam War, that war was the first in American history in which the Reserve components did not play a major role. The failure to mobilize either the Reserves or American society as a whole was a major factor in America's failure to achieve its strategic objectives in Southeast Asia.

To prevent a recurrence of that debacle, the Army chief of staff, General Creighton Abrams, set out to restructure the Army so that it could not be committed to sustained combat without the president and the Congress taking action to mobilize the Reserves, which, perforce, would require mobilizing the country as well. His 1973 Total Force concept called for a closer affiliation of the Reserves with the active force, including the rounding-out of active Army divisions with National Guard brigades. Although General Abrams died in office in 1974, his initiatives were carried forward by his successor, General Frederick C. Weyand, and others, particularly Generals Walter Kerwin and John Vessey.

As a result, 70 percent of the Army's combat support and combat service support units, which are necessary to sustain the Army in the field, are in the Reserve components, including 77 percent of the Army's combat engineers, 77 percent of its hospital units, 71 percent of its supply and service units, 57 percent of its Signal Corps units and 97 percent of its civil affairs units. In addition, the third manuever brigades of two Army divisions that were ultimately deployed to the Persian Gulf were National Guard round-out brigades—the 24th Infantry Division's 48th Infantry Brigade from the Georgia National Guard, and the 1st Cavalry Division's 155th Armored Brigade from the Mississippi National Guard. The 5th Infantry Division, alerted for Gulf duty, was rounded out by the Louisiana National Guard's 256th Infantry Brigade.

The Army was not alone in its dependence on the Reserves. At the time of the Gulf crisis, all of the Navy's combat search and rescue squadrons and logistic airlift squadrons were in the Reserves, as were 93 percent of its cargo handling battalions, 85 percent of its minesweepers, 68 percent of its Seabee mobile construction battalions and 50 percent of its fleet hospitals. In addition, all of the Marine Corps's civil affairs units were in the Reserves, as were 62 percent of its bulk-fuel companies, 50 percent of its force reconnaissance units, 40 percent of its tank battalions, 40 percent of its beach and port operations companies and 33 percent of its heavy artillery.

Fifty-nine percent of the Air Force's tactical airlift was in the Air Guard and the Air Reserve, as was

55 percent of its tactical air support. Ninety-two percent of its aeromedical evacuation personnel were in the Reserve, as were 50 percent of its strategic airlift, 71 percent of its aerial port capability, 69 percent of its engineering personnel, 66 percent of its combat communications, 59 percent of its combat logistics support squadrons and 23 percent of its aerial refueling capability.

Even before the involuntary Reserve component call-ups, volunteers from the reserves were already serving on active duty. During the initial deployments in August 1990, for example, Air Force reservists flew 42 percent of the strategic airlift missions and 33 percent of the aerial refueling missions.

On August 22, 1990, President George Bush signed Executive Order 12717, authorizing the involuntary activation of selected reservists for up to 90 days. The secretary of defense subsequently authorized the call-up of Army, Navy, Air Force and Marine Corps reservists, and the secretary of transportation likewise authorized the call-up of Coast Guard reservists.

By the end of October 1990, the Army had activated 235 Reserve component units with nearly 24,000 soldiers. Approximately 5,000 Navy reservists and 355 units had also been activated, as had 32 Air Reserve units and 5,000 Air Reserve component personnel. Three Coast Guard Reserve units had also been activated.

On November 8, 1990, President Bush announced his intention to build an offensive capability in the KTO, and at the same time authorized additional Reserve call-ups for up to 180 days. This led to the Army's call-up of three "round-out" brigades, Georgia's 48th Infantry Brigade, Mississippi's 155th Armor Brigade and Louisiana's 256th Infantry Brigade, even though the first two units' parent divisions had already deployed.

Two Army National Guard field artillery (FA) brigades—the 142d FA Brigade from Arkansas and Oklahoma, which supported the British 1st Armoured Division, and the 196th FA Brigade from Tennessee, West Virginia and Kentucky, which supported XVIII Airborne Corps—were deployed, as was the Army Reserve's 416th Engineer Command, which served as the theater army engineer command.

The Marine Corps sent substantial portions of its Reserve 4th Marine Division, 4th Marine Aircraft Wing and 4th Service Support Group to the Gulf, including four infantry battalions, elements of two tank battalions, several artillery batteries and composite attack and transport helicopter squadrons.

The Air Force deployed three tactical fighter squadrons, one special operations group, two special operations squadrons, and a tactical reconnaissance squadron. The Navy sent two minesweepers—the USS *Adroit* (MSO 509) and *Impervious* (MSO 449)—two combat search and rescue squadrons, one Seabee battalion, four logistics squadrons and several mobile inshore undersea warfare detachments. For its part, the Coast Guard continued to operate the three Port Security Harbor Defense (PSHD) units it had deployed in October.

On January 18, 1991, there was a third call-up. This one involved primarily individual ready reservists (IRRs) who would serve as fillers in active and Reserve units. At the peak of the mobilization on March 10, 1991, a total of 231,000 reservists had been called to active duty. At the time of the cease-fire on February 28, 1991, more than 100,000 reservists were serving in the KTO, including 37,692 from the Army National Guard, 35,158 from the Army Reserve, 6,625 from the Navy Reserve, 13,066 from the Marine Reserve, 10,800 from the Air National Guard and 281 from the Coast Guard Reserve.

The major shortcoming of the U.S. mobilization effort was the failure of the round-out concept. Instead of deploying with their National Guard round-out brigades, the 24th Infantry Division deployed with the active-duty 197th Infantry Brigade from Fort Benning, Georgia, and the 1st Cavalry Division deployed with the active-duty "Tiger Brigade" from the 2d Armored Division at Fort Hood, Texas. The round-out brigades were not even called to active duty until the second call-up in November 1990, and then they were ordered to the National Training Center for additional training. The Georgia National Guard's 48th Infantry Brigade was certified as combat ready on February 28, 1991, the day the war ended.

Critics of the round-out concept claim it is impossible to train a manuever brigade on a part-time basis. Others point out that a three-month delay in deployability is not unreasonable. Still others claim that the combat readiness of these units was judged unfairly. The debate has yet to be resolved.

The round-out issue aside, the Gulf War provided concrete evidence of the importance of the

Reserve components. In his March 6, 1991, address to the Congress, President Bush declared that the Gulf War victory "belongs . . . to the regulars, to the reserves, to the National Guard. This victory belongs to the finest fighting force this nation has ever known in its history."

Not only were the physical contributions of the Reserves validated, so were their psychological contributions as well. By activating 798 Army, Navy, Air Force, Marine Corps and Coast Guard Reserve component units from more than 2,000 towns and cities in every state across the country, the government almost guaranteed public support for the Gulf War. As General Edwin H. Burba Jr., then commander of U.S. Forces Command, told an audience of reservists, "When you come to war, you bring America with you."

See also AIR FORCE, U.S.; ARMY, U.S.; COAST GUARD, U.S.; LOGISTICS, U.S.; MARINE CORPS, U.S.; NAVY, U.S.

Suggestions for further reading: Department of Defense, *Conduct of the Persian Gulf War: Final Report to the Congress,* "Appendix H: Reserve Component Forces" (Washington, D.C.: USGPO, 1992). For a discussion of the Total Force concept, see "Back to Basics," in Colonel Harry G. Summers Jr., *On Strategy II: A Critical Analysis of the Gulf War* (New York: Dell, 1992). See also David C. Morrison, "Pentagon Counting on Reserves," *National Journal,* September 1, 1990; "The 48th Brigade: A Chronology From Invasion to Demobilization," *National Guard,* May 1991; "Reserve Component Programs, Fiscal Year 1989," *The Annual Report of the Reserve Forces Policy Board* (Washington, D.C.: Office of the Secretary of Defense, 1989).

MORALITY

See JUST WAR; LAW AND ORDER; WAR CRIMES.

MOROCCO

See ARAB LEAGUE; COALITION FORCES; JOINT FORCES COMMAND (JFC).

MRE (MEAL, READY TO EAT)

"Meals, Ready to Eat," or MREs, were the U.S. Gulf War forces' plastic-pouch successor to the canned

C-rations of World War II, the Korean War and the Vietnam War. Officially described as "a single meal food package designed to provide high-calorie and full-vitamin needs to soldiers in high stress environments," the MRE can be heated or eaten cold. With a shelf life of up to four years, each meal provides about 1,300 calories, 50 grams of protein and 160 grams of carbohydrates.

Available in 12 versions, the MRE contains a main course (ham, turkey, beef slices, barbecued chicken and the like), a dessert, crackers with either jelly or peanut butter, a beverage powder such as cocoa or Kool-Aid, and an accessory pack with powdered coffee, cream and sugar, salt and pepper, candy, chewing gum, matches and toilet paper. According to one unofficial survey, spaghetti, beef stew, chicken stew, chicken and rice, and ham slices were among the favorites of soldiers in the field, with omelets and ham at the bottom of the list, along with frankfurters and beans.

Of the accessories contained in MREs, the best-liked were M&Ms and caramels, cocoa and Hershey's nonmelting chocolate. Least liked were applesauce, Kool-Aid and dehydrated fruit.

The plan was to feed each soldier two MREs and one T-ration—a prepackaged meal heated by submersion in hot water—each day. Although the supply system was strained, troops never missed a meal, including special meals on Thanksgiving and Christmas.

Suggestions for further reading: Department of Defense, *Conduct of the Persian Gulf War: Final Report to the Congress,* "Appendix F: Logistics Buildup and Sustainment" (Washington, D.C.: USGPO, 1992); Elisabeth Hickey and Michael Hedges, "Please, Sir, I Want Some MRE: In the Field the Soldiers Make Do," and Betsy Pisik, "Local Chefs Rate Front-line Food," *Washington Times,* February 25, 1991.

MSR (MAIN SUPPLY ROUTE)

See LAND TRANSPORTATION NETWORK.

MUBARAK, HOSNI

See EGYPT.

NATIONAL DEFENSE RESERVE FLEET
See SEALIFT.

NATIONAL DEFENSE SERVICE MEDAL
First authorized in the Korean War and reauthorized during the Vietnam War, the National Defense Service Medal was authorized yet again during the Persian Gulf crisis to recognize one or more days of honorable service in the armed forces of the United States since the beginning of the crisis on August 2, 1990.

Whereas one had to actually serve in the KTO (Kuwaiti Theater of Operations) to be eligible for the Southwest Asia Service Medal, one only had to serve on active duty to be eligible for the National Defense Service Medal.

See also SERVICE MEDALS, U.S.

NATIONAL GUARD
See MOBILIZATION, U.S.

NATIONAL SECURITY COUNCIL, U.S.
The National Security Council (NSC) was created by the National Security Act of 1947 to advise the president of the United States with respect to the integration of domestic, foreign and military policies relating to national security.

During the Gulf War, the NSC consisted of President George Bush, Vice President Dan Quayle, Secretary of State James A. Baker III and Secretary of Defense Dick Cheney. Statutory advisors to the NSC included William H. Webster, the director of the Central Intelligence Agency (CIA), and General Colin L. Powell, the chairman of the Joint Chiefs of Staff (JCS). NSC officials included retired Air Force Lieutenant General Brent Scowcroft, the assistant to the president for national security affairs, and his deputy, Robert M. Gates.

Suggestion for further reading: Bob Woodward *The Commanders* (New York: Simon & Schuster, 1991).

NATO (NORTH ATLANTIC TREATY ORGANIZATION)
See EUROPE.

NAVAL BLOCKADE
See MARITIME INTERCEPTION OPERATIONS.

NAVAL GUNFIRE SUPPORT AND SHORE BOMBARDMENT
See BATTLESHIPS.

NAVCENT (NAVAL FORCES CENTRAL COMMAND)
See SEVENTH U.S. FLEET.

NAVIES, COALITION
Coalition navies were involved in maritime interception operations (MIO) and assisted in antisurface warfare (ASUW), antiair warfare (AAW) and mine countermeasure (MCM) missions during the maritime campaign. Although each nation's contribution varied during the course of the war as ships were relieved on station, the numbers given below are a close approximation of the total naval contributions of the coalition partners.

Country/Mission	Number and Type Ship
Argentina (MIO)	
(ASUW)	1 Destroyer
	1 Frigate
Australia (MIO)	
(AAW) (ASUW)	2 Frigates
	2 Destroyers
	(replaced frigates)
	1 Underway
	Replenishment Ship
Bahrain (MIO) (ASUW)	2 Corvettes
	4 Missile Craft
	2 Patrol Craft
Belgium (MIO) (MCM)	2 Minesweepers
	1 Frigate
	1 Support Ship

Country/Mission	Number and Type Ship
Canada (MIO) (ASUW)	2 Destroyers
	1 Oiler
Denmark (MIO) (ASUW)	1 Frigate
France (MIO) (MCM) (ASUW)	2 Destroyers
	4 Frigates
	2 Replenishment Ships
	2 Hospital Ships
	2 Minesweepers (postwar)
	1 Electronic Intelligence Ship
Greece (MIO)	1 Frigate
Italy (MIO) (AAW) (ASUW) (MCM)	3 Frigates
	1 Support Ship
	4 Minesweepers (postwar)
	1 Helicopter Assault Ship
	1 Destroyer (replaced frigate)
Kuwait (MIO) (ASUW)	2 Patrol Boats
Netherlands (MIO) (MCM) (ASUW)	2 Frigates
	3 Minesweepers (postwar)
Norway (MIO) (ASUW)	1 Coast Guard Cutter
Oman (MIO) (ASUW)	4 Missile Craft
	8 Patrol Craft
Poland	1 Hospital Ship
	1 Salvage Ship
Portugal	1 Transport
Qatar (MIO) (ASUW)	3 Missile Craft
	6 Patrol Craft
Saudi Arabia (MIO) (ASUW) (MCM)	8 Frigates
	5 Minesweepers
	9 Missile Craft
	3 Torpedo Craft
Spain (MIO) (AAW) (ASUW)	3 Frigates
	1 Amphibious Transport
United Arab Emirates (MIO) (ASUW)	2 Corvettes
	6 Missile Craft
	9 Patrol Craft

Country/Mission	Number and Type Ship
United Kingdom (MIO) (MCM) (AAW) (ASUW)	4 Destroyers
	3 Frigates
	5 Minesweepers
	1 Underway Replenishment Ship
	1 Survey Ship
	2 Oilers
	2 Submarines

As noted above, 13 nations in addition to the six Gulf Cooperation Council (GCC) states participated in maritime interception operations. Only U.S., UK, Kuwaiti and Saudi surface combatants were involved in offensive antisurface warfare operations. The GCC navies patrolled their coastal waters and defended coastal facilities. Other coalition navies—those of Argentina, Australia, Canada, Denmark, France, Italy, the Netherlands, Norway and Spain—provided fleet defense for the aircraft carriers and combat logistics forces.

UK, Australian, Spanish and Italian destroyers and frigates were under the operational control of the U.S. antiair warfare headquarters for air defense of coalition naval forces. UK, Belgian and Saudi minesweepers participated in the wartime mine countermeasures mission; after the cease-fire, French, German, Italian, Japanese and Dutch minesweepers joined in the effort to clear the Persian Gulf of mines.

See also MARITIME CAMPAIGN; MARITIME INTERCEPTION OPERATIONS; MINESWEEPING; NAVY, IRAQ; NAVY, U.S.

Suggestions for further reading: Department of Defense, *Conduct of the Persian Gulf War: Final Report to the Congress,* "Chapter 4: Maritime Interception Operations," "Chapter 7: The Maritime Campaign" (Washington, D.C.: USGPO, 1992). Norman Friedman, *Desert Victory: The War for Kuwait* (Annapolis, Md.: Naval Institute Press, 1991) has a listing of coalition naval vessels.

NAVY CROSS

First authorized in World War I, the Navy Cross (along with the Army's Distinguished Service Cross and the Air Force Cross) is the nation's second-highest award for bravery. It is awarded in the name of the president of the United States for extraordinary heroism in an action against the enemy. The act (or acts) of heroism must be so notable and involve a risk of life so extraordinary as to set the individual apart from his comrades.

Two Navy Crosses were awarded to Marine Corps personnel during the Persian Gulf War.

NAVY, IRAQ

"In the Persian Gulf conflict," states the official Department of Defense (DOD) report on the war, "the principal Iraqi naval strength was its ability to conduct small scale, small boat operations, including missile attacks, mine warfare and terrorist attacks against shipping in the northern Persian Gulf. . . . Destruction of the Iraqi surface threat was considered a prerequisite for moving the carrier battle force in the Gulf farther north to bring naval air power closer to targets and to prepare for amphibious operations."

Iraq's inventory of missile boats consisted of 7 ex-Soviet Osa-class boats carrying Styx missiles with a maximum range of 42 miles, and 5 captured Kuwaiti TNC-45 and 1 FPB-57 boats carrying Exocet missiles with a range of 96 miles. The rest of the approximately 165 Iraqi naval vessels were mostly small patrol boats, minelaying boats and such specialized ships as hovercraft, tank-landing ships and auxiliary ships.

Beginning on January 18, 1991, a concerted coalition antisurface warfare (ASUW) operation systematically destroyed the Iraqi Navy. U.S. carrier-based aircraft; maritime patrol aircraft such as United Kingdom (UK) Nimrods; ground-based aircraft such as Canadian CF-18 Hornets, UK Jaguars and UK Lynx; and U.S. Army OH-58D Kiowa helicopters supported the coalition's surface combatants. In addition to the U.S. and the six GCC (Gulf Cooperation Council) navies, 10 other navies participated in the ASUW operation.

Only the U.S., UK, Kuwaiti and Saudi navies engaged in offensive ASUW operations. The remaining GCC navies—those of Bahrain, Oman, Qatar and the United Arab Emirates—engaged in defensive ASUW operations only, patrolling their coastal waters and defending coalition facilities near shore from possible surprise attack. Also engaged in defensive ASUW operations were surface combatants from Argentina, Australia, Canada, Denmark, France, Italy, the Netherlands, Norway and Spain,

which provided fleet defense and protected the aircraft carriers and combat logistics forces.

ASUW operations damaged or destroyed 143 Iraqi naval vessels: 11 antiship missile boats were destroyed and another 2 were disabled, 3 amphibious ships were destroyed, 1 frigate was destroyed, 1 Bogomol patrol boat was destroyed, 116 small patrol boats and auxiliaries were damaged or destroyed, and 9 minelayers were destroyed. In addition, all Iraqi naval bases and ports were significantly damaged, and all northern Persian Gulf oil platforms were searched and secured. Most importantly, no coalition forces were attacked by Iraqi surface vessels.

See also MARITIME CAMPAIGN; NAVIES, COALITION; NAVY, U.S.

Suggestions for further reading: Department of Defense, *Conduct of the Persian Gulf War: Final Report to the Congress,* "Chapter 7: The Maritime Campaign" (Washington, D.C.: USGPO, 1992). Norman Friedman, *Desert Victory: The War for Kuwait* (Annapolis, Md.: Naval Institute Press, 1991) has a list of Iraqi ships and losses, as does Bruce W. Watson, ed., *Military Lessons of the Gulf War* (Novato, Calif.: Presidio Press, 1991). See also *The Military Balance 1990–1991* (London: International Institute for Strategic Studies, 1990).

NAVY, U.S.

The United States Navy, including the Navy Reserve, is the most formidable naval force in the world. During Operation Desert Shield and Operation Desert Storm, the Navy played a crucial role in bringing the Gulf War to a successful conclusion.

In the largest naval deployment since World War II, some 80,000 active and reserve U.S. naval personnel, including 3,700 women and 6,625 of the 18,000 naval reservists recalled to active duty, were deployed to the Kuwaiti Theater of Operations (KTO). NAVCENT (Naval Forces Central Command—i.e., the U.S. Seventh Fleet) comprised some 120 ships, including 6 carrier battle groups with more than 400 aircraft embarked, 2 battleship surface action groups, 13 submarines and the 43 amphibious ships of the Amphibious Task Force.

When the Gulf crisis began in August 1990, the U.S. Navy was already on station with the six ships of its Joint Task Force Middle East, which had been operating in the Persian Gulf since 1949. By August

Part of the USS *Saratoga* **(CV-34) carrier battle group, the guided missile cruiser USS** *Biddle* **(CG-34) was one of the many U.S. warships deployed to the Gulf.**
U.S. Navy photo (CWO Ed Bailey) Empire Press.

7, the aircraft carrier battle groups of the USS *Independence* in the Arabian Sea and the USS *Eisenhower* in the Red Sea, together with their embarked air wings, were also on station, bringing some 164 combat aircraft within striking range of Iraq.

Naval operations in the Persian Gulf War can be grouped into five phases, each of which is discussed elsewhere in more detail. In the initial deployment phase, the role of the U.S. Navy was crucial. Its Maritime Prepositioning Squadrons (MPS) provided essential arms and equipment for the Marine Expeditionary Brigades in the critical first days of the crisis, and its Military Sealift Command delivered some 95 percent of CENTCOM's (Central Command) arms, ammunition and supplies.

Concurrently, during the maritime interception operation (MIO) phase, the Navy's Joint Task Force Middle East was one of the major actors in the coalition's effort to enforce the United Nations sanctions against Iraq. More than 7,500 merchant vessels were challenged, 954 were boarded and 51 were diverted.

During the air-campaign phase, Navy aircraft flew 18,624 sorties, 23 percent of the total coalition combat missions. Navy warships fired 288 Tomahawk land-attack missiles at Iraqi targets ashore, including 8 from the submarine USS *Louisville* (SSN-724) while it was submerged in the Red Sea, and 4 from the USS *Pittsburgh* (SSN-72) while it was submerged in the Mediterranean Sea.

In the fourth phase, in establishing control of the seas the U.S. Navy destroyed the Iraqi Navy. U.S. Navy mine countermeasures operations also allowed the battleships USS *Missouri* (BB-63) and USS *Wisconsin* (BB-64) to move into position to fire some 1,102 of their 16-inch shells in support of the ground campaign.

Finally, in phase five, in support of CENTCOM's deception plan the U.S. Navy Amphibious Task Force's credible threat in the Persian Gulf tied down four Iraqi divisions in coastal defense and persuaded the enemy to hold two armored divisions in reserve.

Two Navy ships, the cruiser USS *Princeton* (CG-59) and the amphibious ship USS *Tripoli* (LPH-10), struck enemy mines, injuring several of their crewmen. Seven Navy aircraft were lost in combat, including two F/A-18 Hornets, one F-14A Tomcat and four A-6E Intruders. Another two fighters and two helicopters were lost in noncombat incidents.

Six Navy personnel were killed in action, and another six died from accidents or other nonbattle causes. Twelve Navy personnel were wounded in action. Eleven Silver Stars were awarded for gallantry in action during the war, 3 Distinguished Service Medals and 18 Legions of Merit were awarded for distinguished service, and 130 Distinguished Flying Crosses were awarded for valor and for meritorious service.

See also AERIAL COMBAT; AIR CAMPAIGN; AIRCRAFT CARRIERS; AMPHIBIOUS TASK FORCE; ARTHUR, STANLEY R; BATTLESHIPS; CARRIER BATTLE GROUPS; CHIEF OF NAVAL OPERATIONS; COMBAT ACTION RIBBON; DEPLOYMENT OF U.S. FORCES; ENGINEERS; JOINT TASK FORCE MIDDLE EAST, U.S.; MARITIME CAMPAIGN; MARITIME INTERCEPTION OPERATIONS; MARITIME PREPOSITIONING SQUADRONS; MARITIME STRATEGIC DOCTRINE, U.S.; MINESWEEPING; SANCTIONS; SEALIFT; SEVENTH U.S. FLEET; SPECIAL OPERATIONS COMMAND CENTRAL COMMAND; TOMAHAWK LAND ATTACK MISSILE.

Suggestions for further reading: Department of Defense, *Conduct of the Persian Gulf War: Final Report to the Congress*, "Chapter 4: Maritime Interception Operations" and "Chapter 7: The Maritime Campaign" (Washington, D.C.: USGPO, 1992); Frank Uhlig Jr., *How Navies Fight: The U.S. Navy and its Allies* (Annapolis, Md.: Naval Institute Press, 1993). Norman Friedman, *Desert Victory: The War for Kuwait* (Annapolis, Md.: Naval Institute Press, 1991) has a listing of U.S. ships in the Gulf War. See also Vice Admiral Stanley R. Arthur and Marvin Pokrant, "Desert Storm at Sea," *U.S. Naval Institute Proceedings*, May 1991; Captain Vincent C. Thomas Jr., USN (Ret.), "The Sea Services Role in Desert Shield/Storm," *Seapower*, September 1991.

NETHERLANDS

See COALITION FORCES; PATRIOT MISSILE.

NEW ZEALAND

See COALITION FORCES.

NIGER

See COALITION FORCES.

NIGHT VISION DEVICES

Coalition forces owned the night in the Persian Gulf War. Their imaging technology, far more advanced than anything available to the Iraqis, turned night into day and allowed aircraft, helicopters and troops to operate around the clock.

Two basic types of night vision devices were used. The first was the ambient light amplifier. Pioneered in the Vietnam War with the starlight scope, this device takes available nighttime light and greatly amplifies it to produce an image almost as good as what would be available in daylight.

Ambient light amplifiers were incorporated into the AN/AVS-6 aviation night-vision system (ANVIS) worn by Army and Marine helicopter pilots and Navy A-6 Intruder attack pilots in the Gulf War. These night vision goggles have a range of seven miles and can operate at altitudes as low as 200 feet. ANVIS consists of a binocular-like objective lens assembly and an 18-mm third-generation image intensifier tube mounted on the pilot's helmet. Although some initial difficulties were reported with ANVIS, including a number of helicopter crashes into steep sand dunes as pilots adjusted to the peculiar desert environment, the night vision goggles provided coalition forces with a decisive edge.

So did the AN/VAS-2 image-intensification driver's viewing system, which was mounted on tanks and armored fighting vehicles, and the AN/PVS-7 single-tube, image-intensifier ground night vision goggles worn by troops. Each infantry battalion had 509 AN/PVS-7s, and each tank battalion had 298 AN/VAS-2s. Also fielded was the AN/TVS-5 second-generation, crew-served, image-intensifier sight used with machine guns or hand-held by individual soldiers for night surveillance.

The second type of night vision system used in the Gulf War was FLIR (forward-looking infrared), a system that employed infrared (i.e., differentiating between the small temperature differences of objects in its field of view) rather than visible light. A FLIR system normally consists of an array of infrared detectors over which an image formed by a lens is scanned, thereby creating a video signal for display on a television-like receiver.

FLIR sights were used on tanks and attack helicopters to detect and engage enemy targets well beyond visual range. They were also used in conjunction with night vision goggles by Marine AV-8B Harrier and F/A-18D Hornet and Navy A-6E Intruder pilots. The Air Force incorporated FLIR technology in its LANTIRN (low-altitude navigational and targeting infrared for night) systems, which are discussed elsewhere in detail.

The Army also used FLIR technology in its AN/PAQ-4 infrared aiming light, which was mounted on M16 rifles, M60 machine guns, M67 recoilless rifles and M72 rocket launchers. The aiming light sends along its line of sight an invisible pulsing beam that can only be detected by those wearing night vision goggles. Two AN/PAQ-4s were issued to each infantry squad.

See also LANTIRN (LOW-ALTITUDE NAVIGATIONAL AND TARGETING INFRARED FOR NIGHT).

Suggestions for further reading: Norman Friedman, *Desert Victory: The War for Kuwait* (Annapolis, Md.: Naval Institute Press, 1991); "Night Imaging Magic Opens Intrepid Manuever Warfare," *Signal*, August 1991; Paul Abrahams, "Darkness Is No Deterrent," *Financial Times* (London), January 31, 1991.

NINTH U.S. AIR FORCE

The Ninth U.S. Air Force encompassed all U.S. Air Force units in the Persian Gulf War. It was also the air component of the U.S. Central Command (CENTCOM) and as such its commander, Lieutenant General Charles A. Horner, served as the commander of CENTAF (Central Command Air Force). He was also the Joint Forces Air Component Commander (JFACC), responsible for coordinating the efforts of some 2,700 coalition aircraft representing 14 separate national or service components.

Lead elements of the Ninth Air Force arrived in Saudi Arabia on August 8, 1990, and by August 14 more than 200 combat aircraft had deployed. They were soon joined by the Ninth Air Force headquarters from its home station at Shaw Air Force Base in South Carolina.

The Ninth Air Force consisted of four provisional air divisions: the 14th Air Division with fighter aircraft, the 15th Air Division with electronic-warfare and command-and-control aircraft, the 17th Air Di-

vision with Strategic Air Command (SAC) bombers and tankers, and the 1610th Airlift Division with Military Airlift Command (MAC) transports.

Ultimately the Ninth Air Force deployed some 50,000 active Air Force, Air National Guard and Air Force Reserve personnel and some 1,200 aircraft to the Kuwaiti Theater of Operations. As detailed elsewhere, it waged one of the most brilliant air campaigns in history.

The Ninth Air Force flew 29,393 combat sorties and dropped 60,624 tons of bombs during the war. Fourteen aircraft were lost in combat. Twenty airmen were killed in action, another six died in accidents, nine were wounded and eight were taken prisoner and subsequently released.

Two Air Force Crosses were awarded to Ninth Air Force personnel for extraordinary heroism, and 50 Silver Stars were awarded for gallantry in action; 864 Distinguished Flying Crosses and 15,938 Air Medals were also awarded.

See also AERIAL COMBAT; AERIAL REFUELING; AIR CAMPAIGN; AIR DEFENSES; AIR FORCE, U.S.; AIRLIFT; AIRPOWER; ATO (AIR TASKING ORDER); CENTCOM (CENTRAL COMMAND); HORNER, CHARLES A; MOBILIZATION, U.S.

NO FLY ZONES
See KURDS; SHIITE REVOLT.

NORWAY
See COALITION FORCES.

NUCLEAR WEAPONS
Iraq's development of weapons of mass destruction, including nuclear, biological and chemical (NBC) weapons, was a major concern of the coalition. Although intelligence estimates were not precise, U.S. Central Command's planning assumption was that Iraq could produce a nuclear weapon by 1992 at the latest. Thus, one of the air campaign's specific target sets included Iraq's NBC weapons research facilities, production capabilities and delivery vehicles.

Although the damage inflicted on these targets was severe, including substantial damage to the Baghdad Nuclear Research center and both of Iraq's research reactors, United Nations (UN) inspection teams and U.S. intelligence sources subsequently discovered that Iraq's nuclear weapons program had not been destroyed by the coalition's air attacks.

As a consequence, United Nations Security Council Resolution 687, which established the cease-fire, specifically required Iraq to identify and destroy all of its weapons of mass destruction. The UN's International Atomic Energy Agency (IAEA) was charged with monitoring compliance with that provision.

Iraq grudgingly accepted the cease-fire agreement, but its cooperation with the IAEA was minimal at best. It stalled, evaded and delayed at every opportunity. One of President George Bush's last official acts was to order the launching of Tomahawk cruise missiles against a nuclear-related factory in Baghdad on January 17, 1993, in response to Iraq's refusal to cooperate with UN inspectors.

Iraqi intransigence continued during the Clinton administration. In July 1993, Secretary of State Warren Christopher warned that the Western allies might again use force if Iraq failed to comply with the UN cease-fire resolution. More recently, in July 1994, the IAEA reported that Iraq was cooperating fully with UN inspectors.

There are unconfirmed reports that during the Gulf War the CENTCOM (Central Command) air staff recommended using small tactical nuclear weapons to destroy 18 Iraqi NBC weapons sites, and that the chairman of the Joint Chiefs of Staff overruled CENTCOM. It was also reported that General H. Norman Schwarzkopf, the CINCCENT (commander in chief, Central Command), recommended that Baghdad be sent a démarche warning that if Iraq used chemical weapons against coalition forces, the United States would respond with a nuclear strike.

See also BIOLOGICAL WARFARE; CEASE-FIRE; CHEMICAL WARFARE; WAR TERMINATION.

Suggestions for further reading: Department of Defense, *Conduct of the Persian Gulf War: Final Report to the Congress* (Washington, D.C.: USGPO, 1992); Anthony H. Cordesman, *Weapons of Mass Destruction in the Middle East* (London: Pergamon Press, 1991); "UN Security Council Resolution 687: Iraq Weapons of Mass Destruction," *Background Brief* (London: Foreign and Commonwealth Office, October 1991); McGeorge Bundy, "Nuclear Weapons and the Gulf," *Foreign Affairs,* Fall 1991; David Albright and Mark Hibbs, "Iraq's Bomb: Blueprints and Artifacts," *Bulletin of the Atomic Scientists,* January/February 1992; Gary Milhollin, "Building Saddam Hussein's Bomb," *New York Times Magazine,* March 8, 1992; David Albright and Mark Hibbs, "Iraq's Shop-Till-You-Drop Nuclear Program," *Bulletin of the Atomic Scientists,* April 1992; Daniel Schwammenthal, "How the IAEA Assists Iraq," *Defense Media Review,* March 1993; Diana Edenswood and Gary Milhollin, "Iraq's Bomb—An Update," *New York Times,* April 26, 1993; Nora Boustany, "U.N. Team Rebuffed by Iraq," *Washington Post,* July 12, 1993. For reports on the possibility that the United States might use nuclear weapons, see Rick Atkinson *Crusade: The Untold Story of the Persian Gulf War* (New York: Houghton Mifflin, 1993).

OAK LEAF CLUSTER

A metallic oak leaf cluster is worn on the ribbon of U.S. Army and Air Force service medals and decorations (except for the Air Medal, on which a metallic number is worn) to denote a subsequent awarding of the same medal or decoration. Subsequent awardings of U.S. Navy, Marine Corps and Coast Guard medals are denoted by a metallic gold star.

OIL FIRES

See ECOLOGICAL WARFARE.

OMAN

A member of both the Arab League and the Gulf Cooperation Council (GCC), the Sultanate of Oman played an important role in the Persian Gulf War.

Located on the southeast coast of the Arabian Peninsula, Oman had an estimated 1991 population of 1,534,000. About the size of New Mexico, Oman has a land area of 82,030 square miles; the tip of its Ruus-al-Jibal Peninsula controls access to the Persian Gulf.

Ruled by Portugal in the 16th century and by the Persians in the 18th century, by the early 19th century the Sultanate of Oman and Muscat (as it was then called) was one of the most influential nations in the region, extending its sway over much of the Persian and Pakistani coasts and as far south as Zanzibar. Under British influence in the 1950s, it established its independence on July 23, 1970, and changed its name to the Sultanate of Oman. It is an absolute monarchy ruled by Sultan Qabus bin Said. With oil reserves estimated at 4.5 billion barrels in 1987, Oman has an economy dominated by oil production. Its capital city, Muscat, had an estimated 1990 population of 85,000.

Oman has several ports and major airfields. In December 1979, the United States began negotiations for the use of these facilities, and in 1980, Bright Star joint military exercises were begun. Funding for improvements to existing air and sea facilities was approved by the U.S. government in 1981, and pre-positioning of U.S. Air Force (USAF) supplies in Oman began in October 1983.

On August 12, 1990, at the beginning of the Kuwaiti crisis, USAF C-130 Hercules transports arrived at Thumrait, Masirah and Seeb air bases in Oman to begin distributing prepositioned supplies. Oman provided construction materials, food preparation facilities and local workers, and it helped correct the transportation problems encountered by the initial USAF units. Oman also provided no-cost host nation support to the coalition, including the establishment of a major hospital there that was staffed by U.S. Army medical personnel. USAF aerial refueling tankers operated from the air base at Seeb, as did U.S. and United Kingdom maritime patrol aircraft.

Oman played a crucial role in maritime interception operations (MIO), and on several occasions ships carrying contraband to Iraq were diverted to the port of Muscat. Oman also participated in amphibious exercises at Ras Al-Madrakah along its coast, as part of the Amphibious Task Force's deception operations.

In addition to allowing the coalition the use of its airfields, ports and facilities, Oman played a direct military role in the Gulf War. The Omani Air Force's 20 Jaguar fighters participated in the coalition's air campaign. The Omani Navy's missile boats and patrol craft participated in the MIO enforcement of UN sanctions against Iraq, and also took part in anti-surface warfare operations in the coalition's maritime campaign.

On the ground, an Omani motorized infantry battalion was part of Task Force Omar, one of the three task forces comprising the Arab/Islamic Joint Forces Command East (JFC-E), which anchored the coalition's line along the coast of the Persian Gulf. During the ground campaign, JFC-E penetrated the Iraqi defensive positions and attacked along the coast directly toward Kuwait City. Its forces entered that city on February 27, 1991, and drove out the Iraqi occupiers. One Omani soldier was wounded in the attack.

See also AIR CAMPAIGN; AIR FORCES COALITION; ARAB LEAGUE; ARMIES, COALITION; COALITION FORCES; GROUND CAMPAIGN; GULF COOPERATION COUNCIL; JOINT FORCES COMMAND; MARITIME CAMPAIGN; NAVIES, COALITION.

Suggestion for further reading: Department of Defense, *Conduct of the Persian Gulf War: Final Report to the Congress* (Washington, D.C.: USGPO, 1992).

101ST AIRBORNE DIVISION (AIR ASSAULT)

The "Screaming Eagles" of the 101st Airborne Division (Air Assault) fought in World War II as an airborne division and in the Vietnam War as an airmobile division. Converted to an air assault division after Vietnam by the addition of an enlarged combat aviation brigade, the 101st is the only such division in the U.S. Army.

Part of the initial XVIII Airborne Corps defensive deployment to the Kuwaiti Theater of Operations (KTO), the first elements of the 101st Airborne Division departed by air for Saudi Arabia on August 17, 1990, from its home station at Fort Campbell, Kentucky. The rest of the division followed by sea.

Commanded by Major General J. H. Binford Peay III, the 101st Airborne Division (Air Assault) consisted of the 1st, 2d and 3d Battalions of the 187th Infantry; the 1st, 2d and 3d Battalions of the 327th Infantry; and the 1st, 2d and 3d Battalions of the 504th Infantry. Organized into three manuever brigades, these battalions were supported by an Aviation Brigade and a Division Artillery.

The Aviation Brigade consisted of two battalions of UH-60 Blackhawk assault helicopters, a battalion of AH-64 Apache attack helicopters, a battalion of AH-1 Cobra attack helicopters, a battalion of CH-47D Chinook medium-lift helicopters and the 2d Squadron, 17th Air Cavalry with OH-58 Kiowa scout helicopters. The 1st, 2d and 3d Battalions of the 320th Airborne Artillery, each with 18 towed 105-mm howitzers, comprised the Division Artillery.

When the ground campaign began, the mission of the 101st Airborne Division (Air Assault) was to penetrate rapidly by air to the Euphrates River, cut the enemy lines of communication (LOCs) between Baghdad and Iraqi forces in the KTO, and destroy enemy forces in the area before turning east to prevent the enemy from counterattacking allied forces.

Augmented by XVIII Airborne Corps's 18th Aviation Brigade, on G-Day (February 24, 1991) the division attacked with its AH-64 Apache and AH-1 Cobra gunships, 60 UH-60 Blackhawk assault helicopters and 40 CH-47D Chinook medium-lift helicopters. The 1st Brigade seized Forward Operating Base (FOB) Cobra, some 93 miles inside Iraq and halfway to the Euphrates, and established there a major logistics base and refueling point.

With its logistics base secure, the 101st continued the attack. In the deepest air assault in military history, the 3d Brigade flew some 175 miles north to seize Area of Operations (AO) Eagle, a 50-mile front stretching from Samawa to Nasiriya along the Euphrates River valley.

By G+2 (February 26), with its establishment of Area of Operations (AO) Eagle, the division had achieved all of its initial objectives, interdicting the enemy's LOCs and blocking the reinforcement of Iraqi forces in the KTO.

But the 101st did not stop there. On G+3 (February 27), the 2d Brigade seized FOB Viper, 200 kilometers to the east of FOB Cobra. Two attack helicopter battalions were the first to reach the Basra causeway across the Euphrates and destroyed every moving vehicle on the causeway, blocking further movement.

With their last escape routes now cut, most of the Iraqi forces were caught between the advancing forces of XVIII Airborne Corps's 24th Infantry Division (Mechanized), the VII Corps and the Euphrates River. The end was at hand, and the next day a ceasefire was declared.

See also XVIII AIRBORNE CORPS; GROUND CAMPAIGN.

Suggestions for further reading: Thomas Taylor, *Lightning in the Storm: The 101st Air Assault Division in the Gulf War* (New York: Hippocrene Books, 1994; Department of Defense, *Conduct of the Persian Gulf War: Final Report to the Congress*, "Chapter 8: The Ground Campaign" (Washington, D.C.: USGPO, 1992); Major James Blackwell, *Thunder in the Desert: The Strategy and Tactics of the Persian Gulf War* (New York: Bantam Books, 1991); General H. Norman Schwarzkopf, *It Doesn't Take a Hero* (New York: Bantam Books, 1992); The Staff of *U.S. News & World Report, Triumph Without Victory* (New York: Times Books, 1992). See also Sean D. Naylor, "Flight of Eagles," *Army Times*, July 22, 1991.

197TH INFANTRY BRIGADE (MECHANIZED)
See 24TH INFANTRY DIVISION (MECHANIZED).

OPERATIONAL LEVEL OF WAR
See AIRLAND BATTLE DOCTRINE; CAMPAIGN PLAN.

ORGANIZATION FOR COMBAT, U.S.
The U.S. organization for combat in the Persian Gulf War was headed by President George Bush as commander in chief and extended to Dick Cheney, the secretary of defense, through General Colin Powell, the chairman of the Joint Chiefs of Staff, to General H. Norman Schwarzkopf, the commander in chief, U.S. Central Command (CINCCENT).

As a joint (i.e., all-service) unified command, Central Command (CENTCOM) had several subordinate component commanders, including an Army component commander (ARCENT), a Navy component commander (NAVCENT), an Air Force component commander (CENTAF), a Marine forces commander (MARCENT) and a special operations component commander (SOCCENT).

The ARCENT commander was Lieutenant General John J. Yeosock, who also commanded the Third U.S. Army. Subordinate to the Third Army was VII Corps commanded by Lieutenant General Frederick M. Franks Jr.; XVIII Airborne Corps commanded by Lieutenant General Gary E. Luck; and the 22d Theater Army Support Command led by Lieutenant General William G. Pagonis.

Under VII Corps was the 1st Armored Division, the 1st Cavalry Division, the 1st Infantry Division (with a brigade of the 2d Armored Division attached), the 3d Armored Division, the 2d Armored Cavalry Regiment and the 11th Aviation Brigade. Also under VII Corps was the British 1st Armoured Division.

XVIII Airborne Corps consisted of the 82d Airborne Division, the 101st Airborne Division (Air Assault), the 24th Infantry Division (Mechanized) with the 197th Infantry Brigade attached, the 3d Armored Cavalry Regiment and the 12th Aviation Brigade. The French 6th Light Armored Division was also under XVIII Airborne Corps's tactical control.

The NAVCENT commander was Vice Admiral Stanley R. Arthur, who also commanded the Seventh U.S. Fleet. Subordinate to the Seventh Fleet was the Persian Gulf Battle Force and the Red Sea Battle Force, together including six carrier battle groups and two battleship surface action groups. Also subordinate to the Seventh Fleet was a Middle East Force commander to coordinate maritime interception operations, the Amphibious Task Force commander, a mine countermeasures force commander and the logistics supply force commander.

CENTAF was commanded by Lieutenant General Charles A. Horner, who also commanded the Ninth U.S. Air Force. Subordinate to the Ninth Air Force was the 14th Air Division with 28 tactical fighter squadrons; the 15th Air Division with 2 1/2 tactical reconnaissance squadrons, 1 1/2 electronic combat squadrons, and Airborne Warning and Control System (AWACS), Airborne Battlefield Command and Control Center (ABCC) and Joint Surveillance Target Attack System (JSTARS) tactical command-and-control units; the 17th Air Division with 3 Strategic Air Command B-52 bomber squadrons and 19 aerial tanker squadrons; and the 1610th Airlift Division with 12 tactical airlift squadrons.

CINCENT's Marine force commander (MARCENT) was Lieutenant General Walter E. Boomer. He commanded The First Marine Expeditionary Force (I MEF). Subordinate to I MEF were the 1st and 2d Marine Divisions, the 5th Marine Expeditionary Brigade, the 3d Marine Aircraft Wing, the 1st and 2d Force Service Support Groups and the attached "Tiger Brigade" from the Army's 2d Armored Division.

Finally, CINCCENT's special operations commander (SOCCENT) was Colonel Jesse Johnson. SOCCENT drew its forces from the parent U.S. Special Operations Command. SOCCENT included the Army's 3d and 5th Special Forces Groups and the 3d Battalion of the 160th Special Operations Aviation Regiment, the Air Force's 1st Special Operations Wing and the Navy's Special Warfare Task Group.

The primary Army and Marine ground combat organization is the squad. Commanded by a sergeant, it may be divided into two fire teams to facilitate fire and manuever. Two or more squads make up a platoon commanded by a lieutenant, and two or more platoons make up a company (a "battery" in the artillery, a "troop" in the cavalry) commanded by a captain.

Two or more company-size units make up a battalion (a "squadron" in the cavalry) commanded by a lieutenant colonel, and two or more battalion-size units make up an Army brigade (a "regiment" in the cavalry, a "group" in the artillery) or a Marine regiment commanded by a colonel.

Two or more brigade-size units make up a division commanded by a major general, and two or more divisions make up an Army corps or a Marine expeditionary force commanded by a lieutenant general. A variant of this structure is the Marine Air-Ground Task Force organization (see MARITIME STRATEGY (IC DOCTRINE, U.S.).

See also CENTCOM (CENTRAL COMMAND); FIRST MARINE EXPEDITIONARY FORCE; NINTH U.S. AIR FORCE; SEVENTH U.S. FLEET; SPECIAL OPERATIONS COMMAND CENTRAL COMMAND; THIRD U.S. ARMY.

Suggestions for further reading: Department of Defense, *Conduct of the Persian Gulf War: Final Report to the Congress*, "Appendix K: Command, Control, Communications (C3), and Space" (Washington, D.C.: USGPO, 1992).

OZAL, TURGUT
See TURKEY.

P

PAGONIS, WILLIAM G(US), LIEUTENANT GENERAL, USA (1941–)

The chief logistician for CENTCOM (Central Command) and the commander of the 22d Theater Army Support Command during the Gulf War, General William G. Pagonis entered the U.S. Army through the Reserve Officer Training Corps at Pennsylvania State University and was commissioned in the Transportation Corps in June 1964.

Volunteering for service in Vietnam in 1967, he commanded the 1097th Transportation Company (Medium Boat) in the Mekong Delta, pioneering the concept of barge-mounted waterborne artillery for

General Pagonis was responsible for creating and directing the enormous logistics network that made victory in the Gulf possible.
U.S. Army photo courtesy of Army Material Command.

riverine operations. After serving in Vietnam Pagonis returned to Pennsylvania State University, where he received a Masters of Business Administration with a major in business logistics.

Returning to Vietnam in July 1970, he served as the transportation officer for the 101st Airborne Division (Airmobile) and, in a unique assignment, as the executive officer of the division's 2d Battalion, 501st Infantry.

Among his significant assignments are commander of the 10th Transportation Battalion (Terminal), director of the Logistics Support Command for U.S. Army Forces (Panama), division support commander of the 4th Infantry Division, and deputy commanding general of the 21st Support Command in Germany. After service in the Office of the Assistant Chief of Staff for Logistics in the Pentagon, General Pagonis was assigned as the director of logistics (J-4) of U.S. Forces Command.

In August 1990, General Pagonis deployed to Saudi Arabia to command the Army Forces Central Command (ARCENT) Support Command, which later became the 22d Theater Army Support Command. With a strength of some 70,000 personnel, during Operation Desert Shield his unit received and moved more than 300,000 soldiers, 110,000 wheeled vehicles, 1,200 armored vehicles and 33,000 containers.

During Operation Desert Storm, the unit moved more than 4,500 truckloads of supplies westward, from the supply bases near the ports to attack positions, in order to sustain the ground offensive. "It was an absolutely gigantic accomplishment," said General H. Norman Schwarzkopf after the war, "and I can't give enough credit to the logisticians and the transporters who were able to pull this off."

Earning the Combat Infantryman Badge for his service in Vietnam, General Pagonis has also been awarded the Distinguished Service Medal, the Silver Star, two Legions of Merit, four Bronze Star Medals (including awards for bravery), five Meritorious Service Medals, three Air Medals and two Commendation Medals.

See also LOGISTICS, U.S.

Suggestions for further reading: Lt. Gen. William G. Pagonis with Jeffrey L. Cruikshank, *Moving Mountains: Lessons in Leadership and Logistics From the Gulf War* (Boston: Harvard Business School Press, 1992); General H. Norman Schwarzkopf, *It Doesn't Take a Hero* (New York: Bantam Books, 1992).

PAKISTAN

See COALITION FORCES; JOINT FORCES COMMAND; YEMEN.

PATRIOT MISSILE

First deployed by the United States in Europe in 1985 as a surface-to-air missile defense system against Warsaw Pact aircraft, the U.S. Army's Patriot system was used in the Gulf War against Iraqi Scud tactical ballistic missiles.

A Patriot battery includes up to eight launchers, each with four MIM-104 missiles and support equipment, including a multifunctional phased-array radar, a weapons control computer, an electric power plant and communications equipment. To achieve an antitactical ballistic missile capability, the computer software, warhead and fuze of the Patriot system was enhanced.

Twenty-one Patriot batteries (132 launchers) were deployed to Saudi Arabia to protect airfields, ports, oil production and refinery facilities, logistics bases, command and control centers and the combat divisions in the field. Four batteries (two American and two Dutch, for a total of 26 launchers) were deployed to Turkey to defend Turkish air bases; none of those batteries was involved in any engagements.

In addition, seven Patriot batteries—four American, one Dutch and two Israeli Defense Force (IDF), for a total of 48 launchers—were deployed in Israel to provide limited area defense of population centers. The Dutch battery was deployed just before the end of the war and was not involved in any engagements.

Of the approximately 600 Patriot missiles deployed, 158 were fired at 47 Iraqi Scuds over Saudi Arabia and Israel.

Hailed at the time as a "Scud buster," the Patriot missile system came under attack from critics after the war.
Central Command Public Affairs.

Hailed at the time as enormously successful, after the war the Patriot system came under intense criticism, much of it motivated by fears that the success of the Patriot antitactical ballistic missile (ATBM) would promote further investment in the Strategic Defense Initiative (SDI) program to develop a defense against strategic ballistic missiles.

Scaling down its initial figures, in April 1992 the Army claimed success in 70 percent of the Patriot-Scud duels over Saudi Arabia and in 40 percent of the duels over Israel. But critics challenged even these figures.

"The Patriot system does not have embedded digital data collection," noted the official Department of Defense report on the war, "therefore a complete quantitative analysis of Patriot effectiveness is not available." But, it went on to say, the system's operational success can be measured qualitatively. "Patriot batteries . . . served as a confidence-building asset to Coalition forces and civilians. The system played an important role in keeping Israel out of the war and strengthened Coalition resolve."

Suggestions for further reading: Department of Defense, *Conduct of the Persian Gulf War: Final Report to the Congress,* "Appendix T: Performance of Selected Weapons Systems" (Washington, D.C.: USGPO, 1992). For criticism of the Patriot, see Theodore A. Postol, "Lessons of the Gulf War Experience with Patriot," *International Security,* Winter 1991–92. For a rejoinder, see Secretary of the Army Michael P. W. Stone's "The Patriot Controversy: Close the Critics' Books," *Christian Science Monitor,* October 16, 1992. See also David C. Morrison, "Patriot Games," *National Journal,* April 25, 1992; and "Patriot Games," *The Economist,* October 10, 1992.

PHILIPPINES
See COALITION FORCES.

POLAND
See COALITON FORCES.

PORTUGAL
See COALITION FORCES.

POWELL, COLIN L(UTHER), GENERAL, USA (1937–)
The chairman of the Joint Chiefs of Staff (CJCS) and the senior officer of the U.S. Armed forces, General Powell was one of the key leaders of the United

One of the most powerful chairmen in the history of the JCS, General Powell was instrumental in the Gulf War victory.
USAF photo (SRA Rodney Kerns) courtesy of OCJCS.

States's Persian Gulf War effort, serving as the principal military advisor to President George Bush, Secretary of Defense Dick Cheney and the National Security Council.

Powell was the most powerful chairman in the history of that office, partly as a result of legislative changes, discussed below, in the authority and responsibilities of the CJCS. But much of his success was also due to his background, personality and experience. An infantry veteran wounded and decorated on the battlefield, he was also wise in the ways of the Washington bureaucracy. He bridged the gap between the uniformed military and the political decisionmakers to an unprecedented degree. The former national security advisor to President Ronald Reagan, Powell had an enormous influence on the conduct of military affairs and was a trusted confidant of both President Bush and Secretary of Defense Cheney.

Powell entered the U.S. Army through the Reserve Officer Training Corps program at The College of the City of New York and was commissioned in the infantry in 1958. In 1962, he served in Vietnam as a senior battalion advisor and as the assistant G-3 (operations officer) advisor to the 1st ARVN (Army of the Republic of Vietnam) Infantry Division in I Corps in the northern portion of South Vietnam. In 1968 he returned to Vietnam, serving as the executive officer of the 3d Battalion, 1st Infantry, 11th Infantry Brigade and later as the G-3 (operations officer) of the 23d (American) Infantry Division in II Corps in central South Vietnam.

In 1972, Powell earned a Master of Business Administration degree from George Washington University, and the following year he was selected as a White House Fellow, serving as special assistant to the deputy director of the Office of the President.

Among his significant military assignments were command of the 1st Battalion, 32d Infantry in Korea; command of the 2d Brigade, 101st Airborne Division (Air Assault) at Fort Campbell, Kentucky; senior military assistant to the deputy secretary of defense; and assistant division commander of the 4th Infantry Division at Fort Carson, Colorado.

In 1983, General Powell returned to Washington to serve as the senior military assistant to Secretary of Defense Caspar Weinberger. In June 1986, he assumed command of V Corps in Germany, only to be recalled to Washington in December 1987 to serve as assistant to the president for national security affairs. Departing Washington in April 1989, Powell then served as commander in chief, U.S. Forces Command at Fort McPherson, Georgia.

On October 1, 1989, General Powell was appointed the 12th chairman of the Joint Chiefs of Staff by President George Bush, and in 1991, after the Gulf War, he was reappointed to a second two-year term as CJCS.

General Powell was able to take advantage of recently enacted legislation (see GOLDWATER-NICHOLS DEFENSE DEPARTMENT REORGANIZATION ACT) that gave the chairman greatly enhanced powers. Instead of being the first among equals among the Joint Chiefs of Staff, as had been the case previously, Powell was clearly in charge and able to

enforce a unified effort among the services to ensure the buildup of personnel, supplies and equipment in the Kuwaiti Theater of Operations.

Although the CJCS is not legally in the chain of command to the field, Secretary of Defense Cheney passed his and the president's orders to General H. Norman Schwarzkopf, the commander in chief, U.S. Central Command (CINCCENT) in Saudi Arabia, through General Powell. As Schwarzkopf later remarked: "Officially, as a commander in chief, I reported to Secretary Cheney, but Colin Powell was virtually my sole point of contact with the Administration. 'It's my job to keep the President and the White House informed,' Powell would say. 'You worry about your theater and let me worry about Washington.' This arrangement was efficient. . . ." Schwarzkopf added:

> And there is no doubt in my mind that General Powell was the best man for the job during this crisis. Not since General George Marshall during World War II had a military officer enjoyed such direct access to White House inner circles—not to mention the confidence of the President. Powell could get decisions in hours that would have taken another man days or weeks.

Although initally hesitant to recommend the use of force against Iraq, preferring to give economic sanctions more time to work, once President Bush decided to use force Powell recommended that it be used decisively and in overwhelming strength. As he told a news conference in January 1991: "Our strategy to go after [the Iraqi] Army is very, very simple. First we're going to cut it off, and then we're going to kill it."

In addition to the Combat Infantryman Badge, General Powell has been awarded three Defense Distinguished Service Medals, the Army Distinguished Service Medal, the Defense Superior Service Medal, two Legions of Merit, the Soldier's Medal for bravery, the Bronze Star Medal, the Purple Heart for wounds received in action, the Air Medal, the Joint Service Commendation Medal, and the Army Commendation Medal.

General Powell retired from active duty in September 1993 and returned to civilian life. He was subsequently made a Knight Commander of the Order of the Bath by Queen Elizabeth II of Great Britain.

See also COMMAND AND CONTROL; GOLDWA-TER-NICHOLS DEFENSE DEPARTMENT REORGANI-ZATION ACT; JOINT CHIEFS OF STAFF (JCS), U.S.

Suggestions for further reading: David Roth, *Sacred Honor* (New York: HarperCollins, 1993); Howard Means, *Colin Powell: Soldier/Statesman— Statesman/Soldier* (New York: Donald I. Fine, 1992); Bob Woodward, *The Commanders* (New York: Simon & Schuster, 1991); Rick Atkinson, *Crusade: The Untold Story of the Persian Gulf War* (New York: Houghton Mifflin, 1993); General H. Norman Schwarzkopf, *It Doesn't Take a Hero* (New York: Bantam Books, 1992). For a contrary view, see Richard H. Kohn's "Out of Control: The Crisis in Civil-Military Relations," *The National Interest* (Spring 1994) and the commentary in the Summer 1994 issue.

PRISONERS OF WAR (POW)

Forty-five coalition military personnel, including 21 Americans, were held as prisoners of war (POWs) by Iraq during the Persian Gulf War. Other coalition personnel held as POWs included two Italian, one Kuwaiti and nine Saudi pilots; seven British Royal Air Force pilots; and five members of the United Kingdom's special operations forces, the SAS (Special Air Service), who were captured while on a mission behind enemy lines. Also held as POWs by Iraq were CBS News correspondent Bob Simon and

With the surrender of more than 86,000 Iraqi soldiers, the care and control of enemy POWs was a major task.
U.S. Army photo courtesy of 24th Infantry Division (Mechanized).

his three-man crew. Repatriated after the war, all reported suffering physical abuse, and the two American female POWs, Army flight surgeon Major Rhonda Cornum and Army truck driver Specialist Melissa Rathbun-Nealy, reported suffering sexual abuse as well.

Coalition forces captured 86,743 enemy prisoners of war (EPWs), including 69,822 who were processed through U.S. facilities. An agreement between the United States and Saudi Arabia provided that the former would transfer custody of EPWs to Saudi Arabia after their registration by U.S. forces. On May 1, 1991, the last EPW in U.S. custody was transferred to the Saudi Arabian government.

The coalition's repatriation of EPWs began on March 6, 1991, and ended on August 22, 1991. A total of 13,418 EPWs refused repatriation, and on August 23, 1991, the International Commission of the Red Cross declared them protected civilians and they were reclassified as refugees.

In April 1993, it was revealed that some 1,000 former Iraqi EPWs had been resettled in the United States and that another 4,000 such resettlements were expected. Other former Iraqi EPWs were resettled in Scandinavian countries, and several thousand were accepted by Iran.

See also WAR CRIMES.

Suggestions for further reading: Department of Defense, *Conduct of the Persian Gulf War: Final Report to the Congress*, "Appendix L: Enemy Prisoner of War Operations," "Appendix O: The Role of the Law of War" (Washington, D.C.: USGPO, 1992). For accounts of the treatment of coalition personnel in captivity, see Rhonda Cornum and Peter Copeland *She Went to War: The Rhonda Cornum Story* (Novato, Calif.: Presidio Press, 1992); Bob Simon, *Forty Days* (New York: Putnam, 1992); Patrick E. Tyler, "American War Prisoners Abused by Iraqi Captors, Pentagon Says," *New York Times,* March 13, 1991; and Andrew Alderson and Grace Bradberry, "Captured Airmen Reveal Full Horror of Gulf War Torture," *The Sunday Times* (London), December 29, 1991. On EPW resettlement, see Jerry Seper, "U.S. Resettles Iraqis," *Washington Times*, April 14, 1993.

PROVEN FORCE JOINT TASK FORCE

See TURKEY.

PROVIDE COMFORT OPERATION

See KURDS.

PSYCHOLOGICAL OPERATIONS

"PSYOPS," or psychological operations, is the term used to describe nonlethal operations—including the use of radio broadcasts, loudspeakers and leaflets—designed to destroy enemy morale and to encourage mass surrender and desertion. All coalition forces, especially those of the Arab nations of the Gulf Cooperation Council, conducted their own psychological warfare operations against Iraq.

Detailed to CENTCOM (Central Command) from SOCCOM (Special Operations Command) in late August 1990, the 4th Psychological Operations Group was responsible for all U.S. psychological operations in the KTO (Kuwaiti Theater of Operations). The group's 8th Psychological Operations Task Force supported the Third U.S. Army in the field with leaflets and radio and loudspeaker broadcasts; its "Voice of the Gulf" radio network went on the air on January 19, 1991, using ground-based and airborne transmitters to broadcast 18 hours a day for 40 days.

Leaflets were the most commonly used method of conveying PSYOPS messages. Some 29 million leaflets with 33 different messages were disseminated in the KTO by aircraft and artillery. Some 66 loudspeaker teams, many from the U.S. Army Reserve, were attached to tactical manuever brigades.

Leaflet and loudspeaker messages were designed to undermine Iraqi morale, provide instructions on how to surrender, instill confidence that prisoners would be treated humanely, and provide advanced warning of impending air attacks, thus encouraging desertion. One effective technique to induce mass defections was to follow the dropping of an earth-shattering BLU-82 15,000-pound bomb near Iraq positions with a dropping of leaflets warning that the next strike would be directly on those positions.

Iraq also tried its hand at PSYOPS with its "Voice of Peace" radio broadcasts by "Baghdad Betty" and "Iraq Jack," as the troops nicknamed the commentators. While listening to the music, the troops were more amused than depressed by the Iraqis' dire warning that "Bart Simpson [evidently unbeknownst to the Iraqis, a TV cartoon character] is making love to your wife."

Suggestions for further reading: Department of Defense, *Conduct of the Persian Gulf War: Final Report to the Congress*, "Appendix J: Special Operations Forces" (Washington, D.C.: USGPO, 1992); Major Robert B. Adolph Jr., "PSYOP: Gulf War Force Multiplier," *Army*, December 1992. See also Charles Paul Freund, "The War on Your Mind," *Washington Post*, January 27, 1991; and Charles Paul Freund, "War's 'Paper Bullets,'" *Washington Post*, February 10, 1991.

PURPLE HEART

The oldest U.S. military decoration, the Purple Heart was first authorized by General George Washington during the American Revolutionary War. It was revived in 1932 for awarding in the name of the president of the United States to any member of the armed forces—or to any civilian national of the United States serving under competent authority in any capacity with one of the U.S. armed services—who is wounded or killed in action against the enemy.

See also DECORATIONS, U.S.

QATAR

A member of both the Arab League and the Gulf Cooperation Council (GCC), the State of Qatar played an important role in the Persian Gulf War.

Occupying a peninsula in the Persian Gulf, Qatar had an estimated 1991 population of 10,387,000. With a land area of 4,247 square miles, it is slightly smaller than Connecticut. Under the control of the Turkish Ottoman Empire from 1872 to 1915, Qatar gave control of its defense and foreign relations to Great Britain in 1916. When the British withdrew from the Persian Gulf in 1971, Qatar declared its independence. A traditional monarchy, Qatar is ruled by Emir Khalifah ibn Hamad ath-Thani.

With proven oil reserves of 3.3 billion barrels, Qatar has one of the highest per capita incomes in the world. Its capital city, Doha, had an estimated 1987 population of 250,000. Qatar has several ports and major airfields.

All GCC states except Qatar granted U.S. forces access to their territory on August 9, 1990; Qatar permitted such access a week later. It also pro-vided host-nation support for coalition medical units, and allowed use of its ports for storage of prepositioned stocks.

Qatar's naval forces participated in the coalition's maritime activities during Operations Desert Shield and Desert Storm, including maritime interception operations, and its air force played a role in the coalition's air campaign. Moreover, the Qatar Mechanized Battalion was part of Task Force Abu Bakr in the Arab/Islamic Joint Forces Command East. It participated in the battle of Khafji in January 1991, and in the ground campaign's attack northward along the Gulf coast through the Iraqi defenses. It also took part in the liberation of Kuwait City.

See also AIR FORCES, COALITION; ARMIES, COALITION; COALITION FORCES; GULF COOPERATION COUNCIL; JOINT FORCES COMMAND; MARITIME INTERCEPTION OPERATIONS; NAVIES, COALITION.

Suggestion for further reading: Department of Defense, *Conduct of the Persian Gulf War: Final Report to the Congress* (Washington, D.C.: USGPO, 1992).

R

RAPID DEPLOYMENT JOINT TASK FORCE (RDJTF)

See CENTCOM (CENTRAL COMMAND).

READY RESERVE FLEET

See SEALIFT.

RECONNAISSANCE

Reconnaissance, a key element in the intelligence collection effort, has as its mission identifying the enemy's strengths and battlefield locations. As discussed elsewhere (see INTELLIGENCE), the coalition's control of the air severely limited Iraqi intelligence-gathering. Iraq's reconnaissance was limited to ground probes by tactical units against coalition positions (see KHAFJI, BATTLE OF).

But for the coalition, and for the United States in particular, reconnaissance was a much more sophisticated affair. Special Operations Forces (SOF) conducted special reconnaissance (SR) missions throughout the Gulf War. British Special Air Service (SAS) personnel infiltrated Iraq to mark targets with their laser designators for air-dropped precision-guided bombs and to capture prisoners for interrogation. Fifty-two medals were awarded to British special operations personnel for their actions in the Gulf War.

U.S. special reconnaissance activities were also extensive. U.S. Navy SEALS (i.e., commandos) and Navy special boat unit detachments maintained a constant presence north of the Saudi town of Khafji and conducted 11 SR missions on the Kuwaiti beaches. At the same time, Army special forces conducted SR missions in support of VII and XVIII Airborne Corps, including analyzing soil conditions to determine whether they would permit passage of heavy armored vehicles. SOF aircraft also conducted SR missions behind Iraqi lines.

The Strategic Air Command (SAC) deployed nine U-2R and Lockheed TR-1 strategic reconnaissance aircraft possessing optical and electronic sensors that could "image" a tank or artillery piece against its background. SAC's nine RC-135 Rivet Joint and E-8A JSTARS aircraft provided reconnaissance from the beginning of the crisis, as did the Navy's electronic reconnaissance squadrons.

The Central Command air component's tactical reconnaissance aircraft included 24 RF-4C Phantoms, six United Kingdom GR1A Tornados and 10 Saudi RF-5Cs.

The war with Iraq was the first in history to make comprehensive use of space systems. As discussed elsewhere (see SATELLITES), early-warning satellites were the primary system for detecting Scud missile launch sites. Multi-spectral imagery LANDSAT satellites provided mapping and warfighting support.

See also ELECTRONIC WARFARE; JSTARS (JOINT SURVEILLANCE TARGET ATTACK SYSTEM); SATELLITES; SPECIAL OPERATIONS COMMAND CENTRAL COMMAND.

Suggestions for further reading: Department of Defense, *Conduct of the Persian Gulf War: Final Report to the Congress* (Washington, D.C.: USGPO, 1992); Eliot A. Cohen et al., *Gulf War Airpower Survey* (Washington, D.C.: USGPO, 1993).

REFUGEES

See CIVIL AFFAIRS; KURDS; SHIITE REVOLT.

REGIMENT

For many years the regiment was the standard military organizational unit. In World War II, for example, a U.S. Army infantry division had a fixed triangular structure consisting of three infantry regiments, each with three infantry battalions. Armored divisions, by comparison, were much more flexible, consisting of three combat commands of no fixed size that could be tailored for specific missions by temporarily attaching the necessary infantry and armor battalions.

Although the term "regiment" was retained for historical and lineage purposes, after the Korean War the Army abolished the old triangular infantry regiments. All combat battalions are still assigned a regimental number—for example, 1st Battalion, 2d Infantry Regiment—but the regiment itself exists only on paper and even the term itself is normally omitted in everyday usage. Thus the 1st Battalion, 2d Infantry Regiment is usually referred to as the "1st Battalion, 2d Infantry" or even abbreviated as "1/2".

In the regiment's place, brigades were formed much like the old combat commands. For example, in the Gulf War the 2d Brigade, 24th Infantry Division was task-organized to include the 1st Battalion, 64th Armor; the 3d Battalion, 69th Armor; and the 3d Battalion, 15th Infantry. The British Army long ago adopted this system, and many of the world's armies have followed suit.

Within the Army only the armored cavalry regiments retain their traditional fixed organizational structure. The U.S. Marine Corps also retains its fixed triangular regimental structure. Each of the several Marine infantry regiments is organized into three battalions (for example, 1st, 2d and 3d Battalions, 5th Marines), and the Marine Corps's artillery is organized into regiments as well.

See also MARINE CORPS, U.S.; ORGANIZATION FOR COMBAT, U.S.

RELIGIOUS SERVICES

Saudi Arabia, the birthplace of Islam, has especially strict religious laws. An early concern of senior U.S. military officers, therefore, was whether Roman Catholic, Protestant and Jewish military chaplains could be deployed with the forces, whether they could openly conduct religious services, and whether Christian and Jewish religious symbols could be openly displayed.

Although this was a matter that attracted much media attention, it turned out to be a non-issue. Although troops were cautioned not to deliberately offend Islamic sensibilities, Bible studies, prayer meetings, prayer breakfasts and church services

were regularly conducted. American Muslim soldiers were permitted to visit Mecca, and Christmas and Passover services were conducted on schedule. The 1st Cavalry Division, for example, had eight concerts of Handel's *Messiah* in the desert on December 23–26, 1990. A Passover Seder was conducted in Bahrain by four Jewish chaplains for 335 soldiers, sailors, airmen, marines and coastguardsmen.

Male and female Army, Navy, and Air Force chaplains were deployed to the Kuwaiti Theater of Operations to minister to the troops. For example, 564 Army chaplains were deployed, including 400 in the active Army, 107 in the Army Reserves and 57 in the Army National Guard. Of these, 492 were Protestants, 63 were Roman Catholics, 6 were Jews and 3 were Orthodox. In the course of the war, chaplains distributed more than half a million Bibles and New Testaments to the troops.

Suggestions for further reading: Chaplain (Major) Granville E. Tyson, ed., "The Gulf War," *Military Chaplains Review,* Summer 1991; Chaplain (Brigadier General) Donald W. Shea, "A Ministry in the Eye of the Storm," *Army,* September 1991.

REPUBLICAN GUARD FORCES COMMAND (RGFC)
See ARMY, IRAQ.

RESERVE COMPONENTS
See MOBILIZATION, U.S.

REST AND RELAXATION (R & R)
See ARMED FORCES RECREATION CENTER BAHRAIN.

ROMANIA
See COALITION FORCES.

S

SANCTIONS

United Nations Security Council (UNSC) Resolution 661, passed on August 6, 1990 by a vote of 13 to 0 (Cuba and Yemen abstaining), imposed a trade and financial embargo on Iraq following its invasion of Kuwait. Binding on all UN members, the resolution forbade all trade with Iraq except in medicine and food. In addition, the transshipment of Iraqi and Kuwaiti oil through pipelines across Turkey and Saudi Arabia was forbidden.

"These sanctions, now enshrined in international law, have the potential to deny Iraq the fruits of aggression," said President George Bush on August 8, 1990, "while sharply limiting its ability to either export or import anything of value, especially oil." Many, including Senator Sam Nunn, the chairman of the Senate Armed Services Committee, and by some accounts General Colin Powell, the chairman of the Joint Chiefs of Staff, felt the UN sanctions could be an effective alternative to war.

Prior to the Kuwaiti crisis, 90 percent of Iraq's oil was transshipped by pipeline across Turkey to the Mediterranean Sea or across Saudi Arabia to the Red Sea, but shortly after the Iraqi invasion of Kuwait both pipelines were closed. On August 25, 1990, UNSC Resolution 665 ordered enforcement of the sanctions by inspection and verification of cargo and destinations of ships in the region.

The coalition's maritime interception operations were the primary means for enforcing the UN trade sanctions. Thirteen nations in addition to the six Gulf Cooperation Council states provided 165 ships to intercept shipping in the Persian Gulf, the Gulf of Oman, the Gulf of Aden, the Red Sea and the eastern Mediterranean. Although Iraq lost 90 percent of its imports and 100 percent of its exports, and had its gross national product cut in half, the sanctions did not cause it to renounce its aggression and withdraw from Kuwait.

In early October 1990, according to Washington Post reporter Bob Woodward, General Powell presented President Bush with two options. One was to continue the sanctions, the other was to build up military forces in the Gulf region for offensive military action. "There is a case here for the containment or strangulation policy," Powell said. "It may take a year, it may take two years, but it will work someday."

"I don't think there's time politically for that strategy," the president reportedly replied, and in November he ordered the massive military buildup in the Gulf that led to Operation Desert Storm and the forced withdrawal of Iraqi forces from Kuwait.

All the while, sanctions continued to be enforced. During the seven months of the Persian Gulf crisis, more than 7,500 merchant vessels were challenged, 964 were boarded, and 51 ships carring more than 1 million tons of contraband were diverted.

The sanctions did not end with the end of the Gulf War. They were continued in order to ensure Iraq's compliance with the terms of the cease-fire agreement. Iraqi adherence has been reviewed every 60 days since the war ended, and as of January 1994, Iraq has been found in violation of the cease-fire agreement's human rights provisions and of the requirement to submit its weapons production facilities to UN monitoring. Although eventually Iraq might be found in full compliance with UNSC Resolutions, the United States might find it politically impossible to lift the sanctions so long as Saddam Hussein remains in power.

As *U.S. News & World Report* magazine noted in its May 17, 1993, issue: "While ordinary Iraqis have suffered fearfully under the international sanctions, smugglers amd clandestine sales of Iraqi oil have kept [Saddam] Hussein and his murderous coterie of hangers-on in relative comfort. . . . Had George Bush listened to the go-slow proponents of sanctions and no use of force, the Iraqi Army might still be billeted in Kuwait City."

See also MARITIME INTERCEPTION OPERATIONS.

Suggestions for further readings: Colonel Harry G. Summers Jr., *On Strategy II: A Critical Analysis of the Gulf War* (New York: Dell, 1992) has a discussion of sanctions and excerpts of Bob Woodward's report. See also Gary Clyde Huafbauer et al., *Economic Sanctions Reconsidered*, 2nd ed. (Washington, D.C.: Institute for International Economics, 1990); "Sanctions on Iraq," *The Economist*, April 2, 1993.

SATELLITES

The Gulf War was the first military conflict in which spacecraft played a major role.

Among the military spacecraft used during the war were the Defense Meteorological Satellite Program (DMSP), the Defense Satellite Communications System (DSCS) and the Global Positioning System (GPS). Three Defense Support Program (DSP) satellites, originally put in orbit to warn of a Soviet ballistic missile attack on the United States, were used to detect the exhaust plumes of Scud missiles.

Two civilian satellites, the U.S. Department of Commerce's LANDSAT and France's SPOT (Satellite Probatoire d'Observation de la Terre), were also used, as were U.S. Department of Defense classified space systems, such as the Keyhole KH-12 photoreconnaissance satellite whose very existence is a closely guarded secret.

Although LANDSAT and SPOT provided useful battlefield imagery, the resolution of the KH-12 has been estimated at two inches in the visible-light spectrum and somewhat more in the invisible band. To say one could read the license plate of an auto photographed from outer space would evidently be an underestimation of the KH-12's capabilities.

In addition to the warfighting support provided by the LANDSAT and SPOT multispectral imagery systems, the Defense Mapping Agency used their images to prepare new maps of the Kuwaiti Theater of Operations that depicted roads, trails and airfields not shown on then existing maps, which were 10 to 30 years old.

See also COMMUNICATIONS AND ELECTRONICS; ELECTRONIC WARFARE; GLOBAL POSITIONING SYSTEM.

Suggestions for further reading: Department of Defense, *Conduct of the Persian Gulf War: Final Report to the Congress*, "Appendix K: Command, Control, Communications (C3) and Space," "Appendix T: Performance of Selected Weapons Systems" (Washington, D.C.: USGPO, 1992); Eliot A. Cohen et al., *Gulf War Airpower Survey* (Washington, D.C.: USGPO, 1993); Norman Friedman, *Desert Victory:*

The War for Kuwait (Annapolis, Md.: Naval Institute Press, 1991); Richard P. Hallion, *Storm Over Iraq: Air Power and the Gulf War* (Washington, D.C.: Smithsonian Institution Press, 1992). For a discussion of classified DOD systems, see William E. Burrows, *Deep Black* (New York: Berkley Books, 1986). See also Kathy Sawyer, "U.S. Spies in the Sky Focus in on Iraqis," *Washington Post*, November 26, 1990; and Kathy Sawyer, "U.S. Planners Rely Heavily on Sophisticated But Limited Electronic Spy Systems," *Washington Post*, February 19, 1991.

SAUDI ARABIA

A member of both the Arab League and the Gulf Cooperation Council (GCC), the Kingdom of Saudi Arabia played a crucial role in the Persian Gulf War. Without its participation and active support, the war quite literally could not have been fought.

Occupying most of the Arabian Peninsula, Saudi Arabia had an estimated 1991 population of 17,869,000. About one-third the size of the United States and with a land area of 839,996 square miles, Saudi Arabia borders on Kuwait, Iraq and Jordan to the north, Yemen and Oman to the south, the Red Sea to the west, and Qatar, the United Arab Emirates and the Persian Gulf to the east.

An ancient nation, Arabia was united for the first time by the Prophet Mohammed in the early 7th century. His birthplace at Mecca and his tomb at Medina are the holy cities of Islam, which some 600,000 Muslims from 60 nations visit each year.

Parts of the country fell under the rule of the Turkish Ottoman Empire in the 18th century, but in 1913 the Turks were overthrown by Ibn Saud, the founder of the Saud dynasty who unified the country under his rule. Oil was discovered in the 1930s, and in 1990 Saudi Arabia's crude oil reserves were estimated to be 225 billion barrels.

King Fahd Ibn Abdul Aziz is the head of state of Saudi Arabia. Its capital city, Riyadh, had an estimated 1986 population of 1,380,000. With major ports at Al-Jubayl and Ad-Dammam, the country also has modern airfields at Dhahran and elsewhere.

Saudi Arabia and the United States have maintained close political and military ties for many years. In 1951, the U.S. Army Corps of Engineers began its involvement in the country with the rebuilding of the airfield at Dhahran, and in 1965 an Engineer Assistance Agreement was signed in which the United States agreed to help construct military facilities in Saudi Arabia, among them King Khalid Military City, which was completed in 1988.

Also in 1951, a U.S. Military Assistance and Advisory Group (MAAG) was established in Saudi Arabia. In 1957, it became the U.S. Military Training Mission, one of the largest security assistance organizations in Asia. Sales of modern U.S. military equipment to the country increased in the 1980s, including F-5 and F-15 Eagle fighters and AWACS (Airborne Warning and Control System) aircraft to the Royal Saudi Air Force.

On August 5, 1990, in the wake of the Iraqi invasion of Kuwait, President George Bush dispatched Secretary of Defense Dick Cheney, accompanied by General H. Norman Schwarzkopf, the commander in chief, Central Command (CINCCENT), to consult with King Fahd. It was a crucial meeting, for without the king's approval it would have been impossible to mount an effective military operation against Iraq. After being assured that the United States would provide sufficient forces to defend Saudi Arabia, and that they would be withdrawn as soon as that mission was completed, King Fahd agreed to the U.S. deployment, which President Bush immediately ordered.

Instead of under a single commander, the Gulf War would be conducted by a dual headquarters: U.S. Central Command (CENTCOM), under the command of General Schwarzkopf; and the Arab/Islamic Joint Forces Command (JFC), under the command of Saudi Lieutenant General Khalid Bin Sultan. Thanks to the efforts of the Third U.S. Army commander, Lieutenant General John J. Yeosock, who had extensive previous experience working with the Saudi Arabian National Guard (SANG), an organization was created to ensure unity of effort. On August 13, 1990, the Coalition Coordination, Communications and Control Integration Center (C^3IC) was formed in the Ministry of Defense and Aviation in Riyadh, the same building that housed CENTCOM headquarters, to serve as the coalition's combined operations center.

In addition to allowing the coalition the use of its airfields, ports and other facilities, Saudi Arabia provided extensive no-cost host-nation support, including some 4,800 tents; 1.7 million gallons of packaged petroleum, oil and lubricants; more than 300 heavy-equipment transporters; approximately 20 million meals; more than 20 million gallons of fuel per day; and bottled water for the entire theater. It also contributed $16.8 billion to the United States, more than any other nation, to help defray the cost of the war.

With some 255 aircraft, the Royal Saudi Air Force (RSAF) was the largest of the coalition's air forces after that of the United States. It included 60 Tornado fighters, 76 F-5 fighters and 63 F-15 Eagles, in addition to tankers, transports and AWACS aircraft.

Integrated into the CENTAF (Air Force Component Central Command) air tasking order, the RSAF flew more than 12,000 sorties, second only to the U.S. Air Force. A Saudi F-15 Eagle shot down two Iraqi Mirage fighters. Two other Saudi aircraft, an F-5 and a Tornado, were lost in combat.

The eight frigates, five minesweepers, nine missile craft and three torpedo boats of the Royal Saudi Navy took part in the coalition's maritime interception operations and in the maritime campaign's anti-surface warfare and mine countermeasure operations.

Under General Khalid, the Joint Forces Command consisted of two corps-size units comprising 193,142 soldiers from 24 countries. Joint Forces Command-North (JFC-N) included the Royal Saudi Land Forces' (RSLF) 4th Armored and 20th Mechanized Brigades, and Joint Force Command-East (JFC-E) included the RSLF's 8th and 10th Mechanized Brigades and the Saudi Arabian National Guard's 2d Motorized Battalion as well as a Royal Saudi Marine Battalion.

Saudi ground forces in JFC-E took part in the battle of Khafji in January 1991. During the ground campaign the JFC, along with the U.S. First Marine Expeditionary Force, conducted the coalition's supporting attack along the Gulf coast to fix the Iraqi defenders in place. Breaching the Iraqi fortifications, JFC units went on to liberate Kuwait City on February 27, 1991.

Forty-seven Saudi Arabians were killed in action during the war, and 220 were wounded in action.

See also AERIAL COMBAT; AIR CAMPAIGN; AIR FORCES, COALITION; ARAB LEAGUE; ARMIES, COALITION; AWARDS, COALITION FORCES; BIN SULTAN BIN ABDUL AZIZ, KHALID; COALITION FORCES; COST; GROUND CAMPAIGN; GULF COOPERATION COUNCIL; JOINT FORCES COMMAND; MARITIME CAMPAIGN; MINESWEEPING; NAVIES, COALITION.

Suggestions for further reading: Department of Defense, *Conduct of the Persian Gulf War: Final Report to the Congress* (Washington, D.C.: USGPO, 1992). An excellent overview of Saudi military operations is David B. Ottoway, "For Saudi Military, New Self-Confidence," *Washington Post,* April 20, 1991.

SCHWARZKOPF, H. NORMAN, GENERAL, USA (1934–)

The commander in chief of the U.S. Central Command (CINCCENT), General H. Norman Schwarzkopf was the overall commander of U.S., British and French military forces in the Kuwaiti Theater of Operations during the Persian Gulf War. With Saudi Arabian Lieutenant General Khalid Bin Sultan, the commander of the Arab/Islamic Joint Forces Command, Schwarzkopf was responsible for the conduct of air, land and sea combat operations against Iraqi military forces.

He took his command to war in August 1990, waging a brilliant military campaign and decisively defeating the Iraqi armed forces. Although there would be some acrimony after the war, among his greatest achievements was the organization of a smooth political-military working relationship with the government of Saudi Arabia and with the Gulf Cooperation Council states.

General Schwarzkopf was commissioned a second lieutenant of infantry upon graduation from the United States Military Academy at West Point, New York, in 1956. In 1964, he earned a Master of Science degree in mechanical engineering from the University of Southern California and taught at West Point until his departure for Vietnam in 1965. There he served as a senior advisor with the ARVN (Army of the Republic of Vietnam) Airborne Brigade from 1965 to 1966. In 1969, he returned to Vietnam to command the 1st Battalion, 6th Infantry in the 23d (American) Infantry Division.

Among his significant assignments were command of the 1st Brigade, 9th Infantry Division at Fort Lewis, Washington; assistant division commander of the 8th Infantry Division in Germany; commanding general of the 24th Infantry Division (Mechanized) at Fort Stewart, Georgia; commander of I Corps at Fort Lewis, Washington; and assistant chief of staff for military operations and plans on the Army General Staff.

General Schwarzkopf, the commander of all U.S. forces in the Gulf, visits his old command, the U.S. 24th Infantry Division.
U.S. Army photo courtesy of the 24th Infantry Division (Mechanized).

During Operation Urgent Fury, the 1983 U.S. invasion of Grenada, Schwarzkopf, then commanding the 24th Infantry Division, was attached to the staff of Vice Admiral Joseph Metcalf, the Task Force commander, and ended up as his deputy commander. On November 18, 1988, Schwarzkopf was promoted to four-star general; he assumed command of the U.S. Central Command (CENTCOM) at McDill Air Force Base in Florida on November 23 of that year.

Although political sensitivities prevented the appointment of a single commander for the Persian Gulf War, Schwarzkopf established a combined command headquarters with Saudi Arabian Lieutenant General Khalid Bin Sultan, the commander of the Arab/Islamic Joint Forces Command, that achieved unity of effort of all coalition forces in the military campaign against Iraq.

Responsible for the air and naval campaigns through his component commanders, General

Schwarzkopf took personal charge of the ground campaign. His shift of the U.S. VII and XVIII Corps several hundred miles to the west to outflank his Iraqi opponents was a masterpiece of military manuever.

And so was the overall ground campaign. Holding the Iraqi forces along the coast of the Persian Gulf with a frontal assault by the U.S. First Marine Expeditionary Force and the Arab/Islamic Joint Forces Command, Schwarzkopf launched a turning movement with his VII and XVIII Corps to envelop the Iraqi military in the field. In 100 hours the ground campaign was over, with the coalition's objective of forcing the Iraqis from Kuwait achieved.

Schwarzkopf relinquished command of CENTCOM on August 9, 1991, and retired from active duty on August 31 of that year. Hailed at the time as one of America's greatest field commanders, his reputation has been somewhat diminished by postwar accounts of his overweening ego and his tendency to lose his temper and ride roughshod over his subordinate commanders.

In addition to the Combat Infantryman Badge, Schwarzkopf's awards and decorations include the Medal of Freedom; the Defense Department, Army, Navy, Air Force and Coast Guard Distinguished Service Medals; three Silver Stars for gallantry in action; three Bronze Star Medals, including one for heroism; the Legion of Merit; the Distinguished Flying Cross; nine Air Medals; three Army Commendation Medals, including one for valor; and two Purple Hearts for wounds received in action. After the Gulf War, he was awarded the French Order of the Legion of Honor and was made a Knight Commander of the Order of the Bath by Queen Elizabeth II of Great Britain.

See also CENTCOM (CENTRAL COMMAND); COMMAND AND CONTROL; GROUND CAMPAIGN; ORGANIZATION FOR COMBAT, U.S.

Suggestions for further reading: General H. Norman Schwarzkopf, *It Doesn't Take a Hero* (New York: Bantam Books, 1992); Roger Cohen and Claudio Gatti, *In the Eye of the Storm: The Life of General H. Norman Schwarzkopf* (New York: Farrar Straus and Giroux, 1991); Bob Woodward, *The Commanders* (New York: Simon & Schuster, 1991); C. D. B. Bryan, "Operation Desert Norm," *The New Republic*, March 11, 1991. For more critical views, see Rick Atkinson, *Crusade: The Untold Story of the Persian Gulf War* (New York: Houghton Mifflin, 1993); Bruce Palmer Jr., "But It Does Take A Leader: The Schwarzkopf Autobiography," *Parameters*, Spring 1993; Gen. Khalid Bin Sultan, "Schwarzkopf Did Not Win the War Alone," *Defense News*, October 26–November 1, 1992.

SCOWCROFT, BRENT

See NATIONAL SECURITY COUNCIL, U.S.

SCUD MISSILES

A direct descendant of the World War II German V-2 rocket, the Scud missile is a Soviet unguided free-fall ballistic missile. It was originally designed in the 1950s to deliver short-range tactical nuclear warheads in situations where pinpoint accuracy was not important.

Originally labeled the SS-1A Scunner or "Scud" for short, in 1965 the missile evolved into the larger and longer-range Scud-B. Replaced in the Soviet arsenal by the SS-23 surface-to-surface missile in 1979, the Scud was passed on to Iraq and other Soviet client states.

Iraq produced two variants of the Scud: the Al-Husayn, with a range of about 600 kilometers, and the Al-Hijarah, with a range of 750 kilometers. These were used to attack Israel and Saudi Arabia during the Persian Gulf War. Mounted on mobile launchers that could be quickly displaced, the Scuds proved to be elusive targets.

Because their CEP (circular error probable—i.e., the radius within which 50 percent of the missiles could be expected to hit) was 3,000 meters, the Scuds were used primarily as an area weapon against cities rather than against specific targets.

Although their purely military value was low, as terror weapons the Scuds had an enormous psychological effect, especially in Israel. As a consequence, the United States deployed a number of Patriot air defense missile batteries to both Israel and Saudi Arabia.

At the time, there was much speculation that the Scuds would carry chemical warheads, but all the Scuds fired during the Gulf War carried conventional explosive warheads. According to official reports, the Iraqis fired 88 modifed Scuds during the war, 42 at Israel and 46 at Saudi Arabia and other Gulf states. Two Israelis were killed in the attacks, and 230 were injured.

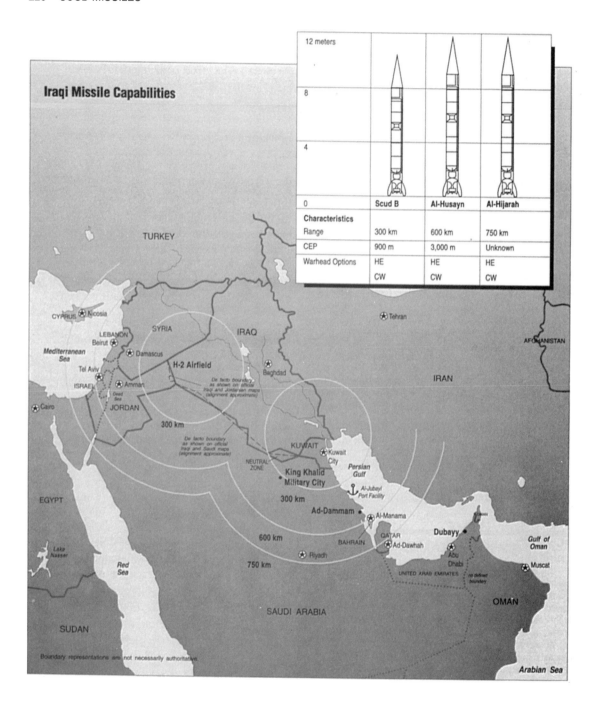

Iraqi Missile Capabilities

12 meters		Scud B	Al-Husayn	Al-Hijarah
Characteristics				
Range		300 km	600 km	750 km
CEP		900 m	3,000 m	Unknown
Warhead Options		HE	HE	HE
		CW	CW	CW

The single most devastating Scud missile attack of the war, however, occurred on February 26, 1991, when a Scud struck a U.S. Army barracks in Dhahran, Saudi Arabia. Twenty-eight American soldiers were killed and 98 were wounded—the greatest loss of U.S. troops in a single action during the war.

According to the postwar *Gulf War Airpower Survey,*

Coalition aircrews reported destroying about eighty mobile [Scud] launchers; another score or so were claimed by Special Operations Forces. But most, if not all, of the objects involved now appear to have been decoys, vehicles such as tanker trucks . . . or other objects that were unfortunate enough to provide "Scud-like" signatures.

"A few [Scuds] may have been destroyed," the study concluded, "but nowhere near the number reported during the war.... Coalition airpower does not appear to have been very effective militarily against this target category."

See also PATRIOT MISSILE.

Suggestions for further reading: Department of Defense, *Conduct of the Persian Gulf War: Final Report to the Congress* (Washington, D.C.: USGPO, 1992); Eliot A. Cohen et al., *Gulf War Airpower Survey* (Washington, D.C.: USGPO, 1993); Richard P. Hallion, *Storm Over Iraq: Air Power and the Gulf War* (Washington, D.C.: Smithsonian Institution Press, 1992); George N. Lewis, Steve Fetter and Lisbeth Gronlund, "Casualties and Damage From Scud Attacks in the 1991 Gulf War," Defense and Arms Control Studies Program, Massachusetts Institute of Technology, March 1993; W. Andrew Terrill, "The Gulf War and Missile Proliferation," *Comparative Strategy,* April–June 1992.

SEABEES
See ENGINEERS.

SEAD (SUPPRESSION OF ENEMY AIR DEFENSES)
See AIR DEFENSES.

SEAL (SEA-AIR-LAND) FORCES
See SPECIAL OPERATIONS COMMAND CENTRAL COMMAND.

SEALIFT
Sealift was the key to victory in the Persian Gulf War. The Achilles' heel of U.S. military operations in the Middle East had always been moving into the region the massive tonnages of tanks, heavy equipment, ammunition and supplies necessary for combat operations. Although the troops themselves could be moved by air, the bulk of their supplies would have to be transported some 8,000 miles by sea. One of the major success stories of the Gulf War was how that was done.

"It was the quickest and largest military sealift buildup since World War II," General H. Norman Schwarzkopf, the CINCCENT (commander in chief, Central Command) told the graduating class at the U.S. Naval Academy on May 29, 1991, "an 8,000-mile, 250-ship haze-gray bridge, one ship every 50 miles from the shores of the United States to the shores of Saudi Arabia." The "sea bridge" concept in the Navy's 1986 Maritime Strategy had become a reality.

Making it a reality was the U.S. Transportation Command's Military Sealift Command (MSC). Its sealift capability consisted of an active force and a reserve force. The active force included the 13 maritime prepositioning squadrons and 11 afloat prepositioning ships discussed elsewhere, and a fast sealift squadron ready force. The reserve force consisted of the 71 ships of the Ready Reserve.

The ready force, Fast Sealift Squadron One, consisted of eight fast sealift ships (FSS). Anchored in U.S. ports with nucleus crews and capable of moving the heavy equipment of a full heavy Army division, the FSSs were activated on August 7, 1990. The first ship arrived at Savannah, Georgia, on August 11 to begin loading the 24th Infantry Division (Mechanized). Sailing on August 14, it arrived in Saudi Arabia on August 27, covering the 8,700 nautical miles at an average speed of 27 knots. According to the analyst Norman Friedman, "It took six more FSSs and three commercial ships to complete the division lift, which closed in Saudi Arabia on September 13, 1990."

For the first time ever, 71 ships of the Ready Reserve Force (RRF), manned by civilian merchant mariners, were activated. RRF activation orders took effect on August 10, involving 18 ships, 17 of which were RO/RO (roll-on/roll-off) ships. During Phase I of the sealift (August–November 1990), 44 RRF ships were activated. During Phase II (November 1990–March 1991), 27 more ships were activated.

Chartered commercial ships, including foreign-flagged ships, also played a major role. Twenty-five cargo ships were reflagged as U.S. vessels, and 187 flew foreign flags. Of the tankers, 47 were U.S.-flagged and 23 were foreign-flagged.

In all, according to the official Department of Defense report on the war, 385 U.S. sealift ships were utilized. By mid-March 1991, with an average of 4,200 tons of cargo arriving daily, some 3,306,569 short tons of cargo and 6,100,00 short tons of POL (petroleum, oil and lubricants) had been delivered to the Gulf. Sealift had moved 95 percent of the cargo needed to sustain U.S. forces in the field, including 85 percent of the dry cargo and 99 percent of the POL. Quite literally, sealift was the lifeline of the war effort.

See also AFLOAT PREPOSITIONING SHIPS; AIRLIFT; DEPLOYMENT OF U.S. FORCES; LOGISTICS, U.S.; MARITIME PREPOSITIONING SQUADRONS; MARITIME STRATEGIC DOCTRINE, U.S.

Suggestions for further reading: Department of Defense, *Conduct of the Persian Gulf War: Final Report to the Congress,* "Appendix E: Deployment," "Appendix F: Logistics Build-Up and Sustainment" (Washington, D.C.: USGPO, 1992); Norman Friedman, *Desert Victory: The War for Kuwait* (Annapolis, Md.: Naval Institute Press, 1991); Captain Douglas M. Norton, USN, "Sealift: Keystone of Support," *U.S. Naval Institute Proceedings,* May 1991. For critical looks at sealift, see Andrew E. Gibson and Commander Jacob L. Shuford, USN, "Desert Shield and Strategic Sealift," *Naval War College Review,* Spring 1991; Maj. Mark L. Hayes, "Sealift: The Achilles' Heel of Our National Strategy," *Marine Corps Gazette,* November 1992.

SEARCH AND RESCUE (SAR)

The responsibility for searching and for rescuing downed coalition aviators, officially called "combat search and rescue" (CSAR), was delegated to CENTAF (Air Component Central Command), which established the Joint Rescue Coordination Center. The head of Special Operations Command Central Command (SOCCENT), who had Army, Navy and Air Force special operations forces under his command, was designated as the commander of combat rescue forces.

"There were 38 downed Coalition aircraft and many downed crew members," noted the official Department of Defense (DOD) report on the Gulf War.

> Several downed crew members ejected over or near heavily fortified Iraqi positions, deep inside Iraq, making rescue attempts impossible due to distances involved and the enemy situation. . . .
>
> Seven CSAR missions were launched. There were three successful recoveries; all rescued crew members were Americans. Kuwaiti partisan forces also recovered a downed Kuwaiti pilot.

Calling CSAR a "disappointment," analyst Richard P. Hallion noted that "only three of sixty-four downed air crews—roughly 5 percent—were actually picked up." One of the failed attempts involved Army flight surgeon Major Rhonda Cornum, who was captured when her rescue helicopter was shot down.

See also PRISONERS OF WAR; SPECIAL OPERATIONS COMMAND CENTRAL COMMAND.

Suggestions for further reading: Department of Defense, *Conduct of the Persian Gulf War: Final Report to the Congress,* "Appendix J: Special Operations Forces" (Washington, D.C.: USGPO, 1992); Richard P. Hallion, *Storm Over Iraq: Air Power and the Gulf War* (Washington, D.C.: Smithsonian Institution Press, 1992); Rick Atkinson, *Crusade: The Untold Story of the Persian Gulf War* (New York: Houghton Mifflin, 1993).

2D ARMORED CAVALRY REGIMENT
See VII CORPS.

2D ARMORED DIVISION

When the Persian Gulf crisis began, the U.S. Army's 2d Armored "Hell on Wheels" Division at Fort Hood, Texas, was in the process of being deactivated. Its 2d Brigade had already stood down, and only its 1st Brigade remained at Fort Hood. Its separated 3d Brigade (2d Armored Division Forward) had been stationed at Garlstadt, West Germany, for some time.

Although the 2d Armored Division itself did not deploy to the Kuwaiti Theater of Operations (KTO), both its 1st and 3d Brigades played significant roles in the Gulf War. When the 1st Cavalry Division, also stationed at Fort Hood, was ordered to the KTO, the 2d Armored Division's 1st Brigade, better known as the "Tiger Brigade," was attached to the 1st Cavalry Division to replace its round-out brigade, the Mississippi National Guard's 155th Armored Brigade, which required additional training before deployment.

After arriving in the KTO, the Tiger Brigade was detached from the 1st Cavalry Division and attached to the 2d Marine Division, where it remained throughout the rest of the war. Meanwhile, the 2nd Armored Division's 3d Brigade was attached to the 1st Infantry Division (Mechanized) from Fort Riley, Kansas, whose own 3d Brigade (1st Infantry Division Forward) had also begun to stand down.

After the war, the decision to inactivate the 2d Armored Division was reversed, and the division once again is stationed at Fort Hood, Texas.

See also 1ST INFANTRY DIVISION (MECHANIZED); 2D MARINE DIVISION.

Suggestions for further reading: J. Paul Scicchitano, "Eye of the Tiger," *Army Times,* June 10, 1991; Tony Clifton, "'Move Forward and Shoot the Things,'" *Newsweek,* March 11, 1991; Steve Vogel, "Hell Night," *Army Times,* October 7, 1991.

2D MARINE DIVISION

Stationed at Camp Lejeune, North Carolina, the U.S. 2d Marine Division was part of the Phase II deployment ordered by President George Bush in November 1990 to build an offensive capability in the Kuwaiti Theater of Operations (KTO). This was the first time the division had been committed to combat since the 1944 Tinian campaign in World War II.

Earlier, the division's 2d Marine Regiment had deployed to the KTO as part of the 4th Marine Expeditionary Brigade (MEB), which became the nucleus of the Amphibious Task Force. When ordered to the KTO, the 2d Marine Division consisted of the 6th and 8th Marine Infantry Regiments, the 10th Marine Artillery Regiment, the 2d Light Armored Infantry Battalion with LAVs (light armored vehicles), the 2d and 8th Tank Battalions, the 2d Assault Amphibian Battalion with AAVs (assault amphibian vehicles), the 2d Combat Engineer Battalion and the 2d Reconnaissance Battalion.

Commanded by Major General William M. Keys, the division included some 4,000 Marine reservists, including Company B (Bravo) of the 4th Marine Tank Battalion, which would destroy some 59 enemy tanks, 32 armored personnel carriers, 26 other vehicles and an artillery piece—the highest kill-rates of any tank company in the war.

After arriving in the KTO in January 1991, the 2d Marine Division took operational control of its "third regiment," the Army's 1st Brigade, 2d Armored Division, better known as the "Tiger Brigade."

With some 20,500 soldiers and 257 tanks, including 185 M1A1 Abrams tanks, the 2d Marine Division was one of the heaviest Marine divisions ever to take the field. Part of the corps-level First Marine Expeditionary Force, on G-Day (February 24, 1991) the 2d Marine Division, in coordination with the 1st Marine Division on its right flank, attacked north through the Iraqi fortifications. On that first day, against sometimes stiff resistance, the division succeeded in breaching two defended defensive belts and establishing a solid foothold inside Kuwait.

By G+1 (February 25), the 2d Marine Division had captured some 5,000 prisoners. On G+2 (February 26), the division began the drive on Kuwait City itself, using the Tiger Brigade to envelop to the west, sealing off an area called al-Jahra. Mutlah Ridge, which dominated the roads leading from Kuwait City, was seized, cutting off the Iraqi retreat and setting up what became known as the "Highway of Death."

The divison's 1st Battalion, 6th Marine Regiment was the first unit to reach Kuwait City, but the division was ordered to halt in place to allow the Arab/Islamic Joint Forces Command to pass through its lines and formally liberate the city.

After the war, the 2d Marine Division returned to its home station at Camp Lejeune, North Carolina.

See also FIRST MARINE EXPEDITIONARY FORCE (I MEF); GROUND CAMPAIGN; MARINE CORPS, U.S.

Suggestions for further reading: Department of Defense, *Conduct of the Persian Gulf War: Final Report to the Congress,* "Chapter 8: The Ground Campaign" (Washington, D.C.: USGPO, 1992); Major James Blackwell, *Thunder in the Desert: The Strategy and Tactics of the Persian Gulf War* (New York: Bantam Books, 1991); General H. Norman Schwarzkopf, *It Doesn't Take a Hero* (New York: Bantam Books, 1992); The Staff of *U.S. News & World Report, Triumph Without Victory* (New York: Times Books, 1992). See also Lt. Gen. William M. Keys, "Rolling With the 2d Marine Division," *U.S. Naval Institute Proceedings,* November 1991. For the exploits of Bravo Company, 4th Tank Battalion, see Lt. Col. J. G. Zumwalt, USMCR, "Tanks! Tanks! Direct Front!" *U.S. Naval Institute Proceedings,* July 1992. For the "Tiger Brigade," see J. Paul Scicchitano, "Eye of the Tiger," *Army Times,* June 10, 1991; Tony Clifton, "'Move Forward and Shoot the Things,'" *Newsweek,* March 11, 1991.

SENEGAL

See CASUALTIES; COALITION FORCES; JOINT FORCES COMMAND.

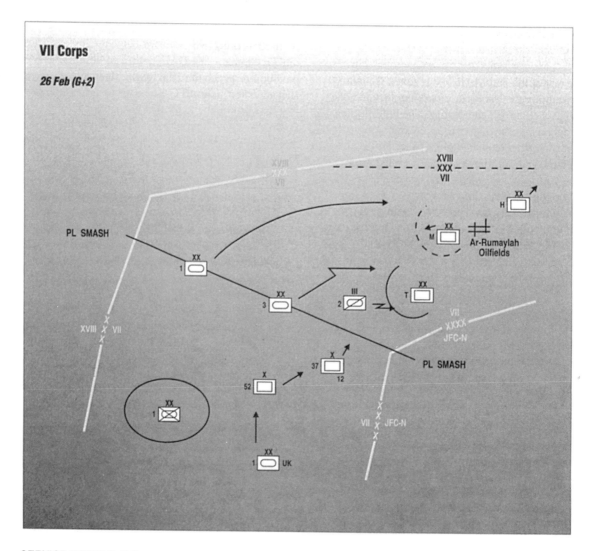

SERVICE MEDALS, U.S.

Unlike "decorations," which are awarded for individual acts of bravery or for meritorious achievement, "service medals" are awarded to recognize military service during a particular period of time or at a particular place.

Two U.S. service medals were awarded during the Persian Gulf War. The National Defense Service Medal was awarded to all individuals who served in the U.S. military, either in the United States or overseas, on or after August 2, 1990. The Southwest Asia Service Medal was awarded to all who served in the Kuwaiti Theater of Operations (KTO) on or after August 1990.

In addition to these U.S. service medals, Saudi Arabia awarded the Kuwait Liberation Medal to all personnel who served in the KTO between January 17 and February 28, 1991.

See also AWARDS, COALITION FORCES; NATIONAL DEFENSE SERVICE MEDAL; SOUTHWEST ASIA SERVICE MEDAL.

VII CORPS

One of the U.S. Army's premier warfighting organizations, VII Corps made the main ground attack in the Persian Gulf War. No stranger to combat, it made the assault on Utah Beach on D-Day in June 1944, and since 1951 it had been stationed in West Germany as one of the crucial components of the NATO (North Atlantic Treaty Organization) defense of Western Europe. In early November 1990, VII Corps was ordered to the Kuwaiti Theater of Operations (KTO) as part of the Phase II deployment implementing President George Bush's decision to build an offensive capability in the Gulf region.

The 146,000-strong VII Corps consisted of the 1st Armored Division, the 1st Infantry Division (Mechanized), the 1st Cavalry Division, the 3d Armored Division, the 2d Armored Cavalry Regiment (ACR), the 11th Aviation Brigade and corps artillery units, including the 142d Field Artillery Brigade from the Arkansas-Oklahoma National Guard. The United Kingdom (UK) 1st Armoured Division was also attached to VII Corps.

Commanded by Lieutenant General Frederick M. Franks Jr., a distinguished veteran of the Vietnam War, the armor-heavy VII Corps was selected to make the main attack of the ground campaign. After shifting some 150 miles to the west to new attack positions, VII Corps would launch an attack designed to avoid most fixed defenses, drive deep into Iraq and destroy that country's strategic reserve—the armored and mechanized divisions of the elite Republican Guard Forces Command (RGFC).

The VII Corps plan included a feint and an envelopment. The 1st Cavalry Division would make a feint toward the Wadi al-Batin in Kuwait, causing the Iraqi forces to believe the main attack would come in that direction. The 1st Infantry Division would breach the Iraqi fortifications on the east of the corps sector and allow the passage of the UK 1st Armoured Division to fix the enemy forces in place. Led by the 2d ACR, the 1st and 3d Armored Divisions would attack around the Iraqi defenses on the corps's western flank.

By G +2 (February 26), the 1st and 3d Armored Divisions and the 2d ACR had already begun their turn to the east to strike the flank of the Iraqi defenses. In the Battle of 73 Easting, the 2d ACR engaged elements of the Iraqi 12th Armored and Tawakalna Divisions, destroying 29 enemy tanks and 24 armored fighting vehicles and capturing 1,300 prisoners.

Meanwhile, the 1st Infantry Division had breached the Iraqi fortifications and was moving to join the main attack. The UK 1st Armoured Division passed through the breach to attack the Iraqi 52d Armored Division in a bitter two-day battle that ended with the capture of the Iraqi division commander and the destruction of 40 enemy tanks.

VII Corps continued its advance on G +3 (February 27). A coordinated attack was made against the RGFC's Tawakalna, Medina and Hummurabi Mechanized Divisions that culminated in their destruction.

VII Corps continued its attack on G +4 (February 28), destroying elements of the remaining Iraqi divisions west of Basra and establishing blocking positions along the enemy's Al-Jahra–Basra main supply route. Offensive operations were ordered to halt at 8:00 A.M. that day.

"In 90 hours of continuous movement," according to the official Department of Defense report on the war, "VII Corps achieved devastating results against the best units of the Iraqi army. VII Corps reported destroying more than a dozen Iraqi divisions; an estimated 1,300 tanks, 1,200 fighting vehicles and APCs [armored personnel carriers]; 285 artillery pieces, and 100 air defense systems; and captured nearly 22,000 enemy soldiers."

After the cease-fire, VII Corps withdrew from the KTO and returned to Germany, where it was deactivated on March 18, 1991.

See also LISTINGS FOR INDIVIDUAL UNITS; ARMY, U.S.; FRANKS, FREDERICK M.; GROUND CAMPAIGN; THIRD U.S. ARMY; UNITED KINGDOM.

Suggestions for further reading: Department of Defense, *Conduct of the Persian Gulf War: Final Report to the Congress,* "Chapter 8: The Ground Campaign" (Washington, D.C.: USGPO, 1992); Major James Blackwell, *Thunder in the Desert: The Strategy and Tactics of the Persian Gulf War* (New York: Bantam Books, 1991); General H. Norman Schwarskopf, *It Doesn't Take a Hero* (New York: Bantam Books, 1992); Rick Atkinson, *Crusade: The Untold Story of the Persian Gulf War* (New York: Houghton Mifflin, 1993); The Staff of *U.S. News & World Report, Triumph Without Victory* (New York: Times Books, 1992); Major William J. Brame; "From Garrison to Desert Offensive in 97 Days," *Army,* February 1992.

NAVCENT COMMAND AND CONTROL

```
                          ┌─────────────────┐
                          │                 │
                          │     NAVCENT     │
                          │                 │
                          └────────┬────────┘
                                   │
            ┌──────────────────────┴──────────────────────┐
   ┌────────────────────┐                     ┌────────────────────┐
   │      NAVCENT        │                     │ Navy Coordinating  │
   │   Representative    │                     │   Group Riyadh     │
   │      Riyadh         │                     │   (NAVCOORGRU      │
   │                     │                     │     Riyadh)        │
   └────────────────────┘                     └────────────────────┘
```

Red Sea Carrier Battle Group (RS CVBG)	Amphibious Task Force (ATF)	Persian Gulf Carrier Battle Group (PG CVBG)

Middle East Force (MEF)	Logistics Supply Force (NAVLOSUPFOR)	Mediterranean Strike Group (MEDSTKGRU)

SEVENTH U.S. FLEET

The Seventh U.S. Fleet was the senior U.S. Navy headquarters in the Persian Gulf War. In August 1990, the Seventh Fleet was named the Naval Component of the U.S. Central Command (NAVCENT), and its commander, Vice Admiral Henry Mauz, took charge of all U.S. naval forces in the Kuwaiti Theater of Operations.

NAVCENT's subordinate commands included the Red Sea Carrier Battle Group, the Persian Gulf Carrier Battle Group, the Amphibious Task Force, the Logistics Supply Force, the Mediterranean Strike Group and the Middle East Force. The Middle East Force maintained operational control over the extensive U.S. maritime interception operations, over

mine countermeasure forces, and over the Middle East Surface Combatant Squadron.

On December 1, 1990, Admiral Mauz was replaced by Vice Admiral Stanley R. Arthur, who commanded the Seventh Fleet throughout Operation Desert Storm.

The largest naval deployment since World War II, NAVCENT included some 80,000 active and reserve naval personnel, including 3,700 women and 6,625 of the 18,000 naval reservists recalled to active duty. The Seventh Fleet comprised some 120 ships, including 6 carrier battle groups with more than 400 aircraft, 2 battleship surface action groups, 13 submarines and the 43 amphibious ships of the Amphibious Task Force.

Underway replenishment, such as that provided by the fleet oiler USNS *Andrew J. Higgins* (T-AO-190), gave the Seventh Fleet enormous mobility and striking power.
U.S. Navy photo (PH1 Scott Allen), Empire Press.

Antisurface Warfare Results

- 143 Iraqi naval vessels destroyed/damaged

  11 Antiship missile boats destroyed
  2 Antiship missile boats disabled
  3 *Polnocny*-class amphibious ships destroyed
  1 *Ibn Khaldun* frigate destroyed
  1 Bogomol PCF patrol boat destroyed
  116 Small patrol boats and auxiliaries destroyed/damaged
  9 Minelayers destroyed

- All Iraqi naval bases/ports significantly damaged
- All northern Persian Gulf oil platforms searched and secured
- No attacks by Iraqi surface vessels against coalition forces

---

During the air campaign, U.S. Navy aircraft flew 18,624 sorties, 23 percent of the coalition's combat missions. Navy warships fired 288 Tomahawk land-attack missiles at Iraqi targets ashore, including 8 from the submarine USS *Louisville* (SSN-724) while it was submerged in the Red Sea, and 4 from the USS *Pittsburgh* (SSN-72) while it was submerged in the Mediterranean Sea.

In establishing control of the seas, the Seventh Fleet destroyed the Iraqi Navy. The fleet's mine countermeasures operations allowed the battleships USS *Missouri* (BB-63) and USS *Wisconsin* (BB-64) to move into position and fire some 1,102 16- inch shells in support of the ground campaign. Finally, in support of Central Command's deception plan, the credible threat of the Navy's Amphibious Task Force in the Persian Gulf tied down four Iraqi divisions in coastal defenses, plus two enemy armored divisions held in reserve.

Two Navy ships, the cruiser USS *Princeton* (CG-59) and the amphibious ship USS *Tripoli* (LPH-10), struck enemy mines, injuring several of their crewmen. Seven Navy aircraft were lost in combat, including two F/A-18 Hornets, one F-14A Tomcat and four A-6E Intruders. Another two fighters and two helicopters were lost in noncombat incidents.

Six Navy personnel were killed in action, and another six died from accidents or other nonbattle causes. Twelve Navy personnel were wounded in action. Eleven Silver Stars were awarded for gallantry in action during the war; 3 Distinguished Service Medals and 18 Legions of Merit were awarded for distinguished service, and 130 Distinguished Flying Crosses were awarded for valor and for meritorious service.

See also AERIAL COMBAT; AIR CAMPAIGN; AIRCRAFT CARRIERS; AMPHIBIOUS TASK FORCE; ARTHUR, STANLEY R.; BATTLESHIPS; CARRIER BATTLE GROUPS; CHIEF OF NAVAL OPERATIONS; COMBAT ACTION RIBBON; DEPLOYMENT OF U.S. FORCES; ENGINEERS; JOINT TASK FORCE MIDDLE EAST, U.S.; MARITIME CAMPAIGN; MARITIME INTERCEPTION OPERATIONS; MARITIME PREPOSITIONING SQUADRONS; MARITIME STRATEGIC DOCTRINE, U.S.; MINESWEEPING; NAVY, U.S.; SANCTIONS; SEALIFT; SPECIAL OPERATIONS COMMAND; CENTRAL COMMAND; TOMAHAWK LAND-ATTACK MISSILE.

Suggestions for further reading: Department of Defense, *Conduct of the Persian Gulf War: Final Report to the Congress,* "Chapter 4: Maritime Interception Operations," "Chapter 7: The Maritime Campaign" (Washington, D.C.: USGPO, 1992); Frank Uhlig Jr., *How Navies Fight: The U.S. Navy and Its Allies* (Annapolis, Md.: Naval Institute Press, 1993). Norman Friedman, *Desert Victory: The War for Kuwait* (Annapolis, Md.: Naval Institute Press, 1991) has a listing of U.S. ships in the Gulf War. See also Vice Admiral Stanley R. Arthur and Marvin Pokrant, "Desert Storm at Sea," *U.S. Naval Institute Proceedings,* May 1991; Captain Vincent C. Thomas Jr., USN (Ret.), "The Sea Services Role in Desert Shield/Storm," *Seapower,* September 1991; Rick Atkinson, *Crusade: The Untold Story of the Persian Gulf War* (New York: Houghton Mifflin, 1993).

SHIITE REVOLT

Encouraged by the U.S. Central Command (CENTCOM) psychological warfare campaign that called for the overthrow of Saddam Hussein, both the Kurds in northern Iraq and the Shiites in southern Iraq rose in open revolt when the Persian Gulf War ended.

Shiite Muslims in the Basra area of southern Iraq and the "marsh Arabs" in the Tigris and Euphrates River delta had long been frustrated by what they saw as neglect by the central government. They attacked government buildings and the local offices of the Baath Party in the area, and for a time controlled much of southern Iraq. But Iraqi military forces loyal to Saddam Hussein soon crushed the revolt.

The Shiite expectation was that the United States would intervene, but, as the *Wall Street Journal's*

Tony Horowitz noted on December 26, 1991, even though units of the U.S. XVIII Airborne Corps were in the area they did nothing to stop the slaughter of Shiite rebels in the town of An Nasiriyah only 10 miles away. Plans to shield the rebels were reportedly drawn up by the Pentagon, much as had been done for the Kurdish rebels in northern Iraq, but the plans were never acted upon. The fear was that intervention would turn into a Vietnam-like quagmire, and that the revolt was a precursor of a radical Islamic state that would ally itself with Iran.

The United States did provide some immediate relief to refugees fleeing the fighting. In March and April 1991, the U.S. 3d Armored Division, aided by a small U.S. Navy contingent, provided humanitarian assistance to some 35,000 Iraqi refugees in the Safwan area in southern Iraq, part of the security zone established at the end of the Gulf War.

Unlike the situation in northern Iraq, where worldwide publicity about the plight of the Kurds forced the United States to reverse its nonintervention stance and institute Operation Provide Comfort, the southern revolt was ignored. Although in April 1991 United Nations Security Council Resolution 688 condemned Iraq's treatment of its people, it did not authorize the use of force to compel the government to stop.

In August 1992, the fighting in Southern Iraq flared again. This time, the United States, France and the United Kingdom decided to do something about it. On August 27, a "no-fly zone" was established for the one-third of Iraq south of the 32d parallel, a zone similar to the one established in 1991 north of the 36th parallel to protect the Kurds.

Barring Iraqi use of airpower to attack the Shiite rebels, the no-fly zone did little to stop the government's use of tanks, artillery and infantry to crush the revolt. Nevertheless, it remains in effect and the Clinton administration has continued to enforce it. In July 1993, U.S. warplanes bombed Iraqi air defense sites in the area.

See also KURDS.

Suggestions for further reading: Tony Horowitz, "Forgotten Rebels: After Heeding Calls To Turn on Saddam, Shiites Feel Betrayed," *Wall Street Journal,* December 26, 1991; Michael R. Gordon, "A New Resolve on Iraq," *New York Times,* August 20, 1991; Carlyle Murphy, "Plan To Bar Iraqi Flights Contains Risks for Allies," *Washington Post,* August

20, 1991; Carlyle Murphy, "Iraqi Exiles Allege New Brutality in South," *Washington Post*, November 21, 1992. For U.S. relief efforts, see Lieutenant Commander Dana C. Covey, USNR, "Offering a Helping Hand in Iraq," *U.S. Naval Institute Proceedings*, May 1992.

SIDEWINDER (AIM-9) AIR-TO-AIR MISSILE

An advanced, short-range, supersonic air-to-air missile fired from coalition aircraft, the AIM-9 Sidewinder uses a passive infrared target acquisition system. During the war, the Sidewinder was modified to include infrared counter- countermeasures.

A total of 16 Sidewinders were fired during Operation Desert Storm, and 5 missed their target. Three were decoyed by flares, 1 was fired "out of envelope" (i.e., outside the performance limits of the system) and 1 was guided through a previously destroyed target. Thirteen missiles, including the 5 that missed, were fired by U.S. Air Force pilots, scoring 8 kills. One was fired by a U.S. Navy pilot and 2 were fired by Royal Saudi Air Force pilots; all three downed their target.

See also SPARROW (AIM-7) AIR-TO-AIR MISSILE.

Suggestions for further reading: Department of Defense, *Conduct of the Persian Gulf War: Final Report to the Congress*, "Appendix T: Performance of Selected Weapons Systems" (Washington, D.C.: USGPO, 1992); Richard P. Hallion, *Storm Over Iraq: Air Power and the Gulf War* (Washington, D.C.: Smithsonian Institution Press, 1992); "Around One-Third of Sidewinders Fired in Gulf Missed, Flares Decoyed Missiles," *Inside the Air Force*, November 15, 1991.

SIERRA LEONE:

See COALITION FORCES.

SILVER STAR

First authorized in World War I, the Silver Star is America's third-highest award for battlefield bravery. It is awarded in the name of the president of the United States for gallantry in action against the enemy.

One hundred and forty-six Silver Stars were awarded during the Persian Gulf War, 74 to Army personnel, 50 to Air Force personnel, 11 to Navy personnel and 11 to Marine Corps personnel.

See also DECORATIONS, U.S.

SINGAPORE

See COALITION FORCES.

6TH FRENCH LIGHT ARMORED DIVISION

See FRANCE.

SLAM (AGM-84E) STANDOFF LAND ATTACK MISSILE

Designed for deployment aboard aircraft carriers, the SLAM (AGM-84E) standoff land attack missile is launched from A-6E Intruder and F/A-18 Hornet aircraft. With a cruising speed of Mach 0.8 and a range of more than 50 miles, the SLAM carries a 500-pound warhead.

The SLAM has an infrared (IR) electro-optical seeker and a computer data link. Using the Global Positioning Satellites to update the missile's inertial navigation system, the onboard computer then points the system's IR seeker directly at the target. The seeker then sends a video image to the controlling aircraft, where the pilot selects a specific aim point and gives the command for the seeker to lock-on.

Seven SLAM missiles were launched during the Gulf War, and the recorded infrared video of the missiles striking their targets provided proof of their exceptional accuracy.

Suggestions for further reading: Department of Defense, *Conduct of the Persian Gulf War: Final Report to Congress*, "Appendix T: Performance of Selected Weapons Systems" (Washington, D.C.: USGPO, 1992); Norman Friedman, *Desert Victory: The War for Kuwait* (Annapolis, Md.: Naval Institute Press, 1991); Richard P. Hallion, *Storm Over Iraq: Air Power and the Gulf War* (Washington, D.C.: Smithsonian Institution Press, 1992); Bruce W. Watson, ed., *Military Lessons of the Gulf War* (Novato, Calif.: Presidio Press, 1991).

SMART BOMBS

See BOMBING.

SORTIES

A sortie is a unit of measure for the number of aircraft taking part in a particular mission. A sortie represents one aircraft making one trip. Thus, 10 sorties could mean 10 aircraft each making one trip or one aircraft making 10 trips.

SOUTHWEST ASIA SERVICE MEDAL

The "campaign medal" for U.S. military personnel serving in the Persian Gulf War was the Southwest Asia Service Medal. It was awarded to "members of the Armed Forces of the United States who participated in military operations in Southwest Asia or in the surrounding contiguous waters or air space after August 2, 1990." Southwest Asia was defined as encompassing the Kuwaiti Theater of Operations (KTO).

A bronze metallic star may be worn on the medal's ribbon to denote each campaign in which the servicemember took part.

See also CAMPAIGNS, U.S. MILITARY; KTO (KUWAITI THEATER OF OPERATIONS); SERVICE MEDALS, U.S.

SOVIET UNION

Even though it was not a member of the coalition, the Soviet Union was the "enabler" of the Persian Gulf War, for without its support the war literally could not have been waged.

As discussed in more detail elsewhere (see STRATEGY, Coalition), in both the Korean and Vietnam Wars the primary focus of the United States was on deterring the Soviet Union (which had the ability to destroy the nation with nuclear weapons within minutes) and only secondarily on fighting the war at hand.) Beginning during the Korean War in 1950 and continuing until the eve of the Gulf War, the United States had stationed the majority of its best-equipped forces in West Germany, including the armor-heavy Seventh U.S. Army and its V and VII Corps, to deter an attack on Western Europe by the Soviet Union and its Warsaw Pact allies.

Politically, the United States had been hamstrung as well, for the Soviet veto in the United Nations (UN) Security Council had prevented the obtaining of UN support for many U.S. foreign policy objectives. Only because the Soviets were boycotting the UN in June 1950 was the United States able to get UN backing for the Korean War, and the Soviets were careful not to make that mistake again.

Thus, it was an act of major significance when on August 2, 1990, the Soviet Union supported UN Security Council (UNSC) Resolution 660 condemning the invasion of Kuwait by Iraq, an erstwhile Soviet ally. Even more telling was Soviet support on August 6 of UNSC Resolution 661, which imposed a trade embargo on Iraq. In the past, Moscow had been one of Iraq's major weapons suppliers, but now Baghdad was cut off not only from new arms and equipment, but also from ammunition and spare parts for existing equipment.

By voting on November 29, 1990, to approve UNSC Resolution 678, which authorized military action against Iraq, the Soviet Union gave its tacit approval to the earlier U.S. decision to pull its VII Corps out of Europe, where it had been stationed for more than 40 years to deter Soviet aggression, and move it to the Gulf region to form the coalition's main attack.

The Soviets were not entirely compliant, however. For example, a joint Iraqi-Soviet peace proposal in February 1991 sought to cancel all UNSC resolutions and to impose an immediate cease-fire in exchange for an Iraqi withdrawal from Kuwait. President George Bush rejected the plan and gave Iraq a 24-hour ultimatum. Over Soviet president Mikhail Gorbachev's objections, the coalition launched its final ground campaign on February 24, 1991.

One hundred hours later, the Gulf War had ended. And 10 months later, on December 25, 1991, the Soviet Union ended as well, as President Gorbachev resigned and the Russian Federation was proclaimed.

See also STRATEGY, COALITION; STRATEGY, IRAQ; UNITED NATIONS.

Suggestions for further reading: Mikhail Gorbachev, "Bush Was Right Not To Destroy Iraq," *Los Angeles Times*, March 4, 1992; Graham E. Fuller, "Moscow and the Gulf War," *Foreign Affairs*, Summer 1991; Elisabeth Rubenfien, "Soviet Military Is Shaken by Allies' Triumph Over Its Former Protege," *Wall Street Journal*, March 4, 1991; Stephen J. Blank, "The Soviet Military Views Operation Desert Storm: A Preliminary Assessment," Strategic Studies Institute, U.S. Army War College, September 23, 1991; Mary C. Fitzgerald, "The Soviet Image of Future War: 'Through the Prism of the Persian Gulf,'" *Comparative Strategy*, October–December 1991; James T. Tritten, "Changing Role of Naval Forces: The Russian View of the 1991 Persian Gulf War," *Journal of Soviet Military Studies*, December 1992. For the Soviet peace plan, see David Hoffman and Ann Devroy, "Soviet Plan Puts Allies in a Bind," *Washington Post*, February 22, 1991; Warren Strobel and Richard C. Gross, "Bush's Dilemma Close To 'Nigthmare Scenario,'" *Washington Times*, February 22, 1991.

SPACE WARFARE
See SATELLITES.

SPAIN
See COALITION FORCES; EUROPE.

SPARROW (AIM-7) AIR-TO-AIR MISSILE
The beyond-visual-range complement to the Sidewinder AIM-9 air-to-air missile, the Sparrow was carried by F-14 Tomcat, F-15 Eagle and F/A-18 Hornet aircraft during the Gulf War.

The Sparrow has a range of about 20 miles and a solid-state infrared homing device. Sixty-seven supersonic Sparrow missiles were fired by the U.S. Air Force and 4 by the U.S. Navy in the Gulf War; they shot down 23 Iraqi aircraft and helicopters.

See also SIDEWINDER (AIM-9) AIR-TO-AIR MISSILE.

Suggestions for further reading: Department of Defense, *Conduct of the Persian Gulf War: Final Report to the Congress,* "Appendix T: Performance of Selected Weapons Systems" (Washington, D.C.: USGPO, 1992); Norman Friedman, *Desert Victory: The War for Kuwait* (Annapolis, Md.: Naval Institute Press, 1991); Richard P. Hallion, *Storm Over Iraq: Air Power and the Gulf War* (Washington, D.C.: Smithsonian Institution Press, 1992); Bruce W. Watson, ed., *Military Lessons of the Gulf War* (Novato, Calif.: Presidio Press, 1991).

SPECIAL OPERATIONS COMMAND CENTRAL COMMAND (SOCCENT)
A sub-unified command reporting directly to Central Command (CENTCOM), Special Operations Command Central Command (SOCCENT) was commanded by U.S. Army Colonel Jesse Johnson. With more than 7,000 personnel, SOCCENT included an Army Special Operations Task Force (ARSOTF) and a separate Army Special Forces Group, a Navy Special Warfare Task Group (NSWTG), the Air Force Special Operations Command Central (AFSOCCENT) and special operations forces from France, Kuwait and the United Kingdom (UK).

ARSOTF consisted of the 5th Special Forces Group, the 3d Battalion of the 160th Special Operations Aviation Regiment, the 528th Special Operations Support Battalion and the 112th Special Operations Signal Battalion. Separate from ARSOTF were elements of the 3d and 10th Special Forces Groups, the 4th Squadron of the 17th Air Cavalry and a Kuwaiti special forces unit.

Among the naval special operations forces deployed for the Gulf War were Navy Special Warfare Group One, SEAL Teams One and Five, Swimmer Delivery Vehicle Team One, Special Boat Unit 12 and a mobile communications team, plus elements from the Kuwaiti Navy and the Kuwaiti Marines.

AFSOCCENT included the 8th, 9th, 20th, 55th and 71st Special Operations Squadrons with MC-130E, HC-130, MH-53J, MH-60G and HH-3 special operations aircraft. The Ninth U.S. Air Force, however, retained operational control of the AC-130 gunships of the 16th and 193d Special Operations Squadrons and the EC-130 Volant Solos from the Pennsylvania National Guard's 193d Special Operations Group.

Some 150 UK Special Air Service (SAS) and Special Boat Service (SBS) special operations forces (SOFs) and some 250 French SOFs were also under SOCCENT's direct command.

Arriving in the Kuwaiti Theater of Operations on August 11, 1990, SOCCENT had as its mission "to conduct special operations in Kuwait, Iraq and Northern Saudi Arabia in support of all phases of the CENTCOM campaign plan." This included providing liaison officers and training teams to the forward combat elements of the Arab/Islamic Joint Forces Command, conducting special reconnaissance of Iraqi forces, conducting combat search and rescue operations and executing such direct actions as raids, ambushes and other assault missions. SOCCENT also conducted signal-monitoring and radio-direction-finding operations against Iraq.

Although much of SOCCENT's operations remain secret, some details have been revealed in postwar media accounts.

See also ADVISORY EFFORT, U.S.; RECONNAISSANCE; SEARCH AND RESCUE.

Suggestions for further reading: Department of Defense, *Conduct of the Persian Gulf War: Final Report to the Congress,* "Appendix J: Special Operations Forces" (Washington, D.C.: USGPO, 1992). See also Melissa Healy, "Special Forces: U.S. 'Eyes' Deep in Enemy Territory," *Los Angeles Times,* February 28, 1991; R. Jeffrey Smith, "U.S. Special Forces Carried Out Sabotage, Rescues Deep in Iraq," *Washington Post,* March 4, 1991; Douglas Waller, "Secret Warriors," *Newsweek*, June 17, 1991; Mark Thompson, "Commandoes Tell Their Gulf War Stories," *Philadelphia Inquirer*, June 21, 1991; Lt. Gen. E. M. Flanagan Jr., "Hostile Territory Was Their AO in Desert Storm," *Army*, September 1991; George C. Wilson, "Secret Warriors," *Army Times*, March 8, 1993. For UK SAS operations, see Christopher Dobson and Alan Coats, "The Secret War," *The Independent*, March 10, 1991.

SQUADRON

In the U.S. Army, a squadron is the battalion-size unit of the cavalry. Commanded by a lieutenant colonel, a squadron consists of two or more company-size "troops."

In U.S. Air Force, Navy and Marine Corps aviation units, a squadron consists of several "flights" of about five aircraft each. It is commanded by either an Air Force or Marine lieutenant colonel or a Navy commander.

STATE DEPARTMENT, U.S.

The U.S. State Department is responsible to the president for the formulation and conduct of U.S. relations with other nations. During the Persian Gulf War, the secretary of state was James A. Baker III.

The State Department played a crucial role in the war. At the United Nations, U.S. Ambassador Thomas Pickering was able to maintain the support of the member states of the Security Council throughout the conflict. And with the help of Secretary Baker's personal diplomacy, the State Department was able to put together the remarkable allied coalition that made victory possible.

Particularly important was the Arab coalition negotiated by State Department ambassadors and diplomats. It included Saudi Arabia and the other Gulf Cooperation Council nations, without which the war could not have been fought. Erstwhile enemies such as Egypt and Syria were also brought together in common cause, and thanks in large measure to Secretary Baker's efforts, Israel was dissuaded from retaliating for Iraqi Scud missile attacks, which were intended to split the alliance.

Through its diplomatic efforts the State Department helped engender the cooperation of the North Atlantic Treaty Organization (NATO) allies, including France and the United Kingdom, both of which provided large military contingents to the war effort.

Also critical was the department's success in obtaining the tacit cooperation of the Soviet Union, which allowed the major shift of U.S. forces from Western Europe to the Persian Gulf.

While receiving high marks for its efforts during the war, the State Department came under heavy criticism for its prewar activities, which critics claimed helped bring about the crisis.

See also COALITION FORCES; COST; GLASPIE, APRIL C.; IRAQGATE; UNITED NATIONS.

Suggestions for further reading: James A. Baker III, "America's Strategy in the Persian Gulf Crisis," *Dispatch*, December 10, 1990; Rowan Scarborough, "State Official Defends Policies Toward Iraq," *Washington Times*, May 22, 1992; Jim Anderson, "Why State Failed To Provide an Ounce of Prevention in the Gulf," *Foreign Service Journal*, January 1991; James Bennett, "Sand Trap," *Washington Monthly*, April 1991.

STEALTH AIRCRAFT (F-117A NIGHTHAWK STEALTH FIGHTER)

Incorporating new technology, composite materials and advanced design that made it practically invisible to enemy radar (hence "stealth"), the F-117A Nighthawk stealth fighter was used during the Gulf War to penetrate dense threat environments such as Iraq's integrated air defense system and to attack high-value targets such as command and communications centers in downtown Baghdad.

The F-117As flew 1,296 sorties, mostly against targets in the heavily defended areas of downtown Baghdad, without the loss of a single aircraft. Carrying two 2,000-pound GBU-10 or GBU-27 laser-guided bombs, they flew approximately 2 percent of the coalition's attack sorties yet struck roughly 40 percent of the strategic targets that were attacked.

Postwar critics have charged that 76 of the 167 laser-guided bombs dropped by F-117As in the first five days of the air campaign missed their targets because of pilot error, mechanical or electrical malfunctions, or weather.

According to the U.S. Air Force, the F-117A had an overall success rate of 80 percent. Of the 1,340 GBU-10 bombs that were dropped, 1,100 hit their target, and of the 760 GBU-27 bombs, that were dropped, 590 were on target. Weather, however, was a limiting factor in the F-117A's effectiveness, causing 340 GBU-10s and 240 GBU-27s not to be dropped.

See also BOMBING.

Suggestions for further reading: Department of Defense, *Conduct of the Persian Gulf War: Final Report to the Congress*, "Appendix T: Performance of Selected Weapons Systems" (Washington, D.C.: USGPO, 1992); Eliot A. Cohen et al., *Gulf War Airpower Survey* (Washington, D.C.: USGPO, 1993); Rick Atkinson, *Crusade: The Untold Story of the Gulf War* (New York: Houghton Mifflin, 1993); Norman Friedman, *Desert Victory: The War for Kuwait* (Annapolis, Md.: Naval Institute Press, 1991); Richard P. Hallion, *Storm Over Iraq: Air Power and the Gulf War* (Washington, D.C.: Smithsonian Institution Press, 1992). *See also* Tony Capaccio, "F-117 Stealth Fighter Hit 80 Percent of Its Targets," *Defense Week*, April 13, 1992. For first-hand accounts of F-117A pilots, see James P. Coyne, "A Strike by Stealth," *Airforce*, March 1992.

STRATEGIC AIR COMMAND (SAC)

At the time of the Gulf War both an independent specified command and one of the major subdivisions of the U.S. Air Force, the Strategic Air Command (SAC) was originally created as America's nuclear strike force. During the Vietnam War, however, its bombers and tankers supported both the tactical ground war and the strategic air war. They would do so again during the Persian Gulf War.

From the beginning of the crisis, SAC's aerial tanker fleet, including 46 KC-10 Extenders and 262 KC-135 Stratotankers, supported CENTAF (Central Command Air Force) operations. SAC also deployed 41 B-52 Stratofortress bombers in support of Operation Desert Storm, as well as 9 U-2R and TR-1 and 9 RC-135 Rivet Joint strategic reconnaissance aircraft. While operating in the Kuwaiti Theater of Operations, SAC's aircraft were under CENTAF's tactical control and were assigned to the Ninth Air Force's 17th Air Division (Provisional).

After the Gulf War, SAC was dismantled. Its nuclear strike responsibilities were transferred to the newly formed U.S. Strategic Command (STRATCOM), and its other functions were allocated to the new Air Combat Command (ACC) and Air Mobility Command (AMC).

See also AERIAL REFUELING; AIR CAMPAIGN; AIR FORCE, U.S.; B-52 STRATOFORTRESS BOMBER; NINTH U.S. AIR FORCE; RECONNAISSANCE.

STRATEGY, COALITION

Coalition strategy, like national strategy, involves the use of the political, economic, psychological and military powers of the coalition's member states to secure the coalition's objectives. The coalition's objectives in the Persian Gulf War were clearly stated by U.S. Secretary of State James A. Baker III.

"From the outset," Baker told the Senate Foreign Relations Committee on December 5, 1990, "the international community has rallied behind four objectives: First, the immediate, complete, and unconditional Iraqi withdrawal from Kuwait. Second, the restoration of Kuwait's legitimate government. Third, the release of all hostages; and fourth, a commitment to the security and stability of the gulf."

While military forces were dispatched to defend Saudi Arabia and the other Gulf Cooperation Council states, the United States launched a diplomatic offensive to garner political support in the United Nations (UN) and to put political pressure on Saddam Hussein to withdraw his forces from Kuwait.

At the same time, economic pressure was applied through UN-mandated sanctions against trading with Iraq and through the coalition's maritime interception operations. Many hoped these economic sanctions would prove sufficient and that the use of force would not be necessary to drive the Iraqis from Kuwait.

In November 1990, President George Bush determined that these political and economic measures by themselves could not achieve the coalition's objectives, and the international community agreed. On November 29, the UN authorized the use of military force if Iraq did not withdraw from Kuwait by January 15, 1991, and President Bush ordered the deployment of an offensive military force to the Kuwaiti Theater of Operations, including the U.S. Army's VII Corps from Germany. This decision to use military force to secure the coalition's objectives was approved by Congress on January 12, 1991.

Not only were the clarity of the objectives and the formal support of Congress major departures from the Vietnam War experience, so was the military strategy by which the war would be fought. Both the Vietnam War and the Korean War before it had been fought on the strategic defensive. The Gulf War, like

World War II, would be fought on the strategic offensive.

After China intervened in the Korean War, the United States abandoned its previous national policy of rollback and liberation, which had governed the conduct of World War II, and instead opted for the policy of containment. Instead of attacking the Soviet Union and its allies directly, this policy called for containing their expansion. While ultimately successful, it had unintended consequences that were not widely perceived.

Unlike the strategic offensive, whose purpose was to defeat the enemy on the battlefield and break his will to resist, the national policy of containment necessitated a change to the strategic defensive. While barring the enemy from achieving military victory, the best possible result under the defensive strategy was stalemate. That is exactly what happened in the Korean and Vietnam Wars. Both wars had to be terminated through prolonged diplomatic negotiations.

But with the end of the Cold War in 1989 came the end of the policy of containment. Again not widely perceived, especially by Saddam Hussein, that meant that for the first time since World War II the U.S. military and its allies were back on the strategic offensive. Once again they could carry the war to the enemy to destroy his armed forces and break his will to resist. And that is exactly what they proceeded to do.

See also AIR CAMPAIGN; GROUND CAMPAIGN; MARITIME CAMPAIGN; MARITIME INTERCEPTION OPERATIONS; SANCTIONS; STRATEGY, IRAQ.

Suggestions for further reading: Colonel Harry G. Summers Jr., *On Strategy II: A Critical Analysis of the Gulf War* (New York: Dell, 1992); James A Baker III, "America's Strategy in the Persian Gulf Crisis," *Dispatches,* December 10, 1990; Lawrence Freedman and Efraim Karsh, "How Kuwait Was Won: Strategy in the Gulf War," *International Security,* Fall 1991.

STRATEGY, IRAQ

Ends and means are at the heart of strategic analysis, and four years after the Persian Gulf War the ends that Saddam Hussein sought with his invasion of Kuwait are still a matter of dispute. Apologists claim it was a defensive move, and some even blame the attack on Israeli provocations. More common, however, are the explanations offered by such analysts as Efraim Karsh and Inari Rautsi, who argue that economic and political pressures exacerbated by the Iran-Iraq War drove the invasion.

Egyptian President Hosni Mubarak believed there was a grand design behind Iraq's invasion. He told *Le Figaro* in October 1990 that Saddam "believed that the invasion of Kuwait would only cause verbal protests and then he could calmly attack the oil wells in the Kingdom of Saudi Arabia and, after swallowing them, attack the oil wells of the United Arab Emirates." Arab expert Laurie Mylroie agrees. "Since becoming president of Iraq in 1979, Saddam seems to have had a grand but simple design, beginning with gaining control of Persian Gulf oil." That grand design, she argues, is to become "an Arab hero."

Saddam's first attempt to achieve his ends was in the Iran-Iraq War. According to Mylroie, "If Saddam had defeated Iran, he would have been in a position to dictate to the Gulf Arabs. If they did not obey he could have attacked them with impunity. . . . Saddam would have controlled world oil supplies [and] would have been among the most powerful individuals on earth." The second attempt, Mylroie argues, was the attack on Kuwait.

While the "ends" of Iraq's strategy remain debatable, the "means" are more easily discerned. Saddam Hussein would pursue the same defensive Fabian strategy that had worked so well against Iran. Laid out some 2,200 years ago by the Roman dictator Quintus Fabius Maximus, the strategy calls for the avoidance of combat. Instead, one seeks to wear down and exhaust the enemy.

This ancient strategy was precisely the one successfully followed by General George Washington in the American Revolutionary War—he avoided becoming decisively engaged by the British regulars and wore them down in a prolonged eight-year campaign. That is also what Saddam Hussein did in his eight-year war with Iran.

But the essential ingredient of a Fabian strategy is time. Time must be on the side of the defender in order to exhaust the attacker's will and erode his base of support. It was in his assessment of "time" that Hussein made his fatal miscalculation.

First, he misjudged the character of President George Bush and the will of the American people. Then he misjudged the strength and cohesion of the allied coalition. Finally, he failed to appreciate the sea change that had taken place as a result of the end of the Cold War, and he consequently overestimated the strength and reliability of his one-time Soviet ally.

"America is still nursing the disasters from the Vietnam War," Saddam Hussein said in a 1990 speech, "and no American official, be it even George Bush, would dare to do anything serious against the Arab nation." As Marine Corps University Professor Norman Cigar noted, "Iraq calculated that, because of its fragile national will, America would not be able to stay the course during a crisis—much less a war. The Iraqis were confident that they understood and could affect opinion in the USA and the West. On the contrary, in general they seemed to have a poor appreciation of Americans."

And the Iraqis had a poor appreciation of their fellow Arabs as well. As Cigar observed, "Iraq also believed that the Arab states were a particularly weak link in the coalition . . . and that their troops would break and run if war ever erupted." Iraq also believed that "Israeli involvement in any manner would trigger popular Arab indignation and compel the Arab governments to . . . end their support for the coalition."

But again Saddam Hussein was wrong. As is true in any coalition, it is the common threat that causes an alliance to coalesce, and the intensity of that threat determines the strength of the cement that holds a coalition together. In the event, the threat posed by Iraq's naked aggression against its Arab neighbor was more than sufficient to hold the Arab coalition together despite Iraq's best efforts to cause it to come apart.

Finally, there was the matter of the Soviet Union. In a perverse way, here is where the Vietnam analogy really applied. Saddam Hussein thought he could fight the Vietnam War all over again. And he did, except that instead of playing North Vietnamese dictator Ho Chi Minh, as he intended, he ended up playing the part of South Vietnamese president Nguyen Van Thieu.

In October 1972, as Henry Kissinger, President Richard Nixon's national security advisor, strong-armed President Thieu into accepting the terms of the "peace" agreement with Hanoi, Thieu said bitterly that compared to the United States, Vietnam was no more than a dot. Its loss would mean little to America, which had its strategies to pursue with

Moscow and Peking. And he was right. In terms of Kissingerian *realpolitik*, America's strategic interests with the Soviet Union and China were far more important than the survival of South Vietnam.

In 1991, Saddam Hussein found himself in exactly the same position. Iraq, too, was no more than a dot whose loss would mean little to the Soviet Union, which had its own strategies to pursue with the United States. Not only did the Soviet Union abandon Iraq, as the United States had abandoned South Vietnam, but it added insult to injury by refusing to exercise its veto in the United Nations Security Council to protect it. Instead, the Soviet Union voted to impose sanctions against its former ally and to use military force to punish Saddam for his aggression.

Iraq's strategy was not only faulty in design and execution, it was inferior in every detail to the strategy of its opponents in the Persian Gulf War.

See also ANTIWAR MOVEMENT; SOVIET UNION; STRATEGY, COALITION; WAR TERMINATION.

Suggestions for further reading: Efraim Karsh and Inari Rautsi, "Why Saddam Hussein Invaded Kuwait," *Survival*, January/February 1991; Lawrence Freedman and Efraim Karsh, "How Kuwait Was Won: Strategy in the Gulf War," *International Security*, Fall 1991; Laurie Mylroie, "Why Saddam Hussein Invaded Kuwait," *Orbis*, Winter 1993; Harry G. Summers Jr., "Iraqi Strategy of Evasion and Delay: Historical Successes," *Los Angeles Times*, January 27, 1991; Norman Cigar, "Iraq's Strategic Mindset and the Gulf War: Blueprint for Defeat," *Journal of Strategic Studies*, March 1992. For Nguyen Van Thieu's remarks, see Arnold R. Isaacs, *Without Honor* (Baltimore: Johns Hopkins University Press, 1983).

SUBMARINES

Although details of the coalition's submarine operations during the Gulf War remain secret, it is known that 13 U.S. submarines were involved, eight of them in surveillance and reconnaissance before the outbreak of hostilities. After hostilities began, five more nuclear-powered attack submarines arrived on station and were under the U.S. Seventh Fleet's operational control. These included the USS *Newport News* (SSN 750), *Philadelphia* (SSN-690) and *Pittsburgh* (SSN 720) in the Mediterranean Sea, and the USS *Chicago* (SSN-721) and *Louisville* (SSN-724) in the Kuwaiti Theater of Operations.

In the first U.S. submarine combat action since World War II, two submarines fired Tomahawk land-attack missiles at Iraqi targets. Submerged in the Red Sea, the *Louisville* fired eight missiles and the *Pittsburgh*, submerged in the Mediterranean, fired four.

In addition, two diesel-powered submarines from the United Kingdom (UK), the HMS *Opposum* and *Otus*, operated in the Persian Gulf, apparently carrying UK special operations forces, including Special Air Service (SAS) and Special Boat Service (SBS) personnel.

See also SPECIAL OPERATIONS COMMAND CENTRAL COMMAND; TOMAHAWK LAND-ATTACK MISSILE.

Suggestions for further reading: Department of Defense, *Conduct of the Persian Gulf War: Final Report to the Congress,* "Chapter 7: The Maritime Campaign" (Washington, D.C.: USGPO, 1992); Norman Friedman, *Desert Victory: The War for Kuwait* (Annapolis, Md.: Naval Institute Press, 1991); Bruce W. Watson, ed., *Military Lessons of the Gulf War* (Novato, Calif.: Presidio Press, 1991).

SUPCOM (SUPPORT COMMAND)

See LOGISTICS, U.S.

SWEDEN

See COALITION FORCES.

SYRIA

A member of the Arab League, the Syrian Arab Republic played an important part in the Persian Gulf War. It supported the key August 1990 League votes to condemn Iraqi aggression, and was one of the first Arab nations to send military forces to the Kuwaiti Theater of Operations.

Located at the eastern end of the Mediterranean Sea, Syria had an estimated 1991 population of 12,965,000. About the size of North Dakota, Syria has a land area of 71,498 square miles. It shares borders with Lebanon and Israel to the west, Jordan to the south, Iraq to the east and Turkey to the north.

The ancient nation of Syria was part of the Turkish Ottoman Empire for four centuries until that empire collapsed at the end of World War I. Divided into the modern states of Syria and Lebanon by the Treaty of Sèvres in 1920, Syria was administered as a French

League of Nations mandate until it declared its independence in April 1946.

The Baath Party seized power in 1963 and continues as the official governing party. The government is dominated by members of the Alawite sect and has been ruled by a military regime headed by President Hafez al-Assad since 1971.

With 28 percent of its territory arable land, and with crude oil reserves of 1.4 billion barrels, Syria has a mixed economy. The capital city of Damascus had an estimated population of 1,361,000 in 1989.

One of the radical confrontation states, Syria took part in Arab attacks on Israel in 1948, 1967 and 1973. Another confrontation with Israel in 1982, after the latter's invasion of Lebanon, ended with a cease-fire in June 1983.

Armed by the Soviet Union, Syria has been widely condemned as a supporter of international terrorism. It was thus an unlikely member of the generally moderate Arab coalition that formed to oppose Iraq in the Gulf War, for Saudi Arabia and Syria had been at opposite poles of the Arab world for more than two decades. But Hafez al-Assad had been a strong opponent of his fellow Baathist leader in Baghdad and had sided with Iran in the 1980–1988 Iran-Iraq War.

Under the command of Major General Ali Habib, Syria's 45th Commando Brigade, with its 122d, 183d and 824th Special Forces Battalions, was dispatched to Saudi Arabia in October 1990. Syria's 9th Armored Division, comprising the 33d and 43d Tank Brigades with approximately 250 115-mm-gun T-62 and 125-mm-gun T-72 Soviet-supplied tanks, followed later, as did the 52d Mechanized Brigade with Soviet BMP armored fighting vehicles and the 89th Artillery Regiment.

Part of the Arab/Islamic Joint Forces Command-North (JFC-N) on the left flank of the U.S. First Marine Expeditionary Force, Syrian forces screened the Saudi border, secured JFC-N's lines of communication and took part in the attack to liberate Kuwait City. Two Syrian soldiers were killed and one was wounded during the fighting.

See also GROUND CAMPAIGN; JOINT FORCES COMMAND.

Suggestions for further reading: Department of Defense, *Conduct of the Persian Gulf War: Final Report to the Congress* (Washington, D.C.: USGPO, 1992). Norman Friedman, *Desert Victory: The War for Kuwait*

(Annapolis, Md.: Naval Institute Press, 1991) has a listing of Syrian forces. See also "In From the Cold," *The Economist*, October 13, 1990; Caryle Murphy, "Syrian Troops Display Unlikely Solidarity With Saudi Arabia," *Washington Post*, December 18, 1990. An excellent overview of Syrian military operations is David B. Ottoway, "For Saudi Military, New Self-Confidence," *Washington Post*, April 20, 1991.

T

T-55, T-62, T-72 TANKS

See ARMOR.

TACTICAL AIR COMMAND (TAC)

In accordance with established U.S. doctrine, the fighter wings, intra-theater airlift wings and other Tactical Air Command (TAC) units deployed to the Kuwaiti Theater of Operations (KTO) came under the command authority of the commander in chief, Central Command (CINCCENT). These units were further assigned to the Air Component Central Command (CENTAF) commander, who also commanded the Ninth U.S. Air Force.

A large part of the Ninth Air Force staff deployed to the KTO from its home station at Shaw Air Force Base in South Carolina. Rather than reconstitute CENTAF Rear at Shaw AFB, on August 12, 1990, Headquarters Tactical Air Command at Langley AFB in Virginia assumed the responsibilities of CENTAF Rear.

After the war, TAC was disbanded and replaced by Air Combat Command, headquartered at Langley AFB, Virginia.

See also NINTH U.S. AIR FORCE; STRATEGIC AIR COMMAND.

Suggestion for further reading: Department of Defense, *Conduct of the Persian Gulf War: Final Report to*

The 3d Armored Division's Chief Warrant Officer Kathy Summers with an Iraqi tank destroyed in the division's attack.
Author's personal collection.

the Congress, "Appendix K: Command, Control, Communications (C3), and Space" (Washington, D.C.: USGPO, 1992).

TANKS
See ARMOR.

TASK FORCE
"Task Force" is a term used to identify an ad hoc organization composed of a variety of military units temporarily assembled under a single designated commander to accomplish a specific mission.

For the U.S. Navy, the "task force" and "task group" are routine subdivisions of the fleet. They, too, have no fixed structure, being tailored for the mission at hand. Unlike those in the other services, however, Navy task forces, such as the Joint Task Force Middle East, tend to be semipermanent in nature.

TELEVISION
See CNN (CABLE NEWS NETWORK); MEDIA.

THATCHER, MARGARET
See UNITED KINGDOM.

3D ARMORED CAVALRY REGIMENT
See XVIII AIRBORNE CORPS.

3D ARMORED DIVISION
Stationed for decades at Frankfurt am Main in West Germany as part of the North Atlantic Treaty Organization (NATO) defense against a Warsaw Pact attack on Western Europe, the U.S. Army's 3d Armored "Spearhead" Division had not seen combat since World War II.

Commanded by Major General Paul Funk, the "Spearhead" division was originally assigned to V Corps. In November 1990, it was transferred to VII Corps and ordered to the Persian Gulf as part of the Phase II deployment ordered by President George Bush. One of the most modern divisions in the Army, it consisted of more than 17,000 soldiers organized into three armor-heavy manuever brigades equipped with M1A1 Abrams tanks and M2 Bradley infantry fighting vehicles. These brigades included the 4th and 5th Battalions, 18th Infantry; the 3d and 5th Battalions, 5th Cavalry; the 3d and 4th Battalions, 8th Cavalry; the 2d and 4th Battalions, 32d Armor; and the 2d and 4th Battalions, 67th Armor.

The 3d Armored Division's aviation brigade consisted of the 2d and 3d Battalions, 227th Aviation, with AH-64 Apache attack helicopters; and Company H, 227th Aviation, with Blackhawk assault helicopters: The division also had a reconnaissance squadron, the 4th Squadron, 7th Cavalry, with M1A1 tanks, M3 Bradley cavalry fighting vehicles and OH-58 Kiowa scout helicopters.

Division artillery consisted of the 2d Battalion of the 3d Field Artillery (FA) and the 2d and 4th Battalions of the 82d FA, with M109 self-propelled 155-mm howitzers; and Battery A of the 40th FA, with Multiple-Launch Rocket Systems (MLRS).

In addition to its Support Command, the division also included the 3d Battalion, 5th Air Defense Artillery; the 23d Engineer Battalion; the 143d Signal Battalion; and the 533d Military Intelligence Battalion.

Part of VII Corps's main attack, on G-Day (February 24, 1991) the 3d Armored Division on the east, together with the 1st Armored Division on the west, followed the axis cleared by the 2d Armored Cavalry Regiment around the western flank of the main Iraqi defensive line. By February 25, VII Corps had completed its envelopment and turned east to strike the second echelon of the Iraqi Republican Guard Forces Command (RGFC).

On February 26, the 3d Armored Division attacked the RGFC Tawakalna Division northeast of Al-Busayyah. Weather conditions were extremely adverse, with winds gusting from 25 to 42 knots and heavy rain and blowing sand reducing visibility to less than 100 meters. Despite the weather, the 1st and 3d Brigades conducted a coordinated attack on the 29th and 9th Brigades of the Tawakalna Division. Spearheaded by the 3d Armored Division's cavalry squadron and a heavy-tank task force, and with five battalions of cannon artillery and 27 MLRS launchers in support, the division succeeded in destroying numerous Iraqi armored vehicles and tanks in intense fighting, effectively destroying the Tawakalna Division.

After a night of heavy fighting, on February 27 the 3d Armored Division's 3d Brigade passed through the lines of the 2d Brigade, which was then in contact with the enemy, and attacked the Iraqi 12th Armored Division. Breaking through the enemy's defenses, the 3d Brigade moved into Kuwait and helped bring the war to a close.

According to official statistics, VII Corps, including the 3d Armored Division, destroyed more than a dozen Iraqi divisions—including an estimated 1,300 tanks, 1,200 fighting vehicles, 285 artillery pieces and 100 air defense systems—and captured nearly 22,000 prisoners.

After the cease-fire, the 3d Armored Division returned to Germany where it was deactivated as part of the Army's post–Cold War drawdown.

See also GROUND CAMPAIGN; VII CORPS.

Suggestions for further reading: Department of Defense, *Conduct of the Persian Gulf War: Final Report to the Congress,* "Chapter 8: The Ground Campaign" (Washington, D.C.: USGPO, 1992); Major James Blackwell, *Thunder in the Desert: The Strategy and Tactics of the Persian Gulf War* (New York: Bantam Books, 1991); General H. Norman Schwarzkopf, *It Doesn't Take a Hero* (New York: Bantam Books, 1992); The Staff of *U.S. News & World Report, Triumph Without Victory* (New York: Times Books, 1992). See also Steve Vogel, "The Tip of the Spear," *Army Times,* January 13, 1992.

3D INFANTRY DIVISION (MECHANIZED)

See 1ST ARMORED DIVISION.

3D MARINE AIRCRAFT WING

The aviation combat element of the First Marine Expeditionary Force (I MEF), the 3d Marine Aircraft Wing (MAW) consisted of more than 50 squadron-size or larger units, including 19 fixed-wing and 21 helicopter squadrons, with some 500 combat aircraft and more than 16,000 personnel.

Commanded by Major General Royal N. Moore Jr., the 3d MAW was stationed at the Marine Corps Air Station at El Toro, California, prior to the Gulf War. Its lead elements deployed with the 7th Marine Expeditionary Brigade (later part of the 1st Marine Division) to Dhahran, Saudi Arabia, on August 14, 1990, and the remainder of the MAW followed soon thereafter.

Flying some 18,000 sorties during the war, the 3d MAW included elements of all three active MAWs as well as the reserve 4th MAW. Helicopter units included four active and two reserve squadrons of AH-1 Cobra attack helicopters, 10 squadrons of CH-46 Sea Knight transport and squadrons of CH-53 Sea Stallion transport.

Among its fixed-wing aircraft were the F/A-18 Hornet, the A-6E Intruder, the AV-8B Harrier STOVL (short take-off and vertical land) jump jet and the EA-6B Prowler electronic countermeasures aircraft. All of their combat missions were coordinated by the air tasking order (ATO) issued by the Joint Forces Air Component Commander (JFACC) at CENTCOM (Central Command) headquarters.

See also AIR CAMPAIGN; FIRST MARINE EXPEDITIONARY FORCE.

Suggestions for further reading: Department of Defense, *Conduct of the Persian Gulf War: Final Report to the Congress,* "Chapter 6: The Air Campaign" (Washington, D.C.: USGPO, 1992); Norman Friedman, *Desert Victory: The War for Kuwait* (Annapolis, Md.: Naval Institute Press, 1991); Richard P. Hallion, *Storm Over Iraq: Air Power and the Gulf War* (Washington, D.C.: Smithsonian Institution Press, 1992). See also Col. Norman G. Ewers, "A Conversation with LtGen Royal N. Moore, Jr.," *Marine Corps Gazette,* October 1991; Lt. Gen. Royal N. Moore Jr., USMC, "Marine Air: There When Needed," *Naval Institute Proceedings,* November 1991.

THIRD U.S. ARMY

The Third U.S. Army was the senior U.S. Army headquarters in the Persian Gulf War, and as such it served as the Army component (ARCENT) for the U.S. Central Command (CENTCOM). Made famous by General George Patton in World War II, in the Gulf War the Third Army was commanded by Lieutenant General John J. Yeosock (except for a brief period from February 15 to February 23, 1991, when it was commanded by Lieutenant General Calvin A. H. Waller). The Third U.S. Army deployed from its home station in Atlanta, Georgia, and established its headquarters in Riyadh, Saudi Arabia, on August 16, 1990.

With more than 300,000 personnel at its peak strength, the Third U.S. Army consisted of the VII Corps and the XVIII Airborne Corps as well as the 22d Theater Army Support Command, which was responsible for much of CENTCOM's logistical support. Also under Third Army command was the 11th Air Defense Artillery Brigade, the 11th Signal Brigade, the 8th Psychological Operations Brigade, the 96th Civil Affairs Brigade, the 513th Military Intelligence Brigade and the 800th Military Police Brigade.

ARCENT COMMAND AND CONTROL

```
                                    ┌──────────────┐
                                    │    ARCENT    │
                                    └──────┬───────┘
   ┌────────────┬────────────┬────────────┼────────────┬────────────┐
┌──────────┐ ┌────────┐ ┌──────────┐ ┌────────┐ ┌──────────┐ ┌────────┐
│DCG LOG/  │ │VII Corps│ │XVII ABN  │ │  DCG   │ │ ARCENT   │ │  VDCG  │
│CG, ARCENT│ │         │ │ Corps    │ │        │ │  Rear    │ │        │
│FWD       │ │         │ │          │ │        │ │          │ │        │
└────┬─────┘ └────────┘ └──────────┘ └────────┘ └──────────┘ └────────┘
```

| DCG LOG/ CG, ARCENT FWD | VII Corps | XVII ABN Corps | DCG | ARCENT Rear | VDCG |

| ARCENT SUPCOM | | LESS OPCOM | | 8th PSYOP | 96 CA | 513th MI | 89th MP |
| 7 TRANS | 11th ADA | 11th SIG | TASOSC | | | | |

ARCENT PERSCOM

Among its forces were some 26,000 female soldiers and more than 78,000 Army Reserve and Army National Guard soldiers, most serving in combat support and combat service support units. Some National Guard combat units also deployed with the Third Army, including the 142d Field Artilley Brigade from the Arkansas-Oklahoma National Guard and the Tennessee-Kentucky-West Virginia National Guard's 196th Field Artillery Brigade.

Although doctrine called for General Yeosock as the Army component commander to develop the ground campaign—just as the air and naval component commanders developed the air and naval campaigns—General H. Norman Schwarzkopf, the commander in chief, Central Command (CINCCENT), chose to retain the Joint Forces Land Component Command responsibility. Schwarzkopf therefore directed the ground combat operations of both the Third U.S. Army and the First Marine Expeditionary Force, but he allowed their commanders to retain the primary responsibility for developing and analyzing courses of action for their respective ground offensives.

Although CINCCENT was responsible for maintaining coordination with the Saudi Arabian ground force command, the Third U.S. Army actually established and operated the Coalition Coordination, Communications and Control Integration Center in the National Defense Operations Center in Riyadh, which served as the link between CENTCOM and the Arab/Islamic Joint Forces Command.

When it came to logistics, CINCCENT gave the Third U.S. Army primary responsibility for supplying certain services and items common to all U.S. forces in the theater, including inland surface transportation, port operations, food, backup water supplies, bulk fuel distribution, munitions, medical and veterinary services and graves registration.

Between January 17 and February 16, 1991, under cover of the air campaign, some 200,000 troops of the Third U.S. Army's VII Corps and XVIII Airborne Corps were shifted westward to attack position along the Saudi-Iraqi border, and Army special forces teams were inserted deep into Iraq to perform strategic reconnaissance. At 4:00 A.M. (Gulf time) on February 24, the ground campaign began. Across a 300-mile front, U.S. Army and Marine Corps and other coalition forces launched the largest ground campaign since World War II.

The 8,508 armored vehicles of VII Corps formed the main attack. XVIII Airborne Corps, with 2,769 tracked vehicles and 1,026 aircraft, attacked along multiple axes while the First Marine Expeditionary Force (with the "Tiger Brigade" of the Army's 2d Armored Division attached) and Arab coalition forces attacked along the Gulf coast. The ground war was over 100 hours after it began. The world's fourth largest army had been decisively defeated.

Third U.S. Army losses were gratifyingly light. Of its approximately 300,000 soldiers, 96 were killed in action, another 84 died from nonbattle causes and 354 were wounded in action. Remarkably, only three

M1A1 Abrams tanks and five M2/M3 Bradley fighting vehicles were damaged by enemy fire. Five Army helicopters were lost in action, including two UH-60 Blackhawks, one AH-64 Apache, one UH-1 Huey and one OH-58 Kiowa.

Seventy-four Silver Stars were awarded to Third U.S. Army personnel for gallantry in action during the war; 24 Legions of Merit were awarded for distinguished service; 23 Distinguished Flying Crosses were awarded for valor and 74 for meritorious service; 37 Soldier's Medals were awarded for noncombat heroism; and 891 Bronze Star Medals were awarded for heroism, 20,005 for meritorious achievement and 6,327 for meritorious service. In addition, 450 Purple Hearts were awarded, 96 postumously, for wounds received in action; 694 Air Medals were awarded for valor, 4,494 for achievement and 555 for service; and 976 Army Commendation Medals were awarded for valor, 68,693 for achievement and 12,009 for service. Combat Infantryman Badges were awarded to 21,775 soldiers, and 3,136 soldiers received the Combat Medical Badge.

See also listings for specific units; ABRAMS M1A1 TANK; AIRLAND BATTLE DOCTRINE; APACHE ATTACK HELICOPTER; ARMOR; ATACMS (M39 ARMY TACTICAL MISSILE SYSTEM); BLACK U.S. MILITARY FORCES; BRADLEY M2/M3 FIGHTING VEHICLE; CAVALRY; COMBAT INFANTRYMAN BADGE; COMBAT MEDICAL BADGE; FIELD ARTILLERY; GROUND CAMPAIGN; HELICOPTERS; INFANTRY; LOGISTICS, U.S.; MLRS (MULTIPLE-LAUNCH ROCKET SYSTEM); MOBILIZATION, U.S.; PATRIOT MISSILE; WOMEN IN THE MILITARY; YEOSOCK, JOHN J.

Suggestions for further reading: Department of Defense, *Conduct of the Persian Gulf War: Final Report to the Congress,* "Chapter 8: The Ground Campaign" (Washington, D.C.: USGPO, 1992); Lt. Gen. Richard L. West, USA (Ret.) et al., *Special Report: The US Army in Operation Desert Storm* (Arlington, Va.: Association of the United States Army, 1991); Lt. Gen. John J. Yeosock, USA, "H+100: An Army Comes of Age in the Persian Gulf," *Army,* October 1991; Charles E. Kirkpatrick, *Building the Army for Desert Storm* (Arlington, Va.: The Institute of Land Warfare, AUSA, 1991); Colonel Harry G. Summers Jr., *On Strategy II: A Critical Analysis of the Gulf War* (New York: Dell, 1992); Field Manual 100-5, *Operations* (Washington, D.C.: USGPO, 1986); Norman Friedman, *Desert Victory: The War for Kuwait* (Annapolis, Md.: Naval Institute Press, 1991); Bruce W. Watson, ed., *Military Lessons of the Gulf War* (Novato, Calif.: Presidio Press, 1991). See also Rick Atkinson, *Crusade: The Untold Story of the Persian Gulf War* (New York: Houghton Mifflin, 1993).

TIGER BRIGADE, 2D ARMORED DIVISION
See 2D ARMORED DIVISION; 2D MARINE DIVISION.

TOMAHAWK LAND-ATTACK MISSILE (BGM-109C/D)
One of the more spectacular technological innovations displayed during the Persian Gulf War was the Tomahawk land-attack missile (TLAM), a stand-off, deep-strike weapon that can be fired from surface ships at sea or from submerged submarines to strike targets ashore in heavily defended areas where the probability of the loss of manned aircraft is too high.

Two variants of the Tomahawk were used by U.S. forces during the war. The TLAM-C (BGM-109C) carried a 1,000-pound warhead, whereas the TLAM-D (BGM-109D) carried 166 BLU-97/B bomblet submunitions that provided armor-piercing, fragmentation and incendiary effects.

With a range in excess of 500 miles, the Tomahawk has a Terrain-Contour Matching (TERCOM) guidance system that uses a radar altimeter to produce terrain profiles at preselected points along the missile's route. These profiles are compared with reference maps in the missile's computer to determine if flight corrections are needed.

As it nears its target, the Tomahawk switches to its more precise Digital Scene-Matching Area Correlation (DSMAC) system, which produces digital scenes of natural and man-made objects and compares them with scenes stored in the missile's computer.

The Tomawawk missile and the Stealth fighter were the only weapons systems used to strike targets in downtown Baghdad during the initial stages of the air campaign, and the Tomahawk was the only system used for daylight strikes against Baghdad during the entire campaign.

Sixteen U.S. Navy surface ships, including the battleship USS *Wisconsin,* and two nuclear-powered attack submarines launched 282 Tomahawk missiles, 64 percent of them during the first two days of the war. Eight Tomahawks were fired from the submarine USS *Louisville* (SSN-724) while it was submerged in the Red Sea, and four were fired from the USS *Pittsburgh* (SSN-720) while it was submerged in the Mediterranean Sea.

Shortly before leaving office in January 1993, President George Bush ordered 45 Tomahawks to be fired at suspected Iraqi nuclear facilities in Baghdad to force Iraq to comply with the terms of the cease-fire agreement. In June 1993, President Bill Clinton ordered the firing of 23 Tomahawks at the Iraqi intelligence services headquarters in Baghdad in retaliation for Iraqi attempts to assassinate former President Bush during a visit to Kuwait.

See also AIR CAMPAIGN; SUBMARINES.

Suggestions for further reading: Department of Defense, *Conduct of the Persian Gulf War: Final Report to the Congress*, "Chapter 6: The Air Campaign," "Appendix T: Performance of Selected Weapons Systems" (Washington, D.C.: USGPO, 1992); Norman Friedman, *Desert Victory: The War for Kuwait* (Annapolis, Md.: Naval Institute Press, 1991); Richard P. Hallion, *Storm Over Iraq: Air Power and the Gulf War* (Washington, D.C.: Smithsonian Institution Press, 1992); John Schwartz et al., "The Mind of a Missile," *Newsweek,* February 21, 1991; Commander Steve Frogget, "Tomahawk in the Desert," *Naval Institute Proceedings,* January 1992. For a critique of the Tomahawk's performance, see Barton Gellman, "Gulf Weapons' Accuracy Downgraded," *Washington Post,* April 10, 1992.

TOW (TUBE-LAUNCHED, OPTICALLY TRACKED, WIRE-GUIDED ANTITANK MISSILE)

Combat-tested in the closing days of the Vietnam War, the TOW was the standard U.S. vehicle-mounted antitank weapon during the Persian Gulf War. It is visually guided to the target by the gunner through the use of thin wires attached to the missile.

With a shaped-charge HEAT warhead and a range of more than 3,000 meters, the TOW was mounted on Marine Corps light armored vehicles (LAVs) and on Army M2/M3 Bradley armored fighting vehicles and HMMWVs (high-mobility multipurpose wheeled vehicles). TOWs were also mounted on Army AH-1 Cobra helicopter gunships and on some Marine Cobra gunships.

While not as technically advanced as the HELLFIRE antitank missile, the TOW proved effective against Iraqi armor. During the battle for Khafji,

for example, a Marine LAV gunner destroyed two Iraqi T-72 tanks with TOW missiles.

See also HELLFIRE MISSILE.

Suggestion for further reading: Norman Friedman, *Desert Victory: The War for Kuwait* (Annapolis, Md.: Naval Institute Press, 1991) has a useful discussion of the TOW missile.

TRANSPORTATION COMMAND (TRANSCOM)

See LOGISTICS, U.S.

TURKEY

Although not officially a member of the coalition, Turkey played an important role in the Persian Gulf War. The political support of President Turgut Ozal was invaluable in building the coalition against Iraq. His decision to close the Iraqi oil pipelines that ran across his country to the port of Ceyhan, a decision that cost Turkey billions of dollars in lost oil revenues, was critical to the enforcement of economic sanctions against Iraq, since about half of Iraq's oil exports ran through Turkey.

Thanks to President Ozal's efforts, on January 17, 1991, the day the air campaign began, the Turkish parliament approved the use by North Atlantic Treaty Organization (NATO) forces of Turkish bases to launch air strikes against Iraq. A planning force from U.S. Air Force Europe's (USAFE) 7440th Composite Wing (Provisional) was already on the ground at the NATO air base at Incirlik, and within hours the Turkish General Staff had approved airspace control, safe-passage procedures and air-refueling tracks.

Under the operational control of EUCOM (European Command) but under the tactical control of Central Command's Joint Forces Air Component Commander, Joint Task Force (JTF) "Proven Force" (i.e., the NATO force in Turkey) included F-15 Eagles for air cover; F-16 Fighting Falcons for day strikes; F-111 Aardvarks for night strikes; EF-111s EC-130s and F-4G Wild Weasels for electronic warfare and suppression of enemy air defenses; KC-135 Stratotankers for aerial refueling; RF-4s for reconnaissance; and E-3B Airborne Warning and Control System (AWACS) aircraft for command and control. B-52 Stratofortress bombers flew from Morón Air Base in Spain and later from RAF Fairford in the United Kingdom in support of JTF Proven Force at Incirlik. A large contingent of the NATO Allied Command Europe Mobile Force (Air) also deployed to Turkey to deter an Iraqi attack. Eighteen West German Luftwaffe Alpha jets deployed, along with approximately 800 personnel. Three German reconnaissance aircraft also arrived with about 125 support personnel. Dutch Patriot missile batteries were sent to Incirlik.

In allowing the use of its base at Incirlik to prosecute the war in northern Iraq, and by massing its own military forces along the Turkish-Iraqi border, thereby tying down Iraqi military forces in border defenses, Turkey was a critical, albeit unofficial, coalition ally.

Suggestions for further reading: Turgut Ozal, "An Unavoidable War," *Washington Post,* January 22, 1991. See also Department of Defense, *Conduct of the Persian Gulf War: Final Report to the Congress* (Washington, D.C.: USGPO, 1992); Brig. Gen. Lee A. Downer, USAF, "The Composite Wing in Combat," *Airpower Journal,* Winter 1991.

24TH INFANTRY DIVISION (MECHANIZED)

Stationed at Fort Stewart, Georgia, as part of the U.S. Army's XVIII Airborne Corps, the 24th Infantry "Victory" Division (Mechanized) was at Pearl Harbor during the Japanese attack on December 7, 1941. It fought its way across the Pacific in World War II, was the first American unit to fight in the Korean War in July 1950, and was the first U.S. heavy division to arrive in Saudi Arabia during the buildup for the Persian Gulf War.

Commanded by Major General Barry R. McCaffrey, the division was alerted to move to the Kuwaiti Theater of Operations (KTO) on August 7, 1990, as part of President George Bush's immediate reaction to Iraq's invasion of Kuwait. Six days later the division began outloading its tanks and heavy equipment from the port of Savannah, Georgia, and by September 7 it had occupied defensive positions in Saudi Arabia to check further Iraqi aggression. The Georgia National Guard's 48th Infantry Brigade was supposed to round-out the division, but that unit was not called to active duty until November 1990. Taking the 48th's place was the active-duty 197th Infantry Brigade from Fort Benning, Georgia.

The 24th Infantry Division's two maneuver brigades consisted of the 2d and 3d Battalions, 7th Infantry; the 3d Battalion, 15th Infantry; the 1st and 4th Battalions, 64th Armor; and the 3d Battalion, 69th

Armor. The 197th Infantry Brigade included the 1st and 2d Battalions of the 18th Infantry and the 2d Battalion of the 69th Armor. In the division's aviation brigade were some 90 helicopters, including 18 AH-64 Apache attack helicopters.

The division's reconnaissance squadron, the 2d Squadron, 4th Cavalry, was equipped with M1A1 Abrams tanks, M3 Bradley cavalry fighting vehicles (CFVs) and OH-58 Kiowa scout helicopters. Division artillery consisted of the 1st, 3d and 4th Battalions of the 41st Field Artillery (FA) and the 2d and 4th Battalions of the 82d FA with M109 self-propelled 155-mm howitzers; and Battery A of the 13th FA with Multiple-Launch Rocket System (MLRS) launchers.

On the eve of the ground campaign the division was reinforced by the 212th Artillery Brigade from III Corps Artillery, the 171st Corps Support Group and the 36th Engineer Group. Now with 34 battalions and some 26,000 soldiers, the Division Combat

Major General Barry McCaffrey (left) directs the 24th Infantry Division's attack into Iraq.
U.S. Army photo (50th Public Affairs Detachment) courtesy of 24th Infantry Division (Mechanized).

Team consisted of 249 M1A1 Abrams tanks, 218 M2 Bradley infantry fighting vehicles (IFVs), 843 M113 armored personnel carriers and 6,500 wheeled vehicles. Fire support included 90 155-mm howitzers, 24 8-inch howitzers and 36 MLRS launchers.

Part of the XVIII Airborne Corps attack, the Victory Division had as its mission striking swiftly and decisively into the enemy's rear and flanks, blocking the Euphrates River valley, preventing the escape of 500,000 enemy soldiers in the KTO and continuing the attack eastward toward Basra to complete the destruction of the Iraqi Republican Guard Forces Command (RGFC).

Evidencing the enormous distances involved in desert warfare was the division's movement over 517 kilometers (320 miles) from its Desert Shield defensive positions in eastern Saudi Arabia to its Desert Storm forward assembly areas in the west. From there it would attack 300 kilometers (187 miles) into Iraq to the Euphrates River, and then 113 kilometers east through the river valley toward Basra, for a total movement of 930 kilometers (530 miles).

Launching its attack five hours early on G-Day (February 24, 1991) because of the successes of XVIII Airborne Corps units on its left flank, by midnight the division had penetrated 75 miles into Iraq. By the close of the day on February 25, against weak resistance from the Iraqi 26th and 35th Infantry Divisions, it had overrun three major objectives and taken hundreds of prisoners.

The 24th Infantry Division's heaviest fighting of the war came on February 26 as it advanced into the Euphrates River valley, when its 1st Brigade came under heavy tank and artillery fire. Opposed by the Iraqi 47th and 49th Infantry Divisions, the Republican Guard Nebuchadnezzar Division and the 26th Commando Brigade, the 24th battled until January 27, when it broke through to capture the enemy airfields at Tallil and Jalibah. When offensive operations ended on January 28, the lead elements of the 24th Infantry Division (Mechanized) were only 30 miles west of Basra, where the division hastily set up defense positions.

On March 2, 1991, following the cease-fire, elements of the Iraqi Republican Guard's Hammurabi Division attempted to break out from Basra, but at the Battle of Rumaylah they were routed by elements of the 24th Infantry Division and fled in panic back into the "Basra Pocket," losing 187 armored vehicles, 34 artillery pieces and 400 trucks in the process.

Moving farther and faster than any other mechanized force in military history, in just 100 hours of battle the "Victory" Division attacked deep into the enemy's flank and rear, severed the enemy's lines of communication through the Euphrates River valley and systematically annihilated the Iraqi 26th Commando Brigade, the 47th and 49th Infantry Divisions and four Republican Guard divisions.

President Bush announced that the 24th Infantry Division (Mechanized) would be the first unit to return home, and on March 6, 1991, the division began its journey back to Fort Stewart, Georgia.

See also XVIII AIRBORNE CORPS; GROUND CAMPAIGN; MOBILIZATION, U.S.

Suggestions for further reading: Department of Defense, *Conduct of the Persian Gulf War: Final Report to the Congress,* "Chapter 8: The Ground Campaign" (Washington, D.C.: USGPO, 1992): See also "A History of the 24th Mechanized Infantry Division Combat Team During OPERATION DESERT STORM"; "24th Mechanized Infantry Division Combat Team Historical Reference Book"; "24th Infantry Division (Mechanized) OPLAN 91.3"; and "The Victory Book: A Desert Storm Chronicle," all from Fort Stewart, Ga: 24th Infantry Division (Mechanized), 1992. Also, Major James Blackwell, *Thunder in the Desert: The Strategy and Tactics of the Persian Gulf War* (New York: Bantam Books, 1991); General H. Norman Schwarzkopf, *It Doesn't Take a Hero* (New York: Bantam Books, 1992); The Staff of *U.S. News & World Report, Triumph Without Victory* (New York: Times Books, 1992); Joseph L. Galloway, "The Point of the Spear," *U.S. News & World Report,* March 11, 1991; James Blackwell, "Georgia Punch," *Army Times,* December 2, 1991.

22D THEATER ARMY SUPPORT COMMAND
See LOGISTICS, U.S.

U

UAV (UNMANNED AERIAL VEHICLES)

See DRONES AND DECOYS.

UNITED ARAB EMIRATES (UAE)

A member of both the Arab League and the Gulf Cooperation Council (GCC), the United Arab Emirates (UAE) played an important role in the Persian Gulf War.

With a land area of 32,000 square miles, the UAE is about the size of Maine. With its capital at Abu Dhabi, the country consists of a barren, flat coastal plain giving way to uninhabited sand dunes in the south. Located on the Persian Gulf, the UAE borders Qatar to the north, Saudi Arabia to the west and south, and Oman to the east.

The UAE is a federation of seven autonomous emirates—Abu Dhabi, Ajman, Dubai, Fujairah, Ras al-Khaimah, Sharjah and Umm al-Qaiwain. These "Trucial States" gave Great Britain control of their defense and foreign relations in the 19th century, and merged to become an independent state, the UAE, on December 2, 1971.

Emirians are a minority in their own country: the UAE's 1992 population was 2,522,325, less than 20 percent of which were Emirians. South Asians make up 50 percent of the population, other Arabs make up 23 percent, and Westerners and East Asians account for 8 percent.

With oil reserves estimated at 98 billion barrels, the UAE is one of the world's major oil producing nations. Oil revenues have given the country one of the world's highest per capita incomes.

During the Gulf War, the UAE provided the coalition with aircraft bed-down facilities, port facilities, hospitals, lodging, food and fuel as well as billions of dollars in cash commitments. Coalition aircraft flew from UAE air bases at Al Ain, Al Dhafra, Al Minhad, Abu Dhabi, Bateen and Dubai, while the 50 Mirage fighters of the UAE Air Force took an active part in the air campaign.

The UAE Navy participated in maritime interception operations and antisurface warfare, and two UAE-flagged ships, the *Vivi* and *Celini,* were con-tracted as support ships for explosive ordnance demolition teams that accompanied the U.S. Mine Countermeasures Group based at the UAE port of Abu Dhabi. The UAE Motorized Infantry Brigade was part of Joint Forces Command-East's Task Force Omar and took part in the liberation of Kuwait City.

Ten UAE military personnel were killed in the fighting and 17 were wounded in action.

See also AIR FORCES, COALITION; ARAB LEAGUE; ARMIES, COALITION; COST; GULF COOPERATION COUNCIL; JOINT FORCES COMMAND; NAVIES, COALITION.

Suggestions for further reading: Department of Defense, *Conduct of the Persian Gulf War: Final Report to the Congress* (Washington, D.C.: USGPO, 1992); Francis Tusa, "Defense No Longer 'Business as Usual' in UAE," *Armed Forces Journal International,* January 1991.

UNITED KINGDOM (UK)

The United Kingdom (UK) played a major role in the Persian Gulf War.

The United Kingdom is a permanent member of the United Nations (UN) Security Council, and its political support was critical, for a UK veto of that body's resolutions would have blocked UN participation in the conflict. And the United Kingdom may have played a critical role in shaping U.S. policy as well. Prime Minister Margaret Thatcher, who was at a conference with President George Bush in Aspen, Colorado, when the crisis erupted, has been credited with stiffening the president's resolve to take strong action to reverse the Iraqi aggression against Kuwait.

The United Kingdom not only sent substantial military forces to the Kuwaiti Theater of Operations (KTO), it also allowed the use of its bases for the prosecution of the war. KC-10 Extender tankers operated from the Royal Air Force (RAF) base at Mildenhall to refuel U.S. aircraft en route to Saudi Arabia. And B-52 Stratofortress bombers flew strike missions from the RAF base at Fairford against Iraqi forces in the KTO, SKYNET, the United Kingdom's

These sailors from the logistical landing ship HMS *Sir Galahad* were part of the Royal Navy's large presence in the Gulf.
U.S. Navy photo (CWO Ed Bailey), Empire Press.

military communications satellite, also supported operations in the KTO.

British forces in the Gulf War were under the overall command of Air Chief Marshall Sir Patrick Hine. The British Forces Commander Middle East for "Operation Granby" (the UK name for Operations Desert Shield and Desert Storm) was General Sir Peter de la Billiere. Except for Special Air Service (SAS) special operations forces, which remained under UK control, UK forces in the KTO were under the tactical command of the U.S. commander in chief, Central Command (CINCCENT).

The Royal Navy, the Royal Air Force and British ground forces participated in the war. The United Kingdom had long had a military presence "east of

Suez," and when the Kuwaiti crisis erupted in August 1990 its "Armilla patrol" in the Gulf region consisted of the Royal Navy destroyer HMS *York*, the frigates HMS *Jupiter* and *Battleaxe*, and the replenishment ship HMS *Orangeleaf*. They were soon reinforced, and the United Kingdom had the largest naval contingent in the Persian Gulf next to that of the United States.

The Royal Navy took part from the start in maritime interception operations to enforce the UN economic sanctions against Iraq, and it conducted the first seizure of a hostile merchant vessel on October 8, 1990. It also played a key role in all phases of the coalition's maritime campaign. For example, on February 24, 1991, two Sea Dart missiles fired by the

HMS *Gloucester* destroyed an Iraqi Silkworm missile aimed at the battleship USS *Missouri.*

With five mine countermeasures (MCM) vessels deployed, the Royal Navy played a particularly active role in MCM operations, taking reponsibility for most surface mine countermeasures. The Royal Navy's Lynx helicopters with their Sea Skua missiles also played a major role in neutralizing the Iraqi Navy, destroying more than a quarter of its warships.

The first RAF squadron of 12 Tornado F3 air defense fighters became operational at Dhahran Air Base in Saudi Arabia on August 12, 1990. A squadron of RAF ground-attack Jaguar GR1As and Nimrod patrol aircraft became operational soon thereafter. During the course of the war, the RAF would deploy some 158 aircraft and helicopters to the KTO; only the United States and Saudi Arabia deployed more.

At the peak of hostilities, some 5,500 RAF personnel, including reservists, were deployed to the Gulf. RAF planners became part of the Joint Forces Air Component Commander's staff and helped plan and coordinate the air campaign.

Six RAF Tornado GR1 attack aircraft were lost during the air campaign, mostly in low-level bombing attacks on enemy airfields. A seventh was lost in a noncombat flying accident.

The first UK ground unit to deploy was the 7th Armoured Brigade, the "Desert Rats" of World War II fame. Some 12,000-strong, the brigade arrived at Al-Jubayl, Saudia Arabia, in October 1990. Initially attached to the U.S. 1st Marine Division, it came under the control of the UK 1st Armoured Division when the latter arrived in-country in November.

Commanded by Major General Rupert Smith, the 25,000-man 1st Armoured Division included the 4th and 7th Armoured Brigades with Challenger tanks, Warrior armored fighting vehicles (AFVs), M109 155-mm self-propelled howitzers and Multiple-Launch Rocket System (MLRS) heavy artillery, reinforced by the U.S. 142d Field Artillery Brigade.

Under the operational command of the U.S. VII Corps, the UK 1st Armoured Division had as its mission passing through the breach in the Iraqi fortifications created by the U.S. 1st Infantry Division, and attacking the Iraqi armored division in its zone to prevent it from moving into the flank of the advancing VII Corps.

On G +1 (February 25, 1991) the UK 1st Armoured Division passed through the breach as planned, then turned right to attack the Iraqi 52d Armored Division. During the ensuing engagement, the UK 1st Armoured Division destroyed 40 enemy tanks and captured some 4,000 prisoners, including the commanders of the Iraqi 48th Infantry Division and 52d Armored Division. One unfortunate incident occurred on G +2 (February 26) when a U.S. A-10 Warthog mistook a British Warrior AFV for an enemy AFV and attacked it, killing nine British soldiers.

After destroying the Iraqi 52d Armored Division, the UK 1st Armoured Division continued the attack on G +3 (February 27), overrunning three Iraqi infantry divisions. The division ended the war astride the enemy's lines of communication along the Kuwait City–Basra road.

"The British . . . have been absolutely superb . . . members of this coalition from the outset," said General H. Norman Schwarzkopf in his post-ground-war briefing. "They played a very, very key role in the movement of the main attack. . . . They did it absolutely magnificently. . . . They just did a great job."

Twenty-five UK military personnel were killed during the war, and another 45 were wounded in action.

In February 1993, it was announced that Queen Elizabeth II had approved battle honors for the troops involved in the Gulf War. The battle honor "Kuwait 1991" went to 15 Royal Navy ships and 10 Royal Fleet Auxiliary vessels. The battle honors "Wadi al-Batin" and "Western Iraq" went to the army, and the battle honor "Gulf 1991" to the RAF.

See also AIR CAMPAIGN; AIR FIELDS; AIR FORCES, COALITION; ARMIES, COALITION; FRIENDLY FIRE; GROUND CAMPAIGN; MARITIME INTERCEPTION OPERATIONS; MINESWEEPING; NAVIES, COALITION; VII CORPS; SPECIAL OPERATIONS COMMAND CENTRAL COMMAND; UNITED NATIONS.

Suggestions for further reading: General Sir Peter de la Billiere, *Storm Command: A Personal Account of the Gulf War* (London: HarperCollins, 1992); Department of Defense, *Conduct of the Persian Gulf War: Final Report to the Congress* (Washington, D.C.: USGPO, 1992). See also the following articles in *RUSI Journal:* General Sir Peter de la Billiere, "The Gulf Conflict," (Winter 1991); Major General Rupert

Smith, "The Gulf War: The Land Battle," (February 1992); Brigadier P. A. J. Cordingley, "The Gulf War: Operating With Allies," (April 1992); Commodore C. J. S. Craig, "Gulf War: The Maritime Campaign," (August 1992) and Margaret Aldred, "Lessons From the Gulf Crisis," (December 1992).

UNITED NATIONS (UN)

The Persian Gulf War was conducted under the authority of the United Nations (UN). Not only did the series of United Nations Security Council (UNSC) resolutions give member nations the legal authority to take action against Iraq, it gave them the moral authority to do so as well. This was particularly important for the Bush administration, which used those resolutions to seek and win congressional approval for the use of U.S. military forces in the Gulf War (see CONGRESS, U.S.).

The UN Security Council is composed of 15 member countries. Five—the United States, the United Kingdom, France, the Soviet Union (now Russia) and China—are permanent members, and each has the power to veto any proposed resolution by voting against it. The other 10 members, representing different regions of the world, are elected for limited terms.

For most of its existence, the UNSC was hamstrung by the political divisions of the Cold War. Only once, in June 1950, was the UNSC able to act to counter aggression—that of North Korea against South Korea. This was possible because the Soviet Union was boycotting the UNSC and was not present to cast its veto, and because China's seat was then held by the Republic of China on the island of Taiwan rather than, as is now the case, by the People's Republic of China on the mainland.

With the end of the Cold War in 1989, this impasse was broken. Both China and the Soviet Union supported UN actions against Iraq, although China abstained on the vote to use force.

Interestingly, as the *Washington Post*'s John M. Goshko noted at the time, the resolution authorizing the use of "all means necessary" deliberately did not invoke Article 42 of the UN Charter. To have done so "likely would have required the council to create a unified U.N. command over all the forces engaged against Iraq." The United States and its principal allies who had deployed forces in the Gulf region wanted "to retain command of their own forces, and for that reason the Bush administration resisted pressures to have the resolution seek some kind of unified UN structure."

See also UNITED NATIONS SECURITY COUNCIL RESOLUTIONS.

Suggestions for further reading: Department of Defense, *Conduct of the Persian Gulf War: Final Report to the Congress,* "Chapter 2: The Response to Aggression" (Washington, D.C.: USGPO, 1992; John M. Goshko, "U.N. Vote Authorizes Use of Force Against Iraq," *Washington Post,* November 30, 1990. For a critical view of UN actions, see Clovis Maksoud, "The Arab World's Quandary," *World Policy Journal,* Summer 1991.

UNITED NATIONS SECURITY COUNCIL RESOLUTIONS

The United Nations (UN) Security Council enacted a series of resolutions concerning the Iraqi invasion of Kuwait. These resolutions are summarized below:

Date	Number	Summary
Aug. 2, '90	660	Condemned invasion. Demanded withdrawal. Adopted 14 to 0, Yemen not participating.
Aug. 6, '90	661	Imposed trade and financial em bargo on Iraq. Adopted 13 to 0, Yemen and Cuba abstaining.
Aug. 9, '90	662	Declared Iraqi annexation of Kuwait null and void. Adopted unanimously.
Aug. 18, '90	664	Demanded immediate release of foreigners held hostage by Iraq. Adopted unanimously.
Aug. 25, '90	665	Called on UN members to enforce sanctions by inspecting and verifying cargoes and destinations. Adopted 13 to 0, Yemen and Cuba abstaining.
Sep. 13, '90	666	Reaffirmed Iraqi responsibility for safety of foreign nationals. Adopted 13 to 2, Yemen and Cuba opposed.
Sep. 16, '90	667	Condemned Iraqi aggression against diplomats. Demanded immediate release of foreign nationals. Adopted unanimously.
Sep. 24, '90	669	Emphasized only special sanctions committee could authorize food and aid shipments to Iraq and Kuwait. Adopted unanimously.

Date	Number	Summary
Sep. 25, '90	670	Expanded embargo to include air traffic. Adopted 14 to 1, Cuba opposed.
Oct. 29, '90	674	Demanded Iraq stop mistreating Kuwaiti and other foreign nationals. Adopted 13 to 0, Yemen and Cuba abstaining.
Nov. 28, '90	677	Condemned Iraq's attempt to change Kuwait's demographic composition and destruction of Kuwaiti civil records. Adopted unanimously.
Nov. 29, '90	678	Authorized UN members to use "all means necessary" to enforce previous resolutions if Iraq does not leave Kuwait by January 15, 1991. Adopted 12 to 2, Yemen and Cuba opposed, China abstaining.
Mar. 2, '91	686	Demands Iraq cease hostile action, return all POWs and detainees, rescind annexation, accept liability, return Kuwaiti property and disclose mine locations. Adopted 11 to 1, Cuba opposed, Yemen, China and India abstaining.
Apr. 2, '91	687	Sets out terms of cease-fire. Adopted 12 to 1, Cuba opposed, Yemen and Ecuador abstaining.
Apr. 5, '91	688	Condemns Iraqi government repression of Iraqi civilian population. Adopted 10 to 3, Yemen, Cuba and Zimbabwe opposed, China and India abstaining.

See also SANCTIONS; UNITED NATIONS.

Suggestion for further reading: The full texts of United Nations Security Council resolutions on the Gulf War are in The Staff of *U.S. News & World Report, Triumph Without Victory,* (New York: Times Books, 1992), Appendix A.

V

VALOROUS UNIT AWARD

First authorized during the Vietnam War, the Valorous Unit Award is presented by the U.S. Army to units of the armed forces of the United States that have exhibited extraordinary heroism in action against the enemy. The unit must have performed with the same gallantry, determination and esprit de corps that would warrant the awarding of the Silver Star to an individual.

Thirteen units received the Valorous Unit Award for their actions in the Persian Gulf War. They include the Third Army's 11th Air Defense Brigade; the VII Corps's 2d Armored Cavalry Regiment; the XVIII Airborne Corps's 18th Field Artillery Brigade; the 3d Brigade, 3th Infantry Division, which was attached to the 1st Armored Division; the 2d Battalion, 34th Armor; the 4th Battalion, 64th Armor; the 1st Battalion, 24th Aviation; the 4th Battalion, 229th Aviation; the 1st Squadron, 4th Cavalry; the 2d Squadron, 6th Cavalry; the 1st Engineer Battalion; the 3d Battalion, 27th Field Artillery; and the 1st Battalion, 41st Infantry, 2d Armored Division, which was attached to the 24th Infantry Division (Mechanized).

V DEVICE

The "V" device is a small metallic attachment to the ribbon of those decorations—such as the Legion of Merit, the Air Medal, the Bronze Star and the Commendation Medal—that can be awarded either for heroism or for meritorious service, to denote that the decoration was awarded for valor.

VETERANS

Some 6,000 veterans of the Persian Gulf War have reported to the Department of Veterans Affairs (VA) that they are suffering from mysterious war-connected ailments, including hair loss, skin rashes, joint pains, bleeding of the gums, and chronic fatigue.

What makes these reports so puzzling is the fact that disease rates for the Persian Gulf War—at least so far—are markedly lower than expected. According to the official Department of Defense report on the war, this was because of "strong command emphasis on preventative medicine, especially regarding environmental threats to health such as prevention of heat injuries; well-trained preventative medicine, environmental health, and bio-environmental engineering officers and specially trained enlisted personnel; a very strong veterinary presence for food inspection; an adequate supply of potable water; a lower than predicted threat from infectious diseases; and minimal contact with indigenous personnel."

In June 1993, Major General Ronald Blanck, commander of the Walter Reed Army Medical Center in Washington, D.C., told a House of Representatives Veterans Affairs subcommittee that he was concerned with the number of soldiers with nonspecific symptoms, the causes of which so far have defied identification.

"The American Legion," reported the *Washington Times* on June 22, 1993, "listed possible causes as inoculations, crude oil, burning oil wells, pesticides, smoke from burning landfills, insect bites, poor sanitary conditions, diesel exhaust and radiation exposure from exploding shells made of depleted uranium." The VA believes the illnesses may have been caused by what physicians call "multiple chemical sensitivity."

In August 1992, the VA established special environmental medicine referral centers in its hospitals in West Los Angeles, Houston and Washington, D.C., to handle cases of unusual symptoms in Persian Gulf veterans. An independent laboratory, paid for partially by the Defense Department, has been established to research the growing number of claims by Persian Gulf veterans, but as of 1994 no specific cause of the illnesses has been found.

See also DEPLETED URANIUM; MEDICAL CARE AND EVACUATION, COALITION.

Suggestions for further reading: Department of Defense, *Conduct of the Persian Gulf War: Final Report to the Congress,* "Appendix G: Medical Support" (Washington, D.C.: USGPO, 1992); "VA Health Care for Persian Gulf Veterans," *VA Fact Sheet,* August 1992; "VA Establishes Referral Centers to Assist Persian Gulf Veterans," *News Release,* Department of Veterans Affairs, August 18, 1992; Frank A. Aukofer, "Gulf War Vets Get Prompt Attention for Mystery Ills," *Washington Times,* June 21, 1993; Jack Dorsey, "Gulf Vets' Illnesses a 'Great Concern,'" *Virginian-Pilot,* August 7, 1993.

VIETNAM WAR

The Vietnam War had a profound effect on the Persian Gulf War. As discussed elsewhere (see STRATEGY, IRAQ), it probably caused Saddam Hussein to misjudge the will and resolve of the United States in the Gulf War. As far as the U.S. military was concerned, the Vietnam War sparked a renewed emphasis on the fundamentals of military art and science and a major renaissance in military education and training.

In the wake of the debacle in Vietnam, conventional warfighting strategy was revitalized, there was a renewed appreciation of operational art and campaign planning, and a renewed stress on tactical manuever. Weapons systems such as the "smart bombs" pioneered in Vietnam were further developed, and new technologies were devised to correct deficiencies revealed in that war.

Most important was the reemphasis on moral integrity among the senior leadership of the U.S. armed forces. All of the generals and admirals and most of the colonels and Navy captains who fought in the Gulf War were Vietnam War veterans. Junior officers in that last war, they saw their seniors temporize with moral issues and fail to speak up when they knew fundamentals were being ignored.

One such moral issue concerned providing "body counts." This requirement was imposed by Secretary of Defense Robert McNamara's "bean counters" in the Pentagon who believed counting enemy bodies was a valid way to measure battlefield success. What it really did was erode the integrity of the officer corps, as leaders were forced to submit false claims in order to protect their careers. Another was the failure of Secretary McNamara to tell the president he thought the war was militarily unwinnable in 1965, even as he began to send American servicemen to their deaths. It would not be until 1984 that McNamara would publicly admit his duplicity. And then there were the Joint Chiefs of Staff themselves, who knew the U.S. had no strategy worthy of the name, knew all the principles of war being violated, yet said nothing.

From Vietnam veterans such as General Colin Powell, the chairman of the Joint Chiefs of Staff, to General H. Norman Schwarzkopf, the commander in chief, Central Command, and throughout the senior officer corps in the Persian Gulf War, there was a deep-seated determination not to repeat those lapses in moral courage again.

Suggestions for further reading: For an analysis of how the U.S. military forged victory in the Gulf War from the defeat in Vietnam, see Colonel Harry G. Summers Jr., *On Strategy II: A Critical Analysis of the Gulf War* (New York: Dell, 1992). See also Al Santoli, *Leading the Way* (New York: Ballantine Books, 1993); Jim Hoagland, "Congress, Bush and the Generals," *Washington Post,* November 22, 1990; Major Mark Clodfelter, "Of Demons, Storms, and Thunder: A Preliminary Look at Vietnam's Impact on the Persian Gulf Air Campaign," *Airpower Journal,* Winter 1991; John D. Morrocco, "From Vietnam to Desert Storm," *Airforce,* January 1992.

W

WALLER, CALVIN A(UGUSTINE) H(OFFMAN), LIEUTENANT GENERAL, USA (1937–)

The deputy commander in chief of the U.S. Central Command (DCINCCENT) during the Persian Gulf War, General Calvin A. H. Waller was commissioned a second lieutenant in the chemical corps through the Reserve Officers Training Program (ROTC) at Prairie View A & M University, Prairie View, Texas, in 1959. In 1978, he earned a Master of Science degree in public administration from Shippensburg State University in Pennsylvania. Earlier, from 1969 to 1970, he served as the chemical operations officer in the J-3 (Operations) Directorate of

The second-in-command of all U.S. forces in the Gulf, General Waller was concerned about an untimely rush to action.
U.S. Army photo courtesy of Dennis Keating, Department of the Army.

Military Assistance Command Vietnam (MACV) in Saigon. Transferring to the armor branch, Waller served as the operations officer and later as the executive officer of the 1st Battalion, 68th Armor in Germany from 1972 to 1974.

Among his significant assignments were senior military assistant to the assistant secretary of defense for manpower, reserve affairs and logistics; commanded the 2d Brigade, 8th Infantry Division (Mechanized) in Germany; chief of staff of the 24th Infantry Division (Mechanized) at Fort Stewart, Georgia; chief of staff, XVIII Airborne Corps at Fort Bragg, North Carolina; assistant division commander of the 82d Airborne Division at Fort Bragg; commanding general, 8th Infantry Division (Mechanized) in Germany; and deputy commanding general and later commanding general, I Corps, at Fort Lewis, Washington.

Appointed DCINCCENT (i.e., the second in command of all U.S. forces in the Gulf) in November 1990, Waller served in that post until March 1991. From February 15 to February 23, 1991, General Waller assumed command of the Third U.S. Army when its commander, Lieutenant General John J. Yeosock, was hospitalized for surgery, but Waller is best known for his warning that Central Command (CENTCOM) was not ready to begin ground combat operations.

On December 20, 1990, Waller said publicly that his troops "will not be ready for combat activities" on January 15, 1991, the United Nations deadline for an Iraqi pullout from Kuwait. The VII Corps was still in transit from Europe, he said, and would not be combat-ready until "sometime between the 15th of January and the middle of February."

His remarks touched off a furor in Washington at the time, but subsequent events proved him absolutely correct. CENTCOM was not ready to launch a ground offensive on January 15, and was just barely ready on February 24 when the ground war actually began.

Like others who served as junior officers in the Vietnam War, Waller would not perpetuate the lack of moral courage of the senior officers of that war who told the president "can do" when the truth was that some tasks could not be done properly.

General Waller's awards and decorations include two Distinguished Service Medals, the Defense Superior Service Medal, two Bronze Star Medals, four Meritorious Service Medals, an Air Medal, the Army Commendation Medal and the Master Parachutist Badge.

In March 1991, General Waller returned to command of I Corps at Fort Lewis. One of the highest-ranking black officers in the Army, he retired from active duty in November 1991.

See also CENTCOM (CENTRAL COMMAND); THIRD U.S. ARMY.

Suggestions for further reading: General H. Norman Schwarzkopf, *It Doesn't Take a Hero* (New York: Bantam Books, 1992). Rick Atkinson, *Crusade: The Untold Story of the Persian Gulf War* (New York: Houghton Mifflin, 1993) argues that Waller was assigned as DCINCCENT to act as a brake on Schwarzkopf's bullying of his subordinates. For the December 1990 incident, see Barton Gellman, "General: U.S. Troops Won't Be Ready," *Washington Post*, December 20, 1990; Eric Schmitt, "Pentagon Seeks To Diminish Effect of Officer's Remarks," *New York Times*, December 21, 1990. See also Frank Trejo, "Gulf General Doesn't Consider Self Hero," *Dallas Morning News*, July 20, 1991.

WAR CORRESPONDENTS

See MEDIA.

WAR CRIMES

On March 19, 1993, the United States submitted a detailed report on Iraqi war crimes during the Gulf War to the United Nations Security Council. Compiled by Army Reserve lawyers from the 199th Judge Advocate Detachment at St. Petersburg, Florida, and the 208th Judge Advocate Detachment in the District of Columbia, it concluded that in Kuwait City alone "a total of 1,082 Kuwaiti civilian deaths could be directly attributed to Iraqi criminal conduct."

"The gruesome evidence," said the report, "confirms torture by amputation of or injury to various body parts, to include limbs, eyes, tongues, ears, noses, lips and genitalia. . . . Some victims were killed in acid baths. Women taken hostage were raped repeatedly. . . . Eyewitnesses reported Iraqis

torturing a woman by making her eat her own flesh as it was cut from her body. . . ."

The official Department of Defense report on the war lists some 17 Iraqi violations of international law, including the Hague Convention of 1907, the Geneva Protocol of 1925, the Genocide Convention of 1948 and the four Geneva Conventions for the Protection of War Victims of 1949. As of this writing, no action has been taken to bring the offenders to trial.

In addition to the inhumane treatment of Kuwaiti civilians, alleged Iraqi war crimes include the taking of hostages, using hostages as human shields, torture and other inhumane treatment of prisoners of war, pillage, ecological warfare and indiscriminate Scud missile attacks against civilian targets.

Antiwar activists, including Ramsey Clark and the New York City–based "International War Crimes Tribunal," have charged that the United States itself was guilty of some 19 war crimes, including provoking Iraq into the war, intentionally bombing civilian facilities and killing soldiers trying to surrender. Because of a lack of substantiating evidence, these charges against the United States have faded from view.

See also ANTIWAR MOVEMENT; CASUALTIES; JUST WAR.

Suggestions for further reading: "Report on Iraqi War Crimes (Desert Shield/Desert Storm," War Crimes Documentation Center, International Affairs Division, Office of the Judge Advocate General, Department of the Army, January 8, 1992; Department of Defense, *Conduct of the Persian Gulf War: Final Report to the Congress*, "Appendix O: The Role of the Law of War" (Washington, D.C.: USGPO, 1992). See also Ramsey Clark, *The Fire This Time: U.S. War Crimes in the Gulf* (New York: Thunder's Mouth Press, 1992); Ellen Yan, "Rights Groups Accuse U.S. of War Crimes," *Long Island Newsday*, November 14, 1991; John Fialka, "A Gulf War Conspiracy?" *Washington Post Book World*, December 27, 1992.

WAR POWERS ACT

See CONGRESS, U.S.

WAR TERMINATION

The paradigm of war for most Americans is the "total war" model exemplified by World War II: The reasons for the war were clearly understood, the war's progress could be followed on a map, and the end result was total victory—the destruction of the enemy nation's armed forces, the occupation of its territory and the trial of its leaders.

The buildup to, and execution of, the Persian Gulf War generally followed that pattern. The objectives were clearly understood and the war's progress was measurable. But the termination of the Gulf War most certainly did not fit that model. There was a cease-fire rather than a total victory, the Iraqi armed forces were not totally destroyed, Baghdad was not occupied and as of this writing, Saddam Hussein remains in power.

The failure to follow the "total war" model left many Americans dissatisfied and unsure whether "victory" had been achieved. U.S. General Norman H. Schwarzkopf fueled that frustration with his re-marks to television interviewer David Frost in March 1991, in which he claimed that President George Bush had ordered an end to the war before the Iraqi military forces could be annihilated. Although Schwarzkopf quickly repudiated his remarks, a cloud has remained over the way the Gulf War was terminated, especially given Saddam Hussein's con-tinued disregard for and violations of the April 1991 United Nations cease-fire agreement.

Unfortunately, the "total war" paradigm appears to be a false model for the post–Cold War world. It raises unrealistic expectations. Almost all wars in the history of mankind have been limited wars, and the Gulf War was no exception. The definition of "vic-tory" in such wars is not the enemy's unconditional surrender but the attainment of the political objec-tives that the war set out to achieve. In the case of the

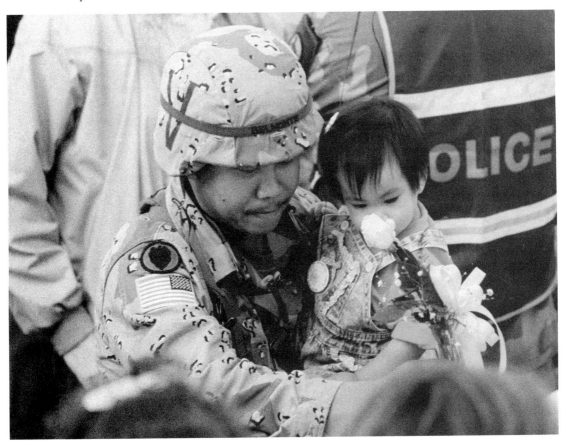

The cease-fire brought U.S. forces home to their families, but Iraqi hostility continues unabated.
U.S. Army photo (Don Teft) courtesy of 24th Infantry Division (Mechanized).

Gulf War, these objectives—expelling the Iraqis from Kuwait, restoring the Kuwaiti government to power, and providing for peace and security in the area— were arrived at in consultation with, and with the approval of, the UN Security Council and the coalition partners.

Why did the coalition not press forward and eliminate Saddam Hussein? The Arab allies in particular did not want to set a precedent of the United States deposing Arab heads of state, and did not want to see a power vacuum develop in Iraq. The Turkish government in particular did not want to see in northern Iraq an independent Kurdistan that might stir rebellion among the millions of Kurds in Turkey. And none of the Gulf states wanted to see created in Southern Iraq an independent Shiite state that would ally itself with the Islamic fundamentalists in Iran.

Those were some of the reasons why the war ended as it did. Other considerations were avoiding the casualties that would have resulted from a drive on Baghdad, and the belief that Hussein would be overthrown in a postwar coup. Yet another reason for the limited war aims was to secure the cooperation of the Soviet Union, cooperation that was vital to the prosecution of the war.

As the former Soviet president Mikhail Gorbachev made clear, such restraint was the key to gaining Soviet cooperation in the war. "Our position was one of principle," Gorbachev said. "Armed action should take place within the guidelines established by the UN Security Council and should not be transformed into a total war against the Iraqi people. . . . The goal established by the Security Council was the liberation of Kuwait, and not the total destruction of Iraq."

"It is worth noting," wrote Army War College professor William L. Dowdy in a 1992 study, "that Saddam Hussein's continuation as the head of the Iraqi government, as exasperating as it is in some ways, is not all bad from the perspective of U.S. interests. . . . His continued presence as head of government rivets the attention and sustains the resolve of his erstwhile enemies and victims in a way a more benign successor would not.

"As long as Saddam is in power yet powerless beyond his borders," Dowdy concluded, "he is much less dangerous than he would be as a martyred hero."

See also CEASEFIRE; KURDS; SHIITE REVOLT; SOVIET UNION.

Suggestions for further reading: Mikhail S. Gorbachev, "Bush Was Right Not To Destroy Iraq," *Los Angeles Times*, March 4, 1992; Harry Summers, "Mission Fulfilled," *Washington Times*, July 9, 1992; Alvin Z. Rubinstein, "New World Order or Hollow Victory," *Foreign Affairs*, Fall 1991; Angelo M. Codevilla, "Magnificent, But Was It War?" *Commentary*, April 1992; William L. Dowdy, "Second Guessing the End of Desert Storm," Strategic Studies Institute, U.S. Army War College, February 27, 1992; Gary L. Guertner et al., "Conflict Termination and Postwar Deterrence," Strategic Studies Institute, U.S. Army War College, February 7, 1991; Jim Mann, "CIA Tells Why U.S. Let Hussein Stay in Power," *Los Angeles Times*, January 8, 1993. For the Schwarzkopf flap, see Ann Devroy and R. Jeffrey Smith, "Bush, Cheney Dispute General on Gulf Cease-Fire," *Washington Post*, March 28, 1991.

WILD WEASEL

Pioneered by U.S. forces during the Vietnam War, the F-4G "Wild Weasel" is an electronic countermeasures (ECM) aircraft designed to destroy, neutralize or degrade enemy radar-directed surface-to-air threats. The "Wild Weasel" is an F-4E/ARN 10 fighter-bomber specially modified to carry the AN/APR-47 Radar Attack and Warning System, which detects, identifies and locates pulsed and continuous wave radar emitters.

Although the aircraft can carry a variety of SEAD (suppression of enemy air defenses) munitions, the preferred ordnance is the HARM AGM-88 high-speed anti-radiation missile.

Sixty-two F-4G "Wild Weasels" were deployed to the Kuwaiti Theater of Operations. Most of them flew out of airfields in Bahrain, but 12 F-4Gs deployed to Incirlik in Turkey. More than 2,700 "Wild Weasel" missions were flown during Operation Desert Storm, with only one combat loss.

See also AIR DEFENSES; ELECTRONIC WARFARE; HARM (HIGH-SPEED ANTI-RADIATION MISSILE); TURKEY.

Suggestions for further reading: Department of Defense, *Conduct of the Persian Gulf War: Final Report to the Congress*, "Appendix T: Performance of Selected Weapons Systems" (Washington, D.C.:

USGPO, 1992); Capt. Dan Hampton, USAF, "The Weasels at War," *Airforce,* July 1991.

WING

A standard organizational unit in the U.S. Navy and Air Force, a wing is commanded by a Navy captain or an Air Force colonel and consists of a number of aircraft squadrons. In the U.S. Marine Corps the equivalent is a Marine aircraft group (MAG), which is also commanded by a colonel. Army aviation units are organized into brigades, battalions and companies.

A Marine aircraft wing (MAW) such as the 1st MAW, which deployed to the Gulf, is comparable to an Air Force air division—it consists of a number of MAGs and is commanded by a major general.

WOMEN IN THE MILITARY

The Persian Gulf War was the watershed for women serving in the military. Although women had served in past wars, especially in nursing and administrative positions, they had not been truly integrated into the armed forces. But that situation changed in the Gulf War.

Women played a vital role in the Persian Gulf War. According to the official statistics, by late February 1991 more than 37,000 female military personnel were in the Kuwaiti Theater of Operations (KTO), making up approximately 6.8 percent of U.S. forces. Roughly 26,000 Army, 3,700 Navy, 2,200 Marine Corps, and 5,300 Air Force women were deployed.

For the first time in American military history, the majority of these women were *not* nurses. They served as truck drivers, military policewomen, helicopter pilots, radio operators, electronic warfare repair technicans, chaplains, and as crew members aboard hospital, supply, oiler and ammunition ships. Women commanded combat support and combat service support brigades, battalions, and company and platoon-size units in the KTO.

Although highly successful, the deployment of women was not without cost. Again for the first time in American military history, none of the women killed or captured on the battlefield were nurses. And for the first time, the casualties included enlisted women as well as female officers. The six women killed in action included Army helicopter pilot Major Marie T. Rossi, helicopter crewman Ser-

geant Cheryl O'Brien, medic Specialist Cindy Beaudoin and supply technicans Specialist Beverly Clark, Specialist Christine Mays and Private Adrienne Mitchell. Another seven women died in accidents or from other nonhostile causes.

Twenty-one women were wounded in action and two—Army flight surgeon Major Rhonda Cornum and truck driver Specialist Melissa Rathbun-Nealy—were captured. One female truck driver from the 1st Marine Division's 11th Marine Regiment struck a mine in Kuwait; receiving no injuries, she and nine other women from that unit received the Combat Action Ribbon for crossing the Iraqi obstacle belt on G-Day. Four other female Marines from the 2d Marine Division received the Combat Action Ribbon for having been engaged by bypassed Iraqi troops and returning fire.

As a result of the Persian Gulf War, opportunities for women in the military were substantially increased—they can now serve as pilots of combat aircraft and helicopters and as crewmembers of naval warships. Overtaken by the Gulf War, the "risk rule" that had prevented women from serving in a combat area was rescinded as of October 1, 1994.

See also ADVISORY EFFORT, U.S.

Suggestions for further reading: Department of Defense, *Conduct of the Persian Gulf War: Final Report to the Congress,* "Appendix R: Role of Women in the Theater of Operations" (Washington, D.C.: USGPO, 1992); Rhonda Cornum as told to Peter Copeland, *She Went to War* (Novato, Calif.: Presidio Press, 1992); Major General Jeanne Holm, USAF (Ret.), *Women in the Military,* rev. ed. (Novato, Calif.: Presidio Press, 1992); Dana Priest, "Women at the Front," *Washington Post,* March 12, 1991; Amy Eskind, "A Post-Gulf Memorial Day, 1991: Arms and the Woman," *Washington Post,* May 26, 1991; Molly Moore, "Women on the Battlefield," *Washington Post,* June 16, 1991; Geraldine Brooks, "The Metamorphosis: Women Warriors Join an Arab Army," *Wall Street Journal,* August 8, 1991. For a critical look, see Sally Quinn, "Mothers at War: What Are We Doing to Our Kids," *Washington Post,* February 10, 1991; Rowan Scarborough, "Women Fall Short on Battle Readiness," *Washington Times,* July 28, 1992. Data on the 10 female Marines in the 11th Marine Regiment was received from their commander, Major J. M. Seng, USMC.

XENOPHON

After the battle of Cunaxa, near present-day Baghdad, in 401 B.C., the Athenian warrior Xenophon led a five-month-long fighting retreat along the Tigris River to reach safety on the shores of the Black Sea. Cited as the most successful withdrawal under fire in history, it was a feat the Iraqi Army was unable to duplicate.

Y

YEMEN

Yemen was one of the few members of the Arab League to openly support Saddam Hussein's invasion of Kuwait. At the time a member of the United Nations Security Council (UNSC), Yemen either opposed or abstained from most of the UNSC resolutions on the war, including those imposing sanctions on Iraq and authorizing the use of "all means necessary" to evict Iraqi forces from Kuwait.

Located on the southern coast of the Arabian Peninsula, Yemen borders Oman to the east, Saudi Arabia to the northeast, the Gulf of Aden to the south and the Red Sea to the west. With an estimated 1992 population of 10,062,000 and a land area of 205,356 square miles, Yemen is about the size of France.

Once part of the ancient kingdom of Sheba and more recently part of the Ottoman Empire, for many years Yemen was divided into the British colony of Aden (after 1970 the People's Democratic Republic of Yemen, the Arab world's only Marxist state) and North Yemen. After two decades of hostility, including open warfare in the 1970s, Yemen was reunited on May 22, 1990.

Although there were demonstrations outside the U.S., British and Saudi embassies in the Yemeni capital of Sanaa in August 1990, and some Yemenis reportedly volunteered to enlist in the Iraqi Army, these acts were seen by the allied coalition as mostly a nuisance. But because of long-standing border disputes between Saudi Arabia and Yemen, and between Oman and Yemen, the latter's alignment with Iraq had to be treated seriously. Although a Yemeni invasion of southern Saudi Arabia or western Oman would have been doomed to failure, it would have distracted attention from the primary Iraqi threat. To guard against that eventuality, the Arab/Islamic Joint Forces Command's Forward Forces Command-'Ar'ar deployed its Pakistani 7th Armored Brigade to cover the Yemeni border.

Suggestions for further reading: Department of Defense, *Conduct of the Persian Gulf War: Final Report to the Congress;* "Chapter 2: Response to Aggression" (Washington, D.C.: USGPO, 1992); Norman Fried-

man; *Desert Victory: The War for Kuwait* (Annapolis, Md.: Naval Institute Press, 1991).

YEOSOCK, JOHN J(OHN) LIEUTENANT GENERAL, USA (1937–)

The commanding general of the Third U.S. Army and concurrently the commander of ARCENT (Army Component Central Command) in the Persian Gulf War, General John J. Yeosock was commissioned a second lieutenant of armor through the Reserve Officers Training Program (ROTC) in 1959 at Pennsylvania State University, where he also received a Bachelor of Science degree in industrial engineering. After serving in Vietnam as a district senior advisor, he earned a Master of Science degree

Commander of the Third U.S. Army, General Yeosock also commanded ARCENT (Army Component Central Command).
U.S. Army photo courtesy of U.S. Forces Command.

in operations research/systems analysis at the Navy Postgraduate School in Monterey, California.

Among his significant assignments were commander of the 3d Squadron, 3d Cavalry at Fort Bliss, Texas; commander of the 194th Armored Brigade at Fort Knox, Kentucky; chief of staff, deputy commander, and commander of the 1st Cavalry Division at Fort Hood, Texas; and assistant deputy chief of staff for operations and plans on the Army General Staff. On March 16, 1989, he was named commanding general of the Third U.S. Army and deputy commanding general of U.S. Forces Command.

One earlier assignment of General Yeosock's that would have particular significance during the Gulf War was his service as project manager for the Saudi Arabian National Guard's modernization program from 1981 to 1983. As a result of that experience, General Yeosock was able to put together the Coalition Coordination, Communications and Control Integration Center that served as the link between Central Command and the Arab/Islamic Joint Forces Command.

Deploying the Third Army headquarters from its home station at Fort McPherson, Georgia, to Saudi Arabia in early August 1990, General Yeosock had responsibility for all aspects of Army combat operations, rear operations and multiservice logistics support throughout the KTO (Kuwaiti Theater of Operations). At the peak of the buildup, General Yeosock commanded more than 330,000 coalition forces, including 303,000 U.S. forces and the British and French ground forces. Hospitalized for pneumonia and gallbladder surgery on February 15, 1991,

General Yeosock returned to duty on February 23, just in time to lead the ground campaign that began the very next day.

At 4:00 A.M. (Gulf time) on February 24, 1991, the ground campaign was launched. Across a 300-mile front, U.S. Army, Marine Corps and other coalition forces embarked on the largest ground campaign since World War II. With the 8,508 armored vehicles of VII Corps forming the main attack, the XVIII Airborne Corps with 2,769 tracked vehicles and 1,026 aircraft attacking along multiple axes, and the First Marine Expeditionary Force (with the "Tiger Brigade" of the Army's 2d Armored Division attached) and Arab coalition forces attacking along the coast, the ground war was over 100 hours after it began. The Iraqi Army, the world's fourth largest, had been decisively defeated.

General Yeosock's awards and decorations include the Combat Infantryman Badge, the Distinguished Service Medal, two Legions of Merit, two Bronze Star Medals with "V" device, the Meritorious Service Medal and the Army Commendation Medal.

General Yeosock returned to Fort McPherson with the Third U.S. Army in March 1991 and later retired from active duty.

See also LOGISTICS, U.S.; THIRD U.S. ARMY.

Suggestions for further reading: General H. Norman Schwarzkopf, *It Doesn't Take a Hero* (New York: Bantam Books, 1992). Rick Atkinson, *Crusade: The Untold Story of the Persian Gulf War* (New York: Houghton Mifflin, 1993) takes a critical look at relations between Generals Yeosock and Schwarzkopf.

Z

ZULU TIME

The military designation for Greenwich mean time, the "Zulu" time zone is used as a common communications reference. The U.S. Central Command (CENTCOM) headquarters in Riyadh, Saudi Arabia, was in the "Bravo" time zone, two hours ahead of Zulu time, and the Pentagon in Washington, D.C., was in the "Romeo" time zone five hours behind Zulu time. An instantaneous electronic message sent from the Pentagon at 1100Z (0600R or 6:00 A.M. Washington time) would be received at CENTCOM at 1300B (1:00 P.M.) Riyadh time.

selected bibliography

SELECTED BIBLIOGRAPHY

Only four years have passed since the end of the Persian Gulf War. If history is any guide, many more books remain to be published on that war. Thus, this bibliography cannot hope to provide the last word on the Gulf War.

Nor is the bibliography meant to be exhaustive. This is a selective bibliography, and the works are primarily those cited as **Suggestions for further reading** in the Almanac itself.

In addition to books, there is an extensive listing of documents and periodicals, for much of the information on the war is still fresh and has not yet been compiled in books and texts.

A deliberate attempt has been made to include diverse points of view in order to provide as broad a perspective as possible on the war. As a result, some of the listed works present strong and parochial views. It is hoped, however, that readers and researchers will find the bibliography as a whole to be both objective and evenhanded.

BOOKS

Allen, Charles. *Thunder and Lightning: The RAF in the Gulf War.* London: Her Majesty's Stationery Office, 1991.

Allen, Thomas B., et al. *CNN: War in the Gulf From the Invasion of Kuwait to the Day of Victory and Beyond.* Atlanta, Ga.: Turner Publishing Company, 1991.

Alpher, Joseph, ed. *War in the Gulf: Implications for Israel.* Boulder, Colo.: Westview Press, 1993.

Amos, Deborah. *Lines in the Sand: Desert Storm and the Remaking of the Arab World.* New York: Simon & Schuster, 1992.

Anderson, Jack, and Dale Van Atta. *Stormin' Norman: An American Hero.* New York: Zebra Books, 1991.

The Armored Fist. Alexandria, Va.: Time-Life Books, 1991.

Aspin, Les, and William Dickinson. *Defense for a New Era: Lessons of the Persian Gulf War.* Washington, D.C.: Brassey's, 1992.

Atkinson, Rick. *Crusade: The Untold Story of the Persian Gulf War.* New York: Houghton Mifflin, 1993.

Aviation Week and Space Technology. *Persian Gulf War.* New York: McGraw-Hill, 1991.

Barakat, Halim. *The Arab World: Society, Culture and State.* Berkeley: University of California Press, 1993.

Blackwell, Major James. *Thunder in the Desert: Strategy and Tactics of the Persian Gulf War.* New York: Bantam Books, 1991.

Bollinger, Lee C. *Images of a Free Press.* Chicago: University of Chicago Press, 1992.

Braybook, Roy. *Desert Storm Air Power.* London: Osprey Military, 1991.

Bulloch, John, and Harvey Morris. *No Friends But the Mountains: The Tragic History of the Kurds.* New York: Oxford University Press, 1992.

———. *Saddam's War: The Origins of the Kuwait Conflict and the International Response.* New York: Faber, 1991.

Carhart, Tom. *Iron Soldiers: How the Men of "Old Ironsides," the American 1st Armored Division, Destroyed the Iraqi Republican Guard During Operation Desert Storm.* New York: Pocket Books, 1994.

Carus, W. Seth. *Ballistic Missiles in the Third World: Threat and Response.* New York: Praeger, 1990.

———. *The Poor Man's Atomic Bomb? Biological Weapons in the Middle East.* Washington, D.C.: Washington Institute for Near East Policy, 1991.

Chadwick, Frank. *Desert Shield Fact Book.* Bloomington, Ill.: GDW, 1991.

———. *Gulf War Fact Book.* Bloomington, Ill.: GDW, 1992.

Cimbala, Stephen J. *Force and Diplomacy in the Future.* New York: Praeger, 1992.

Clark, Ramsey. *The Fire in the Desert: U.S. War Crimes in the Gulf.* New York: Thunder's Mouth Press, 1992.

Clausewitz, Carl. *On War.* Translated by Michael Howard and Peter Paret. Princeton: Princeton University Press, 1976.

Cohen, Eliot A. *Citizens & Soldiers: The Dilemmas of Military Service.* Ithaca, N.Y.: Cornell University Press, 1985.

Cohen, Roger, and Claudio Gatti. *In the Eye of the Storm: The Life of General H. Norman Schwarzkopf.* New York: Farrar, Straus and Giroux, 1991.

Cooke, James J. *100 Miles from Baghdad: With the French in Desert Storm.* Westport, Conn.: Praeger Publishers, 1993.

Cooley, John K. *Payback: America's Long War in the Middle East.* Washington, D.C.: Brassey's, 1991.

Cordesman, Anthony H. *Weapons of Mass Destruction in the Middle East.* London: Pergamon Press, 1991.

———. *After the Storm: The Changing Balance in the Middle East.* Boulder, Colo.: Westview Press, 1993.

Cornum, Rhonda, as told to Peter Copeland. *She Went to War: The Rhonda Cornum Story.* Novato, Calif.: Presidio Press, 1992.

Coyne, James P. *Airpower in the Gulf.* Arlington, Va.: Aerospace Education Foundation, 1992.

Craft, Douglas W. *An Operational Analysis of the Persian Gulf War.* Carlisle Barracks, Pa.: U.S. Army War College, Strategic Studies Institute, 1992.

Crowe, Admiral William J. Jr., with David Chanoff. *The Line of Fire: From Washington to the Gulf, the Politics and Battles of the New Military.* New York: Simon & Schuster, 1993.

Crystal, Jill. *Kuwait: The Transformation of an Oil State.* Boulder, Colo.: Westview Press, 1992.

———. *Oil and Politics in the Gulf: Rulers and Merchants in Kuwait and Qatar.* New York: Cambridge University Press, 1991.

Cumings, Bruce. *War and Television.* London: Verso, 1992.

David, Peter. *Triumph in the Desert: The Challenge, the Fighting, the Legacy.* New York: Random House, 1991.

DeCosse, David E., ed. *But Was It Just: Reflections on the Morality of the Persian Gulf War.* New York: Doubleday, 1992.

De la Billiere, General Sir Peter. *Storm Command: A Personal Account of the Gulf War.* London: Harper-Collins, 1992.

Douhet, Giulio. *The Command of the Air.* Translated by Dino Ferrari and edited by Richard H. Kohn and Joseph P. Harahan. Washington, D.C.: USGPO, 1983.

Dunnigan, James F., and Austin Bay. *From Shield to Storm: High Tech Weapons, Military Strategy and Coalition Warfare.* New York: William Morrow, 1992.

Dupuy, Trevor N., et al. *If War Comes, How to Defeat Saddam Hussein.* McLean, Va.: Hero Books, 1990.

Elshtain, Jean Bethke, et al. *But Was It Just? Reflections on the Morality of the Persian Gulf War.* New York: Doubleday, 1992.

Englehardt, Colonel Joseph P. *Desert Shield and Desert Storm: A Chronology and Troop List for the 1990–1991 Persian Gulf Crisis.* Carlisle Barracks, Pa.: U.S. Army War College, Strategic Studies Institute, 1991.

Esposito, John L. *The Islamic Threat: Myth or Reality?* New York: Oxford University Press, 1992.

Ethell, Jeffrey L. *B-52: Stratofortress.* London: Arms & Armour Press, n.d.

Fialka, John J. *Hotel Warriors: Covering the Gulf War.* Washington, D.C.: Woodrow Wilson Center Press, 1991.

Freedman, Lawrence, and Efraim Karsh. *The Gulf Conflict, 1990–1991: Diplomacy and War in the New World Order.* Princeton: Princeton University Press, 1993.

Friedman, Norman. *Desert Victory: The War for Kuwait.* Annapolis, Md.: Naval Institute Press, 1991.

Gilchrist, Peter. *Desert Storm Sea Power.* London: Osprey Military, 1991.

Girard, Keith F. *Remembering the Gulf War.* Richmond, Va.: Cadmus Communications, 1991.

Grant, Dale. *Wilderness of Mirrors.* Toronto: Prentice-Hall Canada, 1991.

Graubard, Stephen R. *Mr. Bush's War: Adventures in the Politics of Illusion.* New York: Hill & Wang, 1992.

The Gulf War: Military Lessons Learned. Washington, D.C.: Center for Strategic and International Studies, 1991.

Hader, Leon T. *Quagmire: America in the Middle East.* Washington, D.C.: Cato Institute, 1992.

Hallion, Richard P. *Storm Over Iraq: Air Power and the Gulf War.* Washington, D.C.: Smithsonian Institution Press, 1992.

Hawley, T. M. *Against the Fires of Hell: The Environmental Disaster of the Gulf War.* New York: Harcourt, Brace Jovanovich, 1992.

Helms, Robert F., and Robert H. Dorff, eds. *The Persian Gulf Crisis: Power in the Post–Cold War World.* Westport, Conn.: Praeger, 1993.

Henderson, Simon. *Instant Empire: Saddam Hussein's Ambitions for Iraq.* San Francisco: Mercury House, 1991.

Hilsman, Roger. *George Bush vs. Saddam Hussein: Military Success! Political Failure?* Novato, Calif.: Lyford Books, 1992.

Hiro, Dilip. *The Longest War: The Iran-Iraq Military Conflict.* New York: Routledge, 1991.

———. *Desert Shield to Desert Storm: The Second Gulf War.* New York: Routledge, 1992.

Holm, Major General Jeanne. *Women in the Military: An Unfinished Revolution.* Rev. ed. Novato, Calif.: Presidio Press, 1992.

Hufbauer, Gary Clyde, Jeffrey J. Schott, and Kimberly Ann Elliot. *Economic Sanctions Reconsidered.* 2nd ed. Washington, D.C.: Institute for International Economics, 1990.

Johnson, James Turner, and George Weigel. *Just War and the Gulf War.* Washington, D.C.: Ethics and Public Policy Center, 1991.

Joyner, Christopher, ed. *The Persian Gulf War: Lessons for Strategy, Law and Diplomacy.* Westport, Conn.: Greenwood, 1990.

Jupa, Richard, and Jim Dingeman. *Gulf Wars.* Cambria, Calif.: EW Publications, 1991.

Karsh, Efraim, and Inari Rautsi. *Saddam Hussein: A Political Biography.* New York: Free Press, 1991.

Katzman, Kenneth. *The Warriors of Islam: Iran's Revolutionary Guard.* Boulder, Colo.: Westview Press, 1993.

Kelly, Michael. *Martyr's Day: Chronicle of a Small War.* New York: Random House, 1993.

Kelly, Orr. *Hornet: The Inside Story of the F/A 18.* Novato, Calif.: Presidio Press, 1990.

———. *King of the Killing Zone: The Story of the M1, America's Super Tank.* New York: W. W. Norton, 1989.

Al-Khalil, Samiro. *The Monument: Art, Vulgarity and Responsibility in Iraq.* Berkeley: University of California Press, 1991.

———. *Republic of Fear.* New York: Pantheon Books, 1990.

Kinsey, Bert. *The Fury of Desert Storm: Aircraft and Armament.* New York: McGraw-Hill, 1991.

Letters From the Sand: The Letters of Desert Storm and Other Wars. Washington, D.C.: U.S. Postal Service, 1991.

Lowther, William. *Arms and the Man: Dr. Gerald Bull, Iraq and the Supergun.* Novato, Calif.: Presidio Press, 1991.

MacArthur, Brian, ed. *Dispatches From the Gulf War.* London: Bloomsbury, 1991.

MacArthur, John. *Second Front: Censorship and Propaganda in the Gulf War.* New York: Hill & Wang, 1992.

Makiya, Kanan. *Cruelty and Silence: War, Tyranny, Uprising and the Arab World.* New York: W. W. Norton, 1993.

Marr, Phebe, and William Lewis, eds. *Riding the Tiger: The Middle East Challenge After the Cold War.* Boulder, Colo.: Westview Press, 1993.

Matthews, Lloyd J., ed. *Newsmen and the National Defense.* Washington, D.C.: Brassey's 1991.

Mayer, Ann Elizabeth. *Islam and Human Rights: Traditions and Politics.* Boulder, Colo.: Westview Press, 1991.

Means, Howard. *Colin Powell: Soldier/Statesman— Statesman/Soldier.* New York: Donald I. Fine, 1992.

Melia, Tamara Moser. *"Damn the Torpedoes": A Short History of U.S. Naval Mine Countermeasures, 1777– 1991.* Washington, D.C.: Naval Historical Center, 1991.

Miller, Judith, and Laurie Mylroie. *Saddam Hussein and the Gulf Crisis.* New York: Random House, 1990.

Miller, Mark Crispin. *Spectacle: Operation Desert Storm and the Triumph of Illusion.* New York: Poseidon, 1992.

Moore, Captain M. E. H. *Norman Schwarzkopf: Road to Triumph.* New York: St. Martin's Press, 1991.

Moore, Molly. *A Woman at War.* New York: Charles Scribner's Sons, 1993.

Moskos, Charles C. *A Call to Civic Service.* New York: Free Press, 1988.

Muir, Malcolm. *The Iowa Class Battleships: Iowa, New Jersey, Missouri and Wisconsin.* New York: Sterling, 1991.

Munro, Neil. *The Quick and the Dead: Electronic Combat and Modern Warfare.* New York: St. Martin's Press, 1991.

Needless Deaths in the Gulf War: Civilian Casualties During the Air Campaign and Violations of the Laws of War. New York: Middle East Watch/Human Rights Watch, 1991.

Nye, Joseph S. Jr., and Roger K. Smith, eds. *After the Storm: Lessons From the Gulf War.* Lanham, Md.: Madison Books, 1992.

Pagonis, Lieutenant General William G., with Jeffrey L. Cruikshank. *Moving Mountains: Lessons in Leadership and Logistics from the Gulf War.* Boston: Harvard Business School Press, 1992.

Palmer, Michael A. *Guardians of the Gulf: A History of America's Expanding Role in the Persian Gulf, 1833–1992.* New York: Free Press, 1992.

———. *On Course to Desert Storm: The United States Navy and the Persian Gulf.* Washington, D.C.: Naval Historical Center, 1992.

Pelletiere, Stephen C., Douglas V. Johnson II, and Leif R. Rosenberger. *Iraqi Power and U.S. Security in the Middle East.* Carlisle Barracks, Pa.: U.S. Army War College, Strategic Studies Institute 1990.

———. *Lessons Learned: The Iran-Iraq War.* Carlisle Barracks, Pa.: U.S. Army War College, Strategic Studies Institute, 1990.

Perret, Bryan. *Desert Warfare: From Its Roman Origins to the Gulf Conflict.* New York: Sterling, 1988.

Photographers of SYGMA. *In the Eye of Desert Storm.* New York: Harry N. Abrams, 1991.

Porter, Jadranka, *Under Siege in Kuwait.* New York; Houghton Mifflin, 1991.

Prichard, Peter S., and the staff of *USA Today. Desert Warriors—The Men and Women Who Won the Gulf War.* New York: Pocket Books, 1991.

Quigley, John. *The Ruses for War: American Intervention Since World War II.* New York: Prometheus, 1992.

Record, Jeffrey. *Hollow Victory: A Contrary View of the Gulf War.* Washington, D.C.: Brassey's, 1993.

Renshon, Stanley A., ed. *The Political Psychology of the Persian Gulf War.* Pittsburgh: University of Pittsburgh Press, 1993.

Rezun, Miron. *Saddam Hussein's Gulf War.* Westport, Conn.: Praeger, 1993.

Richardson, Doug. *Stealth: Deception, Evasion and Concealment in the Air.* New York, Orion Books, 1989.

Ripley, Tom. *Desert Storm Land.* London: Osprey, 1991.

Romjue, John L. *From Active Defense to AirLand Battle: The Development of Army Doctrine 1973–1981.* Fort Monroe, Va.: U.S. Army Training and Doctrine Command, 1984.

Roth, David. *Sacred Honor.* New York: HarperCollins, 1993.

Rubin, Barry, et al. *Gulfwatch Anthology: The Day-to-Day Analysis of the Gulf Crisis, August 30, 1990–March 28, 1991.* Washington, D.C.: Washington Institute for Near East Policy, 1991.

Sackur, Stephen. *On the Basra Road.* London: London Review of Books, 1991.

Sasson, Jean P. *The Rape of Kuwait: The True Stories of Iraqi Atrocities Against a Civilian Population.* New York: Knightsbridge Publishing, 1991.

Schneider, Dorothy, and Carl J. Schneider. *Sound Off: American Military Women Speak Out.* New York: Paragon House, 1992.

Schwarzkopf, General H. Norman, with Peter Petre. *It Doesn't Take a Hero.* New York: Bantam Books, 1992.

Sciolino, Elaine. *The Outlaw State: Saddam Hussein's Quest for Power and the Gulf Crisis.* New York: John Wiley and Sons, 1991.

Scofield, Richard. *Kuwait and Iraq: Historical Claims and Territorial Disputes.* London: Royal Institute of International Affairs, 1991.

Sifry, Michah L., and Christopher Cerf. *The Gulf War Reader.* New York: Time Books, 1991.

Simon, Bob. *Forty Days.* New York: Putnam's, 1992.

Simpson, John. *From the House of War.* London: Hutchison, 1991.

Smith, Hedrick, ed. *The Media and the Gulf War: The Press and Democracy in Wartime.* Washington, D.C.: Seven Locks Press, 1992.

Smith, Jean Edward. *George Bush's War.* New York: Henry Holt, 1991.

Smith, Major General Perry M. *How CNN Fought the Gulf War: A View From the Inside.* New York: Birch Lane Press, 1991.

Smolla, Rodney A. *Free Speech in an Open Society.* New York: Alfred A. Knopf 1991.

The Staff of *U.S. News & World Report. Triumph Without Victory: The Unreported History of the Persian Gulf War.* New York: Times Books, 1992.

Stapfer, Hans-Heiri. *Mi-24 Hind.* London: Arms & Armour Press, n.d.

Summers, Colonel Harry G. Jr. *On Strategy II: A Critical Analysis of the Gulf War.* New York: Dell, 1992.

Sweetman, Bill. *Stealth Bomber.* Osceola, Wisc.: Motorbooks International, 1989.

Taylor, Thomas. *Lightning in the Storm: The 101st Air Assault Division in the Gulf War.* New York: Hippocrene Books, 1994.

Teicher, Howard, and Gayle Radley Teicher. *Twin Pillars to Desert Storm.* New York: William Morrow, 1993.

Thompson, Loren., ed. *Defense Beat: The Dilemmas of Defense Coverage.* New York: Lexington Books, 1991.

Thornborough, Anthony M., and Peter E. Davies. *F-111: Success in Action.* London, Arms & Armour Press. 1989.

Timmerman, Kenneth R. *The Death Lobby: How the West Armed Iraq.* New York: Houghton Mifflin, 1991.

Trudeau, G. B. *Welcome to Club Scud.* (Kansas City: Andrews and McMeel, 1991)

Tucker, Robert W., and David C. Hendrickson. *The Imperial Temptation: The New World Order and America's Purpose.* New York: Council on Foreign Relations Press, 1992.

Twinam, Joseph W. *The Gulf, Cooperation and the Council.* Washington, D.C.: Middle East Policy Council, 1993.

Uhlig, Frank Jr. *How Navies Fight: The U.S. Navy and Its Allies.* Annapolis, Md.: Naval Institute Press, 1993.

Vogt, William, and Carl Gnam. *Desert Storm.* Leesburg, Va.: Empire Press, 1991.

Warner, John A. III. *The Air Campaign: Planning for Combat.* Washington, D.C.: National Defense University Press, 1988.

Watson, Bruce W., ed. *Military Lessons of the Gulf War.* Novato, Calif.: Presidio Press, 1991.

Wiener, Robert. *Live From Baghdad: Gathering News From Ground Zero.* New York: Doubleday, 1992.

Wilson, George C. *Supercarrier.* New York: Charles Scribner's Sons, 1986.

Witherow, John, and Aidan Sullivan. *War in the Gulf.* London: Sidgwick, 1991.

Woodward, Bob. *The Commanders.* New York: Simon & Schuster, 1991.

Wormuth, Francis D., and Edwin B. Firmage. *To Chain the Dogs of War: The War Powers of Congress in History and Law;* Urbana: The University of Illinois Press, 1989.

DOCUMENTS, REPORTS AND PERIODICALS

Abrahams, Paul. "Darkness Is No Deterrent." *Financial Times* (London), January 31, 1991.

Adams, James. "The Real Lesson of the Gulf War." *Atlantic.* November 1991.

Adams, Jerry, et al. "The War Within." *Newsweek,* February 4, 1991.

Adolph, Robert B. Jr. "PSYOPS: Gulf War Force Multiplier." *Army,* December 1992.

Albright, David, and Mark Hibbs. "Iraq's Bomb: Blueprints and Artifacts." *Bulletin of the Atomic Scientists,* January/February 1992.

———. "Iraq's Shop-Till-You-Drop Nuclear Program." *Bulletin of the Atomic Scientists,* April 1992.

Aldred, Margaret. "Lessons From the Gulf Crisis." *RUSI Journal,* December 1992.

Allen, Henry. "The Gulf Between the Military and the Media." *Washington Post,* February 21, 1991.

Anderson, Jim. "Without A Compass: Why State Failed To Provide an Ounce of Prevention in the Gulf." *Foreign Service Journal,* January 1991.

Arkin, William M. "The Desert Glows—With Propaganda." *Bulletin of the Atomic Scientists,* May 1993.

Arthur, Stanley R., and Marvin Pokrant. "Desert Storm at Sea." *U.S. Naval Institute Proceedings,* May 1991.

Assembly of the Western European Union. "Document 1244: European Security and the Gulf Crisis." Paris, November 14, 1990.

———. "Document 1248: Consequences of the Invasion of Kuwait: Continuing Operations in the Gulf Region." Paris, November 17, 1990.

———. "Document 1268: The Gulf Crisis—Lessons for Western European Union." Paris, May 13, 1991.

Aukofer, Frank A. "Gulf War Vets Get Prompt Attention for Mystery Ills." *Washington Times,* June 22, 1993.

Babcock, Charles R. "Temperamental Helicopter Joins Battle." *Washington Post,* February 20, 1991.

Bacon, Edwin. "Military Reform and Soviet Analysis of the 1991 Gulf War." *Journal of Soviet Military Studies,* June 1992.

Baker, James A. III. "America's Strategy in the Persian Gulf Crisis." *Dispatch,* December 10, 1990.

Batcheller, Gordon D. "The Eclipse of the Joint Chiefs." *Marine Corps Gazette,* July 1991.

Baram, Amatzia. "Israeli Deterrence, Iraqi Responses." *Orbis,* Summer 1992.

Barnes, Fred. "The Unwimp." *The New Republic,* March 18, 1991.

Bennet, James. "Sand Trap." *Washington Monthly,* April 1991.

Bien, Lyle J. "From the Strike Cell." *U.S. Naval Institute Proceedings,* June 1991.

Bingham, Price T. "Air Power in Desert Storm." *Airpower Journal,* Winter 1991.

Bin Sultan, Khalid. "Schwarzkopf Did Not Win the War Alone." *Defense News,* October 26–November 1, 1992 (reprinted in the *Chicago Tribune,* November 7, 1992).

Blackwell, James. "Georgia Punch." *Army Times,* December 2, 1991.

Blank, Stephen J. "The Soviet Military Views Operation Desert Storm: A Preliminary Assessment." U.S. Army War College, Strategic Studies Institute, September 23, 1991.

Bolger, Daniel P. "The Ghosts of Omdurman." *Parameters,* Autumn 1991.

Boo, Katherine. "How Congress Won the War in the Gulf." *Washington Monthly,* October 1991.

Boustany, Nora. "U.N. Team Rebuffed by Iraq." *Washington Post,* July 12, 1993.

Brame, Major William J. "From Garrison to Desert Offensive in 97 Days." *Army,* February 1992.

Brooks, Geraldine. "The Metamorphosis: Women Warriors Join an Arab Army." *Wall Street Journal,* August 8, 1991.

Brown, Dallas. "Too Many Blacks in Combat?" *Washington Post,* July 30, 1991.

Brown, Malcolm W. "The Military vs. the Press." *New York Times Magazine,* March 3, 1991.

———. "Steps to Avoid Own Side's Fire Studied in U.S. *New York Times,* May 18, 1993.

Bryan, C. D. B. "Operation Desert Norm." *The New Republic,* March 11, 1991.

Bundy, McGeorge. "Nuclear Weapons and the Gulf." *Foreign Affairs,* Fall 1991.

Bush, George. "Why We Are in the Gulf." *Newsweek,* November 26, 1990.

———. "The Persian Gulf War: Text of President Bush's Address to Joint Session of Congress." *Washington Post,* March 17, 1991.

Butler, Katherine. "Operation Desert Storm: The Logistical Story." *Government Executive,* May 1991

Canan, James W. "The Electronic Storm." *Airforce,* June 1991.

Caporale, Louis G. "Marine Corps Historical Notes From the Gulf War." *Marine Corps Gazette,* December 1991.

Childers, Erskine B. "Gulf Crisis Lessons for the United Nations." *Bulletin of Peace Proposals,* June 1992.

Cigar, Norman. "Iraq's Strategic Mindset and the Gulf War: Blueprint for Defeat." *Journal of Strategic Studies,* March 1992.

"Civil Affairs in the Persian Gulf: A Symposium." U.S. Army JFK Special Warfare Center & School, Fort Bragg, N.C., October 1991.

Clodfelter, Major Mark, USAF. "Of Demons, Storms, and Thunder." *Airpower Journal,* Winter 1991.

Codevilla, Angelo M. "Magnificent, But Was It War?" *Commentary,* April 1992.

Cohen, Eliot A. "After the Battle." *The New Republic,* April 1, 1991.

Cohen, Eliot A., et al. *Gulf War Air Power Survey.* Washington, D.C.: USGPO, 1993.

Collier, Peter. "The Other War They Lost." *Second Thoughts,* Spring 1991.

Collins, John M. "Iraqi Options Early in the Persian Gulf Crisis." *CRS Report for Congress,* August 14, 1990.

———. "Military Geography of Iraq and Adjacent Arab Territory." *CRS Report for Congress,* September 7, 1990.

———. "High Command Arrangements Early in the Persian Gulf Crisis." *CRS Report for Congress,* September 21, 1990.

———. "Desert Shield and Desert Storm: Implications for Future U.S. Force Requirements." *CRS Report for Congress,* April 19, 1991.

Collins, Joseph. "Desert Storm and the Lessons of Learning." *Parameters,* Autumn 1992.

Connaughton, R. M. "The Principles of Multilateral Military Intervention and the 1990–1991 Gulf Crisis." *British Army Review,* August 1991.

Cooper, Kenneth J., and Elsa Walsh. "On U.S. Campuses, A Faint Anti-War Cry." *Washington Post,* February 22, 1991.

Cordingley, Brigadier P. A. J. "The Gulf War: Operating With Allies." *RUSI Journal,* April 1992.

Covey, Lt. Cdr. Dana C., USNR. "Offering a Helping Hand in Iraq," *U.S. Naval Institute Proceedings,* May 1991.

Craig, Commodore C. J. S. "Gulf War: The Maritime Campaign." *RUSI Journal,* August 1992.

Cushman, John H. "Command and Control in the Coalition." *U.S. Naval Institute Proceedings,* May 1991.

Dannreuther, Roland. "The Gulf Conflict: A Political and Strategic Analysis." *Adelphi Paper 264.* International Institute of Strategic Studies, Winter 1991/1992.

De la Billiere, General Peter. "The Gulf Conflict: Planning and Execution." *RUSI Journal,* Winter 1991.

"Desert Storm: January 17–February 28, 1991." *Stars and Stripes Commemorative Edition,* n.d.

Dionne, E. J. Jr. "This Time, No Fixation on Hostages." *Washington Post,* December 17, 1990.

Dobson, Christopher, and Alan Coats. "The Secret War." *The Independent,* March 10, 1991.

Donnelly, Tom. "Road to Baghdad." *Army Times,* January 25, 1993.

Dorsey, Jack. "Gulf Vets' Illnesses a 'Great Concern.'" *Virginian-Pilot,* August 7, 1993.

Dowdy, William L. "Second-Guessing the End of Desert Storm," U.S. Army War College, Strategic Studies Institute, February 27, 1992.

Downer, Brig. Gen. Lee A., USAF. "The Composite Wing in Combat." *Airpower Journal,* Winter 1991.

Drozdiak, William, and R. Jeffrey Smith. "French Decision Makes Coalition Possible." *Washington Post,* January 17, 1991.

Duke, Lynne. "Gen. Powell Notes Military Enlistment Remains Matter of Individual Choice." *Washington Post,* November 28, 1990.

Easterbrook, Gregg. "Operation Desert Shill." *The New Republic,* September 30, 1991.

Edenswood, Diana, and Gary Milhollin. "Iraq's Bomb—An Update." *New York Times,* April 26, 1993.

Eskind, Amy. "A Post-Gulf Memorial Day, 1991: Arms and the Woman." *Washington Post,* May 26, 1991.

Ewers, Colonel Norman G. "A Conversation With LtGen. Royal N. Moore, Jr." *Marine Corps Gazette,* October 1991.

"The Failed Anti-War Movement." *VFW Magazine,* August 1991.

Fialka, John. "A Gulf War Conspiracy?" *Washington Post Book World,* December 27, 1992.

"Field Artillery Desert Facts." *Field Artillery,* October 1991.

Fitzgerald, Mary C. "The Soviet Image of Future Wars: 'Through the Prism of the Persian Gulf.'" *Comparative Strategy,* October–December 1991.

Flanagan, Lt. Gen. E. M. Jr. "Hostile Territory Was Their AO in Desert Storm." *Army,* September 1991.

"The 48th Brigade: A Chronology From Invasion to Demobilization." *National Guard,* May 1991.

"43 Days: Images of the War," *The Sun,* March 10, 1991.

Fotion, Nicholas G. "The Gulf War: Cleanly Fought." *Bulletin of the Atomic Scientists,* September 1991.

Frantz, Douglas. "Military Gets to the Gulf 'Fastest With the Mostest.'" *Los Angeles Times,* December 30, 1990.

Franz, Wallace. "Defeating the Iraqis: Saddam's Troops Are Not Ready for a War of Manuever." *Armor,* January–February 1991.

Freedman, Lawrence, and Efraim Karsh. "How Kuwait Was Won: Strategy in the Gulf War." *International Security,* Fall 1991.

Freund, Charles Paul. "The War on Your Mind." *Washington Post,* January 27, 1991.

———. "War's 'Paper Bullets.'" *Washington Post,* February 10, 1991.

Froggett, Commander Steve, USN. "Tomahawk in the Desert." *U.S. Naval Institute Proceedings,* January 1992.

Fuller, Graham F. "Moscow and the Gulf War." *Foreign Affairs,* Summer 1991.

Gagner, Frank. "Black Art Electronic Systems Prove Merit in Gulf Air War." *Signal,* April 1991.

Galloway, Joseph L. "The Point of the Spear." *U.S. News & World Report,* March 11, 1991.

Garfinkle, Adam. "The Gulf War: Was It Worth It?" *The World & I,* October 1991.

Gellman, Barton. "General: U.S. Troops Won't Be Ready." *Washington Post,* December 20, 1990.

——. "Allies Prevented War of Attrition With Deception." *Washington Post,* February 28, 1991

——. "U.S. Bombs Missed 70% of Time." *Washington Post,* March 16, 1991.

——. "Gulf Weapons' Accuracy Downgraded." *Washington Post,* April 10, 1991.

——. "Allied Air War Struck Broadly in Iraq." *Washington Post,* June 23, 1991.

Gibson, Andrew E., and Commander Jacob L. Shuford, USN. "Desert Shield and Strategic Sealift." *Naval War College Review,* Spring 1991.

Gitlin, Todd. "Student Activism Without Barricades." *Los Angeles Times,* December 23, 1990.

Goldman, John J. "Iraq Tells of Chemical Arms Cache." *Los Angeles Times,* April 19, 1991.

Gorbachev, Mikhail S. "Bush Was Right Not To Destroy Iraq." *Los Angeles Times,* March 4, 1992.

Gordon, Michael R. "A New Resolve on Iraq." *New York Times,* August 20, 1992.

Goshko, John M. "U.N. Vote Authorizes Use of Force Against Iraq." *Washington Post,* November 30, 1990.

Gottschalk, Marie. "Operation Desert Cloud: The Media and the Gulf War." *World Policy Journal,* Summer 1992.

Greenway, H. D. S. "Gulf Cover-up Evidence Said Lacking." *Boston Globe,* October 21, 1992.

Grier, Peter. "Iraq's Chemical Weapons Found To Be Potent." *Christian Science Monitor,* January 23, 1992.

Guertner, Gary L., et al. "Conflict Termination and Post-war Deterrence." U.S. Army War College, Strategic Studies Institute, February 7, 1991.

"The Gulf Crisis." *France Magazine,* Spring 1991.

"The Gulf War." International Security Council, Washington, D.C., January 17, 1991.

Halliday, Fred. "Historical Antecedents to the Present Crisis." *RUSI Journal,* Autumn 1991.

Hampton, Capt. Dan, USAF. "The Weasels at War." *Airforce,* July 1991.

Hayes, Major Mark J. "Sealift: The Achilles' Heel of Our National Strategy." *Marine Corps Gazette,* November 1992.

Head, William. "Air Power in the Persian Gulf: An Initial Search for the Right Answers." *Air Force Journal of Logistics,* Winter 1992.

Healy, Melissa. "Special Forces: U.S. 'Eyes' Deep in Enemy Territory." *Los Angeles Times,* February 28, 1991.

Heidenrich, John G. "The Gulf War: How Many Iraqis Died?" *Foreign Policy,* Spring 1993.

Hickman, William F. "Confrontation in the Gulf: Unintended Consequences." *Naval War College Review,* Winter 1991.

Hoagland, Jim. "Congress, Bush and the Generals." *Washington Post,* November 22, 1990.

Hockstader, Lee. "Media Ouster Cuts Off West's View of Iraq." *Washington Post,* March 9, 1991.

Hoffman, David, and Ann Devroy. "Soviet Plan Puts Allies in a Bind." *Washington Post,* February 22, 1991.

Holzer, Robert, and Neil Munro. "Microwave Weapon Stuns Iraqis." *Defense News,* April 13–19, 1992.

Hopkins, Robert S. III. "Ears of the Storm." *Airforce,* February 1992.

Horowitz, Tony. "Forgotten Rebels: After Heeding Calls To Turn on Saddam, Shiites Feel Betrayed." *Wall Street Journal,* December 26, 1991.

"How We 'Kicked His Butt.'" *Army Times,* March 11, 1991.

Hurley, Matthew M. "Saddam Hussein and Iraqi Air Power." *Airpower,* Winter 1992.

Hutchison, Robert, and Sean Ryan. "Saddam's Oil 'Time Bomb' Ravages Fish and Bird Life." *The Sunday Times* (London), February 21, 1993.

Hyde, James C. "Defense Contractors Serve on the Front Lines of Operation Desert Storm." *Armed Forces Journal International,* March 1991.

"In From the Cold." *The Economist,* October 13, 1990.

Inman, Bobby R., et al. "Lessons From the Gulf War." *Washington Quarterly,* Winter 1992.

"Iraq: A Special Report." *Jane's Soviet Intelligence Review,* October 1990.

Jackson, Brendan. "Air Power." *RUSI Journal,* August 1992.

Jeambar, Denis, and Christian Makarin. "Le 'Scandale' Chevènement." *Le Point,* September 10, 1990.

Jenish, D'Arcy, and Dale Grant. "The Man With the Golden Gun." *Macleans,* April 22, 1991.

Jones, John F. Jr. "Giulio Douhet Vindicated: Desert Storm 1991." *Naval War College Review,* Autumn 1992.

Judis, John B. "The Strange Case of Ramsey Clark." *The New Republic*, April 22, 1991.

Al-Khalil, Samir. "Iraq and Its Future." *New York Review of Books*, April 11, 1991.

Kamen, Al. "Kurds Hope To Attain Autonomy," *Washington Post*, March 22, 1991.

Kaplan, Fred. "Beast of Battle." *Boston Globe Magazine*, July 21, 1991.

Kaplan, Robert D. "Tales From the Bazaar." *Atlantic*, August 1992.

Karsh, Efraim, and Inari Rautsi. "Why Saddam Hussein Invaded Kuwait." *Survival*, January/February 1991.

Kedourie, Elie. "What's Baathism Anyway?" *Wall Street Journal*, October 17, 1990.

———. Iraq: The Mystery of American Policy." *Commentary*, June 1991.

Keegan, John. "The Lessons of the Gulf War." *Los Angeles Times Magazine*, April 7, 1991.

Kelley, P. X. "The Amphibious Warfare Doctrine." *U.S. Naval Institute Proceedings*, January 1986.

Kelly, Michael. "The Rape and Rescue of Kuwait City." *The New Republic*, March 25, 1991.

Keys, Lt. Gen. William M. "Rolling With the 2d Marine Division." *U.S. Naval Institute Proceedings*, November 1991.

Kirkpatrick, Charles E. "Land Warfare Paper No. 9: Building the Army for Desert Storm." Institute of Land Warfare, Association of the U.S. Army, Washington, D.C., November 1991.

Kitfield, James. "Civilian War." *Government Executive*, December 1990.

Kochansky, Peter N. "3 Years Later, Gulf War Death Toll Unknown." *San Francisco Examiner*, July 31, 1993.

Kohn, Richard H. "Out of Control: The Crisis in Civil-Military Relations." *The National Interest*, Spring 1994.

Krauthammer, Charles. "The Lonely Superpower." *The New Republic*, July 19, 1991.

Krulak, Charles C. "CSS in the Desert." *Marine Corps Gazette*, October 1991.

"The Kurdish Problem in Iraq." *Background Brief*. London: Foreign and Commonwealth Office, May 1992.

Lacayo, Richard. "Did Bush Create This Monster." *Time*, June 8, 1992.

Lancaster, John. "Logistical Shortcomings Of 'Desert Storm' Cited." *Washington Post*, December 31, 1991.

Layne, Christopher. "Why the Gulf War Was Not in the National Interest." *Atlantic*, July 1991.

Lewis, Bernard. "Rethinking the Middle East." *Foreign Affairs*, Fall 1992.

Lewis, George N., Steve Fetter and Lisbeth Gronlund. "Casualties and Damage From Scud Attacks in the 1991 Gulf War." Defense and Arms Control Program, Center for International Studies, Massachusetts Institute of Technology, March 1993.

Lopez, George A. "The Gulf War: Not So Clean." *Bulletin of the Atomic Scientists*, September 1991.

MacLeod, Scott. "In the Wake of 'Desert Storm.'" *New York Review of Books*, March 7, 1991.

Maksoud, Clovis. "The Arab World's Quandary." *World Policy Journal*, Summer 1991.

Malone, William Scott, David Halevy and Sam Hemingway. "The Guns of Saddam." *Washington Post*, February 10, 1991.

Mann, Jim. "CIA Tells Why U.S. Let Hussein Stay in Power." *Los Angeles Times*, January 8, 1993.

Milhollin, Gary. "Building Saddam Hussein's Bomb." *New York Times Magazine*, March 8, 1992.

The Military Balance 1990–1991. London: International Institute for Strategic Studies, 1990.

Milton, T. Ross. "Strategic Airpower: Retrospect and Prospect." *Strategic Review*, Spring 1991.

Moore, Molly. "Women on the Battlefield." *Washington Post*, June 16, 1991.

Moore, Lt. Gen. Royal N. Jr. "Marine Air: There When Needed." *U.S. Naval Institute Proceedings*, November 1991.

Morin, Richard. "Marchers in D.C. Liberal, Educated, Survey Finds." *Washington Post*, February 27, 1991.

Morrison, David C. "Pentagon Counting on Reserves." *National Journal*, September 1, 1990.

———. "Patriot Games." *National Journal*, April 25, 1992.

Morrocco, John D. "From Vietnam to Desert Storm." *Airforce*, January 1992.

Muir, Daniel J. "A View From the Black Hole." *U.S. Naval Institute Proceedings*, October 1991.

Munk, Erika. "The New Faces of Techno-War." *The Nation*, May 6. 1991.

Murphy, Caryle. "Syrian Troops Display Unlikely Solidarity With Saudi Arabia." *Washington Post,* December 18, 1990.

———. "Plan to Bar Iraqi Flights Contains Risks for Allies." *Washington Post,* August 20, 1991.

———. "Iraqi Exiles Allege New Brutality in South." *Washington Post,* November 21, 1992.

Mylroie, Laurie. "Why Saddam Hussein Invaded Kuwait." *Orbis,* Winter 1993.

Naylor, Sean D. "Iraqi Fire: Big Guns, Bad Aim." *Army Times,* January 14, 1991.

———. "Friendly Fire: The Reckoning." *Army Times,* August 26, 1991.

Neuhaus, Richard John. "Just War and This War." *Wall Street Journal,* January 29, 1991.

"Night Imaging Magic Opens Intrepid Maneuver Warfare." *Signal,* August 1991.

Norton, Captain Douglas M., USN. "Sealift: Keystone of Support." *U.S. Naval Institute Proceedings,* May 1991.

Nunn, Sam. "Military Reform Paved Way for Gulf Triumph." *Atlanta Constitution,* March 31, 1991.

Nye, Joseph S. Jr. "Why the Gulf War Served the National Interest." *Atlantic,* July 1991.

Oberdorfer, Don. "Missed Signals in the Middle East." *Washington Post Magazine,* March 17, 1991.

O'Neill, Bard E., and Ilana Kass. "The Persian Gulf War: A Political-Military Assessment." *Comparative Strategy,* April–June 1992.

Ottoway, David B. "For Saudi Military, New Self-Confidence." *Washington Post,* April 20, 1991.

Owens, Mackubin Thomas. "Desert Storm and the Renaissance in Military Doctrine." *Strategic Review,* Spring 1991.

Ozal, Turgut. "An Unavoidable War." *Washington Post,* January 22, 1991.

Palmer, Bruce. "But It Does Take a Leader: The Schwarzkopf Autobiography." *Parameters,* Spring 1993.

Palmer, Michael A. "The Navy Did Its Job." *U.S. Naval Institute Proceedings,* Naval Review 1991.

———. "The Storm in the Air: One Plan, Two Air Wars?" *Air Power History,* Winter 1992.

Pasternak, Douglas. "Minimize Casualties: Technology's Other Payoff." *U.S. News & World Report,* February 11, 1991.

"Patriot Games." *The Economist,* October 10, 1992.

"Patrolling the Persian Gulf." *Bulletin: The United States Coast Guard Magazine,* March 1991.

"The Persian Gulf Crisis: Uses of National and International Power in the Post–Cold War World." U.S. Army War College, Strategic Studies Institute, April 1991.

Pope, Sterett, and Raghida Dergham. "Shifting Sands: Arab Alliances and the Gulf Crisis." *the inter dependent,* no. 4, 1990.

Postol, Theodore A. "Lessons of the Gulf War Experience With Patriot." *International Security,* Winter 1991–1992.

Preston, Anthony. "Naval Lessons of the Gulf War." *Asian Defense,* January 1992.

Priest, Dana. "Women at the Front." *Washington Post,* March 1, 1991.

Quinn, Sally. "Mothers at War: What Are We Doing to Our Kids?" *Washington Post,* February 10, 1991.

Record, Jeffrey. "AF's Future Bright After Stellar Gulf Showing." *Air Force Times,* March 11, 1991.

Reference Text: Forces/Capabilities Handbook. Vol. 2, *Weapons Systems, Academic Year 1990.* Carlisle Barracks, Pa.: U.S. Army War College, 1989.

"Reserve Component Programs, Fiscal Year 1989." In *The Annual Report of the Reserve Forces Policy Board.* Washington, D.C.: Office of the Secretary of Defense, 1989.

Richards, Evelyn, and Charles R. Babcock. "Half-Tank, Half-Taxi Bradley Proves Its Worth in Battle." *Washington Post,* March 15, 1991.

Rigdon, Joan E. "Students Prepare To Dodge a Draft that Doesn't Exist." *Wall Street Journal,* February 27, 1991.

Ripley, Tom. "Operation Provide Comfort II." *International Defense Review,* October 1991.

Roberts, Roxanne. "The Silence of the Diplomat." *Washington Post,* March 15, 1991.

Roberts, Tom, and Gary O'Guinn. "Persian Gulf Makes 'Just War' Debate No Longer Academic." *Washington Post,* February 2, 1991.

Rojo, Alfonso. "Bombed Plant 'Nuclear Site Not Milk Factory.'" *The Guardian (London),* March 11, 1991.

Ross, Robin. "Some Early Lessons From Operation Haven." *RUSI Journal,* Winter 1991.

Roy, Robert J. "Combat Operations Garner Unmanned Aerial Support." *Signal,* April 1991.

Rubenfein, Elisabeth. "Soviet Military Is Shaken by Allies' Triumph Over Its Former Protege." *Wall Street Journal,* March 4, 1991.

Rubinstein, Alvin Z. "New World Order or Hollow Victory?" *Foreign Affairs,* Fall 1991.

"Sanctions on Iraq." *The Economist*, April 2, 1993.

Sawyer, Kathy. "U.S. Spies in the Sky Focus in on Iraqis." *Washington Post*, November 25, 1990.

————. "U.S. Planners Rely Heavily on Sophisticated But Limited Electronic Spy Systems." *Washington Post*, February 19, 1991.

Scarborough, Rowan. "State Official Defends Policies Toward Iraq." *Washington Times*, May 22, 1992.

————. "Women Fall Short on Battlefield Readiness." *Washington Times*, July 28, 1992.

Schmitt, Eric. "Pentagon Seeks To Diminish Effects of Officer's Remarks." *New York Times*, December 21, 1990.

Schneider, William. "The Lessons of Iraq." *American Enterprise*, 1991.

Schwammenthal, Daniel. "How the IAEA Assists Iraq." *Defense Media Review*, March 1993.

Schwartz, John, et al. "The Mind of a Missile."*Newsweek*, February 18, 1991.

Schwarzkopf, H. Norman. "Strategy Behind Desert Storm." *Washington Post*, February 28, 1991.

Schwelien, Michael. "CNN: Television for the Global Village." *World Press Review*, December 1990.

Scowcroft, Brent. "We Didn't 'Coddle' Saddam." *Washington Post*, October 10, 1992.

Sharp, Walter G. "The Effective Deterrence of Environmental Damage During Armed Conflict: A Case Analysis of the Persian Gulf War." *Military Law Review*, Summer 1992.

Shea, Donald W. "A Ministry in the Eye of the Storm," *Army*, September 1991.

Shenon, Philip. "Vehicles Roam the Front To Detect Gas Attacks." *New York Times*, February 24, 1991.

Shichor, Yitzhak, "China and the Gulf Crisis: Escape From Predicaments." *Problems of Communism*, November/December 1991.

Shrader, Charles R. "Friendly Fire: The Inevitable Price." *Parameters*, Autum 1992.

Simmons, Edwin H. "Getting Marines to the Gulf." *U.S. Naval Institute Proceedings*, May 1991.

Smith, R. Jeffrey. "U.S. Special Forces Carried Out Sabotage, Rescues Deep in Iraq." *Washington Post*, March 4, 1991.

Smith, R. Jeffrey, and Evelyn Richards. "Numerous U.S. Bombs Probably Missed Targets." *Washington Post*, February 22, 1991.

Smith, R. Jeffrey, and John Goshko. "Ill-Fated Policy Originated Shortly After Bush Took Office." *Washington Post*, June 29, 1992.

Smith, Major General Rupert. "The Gulf War: The Land Battle." *RUSI Journal*, February 1992.

Smith, Vern E. "The Whole World Is Watching." *Sunday Times Magazine* (London), October 7, 1990.

Snyder, Michael R. "The USCG's Forward-Deployed LEDETS." *Seapower*, February 1991.

"The Soldier Armed: AH-64A Apache Attack Helicopter." *Army*, April 1991.

Steele, Dennis. "New Technology Targets Friendly Fire Deaths." *Army*, April 1993.

Stein, Janice Gross. "Deterrence and Compellence in the Gulf, 1990–91." *International Security*, Fall 1992.

Stephens, Mitchell. "Why the Protest Against the Gulf War Fizzled." *Long Island Newsday*, March 27, 1991.

Stone, Michael P. W. "The Patriot Controversy: Close the Critic's Books." *Christian Science Monitor*, October 16, 1992.

Stork, Joe. "The Gulf War and the Arab World." *World Policy Journal*, Spring 1991.

Strategic Survey: 1990–1991. London: International Institute for Strategic Studies, May 1991.

Strobel, Warren, and Richard C. Gross. "Bush's Dilemma Close to 'Nightmare Scenario'." *Washington Times*, February 22, 1991.

Summers, Harry G. Jr. "Western Media and Recent Wars," *Military Review*, May 1986.

————. "Victory Is Military—and Political." *Los Angeles Times*, January 17, 1991.

————. "Some Notions of Naysayers Bite the Dust." *Los Angeles Times*, January 21, 1991.

————. "Allied Forces To Target Iraq 'Center of Gravity.'" *Los Angeles Times*, January 22, 1991.

————. "As the History of Warfare Makes Clear, Potential for Catastrophe Remains Great." *Los Angeles Times*, January 23, 1991.

————. "Allied Successes Score in War's Political Dimension." *Los Angeles Times*, January 24, 1991.

————. "Iraqi Strategy of Evasion and Delay: Historical Successes." *Los Angeles Times*, January 27, 1991.

————. "When it Comes to Artillery, U.S. Is Outgunned by Enemy Weaponry." *Los Angeles Times*, January 30, 1991.

————. "Fog of War Triggered Iraq's Attack on Khafji." *Los Angeles Times*, February 1, 1991.

———. "Even Civil War Had Friendly Fire Victims." *Los Angeles Times*, February 3, 1991.

———. "As Observers and Critics, Media Play Vital Roles in Time of War." *Los Angeles Times*, February 4, 1991.

———. "Checklist for Cheney and Powell: Mission, Enemy, Terrain and Troops." *Los Angeles Times*, February 6, 1991.

———. "'Collateral Damage' a Familiar, Often Intended, Part of War." *Los Angeles Times*, February 8, 1991.

———. "Body Count Proved To Be a False Prophet." *Los Angeles Times*, February 9, 1991.

———. "AirLand Battle: Next Stage is Critical." *Los Angeles Times*, February 11, 1991.

———. "This Time Out, the American Strategy Includes Victory." *Los Angeles Times*, February 13, 1991.

———. "War, It Turns Out, Has a Language of its Own." *Los Angeles Times*, February 15, 1991.

———. "Baghdad's Sudden Interest in Peace No Surprise." *Los Angeles Times*, February 16, 1991.

———. "Credo on Ground: Speed, Surprise." *Los Angeles Times*, February 18, 1991.

———. "Penetration Attack Could Launch Ground War." *Los Angeles Times*, February 19, 1991.

———. "Without Air Mastery, Hussein Loses Mobility." *Los Angeles Times*, February 20, 1991.

———. "Bush Asserts Himself as Commander in Chief." *Los Angeles Times*, February 22, 1991.

———. "Snookered in Vietnam and Korea, U.S. Learns a 'Peace Talk' Lesson." *Los Angeles Times*, February 23, 1991.

———. "God of War Will Force Withdrawal as Hussein Sidesteps Other Options." *Los Angeles Times*, February 24, 1991.

———. "Mubarak's 'Paper Tiger' Label for Iraq Appears Right." *Los Angeles Times*, February 25, 1991.

———. "Hussein's Deceits Fall on Deaf Ears." *Los Angeles Times*, February 27, 1991.

———. "Military Support Services Proved Their Worth in Supplying Victory." *Los Angeles Times*, March 1, 1991.

———. "Putting Vietnam Syndrome to Rest." *Los Angeles Times*, March 2, 1991.

———. "Strategic Bombing: Terrorist Act or Necessary Force?" *The World & I*, September 1991.

———. "Mission Fulfilled." *Washington Times*, July 9, 1992.

Terrill, W. Andrew. "The Gulf War and Ballistic Missile Proliferation." *Comparative Strategy*, April–June 1991.

Thomas, C. J. D. "How Israel Saw Iraq During the Gulf War." *RUSI Journal*, Winter 1991.

Thomas, Vincent C. "The Sea Services Role in Desert Shield/Storm." *Sea Power*, September 1991.

Thompson, Air Vice Marshal C. J. "Air Power in Operation Granby—The Lessons So Far." *RUSI Journal*, Winter 1990.

Thompson, Jake. "Glaspie Twisting Slowly, Slowly in the Wind." *Washington Times*, March 13, 1991.

Thompson, Mark. "Commandoes Tell Their Gulf War Stories." *Philadelphia Inquirer*, June 21, 1991.

Toolis, Kevin. "The Man Behind Iraq's Supergun." *New York Times Magazine*, August 26, 1990.

Trejo, Frankl. "Gulf General Doesn't Consider Self Hero." *Dallas Morning News*, July 20, 1991.

Tritten, James J. "The Changing Role of Naval Forces: The Russian View of the 1991 Persian Gulf War." *Journal of Soviet Military Studies*, December 1992.

24th Infantry Division (Mechanized). *A History of the 24th Mechanized Infantry Division Combat Team During OPERATION DESERT STORM*. Fort Stewart, Ga., 1992.

———. *24th Mechanized Infantry Division Combat Team Historical Reference Book*. Fort Stewart, Ga., 1992.

———. *24th Infantry Division (Mechanized) OPLAN 91.3*. Fort Stewart, Ga., 1992.

———. *The Victory Book: A Desert Storm Chronicle*. Fort Stewart, Ga., 1992.

Tyson, Granville E., ed. "The Gulf War." *Military Chaplain's Review*, Summer 1991.

"UN Security Council Resolution 687: Iraq Weapons of Mass Destruction." *Background Brief*. London: Foreign and Commonwealth Office, October 1991.

U.S. Congress. House of Representatives. Committee on Armed Services. *Crisis in the Persian Gulf: Sanctions, Diplomacy and War*. 101st Cong., 2d sess, 1990.

U.S. Congress. Senate. Committee on Armed Services. *Crisis in the Persian Gulf Region: U.S. Policy Options and Implications*. 101st Cong., 2d sess, 1990.

U.S. Congress. Senate. Committee on Governmental Affairs. *Pentagon Rules on Media Access to the Persian Gulf War*. 102d Cong., 1st sess, 1991.

U.S. Department of the Air Force. *Air Force Manual 1-1: Basic Aerospace Doctrine of the United States Air Force.* Washington, D.C.: USGPO, 1984.

———. *Air Force Manual 1-1: Basic Aerospace Doctrine of the United States Air Force.* Washington, D.C.: USGPO, 1992.

———. *Reaching Globally, Reaching Powerfully: The United States Air Force in the Persian Gulf War.* Washington, D.C.: USGPO, 1991.

U.S. Department of the Army. *Field Manual (FM) 46-1: Public Affairs Operations.* Washington, D.C.: USGPO, 1992.

———. *Field Manual (FM) 100-5: Operations.* Washington, D.C.: USGPO, 1986.

U.S. Department of the Army. Office of the Judge Advocate General. *Report on Iraqi War Crimes (Desert Storm/Desert Shield).* Washington, D.C.: War Crimes Documentation Center, International Affairs Division, January 8, 1992.

U.S. Department of Defense. *Conduct of the Persian Gulf Conflict: An Interim Report to Congress.* Washington, D.C.: USGPO, 1991.

———. *Conduct of the Persian Gulf War: Final Report to the Congress.* 3 vol. Washington, D.C. USGPO, 1992.

———. "Press Release 241-92: Pentagon Adopts Combat Coverage Principles." Washington, D.C., May 21, 1992.

U.S. Department of Veterans Affairs. "News Release: VA Establishes Referral Centers to Assist Persian Gulf Veterans." Washington, D.C., August 18, 1992.

U.S. Department of Veterans Affairs. "VA Fact Sheet: VA Health Care for Persian Gulf Veterans." Washington, D.C., August 1992.

U.S. Marine Corps. *FMFM 1-1: Campaigning.* Washington, D.C.: USGPO, 1990.

———. *FMFM 1: Warfighting.* Washington, D.C.: USGPO, 1989.

"Victory in the Gulf." *Washington Times,* March 22, 1991.

The White House. "Executive Order 12727: Ordering the Selective Reserve of the Armed Forces to Active Duty." Washington, D.C., August 22, 1990.

———. "Executive Order 12728: Delegating the President's Authority to Suspend Any Provision of Law Relating to the Promotion, Retirement or Separation of Members of the Armed Forces." Washington, D.C., August 22, 1990.

———. "Executive Order 12733: Authorizing the Extension of the Period of Active Duty of Personnel of the Selected Reserve of the United States." Washington, D.C., November 13, 1990.

———. "Executive Order 12743: Ordering the Ready Reserve of the Armed Forces to Active Duty." Washington, D.C., January 18, 1991.

———. "Executive Order 12744: Designation of Arabian Peninsula Areas, Airspace, and Adjacent Waters as a Combat Zone." Washington, D.C., January 21, 1991.

———. "Executive Order 12750: Designation of Arabian Peninsula Areas, Airspace and Adjacent Waters as the Persian Gulf Desert Shield Area," *The White House.* February 14, 1991.

Wilkerson, Isabel. "Blacks Wary of Their Big Role in Military." *New York Times,* January 25, 1991.

Williams, Pete. "The Press and the Persian Gulf War." *Parameters,* Autumn 1991.

Wilson, George. "Secret Warriors." *Army Times,* March 8, 1993.

Yan, Ellen. "Rights Groups Accuse U.S. of War Crimes." *Long Island Newsday,* November 14, 1991.

Yeosock, John J. "H + 100: An Army Comes of Age in the Persian Gulf." *Army,* October 1991.

Young, P. Lewis, "Diego Garcia: Its Role in the US Gulf Security Policy." *Asian Defense,* July 1992.

Zoglin, Richard. "Live From the Middle East." *Time,* January 28, 1991.

Zugschwert, John. "Apache Earns Wings in Desert Storm." *Defense News,* April 8, 1991.

Zumwalt. Lt. Cdr. J. G., USMCR. "Tanks! Tanks! Direct Front!" *U.S. Naval Institute Proceedings,* July 1992.

SUBJECT INDEX

Boldface page numbers indicate extensive treatment of a topic.
Italic page numbers indicate illustrations or captions.
Page numbers followed by m indicate maps.
Page numbers followed by t indicate tables.

ARMAMENTS INDEX

Boldface page numbers indicate extensive treatment of a topic.
Italic page numbers indicate illustrations or captions.
Page numbers followed by t indicate tables.